S0-AKZ-143

THIS BOOK BELONGS TO

Roselyn Benon

SELF PORTRAIT WITH FRIENDS

Self Portrait with Friends

The Selected Diaries of
Cecil Beaton
1926-1974

Edited by
Richard Buckle

Times
BOOKS

TO EILEEN
a friend for all seasons
with gratitude
and love

Published by TIMES BOOKS, a division
of Quadrangle/The New York Times Book Co., Inc.
Three Park Avenue, New York, N.Y. 10016

All photographs copyright by Cecil Beaton
Copyright © 1979 by Cecil Beaton
Copyright © 1979 in the Introduction and compilation by Richard Buckle

All rights reserved. No part of this book may
be reproduced in any form or by any electronic
or mechanical means including information storage
and retrieval systems without permission in writing
from the publisher, except by a reviewer who may
quote brief passages in a review.

First published in Great Britain in 1979
by Weidenfeld and Nicholson.

Library of Congress Cataloging in Publication Data

Beaton, Cecil Walter Hardy, Sir, 1904–
    Self portrait with friends.

    Includes index.
    1. Beaton, Cecil Walter Hardy, Sir, 1904– 2. Photographers—England—
Biography.
I. Buckle, Richard. II. Title.
TR140.B4A325 1979   770'.92'4 [B]   79-51451

Manufactured in the United States of America

Contents

Illustrations

Acknowledgements

Sir Cecil Beaton wishes to thank Miss Eileen Hose for her help over research and the assembling of illustrations: she has been as indispensable and thorough as ever. He thanks the Beaton Studio, Sotheby Parke Bernet, for allowing him to reproduce most of the photographs (only those of the Royal Family remaining in his copyright). Richard Buckle is grateful to Mrs Anthony Harris for her work in typing and photocopying, and for her encouragement. Mr John Curtis suggested the third word of the title. Mr Benjamin Buchan of Weidenfeld and Nicolson saw the book through the press.

Introduction

When he was a schoolboy at Harrow Cecil Beaton began a Diary which he continued until, at the age of seventy, he lost the use of his right hand. The Diary fills over a hundred and fifty volumes. Some of these are school exercise books, others are artists' sketchbooks or handsome folios. It is easy to understand why the Diary was written. Started because Beaton had no close friend or relation to whom he could pour out his hopes, fears and dreams, it became, when life grew more exciting, a way of snatching at the fleeting moment – of pinning down 'le vierge, le vivace et le bel aujourd'hui'. Then there was Beaton's determination to waste none of his gifts. He knew he could write, besides being able to draw and photograph; and his idea of relaxation after long hours of taking photographs for money, or designing a play, or supervising fittings at the costumier, or going to parties, was to cover pages of the Diary with accounts of what he had done and seen. Like Proust, with his rearguard action against lost time, and like Casanova, reliving his youthful conquests in the lonely impotence of old age, Beaton wanted to hoard experience. Yet, unlike the memoirs of the Venetian amorist, Beaton's Diary was not a record of 'emotion recollected in tranquillity'; nor was it, like *A la Recherche du temps perdu*, a conscious work of art. We must seek closer comparisons.

Although in the early frantic years, when Beaton was making his name in the world, he left gaps in the Diary to be filled after a few weeks or even months had passed – and some gaps were never filled – what he wrote was mostly 'Stop Press News', a daily bulletin issued (to himself) on 'the morning after'. Should Beaton therefore be judged alongside diarists like Pepys and Greville or letter-writers like Mme de Sévigné and Horace Walpole? Less political than the former two, he was less aware of his audience than the latter: he falls betwixt and between. Even if we compare him to the contemporary diarists Harold Nicolson and Chips Channon, with whom he had something in common, the difference is more striking than the similarity. Every human being is unique, but among recorders of current events – journalists, we might call them, whether they leave us journals, or letters, or a series of articles in a newspaper – Beaton stands alone. Neither Sévigné, nor Pepys, nor Walpole, nor Greville, nor Nicolson, nor Channon met – and photographed – such a diversity of men and women, travelled in five continents during a world war, or spent a year in Hollywood designing the most successful musical film of all time.

The range of Beaton's talents and the variety of his experience would have availed him nothing as a diarist without the gift for self-expression in words. He was a careless, impatient writer who 'scarce blotted a line': that is the price we pay for the boon of immediacy, for receiving dispatches from the field of battle. I recall, however, travelling on the train from London to Salisbury with Raymond Mortimer while he read one of Beaton's newly-published volumes; and Mortimer, so fastidious a writer himself that he has barely, in a long life, published one book, kept exclaiming aloud at the zest and colour of Beaton's style.

After his illness it was hard, if not impossible, for the busy Beaton to 'improve each shining hour': enforced idleness brought him near despair. Then he asserted his will-power. Before long, with his left hand, he began first to sign Christmas cards, then to write short letters, then to draw, then to use water-colours, then to paint in oil and even to take photographs again. But the Diary was given up for good.

A Note on the Text

Cecil Beaton published six volumes of selections from his diaries: *The Wandering Years* (1961), *The Years Between* (1965), *The Happy Years* (1972), *The Strenuous Years* (1973), *The Restless Years* (1976) and *The Parting Years* (1978). I thought it best to omit all the youthful diaries describing schooldays, Cambridge and the unhappy years in the City, for these – of which only a tithe has been published – are very profuse and might form a book on their own. In choosing what to reprint from the remainder I have omitted most of the 'travelogues' – that is, descriptions of holidays abroad – while trying to mention the author's principal journeys in my introductory notes to each section. I have included passages from three other books, which, like most of the Diaries, are now out of print: *Ashcombe* (1949), *It Gives Me Great Pleasure* (1955), and *Cecil Beaton's Fair Lady* (1964). I should have liked to ask leave to include many unpublished entries from the Diaries, but, in the interests of space, confined myself to two: one is about Princess Margaret's impromptu tea with Beaton at Broadchalke, and the other about the exhibition of 'Beaton Portraits' at the National Portrait Gallery, and the Queen Mother's visit to it. That this show was of historic importance, as well as being the summing-up of Beaton's career as a photographer, could hardly be guessed from the paltry paragraph on page 82 of *The Parting Years*, and I was determined to remedy this defect.

The description of Beaton's 'one night stand' at Norfolk, Virginia, in the course of his lecture tour, reprinted, with cuts, from *It Gives Me Great Pleasure*, may seem more deliberately composed than other long episodes in the book, but it is based on the Diary none the less.

My subdivisions differ considerably from those in the previously published Diaries, but I have made no alterations in the text.

R.B.
Wiltshire, 1978

1

Life Begins
1926–9

At Cambridge the dramatic societies had provided C.B. with an escape route from the dullness of middle-class family life into the glamorous world where he felt he belonged. He designed Volpone *for the Marlowe Society, and photographed* The Duchess of Malfi *for* Vogue. *He designed Pirandello's* Henry IV *and played the principal female role himself. He appeared in comic review sketches.*

A year or two 'in the City' proved disastrous, but C.B. worked at home on his photography, with his sisters as guinea-pigs. In February 1926 his family moved from 3 Hyde Park Street to 61 Sussex Gardens. That August he went to Venice and even managed to show Diaghilev his designs.

It was Allanah Harper who introduced C.B. to a new world of intellectuals and bright young people. He photographed them in a novel way, and they liked the results. The Sitwell family encouraged him. In August 1928, Duckworth accepted his Book of Beauty. *His introduction to Wiltshire, during a weekend with Lady Grey and her son Stephen Tennant, led to his meeting Edith Olivier and Rex Whistler; but he was ducked in the River Nadder by fellow guests at the Wilton ball. He paid his first visit to New York, and was employed by* Vogue.

7 December 1926

Allanah was to bring Edith Sitwell to lunch. Afterwards, I'd take photographs.

Edith arrived, a tall, graceful scarecrow with the white hands of a medieval saint. At first I felt she was 'making conversation', but soon she relaxed completely. She told stories with measured flourish and effect. A great actress, she can keep a room in fits of laughter.

I had expected Edith Sitwell to be ethereal and beyond worldly concepts. But to my surprise, she embarked upon a pungent assessment of people and events. She fired comic broadsides at Drinkwater and Squire, also shaking a little pepper on Ethel M. Dell, Hannen Swaffer and Tallulah Bankhead.

Gradually, I found her formidable aspect less striking than her sympathetic girlishness. In spite of her cadaverous appearance, her complexion is as fresh as a convolvulus, and she has a disarming girlish manner of not being able to contain her laughter.

Lunch was a success. Edith ate heartily of a piping hot fish *soufflé* which was a triumph, except that it had bones in it. Manley (our butler) offered red or white wine at the same time, and to make matters worse had placed the bottles on a mingy little tray he had picked up from heaven-knows-where. Edith, when approached, entolled in her bell-clear voice, 'White, please.' During dessert she recited a bit of Gertrude Stein's 'Portrait of Tom Eliot': 'Silk and wool, silken wool, woollen silk.' How precisely and richly she spoke. She could make any rubbish sound like poetry.

I could hardly contain my impatience and delight as we went up to my sisters' bedroom for the afternoon's photography. She posed instinctively. No matter how many positions I had already taken, I felt loth to call a halt. Surely this was an unique opportunity. I must perpetuate the image in front of me, of a young faun-like creature sitting against my leaping-fawn design, looking surprisingly Victorian in her crudely-cut Pre-Raphaelite dress, with her matador's jet hat, and necklace, her long medieval fingers covered with enormous rings. When the hat was discarded, she became a Brontë heroine, and her pale silken hair fell in rats' tail wisps about her face, while the big teapot-handle bun made the nape of her neck appear even more impossibly slender.

As the afternoon wore on, I suggested more exotic poses. I even persuaded her to asphyxiate under the glass dome. She became quite hysterical kneeling on the floor, her knees and joints popping and cracking. A Chinese torture she called it, but loved it all the same.

I, meanwhile, had my own agonies. The camera kept going wrong, the film got stuck and couldn't be wound further. I excused myself, crossed the landing to my room, pulled down the blind and unrolled the film.

At last Edith left to 'finish a poem' she was in the middle of. I caught an approving twinkle in her eye as she left. It meant that we were going to be friends. I remembered a letter Kyrle [Leng] had written to me in answer to a *cri de cœur* of mine. I had begged for his advice. 'What on earth can I become in life?' He had replied: 'I wouldn't bother too much about *being* anything in particular, just become a friend of the Sitwells, and wait and see what happens.'

After today's photographic session my eyes ached from looking into the unshielded photographic bulbs. I could see wiggling scarlet and green worms everywhere. Hastily I changed for dinner, as Billie Williams was taking me to the ballet.

What a rush life has become!

9 December

The telephone bell rings all day long. It seems that the young girls I've lately
come in contact with have nothing better to do than to call me: 'Take me out;
take my photograph again and let me bring Tanis, Meraud, Honey and Rosamond ...'

I'm generally in a compliant mood. If there is any complaint, it's simply
that I spend too much time on the drudge work connected with photography.
Lately, however, I've been giving Selfridge's photographic department nearly
all the developing. This morning I traipsed there for the fifty millionth time
to get the results of Edith Sitwell. The camera had leaked: light got in and
spoiled a number of negatives. It would!

Soon after lunch, Inez brought Honey, Rosamond, etc., to be photographed.
After almost every pose the camera got stuck; I had to go into my darkened
bedroom and tug at the film.

Inez, very businesslike, suggests that I give her a commission on each girl
she brings to be photographed. It sounds all right to me.

The girls sat round in various stages of *décolleté*, as I like to take bare
shoulders. With everyone in her slip, the room looked like a dormitory. (When
I was photographing the Du Maurier sisters, outspoken Daphne said it looked
like a brothel.) Inez chatted and smoked cigarettes, sometimes holding the
lights above the girls' heads for me.

We had a riotous afternoon. Inez's friends kept saying they hadn't enjoyed
themselves so much for ten years; in fact, not since the last time they'd been
photographed. Meanwhile, I tried to keep my head and bring into play all the
stunts and tricks I've developed.

18 December

There were endless photographs to be done. A glut of Tanis Guinness turned
out beautifully. I love her fat face, her enormous eyes with tulip-petal lids.

I sat for hours under a light, retouching prints with pencil and paint. Then
I steamed them over a kettle in the cook's den downstairs; mounted them with
secotine and put the cards to press under the leg of some heavy furniture. Then
more hours enlarging: I persisted in making endless prints of the same picture
until I got one worthy of being sold.

I stopped at ten o'clock, as I was invited to Madge Garland's bottle party.
Mum knew I was going out, but we had to keep it from Dad. Last night Reggie
had been stupid enough to stay on at a nightclub until five o'clock. Dad is
generally a sound sleeper, but by some misfortune he woke up and heard Reggie
returning surreptitiously. There was a terrific row. I had difficulty getting away
unnoticed. Mum kept *cave* for me. I couldn't stop laughing at the sight of her
in her nightgown, face soused in grease and terrified eyes beckoning me to come

on or go back. She allowed me to take a bottle of champagne to the party, as it's Christmas.

20 December

The Christmas rush is on. Everyone wants last-minute photographs taken for presents. I am up to my navel in work. This morning was such a pandemonium I hadn't a jiffy to shave or dress smartly. I grovelled on the floor in a dirty old sweater and flannel trousers, mounting and retouching masses of prints. The pink work room got strewn with rubbish. My mother came to the door, looked and sighed woefully, 'This room will never be the same again.'

Anyway, I did a good day's work and sent off several large packages, including the glass-eyed woman's order.

14 January 1927

Today is my twenty-second birthday. Yet the last few years have meant so little to me, compared with my early life. How impressed one was, how cut with emotions as a child! Now I feel that life has slowed down to half pace. I'm rather thick-skinned, and things don't seem quite as important or vital as they once were. Life has become more or less routine.

Twenty-two, damn it! Hell take it! Or no! I do believe it is twenty-three! Yes, I was born in 1904. Good Lord, I'm twenty-three!

In my suit of plus fours, I felt like a new person. I then went hunting for a place to use as a photographic studio. Now that my photographs have become well known, I can make a great deal of money if I start in a business way.

I went to estate agents. I'd like a mews in Mayfair, an amusing place where I could not only click away but also paint and read and telephone my friends. I want to do the place up to look like my own, with cages full of chirping birds.

Wiltshire: 15 January

I was met at Salisbury station and motored through the dusk to Wilsford Manor. It turned out to be a greystone manor house, with parrots, lizards, Morris chintzes, and flagstones. The long, panelled drawing-room created a comfortable and informal air with its enormous soft chairs, bowls of fat hyacinths, sweet-smelling freesias and an untidy litter of books.

Lady Grey, plump finger tips in the air, beamed her greetings, eyes bright and small. [Her son] Stephen wore plus-four trousers and a lizard-skin belt. Zita and Baby Jungman both looked countrified in wool and tweeds. Dolly Wilde [niece of Oscar], raven hair shingled, and oyster face plastered with powder, wore vitriolic purple and reclined like a decadent Roman empress.

We sat on the floor in front of a great log fire, at which an extravagantly exotic scented elixir was burnt in a long-handled spoon. I felt awed by Lady

Grey, gracious and queenly as a fairy godmother. But soon she left the young people to themselves.

Stephen talked like a rocket going off. Dolly, never expecting that she might have inherited her uncle's wit, continually managed to say clever, funny things as if by a fluke. Her eyes widened with astonishment at each *bon mot*, and she exploded as heartily as anyone in the ensuing laughter. Baba [Eleanor] Brougham hunched her shoulders, chuckled in spite of a cold and encouraged cleverness with, 'Oh, that's good! Oh, my! That's very witty!' Baby tossed a strand of flaxen hair out of her eyes and chuckled contagiously; Zita looking like Trilby with her page's cap of hair, had a gentle quiet voice like honey, or milk that is slightly off. I love them both.

Steven Runciman added a note of erudition. He told historical anecdotes, including a grotesque account of Louis XIV's heart. It seems that, many years after the Sun King's death, his heart was transported to England with much ceremony and reverence. While being exhibited on a salver at some reception, it was mistaken for a little cake and eaten by a short-sighted clergyman!

At dinner, I warmed to Lady Grey when she regaled us with nonsense. She told about the woman who wanted to have diamonds put in her teeth so that she could even say. 'Good morning' brilliantly.

Afterwards we played a game of 'Analogies'; also various word games, including one called 'Interesting Questions'. I was very bad at that, being so ill-educated. But, by dint of being funny instead of knowledgeable, I managed to come out fairly well. Steven Runciman wrote about me: 'My Mother: Lady Colefax. My Father: Cardinal Mazarin. My Teacher: Leonardo da Vinci. My governess: a piece of porcelain. My skeleton in the cupboard: a kind heart. What would I save from the fire: myself.'

I considered this weekend the beginning of a new life. At last I found myself among people with kindred interests. Moreover these people seemed to like me, whereas at home I feel misunderstood, somewhat of an idiot and a nuisance. Undressing in front of the fire that glowed welcome to me in this strange Honeysuckle Bedroom, I was happy and thankful after so many months of having fought desperately. If I hadn't made a move from the Holborn office I should still be at odds with the world – miserable, unsuccessful and undeveloped.

August 1928

I found that Osbert and Sachie [Sitwell] were in London. Osbert asked me to dine with him and Rex Whistler at Boulestin's, the prettiest restaurant in London, with its deep yellow varnished walls, cloudy mirrors and Dufy designed silks. We sat on *banquettes* and in the most leisurely and epicurean manner, enjoyed Osbert's talk, the cheese sauces and red wines. Osbert has very early in life acquired the grand manner without pomposity. He tells a story with interruptions of 'Huh Huh' as he himself enjoys the humour and looks quickly from one face to another for approval. He is generous in his appreciation of others' attempts at wit, snorting with painful grunts of suppressed laughter during an imitation of some new friend or rival.

When leaving, Osbert fell up the stairs and said, somewhat surprisingly, 'That means good luck.' It seemed so out of character.

Rex and I hadn't seen one another for months, so that there was so much to discuss that we could not now call a halt to the evening. In fact, when Osbert was bundled into a taxi-cab an impetus was given to the outpourings on many subjects in which our host could not have shared. Yattering so volubly that we were oblivious of the direction in which we were going, we walked until I got a hole in my sock. Then we sat on spiked railings, and unaware of the chiming of clocks, gossiped about friends: Stephen's relapse of health, his strange relationship with his mother, his recent friendship with Siegfried Sassoon, a paradoxical combination of characters, the one so flamboyant and the other so retiring.

We talked of Edith Olivier, with whom Rex had just been staying. Edith, at the best of times, likes to lie on a chaise-longue with her head lower than her legs, while she reads or converses in her sibilant, jerky tones. This time, Edith, having cracked her knee-cap, lay prostrate on her terrace while she read the proofs of her new novel, *As Far as Jane's Grandmother's*.

We discussed Osbert's vicissitudes with his father, who, with his ivory complexion and ginger beard, looks like a Victorian Tintoretto. It seems that, much to Osbert's exasperation, the father's extravagance is now manifesting itself in the removal of an ornamental lake from one side of the Renishaw park to the other.

Rex has a *bonté* towards mankind. Curious about all aspects of his world, he finds the complicated behaviour of some of his friends completely baffling, but his interest in gossip is never malicious. Rex, so romantic with his luminous face, Roman nose, and large crown to his head, exudes warm-heartedness and sympathy, but he is a strangely remote person. I doubt if many people even impinge on his inner feelings. He seems to accept me as a new bosomer, but I wonder if, apart from his deeply reciprocated devotion to Edith, he has really loved anyone.

Wilton: Summer

The festivities were to celebrate the coming-of-age of Lord Herbert. Edith Olivier had asked me to stay in her house in the Park for the event. After dinner our party walked along the river and over the illuminated Palladian bridge, across the smooth lawns to the house. In the gloaming the Inigo Jones façade looked its most noble with the long range of tall lighted windows.

It was a grand occasion, and I was overawed. I remember Mr Rudyard Kipling with his plebeian moustache; his flat chest was pasted with medals. And a more handsome couple could seldom have been seen than Lord and Lady Anglesey! she looking so cool and wistful, with white face and black hair, and carrying the weight of the world and a tall spiked tiara on her poetical head.

I walked on the lawns in a dream.

How beautiful the night scene was! How calm and visionary! But my reveries were short-lived. Suddenly they became a nightmare.

Out of the darkness a group of tail-coated young men surrounded me and, without a word of explanation, highjacked me across the lawns at enormous pace towards the river. I remember my head was raised in a Guido Reni agony which seemed to be unending. In the panic that assailed me, the emotions of humiliation and shame were stronger than those of fear. The black night whirled past me, bat-like, as the phantasmagoria journey continued, until abruptly, with a vicious thrust from all my attackers, I was catapulted into the darkness. With a tremendous splash and plopping of stones, I found myself standing hip deep in the Nadder. Too stunned to know what to do, in my startled misery, I merely stood silent. This had the effect of a clever ruse: my enemies now became somewhat apprehensive lest their treatment of me should have ended in my complete disappearance. The group above me on the river bank murmured, 'Do you think the bugger's drowned?' I continued to stand motionless in the water. Someone – I think it was Roger Chetlock – shouted, 'Are you all right?' I did not answer. More murmurs. But perhaps I feared further retribution, if some would-be rescuer were to plunge after a supposedly drowning man and find him no worse off than wet to the white waistcoat. 'Where are you? Are you alive?' Eventually, in a rather dead voice, I replied, 'Yes, the bugger's alive,' and I trudged up the stones and mud into the comparative light of the lawns. My attackers had vanished.

The night was still comparatively young. I was determined not to leave the ball. While the water ran down my legs and oozed out of my shoes, I remained by a window of the Double Cube room making conversation to an eminent Field Marshal ... Later I danced with some of Edith's young nieces. They did not seem to notice my damp trousers, or that the squelching soles of my feet dragged without their accustomed smoothness across the parquet.

Walking home, as dawn lightened the skies, down past the river that I had come to know so intimately, I joined airily with the others in a post-mortem on the party. 'Yes, it was a glorious ball. The best I've ever been to.' About one thing I was determined: the incident would never be mentioned by me. So far as I was concerned, it had never taken place. Although Edith's servant must have been surprised to find my soused clothes next morning, she did not draw my attention to them, nor did Edith ever allude to my shame; and her tact increased my love.

New York: November 1929

Little white cubes shone in the sun, tug-boats began the slow business of herding a giant up river to its Manhattan pier.

There were crowds waiting to welcome everyone but me. Fellow passengers pushed excitedly.

'Excuse me for doing you out of your place, but I'm crazy to see my mother!'

'Ah, that's my wife!'

The taxi drive was a trail of shocks. New York's tall buildings were lost somewhere overhead. It became dark en route to the hotel, and the scene turned to a frozen fireworks display. From my eighteenth-floor bedroom window the view appeared even more dramatic: the Hudson shining in the distance below, stars shining, brightly-lit buildings contrasted against shadowy edifices in the foreground, and rose-coloured church steeples.

7 December

Friday is a bad day for me. It marks the end of the week, and the hotel bill arrives. This week my bill seemed much higher than before. There are very few cheques left in my letter of credit book. It is terrifying and depressing. I have begun to loathe the Ambassador Hotel. 1805 is a nice room, but even if the numbers *do* add up to my lucky number fourteen, it has been a jolly expensive fourteen.

Suddenly the telephone went: Mrs Chase bid me go round to *Vogue* and see her at once. The photographs I had taken for them of Natica, Condé Nast's daughter, were admired. I felt relieved, as I have been here already a month, and it's time I started to work in real earnest.

I met Mrs Chase's second-in-command, Mrs Snow, who is the American editor. This meeting was very satisfactory. Mrs Snow, looking like a fox terrier, seemed pleased with me, and we arranged that I should do various jobs for her. Around her sat Miss Margaret Case and Miss Voght, taking down notes of what I was to do. My assignments included an article on New York's night life, for which I would be taken to various joints and have an opportunity to meet Erickson, as he is to do the illustrations. I would also write another article on theatres, to be illustrated with my drawings. *Vogue* would supply tickets for all the plays I hadn't seen. I wish this had been arranged before, so that I could have saved my fast depleting dollars!

Mrs Snow has the most satisfactorily ordered life. She is never flustered by the vast amount of work to be done at the office, yet has time to devote to her husband and children, a house in New York and another in the country, while still she manages to travel in Europe. It seemed typical of her to plan three different evening-entertainments for me – one to be passed in a lounge suit, another in black tie, and the third in tails! She said, 'Well, that night you'll go to the movies after dining at the Caviar. You can try Casanova later. And this will be a good night to go to Harlem.' The itinerary was as carefully balanced as if a gourmet should say, 'Well, after the juicy steak, a little *soufflé* should be washed down with a glass of Château Yquem.'

8 December

I was asked down to Long Island to spend the day with the Harrison Williamses, whom I had never met. The prospect was terrifying. I waited in the lobby of my hotel to be picked up by an unknown quantity with a motor car.

The car turned through tall gates and made a semi-circle along the gravel drive, stopping before a sumptuous country house. I noticed odd, crate-like structures of canvas and wood littered all over the garden. It seemed as if a circus were pulling up stakes. But on inquiry I found that box trees (a sign of antiquity on Long Island) were put under these tents for winter protection, making the garden an eyesore for four months of the year.

The house was new and neo-Georgian, filled with English Hepplewhite and Sheraton. Among the paintings were a fine Bronzino and two Tiepolos.

Our host and hostess greeted us. Mrs Williams is fascinatingly beautiful, like a rock-crystal goddess with aquamarine eyes. She moved with pristine and smiling ease among dozens of guests. Harrison Williams has a wrinkled parchment face, a blunt mouth and tired Chinese eyes that have seen everything. His low, deep voice crackles like coke. Although I had little chance to get to know what sort of a man this great mogul was, he seemed extremely sympathetic and was obviously somewhat aloof and only tolerably amused by his guests. I must admit that, for the most part, they rather put me off.

Knowing nothing about stocks and bonds, I thought I should go mad listening to market quotations about what shares went up or were going down. Most of these people seemed to treat a hundred thousand dollars as a mere bagatelle. The loss of a million was another matter: 'Oh I've known people commit suicide when that has happened.' This depressed me very much indeed: I, who have about twenty pounds left out of the two hundred I brought to the States with me!

After lunch came tennis in the new glass-domed enclosure which is artificially lit so that people can play all night if necessary. Also enclosed here were a huge swimming pool and gymnasium. I feared the standard of tennis would be far higher than mine; as indeed it turned out to be. I watched in awe and silence while the Parrot [C.B.'s nickname for one of the guests] slammed volleys and yapped, 'Atta-boy!'

More people arrived for dinner – all celebrities of Long Island, all indefinite in appearance and definite in thoughts. They emanated self-assurance, and I felt alarmed by everyone except one fat old Mrs Tiffany, a terrific personality whom everyone calls Nannie. She was amusing and shrewd; she had a wry sense of humour. She talked like a lady in a play, offering her formula for getting thin: for three days now, she had had nothing but hot and cold water and the juice of one orange.

On my left at the dinner table was a Mrs Henry Russell. Earlier in the day she had taken no notice of me, but now seemed flattered that I should ask so many questions about the people present. She was a mine of information. That hard woman there recently married a prince and was keeping him penniless. The overtired lady, with bloodless lips and incessantly blinking eyes, had a debutante daughter who needed closer chaperoning than she had received.

After dinner there was more talk of bull and bear markets, also bridge. Mrs Williams, Nannie Tiffany and myself begged off. We made conversation. I warmed to a sense of *entente* with our hostess: she was so unlike the others. She radiated serenity and sympathy; she seemed utterly selfless. Without her, I would have felt at a loss, hobnobbing with the weightiest names of Wall Street. As a matter of fact, what good did it do when one had nothing in common with them?

I sank into a car and was driven back through miles of Long Island bleakness to New York. I hoped I would see Mrs Williams again, as I felt we should become friends. If only she weren't so rich, so sought after, it might be easier.

In my hotel room, the windows were all shut, the steam heat terrific, my puny vase of cheap flowers was quite dead. I found urgent notes and telephone messages from Elisabeth Marbury asking me to meet Amelia Earhart.

Quite a glut of sitters – and impressive ones too. At this afternoon's session I was amazed at my own patter: Don't budge an inch, I beg you. That's fine. I do thank you for keeping so still. Now lower your chin – lower, much lower. You see, with this little camera I'm like a dog looking up at you. Still a little lower. Don't worry about the double chins. I'll knife them later. Pretend you're looking down a well. Good; perfect.

Dear old Mr Frank Crowninshield appeared and, to my great delight, raved about my photographs. He liked some of the paintings, too. I felt that praise from the editor of *Vanity Fair* augured well. Gosh, it was good to hear him enthuse so extravagantly: myself, Steichen and de Meyer the *only* photographers: 'But it's so amazing that you can do things like this with a toy camera.' And he stayed three times as long as he had intended.

At sea: 5 April 1930

I don't think I slept for more than a few hours during the last week in New York. I've started a very bad cold now. My throat feels relaxed and sore, the boat rocks up and down. After two days of semi-coma in an airless inside cabin, I staggered from my bed this morning, dressed in plus fours and managed to walk to my chair on deck without being ill. There I met Noël Coward and Mrs Venetia Montagu, whom I had always imagined to be charming and interesting people.

At once they attacked me. 'Why do you write such malicious articles? Why do you say such nasty things about Mr Coward?'

I staggered, my knees quaked. 'You must please not attack me now. I am feeling ill.'

'You must expect to be attacked if you write such horrible things.'

They told me my writings were impertinent, malicious, mean, full of untruths and utterly superficial. They exaggerated, of course. But there was so much truth in what they had to say that I could not deny it. The blows came raining down upon me.

Mrs Montagu is the sort of woman I admire: tall, *raffinée*, gaunt and grey-haired with a hawklike profile. There are few good books she hasn't read and remembered, never forgetting the name of a character or the gist of a situation. At crossword puzzles and writing games she is quicker than anybody else.

As for Noël Coward, the truth is that I've wanted to meet him for many years. I admire everything about his work: his homesick, sadly melodious tunes, his revues, his witty plays, his astringent acting.

Why, then, have I hated him? Perhaps for the very reason that I've not known him before and wanted to. I hated him personally, out of pique. I was envious of his success, of a triumphant career that seemed so much like the career I might have wished for myself.

Since my friends in New York had told me how *unmalicious* I was, I could now hardly believe my ears. Mrs Montagu lashed out at me, determined to give me a lesson for several reasons: (a) because she disliked me and (b) because I obviously needed putting in my place. Coward showed more aplomb, investigating me out of a detached curiosity. Yet both came to the same conclusion: I was flobby, flabby and affected.

I moaned tragically, 'But believe me, I'm a wad of guts and gristle.'

They died of laughter. They mimicked me: 'Oh, it's too, too luvleigh!' My arms were said to fly in the air. This I thought was going too far! I denied it. My walk was said to be undulating, my clothes too conspicuously exaggerated.

I felt speechless with inferiority. I had wanted enormously to be liked by Noël Coward, and now he thought nothing of me. I thought nothing of myself. My gloom was total.

It will be so unsatisfactory to break an acquaintance like this, without convincing them both that I'm not as low as they think me. There may never again be a further chance of making explanations, excuses or amends.

I arranged to do a drawing of Noël Coward and went to his cabin.

'We've been absolutely beastly to you,' he admitted. 'But you've shown spirit and let's hope you've learnt a lesson. It is important not to let the public have a loophole to lampoon you.' That, he explained, was why he studied his own 'façade'. Now take his voice: it was definite, harsh, rugged. He moved firmly and solidly, dressed quietly.

'I see.'

'You should appraise yourself,' he went on. 'Your sleeves are too tight, your voice is too high and too precise. You mustn't do it. It closes so many doors. It limits you unnecessarily, and young men with half your intelligence will laugh at you.' He shook his head, wrinkled his forehead and added disarmingly, 'It's hard, I know. One would like to indulge one's own taste. I myself dearly love a good match, yet I know it is overdoing it to wear tie, socks and handkerchief of the same colour. I take ruthless stock of myself in the mirror before going out. A polo jumper or unfortunate tie exposes one to danger.' He cocked an eye at me in mockery.

2

Hollywood
1930–31

Friendship with Anita Loos, author of Gentlemen prefer Blondes, *gave
C.B. an introduction to Hollywood. He met and photographed many stars
of the silent screen; and there were other adventures in the booming film
colony. With two dozen other guests he stayed at Saint Simeon with William
Randoph Hearst.*

*C.B. also went to North Africa with George Hoyningen-Huene, a photo-
grapher who taught him much.*

December 1930

I travelled from New York with Anita Loos and her husband, John Emerson,
to spend Christmas in Hollywood. Anita, at the age of sixteen, wrote the
scenario for Mary Pickford's film *The New York Hat*. Ever since, she'd been
one of Hollywood's most popular citizens. So I was assured of seeing the film
metropolis under good auspices.

On board the train were exclusively film folk. The talk centred almost entirely
on the 'recent advent of talking pictures'. Someone bet that Garbo would be
no good in talkies; her downfall was certain to be as rapid as her rise. John
Gilbert's reedy voice had caused him to be eased out of his contract. Clara
Bow, it seemed, was suffering from appendicitis.

For three days we ate enormous tenderloin steaks in the confines of a metallic
dining car. In Chicago, a frenzied porter wheeled a barrow most painfully into
the back of my legs. At Las Vegas, John Emerson bought a bow and arrow
from an Indian. And at San Bernadino we alighted from the train.

A car and chauffeur had been sent by Mr Joseph Schenck. The limousine
had been given to Mr Schenck as a birthday present from Al Jolson. Five years
previously, it had won first prize for its body in an exhibition of modern art
in Paris. It was decorated with inlaid woodwork, engraved glass and tortoise-
shell. The seats and carpet were woven with a design of paradise birds whisking
among futuristic globules.

It was a relief to be out of the train, whizzing along in comfort. The daylight faded. The sky turned to copper. In the distance, mountains were purple; a warm and velvety evening air was heavy with the smell of orange blossoms. I sniffed happily, but felt a stab of longing for some sort of love affair, so that the palm trees and warm evening could be appreciated even more.

We were keyed up to observe everything. A huge electric sign read, 'Ye Olde Gas Shoppe'. There were many such 'shoppes', with Merrie England propaganda abundant. On we sped, past wooden bungalows, imitation Spanish haciendas, and weird constructions where the traveller stops for ice cream. These were decorated to look like gigantic ice grinders, or puppy dogs or dolls with hats and yellow curls.

Every little bakery had been built like a windmill, theatrically illuminated. Gardens were inhabited by pottery elves and gnomes with long beards and red caps. We passed the Hansel and Gretel kindergarten school for girls and boys. Perhaps it was these children who had been allowed to run amok with their whimsy, creating a dotty never-never land.

The chauffeur explained that Hollywood Boulevard was being officially renamed 'Santa Claus Lane' for the holidays. Its sidewalks were lined with huge Christmas trees, all tarted up by vari-coloured lamps.

John Emerson mopped his brow. 'Phew, the heat!' We all felt breathless in the sultry, subtropical humidity.

All at once there was excitement. Coming towards us a lorry, equipped with spitting blue lights, towed in its wake a giant sleigh on wheels. Merry Christmas! In the 'one-lorry open sleigh' a group of Eskimo, wearing white fur, sat placidly enduring an artificial snowstorm. The lorry men whipped themselves into an arctic hysteria, shovelling mounds of white confetti through a wind machine that spewed clouds of white over Nanook and Nanette. This was Hollywood! If anyone doubted it, a rival lorry driven by outraged puritans proclaimed: 'The Lord Jesus came to save sinners, not to worship Santa Claus in Hollywood!'

We arrived at our hotel. The Roosevelt turned out to be a mock Moorish conceit with patio, fountain, and shawl-draped balconies. Its lobby was crowded by desperate blondes in black satin, osprey and furs. Though the climate varies little the year round, Hollywood ladies insist on wearing the same season's clothes that are being worn in the East. Little matter if the December sun is broiling.

Apollos and Venuses are everywhere. It is as if the whole race of gods had come to California. Walking along the sidewalks with Anita, I see classic oval faces that might have sat to Praxiteles. The girls are all bleached and painted with sunburn enamel. They are the would-be stars who come to Hollywood from every part of America, lured by hopes of becoming a Mary or Doug, a Joan Crawford, Gloria Swanson, Richard Barthelmess or Gary Cooper, whose autographed pictures are part of nearly every shop window display. Few of the hopefuls ever 'make it'; some are realistic enough to admit their failure, in time to leave before their savings have been exhausted. The diehards hang on, buoyed by empty prospects and promises, eking out a piecemeal existence by working at 'drive-in' quick-lunch counters or as shoe shiners.

Some of the women, accepting their failure to dazzle on the silver screen, mate and make babies which they are convinced will become a gold mine like Jackie Coogan. They encourage them to be tarts out here from the age of five. Younger still: by the time a brat is three or four, it has been mercilessly trained in the art of sophistication and artificiality. Cheeks are painted, noses powdered, hair permanently waved. The girls are dressed in tight-fitting little frocks, so short as to barely cover their rumps. In doorways, elevators and lobbies, mothers and aunts can be seen titivating their prodigies. They moisten fingers and smooth plucked crescent brows; they encourage the lashes backwards.

One little horror of six took our breath away. She was coming out of a draper's shop with her mother. Her sausage curls were peroxided canary yellow to match her mother's tresses. Her eyes were large and blue, her cheeks had been painted like blushing roses. A frilly pink bonnet surmounted the head, while the tiny body had been squeezed into a skin-tight, sleeveless frock. To complete the picture, a *corsage* of blue and white flowers was pinned to her little chest, and coral bead bracelets dangled from each dimpled wrist. We stared so hard that both the tot and her mother became self-conscious.

Whimsicality soars to new heights. Beauty shops advertise 'face exchange' or 'face aesthetics'. In the household stores, hand-painted velveteen cushions are decorated with lake-side scenes of bewigged love-making, or stuck with bas-relief roses of acid-tinted putty. One cushion was affixed with a small statue possibly made of chewing gum; another depicted two pseudo-classical nude figures clasping one another on a draped 'couch'. Both these art works were exhibited as being 'suitable for milady's salon'.

Weary from window-shopping, we sit down on a sidewalk seat that advertises a dentist, a doctor or a funeral parlour.

Inside the Paramount film studio, the stars' dressing-rooms are built with façades of various styles of architecture. Thus, when occasion demands, they can be used as backgrounds for films about England, Holland, Germany or Russia.

I soon discovered that most buildings had no interiors, were merely shells of Civil War plantations and Istanbul nights.

In an enormous cafeteria, actors, producers, cutters, photographers, caption-writers and scene-writers had congregated for their salad-and-coffee lunches. An old monk in medieval habit was scrutinizing the menus through pince-nez. A dowager duchess, in ball dress and tiara, sat eating spaghetti by herself. There were Hugo-esque beggars, Dickensian executioners, creole beauties in crinolines and hospital nurses from 1914.

I was introduced to a series of people whose names I knew from the movie magazines I'd been reading. 'Meet Mr Lubitsch.' A cigar twisted from one side of his mouth to the other, while I remembered his *The Marriage Circle*, the first good film I ever saw. 'Meet Mr Richard Arlen.' A nice, clean-looking young man wrinkled his forehead and smiled. 'This is George Bancroft.' The twinkling tadpole eyes didn't seem a bit thuggish off the screen.

A Mr Al Kaufman now took me to see the man who made *Wings*. He was busy producing his next picture, which featured Gary Cooper. A shot was in progress. Over and over again, Gary Cooper had to address Fay Wray as 'Miss Calhoun'.

Cooper is warm and friendly with everyone. The electrician offered him a cigar. 'Are they all right?' 'They should be: the three of them cost twenty-five cents.' Gary lit up, and the cigar did not explode.

This ingenuous cowboy's success has sky-rocketed. He started in the business only three years ago, and now it saps him entirely. He pines to get away but can't. He can't even spend his money. He longs for the sun to stop shining, but it never does. 'Terrible weather this, for the day before Christmas.' The sun was broiling hot.

On the next set, a 1914 wartime party was in slow progress. The men strutted about in khaki; the women we had already seen in the cafeteria, wearing aigrets and beaded tunic dresses.

On another stage, William Powell was being extremely serious in a typical detective drama. Immaculately dressed, he sat at a desk and frowned. His cool white hands were crossed. He spoke in a rich, unctuous voice, due perhaps to the relish with which he enjoys his great success.

While various technical gadgets were adjusted before a new take, Powell talked shop to bystanders. 'Why is it that Barrymore is so lousy nowadays? I haven't seen *General Crack*, but I hear he surpasses himself in over-acting. I suppose he's up to his old tricks.' An imitation of the old tricks convulses electricians and prop men with sycophantic laughter.

Encouraged, Powell went on to discuss the interpretations of another famous actor. 'He's acting in an eighteenth-century play, isn't he? I suppose that means he does the snuff business.' There followed an imitation of snuff-taking.

An electrician, lying in the gantry above, roared with laughter and shouted, 'The pansy!'

'Okay,' the director bellowed. And they proceeded with the next scene.

Anita took me to United Artists about photographing Lilian Gish. But the film had been finished, and the publicity man doubted if Gish would ever make another 'talkie'. So by witnessing peradventure that defiant little spinster, wrapped in a squashed strawberry-coloured shawl and walking with such martial tread back to her dressing-room, I had been present at Gish's exit from the screen world!

What an exquisite artist! What a genius to have made her way so delicately and forcibly among such crashing vulgarity all these years. The memory of her in *Orphans of the Storm* is still for me a strangely intimate one. We were shown the 'stills' of the new *Swan* film and they look terrible! They have modernized the story, the fools, and I gather the picture will be a big flop.

Later I had occasion to hear Gish's criticism of Hollywood's trend. 'With the talkies stars are treated with less artistic authority. During the making of the *Swan* I was considered a novice, and my years in the business counted for nothing. I had thought it such an inspiring idea to call the studio United Artists. But they weren't united or artists. I don't want to make another talkie. I shall become a little old maid, looking after my invalid mother, going through the linen and counting the glass.'

Christmas Eve in a film studio must be seen to be believed. On Wellman's new film, we were given a demonstration of the director-genius at work. He did weird gymnastic exercises; he mouthed, gesticulated, swayed and switched coloured lights on and off. Finally he screamed, 'All right! Stop! God, this scene is a bastard!' The 'bastard' entailed much moving of cameras and sound apparatus while a pretty German spy was busy doping the hero home on leave, so that her accomplice could get hold of the secret papers.

It was very nearly the end of the day's work. Yuletide exaltation became exaggerated. Wild-eyed stenographers were whisked under doorways to be kissed beneath sprigs of mistletoe. One young man, a total stranger to me, rushed up and asked, 'How are you going to spend your Christmas?' When I said I didn't really know, he almost shed a tear for the poor limey bum. A stenographer rushed into the room, picked up the telephone and barked, 'Hello, you silly sucker. Merry Christmas to you!' Then she hung up.

The whistle blew. The studio became a scene of pandemonium as its inhabitants, laden beneath mountains of fancily wrapped packages, rushed forth like school children let out for their holidays.

2 January 1931

Anita, John and I were invited to stay at W.R. Hearst's ranch for New Year's Eve.

We were to take Hearst's special train, leaving Los Angeles at eight o'clock in the evening. The train would arrive at its destination around two in the morning; but we could sleep as long as we wanted to, and, when everyone was awake, there'd be a communal drive out to the ranch.

The party assembled at the station. Everyone was in high spirits. Tough blondes, hams and nonentities mingled with directors and magnates. Eileen Percy, the gay spark of the crowd, wisecracked, laughed hilariously, swished round on one heel and boxed anyone within reach.

W.R. had taken a train from New York. His car was now slowly linked to the private train that would transport our raucous mob. An official hurried along, carrying a huge bouquet. Flashlight photographers sought out Marion Davies. They love her because she is unlike any other star. Not a bit stagey, she doesn't clasp a bouquet and smile with shut eyes and raised brows for the cameras. She is genuinely surprised by the bouquet: 'Oh, but how nice.'

We were all ravenously hungry and made a dash for the dining car. Hearst, Marion and Ambassador Moore were edging their way along the corridors. Marion dined quietly with Hearst, and only occasionally dashed across to whisper to her girl friends about how she had lost a bracelet or had her hair dyed a different colour.

I ate in the company of two blondes: Eileen Percy, gayer now than ever, and Julianne Johnston, a nice film actress with no particular personality. With us was Colleen Moore. I had seen pictures of Colleen looking pretty and cute. Now she was here in the flesh. I marvelled. It is one of the tricks of fate that Colleen Moore photographs so well. She looks utterly different in the flesh and I couldn't keep my eyes off her.

Colleen Moore said not a word during dinner. Afterwards we joined Anita and John. I had a spurt of vitality and was in good form while describing a brawl at Zoe Akins' party, when someone knocked a goldfish bowl on to Gloria Swanson's chinchilla coat. The blondes and even Colleen Moore screamed hilariously, spurring me on to fresh sallies.

Later in the evening, John took a redhead in tow and brought her to Anita's compartment for laughs. I have never heard such laughs. Miss Stork (we found out her name) was quick and witty, and so dirty that we yelled in an agony of laughter.

At last Anita and John, their ribs aching, decided to go to bed. I was to share a compartment with a natty little counter-skipper named Eddie Kane. The compartment reeked with fumes of alcohol. Eddie and an old-girl actress were rather tight, talking over-emphatically to one another. At last she tottered off. The beds were made up, and in the space of a few square inches we undressed. We spun a coin; I won, and slept on the lower bed. 'Good night, old man,' Eddie said. I replied, with as much energy and spirit as I could muster, 'Good night, old man.'

A tap on the door. The porter's voice saying, 'It's after nine o'clock and Mr Hearst is up,' was a command for us all to get ready. The king had arisen; now his minions must rise.

The awful Eddie Kane made early-morning noises. He dressed and departed, looking both pathetic and smart.

I joined Anita and John. After a slight delay, we started off in a motor for the ranch. There were about ten cars in all; and the party dribbled up to the ranch in twos and threes.

The air was sharp and crisp, with a tang in it. We admired glorious scenery, we gaped at enormous green hillsides that made remembered mountains seem like molehills.

At length the car shot through a gate, and we were on the grounds of the estate. A sign warned: 'Danger! This road dangerous to pedestrians on account of wild animals.' Soon we passed herds of buffalo, striped zebra, deer and antelope, exotic birds that looked like white ostriches.

Abruptly, in the distance, at the top of a tree-spotted mountain, we caught sight of a vast, sparkling white castle in Spain. It was right out of a fairy story. 'Gosh,' I said. The car moved closer and closer to the vision. Through the cypress trees we could distinguish statues. And then we had arrived.

The sun poured down with theatrical brilliance on tons of white marble and white stone. There seemed to be a thousand marble statues, pedestals, urns. The flowers were unreal in their ordered profusion. Hearst stood smiling at the top of one of the many flights of garden steps.

As we stepped out of the motor the housekeeper, a white-haired, dark-eyed woman, came forward and shook hands. Then we were shown to our quarters, with footmen conducting us.

My room seemed gigantic. There was a carved gilt ceiling; great, hewn Jacobean beds with gold brocade covers; old, tinselled velvets hanging on the walls. The view from the window revealed a panorama of pale green mountains, blue, misty hills and a silver sea in the distance.

I walked outdoors. The castle consisted of a main building and five outbuildings. The main portion loomed like Wells Cathedral, with an assembly-room and a dining-room both the size of a great church. The outbuildings were almost as impressive.

John and Anita's accommodation was even better than mine. Brocade lined the walls of their sitting-room from floor to ceiling. It would have bankrupted you to buy one square foot of the material for a cushion. The Italian furniture was of museum quality. The ceiling, like the one in my room, had been carved with full-sized gilt angels. And the bed, an affair of oak tooled to resemble drapery, had the most elaborately embroidered coverlet upon it.

We went outdoors and toured the formal terraces, then wandered in the vast garden. Some of the statues, I noted with surprise, were not up to scratch, even cheapjack. Perhaps it was by intent; we'd been so overpowered by Dona-tellos and Della Robbias that it made the place come alive to see a nymph with bobbed hair eating an apple, or three very obviously Victorian graces playing together.

Inside the cathedral-like assembly-room the party now gathered, all bemoan-ing the non-arrival of their bags. Some stood in awe at the grandeur of their surroundings. Those who didn't, the tough blondes and nonentities, had been here before. Blasé, they made efforts to explain what certain pieces were, where they came from and their date. This aesthetic assessment ended in shrieks of ribaldry. In fact, Eileen Percy was already making whoopee, rushing about with a sword she had picked up for an impromptu bacchanale.

The lunch table looked like a scene in some epic film about the lives of the Caesars. A never-ending length of table was literally covered with food – bottles of pickled fruits of all descriptions, chutneys, olives, onions, squares of every kind of cheese, bowls of fresh fruit. Purple glass goblets, vivid hanging banners and urns of poinsettias completed a Lucullan sight. The food turned out to be as good as it looked. I gobbled away, while the blondes became increasingly hilarious as they planned a cockeyed New Year's Eve.

Trunks arrived. I retired to shave and put on entirely new clothes. In doing so, I lingered too long. Feeling spick and span, I came down from my Jacobean magnificence to join the party but could find no one. Every guest had dis-appeared.

I wandered about, rather unadventurously trying to explore. Occasionally, a secretary hurried through the marble garden. I got out my camera and spent an hour or so trying unsuccessfully to photograph myself with a timing gadget. It kept going off prematurely, clicking the shutter before I could even get into position. Still no one. I wrote a long Hollywood letter home, skimmed through newspapers, ate chocolates and nuts, smoked cigarettes.

At last I found some of the party drinking in the kitchen. The blondes were in riding breeches and bright-coloured sweaters. They had had a glorious ride. Secretly, I wished I'd been with them, though years had elapsed since I last rode a horse. It also turned out that I'd missed joining the throng when they went to watch the animals being fed in W.R.'s private zoo.

The sun now set; the lights in the garden were put on, illuminating the swim-ming pool. I went indoors and found Marion Davies arranging the placement for dinner. She was wearing Wedgwood blue, which accented her white, freckled skin, her drooping aquamarine eyes and shining, pearly teeth.

Marion Davies is pretty as a Greuze, and what a character! She is kind, humble, shrewd, blindly generous and madly inconsequential. When I photo-graphed her a few weeks ago in New York, we wanted a bare shoulder which the small neck to her dress would not allow. In spite of its being a new dress, worn for the first time, she seized a pair of scissors and ripped it down.

Marion is never alone, always surrounded by a gang of twenty or thirty hangers-on. In New York, her party kept arriving at the theatre so late they once trooped in ten minutes before the final curtain. When she went to Europe last year, she took a retinue of twenty-six people who could buy anything they liked and charge it up to her. The scent bills alone came to thousands of dollars. But then, Marion must spend more money than anyone else in the world. . . .

'Marion is most attentive to all sorts of people,' Anita later remarked. 'I've often gone into a shop where she knows the salesgirl, and the salesgirl says, "I had a post card from Miss Davies this morning".'

A very ordered party went out on to the terrace to see Marion's latest picture. The cold air sobered us up. Or perhaps it was the dull film. I wondered why Marion should spend her time making such bad movies. The production of this one seemed particularly poor. I went to sleep once or twice, but a blonde Miss Lloyd nudged me incessantly.

Indoors, the mob crowded the assembly-room and waited for midnight. We drank champagne, tried to be hilarious, exchanged kisses all round. But the party was so large that many of the guests remained strangers one to the other. Bells ringing, sirens going off and a whining moan in the distance announced that the New Year was in. Eileen Percy put a cushion on her head, then turned somersaults in front of the colossal chimney grate. Colleen Moore drank silently. Marion had sudden spurts of energy, did a Charleston, shook her hands frenziedly, then hurried out of the room to consult with Hearst. Gradually, all hopes of an orgy disappeared. We dwindled to bed.

3

Ashcombe
the 1930s

Through Edith Olivier C.B. found his dream house, hidden among the Wilt-shire Downs. It was to be his home for fifteen years. He bought furniture in Vienna and Venice. He published his first book, Beaton's Book of Beauty, *with drawings and photographs by himself.*

Spring 1930

During the spring of 1930 I happened to be staying with Edith Olivier at the Dayehouse in Wilton. Her small Gothic dwelling, filled with a strange assortment of objects collected over a long period of years, crowded with books and pictures and all kinds of visitors, was, to me, as to many other young people at the beginning of their careers, a spiritual home. There was always reading aloud, sketching, visiting of interesting neighbours and nearby beauty-spots, and a lot of laughter. Edith Olivier was born one of a family of ten in the Rectory of Wilton. Here she lived a life of Victorian conventionality, doing good works in the ancient borough. After the death of her stern father, when she moved to the small house, formerly a dairy, in the Great Park of Wilton House, she discovered a talent for writing and for entertaining. The long room in which we sat was full of the books which she and her friends had written, and the paintings her friends had given her.

On this particular visit, Rex Whistler and I were her weekend guests. Rex, whose superabundance of charm and coziness made us all vie for the privilege of including him among our intimates, had become Edith's greatest friend, and had come to the Dayehouse to relax after the exertion of completing his first great commission, the murals at the Tate Gallery. On the Sunday afternoon, for no particular reason, except that in our hostess we had always a ready accomplice, we decided to transform Edith into the sort of woman whom Toulouse-Lautrec would use as his model. Edith was made to wear dozens of necklaces, a long, tight-fitting leopard-skin dressing-gown which I owned, and a huge picture hat trimmed with full-blown roses ravished from her garden beds. To complete the transformation, we decided Edith must submit to having her face outrageously painted. The lips forthwith became enlarged with sensuous curves of cerise paint and we covered the eyelashes with hot molten wax. I remember Rex whistling as he daubed Edith's cheeks with magenta rouge.

Conversation at the Dayehouse never flagged. At this very moment a discussion sprang into being as to the relative merits of the various counties of England. Soon we forgot that Edith had been metamorphosed and it did not strike us as paradoxical when this painted houri, as the daughter of Wilton's rector, opined, with her own particular emphasis of voice and gesture, that positively no county was as wonderful as Wiltshire. 'From Salisbury to Marlborough we are situated so high that if eyesight were strong enough, you could see across the great vale of Europe to the Ural Mountains. Here you have the impression that you are above the world.' Waving her arms about in her typically flamboyant manner, Edith elaborated her theme. Then suddenly she asked us:

'Who are the first architects of Wiltshire?' Without waiting for our attempted replies, she continued, 'Why, the trout streams!' She nodded her head and shook a finger that had been covered with theatrical rings. 'Yes, by carving the hills and valleys, the trout streams have created the vales of the Wylye and the Nadder!' She readjusted the enormous rose-covered hat. 'And what could be more apt than to call Salisbury Cathedral "that Minster most perfect of all shrines", but, mark you! not only is there Salisbury Cathedral, which was built in twenty years as one gigantic conception, and, mind you, that was long, long before the days of great architects, not only is there the glory of Wilton House and Stourhead and the palace at Clarendon, and the castle at Longford, but there are all the wonderful small houses scattered about Wiltshire's highlands and meadows. Don't you feel, Rex, under your very feet, the lingering vibrations of the prehistoric life of Avebury and Stonehenge? And the life of thousands of years ago when these green roads led, from this central point, to the gold and tin mines of Cornwall and to the lead mines of Wales? Of course you do, Cecil. Even strangers, who remain here but a short time, become conscious of that mystical feeling and immense dynamic power. Oh, no other county can compare with Wiltshire!'

Without knowing that I was thinking aloud, I wondered if perhaps I could ever own a cottage in such wonderful surroundings. With her customary optimism, Edith asserted that she felt certain I could. 'Small houses are difficult to find, but Stephen Tomlin, the sculptor, on a walking-tour in the downs recently discovered a deserted house, among the trees of Cranborne Chase, and when he looked closer he saw that there was a grotto in the garden.'

'A grotto? A grotto?' The word conjured up pictures of baroque fantasies, for which, at that time, influenced by the Sitwells, we all showed much enthusiasm.

There and then we got into Edith's small motor car and set off on our quest.

We called at Tomlin's studio at Swallowcliffe, where the sculptor was working
on a large garden figure of Pomona. He seemed somewhat baffled at Edith's
appearance, but since she did not mention it, he made no allusion to 'La
Goulue'. Edith insisted that Stephen, in his overalls, should guide us to the
hidden house.

'I don't know if I should ever be able to find it again,' he said. 'It was a
sort of "Grand Meaulnes" place.'

'But you said it had a grotto!'

'Yes, it had a grotto.'

We motored along the main road towards Shaftesbury, then suddenly turned
off to circle through narrow lanes that mounted high into the downland. The
pathways became rough and overgrown, and a few rabbits bolted at our
approach.

'It can't possibly be this way. Nobody would live up here,' remarked Rex.

'We'll get lost!' Perhaps it was the heavily-painted eyes that gave Edith such
a look of extreme alarm. 'We'll never be able to find the road back.'

Stephen Tomlin remained composed. 'I believe this is the right way. It was
almost on the borders of Dorset. I remember seeing that clump of trees there,'
he pointed. 'It's called Wingreen, and is said to be a pre-Druidical burial
ground.' We found ourselves motoring over the side of the downs at a perilous
angle. 'I think we must keep quite calm and make towards that landmark,'
Stephen continued. The car bumped uneasily. Eventually he said, 'I believe
we're there; if we go down that steep bridle-path we'll find the house down
among those trees.'

With intense excitement we got out of the motor. Below, stretching to the
distant sea, lay an extraordinary sylvan carpet. There were hills wooded with
a variety of beautiful trees. Among a cluster of ilex trees a coil of smoke arose.
We walked down the rough track of white chalk and flint stones which was
bordered with nettles and yellow tansy. After we had descended for nearly half
a mile we came to an arcade of low hanging beech trees, and an archway of
pink brick faced with stone. None of us uttered a word as we came under the
voluted ceiling and stood before a small compact house of lilac-coloured brick.
We inhaled sensuously the strange, haunting and rather haunted atmosphere
of the place.

High around us on three sides was a feathery wall of wooded downland. The
valley was screened from sight by limes, while the house itself stood half
shrouded by some melancholy drooping ilexes. Opposite, an L-shaped building, the former stables, with rounded windows and elaborate stonework,
resembled an orangery. The overgrown nettles, brambles and the straggling
bushes produced a curiously slumbrous effect as if these were the outhouses
of the Palace of the Sleeping Beauty.

Our admiration was interrupted by the sudden appearance, across the courtyard, of a small man in leggings and a green hat; a chained dog barked. Rex,
Stephen and myself hung back from approaching the stranger, but Edith, in
her fantastic motley, simpered forward, and in her most sibilant and delicate
tones, wondered if the house were empty, and if we could have a look over
it. The resident gamekeeper, as he turned out to be, appeared less surprised
at the apparition confronting him than might have been expected. Yet, though
Edith used all her wiles to charm him into showing us his Arcadian abode,
he explained in the broadest Wiltshire accents that his master was a very fierce
man and that nobody was allowed near the place.

Raising his voice while we three men cowered in the background, he roared:
'If I'm so much as *seen* tarking to ye, Oi'll be given the sarck!'

Edith continued undaunted. 'Couldn't we even peep through a window?'

'No, not even thaurt.'

'But isn't it true you have a grotto here?'

'Yes, we have a grotto, but I can't show you thaurt.'

After we had learned that the place was called Ashcombe, the nearest village
was Tollard Royal, and the property belonged to a man named Borley who
lived at Shaftesbury, there was nothing for us to do but return up the long
white cart-track. I do not know if the others spoke during the trek up the hill.
I was perhaps vaguely conscious of their eulogies, but I was almost numbed by
my first encounter with the house. It was as if I had been touched on the head
by some magic wand. Some people may grow to love their homes: my reaction
was instantaneous. It was love at first sight, and from the moment that I stood
under the archway, I knew that this place was destined to be mine. No matter
what the difficulties, I would overcome them all; considerations of money, suit-
ability, or availability, were all superficial. This house must belong to me.

I wrote to Mr Borley of Shaftesbury asking him if he would be willing to
sell, or rent, the small house at Ashcombe. In order that I should not give
the effect of affluence, I wrote on a small sheet of extremely thin tracing paper.
Perhaps this created an effect of abject poverty: the note received no response.
After a while I wrote again, this time on some rather pretentious stationery
that I had ordered from Frank Smythson of Bond Street.

'Do you refer to the cottage or the house in the valley?' came back the query
So great was my excitement that I could not trust myself to speak intelligently
to this unknown man who held in his palm for me the most prized possession
on earth: Edith Olivier boldly took upon herself the heavy responsibility.

'We don't quite know which house you mean,' she explained into the telephone. 'You see, your gamekeeper would not allow us to remain. May we come
over with you and have a peep?'

'There's no harm in looking,' replied Mr Borley, 'but I doubt very much

if it's worth your while. The place is all right for the purpose we put it to;
a gamekeeper lives in part of the house, looking after my pheasants and par-
tridges, but it's not really habitable. However, if you wish to come over just
for an inspection, then by all means. . . .'

Mr Borley, a large and prosperous elderly man without much imagination
but with a sound practical sense, accompanied us when, a few days later, we
made again the adventurous journey through the winding pathways that led
to the summit of the downs. Perhaps fortunately, as it turned out, Edith's car
stuck on a hill when nearing our goal and refused to budge forward an inch.
For a moment this was an alarming hitch, for had we not been warned of Mr
Borley's ferocity? Indeed, he did not seem at all pleased as Edith, in desperation, but in vain, pressed every knob on her car, including that of the horn.

'Well, it's no good going back since we're thus far,' suggested Mr Borley.
'We'd better foot the rest.'

The scale and descent of the precipitous slopes was strenuous. From the
summit of the downs, the house seemed to be buried among the trees, but
when one looked from its windows into the valley below one realized that it
was perched at least six hundred feet above the sea.

Inside the little house we were surprised to find such elegant proportions.
A lobby hall reached the whole height of the house, and the simple staircase,
of white painted wood, was of a Chinese Chippendale design. None of the rooms
possessed the disadvantage of being cottagey, and each window seemed to have
a more dazzling view than the last; those looking north gave on to the green
court and the entrance arch of the L-shaped stable; those facing south commanded Elysium itself.

The house was indeed in a state of decay. Everywhere were signs of dis-
integration, but ruin fires the imagination, and my mind was filled with pictures
of what the future could provide. We walked along the rubble of what, one
day, could be made into a garden. An old brick wall was being pulled down
by a rambling lilac, some stone steps indicated where a terrace might have been
and could be rebuilt. We inspected the grotto. It was very dilapidated – but
a grotto nevertheless.

Even on this visit there was no time to linger admiringly, for we must needs
follow the business-like landlord on his cursory tour of inspection. 'This is
used for hatching out the pheasants' eggs; the disused stables are now a storehouse for the coops and stacks of grain; this is the kitchen, here the larder.'

In my mind I was planning that this should be my studio, and here, with
a front-row dress-circle seat of the Keatsian valley, my bedroom. That there
was no electric light, no water system and no plumbing whatever, was of little
consequence to me. We had seen all over the demesne, and I was in a haze
of ecstasy.

Although Mr Borley was reluctant to sell the property to me, it was eventually settled that I should rent these buildings for seven years. In view of the elaborate alterations and improvements I was about to embark upon, the charge would be a nominal one of fifty pounds per annum.

Summer 1930

With the satisfaction of knowing that the builders were at work at Ashcombe, and the printers on my book, *Beaton's Book of Beauty*, I went off to join Anita [Loos] in Vienna. Here antiquaries were ransacked for cheap baroque chairs and consoles for my new home. Oliver Messel joined us; and with him a tall, gangling young man, with the face of a charming cod-fish, named Peter Watson. Of all my recently acquired friends, he was to strike the deepest and rarest chord of sympathy. Peter's acute sensibility, subtlety of mind, wry sense of humour and mysterious qualities of charm made him unlike anyone I had known. Not that we took to one another at first sight. To begin with, when we went *en masse* to beer halls and fêtes, we were merely civil. I did not recognize his virtues, and asked Oliver if the newcomer was not a bit of a bore. But one morning, when Peter decided to come out with me on a sight-seeing expedition, and we stood in stiff silence coming down in the hotel lift, he caught sight of me, and I caught sight of him, each glancing surreptitiously at the other in the looking-glass. We burst into laughter, and arm-in-arm walked off into the Vienna side-streets to become the greatest friends. We stimulated one another. Whereas I gave Peter his first glimpse of a modern painting – a Matisse at the Leicester Galleries – he taught me an appreciation of music. Before meeting him I had heard of the composer Strauss, but had not yet discovered that he could be either Johann, Richard or Oscar.

Oliver and Peter were going on to Venice, and it did not take much persuasion on their part to make me join them. Here, in the dank alleyways, I foraged for junk and bought for Ashcombe old painted doors and cupboards, and stone ornaments, to be sent home by *Petite Vitesse*.

With a feeling of almost complete contentment, I returned to England to correct proofs and work on my new acquisition. Rex pencilled designs for a doorway, with a pineapple in its broken pediment, for urns for the parapet and a chimney piece for the sitting-room; these were given to a local stone-mason. But since bona fide antiques were beyond my financial reach, ingenuity and the Caledonian market had to come to my rescue for the furnishing of the house. Even carpets and curtains cost more than I could afford. Materials were put to uses never intended. 'Animal baize', as the felt is called which covers pantomime zebras and leopards, provided excellent carpeting, and other theatrical materials, originally invented to last for the run of a play, had to stand the test nobly as curtains and sofa coverings.

The wild winter's evening arrived eventually when Rex, Oliver, Peter and I ventured down the steep chalky hill of the valley to spend the first weekend at Ashcombe. We savoured the chill smells of paint and freshly carpentered wood, combined with the warm smell of calico, new rugs, and crackling log fires. The small habitation, for so long abandoned to its loneliness, suddenly became alive and took on its own personality. It was unlike any other abode, admittedly fantastic and strange with its bright colours and silver trumpery, but to me, at any rate, infinitely charming.

Edith Olivier joined us; and together with the cheerful bucolic creatures who were to work with devotion in house, kitchen and garden, ran out into a wintry holocaust, danced around a bonfire, fell in the mud, and toasted the future in champagne.

Ashcombe became lived in. Imported plants grew in pots, chickens browned and crackled in the unreliable antiquated oven. In addition to the favourite kedgerees, haddock and kipper dishes, we enjoyed the novelty of sweet potatoes and shadroe from America, and the luxuries of brandied fruits and cigars from Fortnums. Lorries, bringing more curious pieces of furniture, were lost in Brontë-esque storms, but finally bumped over the hazardous descent through the downland, churning up the courtyard into a playground of mire.

By degrees the stables became a studio, fashionably decorated white upon white; my bedroom acquired circus murals painted by friends. Whatever decorative folly was perpetrated, the mood of this remote and poetic spot remained unharmed. Ashcombe always retained its time-haunted peacefulness. Of course, the chimneys smoked, but I was happy.

Christmas-time saw the first family party. My father was quite baffled by the décor, and tripped over the dais on which my Carousel bed was poised. Rubbing a sprained ankle, he complained that for his taste the house was too full of booby-traps; by degrees my mother, forgetting Ashcombe's impractica-bilities and its remoteness, made suggestions for next summer in the garden; while Aunt Jessie, with eyes twinkling, ooh-ed and ah-ed to my heart's delight.

The *Beauty* book appeared: although it ignited perhaps less of a blaze than I had hoped, Lady Cunard added to the conflagration by throwing her copy into the fire. Her luncheon guests were astonished to watch her thrusting a poker through the burning covers as she exclaimed in a high canary squeak, 'He calls me a hostess, that shows he's a low fellow!'

Guests arriving at Ashcombe for the first time would appear with that vague look in their eyes as if they could hardly believe that their long pilgrimage was at last at an end. To find the whereabouts of the house, even from the most detailed instructions, was always an accomplishment, for strangers would find themselves mountaineering without any conviction that their perseverance would end in reward. Suddenly as the wanderer in the desert sees water in the distance, so would my mountaineers be heartened by the sight, at the crossroads of some five or six country lanes, of a clump of milk cans for which they had been told to keep a look-out. Their spirits were raised. They would then attempt the ascent in front of them, to be followed by the precipitous descent of the broken-down cart-track. Boulders of chalk would hurtle downwards at their approach, frightening a multitude of rabbits, who, catching alarm, would dart in all directions. The motor car, with brakes hot and smoking after the prolonged and unaccustomed effort, would disgorge its passengers underneath the beech trees. They would be faced by the back of a tumbled-down studio building with corrugated-iron roof, a litter of packing-cases, broken statues and discarded junk. With spirits somewhat lowered by this spectacle, they would proceed under the vaulted archway of the stable building. A hanging lamp would rattle in the draught. Suddenly they were comforted by the sight of neatly-mown lawns, a fluttering of white doves, and, facing them, the small dolls'-house with its open front door. Perhaps a figure dressed in a black crinoline would come out of the doorway on her way to be photographed: a friend arriving from America was startled to find Miss Tilly Losch, dressed as a Meissen shepherdess, posturing among a flock of sheep. Perhaps Dorothy, the maid, now dressed in purple and looking like a character out of Dickens, would appear with a tray, but more probably the host, wearing a Tyrolean suit, would dash out to give an exaggerated welcome.

The visitors to Ashcombe were often to be seen in unconventional garb. I used to encourage my guests to bring fancy costume in their luggage so that I could photograph them against my romantic background. No one need be surprised if my five-year-old nephew ran out of a thicket with bow and arrow dressed as Robin Hood.

When Miss Ruth Gordon was appearing in Farquhar's *The Country Wife* at the Old Vic Theatre, she brought with her for a weekend her entire wardrobe of Restoration Comedy clothes, ranging from period night-gowns to ball-dresses which Oliver Messel had designed for her. She spent her entire visit in costume, being photographed having her breakfast in bed, attending the bird in its cage, sweeping the front door-step, feeding the hens, swinging on a Fragonard swing, peering through windows, and lastly, wearing fantange and corset, cleaning her teeth preparatory to going to bed at night.

Once the eccentric and wonderful Marchesa Casati came over for tea from Crichel on one of the coldest days of the winter. For her initial visit to Ashcombe she elected to wear a huge cowboy hat of straw, a gold brocade coatee, white flannel tennis trousers; and her stockingless feet were shod in cork-soled sandals. On her way through the icy snow to see the signs of snowdrops in the bare woods she made a delightfully incongruous picture.

Lady Ottoline Morrell used to appear wearing particularly resplendent attire with large picture hats, lace shawls, yellow brocade skirts and many rows of pearls, and so accustomed did one's eye become to the more fancifully-dressed guests that when Mr H.G. Wells was brought over one Sunday wearing a Homburg hat and pin-stripe suit, one felt he was the man from Mars.

My guests, before leaving my house for the first time, were made to trace the outlines of their hands on the walls of one of the bathrooms. By degrees an extraordinary collection was achieved. As one lay sousing in hot water one could ruminate upon the characteristic traits shown in these significant and life-like shapes and in the choice of position or proximity to others chosen by their owners on the wall, and later, on the ceiling.

When every other room was furnished, my own bedroom still remained large and empty. A major undertaking of decoration lay ahead, and my financial resources were now at a low ebb. A rainy weekend supplied the solution. It happened that all my guests were painters and since the weather was too inclement to tempt us out of doors, the Sunday was dedicated to transforming my bedroom into a circus-room. The room was to be painted in garish colours with niches filled with circus performers, with baroque emblems, barley-sugar poles and flowered mirrors. Each guest set to work on the white walls to contribute his own panel. Rex Whistler painted a superb 'fat woman', Lord Berners a Columbine with performing dogs (a very ungainly mastiff was caught in the agonizing act of jumping through a paper hoop), Christopher Sykes painted a tumbler, upside down, balancing, among other objects, a goldfish bowl on his feet. Oliver Messel created a small negro, naked except for a pink flamingo ostrich feather worn on his head. Mme von Bismarck pictured an equestrienne on a flower-dappled circus pony, and her husband decided to portray 'the strong man of the Fair' with volute mustachios, tattoo marks, heavy ball-weights and chains. However, Yorck Bismarck eschewed the traditional circus manner of carefully finished realistic painting for the more modern slapdash strokes of the brush, and the next weekend Rex Whistler could not resist touching up the flowing chevelure and mustachios, the better to conform with the other murals.

'Please don't, Rex!' I pleaded. 'There'll be hell to pay if Yorck ever discovered you've touched the thing.'

But the temptation was too great. Rex was unable to resist repainting, meticulously and realistically, the crisply waving hair, the mustachios, then, of course, the column-like throat, the brawny chest, and so on down the whole over-muscular body. Unfortunately, it so happened that the Bismarcks drove over from Biddesden the following Sunday to admire their handiwork. Although my strong man had been made into a work of art, the Bismarcks were enraged at the indignity committed upon him, and a nasty situation was created in the artistic world, of which reverberations were heard for many weeks to come.

Rex also made designs for my four-poster bed, which was built by Savages, the circus-roundabout-makers of King's Lynn. Father Neptune at the bedhead was flanked by cupids and subaqueous plants. The canopy was held aloft by barley-sugar posts of brass. We were only disappointed that, at any given moment, the bed could not be made to revolve to the accompaniment of steam music.

June 1931

Alice Astor [later von Hofmannsthal], Freddie Ashton and Ivan Moffat [Iris Tree's son] arrived to stay another weekend.

Freddie entertained us with brilliant, spontaneous imitations, each a choreographic gem in itself. He is a born mimic, relying on gesture to create a devastating caricature of a person or situation. We sat amazed as he ran through a repertory from Sir Thomas Beecham to an Edwardian lady and Sarah Bernhardt. This display was deft, professional, done without shyness or blunder. His sure hands created improvised effects from whatever his eye lighted upon, with the certitude that only an artist can possess. The lid of a coal scuttle served many purposes, becoming a picture hat, then a garden basket in which the Edwardian horticulturist gathered her specimen flowers.

The Bernhardt impersonation was a cameo of one of the actress's stage *tours de force*, during which she acted a dramatic scene while arranging an elaborate bouquet of flowers in a vase without even looking. Her back to the public but head turned towards the arc lights, she selected each bloom, placed it with careful precision until the arrangement was finished, then stepped back with grandiose gesture to admire the effect. The audience applauded wildly.

Freddie's performance prompted Ivan to discuss how much children sensed of everything that was happening. No doubt Freddie never actually *saw* Bernhardt arranging those flowers, but even in his perambulator he must instinctively have known she was doing it and that the audience would applaud. Just so, Ivan at the age of three knew that his mother, pouting and frowning and moaning, was only pretending to concentrate for his benefit. It is true that all children seem astonishingly intuitive, and will automatically be aware, even at a distance, that things about which they should be ignorant are being discussed.

Freddie said he considered that he had been living all his adult life on investments from boyhood. In illustration of this, he was able to convey with exceptional *éclat* the romance that some Brazilian woman had had for him in his youth, when he lived in South America. He recalled how a certain disdainful woman had behaved after being given the honour of dancing with the Kaiser.

He mimed the way this same woman made conversation with the British Minister at a garden party in Buenos Aires, and how she turned her head beautifully for the waiting photographer. He also described the stance of Edwardian beauties, their heads held high, their chins proffered slantwards to reveal to perfection the line of neck and throat.

4

First Meeting with Greta Garbo
1932

On their first meeting, C.B. and the unapproachable, mysterious queen of Hollywood got on like a house on fire.

Hollywood: February

Once more I arrived in this arc-lit, slightly macabre suburbia. By now, I was no longer a stranger, and could call friends with whom I felt at home. I became absorbed in their tales of the film industry. The conversation always seemed to revert to Garbo; her hermit-like independence, her unconventionality in this most conventional of all worlds.

For years now Garbo had become quite an obsession with me. Her screen image haunted me. I collected her every published photograph, and now in a valiant, though doomed, attempt to take my own pictures of her, pestered Howard Strickling of the MGM Publicity staff. Instead of flatly discouraging me, he held out hopes. She had gone to the mountains to get some rest, but was due back tomorrow.... Meanwhile, Miss Shearer was offered on a plate, or Miss Crawford....

Garbo's Nordic blood may be a reason for her tendency towards morbidity, and being so highly strung, together with her sadness at finding herself in a trap, she periodically gives way to bouts of complete despair. It is then that she locks herself up without seeing even her maid for days; for two years no one crossed the threshold of her home.

My chances of capturing the butterfly were becoming more slender each day. Yes Garbo had returned, and had been busy on some retakes, but these were now about to come to an end. I was resigning myself to leaving Hollywood with my mission uncompleted. Funds were running rather low, and Howard Strickling's prevarications became exhausting.

However, when an English couple, Eddie Goulding, the director, and his wife, the former ballroom dancer, Marjorie Moss, suggested my leaving the hotel and coming to their house for a few days, the invitation was accepted with alacrity – particularly since Eddie had directed Garbo in *Grand Hotel*, and was one of the few people she visited at weekends. 'We never know if we should expect her, but she generally rings up at the last moment to ask if she can come along for cold Sunday supper.'

My turret bedroom was reached by circular steps, in this typical 'Spanish-type' mansion. Marjorie mothered me in her disarming nasal voice, which sounded particularly Cockney in Hollywood: Eddie was entertaining in his exaggerated British bulldog bass. I drove a hired car to the various studios and to the 'Army and Navy Stores'. Here was a treasure-trove of men's clothing that could be worn with impunity only in Hollywood or at Ashcombe. I bought vast quantities, at almost negligible cost, of football vests, exotic footgear, the scantiest shorts in all colours and in white sharkskin; I could not resist one particularly beautiful white kid jacket.

Sunday arrived, my last day before returning home via San Francisco. Would Garbo 'drop in', and would I be included in the spontaneous party? Yes, she *had* telephoned, but she didn't want to meet me. She usually hid from English people, and she said, 'He talks to newspapers.' Crushed with defeat and dejection, I tried to telephone a mutual friend; if it was not permitted to pass the evening talking to Garbo, then it could be spent talking *about* her. The friend was out. The call was repeated all the afternoon. So I slept. I woke. Still no reply from the mutual; and, for want of anything better to do, I took a long hot bath. I dressed myself, choosing to wear, for the first time, the pristine white kid coat, the sharkskin shorts, and new white shoes and socks.

Then I looked out of the window. In the garden below my host and hostess were gossiping. With them was a visitor. Garbo was sitting cross-legged on a white garden seat, smoking a cigarette held high in two definite fingers. I could not hear their conversation, but the Gouldings seemed animated, and Garbo wore a sort of Olympian smile with quizzically raised eyebrows and lowered lids.

Garbo, too, was all in white, wearing a thick woollen sweater, shorts, and half an eggshell on her back-scraped hair. Her waxen complexion and her thighs were sunburnt to a rich biscuit colour.

If a unicorn had suddenly appeared in the late afternoon light of this ugly, ordinary garden, I could have been neither more surprised nor more amazed by the beauty of this exotic creature.

I was overcome by stagefright when the introduction was made, but finding myself confronted by such an understanding smile, something so sympathetic and encouragingly helpful, I was able to continue to breathe. A deep, familiar voice cooed at me, and bade me sit by her on a leather pouf.

The situation became even more piquant when the voice showered me with compliments, 'But you're so yorng? How do you stay so yorng? Are you like one of those people that never grow up? I know a man who is fifty who still looks so yorng; and you're so white. If only I could draw you like that.' I held on to her hands.

The voice continued, 'You're so beautiful.' 'But *you're* so beautiful,' was my lame reply. 'No, you should never return a compliment.' This was a moment of danger. But after a flicker of displeasure passed across those brows, my solecism was forgiven. It was accepted – while a huge tumbler of orange juice and champagne was proferred by Marjorie. It tasted like nectar.

Even if Garbo would not allow me to give vent to eulogies I could now drink in every detail of her beauty. This marvellous gay creature had the sadness of Deburau, the clown – a resemblance accentuated by her pale face, her deep-set darkened eyelids and skull cap. There was an incredible sensitivity about the modelling of the nose, as if she were able to savour exquisite perfumes too subtle for other human beings to enjoy. Her lips, bereft of lipstick, were like polished shells, and when she gave her big generous smile, her teeth showed square and shining.

Conversation then continued without any of the polite preliminaries of strangers. We talked nonsense as if we had known one another forever. 'In short, these are the nicest Indian shoes I have ever seen in my life, and I have not seen many! But are we dressmakers that we talk of clothes?'

The Gouldings must have been surprised to find that, from now on, they hardly existed in the presence of their guests. Yet they were not resentful. And although I could never be grateful enough to them for bringing about this meeting, how could they now be paid more than desultory deference?

Garbo told us about her coloured maid, whose husband had cold feet at night. The maid undresses in the dark. She described a woman who had an oversize Adam's apple, and how some men have such big 'Ardumms arppless' that they go up and down when they swallow. 'Oh, it's pathetic; how can you laugh at human beings?'

We all moved to the bar for more nectar. On the way Garbo and I crab-walked with arms round each other's waists, and much friendly hand squeezing. She pervaded a scent of new-mown hay, and of freshly-washed children. 'Show Greta your hands,' Marjorie piped. My hands were carefully scrutinized. Garbo said hers were kitchenette hands and laughed. 'I play the most sophisticated women without a manicure.'

We all drank a great deal of this cold, refreshing, very intoxicating drink. Garbo was inspired to hop about the room gesticulating and giving spontaneous impersonations of grandiose actresses, quoting snatches of poetry or prose that came into her head.

A huge vase of yellow roses freshly sprayed with water had been placed on the bar. 'Oh, who put the dew on them?' Garbo picked a rose and kissed it, fingered it with an infinite variety of caresses and raised it above her head.

As she looked up at it, she intoned, 'A rose that lives and dies and never again returns.' Suddenly with wild eyes and a deep look of astonishment she asked, in her hushed 'mystery' voice. 'How is one to know?' She supplied the answer, '*Je ne sais pas*', then burst into laughter apologizing for her accent. 'Oh, my poor few words that I know of French!' Then like a celestial parrot she repeated, 'For thee and thine' (pronounced with a thick Scandinavian 'Th').

We were bidden by Marjorie to partake of the collation appetizingly laid out in the enforced absence of the servants. 'Och! Lobster Americaine!' The spontaneous picnic was applauded. The parrot kept repeating the words 'Lobster Americaine' and made them sound extremely comic. She helped me to lettuce. 'I'm no *hausfrau*,' she said, but did an imitation of a dainty lady with little finger perched in air; this dainty lady then started to embroider a table napkin, before becoming extremely interested in the sex of two cold chickens.

We all ate enormously. Talking of the food of different countries it became apparent that Garbo has a highly sensitized palate, with an uncanny instinct for the most sophisticated tastes.

Suddenly something untoward has happened. The air is electric. Eddie is severely reprimanded. It seems he has said something insensitive, and unsuitable. Garbo has a rooted dislike of 'loose language' – slang such as 'honey' or 'swell' – and cannot understand educated people wanting to talk like the electrician and the 'prop' man. Worst of all to her are schoolboy jokes, particularly those to do with the posterior portions of the anatomy. Eddie has idiotically proclaimed that if Garbo didn't do his bidding as director he'd turn her upside down and give her a smacking where she sits upon. Fortunately this tiff quickly passed off and Garbo was asked if she would like to go upstairs and see my photographs of Ashcombe where I wished she would come and live for ever. The parrot replied, 'Absolutely Adolphe.'

'Are you happy?' she asked.

'Yes.'

'It's so easy to say Yes.'

'And you?'

She sighed. 'Tomorrow I got to work with a lot of people who are dead. It's so sad. I'm an onlooker. I've passed being active in life. It's not a question of time and age – but it's just what you are yourself. One doesn't do the things one doesn't want to do.'

Twilight had passed; the curtain breezed in by the window. 'Is that a ghost? Ssh!' We ran downstairs and the hilarity continued. We all danced to the 'rardio'. Garbo in imitation of Douglas Fairbanks swung from the cross beam and Spanish rafters. Marjorie, as light as thistledown, did a ballroom dance. Then in turn we did improvisations to Strauss waltzes, Rachmaninoff, *The Lost Chord* and *Wunderbar*. Garbo, as a policeman, arrested me for some importunity. The lights were turned out and our bacchanalia became wilder in the firelight.

Suddenly the dream was over. It was time for Garbo to leave. It was very late, daylight had reappeared, and she had to be at the studio in a few hours. She was at the wheel in a rather shabby, big motor car. We put our hands through the windows. I was due to leave California, but if she would see me again, I would stay. 'Can't I come and eat spinach with you tomorrow – no, today – at the studio at the lunch interval?' 'No.' Surely this cannot be the end? Shall we never meet again? Will we be able to communicate in some way? In desperation I seized hold of a feather duster with a long handle, a curious object that was lying by her side. 'Can I keep this as a memento?'

'No.'

'Then this is Goodbye?'

'Yes, I'm afraid so. *C'est la vie!*'

The Gouldings were rather too baffled by the evening to talk about it. I could hardly believe what had happened. The only concrete proof was the yellow rose which she had kissed, and which I now took up the turret stairs to keep pressed between the pages of my diary.

5

New Friends Abroad
1933–6

In Paris C.B. made friends such as Pavel Tchelitchev, Picasso, Jean Cocteau, Marie-Louise Bousquet, Christian Bérard, Gertrude Stein and Alice B. Toklas, some of whom influenced his work and thought. In 1934 he went to Madrid with Tchelitchev. He stayed in Austria with Raimund and Alice (Astor) von Hofmannsthal. He went on a motor tour of Hungary and Dalmatia with David Herbert. C.B.'s first ballet, The First Shoot, *a collaboration with Frederick Ashton and William Walton, was included in Cochran's 1936 revue* Follow the Sun. *Then came the ballet* Apparitions, *with Ashton, for the Sadlers Wells Ballet and* Le Pavillon, *with Lichine, for de Basil's Ballet Russe.*

C.B.'s sister Nancy married Hugh Smiley, his sister Baba married Alec Hambro. His brother Reggie was killed by falling beneath an underground train. His father died.

Rome: 1933

It was while staying with Gerald Berners in his house overlooking the Forum that I saw the apricot light, clear skies and parasol pines of Rome for the first time. Rome does not take strangers to its bosom, and the malice of society in the eternal city was a bit alarming, but painting expeditions, the panoply surrounding the church, Firbankian intrigues, and the eccentrics of the English Tea Room were all part of the general enjoyment. En route for home there was a three-week stop-off in Paris. This coincided with Edward James's controversial new season of ballet, with Kurt Weill writing music for *The Seven Deadly Sins* and Lotte Lenya rasping it out: also Pavlik Tchelitchev, the Russian painter designing transparent scenery for *Errante*.

Tchelitchev at first intimidated me (he could be devastating in his disapproval) but soon cast an almost hypnotic influence over me. Under his spell my photographs became 'neo-romantic'.

One particular evening he exercised himself on a variety of sacred and profane subjects. He started with colour. Grey: certain greys were gritty and dry to him. Mantegna's colours are so dry he feels they pop and crack, giving the spectator the feeling of being able to break off with equal ease the drapery, the mountains, or Christ's feet and legs.

With his histrionic brilliance Pavlik makes even the simplest anecdote a marvel. He whispers and then shouts; he becomes alternately a bull or a child.

Pavlik rehashed an argument with Virgil Thomson about music. V.T. said the only noise that frightened people today was a siren. Pavlik objected. 'Some sensitive people are frightened by the flutter of a falling piece of paper, the whisper of a breeze through a window.'

He tells how most people (if no one is around) will touch the private parts of statues in the museum; and in consequence these parts have continually to be washed! He embroiders on this assertion, relating an encounter with Etienne de Beaumont among the statues – all the more exciting an adventure because nothing happens. He conjured up a bad picture in some remote museum, painting it with a few deft verbal strokes that endow it with imaginative immortality.

Pavlik's imitation of Kshessinskaya in her heyday as ballerina and Czar's darling was accompanied by many twirls and arm flourishes. The subject transports him: he takes to his feet and executes several elaborate arabesques. The impression is that of a bluebottle – darting, resting, then off again on its tormenting flight. And this bluebottle was dressed as follows (Pavlik evoked the costume with gestures): a tutu made of thousands of yards of the most expensive pink silk tulle; over this, black lace; then a bitter-almond-green satin corsage, with a huge pink rose at the breast; neck and chest a dazzle of diamonds, ears heavy with enormous cabochons, elaborately coiffed head sprouting black and white aigrets. It was a performance of sublime ridiculousness. But so intense and successful was his determination to conjure up this phenomenon that the monk-like Slav transcended his outward appearance and, in fact, *became* this pampered esoteric plaything of a forgotten age.

It was during this visit, despite the danger of being considered disloyal, that I first became a devoted admirer of Pavlik's great rival Christian Bérard. From the moment we met, Bébé gave me his open hand. When George Huene took me to see Jean Cocteau smoking opium I considered that adult life could reach no higher.

Paris

Paris artists and writers seem to have infinite leisure so that one never has the impression of interrupting the tenor of their day or night. Colette had covered reams of blue stationery with enormous calligraphic scrolls with the choice of a dozen fountain pens at her elbow, when she carefully cleared away her tray to give full attention to her visitor. Likewise Gide was content to ignore the ringing of the doorbell while he allowed me to spend a morning in his company.

When first I met Picasso, he greeted me in his quiet dignified manner, with a twinkle of liquid amusement in his brilliant eyes. It somewhat surprised me to see him wearing the most conventional and elegant of blue suits, with a white shirt. On the first sight his surroundings struck me as being like that of a typical doctor's waiting-room. The current fashion of stripped panelling, whitened woods and vague baroqueries was so universal that these plain walls and bold mahogany furniture came as a disappointment. But by degrees I acquired a new vision and noticed that every piece of furniture was of eclectic simplicity. Noticing my growing enthusiasm he demonstrated the ingenious craftsmanship of the various pieces; how a low stool turned into a pair of steps, or a desk possessed hidden levers, drawers and lids, and that the curious objects on tables and chimneypiece had been made from matchboxes, by piecing together pieces of menus, lottery tickets and playing cards, or part of a leather bicycle seat.

Surely it was a privilege to be given a secret glimpse of his seldom-used salon? Shutters were thrown wide to reveal a white panelled room stacked with vast portraits of his wife, some like Ingres, others Cubistic. The large armchairs were covered in white linen. Suddenly Picasso indulged in a piece of legerde-main as he danced towards one of the chairs and in a bold gesture ripped off its cover to disclose a shining conch-shell of orange. One by one he threw off other covers to reveal chairs upholstered in brilliant satins that somehow reminded me of those sugared cushion-sweets of one's childhood. With a flick of his arm he conjured up a hot-yellow conch: then another butcher blue. Yet another crimson, and now an emerald green, Picasso's eyes flashed with excited enjoyment as each new colour appeared. These were the real colours of Spain, bold, unconforming and startling. It gave me an indication of a whole taste of which I had never before been conscious.

Summer 1935

Tilly Losch asked me to help her with her costume for the Oriental Ball. It soon became my work of the morning. Endless telephoning. What is the address of the woman who is so good at make-up? Daisy would know but is out. Iya knows it. Iya is away. Boris would know, or Natasha, or Nabokoff.

We then went in search, and at last found, near the Musée Grévin, that curious little circus shop called Poupineau. Here we revelled in the glories of spangle and tinsel.

Tilly has a smouldering, Slavic face. In costume as an *ouled naïl*, her appearance becomes barbarically *fatale*. Unfortunately she is completely helpless – either lazy and spoilt or else clever at getting things done for her. After creating her costume the whole morning I said, 'Now you are complete. All you have to do for the Ball is glue a sequin between your brows.' Tilly whimpered, 'But how can I do that? Won't you come to the hotel and bring some glue?'

Lunch *chez* Noailles was not at all what I had expected. I imagined that the two children, Marie-Laure and myself would sit rather embarrassedly discussing generalities and veering towards our mutual object of affection. But no, it proved to be a lunch-party *manqué*, with an empty place for the hostess. Just before lunch, Marie-Laure received news that René Crevel had attempted suicide and she rushed off to his bedside in the hospital.

All day long the telephone buzzed. Harassed conversation alternated between the dying man and tomorrow's costume ball.

'*C'est effroyable! O, ma robe, c'est une merveille! Pauvre petit garçon. O, ma robe!*' There was a scene at Karinska's emporium in the afternoon, with everyone turning up for a minute to try on a turban and discuss the unhappy news.

Later in the evening, in Bébé's cluttered room at the First Hotel everyone talked of René. Tony Gandarillas arrived from the hospital, panting for a palliative. This *would* happen just as he came to Paris for a few days' holiday. 'It is too much. I've been through this too many times before. All my friends commit suicide.'

Later, at Marie-Blanche de Polignac's, we heard that the attempted suicide had succeeded: after dying all day long, René eventually expired.

In spite of the tragedy, the evening turned out to be just the sort I like best. The two Polignacs, Bébé, Boris Kochno [Diaghilev's former secretary] and I sat down to a rare dinner. There was lamb cooked in maize, so delicious that I could not believe such things existed. The sauces were unbelievable, the atmosphere of the house equally sympathetic. Bébé's murals, influenced by Raphael, in the dining-room are his best things. We looked at the lovely, loved collection of Madame Lanvin [mother of Comtesse Jean de Polignac] – Renoirs, Degas, Stephens and ravishing small Boldinis. We talked of the solid charm of English country houses, browsed through snapshot albums, admired the pretty objects throughout the house.

The others went off to a party at the British Embassy, and for the rest of the evening I was with Bébé. We stopped at Maxim's, talked of Marie-Laure, were charmingly interrupted by Figgi Ralli and Igor Markevitch. Then, back to the First Hotel until four o'clock in the morning. Bébé smoked and talked with the avidness of a haunted creature, desperate to rid himself of some devil. 'You do like me, Cecil, don't you?' My reply was such a relief that it went through him like an electric shock. 'That's over. Good! Now we continue.'

Bébé's sensitivity and intensity are beyond compare. He talked inspiredly of his hobbies of collecting – *objets d'art*, terra cottas, rare books – and of reading the cheapest American magazines, devouring the detailed lives of movie stars. He praised Eduard Bourdet for being such a gentle and inspiring collaborator in the theatre and we both eulogized the photographs of Cartier Bresson. Bébé also talked of Boris, while Boris slept. It seems that Boris, about to organize a new ballet season, hadn't turned up for an important date with Markevitch and Dali. Bébé loves Boris, but minds very much that Boris is disorderly and unpunctual, throwing away so many of his important chances.

I haven't known Bébé for long, but I already understand him. I love him for the rocklike character that fundamentally, and in spite of all his superficial nonsense, he really is.

This afternoon I went to see Gertrude Stein in her new apartment on the Rue Christine.

Oddly, I had never imagined Miss Stein's apartment would be so impressive, though there was no reason to believe otherwise: whenever we met, I'd always been particularly struck with her sense and taste. Here now was the expression of a *goût impeccable*. Tall ceilings, panelled walls and high windows delighted the eye. Each piece of furniture seemed solid and beautiful in design. There was no *chichi* or vulgarity anywhere. The Misses Stein and Toklas live like Biblical royalty: simply, yet in complete luxury.

A well-scrubbed, apple-cheeked maid opened the door. Miss Toklas was sewing in her bedroom. She did not move, determined to spend the afternoon there. This plan succeeded admirably, except when explanations were necessary to a workman who had come to mend a latch.

Miss Stein took me on a tour of inspection. I noticed her low-heeled brown shoes, as highly polished as the furniture in the various rooms. 'This,' she gestured, 'is where we have some of our pictures.' Over the fireplace was an enormous portrait of a woman by Cézanne. Hung in front of a huge looking-glass was a full-length Picasso nude; while his portrait of Gertrude Stein occupied the space above a beautiful brown and gold cabinet, its colours reflecting those of the painting.

A few unique objects were displayed: a portrait of Voltaire done with pin-pricks, a china cherub fallen asleep with his head resting on a skull. Cut azaleas were in bowls; bluebells sprouted from earthenware vases. The copybooks in which Miss Stein writes all her works had been placed in orderly readiness. Fuss, bother and discomfort seemed eliminated from an apartment whose great strength resides in its uniformity.

The curtains were made of glazed white linen with a waxy, dotted-leaf motif. Ubiquitous brown carpets and brown wood furniture with brass ornamentation created a bold background for the petit-point chairs, embroidered by Miss Toklas from designs Picasso had drawn on to the canvas.

Juan Gris is another of Stein's masters. When she lives with pictures that continue to be good, then she knows they are great. 'There's no doubt about it. There are no ifs and ands. If I live with a man I know so. There's no *parti pris*. It's just definite, and Juan is great.'

Gertrude held on to Pepé, the dog, standing against the blue and white wallpaper depicting pigeons on the grass, alas.

I photographed also Toklas at her sewing. Determined not to talk this afternoon she nodded by way of understanding and said, 'Interior'.

August

After a night journey to Salzburg, came the excitement of arriving at Schloss Kammer, on the edge of Lake Kammer. In this somewhat uncanny, mountainous landscape, an enormous quantity of curious people have gathered to create a world of their own under the aegis of Alice von Hofmannsthal and Eleanor Mendelssohn, who with their families share the castle.

Kammer has a strong personality – ruthless, sometimes morbid. However much Alice may redecorate the rooms or alter the construction of house and gardens, the atmosphere remains unchanged. Sometimes a shadow falls over the gayest parties. Guests find themselves miserable and never return. Others, like myself, are stimulated for a while. But however much one has enjoyed a visit, it is always as though a cloud has lifted when one leaves.

This summer the castle became a sort of kindergarten for extraordinary grown-ups; long, hilarious discussions; incongruous groups for lunch, for tea, for swimming, for sightseeing. We rode and went shooting in the mountains. At night on the lake, we ate gay dinner on rafts by torchlight, with music provided from adjoining barques.

Apart from the superficial gaiety, jealous intrigue and romantic complications flourished. Scarcely a day but provides a dozen situations for a play, or material for a novel. Lawyers create dramatic scenes to keep X or Y from buying up part of the castle. Complete strangers arrive to stay, and only after two or three days does Eleanor get around to asking their names. Guests arrive in hoards to find neither host nor hostess. The wife of a composer, upon being expelled from the castle, flounced out, rudely exhibiting her behind.

Raimund, a power-station of energy, laughingly relates that Alice must cope with three vans of furniture just arrived from America. The shipment has already crossed the Atlantic three times. One of the tables, intended for her London house, didn't fit; and so it was sent back to Rhinebeck, but there they decided it could go well in Schloss Kammer. Now Alice is being kind to the customs appraisers, shaking hands and saying, '*Guten Tag*', and seeing that they are forthwith made drunk on the local wine.

'Alice has a new wheeze,' Raimund confides. 'It is telephone shopping. The other day, while several people were gathered in her bedroom, she took up the telephone and acquired more furniture, including some painted peasant tables and cupboards, circa 1790. "Hullo," says Alice, "have you something with birds painted on it?" A pause, while the man in the antique shop hunts around. Then he comes back and says, "No, but we have a pretty chest with deer on the drawers." '

Margot Oxford motored over to lunch today. She talked about 'her queen', her Alexandra. Alexandra was so *beautiful*, so interested in people and not a bit stuck up. When it was time for Margot to settle down to the business of an autobiography, she sent a letter to 'her Alexandra' asking for permission to write about their friendship. In reply came a telegram saying, 'Of course, any damn thing you like. Love A.'

Margot's mind is as alive and alert as that of Ivan Moffat, the youngest guest at the Schloss. But she boasts the advantage that only older persons have – experience. And she can say, as only more mature people do, exactly what is on her mind. Margot will never do anything she doesn't wish; her mind cannot be exhausted by complicated half-truths. On leaving, she turned to her host with a candid, 'It's been most enjoyable. Thank you, sweet Raimund. Please ask me a little more often.' The diminutive shaved off any rudeness, while the tragedy of age and the cleverness remained.

Paris: Spring 1936

Jean [Cocteau] lives at the Castille, which is visible from my hotel room. As a result of a telephone call, we waved towels and handkerchiefs at one another from our balconies.

After this semaphore, he became ill. For several days he could not sleep, eat or smoke opium. His throat was completely constricted. At last someone puffed opium smoke into his mouth; and like a galvanized corpse he staggered from his bed, and gave a virtuoso performance that was full of ideas, wit and poetry.

Looking like cheese, Jean came out to the ruins of the Paris Exhibition to be photographed. It was very cold. His nose turned purple, making the rest of the face seem even more grey, green and yellow. But the low temperature did not chill his volubility. Indeed, I could hardly persuade him to stop talking long enough for exposures to be made.

Like all ruins, this discarded playground is strange and very romantic.

Jean is having a hard time: his recently completed play was rejected by Jouvet and Bourdet. Jean feels all France to be against him, rails that he alone has not succumbed to the perils of cheap success and vulgarity.

As for the play, it is said to be unlike anything else he has written. No metaphysical characters, just five members of an ordinary family. It is only their wickedness, viciousness and meanness that make them appear extraordinary. Marcel [Khill], to whom Jean read the play, was so horrified that his face swelled and broke out in spots. Glenway Westcott heard it the next night. He told me the audience would roll in the aisles; but he thought the play eminently actable and translatable into German and English – a thoroughly well-constructed piece of work in the Bernstein manner.

I should like to make a catalogue of Jean's qualities and characteristics.

Where to begin? His physical appearance: a fakir-thin body is held up by legs as thin as a sparrow's; yet curiously, he has flat feet. His hands seem so brittle you are afraid a sharp blow may crack them off. The fingers taper, can bend backwards. The nails are discoloured and slightly dirty (a sign of the dope addict's *laisser-aller*). As with most artists, the eyes communicate their owner's deepest secrets. As silent as Jean's mouth is talkative, the dilated pupils of his bulging fishy eyes, anguished and tortured, aghast and helpless, seem to be looking into another existence.

Charm, childish exuberance and longing to please are Jean's greatest personality assets. He is completely unselfconscious during conversation, chuckling with an infectious gaiety. Sometimes he will nervously thump his listener's chest and shoulders as though to assure himself of riveted attention.

Famous are Jean's annihilating descriptions of people with whom he is displeased. 'When that ballerina misses a step,' he exlaims acidly, 'she creates the same embarrassing effect on her audience as an old woman who bends down to pick up something and lets off a loud report.'

Jean's surroundings are a typical reflection of his personality. There is a tingling aliveness about his room. Even the bad photograph of Daisy Fellowes is now justified, for he has cut it to make her look like a bird and has stuck real feathers on her. Black drawing boards are covered with chalk scribblings – his engagements, random drawings or ideas. There are plaster heads decorated with wax tears.

In spite of the darkness of Jean's room, it has comfort and great organization. A high desk serves for drawing; a bedside table holds equipment for smoking. Neat files of letters and photographs in portfolios permit him to find things quickly. His india rubber is never lost. In evidence are the drawings, always displaying an easy flow of line and imagination. Two sailors playing games with one another suggest the celestial regions to which lust can be elevated. (A more earthy illustration is provided by the indecent postcards strewn about.)

If a stranger looks at the objects in the room, he will perhaps guess Jean's unhappy side – the great disasters, the personal tragedy of being abandoned by lovers. There is a lurking sentimentality in the crimson wools, a death-like aura about the life masks of his head and hands, a secretly depressing claustrophobia in this atmosphere redolent of the seminal smell of opium.

But Jean himself is unmistakably alive, frenziedly so. No one can doubt his supreme intelligence, wit and authority. When the master expresses himself, it is always a very special performance, matinee or evening. Nor is he showing off; rather, he merely discourses with his disciples.

It is interesting when an artist has sufficient strength of personality to be *outré*, yet accepted by the most conservative elements of society.

My former disappointment and bitterness at not having worked for Cochran had long since been forgotten; now once more he approached me: this time, the offer to decorate a ballet – which Osbert [Sitwell] had written upon a sheet of Renishaw Hall writing paper – was definite. The subject of the work involved the love complications at an Edwardian pheasant shoot. Willie Walton had composed the perversely lyrical music – and this was to be the first of many collaborations with Frederick Ashton.

Over lunch in a Soho restaurant Fred [Ashton] and I discussed the proposed sets and the costumes, and used the menu for pencilled suggestions. More menus were called for. Before the hors d'œuvre had been cleared, Fred remarked somewhat wryly, 'You have finished your work – it has taken twenty minutes. I still have all mine to do.' His face then crinkled into that wonderfully disarming laugh.

A few weeks later, the stage curtains parted to reveal my first living picture in the theatre. It was a moment of exaltation for which the long wait had been well worth while.

6

Royal Romance
1935–6

C.B. drew and photographed Mrs Simpson, and paid two visits to her at Château Candé, during the second of which he pre-photographed her wedding to the Duke of Windsor.

Autumn 1935

Though nothing about Mrs Simpson appears in the English papers, her name seems never to be off people's lips. For those who enjoy gossip she is a particular treat. The sound of her name implies secrecy, royalty, and being in the know. As a topic she has become a mania, so much so that her name is banned in many houses to allow breathing space for other topics.

Five years ago I met Mrs Simpson in a box with some Americans at the Three Arts Club Ball. Present were Thelma Furness, her sister, Mrs Gloria Vanderbilt, and a lot of other people. Mrs Simpson was introduced as being a vague relation to me by marriage: her husband, Ernest Simpson, being the brother of Mrs Kerr Smiley [aunt of my brother-in-law Hugh]. Mrs Simpson seemed somewhat brawny and raw-boned in her sapphire-blue velvet. Her voice had a high nasal twang.

About a year ago, I had an opportunity to renew acquaintance with Mrs Simpson. I liked her immensely. I found her bright and witty, improved in looks and chic.

Today she is sought after as the probable wife of the King. Even the old Edwardians receive her, if she happens to be free to accept their invitations. American newspapers have already announced the engagement, and in the highest court circles there is great consternation. It is said that Queen Mary weeps continuously.

I am taking bets that the marriage will not happen this year.

Now I was to photograph her. Mrs Simpson was punctual, arriving at my studio rather shyly (although she has acquired considerable assurance since the recent developments).

She had scarcely arrived when the telephone rang for her. It seems that incessant callers make demands upon her all the time. 'Will you lunch?' 'May I come in for a cocktail?' To accept all this lionizing required careful arranging, which she manages well. She has learned how to keep people at a distance: 'Wait till I get home and look at my book.' 'My secretary will give you a ring in the morning.' Her voice seemed quieter.

Our photographic sitting was not particularly eventful, except that I found it difficult to avoid making remarks which might be misconstrued. For instance, as background I suggested scrolls of ermine pinned on a white cloth. She immediately responded with, 'Don't do anything connected with the Coronation for me. I want none of that now.' And again, when I asked her to lower her chin 'as though bowing', the unfortunate simile caused her to look sharply at me.

Whatever fantastic changes have taken place in Mrs Simpson's life, she has obviously suffered. There is a sad look to be seen in her eyes. The camera was not blind to this. We worked well together for a long time, and made a date so that I could do some drawings.

Two afternoons later, I went to her house in Regent's Park, bringing my sketching paraphernalia and the proofs of the recent photographs. There was a policeman at the end of the road; but then, there generally is in most London streets. The house has been rented furnished, but has a few temporary additions by Syrie Maugham, and Mrs Spry contributes her arrangements of expensive flowers mixed with bark and local weeds. This day Mrs Simpson looked immaculate, soignée and fresh as a young girl. Her skin was as bright and smooth as the inside of a shell, her hair so sleek she might have been Chinese.

The afternoon was successful, in spite of the fact that none of my sketches quite came off. Mrs Simpson proved an exceptionally difficult woman to draw. I found nothing facile to catch hold of and soon discovered that even the slightest impression was devilishly difficult. Still, we had a lot of fun, discussing London and various personalities we knew in common.

She spoke amusingly, in staccato sentences punctuated by explosive bursts of laughter that lit up her face with great gaiety and made her eyebrows look attractively surprised.

I worked while she talked. Mrs Simpson glanced about the pale white and olive green drawing-room. 'I would do more with this place if I were staying here longer. But I've only got it for such a short time more.'

Suddenly I asked, 'Where will you go for the Coronation? A flat again?'

'A flat is much easier to run,' she considered. 'This is so far away. I'd like Claridge's, but there is the disadvantage of public exits.'

I said, 'But in any case, wherever you are, I should think there'll be crowds of Americans waiting outside for a look-see. That is, if I know anything from my American papers.' Then I hazarded, 'Do you realize how much people talk about you? Do you know that as a topic I have banned you?'

'Yes. Yes.'

From that moment onwards, there was practically nothing we did not discuss. She said, 'After this, I think I must call you Cecil. And I don't want you to call me by that name of Mrs Simpson, which the American yellow press has made me loathe.'

Yes, her private life had been taken away from her. People stared and hung about all the time. The King minded greatly for her sake. And what absolute nonsense all this was about marriage. How could English people be so silly? They hadn't gossiped before the American newspapers got hold of it. There was no question of marriage.

I said, 'I've made bets against it. But maybe you'll ruin me.'

She replied, 'No. I expect I'll be very poor and you'll clean up.'

We then discussed the possibility of my photographing the King. Wallis said, 'You mustn't put any background in, he'd hate it.' At which the door opened and the butler announced, 'His Majesty.'

Wallis gave a caw of surprise. 'Oh sirrr,' she drawled, 'we were just talking about you. Oh, you've got what the *Daily Express* calls your coif today, sirr.'

The King, in bright spirits and not nervous at all, laughed and examined my photographic proofs laid out on the sofa. Quickly he gave his definite opinion as to which were good and which were not.

Jokes and laughter ensued. 'I like this,' the King commented; 'that one, too. In fact, all these are good. I want the lot.'

'Oh, sir, wouldn't that be too much of a Wallis collection?'

'Ha, ha!' And we all laughed.

'No, I don't think Cecil likes this one, sir. It's hard, like granite.'

His Majesty repeated several times, 'Funny kind of granite.'

'Now sir, won't you sit down and have a drink? Let Cecil do a quick drawing of your profile.'

In a trice the King, holding a whisky and soda, was sitting *en profil* and talking of the events of the day as reported in the *Evening News* – the Spanish revolution, unemployment in South Wales, Mr Ernest Brown's incessant quotations from the Bible.

The King has an enormous store of general knowledge. He never forgets names, remembers statistics. He knows, too, the average man's tastes and inclinations, is himself a kind of average man *par excellence*. He will be a very popular King, as one instinctively respects him.

Quips and sallies were rather broad. The King observed that Ataturk must have taken his title as President of Turkey from the American 'Attaboy'. But, however trite his humour, he betrayed no interest in gossip or personalities.

We were shown the snapshots of the Nahlin cruise along the Dalmatian coast, with both the King and Wallis wearing shorts. 'That's sweet, isn't it? That's

Corcula or however you pronounce it. And that's when we came ashore in Turkey. We weren't announced, but they all came down to greet us. Do you remember it? It was swell.'

Into this atmosphere came Wallis's aunt, lately arrived in England. She added to the general wisecracking, relating the story of her boat trip (during which, as Wallis had earlier told me, she listened to people talking about the pros and cons of the King's possible marriage to her niece).

A silver tray was brought in. On it were eight different varieties of hot hors d'œuvre, also green grapes stuffed with cream cheese. The King talked very fast, darted around the room, rang bells, busily untied parcels with red, slightly horny hands that looked surprisingly like a mechanic's. He had a bad cold and wore a heavy silk jersey. Wallis's eyes sparkled; her brows lifted in mock-pain; her mouth turned down at the corners as she laughed. The aunt sat back quipping.

At last the King (like a child whose before-dinner play hour had come to an end) was told that we must all go. Wallis, who had only a few minutes to dress for Emerald Cunard's dinner, was already beginning to unbutton her dress.

New York: Winter

I watched and listened to old Mrs Vanderbilt, the Queen of New York. Towards the end of lunch she told me how upset she was about the King's abdication. First, she produced a small bag. Then, from inside, she whisked the wherewithal to make her nose clown-white. Ridiculously, she began covering her entire face with ugly blobs of powder. The chin received another heavy patch. During the story-telling, by dint of gradual smoothing away, a natural face appeared from under its heavy coating. 'Oh, I can't tell you how I have suffered! I can't tell you what the family means to me. I was the first person to be received by the late King after his illness. I was summoned to tea with Their Majesties and we talked and talked and talked. I kept waiting to be dismissed. But no, we talked until I began to get a little faint. My head drooped; I said, "Ma'am, am I not keeping you? Must I not go?" And the Queen said, "Oh no, if you *have* to go that is different, but if you can, please stay." And do you know, I had arrived at the Palace at five o'clock and by the time I left it was – six o'clock. Oh, they've been so wonderful to me. I could lay down my life for that family.'

Spring 1937

I meant to take the train to Touraine, thus offering myself the enjoyment of reading *Le dernier des Villavides*. But the day proved too beautiful, with spring far advanced. I motored instead, feeling more than compensated by a countryside blossoming with lilac, fruit trees and chestnut. I also saw Chartres for the first time; and the Palace at Blois and a few châteaux along the Loire.

Château Candé is situated on high, commanding a view of miles of green country. Tall poplars and willows grow in platoons. The château itself, begun in the sixteenth century, has seen many subsequent additions in the intervening years. It is feudal and rather ugly, with high towers, pointed turrets and heavily embellished Gothic doorways. But the house is run with a modern luxurious comfort that would make a Long Island millionaire envious.

I arrived to find Wallis looking rested after her long incarceration here. Mr and Mrs Herman Rogers and Mme Bedaux joined us. All were thirsting for news of the outside world. To the accompaniment of cocktails, chatter was of people and clothes and the 'Buick of which you've read so much'. Then it was late, and time to change.

My rooms were Empire, decorated in striped satin. From the bathroom, with its sunken bath, came clouds of red carnation scent.

A footman waited to conduct me to the underground vault where dinner was to be served. Hams and salami sausages hung from hooks in the ceiling. In dim candlelight we were royally waited on by a solicitous butler (who really overdid his act) and three footmen. The chef used to be with the Duke of Alba, who must have regretted letting him go. There was a superb variety of wines and everyone's spirits rose.

The women had dressed to the nines, all in reds. Wallis sported a new jewel in the form of two huge quills, one set with diamonds, the other with rubies. Her dress showed to advantage an incredibly narrow figure, narrower since the abdication.

The atmosphere was one of suppressed excitement. Rogers said that though the worst was over, the strain on Wallis became greater as the wedding day approached. Her divorce goes through this week; and after the Coronation, they will undoubtedly be married without further delay. Still, no mention could be made of the date or details.

After dinner we went across a courtyard to a games pavilion. Billiards ensued, then were abandoned for conversation. At midnight the Rogers said goodnight, leaving Wallis and me to talk in full earnest until nearly dawn.

I was struck by the clarity and vitality of her mind. When at last I went to bed, I realized that she not only had individuality and personality, but was a very strong force as well. She may have limitations, she may be politically ignorant and aesthetically untutored; but she knows a great deal about life.

Some people maintain that Wallis obviously possesses little insight into British character and customs. Certainly I got the impression that she has been taken as much by surprise by recent events as anyone else. Though her divorce proceedings had already begun, I don't believe she had any clear intentions of marriage. If the King ever said to her, 'What about your wearing that little crown?' she more than likely laughed and replied, 'Let's talk about it after your Coronation.'

Of the abdication, she told me she had known less than anybody. It had been impossible to talk freely with the ex-King on the telephone, as the wires were constantly tapped. But two things, she confided, had not been generally known. One was that the ex-King had told Mr Baldwin he would be willing to let the matter of his marriage hang fire, to be discussed again six months after his Coronation. Secondly, during the entire period of these discussions, Mr Baldwin held in his possession papers which had been signed by Wallis, to the effect that she was willing to stop divorce proceedings against her husband.

It wasn't just tactfulness, I am sure, that prevented Wallis from airing any grievance she might have against Mr Baldwin or the so-called friends who 'welshed' on her when the situation altered. She said, 'It has only shown me *who* among my friends *are* my friends.' She is bitter towards no one.

As for her future, she seems determined that she and the Duke will 'work things out'. Obviously she has great admiration for his character and his vitality; she loves him though I feel she is not *in* love with him. In any case, she has a great responsibility in looking after someone who is temperamentally polar to her but yet relies entirely upon her.

Our conversation in the abstract was most interesting. I became sleepy and soft from time to time, perhaps saying things without careful consideration. Thereupon, Wallis, quick as a flash, would contradict or challenge me, observing, 'No, I don't agree with you. I've always found that in life people may be given this but they do that.'

She twisted and twirled her rugged hands. She laughed a square laugh, protruded her lower lip. Her eyes were excessively bright, slightly froglike, also wistful.

Candidly, she concluded that she had always been much alone in her life. Perhaps this isolation helped her now. She confessed that it had been difficult for her not to give way and hang herself on one of the many pairs of antlers in the room in which we sat. But her control surprised her. She was, she said, very like a man in many ways; she has few woman friends, and Katherine Rogers, the most intimate among them, has likewise, I think, a man's mentality. Yes, both the Rogers had been wonderful friends and had borne the brunt of her hysterics; but a great deal of her time had none the less been spent by herself in her bedroom.

The next morning, Sunday, was given over to preparations for the photography. A manicurist and hairdresser arrived from Paris. Her hair was set in a new way, with waves flowing up instead of down.

After lunch, our camera session started with 'romantic' pictures in the shade of sunlit trees, where the thick grass was covered by daisies. A greyhound came in useful, together with bunches of gorse and broom. Wallis was terrified of treading in the long grass where her dog, Slippers, had recently been fatally bitten by a viper, but tread she did.

The photography went on for many hours. Birds sang; conditions, and settings and organdie dresses were ideal. We mounted a Gothic turret to Wallis's bedroom, where the *boiseries* made a good background, for a succession of clothes which were put on and off with the speed of a quick-change artist. Jewellery was produced in unostentatious driblets. It impressed me to see some big historic stones, including a pair of diamond pear-shaped clips the size of pigeons' eggs. Wallis, helpful and serious, purposely dropped her usual badinage.

On the desk, dressing table and bedside table were informal pictures of the Duke, signed 'To Wallis – David.' Over a number of these pictures hung little enamel or palm crosses.

Regularly, like the chimes of a clock, the telephone rings: at seven o'clock and again at ten. For the Duke still enjoys his long telephone conversations. At frequent intervals the press also rang up to make inquiries. Wallis seemed to be at pains to please them. She continually remarked to whoever answered, 'Be careful to be nice: So-and-So is very important.' Once we laughed when someone asked for proof that Mrs Simpson was really there, as a report published in America had authenticated her return to Baltimore!

After dinner, Rogers showed a series of cine-Kodak films which he had taken intermittently since 1924.

The first setting was China, at a time when Wallis had again been staying with the Rogers during six months of divorce proceedings against Spencer. The women wearing knee-length dresses and boudoir caps or bandages on their foreheads, and gambolled and laughed coyly. The men were in immensely tight trousers and high collars. In one sequence Wallis hilariously kissed Rogers, laughed into the camera and then continued her attack.

There were scenes at the races, also intimate glimpses of the English colony with Wallis, as ever, the life and soul of the gatherings. She seemed much less individual then, her hair thicker, her head bigger, her body fatter.

This was followed by glimpses of the Simpson–Rogers friendship with the Prince of Wales and future King. They appeared, a jovial group, in Budapest and Vienna. In the south of France, they splashed and frisked in a turquoise sea. They picnicked on rocks, snapped one another, rowed in collapsible boats, ate lunch.

Then came the *Nahlin* cruise, showing the Royal party steadfastly roughing it at sea. The King, with Wallis at his side, went round asking questions of the crew, of anybody and everybody. He seemed a wizened little boy, distinguished by untidy golden hair and a brown, naked back.

But an unique film showed the Simpson–Rogers visit to Balmoral. Here, against the Highland setting, more candid shots of the turreted castle, which caught the King demonstrating to his guests an Austrian game by shooting some kind of arrow through the air. Lord Louis Mountbatten tried after him, then the Duke of Kent. They fared badly, making everyone laugh. As they sat on the terrace waiting for lunch, the ladies looked untidy and relaxed. The Duchess of Sunderland seemed enormous in a dowdy hat; Mollie Buccleuch was made to look very squat in tartans. Neither Mary Marlborough nor a begoggled Edwina Mountbatten were flattered by the camera; only the Duchess of Kent looked romantic with her hair untidily blowing and tied with a baby bow of ribbon. Every few feet of film, the King appeared with Wallis. She looked very different from the others, neat and towny in smart clothes and a black felt hat. In the background, the Rogers laughed and ran round in circles.

One sequence showed the King in a huge hood and cloak, lying in wait on the moors. He munched an apple, asked questions of the old retainers, helped the stalkers to put the victim deer on the pony's back. . . .

After Rogers' cine-Kodak, we discussed the 'stills' I had taken earlier in the day. There were inquiries as to the proper use of these pictures. Some must be allowed to the general press, for Wallis has got used to her publicity now.

We exchanged goodnights, and the weekend was over. It has given me much to muse upon. The Rogers, I concluded, are nice – but in spite of being wary, not very intelligent and apt to be fooled. Still, they're loyal friends. Wallis appreciates this, and throughout her success she has always insisted on the Rogers being included in social invitations.

Next morning, the over-solicitous butler and footmen were lined up at the door to salute my departure. I concluded that, for Mrs Simpson, events might have been worse. If she has not been fated to wear a crown, she is still loved by an abdicated King and will soon be married to him. It won't be so bad to be called the Duchess of Windsor.

3 June

I took a very early train to Tours. When I arrived at the château, swarms of journalists and their vans and motor cycles waited outside the gates.

Mrs Spry and her assistant Miss Pirie, two laden Ganymedes, calmly went about their business of decorating the whole château with magnificent mountains of mixed flowers. Rogers with his typewritten lists busily handled the telephone, and the press.

Wallis hovered about in yellow, slightly more businesslike than usual; with her face showing the strain: she looked far from her best. The Duke, by contrast, seemed radiant – his hair ruffled gold, his complexion clear and sunburnt, his blue eyes transparent with excitement. Marriage in Westminster Abbey should have been his birthright yet now he beamed contentedly at the impromptu wedding arrangements set up in the music room. The piano had been taken out; and thirty-two chairs placed in the room. Wallis inquired, 'We don't have to shake hands with everybardee, doo weeh?'

A car drove up. Great consternation and activity were occasioned by the arrival of the clergyman who (out of the blue and at the eleventh hour) had volunteered to marry the loving pair. This obscure Darlington vicar had felt it an injustice that the Duke should be denied a religious ceremony, and sent through the post a letter to that effect. As with all the other letters, it was personally opened by the Duke. And so, out of provincial obscurity, a vicar had been hied to Château Candé to be the centre of world interest.

The Duke was interested in everything he had to say, and spent much time discussing arrangements with him.

Now the clergyman wanted an altar, of course. The château was scoured for a suitable table. 'What about the one with the drinks on it, or the chest from the hall?' In the confusion someone knocked over an Italian lamp and cracked it. The Duke became greatly perturbed, and tried forthwith to mend it.

At length the chest from the hall was chosen. It promised to be just the thing: a heavily-carved, vastly ornate affair of no particular period, with a row of fat caryatids holding up bogus Renaissance carving.

Wallis, rather harassed but not too harassed to laugh, wondered about an altar cloth. Pointing to the caryatids, she drawled, 'We must have something to cover up that row of extra women!'

'Oh, I've got a tea cloth,' Wallis suddenly exclaimed.

The tea cloth was produced from the bottom of an already-packed linen trunk. Wallis's Cockney maid, furious at having to unpack the trunk, whined, 'If it's as much trouble as this getting married, I'm sure I'll never go through with it myself.'

Wallis explained, 'I couldn't let the poor girl be put off matrimony for life. I felt duty-bound to say,"Oh, it isn't always as bad as this – only if you're marrying the ex-King of England!"'

The altar cloth was spread. Mr Allen, the solicitor, a rather sheepish expression on his face, trooped in with two heavy candlesticks to be placed on the altar.

Wallis remonstrated, 'Hey, you can't put those out: we want them for the dinner table tonight.'

More flowers were brought in. Mrs Spry, robin-like in a picture hat and overalls, sentimentally broke off a branch of laurel: 'I'm going to make the flowers as beautiful as I can. I'm so glad they've both got what they want with this religious ceremony. I'd do anything for her. I adore her. So did all my girls when they arranged flowers for her in her Regent's Park house and didn't know who she was.'

The parson now allowed the photography to begin without further delay. The electricians had fixed up the lights in Wallis's bedroom, and we started with pictures of the Duke alone. He turned himself into a pliable, easy-to-pose subject, doing his best to make things less difficult. The only taboo: he would not allow himself to be photographed on the right side of his face, preferring the left as it showed the parting in his hair. Though somewhat wrinkled, he still seemed essentially young for all his forty-three years. His expression, though intent, was essentially sad, tragic eyes overruling the impertinent tilt of his nose. Those eyes, fiercely blue, do not seem to focus properly, and one is somewhat lower than the other.

Photographing the bridal couple together proved more elusive. It developed that nowhere in the château was there a crucifix to place upon the improvised altar. The British Embassy in Paris must get one; which meant that the Duke himself had to telephone to Lloyd Thomas about the matter. Wallis, wearing a black dress and her huge diamond pear clips, was meanwhile waiting impatiently to be photographed with him. She became perturbed at the delay. The Cockney maid telephoned to his room: 'Is that your Royal Highness? Well, will you please come down right away?' When he finally did appear, Wallis let him see she was annoyed. After a preliminary argument he apologized. Then the two sat hip to hip on the pouf, his far hand round her waist while I clicked away.

There was a lunch interval before we settled down to taking pictures in the wedding vestments. The other guests on hand were whisked off to a restaurant in some neighbouring town by M. Bedaux – a strategy designed to get them out of the way. Our own meal was served out on the terrace under the trees. The Duke never eats much lunch, but today had strawberries and cream while Wallis, Rogers, Dudley Forwood the equerry, and myself ate curried eggs and rice, kidneys and other dishes.

At the beginning of lunch, Wallis asked that the large sunshade on the terrace be lowered. The Duke rose from the table to do it himself. Footmen hovered impotently as he called, 'Is this the right height? Six inches lower?'

Lunch conversation was light and witty. At times the Duke roared and wrinkled up his face so that it looked like last year's apple.

Then he went off to change into his morning coat.

Upstairs, in the bathroom-dressing-room, hung Wallis's hard blue wedding dress. On a stand by the window was her hat, of matching feathers with a tulle halo effect.

With Wallis in costume, we were now ready to take the wedding pictures. 'Oh, so this is the great dress? Well, it's lovely, very pretty,' admired the Duke.

To avoid possible sightseers with telescopic lenses, we had to confine ourselves to certain shielded parts of the house. The most successful pictures were those taken on the steps and terrace of the medieval porch.

As misfortune would have it, Forwood brought some bad news just as the bridal couple posed at a turret window. Through the lens I saw the Duke become worried, frowning and contorting his face until he looked as tortured as a German gargoyle. Wallis, too, seemed troubled. The Duke opined, 'That's one point I will stick to. I'm certainly going to have my way on that. After all, I *am* English!'

It was painful. I couldn't very well interrupt and say, 'Please look pleasant.' I took several unflattering but illuminating pictures. Then the mood changed for the better again, as Wallis suggested, 'Let's remember now, we're having our pictures taken.'

The sun poured down beneficently. I was glad to be getting what I knew would be good results, since the day's earlier efforts hadn't augured well. But at last there was no excuse to go on; and so the bridal pair changed their clothes.

The Duke reappeared in a bright blue suit that made his complexion even more rubicund, his hair more flaxen. The latest batch of mail was carried across the lawns to him. Great joke: 'Old Carter with the mail.' I took pictures of the Duke with Carter and the mail tray piled high, every letter bearing the Duke's profile.

Wallis decided to rest. I wandered about the house. Another photographer, who formerly worked for Vandyk, had taken a few shots when my sitting was over. The Duke and Wallis laughed, as he was old-fashioned and chose the darkest, most over-ornamented room in the house to feature them, standing bolt upright against an enormous fireplace. This photographer now came up to me and gave me his card, saying he knew no reason why there should be enmity between rivals. I looked on him with condescending superciliousness. Later, I had reason to think differently.

The guests came back for tea, staggering after their enormous lunch. Baba Metcalfe confided to me her quiet amazement at the Duke's unalloyed high spirits. He had made no mention of England or his family (and I said nothing of the momentary pique at the turret window). But, even as Baba spoke, the Duke seemed once more preoccupied with things other than at hand. He stood on the lawn with his back to us, head lowered while he stared into space. He stood still long enough for me to click the camera for an introspective photograph. Beyond him the dogs wandered about, ignored for the day – the greyhound, the saluki, the endless cairns.

Tea was on now. Wallis's Aunt Bessie officiated. The Duke talked earnestly to the parson. The Metcalfes looked calm; Sir Walter Monckton smiled nicely; Allen wore a grave air. Rogers admitted that he had a headache and was in a bad temper, though his press announcements were about at an end. Mme Bedaux persisted in saying inconsequential things. She has been staying in the same house with the Duke for weeks; yet this morning she greeted him with a fatuous bob of the head, 'Nice to see you again.' M. Bedaux hovered about.

Forwood seemed pooped but alert. He confided to me how deeply hurt the Duke was because certain of his personal friends had not materialized for the wedding.

It was soon time for me to be leaving, with the suitcase I had packed in case they relented and allowed me to stay for the wedding tomorrow. But that proved impossible. Only four representatives of the press had been invited; and I could scarcely be permitted to stay when so many intimates had been excluded.

On leaving I kissed Wallis goodbye: not because she encouraged me to, but I felt moved by all that was happening.

I came away with photographs that, had they been for sale in the open market, would have commanded a fancy price. With the *Queen Mary* sailing tonight, prints would arrive in America a whole week before the press photographs tomorrow. One agent told me that fifteen hundred pounds had been paid for the first Coronation pictures; and these were of equal historical interest. But my *Vogue* contract precludes such negotiations. The bulk of my work was exclusive to them. However, Mrs Chase had agreed that any photographs that *Vogue* did not want could be given to the general press.

This called for a certain celerity. I was pent-up in the train coming back to Paris. By the time I grabbed the aeroplane to London early the next morning, I fancied myself being presented with a cheque that would enable me to clap a new roof on the studio at Ashcombe; the rough chalk road down the valley could be made navigable! I'd give presents to my mother and all my friends.

Still counting chickens, I landed at Northolt and rushed to a conference with *Vogue*. But even as Miss Joseph, at home, was bargaining with the press about the price of pictures I might or might not have left, surprise overtook us. There was already a large photograph in the *Evening Standard* of the Duke and Duchess of Windsor standing bolt upright against an enormous fireplace in a dark, over-ornamented room. The old-fashioned photographer had seized the day! His effort was already being radioed to the USA, with prints on board the *Queen Mary*. I felt like a hare outrun by a tortoise.

7

England and New York
1937–8

Rex Whistler had become a close friend. In New York C.B. visited Mrs Patrick Campbell, a queen of the stage in exile. He published Cecil Beaton's Scrapbook.

London: September 1937

Dinner with Rex [Whistler]. There could scarcely be a nicer way of spending time. More than any among all my friends, Rex has an aura which improves the more you are with him and the older he becomes. His sense of repose, no doubt, springs from an unruffled, poetic and calm interior world. Rex has a tawny elegance; though he may sum up contemporary situations and passing foibles with understanding and wit, his atmosphere is nevertheless that of an older man of another century.

Perhaps this anachronistic solidity is the very reason for Rex's being more laurel-crowned than almost any young painter today, especially by the older generation of cultured aristocrats. And recognition has come to him in spite of his putting every obstacle in its way: Rex makes himself almost impregnable, hardly ever answering letters or the telephone.

I called for him at Brook House. He was exhausted, looking very grey and white as he worked on the grey and silver decorations of landscape and motifs for Edwina Mountbatten's boudoir. I didn't envy him. The prospect of having to complete the details he has already mapped out for himself would fill me with despair.

It was only after he had eaten a little and drunk a lot that Rex felt able to expand. He then regaled me with characteristic personal descriptions of his weekend stay with the King and Queen at Balmoral.

His great interest, quite naturally, had been in the objects, furnishings and gardens of the castle. All seemed a blazing brightness of colour. Hundreds of vases held Victorian bouquets of flowers that had been freshly and brilliantly arranged. Bright gilt clocks, glass-domed *objets d'art* and albums abounded. The carpets were brilliant flowered or plaid.

The garden struck Rex as being peculiarly fantastic, with many leaden statues of John Brown, of stags, deer and dogs. The emerald-green lawns were studded with Wellingtonias, each planted by some illustrious name.

In preparation for the royal event, Rex had borrowed a wrist-watch so that he could be on time for meals. But the equerries proved indefatigable, tapping on the door to announce, 'It'll be all right if you come down in five minutes' time.'

The hours had been long. Everyone came down for breakfast at eight o'clock or eight-thirty (I forget which). This in spite of the fact that, on the night of the Ghillies Ball, no one went to bed until three in the morning.

The Ghillies Ball was held in an enormous Gothic hall. Here they danced ceaselessly throughout the night. The King and Queen jigged with great abandon. The Queen ducked under huge ghillies' arms in the various complications of the reels. Pipes squealed, people hooted and laughed. The complicated footwork of the prancing men was displayed to advantage by virtue of their spats. Even old Princess Marie Louise twinkled her toes by the hour. Rex commented on how surprisingly independent and assured all the Scots were, communicating a staunch feeling of being as good as anybody, surpassed by no man.

New York: 1938

Mrs Pat [Campbell] is a great woman, triumphing over the sordid difficulties of poverty and age by a resolute sense of beauty and poetry. For today's sitting she wore black velvet and artificial pearls. She brought with her the white Pekinese dog to which she is so inordinately devoted that she will not return to England (dogs must remain in quarantine for a year before entering the British Isles).

In appearance, Mrs Pat seems a prototype of a stage duchess. But after the hot lights had played on her for a while, she began to disintegrate. There was something ghastly about her dirty white gloves, her fallen chins and the tragic impedimenta of age. She bellowed like a sick cow, throwing her hands to the skies, 'Oh, why must I look like a burst paper bag? Why must I have all these dewlaps? Why can't I be a beauty?'

I took Mrs Pat to lunch at Voisin's. She was in good form castigating Orson Welles's production of *Julius Caesar*: 'They have no reverence, those boys. They speak the lines as if they had written them themselves. You can't recite the *Song of David* spontaneously. You must recite it as David. Mr Welles's Brutus is like an obstetrician who very seriously visits a lady in order to placate her nerves.'

As only an artist can be, she is canny and clear in her observations about people: 'Lilian Gish may be a charming person, but she's not Ophelia. She comes on stage as if she'd been sent for to sew rings on the new curtains.'

Kirsten Flagstad 'walks meaninglessly around the stage, like a wardrobe at a séance.'

About Violet, Duchess of Rutland (whose recent death robbed us of a landmark) Mrs Pat said, 'She was the most beautiful thing I ever saw. In my day, beauties were poetic looking. They wore long, pre-Raphaelite tea gowns. They moved and spoke very slowly, giving the impression that they had just been possessed.'

In the corridor outside my room I could hear a booming voice coming nearer. '2645, 2645, 2645.... Ah! Here we are. Can I come in? Are you expecting me?'

Mrs Pat arrived, swathed in furs, wearing a feathered hat and the usual black velvet dress with train. She brought with her the proofs of the pictures I had taken; also, for my inspection, a selection of old photographs of herself as she used to be. These documents attested such beauty that it was almost frightening to compare them with what they have turned into. 'Look,' she moaned, 'at the beauty of that neck, at that line of cheek. And look at me now, all wind and water.'

The early pictures depicted a magnolia beauty with dark hair and prune eyes, communicating an acute sensitiveness and delicacy. Mrs Pat inveighed: 'Oh God, how can You be so unkind as to do this to me? Why must we all become ugly? I don't know how some women stand it. Why don't they commit suicide?'

She was apparently comforted by my photographs. I didn't dare protest what I thought – that they were really quite ordinary. To Mrs Pat, they seemed the distillation of magic. 'Oh, that shadow under the jaw! You're a genius to put in that shadow. And no one has taken such a photograph of gloved hands. Those gloves are alive. Look at the depth between the thumb and first finger. That's what everyone wants to have!'

She was likewise delighted with the photogenic qualities of Moonbeam, who, according to my spy, David Herbert, had been the cause of trouble a day or two ago. David, having taken Mrs Pat out to dinner, brought her back to her hotel in a taxi. When the driver discovered that Moonbeam had wetted the floor of the vehicle he remonstrated vehemently with Mrs Pat. To placate him, she held Moonbeam high and wagged a finger at the culprit, cooing, 'Who would have thought the old dog had so much pee in him?'

Abruptly, Mrs Pat broached the irrelevant subject of money. 'Now I've brought you forty dollars for these pictures.'

I remonstrated with her. I had no intention of her *buying* any photographs. They were meant as a tribute.

Mrs Pat insisted on paying. She said, 'It's rather affected of you to go on like this, you know. I shall give you *thirty* dollars, then. I can afford it. I have a rich pupil now.'

'Now tell me about your life at the moment,' I asked.

'I am poor but I'm not afraid of being poor. I could easily have been rich if I'd been just a bit vulgar or broken a little dog's heart. You can understand my giving up a career for Moonbeam, can't you? I couldn't go back to England and let that little dog die! Anyway, I live in an old-fashioned hotel, a red brick building full of old people who adore me. They look after me so kindly; they adore Moonbeam. I have two rooms with french windows and a high ceiling. And I don't have to hear other people's bath water!'

It was in her present hotel that John Gielgud visited her. He felt so sorry for her poverty that he offered to lend her money, then sent fruit and all sorts of food she couldn't eat. He wept for her, which she thought silly. She had no wish to be pitied. She said, 'Get along with you. Pull yourself together. You're too hysterical on and off the stage.' Wiping his eyes, Gielgud replied, 'Those are Terry tears.'

Mrs Pat on love: 'Oh, I was loved once. But it didn't work. The French have a proverb, "Become like honey and the flies eat you".'

Mrs Pat said she was having an anxious time trying to find someone who could write the necessary explanation about herself and Shaw, for the publication after their deaths of Shaw's letters to her. Gaps in the correspondence must be filled in; it must be understood that this was not just the gaga drivellings of a writer to any actress. The editing had to be done with understanding, reverence and taste. 'It's difficult to find someone who will not throw these letters to the ground so that you have to stoop to see them. We want them on a pedestal just at eye level! I believe we have got hold of an Irishman; and, you know, Irishmen are never vulgar!'

She talked about her difficulties in the theatre. Only today she had had such a bad snub. Someone had asked her to take the part of a drivelling old woman of a hundred and two. 'It is very difficult to be a hundred and two convincingly. Even at my age I can hardly move. But to be a hundred and two and drool at the mouth is too horrifying. It is surely better that I remain a legend!'

The legend went on to talk of her big opportunity, when she played Mrs Tanqueray. 'I never got my chance until I had two children. Then, straightaway, I went right to the top. It's a question of taste and not experience. [George] Alexander knew I had had no training, but he always listened to me. He told me to lose my temper in one scene and brush all the photographs from the piano on to the floor. But I replied that I could never lose my temper or do ugly things with my hands. In the play, I was supposed to be a musician: no musician would put frames on the piano! And again, at rehearsal, he told me to strum the piano. I said, 'I *never* strum. My mother locked the keyboard and only let us open it if we were going to *play*.' Alexander then said to me, 'Well, *play* then.' But it so happened that my teacher had discovered the third finger of my right hand was weak. I must rest it a while. In the interim, he'd been teaching me an arrangement by Bach, for left hand only. Thus, in front of Alexander, I held a book high in my right hand, adopted an expression of complete disdain, and played the piano with my left hand until the poor man was eventually able to gasp, "That's enough, Mrs Campbell!"'

Mrs Pat has made a study of being absent-minded. When the telephone rings, she calls, 'Come in.'

It was Mrs Pat's seventy-third birthday. Some gardenias and a cablegram from England paid homage to her great character, to an actress who had been loved by Shaw, who had brought a new influence to the theatre and was now a waning one. Moonbeam, who would never be in quarantine, snoozed contentedly in his basket.

8

French Scenes
1938–9

With David Herbert, C.B. went on a long cruise on Mrs Reginald Fellowes's yacht, visiting Turkey and the Greek islands. After a stay in Venice, he went to Tamaris in the South of France, where Bérard painted his portrait.

Tamaris: Summer 1938

Bébé [Bérard] has an elementary quality. It is one of his many virtues. No one could be more highly civilized and, to use a word I hate, *sophisticated*; yet his instincts, reactions and gestures are those of someone utterly primitive. When he is in his room and thirsty, it is unnatural for him to pour mineral water from the Vittel bottle into a tumbler – he drinks straight from the bottle. Instead of spreading butter on bread with a knife, he will dip his bread into the butter dish.

For his work, Bébé is without paraphernalia. Here in the hotel, the bed has been taken from the room he uses as a studio. On the bedside table lies his paint palette; on the mantelpiece his canvas perches, somewhat rickety. But Bébé finds this emptiness full, making me aware of how an unfurnished room can stir the imagination.

Bébé's preparations are animal. He smears the paints with his hands, never bothering to screw the tops back on paint tubes. Colours are squeezed directly on to ever-thickening mountains of paint. He recognizes and justifies a sloppiness that in others would be inexcusable: 'If I am careless and dirty and drop everything, it is all right. I can spatter filth about the floor, and it will not be repulsive. But when Francis Rose leaves a pair of bedroom slippers lying about, it seems as unprepossessing as a dirty comb.' This paradox is true enough. Bébé seldom washes; he never sleeps *in*, but *on*, his bed. His clothes are filthy. Yet he is never revolting, never unpleasant. His personality and temperament outweigh all disadvantages.

When he works on my portrait, I notice that Bébé's every stroke of the brush, every daub, is the result of intense concentration. After each bout of work, lasting perhaps fifteen minutes, he sinks exhausted on his bed. There must then be an intermission, time to smoke an opium pipe.

One of the reasons Bébé has been so aghast at the thought of war is that he realizes he must be disintoxicated before being called up. Otherwise his long-drawn-out death would be one of the greatest suffering. He showed me his registration card: '*Bérard – numéro such-and-such-soldat. In the event of war report immediately....*'

Bébé's bedroom looked like the scene of an alchemist's nightmare. Casseroles had been brought out; spirit lamps flickered. A shirt was sacrificed and torn in shreds. Two lady friends now appeared, volunteering to do the cooking for him, while he worked on my portrait in the adjoining room. Strange odours of earth and opium wafted in to us – Picasso says opium is the cleverest smell. Soon every piece of furniture was covered with steaming casseroles of brown liquid. This would be passed through the sieve of the torn shirt. The residue left in the cloth was squeezed dry and set aside for future leaching, while the filtrate was boiled down.

One can buy opium in the final form; but glycerine, morphine and heaven-knows-what are often added as adulterants, so that it is only safe to prepare the product oneself. I wondered why the very process did not put Bébé off the stuff forever – the smells were sickening, the brown liquids looked extremely unpleasant.

Busily the two cooks fidgeted, giggled and fluttered. Bent double over their witches' brew, they reminded me of Nancy and Baba as children, making fudge on rainy days. And when, in extremis, the *pot de chambre* was whisked from its little wooden home to provide another receptacle for the slimy liquid, my imagination could not be curbed.

Today's war news seemed less acute. Mr Chamberlain, aged sixty-nine, has taken an aeroplane for the first time and flown to confer personally with Hitler. While these conferences are on, war cannot be started.

After the anxiety and gloom of last night, our present happy mood continued. The pendulum had swung violently back to gaiety, the evening became a bacchanalia.

After dinner at Denise's, John Sutro released his pent-up emotions, bursting forth with a spontaneous programme of improvisations, recitations, mock-Alexandrine peace orations, Restoration plays, folk songs and what you will. His plays in rhymed couplets were inspired; his impromptu Shakespearean scene proved the best I had even known him to do. Bébé entertained by executing a ballet imitation of a butterfly fluttering over flowers; or could it have been a moth in a wood? He skipped about on minute feet, a fantastic sprite with red beard and twinkling almond eyes. John provided the score, whistling like an inspired bird. Challenged, I danced with Denise to Brahms waltzes and Liszt.

Oliver Messel arrived with Peter Glenville. Bébé said, 'Now Oliver, do some new imitations. You've done the same ones for ten years, and you must get something new in your repertoire.' Oliver looked astonished.

Towards the end of the evening, our entertainment became more ribald. We resorted to a number of *Folies Bergère* spectaculars: *Les Folies Nues, Les Pays, Les Fleurs, Les Vices*, etc.

Some French political journalists arrived unexpectedly. God knows what they thought as they witnessed the scene in Denise's drawing-room, with the company dressed in anything to be found in the hallway – umbrella stands, garden chairs, a globe of the world, tennis nets, rugs and cacti.

This morning Bébé painted like someone in the throes of medieval torture. He did not talk during the sitting. He groaned, whispered, sighed, whimpered, stamped his feet, jerked backwards and forwards, lunged with noisy intakes of breath. 'You don't *know* how difficult it is! Oh God, oh God! Ah, *je vois. Non, ce n'est pas ça! O, Dieu!*'

It was both a revelation and a lesson to me. Even so lightly painted a portrait as mine was a tribute to Bébé's agony.

After a long bout, he rested to smoke a pipe. I said, 'I'm so sorry you have suffered as you did today.'

He replied, 'It's all I like in the world!'

9

The End of an Epoch
1939

C.B. published his parody of Edwardian memoirs, My Royal Past. *His romantic photographs of the Queen at Buckingham Palace marked 'the end of an epoch', as she was to comment thirty years later. When war was imminent, C.B. hurried back from a visit to Gertrude Stein.*

London: July 1939

The telephone rang. 'This is the lady-in-waiting speaking. The Queen wants to know if you will photograph her tomorrow afternoon.'

At first, I thought it might be a practical joke – the sort of thing Oliver might do. But it was no joke. My pleasure and excitement were overwhelming. In choosing me to take her photographs, the Queen made a daring innovation. It is inconceivable that her predecessor would have summoned me – my work was still considered revolutionary and unconventional.

A rush of organization had to start forthwith. Telegrams were sent off summoning electricians and operators.

I arrived at the Palace soon after ten o'clock the following morning, to choose the rooms in which the photographs would be taken.

Following a scarlet-liveried page down miles of the dark-red carpeted corridors of the Palace, hung with petunia-crimson cut-velvets, I was in the clouds. We passed rows of family portraits, busts on columns, and gilt chairs. Housemaids, busy with their dusters, hurried through baize doors. Groups of grey-haired, be-medalled servants stood in posses at the end of an enfilade. Through the door of a small dining-room, I saw crumbs on a white linen table cloth.

The superintendent made himself congenial, and showed me the Rembrandts, Le Nain, Vermeer, and other pictures in the long and ugly railway-station gallery; also the Boucher tapestries, French furniture, and objects of art that during the past twenty years Queen Mary has collected to replace the Victorian stuff gradually being weeded out.

The Palace is now a happy combination of Regency and Edwardian. I admired a certain Louis Quinze desk, as it proved to be one of the treasures of the Palace. Moss Harris, the antiquary, had offered Queen Mary fifteen thousand pounds any time she wished to sell it.

The superintendent opened the double doors to various drawing-rooms, the throne room, the small sitting-rooms. He explained that workmen and artisans, non-stop throughout the year, are making repairs or renovating some aspect of this huge ensemble – the superintendent has forty men under him.

He confessed, 'We have a lot to do matching the silk on the walls. Do you see how it has faded behind these pictures? We have a great deal of the material, but it must be the same tone as where it has faded. Look at these sofas: also upholstered in the same material. Look at this patch. We've had that bit of silk out in the garden to fade it in the sun; but even so, it looks different from the rest. These repairs go on all the time. After every party we find someone has slashed a sofa with his sword.'

Through the windows, I could hear the changing of the guard. The commands of the officers, shouting to their men, sounded like someone retching. Throughout the Palace, I noticed, one has no feeling of remoteness from the people. The garden, though enormous, hums with the distant burr of traffic. Through the windows of many rooms, one can see the curious crowds waiting beyond the railings.

The Deputy Master of the Household suddenly appeared. He cleared his throat, seeming like so many courtiers, who enjoy communicating their nervousness to suitably terrified 'outsiders', and explained, 'Uh-huh-Her Majesty wanted to see you-uh-huh – about – uh-huh – choosing the dresses for this afternoon's pictures. I'll try and get you in quickly, because as a matter of fact I know the Queen – uh-huh – has got the – uh-huh – hairdresser at eleven.' By the time we had waited outside the Royal apartment and I was at last bidden into the presence, any self-confidence I might possibly have assumed had been knocked out of me. My mouth was dry. When the mahogany doors were opened, I felt I was being precipitated on to a stage without knowing any of my lines.

The Queen was in the act of moving towards a desk. All about her, a blue haze emanated from the French silk walls embroidered in bouquets of silver. The room seemed a pointillist bower of flowers – hydrangeas, sweet peas, carnations.

The Queen wore a pale grey dress with long, fur-edged sleeves.

She greeted me, smiling and easy. Nevertheless, I felt myself standing stiff, my knees shaking. 'It is a great happiness for me, Ma'am.'

'It is very exciting for me.'

We discussed dresses. 'You know, perhaps the embroidered one I wore – in Canada ...?' A slight hesitation prevented the remark from being conceited, for the Queen must have known I was aware of what she wore on her Canadian tour.

The Queen made other tentative suggestions: 'And I thought, perhaps, another evening dress of – tulle? And a – tiara?' All this wistfully said, with a smile, and raised eyebrows. The charm of manner was so infectious that, no doubt to the Queen's astonishment, I found myself subconsciously imitating her somewhat jerky flow of speech, and using the same gentle, staccato expressions. I wrinkled my forehead in imitation of her look of inquiry as I asked if – perhaps – as much jewellery as possible could – be worn? The Queen smiled apologetically – 'The choice isn't very great you know!'

I went away in high spirits and full of hopes for the afternoon.

In a corner of the semi-circular music room, with its lapis columns, a great group of men were preparing the lights. Others had already set up a platform, and a screen with my backgrounds hung on it.

The superintendent had told me that I wouldn't be allowed much time with the Queen. In fact, he explained, not since the late King George's reign had any photographer been allowed to take pictures for more than twenty minutes.

Thus, at last, when a rush of pages and a hustle in the corridor preceded Her Majesty's entrance in ruby-encrusted crinoline of gold and silver, I began to photograph with monkey-like frenzy. This seemed to amuse my sitter.

We photographed now from room to room. The electricians and the camera assistants could hardly keep up with us. Nevertheless, the sitting went with such ease and rapidity that I beamed even as I sweated with the effort. The Queen smiled as freshly as ever. In fact, she said, 'It is so hard to know when *not* to smile.' She tidied her shoulder straps meticulously and placed her fan just so. She was gamely prepared for another picture to be taken.

It was only when the plates had to be reloaded that I could possibly allow Her Majesty to change into another dress. I apologized for my over-enthusiasm and expressed the hope that the results would justify this behaviour.

The Queen disappeared, then reappeared in spangled tulle like a fairy doll. She admitted with a smile, 'I changed the tiara. And these diamonds – are they all right?' They had been given as a coronation present by the King: two rows of diamonds almost as big as walnuts.

Then, after the diamonds, the Queen produced three rows of enormous pearls. 'Are three rows too much?' I protested. But a little later Her Majesty removed all but one row, saying with a chuckle, 'I think three *are* too much!'

The camera devoured plates with gluttonous rapidity. The Rolleiflex did service whenever the big camera was not ready. Pictures were taken of the Queen against my old Piranesi and Fragonard backgrounds, with flowers from her rooms padding the sides of her chair. We also took shots against the pillars of the drawing-rooms, in doorways, on sofas and against the precious Louis Quinze desk.

The sun now came out, encouraging the hope that I might be able to take photographs outside. What about – a garden party dress – on the terrace? The Queen assented. In ten or fifteen minutes we would meet downstairs.

While I waited, a tea tray was brought to me in the lapis drawing-room. My superintendent friend came in and said, 'Do you realize you are the most fortunate young man I've ever known? Why, you've had three hours of the Queen's time already. Do you mean to say she's gone off to change once more? Why, she hasn't had her tea yet, has she? Well, it means the poor King will have to have his tea alone!'

Never has tea tasted better. The bread and butter was like angel cake. Yes, I was a fortunate young man. I smiled to myself, recalling the little comments the Queen had made during our indoor sessions. When I ran out of Rolleiflex films, someone was sent to Heppels for more. The films arrived very soon. Her Majesty exclaimed, 'Never have I known such celerity.' Again, when we tried consciously to arrange her hands on her lap, they became self-conscious. Abandoning all efforts to put one hand on top of the other, the Queen said, 'I'm afraid your instructions were too rigid.'

I waited on the terrace. The Queen appeared, smiling and laughing in a sudden gust of wind. She was wearing a champagne-coloured lace dress and hat. She carried a parasol.

She walked down a flight of steps while I ran about with my small camera.

The lawns of the Palace were fitfully strewn with sunlight; the atmosphere seemed strange and timeless. I felt that our expedition to the lake, to photograph by the water's edge, was something outside reality.

The Queen talked gaily. 'I am interested in your photography. You have such a high standard. Can you do a lot afterwards? Can you take out a whole table?'

'A table is a bit much, Ma'am. But I can slice people in half.'

'How the King will laugh when I tell him you photographed me directly against the sun. We have to spend our time running round to face the sun for the King's snapshots.'

Her Majesty halted suddenly on the lawn. 'Do you realize we are in the Sacred Circle?' On the grass a white circle had been painted. 'This is where all the Bishops assemble at the Garden Party and wait to be received.' How disappointing for ten thousand people that yesterday the rain had wrought havoc! The Queen commented that for ten days they had listened to the hammering of the tents being erected. Now they would listen for nearly as long while the tents were being pulled down.

Photography continued beneath a giant stone vase, in a summer house of tridents that came, it seems, from the Admiralty. We then took pictures from under the trees against the water, with the Palace in the distance.

'Will my parasol obliterate the Palace?'

'It is a very big Palace.'

'That central part is the original Buckingham House.'

In the filtered light, it looked as though it were made of opals. We stood for a moment listening to the distant roar of traffic. The evening sun was beginning to lose its power. Soon the sky would become rose-coloured; as if, as the Queen said, 'Piccadilly were on fire every night.'

We walked back to the Palace, where tired and baffled officials clustered by the door.

Downstairs, in the circular hall, I took my leave. As mementoes of the honour, there would be a hundred negatives. But in my pocket was hidden, scented with tuberoses and gardenias, a handkerchief that the Queen had tucked behind the cushion of a chair away from the onslaught of the camera. I had stolen it. It was my particular prize, one which would have more romance and reality than any of the photographs.

Bilignin, Bellay, Ain: August

This house [of Gertrude Stein and Alice Toklas] has an atmosphere that every artist must respond to. It is an invitation to work in ideal conditions. Colours, sounds and smells combine to produce an impression of complete simplicity and harmony. Here everything necessary is at hand, nothing more. The whole day may be spent idling or working, as one pleases. The house was built *circa* 1649 when domestic architecture in France was good. It is solid, boldly proportioned. Each room is as satisfying as the solution of a mathematical problem.

Throughout the house, there are few objects. But each object is of merit. There is nothing to offend the eye. A polished perfection dominates this rusticity. The cakes of soap in the bathroom are placed in rigid, sharp-edged precision. The food is the best food, for Alice has not only a *cordon bleu* but watches her cook with a rapier eye. The plates and the goblets are bold and beautiful.

In the terrace garden, frail China-pink roses bloom between the borders of box hedges. Wisps of ivy climb over the gnarled stone parapet. At intervals along it are three small pavilions as simple as a Noah's ark house, but with the proportions and textures and colours of the best relics of the fifteenth century. The distant mountains and poplared valley are constantly changing throughout the day, as clouds gather or the sun shines.

Gertrude is delighted here. 'Yes, it *is* nice. Yes, it is *very* lovely.' She beams with enjoyment as she snatches a handful of weeds from the rose bush.

Alice wakes at five each morning. She puts on a cretonne smock, then sets

about the task of collecting vegetables from the garden, planning the meals
for the day and arranging the flowers. By eight, she is wandering with a large
basket over her arm and a cigarette wobbling between her lips. By nine o'clock,
the vases have become the most esoterically arranged still-lifes. I know no one
who arranges flowers better than Alice. They have an architectural quality.

'She wasn't a servant [said Gertrude Stein of a former retainer]. She had
never been trained. She was only good at making a bed. She was the best maker
of beds we have ever had.'

I had not realized there could be such difference in the way a bed was made.
But then, I am English. The French have a ritual of bed-making. The mattress
is thrown one way one day, another way the next. The sheets are drawn tight
as a board over this newly-aired mattress, then tucked in by half the length
of the whole sheet. Gertrude and Alice, when they come to England, have great
difficulty sleeping in beds made by the servants in even so well-ordered a house
as Gerald Berners's. And Francis Rose's mother used to weep tears of rage
when she came to England, as she could get no one to make the bed properly.

There is no one more alarming than an optimist. Gertrude Stein is a great
general and a great optimist. She will not hear of war talk. It is almost a breach
of etiquette to mention the fact that events look black or the prospect horrifying.
'Oh, no, no. War isn't logical, no one wants a war. Yes, of course Hitler is
making a speech tomorrow. He's always making a speech. Of course, Roosevelt's going to talk. Ha, ha, he's always talking. No, no, things aren't serious.
Last year they were serious, yes. But last year, the postman had been called
up by this time. He hasn't been called this year, and they're perfectly calm
down at the village.'

The 'General' faced reality when at last the butcher telephoned this morning,
to say that the soldiers had requisitioned all the meat and he could not supply
the joint that had been ordered. The household became panic-stricken. Gertrude now felt she could no longer take the responsibility of our being there.
Francis Rose, with nowhere to go, has tried to influence me to join him at Jean
Hugo's. I do not wish to get further away.

10

Early War Years
1939–40

C.B.'s mother found a house, 8 Pelham Place, South Kensington, which was useful as a base while he worked as photographer for the Ministry of Information, and which remained his London home until 1974. From this he escaped, when he could, to the isolation of Ashcombe. Lady Diana Cooper, a friend of several years' standing, became an even closer one. The war brought C.B. a different kind of sitter. He published History Under Fire, *with a text by James Pope-Hennessy.*

Ashcombe: September 1939

I feel frustrated and ashamed. This war, as far as I can see, is something specifically designed to show up my inadequacy in every possible capacity. I am too incompetent to enlist as a private in the army. It's doubtful if I'd be much good at camouflage – in any case my repeated requests to join have been met with, 'You'll be called if you're wanted.' What else can I do? I have tried all sorts of voluntary jobs in the neighbourhood, helping Edith Olivier organize food control, and the distribution of trainloads of refugee children from Whitechapel. I failed in a first-aid examination after attending a course given by a humorous and kindly doctor in Salisbury. Now I start as night telephonist at the ARP centre in Wilton.

8 Pelham Place: 11 May 1940

It was a particularly idyllic early evening. Cyril Connolly paid a visit. London was looking defiantly beautiful, its parks with their blue vistas of Watteauesque trees – so different from the trees that grow in the country – and its gardens behind the railing a mass of lilac and blossoming trees. As Cyril was about to leave, we stood at the front door enjoying the opalescent evening light. The sun made the barrage balloons very bright gold, and the Gothic towers of the Victoria and Albert Museum at the end of the road and the peach blossom trees in the Emlyn Williams's garden opposite were seen in an apricot haze. We remarked on the paradox of the scene. Nothing here was indicative of the turmoil in the world today, a turmoil created by one gangster. We could feel the peace and repose of the evening so forcibly that it was almost tangible, or something that one could eat.

I dined with Loelia Westminster. After six months she had thrown aside the dust covers and re-opened her drawing-room. To celebrate this great event she gave a party. We all felt the dinner to be so excellent that we wanted to keep the menu in an album, as an archaeological specimen showing that this was the meal that we, in England, were fortunate enough to enjoy even after six months of war effort. Perhaps it would be the last of its sort. Anyhow, while we could, we would be as gay as possible. We went out to night clubs and danced all night. When we came back to our beds Germany had invaded Holland, Belgium and Luxembourg. Hell had broken loose.

September

I often forget the address to which I have to go, so that a taxi driver looks on superciliously while various doorbells are rung in vain. Today no such difficulty: No. 10 Downing Street is a number even I could not forget. I was going for the Minister of Information to photograph Mrs Churchill – possibly the great man as well: but that was indefinite. A breathless skivvy showed me up to the secretary's room and left me. For the first half-hour I beguiled myself prowling around, looking at the stacked files of newspaper articles and accounts of speeches, and the boxes with their ordered headings. It was enjoyable to note the presents sent to the Prime Minister from fans, with letters thanking him for what he was doing for the nation. But I was anxious to get to grips with my electrician, already established in the drawing-room, so in a fever I used the house telephone to ask to be freed from my imprisonment.

The suite of rooms where the pictures were to be taken had tall ceilings, with long windows looking on to herbaceous borders. Here, in the heart of London, bees were wafting in through the open curtains, and the quiet was a country quiet. It was the hottest day of the loveliest summer (climatically) we remember, and the rooms were a delight with sun streaming in from beneath the blinds on to bowls of sweet peas from Chartwell. There were some fine English portraits, Adam fireplaces and Georgian silver. Mrs Churchill has typically arranged the rooms with her usual pale colours of pistachio green and palest salmon pink. Pamela [Mrs Randolph Churchill], enormous with child, announced the imminent arrival of Mrs Churchill who appeared with her hair set for the occasion like Pallas Athene. Mrs C. announced that Winston was not able to be photographed. He was inspecting New Zealanders somewhere. This was a disappointment but, at the same time, a relief. If I had felt that, at any moment, he might come through the door I would have been most uneasy, for he has a paralysing effect on me.

Mrs Churchill, a bright, unspoilt and girlish woman, is full of amusing and shrewd observations about people and the afternoon's photography passed breezily and easily. She insisted on showing me the whole house, and I was an avid sightseer. The three reception-rooms give on to a small passage room which Philip Sassoon turned into a dining-room where Mr and Mrs C. have their evening meal, the big parties taking place in the panelled hall next door. Mrs C.'s own bedroom with chintz flowers is as pretty as any country bedroom, and all the corridors and bedrooms look like part of a manor house. On the pale-coloured walls were Sickert sketches and Nicholson still-lives, family photographs and Victorian sketches. The Prime Minister's bedroom was simplicity itself. A small single bed; some drawings of his family and his mother by Sargent; a bedside table mounted with telephones galore; boxes of cigars; a wash basin with shaving soap and brushes in evidence; a few books; some files of Parliamentary speeches, and that was all – except for the view from the windows on to the Horseguards Parade and the Admiralty. Mrs C. pointed out a truck full of pigeons. These are being trained in case all else fails. Pigeons to send last-minute SOSs – in extremes we revert to the primitive.

While we had a break from photography for tea Mrs C. talked of the terrible days when France was cracking and Winston had to keep bolstering up the French. But Winston had been so convinced of France's weakness that he had to refuse them the help of all our own fighter squadrons lest we ourselves be wiped out. They are, Mr and Mrs C., both pro-de Gaulle, whom they consider a great engineer-officer responsible for many new methods of mechanized warfare. He is full of courage, the maker of many magnificent speeches, but a difficult man to get along with.

Mrs Churchill recalled having sat next to the General at luncheon. During one of the many silences Mrs Churchill pondered on how difficult must be the life of Madame de Gaulle. Her daydreams were interrupted by the General addressing her: '*Vous savez*, Madame, it must be very difficult, Madame, being the wife of Mr Churchill.'

12 October

James [Pope-Hennessy] is writing a book called *History Under Fire* for which I am doing the photographs. Besides the vandalistic damage, we must show the tenacity and courage of the people, and we do not have to look far. Signs are posted: 'We have no glass, but business continues.' As soon as the worst rubbish is cleared away, the notice appears 'Open as usual'.

Londoners have had one month of this so far, and they must look forward to a whole winter of it. The planes arrive each night at dusk. One hears the drone, then the bangs, crunch, zumphs of the bombs. The AA gunfire, which is gay and heartening, is like a firework fiesta: and then an interval. During the lull one tries to read a book, but one's thoughts wander, and soon the hum of more approaching planes is heard. The zumphs come perilously near, and one leaves the chair for a vantage point under the lintel of a door. The restless night continues.

By degrees many people have grown accustomed to being frightened. For myself, most evenings I have beetled off to the Dorchester. There the noise outside is drowned with wine, music and company – and what a mixed brew we are! Cabinet ministers and their self-consciously respectable wives; hatchet-jawed, iron-grey brigadiers; calf-like airmen off duty; tarts on duty, actresses (also), *déclassé* society people, cheap musicians and motor-car agents. It could not be more ugly and vile, and yet I have not the strength of character to remain, like Harold Acton, with a book.

In the infernos of the Underground the poor wretches take up their positions for the night's sleep at four o'clock in the afternoon. The winter must surely bring epidemics of flu, even typhoid. The prospect is not cheering, and Churchill makes no bones about the ardours of the future. The electric trains are bombed, so typists fight their way on to extra buses. Telephone exchanges are out of order, and hardly a clock has its face intact. Yet the life of the city manages, more or less, to continue as if in normal times. Nothing can really dash the spirits of the English people, who love to grumble, and who, in spite of their complaints, are deeply confident of victory.

The prospect of photographing the Prime Minister next morning prevented me from sleeping most of the night. I knew it would be a difficult job, but it was most important that I should succeed. As with anyone whom I enormously revere, I am always paralysed with shyness in the presence of Churchill, and I knew I wouldn't be able to wear down his gruff façade in the short time that had been allotted for the sitting.

It was a cold grey morning and Dorothy, the maid, was slow in bringing the wretched little pot of hot shaving water (we have been two months without a bath at home – still no gas!), and I was late in starting off. When I got to No. 10 they were all rather feverish, Mrs Hill, Churchill's secretary, saying she had tried to call me to come earlier but my line was always busy, and now the Prime Minister was already in the Cabinet room and would not allow the lights to be rigged up there while he was working. Would we like to fix up something somewhere else? I was whisked down to see Mrs Churchill. On my way I noted that the symbol of Western survival had evidently hurried out of his tub that morning, and there was a trail of wet feet along the corridor, together with damp bath towels and a dripping sponge on a window-sill. Far from being surrounded by footmen or valets who ministered to his needs, Churchill has to manage his own bath, and however late he might be for a Cabinet meeting or an audience with the King, there are no short cuts even for his daily ablutions. Very feverish and excited Mrs C. seemed to be and said, 'You must come and see Winston right away.' Before I demurred that my preparations were not complete, all a-flutter, all flurries and staccato darts and jabs, Mrs Churchill put her head around a succession of mahogany doors. 'Is the Prime Minister in there?' Further doors leading to Adam rooms were opened, and from the final secretary's room I was able to catch my first glimpse of our goal. Through a double door, heavily lined, and framed by a couple of white columns, at the centre of an immensely long table, under an eighteenth-century portrait hanging above the noble chimneypiece of white marble, sat the Prime Minister. The huge Cabinet table stretched to left and right. The tall windows were, here and there, pasted with improvisations of brown paper. Mr Churchill appeared immaculately black, white and pink; fat, white, tapering hands deftly turned through the contents of a red leather box at his side. A vast cigar was freshly affixed in his chin. He was deeply engrossed.

But Mrs Churchill's entrance broke the solemnity of the atmosphere. All smiles and femininity, Mrs Churchill beamed, 'You know Mr Beaton, don't you? He's come to take a photograph of you.'

'Ah, yes!' He pierced me with his cold blue eyes, and barked, 'I hear you're very clever!'

The interruption was obviously displeasing and who, indeed, would wish to be deflected from the business of running a war by a photographer? The Prime Minister grumbled gruffly, inarticulately, huh-hummed. In desperation I threw down my trump card. The first photograph, just rushed through, of his grandson, Winston Junior. The atmosphere lightened for an instant, but then what else to do but leave the presence immediately, for what use is a photographer without a camera or light? Mrs Churchill had disappeared, smiling, into thin air, perhaps as embarrassed as I, perhaps oblivious. I made a hasty retreat and threw myself on the mercies of understanding and competent secretaries. Where could we most easily and quickly fix up the lights? No. 10 is now a nutshell, most of the furniture and pictures are gone, only a few secretaries' rooms have the necessities.

Mrs Hill, always kind and helpful, hurried from her silent typewriter opposite the Prime Minister to whisper that perhaps the reception room would be most suitable, but we must hurry as there was an eleven o'clock appointment. In a frenzy we tried to arrange the necessary paraphernalia, but the devil was in my Indian assistant, Haupt, today, and the lights would not go on. The big antediluvian camera was still buried in its case, and even the procedure of unpacking it was a lengthy one. Already panicking at the thought of the rush there would be at the last moment, I compromised on making a half-hearted arrangement of portable lights and smaller camera trained on to a yellow marble pillar in an upstairs room. Haupt and I then hurried down to the ground floor to await our fate outside the Cabinet room armed, just in case, with a Rolleiflex and some flash bulbs.

At ten minutes to eleven o'clock we were still waiting outside the mahogany door. Senior secretaries, who were playing their important roles in fighting the war, passed by. I noted with relief that they all seemed cheerful and at ease. Perhaps the war was not going so badly after all. At eleven o'clock the butler took a glass of port into the Cabinet room, and came back confiding that the Prime Minister had just started dictating to Mrs Hill.

The Whip, David Margesson, appeared and talked about the latest air-raid damage: minor secretaries crossed and recrossed the hall. It was 11.10. At 11.20 some more Government servants appeared. Without doubt the Prime Minister must leave at 11.25. He had a Cabinet meeting at 11.30!

Mrs Hill, white and worried, put her head around the mahogany door. 'No time to go upstairs. Would you just come in here and take a few pictures now?'

I went into this noble room again. Churchill, still with cigar in mouth, looked so lonely and alone in this large room. This would make an aptly symbolic picture. From my distant vantage point, I clicked my Rolleiflex, and Haupt let off a flash. This surprised the Prime Minister. Although his sentences were not perfectly formed, I would hazard that the following would be an interpretation of the barks, wheezes and grunts that turned my blood cold: 'Hey, damn you, young fellow, what the hell are you up to with your monkey tricks? Stop all this nonsense! I hate candid camera photographs! Wait till I'm prepared: the glass of port taken away, my spectacles so – this box shut, the papers put away thus – now then – I'm ready, but don't try any cleverness on me!'

The PM settled himself and stared into my camera like a bulldog guarding its kennel. Click! 'One more, please.' By slow degrees I stealthily stalked my prey, coming at last within close range of him on his left side. He glowered into the camera, and by slow degrees dissolved into half a smile. Good humour prevailed. 'Sorry I can't go upstairs to the lights, but come again – come another day!'

By now three minutes must have ticked away on the clock. Dare I venture? 'Would you turn this way?' To my intense relief he turned his head and in reply again I clicked the camera. 'But come again another day. I'd like to see something that isn't just another photograph.' He rose from his chair. I asked, 'May I take a flash of you as you walk along the corridor outside towards the front door?'

'Certainly, so long as you don't photograph me putting on my coat and hat – no fooling about!'

We are in position; the PM, ready for the day's business, was about to make his stately progress along the hall. The flash went off twice. I moaned an aside to Haupt, 'But that was a double flash!' The PM stopped. 'Does that mean it's ruined? Does that mean it won't come out?' 'Yes, sir.' And once more he turned on his heel and walked back the length of the hall to repeat the exodus for me.

30 December

The city was still in flames after last night's raid when eight Wren churches and the Guildhall were destroyed. It was an emotionally disturbing experience to clamber among the still smouldering ashes of this frightful wasteland. It was doubly agonizing to realize that, had precautions for fire-spotters been taken, much of the damage could have been avoided. But it was too late, and some of the best churches have gone with little to indicate what was there before.

St Bride's in Fleet Street is now just a gutted orangery; St Andrew-by-the-Wardrobe, a hideous black mass with a molten copper roof like a blanket pall over the charred remains. No signs can be found of Gog and Magog at the Guildhall, and only a few baroque memorial tablets with sorrowing cupids and skulls remain at St Vedast's.

In the biting cold with icy winds beating around corners, James P.H. and I ran about the glowing smouldering mounds of rubble where once were the printers' shops and chop houses of Paternoster Row. We have trundled under perilous walls, over uncertain ground which, at any moment, might give way to the red-hot vaults below. We have known Ypres in the heart of London. We could not deny a certain ghoulish excitement stimulated us, and our anger and sorrow were mixed with a strange thrill at seeing such a lively destruction – for this desolation is full of vitality. The heavy walls crumble and fall in the most romantic Piranesi forms. It is only when the rubble is cleared up, and the mess is put in order, that the effect becomes dead.

We went to St Paul's to offer our prayers for its miraculous preservation. Near the cathedral is a shop that has been burned unrecognizably; in fact, all that remains is an arch that looks like a vista in the ruins of Rome. Through the arch could be seen, rising mysteriously from the splintered masonry and smoke, the twin towers of the cathedral. It was necessary to squat to get the arch-way framing the picture. I squatted. A press photographer watched me and, when I gave him a surly look, slunk away. When I returned from photographing another church, he was back squatting and clicking in the same spot as I had been. Returning from lunch with my publisher, my morning's pictures still undeveloped in my overcoat pocket, I found the press photographer's picture was already on the front page of the *Evening News*.

Bognor

Duff [Cooper] has been ill for some days with a cocci infection. Three doctors have been brought in to look after him. At last his temperature is normal,

though he has become deaf in one ear, and he is sufficiently recovered for Diana
to send me a wire to come after all to Bognor.

The small Regency House in Bognor has been part of her life since her childhood holidays. Later her mother bought the beloved property, and now it is
Diana's haven. Although even here the sirens sound thirty times a day and
night, it is a comparatively peaceful existence for her running the place as if
it were a farm.

Diana has bought a cow called Princess – a feminine equivalent of Ferdinand,
for there never was so clinging and affectionate an animal as Princess. Twice
a day Diana milks her, at 7.30 am and 6 pm. Princess delivers enough milk to
keep the household and to make one large cheese every other day. The goat,
less docile, produces milk that makes equally good cheese. Diana's hens produce ten eggs a day, and the pigs, named after the St John Hutchinsons, their
children and children-in-law, are extremely clean for pigs.

But there is no nonsense about Diana posing in Le Hameau. 'To begin with,
it gave me a mental hernia to put my hand inside a rabbit and pull out its
insides. Now I give a good tug and don't mind, and it's the same skinning
a hare.' It is hard work. Every day, by breakfast time, Diana has been looking
after the farm for two hours. After breakfast she motors into Bognor with a
trailer attached to the car to see about a hen house, or she collects swill from
the neighbours, or the fish for the pie from the bus stop.

The latter part of the morning is spent in the dairy with large bowls of blue
and white china, butter muslin nets and spotless efficiency. Here she sets about
the technical jobs of cutting whey, taking temperatures and heating to certain
degrees large bathtubs of milk, which with the addition of rennet drops from
a calf's innards will be eventually turned into the required number of cheeses
and arranged in rows on the storeroom shelf.

Like everything she takes up, Diana works with enormous, business-like enthusiasm. Many amateurs set about their latest hobby with most elaborate
equipment, little patience and no knowledge. Not Diana: her house is now
littered with dog-eared, second-hand textbooks on bee-keeping, on chickens,
cows, goats. Her equipment consists of improvised utensils. A tinselled red
embroidered Mexican saddle bag is filled with heavy stones. This, she considers, placed together with a log of wood on a wooden tray, makes a suitable
enough press for the cheeses.

The guests – who may come down to keep her company while the Minister
is busy at his desk – help bring the swill pails, add bone meal to the animals'
fodder, or measure the dairy nuts for Princess. Diana makes all these chores
such fun, and gives the impression that the animals' food is every bit as good
as her own. Diana galvanized me into collecting in sacks some hay she had
earlier cut from a neighbour's field. The job was a pleasant form of relaxation

and an accompaniment to conversation, but, that task finished, there were many more to do while she fed the Khaki Campbells – her latest addition to the farm: a dozen ducks.

At the end of a long day she cooks the dinner. We sit at a table covered with pale lime green macintosh. The fish pie is highly flavoured with a lot of onions. The news is turned off directly the raids start.

Moments of pleasure and relaxation are savoured to the utmost in this cluttered personable house – so live a picture of its owner – with the pale limedrop cushions, the grey-lilac walls, the Empire mirrors and candlesticks, the taffeta-bowed muslin curtains and the cases brimming over with books. It is a house feminine in its colour but broad in its effects. There is no time for arranging nick-nacks for, as soon as *The Times* crossword puzzle has been completed, there is some mending to be done. Diana sews some yellow fringe from discarded dining-room curtains. She picks at the yellow braid and twists it around thumb and little finger in the professional way that drapers' assistants had perfected when she watched them, awestruck, as a child. Enough twilight remains for Duff to read aloud some stanzas of Andrew Marvell, and to compare Cowper's description of Cromwell to Hitler. Then early bed and a lot of books on the counterpane.

Diana has always been attuned to the time and circle she adorns. Today she is beautiful in the only way she could be admired at this moment. Wearing dungarees of blue canvas, flecked and splashed in many colours, her head tied up in a kerchief over which she wears a straw hat, she manages artlessly to look as beautiful as she did in *The Miracle*. Hard-working and vital, close to essentials and yet, in her simplicity, so highly civilized.

It is a lovely picture: Diana in her garden grown wild with gangling flowers blossoming under the rees, or scything the paddock; Diana, painstakingly putting entries into the farm ledger or, after carefully reading the instructions supplied by the local decorator, successfully hanging paper on the walls of an improvised guest room.

11

With the Royal Air Force
1941-2

C.B. toured the country, photographing both Fighter and Bomber bases for the Ministry of Information. He wrote and published Time Exposure *with text by Peter Quennell, and* Air of Glory. *He designed costumes for the films* Major Barbara, Kipps *and* The Young Mr Pitt.

Hugh Francis told me he would authorize my making a complete study of the RAF. Apart from the uses he would make of the photographs, I should write a fictional composition, written for propaganda. (This resulted in Hutchinson's publishing *Winged Squadrons*, drawn from my diaries.) At last, I felt, I was able to do something to assuage my pangs of guilt at being unable to make a more worthwhile contribution.

Tangmere: April 1941

Fighter pilots have a daredevil *bravura* quality, and seem to be rakishly gay and heroic in an offhand way. They are the more reckless ones, slightly temperamental, perhaps even a bit selfish – but only in comparison with the rest of the RAF, for selfishness, as known in the outside world, cannot exist here.

Though the fighter pilot generally flies alone he is always a part of the squadron, he is often flying in formation, and receives his instructions from the squadron leader or wing commander. However, we have the impression that the fighters are the tough ones, irresponsible young sparks who might risk all for a lark. But the daredevil who, without reckoning the odds, would go 'flat out', would 'shoot up' his aerodrome, diving down between the refuelling bowsers, has long since gone. Erratic feats of devil-may-care recklessness are less admired today than the calculated courage of the new type of hero with his 'cold guts'. His bravery needs no aids. His attitude, without heroics, even a little cynical, is sobered by his sense that so much depends upon him.

Under fine-weather conditions any fool can fly a straight course. To manœuvre a Spitfire in rough weather for an hour is as fatiguing as any normal day's work.

Although so much can happen within the few split-seconds of combat, the fighter is rarely more than an hour and a half in the air. Most of his time is spent waiting near his Spitfire 'at readiness' from dawn to sunset.

These young pilots stand about in loose attitudes, flexing the muscles of a leg, kicking a corner of the door with a heavy foot, or tossing a pencil in the palm of a hand that has a piece of sticking-plaster on it. Intent on nothing particular, they are absorbed by the waiting. Yet this lassitude is neither as casual nor as utterly carefree as it seems. At any moment the alert may sound – and then all hell breaks loose.

Hallo! What's this? One of the squadron back already?

'What happened to you, McCarthy?' McCarthy, of the large, pale moustache, is 'browned off'. The door of his machine had come unhinged and might have flown off, hitting his tail. So he'd had to turn around, hanging on to it with all his strength. He settles down in resignation to read a detective novel until the others return.

A dramatic silence pervades the operations room with the flashing lights of its batteries of telephones through which come information, orders and inquiries to the controller. The men working here are older, now considered unfit for operational duties although, having been previously through similar combats, they are able to give confidence to the younger men fighting in the sky.

The pilots, when many miles away over enemy-occupied territory, are comforted if they know the controller on duty and recognize his voice. The controller can become a sort of godfather to the fighter pilots – a sympathetic link with the ground; they like to hear the deep, pleasant voice which warns them: 'Bandits behind you, but don't worry', and in answer to their, 'I think I'd better come home', replies: 'Yes, come home right away.'

Though conversing with one another in the air is not encouraged, for it may add confusion and their bad language prove embarrassing to the WAAFs in the 'Ops' room, the fighters can often be heard calling to one another on their radio sets: 'Look out for your tail!' 'You take that one on the right, I'll take this.' Leslie, with his tombstone teeth and mop of yellow straw hair, is recognized, when soaring above the clouds, by his imitation of Donald, the squadron's mascot duck. It never fails to send a shiver down the spine when you hear the cry 'tally-ho' as the fighters dive to engage the enemy.

One by one the returning aircraft circle before landing. An intelligence officer is there to interrogate the fighters as, with surprising agility, they jump from the cockpit. As all men when they arrive from the skies, they appear a little remote from this planet. They have acquired the ecstasy that only pilots know. They have become a particle of the great kingdom of the skies – attained the sense of freedom of a bird. This has been achieved by complete mastery of the aircraft and the element in which they fly. Now, ambling along towards the hangars, harness thrown over their shoulders, they smile the smile that conveys more sentiment than a whole host of words.

The questions surprise them. 'How many does that make? How many missing?'

'Yes, I got one, but Brownie's not back, nor Leslie.'

'Anyone see what happened to Brownie?'

'Someone saw him shot down in flames.'

'See him bale out?'

'No. Don't think he got his hood open.'

'How bloody!'

Another aircraft circles above. It must be Leslie! Yes, it is. Leslie appears, straw thatch on end, in such a state of wild exultation that his very teeth are flashing as he punches the air.

'Oh, boy! Oh, boy! Never had such a time! I got two, two down. Never had such a wonderful ten minutes in my life. Oh, boy! Oh, boy!'

Mildenhall

These dark grey weeks spent at a bomber station have given me an appalling sense of guilt. Not only am I a stranger and one who is incapable of sharing the dangers of this terrifying life, but I am an interloper prying into the private existences of these airmen.

Hugh Francis suggested that a picture 'feature' – hackneyed enough in idea, but, none the less, one to be approached with sincerity and freshness – would be to show 'a day in the life of a bomber pilot'. Initially to find the right type was hard enough, but then to assuage his natural aversion to being picked out for prominence from his fellows created a tougher problem. However, when the CO suggested we should use Robert Tring as our star – he was handsome, nineteen years old and had brought back his crew and aircraft, B for Bobby, from twenty-nine bombing trips over Berlin – Bobby could not demur with impunity.

B for Bobby was, in fact, an excellent choice with his photogenic, cat-like features, rather wild, dark eyes, and black silken curls. But to see him, as I did for the first time, sitting bolt upright in his cell-like room, legs folded, with *Tarka the Otter* held in his slender, feminine hands, you would never suspect that he had enough strength of muscle to take up, and bring down, a heavy Stirling bomber. Yet Bobby is one of the most steady and reliable pilots of the squadron. The son of a clergyman from the Cotswolds, his is the dark quiet voice of the scholar. He is the perfect antithesis of the brutish type our enemy produces.

Slowly he went to the basin, washed his hands, and brushed smoother his

C.B. in 1924; Summer holidays at Sandwich

Edith Sitwell

Rex Whistler

John Gielgud as Romeo, 1930

Jean Cocteau, Gare des Invalides, Paris, 1933

Gary Cooper

Gertrude Stein and Alice B. Toklas

The Duke and Duchess of Windsor, 1936

hair. He looked abashed that this action should seem worth recording. Again, before lunch in the mess, when he drank from a pewter tankard, he seemed surprised that this conviviality should warrant more pictures.

After lunch Bobby and all the crews on tonight's raid were given their preliminary briefing. Every available inch of wall is covered with large-scale maps and photograph mosaics: the balloon barrages, the known ground defences and hostile fighter bases are indicated by blobs of purple ink; threads are stretched over the route the bombers are to take. Seventy-five per cent of the bomber's work must be done before he leaves the ground, so he must be of a patient, persevering disposition, ready to take infinite pains over his preparations.

So great is Bobby's absorption that he has now become quite oblivious to the camera's presence. No lecturer ever had a more attentive audience than the senior intelligence officer. Heads crowd close together around him, intent, earnest, solemn; they are surely those of mere schoolboys. Their faces and hands are smooth and pale without any suggestion of down upon them. Rows of cats' eyes peer up at a blind which is suddenly pulled down on which the details of tonight's target – the Ruhr – are flashed by the vast epidiascope. The navigators are given their special conundrums and immediately start to make their calculations, and to copy the various codes and cyphers to be used. They must recognize the fake German towns – and not release their valuable load on dummy targets.

These youths are quite objective about their task: they do not feel hatred for the individual German. How can he hate someone he does not know? Bobby asks. Yet he will have no mercy for the enemy, knowing he will show none for them. Incentive for revenge is given when a submarine sinks a ship without warning, or a friend is shot down on his parachute; but in most cases the assault is an impersonal one.

The crew ask few questions. They show little interest in why this certain target has been selected; they just get on with whatever they have to do and make every effort to ensure good results. Thus the explosion from an effective hit causes them satisfaction, for a technical feat has been accomplished. But they do not like to think too much about the punishment they inflict.

The weather is rough again – perhaps too rough for tonight's sortie: nothing to do but wait for further reports to come in. This tension of anticipation has a frustrating effect to which no pilot becomes totally inured, however hard he tries to accustom himself. Sometimes a pilot will remain keyed-up for weeks before it is possible for him to play his part.

By now Bobby is showing distinct signs of becoming tired of me. In fact, by the way he chain-smokes and casts a slightly haunted look out of his stag's eyes, I wonder if he is not showing signs of over-fatigue and nervous stress.

But one more trip and Bobby will be leaving this station. He wishes to be sent 'out' East, but it's more likely that he will be posted to a training school to become a flying instructor.

The wind has blown away some fog. The Met people now seem to think conditions are becoming more favourable.

'We'll be on tonight,' says Baker, who puts his head around the door, then is gone. Baker is Bobby Tring's second pilot, the heavy Etruscan type, with a shock of black silk fringe falling to his jet-black eyes. Sitting by Bobby's side in his heavy leather suit, he has been a monolith of strength throughout the perils of the past twenty-nine trips.

The Met people were right and the 'big trip' is on: those valued and terrible jewels of destruction, the enormous torpedo-shaped bombs, have been taken from the prison-like vaults where, in the silence of the tomb, they lie in row upon row, rack upon rack, and are now placed in readiness in the under-belly of the aircraft.

The crew-room is crowded and full of smoke for the final briefing. The weather expert gives his latest information and last words of advice. The navigators put maps, dividers, and protractors into their satchels. The crews stand about, fastening the clasps or pulling at the straps of their parachute harness, buckling on the life preservers, or adjusting the electric tubes of their 'hot suits'. They are laughing and in high spirits.

The provisions for the trip are handed out, carefully selected Christmas packages: energy pastilles, chewing-gum, raisins, chocolate slabs. The scene is as light-hearted as that of the locker-room before a preparatory school football game.

'What's happened to my gloves?' asks Bobby's gunner, a tough-looking little runt from Lancashire with a face that screws up like rubber when he smiles. The missing gloves are found. Then a pair of white silk ones (one had forgotten that sort since the days of juvenile dancing classes) is put on; over these he wears the leather gloves, and on top the fur. A ten-foot scarf is coiled around neck and shoulders. Bobby, serious and somewhat aloof, still wears his service cap, for he does not wish to be photographed in a helmet and will only put it on when once in the cockpit.

Outside they lie about on the ground, looking suddenly like strange Bank Holiday-makers, waiting for the lorry to come back to take another load to the dispersal points. Bobby is taking a light from Baker, their last cigarette for an unconscionable time.

'Wonder how much we'll see tonight?'

'From the look of it we'll be lucky if we see the Rhine.'

I now realize that in any further photograph I take it would be tactful to make Bobby's presence only incidental.

The lorry's here. In their cumbersome harness the young men clamber up and are jostled together, laughing, jerking up their thumbs and generally behaving as if they were getting a lift as far as the local Odeon, instead of for a journey of 1,100 hazardous miles.

Arrival at the aircraft seems as vague and casual as if no definite time were set for the take-off. But there is no hitch or delay. The ground crew have put their final touch to the vast machine that towers, like some prehistoric beast, against the grey-blue sky streaked with apricot-coloured islands. Daylight is waning, but the decline is gradual, and you are barely aware of it before semi-darkness envelops you.

Two of the crew are standing rather stiffly against the hedge, with their backs to us; then they come towards us and burrow into the bowels of the aircraft.

Aloft in the cockpit, at a height where the top windows of a tall house would be, Bobby at last straps on his helmet. The navigator is laying out his chart, adjusting his astrograph, arranging his sextant and numerous papers and bundles into position. The wireless operator is tuning up his set; the second pilot testing his RT, while the engineer checks his instruments. In his protruding glass 'blister', the rear-gunner, with barrels depressed to their fullest extent, takes a careful look to see that no one is 'in line', and fires a burst of fiery sparks to make sure his guns are working correctly.

'He's taking no chances,' an officer standing by explains.

'Don't blame him either,' smiles another.

As the airscrews jerk and, one after the other, the four engines roar, the wall of noise becomes deafening. The wind of their power flattens the grass and drives away stray leaves, twigs, dust, and some old canvas covers in the slip-stream. The ground crew, their flapping trousers flattened to one side of their legs as the engines rev up ever more furiously, are standing on the side lines and, like comic people in an early cinema farce, are quivering paralytically, their hair on end. The vast chocks are pulled aside. The prehistoric beast is navigated into position for the take-off. From the control tower the instructions are given to stand by. The first monster crawls forward, gathers speed, rushes to the boundary of the airfield, and rises with a roar. Another has taken up its position and starts its run, along, now off. One by one the 'giants with stings in their tails' have circled the pale night and float like a slow-moving frieze against the sky.

Those of us who are left behind can only guess what the experience must be for those who undertake this awful journey. We see the men who come back and we receive their travellers' tales: we hear them discussing amongst themselves the excitement and terrors of that nine or twelve hours' ordeal. Time itself becomes a black eternity as the aircraft, without even giving its passengers the comforting sensation that they are in motion, bores its way through the night.

('Will there really be a morning – is there such a thing as day?') We know that the heating apparatus often 'packs up', and in an attempt to relieve with some counter-pain the agonies of frostbite and lack of oxygen these boys have butted their young heads on the metallic floors of the aircraft.

Meanwhile, in the control room, situated at the top of a sort of land light-house, the signals and reports come in. To avoid being located by their radio, the bombers seldom break wirelesss silence on the outward journey, but they must send a message when their mission is completed. To this polished, rather empty operation theatre of a room, the dramas of the raid are relayed.

In Shakespeare's wars night was quiet for men and animals, and the birds slept. This war knows no such night; the crepitations of darkness are shattered by the bestial shriek of enemy bombs, or, as we now hear, the magnificent roar of returning friends – the giant Stirlings circling above.

How long must we wait until they are all back? This is the zero hour of suspense; soon the vigil will be over; we will hear of their achievements and of the price that has been paid.

Up on a vast board the arrivals are chalked; there are still half a dozen to return, but already the lorries will have brought back from the dispersal points the first crews who, peeling off layers of gloves, jackets and scarves, explode into the guard room. Accustomed to being buffeted by various vibrations in their cramped confines, they tell you how wonderful is the moment when the engines are switched off, the noise is over, and they can drop out and pull deeply at a cigarette. With hair awry, these boys are still part of the nightmare that has engulfed them. After the hours of inspissated darkness, interrupted only by blinding flashes of deadly light, they screw up their eyes on coming into the unshielded lights, and appear as if waking from a deep sleep. Here they are – yes, the same men whom (secretly) you prayed for at their outset at sundown. But the interim has told its tale and every one of them has aged by several years.

However, soon their tongues are loosened, and they tell one another, with an exuberant relish, of their adventures. For the time they quite forget that 'brave men hide or make excuses for their deeds'.

'We gave the Hun a pasting all right – took him by surprise – must have had too good a dinner, for it was some time before he started any "flak".'

'Thank God!' says one of the men as he flings his helmet on a bench. 'But they're bastards. Don't know how they do it. We fly so high that it takes their "flak" a minute and a half to reach us, yet by the time we've travelled a mile and a half on anything but a straight course, there's the stuff waiting to meet you! And doesn't it just bump you about when it hits you!'

The CO moves among them. He learns that the squadrons hopped over clouds on their way out; they expected to have to fly low over their targets, but in the end the clouds had parted to show the way for the bomb-aimers.

The CO hides his relief, and casually asks, 'Any news of B for Bobby, or D for Donald?'

'No, sir.'

The crews are now wolfing sandwiches and meekly saying 'thank you' for the thickly-sugared milk and coffee from the urn.

A gaunt, ghostlike youth tumbles in, his face of a grey pallor.

'Feugh! I've never sweated so much in one night! For sheer sweat this trip takes the cake! I thought those photographs that you took of us, Beaton, were going to be our memorial. Jerry got us in a cone of lights, and did he jib us about, eh? I certainly thought it was our last "ops" – the worst I've had yet!'

The flight sergeant returns, 'B for Bobby just down, sir,' and before long Bobby Tring strolls in, still very erect, but with the look in his eyes even wilder. He wears his peaked cap on the back of his curly head and smokes nervously.

Soon the formal interrogation has started. The epic legends of the night are pieced together. At one table they discuss the fighter opposition met on the raid, and how L for London had pinpointed a factory with a load of incendiaries. A senior intelligence officer points with a pencil to the map in front of him. 'And here, how was the "flak"?'

Bobby, leaning on the palm of his hand, with wrinkled forehead, mumbles, 'Pretty bad, sir, really pretty bad.'

The older man wrinkles his forehead in sympathy and nods. 'Still here,' he said, again pointing. 'Over Holland at this point it would be fairly quiet, wouldn't it?'

'Oh, no, sir!' affirms Baker, the second pilot, and the others join in. 'Not a bit of it, regular Fifth of November firework display.'

'Hm! And there – did you make that target?'

'Yes, sir; we had to make a second run though. But I think we can be certain of it,' says Bobby, drawing deep on his cigarette.

'Oh, yes! We got that all right,' corroborates the rear-gunner in his Lancashire accent. 'Yes, sir, we got that one – and what a flame that dump made!'

Again the CO turns to a corporal. 'Any news of D for Donald? – must be getting short of petrol now.'

'Nothing's come in yet, sir.'

At another table a group is arguing about the colour of the 'flak' at Gelsenkirchen. 'It was red, definitely.'

'No, I'd say pink.'

'Absolute rot! It was orange with a white centre.'

'Aw! You mean pink with green spots.'

January 1942

Wet feet – cold feet all day long – in the snow and in railway carriages going to and from a Ministry of Information job. Particularly discouraged to arrive at night at Denham to find no John Sutro to meet me, as arranged, at the station. Waving a lantern in an endeavour to find a telephone box, like Lear on the heath, I staggered down a snowy road. At last a pair of headlamps, a call from the darkness, and I was saved. John motored me to his temporary home where we found his wife, Gillian, waiting for us in front of a glowing hearth. With her was Noël Coward, who is preparing his film *In Which We Serve* at the neighbouring studios.

Although each time we have met we have become friends Noël and I have never got along well. In between meetings we have said bad things about one another and obviously they have been repeated. It's true that I have been bloody about him, and I have never quite known why I should have felt so intolerant and bitter. There was no reason to be that jealous of him. It isn't that we cross one another's paths. I don't resent successful people as a rule. However, here we were irrevocably face to face and, as usual, and, of course, we were pleased to see each other.

Noël was extremely generous and, at once, said some kind things about my recent work. I was pleased. Life suddenly had a glow as I sat in my socks, my shoes baking by the huge fire. The very cockles of my being were thawed even more by the praise than the embers or the cocktails. However, after two enormous Martinis I felt I should keep a check on myself in case I should say something that could be taken in evidence against me by my new-found friend. This was ungenerous of me because the white flag had been accepted by us both, and Noël was being completely frank and opening himself up to me on a platter. Who was I to hold back? A lot more gin loosened any remaining constraints I had.

Soon an extraordinary evening, which the Sutros watched in comparative silence, was under way. Suddenly I confessed, 'I've never really minded your being bloody about me, but it has baffled me that a person of your perspicacity should have shown no interest in me.' To which he answered, 'Don't you believe it, sister, I've been madly interested in you! But I've been a fool, I've misjudged you. The war has shown how wrong I've been. You've done a great job – you've earned great respect in the RAF; and it just shows what a mistake I made. You've been yourself always, and how right you've been! I've been hiccuping off at the outbreak of the war, thinking it was a wonderful thing to give up those two plays that were already in production to do a job that anyone else could have done. You've done much better than I by just sticking to your guns: people respect you more for that. You used to stand for everything I dislike. I've been beastly about you being Elsa Maxwell's darling and Elsie

Mendl's puss. But I've been wrong. Let's be buddies! Life's going to be tough for us all for the next years of the war, and much tougher after the war, and it's better that people like us should be friends rather than enemies because we really have so much in common – powers of observation, wit, industriousness and professionalism. Ring me up, or I'll telephone to know what you're doing at the last minute, and come to stay here, while we're making this film, in my guest room any night you're free.'

I asked Noël about his method of writing plays, but he elaborates little on the birth pangs of creation for the reason that there are none, or if so, they are not interesting to him. 'If I type easily then I know the stuff is good!' The way he goes over the appalling obstacles of play construction is done with the ease of a surf-rider skimming the Honolulu waves. He spoke with emotion of his childhood when his mother took him to the pit to see Gertie Millar, Gracie Leigh and the other stars of his formative period. He is first-rate when discussing the theatre in any of its branches. He dismisses Broadway as of little interest. I asked, 'And Geo. Kaufman – what do you think of him?' 'Nothing – why, do *you*?' Broadway is too easy meat for Noël. He admitted to having had such success during the last fifteen years that he wouldn't think it terrible if a bomb killed him today. '*Blithe Spirit* is a bloody good play, and *Private Lives* will always be revived and will go into the history of comedy like a play by Congreve or Wilde.'

14 January

Thirty-eight! 14 January 1904, I was born thirty-eight years ago! I've never liked birthdays – not even at fourteen did I want to be older. But birthdays used to be a festivity – now another nail in my coffin. Was busy this morning – didn't have much time to think about it.

Lunch with Cecil Day Lewis who talked about the way he writes poetry: gets a clue line, writes it in a notebook. Later, when he has a stomach-ache that denotes it is time for him to deliver, the poem is evolved around this line. Half of poem is due to the way he works it out – half inspiration – half technique (or idiom).

24 January

Margot Oxford said she was not fond of Sibyl Colefax of the dark curly hair. 'I don't care who people know, and it is so tiresome that Sibyl is always on the spot. One can't talk about the birth of Christ without that Astrakhan ass saying she was there in the manger.'

It was here at the Savoy that Ivor Novello had recently gone up to Margot's table and introduced himself. Margot looked nonplussed, then uttered: 'Novello? Novello? Ah yes! You smile too much and Eddie Marsh loved you!'

Now that my RAF book has been sent to the printers I am looking around for my next job. My ambition is to be sent to the Near East. Randolph Churchill, on leave, was enthusiastic and helpful. I go to see Brendan Bracken on Wednesday, and there is a chance that the Ministry of Information may send me to Cairo to take photographs and do articles for another book. It is a thrilling prospect, and there is now a star shining brightly in front of me.

12

The War in the Middle East
1942

From Cairo C.B. made excursions into the Western Desert, to Iran, Iraq, Palestine, Transjordan and Syria. As Rommel advanced on Egypt, he returned home via the Sudan, Lagos and the flesh-pots of Portugal. He published Winged Squadrons.

Cairo: March 1942

Many of those in high authority have been out here for more than three years. To an outside observer like myself that seems far too long. In this war, fresh ideas come so fast that even a man capable of adapting himself to new ways of thinking is soon apt to get 'behind the times'. Moreover, the clammy heat squanders a man's patience and plays upon his moral fibre as relentlessly as on his physique: unless he resigns himself to running in low gear his nerves are soon frayed and the Kipling epitaph applies: 'Here lies the fool who tried to hustle the East.' Thus, the Cairene climate, producing a *laissez-aller* policy, procrastination and delay, is a great ally to Hitler.

I was bidden to eight o'clock breakfast at 'Air House'. This official residence of the Air Officer Commanding-in-Chief Middle East is where he lives and entertains any distinguished RAF commanders in transit or on a visit to Headquarters. It looks like a house you would find at Godalming, and its drawing-room and dining-room suites are furnished with a strange 'unlived-in' formality. Park and de Crespigny, the AOCs of Egypt and Iraq respectively, had already finished breakfast when I arrived, and Tedder came down saying, 'Shall we nibble?' What sort of a man is this who has one of the most responsible jobs out here? He looks like a bilious schoolboy. His complexion is sallow and rather dry with very small wrinkles. Thick hair, twinkling eyes, bat's ears and wiry body, with legs that stretch back at the calf like a bow. It is impossible to believe that this coltishness belongs to someone of fifty-two. He does not wish to impress – rather to put everyone at ease, so that talk will be at its most natural and interesting. He puffs at his pipe, smiles with his eyes, and invites you to a conspiracy of friendship. He is, you feel, always storing up impressions, and the opinions of anyone with whom he comes in contact are grist to his mill.

Tedder has been accused of being too full of charm, of not being forceful enough. He is a man of undoubted charm, but I would not like to cross him. He can suddenly become granite, as he did when describing some of the remarkable things against heavy odds that the RAF boys had achieved out here in the desert, and in Malta, from where he had just returned.

I was somewhat anxious lest he should give me technical instructions that would be above my head, or that he might discuss warfare in the Near East as if I were as knowledgeable as some recent American woman journalist had been. But, knowing that someone else was in charge of my programme, he showed me crayon sketches he had done of the bombing of Malta. Although quite naïve in technique these little pictures gave a better impression of these war scenes than the press photographs. Tedder always carries this small notebook in his breast-pocket, and produces it when he sees something he'd like to record as a 'souvenir'. 'You're going to Syria? Well, hurry up and get there before the spring flowers are over.' This remark surprised me pleasantly. 'Yes, the wild flowers are a bit late already, but they're amazing – in one square yard of rock garden I counted twenty-seven different varieties.'

After the comparative 'austerity' of England, Cairo presents a luxurious façade with ultra-fashionable Egyptian, Greek and Syrian women giving lavish entertainments, servants without number, and none of the usual restrictions. The torrent of optimistic war news in the Anglo-Egyptian newspapers gives many of the English people here the complacent feeling that the war will be over in two months. Even Churchill's speeches are not given in full if the import is not sufficiently encouraging. This policy of pap feeding is aimed, it is said, at 'heartening' the Egyptians. But surely we have a grim enough example from France of what happens when the newspapers refuse to face the gravity of events?

The Desert

Derek Adkin is to be my conducting officer while I am with the RAF in the desert. This is a godsend, for Derek has toted me around so many air stations in England – and he knows my interests and how to intervene as soon as I am getting out of my depth. Today Derek and I went shopping for necessities and commodities for the desert trip. There is so much to buy that it seems like marriage, getting a trousseau, and setting up house.

Once you have shown your passes and are admitted into the fraternity inside the barriers of the desert – yes, there is a barbed-wire entrance to the desert

– the newcomer, no matter to what Service or Allied nation he belongs, will be received, without question, not only as an honoured guest, but as a long-lost friend. No matter to what strain the cookhouse has already been put by the difficulties of communications, invitations to share what rations remain will always be pressed, even if an acceptance means your host 'tightening his belt' or 'going dry'.

The bedouins, in the wadis near the shore, watching the battle wage backwards and forwards along the tableland, consider the protagonists mad. They see first one army and then another retiring in haste, leaving behind a wonderful amount of loot. The bedouins steal forward and sell their spoils to the conquering army. A few months later the victors are vanquished; again the Arabs find great booty. They are the only people, so far, to win on this hazardous chessboard, where invariably the winner loses with his long lines of communication. Only the Arabs understand how to live here in the desert. They have learnt little else. After the battle, in which tanks are set on fire and their occupants fried alive, the fluid field of battle moves on, and the Arabs arrive to pick up, among the useless relics and impediments of destruction, the gold rings, wrist-watches, cameras and souvenirs from the stiffened bodies lying in the sun. They will sell the silver strap of a wrist-watch that is worth fifteen guineas for a few pounds of sugar. Occasionally they are punished with the loss of an eye, hand or arm; for the Germans sometimes leave behind them fountain-pens and Thermoses which, when opened, ignite the secret fuse – then bang!

I came to the desert thinking I was nearer to war; yet even here war seems distant.

Where then is war? In Whitehall, where the planning is done, thousands of miles from the sound of the guns, it necessarily seems remote. Here I see how much spade work goes on continuously behind the lines, the running of maintenance units, of repairs to telephones and cars, the arranging of the never-ending difficulties of transport. I see how many hours of dreary waiting and inconvenience must be endured each day, or how much time can be spent repairing an accumulator or a lorry, bringing in trays of tea, or doing chores that make life here similar to what it might be back home. I see that human existence in the desert has not the proportion of the surroundings. Yet I realize that all these aspects are as real a part of war as another.

'I've never had so much fun as now', said a friend of mine while firing at the Germans, but he was carried away by his enjoyment and was soon taken prisoner. Can he be considered a more intrinsic part of war than the orderly lighting the Primus stove? The chores are as actual a part of war as the excitement.

Halfaya Pass

Now to the forward areas. The packing up was like moving house. Bags, folding beds, Primus stoves, provisions, water cans. Derek and I took crates of drink. We bumped and banged, ricocheted from rocks into potholes. The hideous roads seemed endless, with many miles of scrub and muck extending as far as the eye could see.

Quite unexpectedly, and within a few minutes, I was given my baptism of sand. Hot winds blew particles into every crevice of the sealed car, into one's throat, eyes, nose. The wheels of the car added their individual dust storms and the sand poured over the mudguards like clouds of sulphurous smoke. Sometimes it was impossible to see even a few yards ahead, but occasionally patches of road were clear. When the storm was at its worst, the smell was, according to Derek, like new linen.

The sandstorm had abated when we got to Sollum, a badly-bashed fishing village. The waves were washing through the skeleton of a wrecked ship by the shore. The houses were pockmarked with shell wounds, and not a roof remained. We drove by hairpin turns up Sollum Pass, past long-haired, immaculate, turbaned Indians, running glibly over Halfaya Pass in pistachio-green tanks. The relics of the battle of Halfaya are now half-buried in sand. A clothing stores must have been blown up; hundreds of shirts, neatly folded, were strewn on the sand; some tanks were blown up, so that a rhythm of circular discs stood in diminishing recession. The ground was littered with ammunition, gas masks, water-bottles, old boots and letters. The surrealist painters have anticipated this battleground with its eternal incongruities: the carcasses of burnt-out aeroplanes lying in the middle of a vast panorama; overturned trucks; cars that have been buckled by machine-gun fire, with their under parts pouring out in grotesque, tortured shapes: some unaccountable clothing blown into the telephone wires, or drapery in a tree seen against sunsets of bright, unforgettable colours.

A north-country soldier was wandering casually among the graves of the German soldiers, their topis, rotting in the sun, thrown over the crosses that bear the beastly swastika. A beer bottle, with a piece of paper inside, upturned with its neck dug into the sand, was all there was to identify the young man who had died in obedience to the Fuehrer – 'Adolf Gross, born 14.11.19, died June 1941'. The north-country soldier put back the bottle. 'It makes you think,' was what he said.

One of the worst aspects of desert life is the men's lack of reading matter. However conscientious they are about their duties, much of their time necessarily must be spent 'hanging about being bored'. In the whole of the Middle East there is a shortage of books (such a thing as a Baedeker is nowhere available). The paper shortage is worse than it is in England, and transport cannot be spared for the printed word. Randolph Churchill has worked wonders by not only inaugurating, within a week, and editing a *Desert Press Review*, but by devious means, seeing that it has reached even the most remote outposts.

Air Chief Marshal Coningham welcomed us in his immaculate trailer. Of its interior he is justifiably proud: no grain of sand had penetrated past the meat-safe mesh of the entrance. In leather frames were photographs of his good-looking wife, like Norma Shearer, and family. The atmosphere was peaceful, as if he had everything in control, a most encouraging feeling. Huge, good-looking, strong, sunburnt like an apricot, with a wide column of neck and massive chest. When he talks he shows his lower teeth – there is a gap between the two front teeth. When he laughs, the upper row appears small and in bad condition. In every other way Coningham gives the impression of perfect health. His bright clear eyes turn up slightly at the outer corners. He sits, a colossus at his desk, and waves his arms in broad masculine gestures.

He considers Cairo a bad place for a headquarters. English people cannot fight against the climate and sooner or later become static. Yet, on account of communications it seems impossible to transfer to Heliopolis or Alexandria. He described the desert, without trees or water, as an ideal battleground. He quoted the German General von Ravenstein who, when taken prisoner, called it 'the tactician's paradise and the quartermaster's nightmare'. Not more than one man out of every 500 is ill, that is 0.2 per cent. Of the difficulties he encountered in the desert one of the most frequent was the wish of the men to 'build themselves in'. Whenever he found someone made himself a cement floor to his tent, Coningham would move the camp a mile farther on. The men should be mobile at a few hours' notice and feel that they are nowhere permanently. For the Germans, with their Teutonic orderliness, it was even more difficult. Each time they move camp they start lining little pathways with stones, so soon (we hope) to be abandoned. To keep them in good mental health, Coningham insists that his men work every hour of daylight so that they are pleased to go to bed: with nothing to do but try to look for ticks and scorpions they would become so apathetic that they would not even walk the necessary mile to their mess for a hot meal, but would prefer to open, on the spot, a tin of bully beef for their lunch. Fortunately we had troops here before the war who have the instinct of the desert by now.

But the desert absorbs so much it alone is the victor. To fight here is like trying to fill a bath without a plug, where everything gets washed down the pipe. Two hundred thousand gallons of petrol are devoured each week, 80,000 vehicles are maintained in the knowledge that each can survive only about six months' duration. The waste was terrible; especially on aeroplane machines, which had continuously to be overhauled. A man returned from a raid on Benghazi with, it was discovered, eighty pounds of dust in the wings of his aircraft. He said he thought it felt rather 'soggy'.

Stirling and the Long Range Desert Group, the highwaymen of the desert, have made a legend for themselves with their extremely scientific, yet romantic, pirate-story adventures. Sometimes for months on end they patrol the desert ocean in armoured vehicles equipped with radios. Often they penetrate miles behind the enemy's lines, take him by surprise at night, burn army lorries, destroy tanks, and blow up vital equipment. This war is one of machines and technical efficiency: it allows little scope for individual escapades by groups of men. But the very specialized warfare that the Long Range Desert Group have perfected is an exception. It is one which the Germans, thus far, have ignored or have not dared to undertake.

Stirling, Ramsay and the other officers seemed to be a serious, sophisticated lot – like members of an Olympian club. The easy laughter and child-like ragging that whiles away time in many messes was absent. A most impressive group, too dedicated for small talk, they plot and carry out a primitive and savage form of warfare with a buccaneer's courage and a philosopher's mental refinement. The men, coming from all walks of life – chauffeurs, bricklayers, policemen, professional soldiers – were drilling in the heat of the day with as much precision and smartness as if they were outside Wellington Barracks square.

Clump, clump, clump. A patrol commander came in, heavily-bearded, covered with sand, matted hair on end, sunburned so that the white shining teeth were his most brilliant feature. He had just returned from an expedition of many month's duration yet his fellow officers welcomed him as if he had returned from short leave. 'Had a good time?' 'Everything go well?' No doubt on account of the stranger in their midst, few questions were asked. Everything was taken quietly as a matter of course. Yet, undoubtedly, this man had come across tremendous excitements. Lunch over, the newcomer took us round to see his men. A more grotesquely assorted, more frightening-looking bunch of bandits it would be hard to imagine. Bearded, covered with dust, with bloodshot eyes, they were less of the world of today than like primeval warriors, or timeless inhabitants of a remote hemisphere. One apparition with ginger matting for hair, and red eyes staring from a blue-grey dusty face, looked no more human than an ape. They were now avidly reading the mail that had arrived during their long absence. One man, who had been a professional swimmer, chuckled as he read aloud: 'I cannot wait until after the war, when we can get married and live together for always.' Cairo demands too little of a man, and the desert too much. Existence in the desert is, in its way, as

unnatural as that of Cairo, for a false reality prevails. The desert is an unnatural habitat for the average human being. It may be possible to dominate
your surroundings for a certain length of time. But after a long spell you may,
though physically healthy, grow mentally lax.

Yet although there can be no more wasteful, heartless and purposeless theatre
of war than the desert, still it possesses advantages. It is a healthy battleground,
unlike the disease-spreading mud and miasmas of the 1914 trenches: most men
are physically fitter than ever before in civilian life. Life here is primeval, and
from this very simplicity seems to spring a new contentment. Often the men
become so contented that they are said to be 'sand happy'.

Geoffrey Nares, the son of Owen Nares, the matinée idol, whom I knew in
theatrical circles, suddenly appeared as if from nowhere. He is much changed
from the elf-like boy I used to know. He is now captain of an armoured car.
He told me that in the desert he was continuously frightened. During a patrol
through all the hours of daylight, he must watch the enemy through field-
glasses. Sometimes during an entire day he would be lucky if he could snatch
a cup of tea.

Geoffrey told me how for months his men had perched on a little hill facing
the enemy. They had come to think of it as 'their' hill, but one day the Germans
brought up a big gun and forced them to retreat. In the excitement one of Geoffrey's men left behind an enamel plate. When later the fortunes of war changed
and they were able to throw the Germans back from the hillock, they found
a little pile of German magazines, on which was the plate bearing the message:
'You left this behind you – Fritz.'

Cairo

Geoffrey is here on leave, and I have seen a lot of him. He does not seem to
know what to do with his days – the days to which he had looked forward
all those months in the desert. Maybe Geoffrey has always been a sad, striving,
rudderless young man. I knew him at first when, dabbling on the stage, he
appeared with my friend Caroline Paget. They struck up a romantic friendship.
However, the moment war was declared, though hating the idea, he joined the
army. He did well. He is now a grand officer in a grand regiment. Yet he still
seems to be lost.

While we sat at a café or restaurant table Geoffrey, with his attractive, sallow,
tired baby's face and dark, melting eyes, talked obsessively of his life in the
desert. Most men there pass the time wondering what it is they most look forward to on their leave: luxury, comfort, food, sex life, or drink. Yet whenever
Geoffrey heard the troops discussing their future, their one desire, no matter
how poor their conditions had been, was that life after the war should be exactly

the same as it used to be. They don't want a 'better world'; they dream only of the old days.

The night before his leave was up Geoffrey and I dined together: he looked particularly poignant, his large brown eyes deep pools of sadness. As we got into the hotel lift to go to our rooms he appalled me by saying, 'Goodnight! I shall never see you again – give my love to Caroline and all those people.' (Geoffrey's premonition was correct. He died in hospital a few months later.)

Friday 29 May

Dudley Barker asked excitedly, 'Do you want to take some action pictures?'

'Then it has started in the desert?'

'Yes, this morning.'

This was how I heard that Rommel had attacked. One of the Anglo-Egyptian secretaries squeaked up, 'Oh, I can't get a thrill out of the desert any longer. It's always a case of someone going backwards or forwards.'

Saturday 6 June

The news from the desert still is that we are locked in a death struggle with the enemy. The losses in men and machinery must be colossal, but this seems quite remote from the war that the Egyptians see. They only take the war seriously if it means they are able to do just a bit more profiteering.

Beirut

Joan Aly Khan is a subtle and kind creature. To find myself sheltering under her roof is one of the greatest strokes of good fortune I have ever enjoyed. We talked of the Syrian campaign, of the Free French difficulties, of Spears's mission which, starting as a liaison organization, is now almost a local government, while Spears is invested as minister. He has a brigadier as his military attaché and a staff of some really first-rate, hand-picked men. In certain circles Spears is unpopular, and the plea has been heard that Syria should be 'French without Spears'.

Ali, who works as secretary for General Catroux, came in depressed at the news: 'The Libyan battle has been lost by us – we have announced as much on the radio.' There had been no indication that things were not going well: the campaign started so successfully, but now it is likely that we shall lose Tobruk in less than a month, for the Navy can't afford to supply it. What then is there to prevent Rommel from making a nice straight run to Cairo?

Thursday 25 June

While I was in my bath, the angelic Joan shouted, 'You can go on Misery tomorrow, if you want.' Action, splendid! Determined Joan had managed to get me on the Egyptian transport MISR passenger aeroplane to Cairo.

Shepheard's Hotel, Cairo

Cairo is full of rumours. Stories of reinforcements are encouraging: a convoy is said to have arrived at Suez just at the right time; de Gaulle is reported to be flying in, and Wavell, too, is on his way. Shepheard's Hotel is already lousy with generals; General Messervy in the telephone booth, General le Gentilhomme standing by the revolving doors with General Catroux, General Ritchie coming out of the wash-room. There is a great deal of talk as to who must be punished for the fiasco in the desert. The Egyptians have behaved surprisingly well and have not panicked in the face of unpleasant news. In fact Cairo, outwardly, seems quite calm.

Lilia Ralli has appeared from Alexandria where tearfully she bade goodbye to her parents: 'They are too old to be chased about by Rommel,' she cried. She described Alexandria as a dead city: all Wrens and sailors evacuated; roads without traffic; windows open on to empty rooms; telephone bells ringing unanswered.

Derek Adkin turned up with stories of the retreat. Yes, it was sad leaving the 'Ritz' at Bagush, the camp which we had considered our desert home, and awful to have to blow up the recently-built cookhouse of which they were so proud.

Randolph [Churchill], who was smashed up in a motor accident in the desert, is out of the hospital for the first time today. I had dinner off a tray by his bed. He was at his most enthusiastic for four hours on end, shouting with relish, 'The situation's splendid!' He'd like to see the Germans come to within fifty miles of Cairo, then, with their long transport lines, be cut off. He said he was glad I was going home soon so that I could tell 'them' what had happened at Tobruk; but when I asked him what did happen at Tobruk he was unable to answer. Randolph's stout heart makes me feel ashamed of my anxieties. Just to hear such exuberance is encouraging.

28 June

The German radio announced that their armies would be in Alexandria on the 6th and in Cairo by the 9th. The front lines are so near that the journalists go up to the battle for the day.

29 June

The Germans have announced the fall of Mersa Matrûh. All army and air force personnel must remain indoors after eight o'clock. Cairo, at last, seems in a state of alarm with queues outside the banks and crowds milling in front of the shops that sell luggage. Rumour is rife: forty tommy-guns were found in a priest's house. In offices everyone is busily burning documents: black charred pieces of paper drift down from the chimneys – a storm of black cinders, a hail of funeral confetti; the air thick with a pungent, peppery smell of burning. Out of doors there are more braziers heaped with piles of smouldering paper.

Tuesday 30 June

Cable came from Air Ministry requesting I do job in Lisbon on way home: this makes my departure seem more probable. *Later:* Houghton came in again. 'Look here, you're in luck, Beaton! You can get a plane to Lagos on Thursday.' The photographs of my Palestine–Persia trip arrived and there was a lot of ordering and captioning to be done.

13

English Interlude; A Near Escape
1942-3

C.B. designed the costumes for Shaw's Heartbreak House *and worked with Edith Evans. He narrowly escaped death in a plane crash. He published* Near East.

8 August 1942

Edith Olivier's hair has become white. We shall soon forget that she was all these years the dark-haired gipsy for ever on the move, laughing and scratching her scalp. The white hair, while being more becoming, is not so striking. She appears more of a conventional little old lady and less the violent character that her conversation still proves her to be.

While staying with Edith in the park at Wilton, I walked one afternoon, while she was out at a meeting, to the Close at Salisbury. Here I wished to feast my eyes again upon the rosy brick façade of the Wren school that, together with Mompesson House, and twenty other exquisite small houses, is part of the most beautiful domestic architecture in England.

It was a leisurely afternoon, and so peaceful that it gave me the feeling that often accompanies such an unexpected pause – that of presaging great activity – which is exactly what it did. Returning to the Dayehouse, I found Edith at her door, bidding *au revoir* to someone from the Women's Institute. Edith saw me and called, 'The King and Queen want you to photograph an unexpected visitor with them tomorrow – you must go up to London by the earliest train.'

I had been working on my Middle East book and had not taken photographs for some weeks. In my mind I felt so far away from photography that this summons came as rather an upheaval. My night's sleep was punctuated with half dreams in which all the usual fears had eventuated, with fuses blowing, lamps falling and confusion reigning in the subsequent darkness.

Sir Eric Miéville rang me at Pelham Place to say the visitor, though expected, might not arrive: the aeroplane had left Iceland but there had been fog, though now it had lifted. On getting to the palace there was still secrecy, but eventually

I was told that the expected arrival was that of Mrs Roosevelt. Messages kept coming through. As I waited I was treated to a furlong by furlong account of Mrs Roosevelt's progress as if she were a Derby favourite. 'She's coming round now – she's at Tattenham Corner – she's leading by a head – she's getting closer – now a straight run for it and she's here!'

The royal family came in quietly and shyly, the King showing restrained embarrassment by a muscle moving in his cheek, the children meek with furtive side-long glances. The Queen smiled blandly and said, 'Mrs Roosevelt is just taking her hat off. After she's had a cup of tea, we'll come in again right away.'

The lamps stood in readiness in the Bow room – its walls decorated with rather pretty gilt medallions containing copies of Winterhalter portraits. The glass cupboards, because of bombing, were bare of china and the fireplace was empty. The palace has conformed to wartime strictures and sets an example in austerity. The temperature in corridors and many of the rooms was little above freezing. There were no flowers in vases. It very likely *is* true that the King allows himself only a few inches of bath water, but this somewhat dour atmosphere did not make my job of picture-making any the easier.

After a slight interval the royal party, with their tall powdery-haired, powder-faced guest, swept in. Hurriedly I stage-managed a group around the chimneypiece. A few suggestions from the King were graciously acknowledged. At last we were ready. 'Now still! Quiet, please!' Whereupon Madame President turned this way and that – her head high in the air while she shouted, 'I haven't put a comb through my hair since New York. I haven't had any powder on my face since leaving Washington. Now that's very nice of you to arrange to have him for dinner – I didn't know where I'd contact him!' Meanwhile, the family smiled nervously and the youngest child tittered. I asked for quiet, and waited by the huge camera with trigger poised. I felt like an old-fashioned Victorian photographer trying to take an exposure of a scalded cat. Mrs Roosevelt leant forward this way and that, threw her head back, and kept up a monologue while I waited with the trigger poised in helplessness. I shouted hopefully, 'Still! One second's exposure!' Yet Mrs Roosevelt talked!

It was much later, after reading of it in the press, that any of us realized that Mrs Roosevelt has become somewhat deaf, and this, of course, had been accentuated by the recent throb of aeroplane engines. I now realize that this deafness gives her the expressionless voice and the baffled look that these unfortunates possess.

Personal vanity is something of which Mrs Roosevelt is not conscious. Obviously it made no difference to her how she looked in these pictures. It seemed ridiculous that I should ask her to cross her feet, lower her chin and moisten her lips. Mrs Roosevelt was much more interested in going upstairs in order straightaway to write her column 'My Day' – which, in fact, is what soon she did. In any case the wife of the President of the United States was under the impression that a movie camera was in use and that she must portray animation.

After her exit, the royal family were photographed in turn. The photographs primarily are for official purposes, and one must not take a chance on their not being technically perfect. So, instead of taking informal pictures with ordinary lighting and candid camera, a barrage of enormous lights, with clumsy electrician attendants, is brought in. The lamps stand six feet from the ground and cannot, with safety, be raised more than nine feet. The blaze of ubiquitous light that they create is unlike life: it is the sort of glare you see only on an amateur stage. Not only must one try to regulate the lights in a bold and original way, but one must try to disassociate one's self from all those groups of royalty that have differed little since Queen Victoria's early days. To prevent these well-trained sitters from regimenting themselves into a rigid composition that is not merely a pastiche of the past, provokes a great challenge. I knew that today I was not meeting this challenge. In a desperate effort that some unexpected felicity would eventually arrive to save the situation, I exposed dozens of negatives that I knew would never be of interest. Quantity does not necessarily improve quality. The bolt from heaven never arrived.

The King was amenable, but I found myself completely uninspired. The lights would not do my bidding, although there in front of me were great possibilities, provided by the raw, bony, medieval aspects of that handsome face. I could only fall back in desperation on a Bond Street 'camera-portraitist' form of flattery!

While waiting for a brainwave, I played for time by scrutinizing an enormous Chinese vase covered with dragons. 'This is a strange object but it casts nice shadows.' 'Isn't it hideous!' remarked the King. 'Where did it come from, I wonder?' After we had surveyed it for some seconds in silence the King ventured, 'It's Chinese, I suppose.' The delay before continuing the photography could be no longer protracted.

The Queen was as sympathetic and full of charm as ever. Princess Elizabeth has developed her mother's smile. The two Princesses, posing together, reminded me of the beginning of my career when I used to photograph Nancy and Baba as school children.

Emerald Cunard has returned to bombed London from her native America with the feeling that she has now come back where she belongs.

Now she has made a life for herself at the Dorchester in two rooms that are overfilled with outsize Buhl and ormolu furniture left over from her more spacious existence.

Since she is about the only woman attempting to entertain in London it is not difficult for her to ensure Cabinet ministers and war leaders to drop in on their way home for a drink, or to sit at her dinner table, together with groups of writers, painters and decorative women.

Emerald's frivolities are so entertaining that her audience is apt to ignore the scholarly mind which is her *raison d'être*. In effect, the play-acting with friends during the evenings is only a preliminary for her real life of the mind. After her last guest has gone Emerald will read for six or eight hours until long after dawn has lightened her taffeta curtains. 'But he's not a cultured man,' she explodes about some successful playwright. 'I don't suppose he knows one word of an ode of Horace!' Returning from an American play that was enjoying enormous success, she whispers with disgust, 'It's for the servants! Really, we can't watch people trying to lift up a Scot's kilt to see what's underneath. We all know what's underneath: it can't be anything new! It isn't as if it were a sea anemone or a salamander.'

Emerald has recently been telephoning to me a great deal. It was, at first, a shock to wake to answer the bedside bell at four o'clock in the morning. But Emerald is lonely, and after a moment's readjustment, I lie listening in the dark until I am so entertained by some of her remarks that I switch on the light and make a note of them.

Without her exquisite sense of timing her remarks lose much of their effect, but here are a few of her aphorisms:

'Only a brilliant man knows how to be ridiculous.'

'Oh, it was a most Lenten existence.'

'Life and art never overlap.'

'A witty woman can never keep a man. She can't afford to laugh at the wrong moment.'

'Never be sincere. The whole structure of society falls if you start to be sincere, and you can hardly ever afford to tell the truth. Very seldom can a wife tell the truth to her husband. It's much too dangerous. You must always live in a very rigid convention.'

Recently Emerald has fallen in love, and for hours she will talk in veiled terms of her unrequited romance. Tonight she held forth on the subject:

'The greatest men I have ever known have never been able to put up with love. Why? It's so distracting – and great men must never be disturbed at their work. George Moore used to sit all day in front of his papers, and if anyone called at his house he would tell them to go away. He couldn't see anyone before sundown. One afternoon Mary Hunter arrived in Ebury Street and saw him, through the open window, having his tea. (He never had his tea in the drawing-room, but down in the dining-room).) She heard him saying to the maid who had announced her arrival, 'I could not be more devoted to Mrs Hunter, but please tell her I don't want to see her.' The poor woman never recovered.'

'I think it better to be feared than loved. I remember Sir Thomas Beecham used to say, "I pray that one day I may be sent to prison so that I may spend some weeks undisturbed." On many occasions he nearly got his wish, but he's resentful of people who love him. He's very grudging. He said, "I owe that woman a lot." "Why?" I asked. "She gave me my very first Bible." "When was that?" "At the time I must have been sixty-five. I owe her a lot, but I cannot love her."'

Discussing a well-known *amoureuse*, Emerald said, 'She knew all the arts of seduction. She would often display her tongue: she didn't put it out, but she'd let one have a tantalizing peep – just so that one should know she had a tongue. You forget that most people do have tongues because you never see them, but a tongue is a charming addition if you like a person.' 'And what about teeth?' I asked. 'Oh, teeth should never be a reality, only an indication.'

Emerald would then say, 'Now, when will you come to dinner? I'll read out to you those who are coming on different nights. Now, do you want to be impresssed? Laura Corrigan and Chips always want to be impressed.'

After an hour and a half's conversation Emerald would suddenly say, in a sweet and formal voice, 'Well, I'll say goodnight to you, and send you much love.'

Emerald has an unconventional way of introducing her guests to one another. Sometimes she explains: 'This is Poppy – everybody loves little Poppy.' 'This is our great poet from the Foreign Office.' Once she had nothing to say about one guest except that her mother had been killed on the Underground.

Tonight Lord Wavell, a newcomer to Emerald's circle, was the figurehead for whom the gathering was being celebrated. The Field-Marshal looked a little nonplussed when Emerald introduced a bald-headed man: 'This is Gerald Berners – he's a musician, and a saucy fellow.' 'This is Dr Stewart, a worldly prelate, the final authority on Pascal and a professional beauty.'

But the small party, under the aegis of such a brilliant *entrepreneuse*, soon acquired its own impetus, and before the synthetic ice-cream arrived we had recitations of Ronsard from Leslie Hore-Belisha, followed by large slices of Browning and Dowson from the Field-Marshal himself. Gerald, perhaps determined to act up to his sobriquet, seemed intent on lowering the tone of the party and contributed a child's nonsense rhyme about Pussy Cat. When conversation turned to famous last lines ('Mehr Licht') Gerald croaked Schubert's last words, 'Don't let poor Tauber starve.'

Ashcombe: 5 November

Mummie hurried into my room. She pulled the curtains earlier than usual. No nonsense about lying in bed – however late I'd been writing last night. This was worth waking up for: the most exciting event of the war – the turning point: 'Wonderful news! Rommel's army on the run – in full retreat!' The whole look of the war suddenly changed.

Bognor: 26 July 1943

We were just about to go to bed on Sunday night – standing up, lingering at the door, discussing morning trains, when the telephone bell rang. 'That's bad,' said Diana [Cooper], the pessimist, pulling a face, as she went to answer the summons. It was Freda Casa-Maury. Diana shouted, 'Mussolini's resigned.'

The bombshell has really churned us up in a way that no other piece of news has since the collapse of France! (Only this time the churning is of a different kind!) I felt weak, and slightly tearful, but the others were just gay, smiling like children, and being absolutely enchanting in their happiness. Duff opened a bottle of champagne, and we sat for half an hour while the clock ticked very slowly towards the BBC midnight news. Raimund [von Hofmannsthal] exclaimed, 'Oh, you British are so extraordinary! Here's this wonderful piece of news – and your radio wouldn't dream of interrupting a programme of gramophone records with it. In America the news will by now have been given over and over and over again.' Duff beamed. He did an imitation of Mussolini meeting Hitler for the thirteenth time and saying, 'I must have *una, due, tre ... divisioni!*' We roared with laughter. Diana was like a young girl. She said this was one of the greatest moments of her life. She looked radiant. Duff said he thought the King would make Badoglio successor, then send for someone and surrender. He thought it 'all up' with Italy within the next week, that now we had the Mediterranean we could hammer Germany and the Balkans from Italy, and the effect on German morale would be immense. Bertram Kruger, beaming, said, 'It's all over.' Duff, still beaming, said, 'No – we mustn't go as far as that.'

The clock ticked, they played Delius, and an announcer made a boring commentary. At last midnight. We raised our glasses at the wonderful news. The beginning of the end! It was as Duff had anticipated – Badoglio was in Mussolini's place.

London: Autumn

Edith Evans lives in Albany, a suitable place for her with its collegiate dignity and somewhat dour feeling of repose. I arrived punctually at four o'clock. Edith answered the door and was apologetic – the fire hadn't been lit long – part of the furnishings had been blitzed – the flat was not as she wanted it to be

– and yet she burst out laughing and in a sing-song voice continued, 'Why should I *apologize* for all these things – why should I be so *silly*?'

Now we sat to discuss *Heartbreak House* – its mood and atmosphere. Beaumont had told Edith he wanted to do something to lift the play, give it a height – even in the scenery. 'That's right, we must heighten everything!' Edith promised. 'The play's very long, and unless we can mesmerize audiences by the atmosphere they will become tired. Shaw has got such a mighty brain that he could talk or listen to discussions for eight hours on end, but if audiences are conscious of being indoors listening they soon need a sandwich. We must make them feel we're out in a garden, in the evening, sitting doing nothing. A garden gives you patience and repose; in the twilight you can sit and do nothing sometimes for an hour even! We must create that "evening in the garden" effect, then no one can be bored! No one is bored in a garden! And we must all concentrate hard. We must listen – and *think*!'

Talking about Hesione Hushabye, Edith said she felt she was not well-mannered or bad-mannered, but a complete 'original'. She saw her in flowing draperies but discarding their grandeur – screwing up her arms, and going to sleep in public lying back in a huddle with legs twisted. Edith shouted, 'She must gather up the sleeves of her lovely tea gowns, and wave!' It is by such touches that Edith brings her characters to life.

Edith now set about trying to convince me that H.H. *must* have black hair. 'These two sisters must really be something! They're just a little past their prime, but they must be stunning!' For Edith, with her pale skin and irregular features – for Edith, of all people, to face up to a black wig sounded hell to me, but I was determined to keep an open mind. 'Oh, of course if I wear a dark wig I alter my entire skin pigment. You'll never know I'm wearing a wig – the audience will think I've dyed my hair, for it will look so natural. It will, in fact, be made up of all colours and there will be very little extra hair. Always when I have wigs made I say, "Remember, only half the usual amount of hair!" and when I wear a wig in a play it isn't just something I put on like a hat: it becomes part of me. I do my own hair – dress it on myself. Sometimes in front of the audience a curl falls out of place, and it is very effective to do it up as part of my acting. No – I don't want to have my own coloured hair – it's mouse – mouse – mouse. Don't let the audience associate Mrs Hushabye with Edith Evans! Let me assume beauty with your lovely dresses and a dark wig. I'll not fail over that at any rate: if I feel satisfactory there is no limit to what I can seem to be!' Edith was not just arguing for argument's sake; this was the result of deep convictions.

Apropos Edith's performance of Millamant she said that others too often have the wrong conception of the eighteenth century. 'It wasn't just finicking daintinesses with little fingers raised, snuff-pinching and fluttering of fans.

Why, the climate hasn't changed! Women nowadays are seldom hot enough to want to fan themselves! A fan should be used for poking the fire or, at best, making an aside behind, but it should never be used for fanning. A parasol, too, was useful for poking people.'

Edith talked about breathing spaces in plays: Shakespeare gave his actors plenty of breathing space before they went over their hurdles. 'Shaw makes you take your hurdles too quickly – one after another without interval.' She laughed at herself guiltily for using analogies about racing – 'As if I know anything about horses!'

I left Brighton, where I was recuperating from a stone in the gall bladder, for one day in London to fit dresses for *Heartbreak* and to see Edith Evans about her bloody black wig. I arrived for the first stage rehearsal. Edith was in a great state of subdued, pent-up thrill at being, at last, able to get going on this new production. In her excitement at jumping the next hurdle, Edith had forgotten all about Gibraltar, from whence she has just returned after appearing in a revue for the troops.

It was tremendously interesting to watch her looks of complete concentration when, wearing spectacles and appearing particularly plain, she listened to the director's instructions while keeping an eye on Isabel Jeans (who plays the sister) rehearsing by herself in a corner. (Isabel never relaxes – she is like a peahen, with the over-nervousness of a greyhound.)

John Burrell, the director, conducted the rehearsal for five hours on end. Burrell seems very sure of getting the effects he wishes, but today it seemed to me that the leading actors are such definite personalities that they were merely playing themselves. Maybe their characterizations will appear later. Only the minor actors seemed to become characters and not just personalities.

Edith said that a few of the things she was doing were right – that, by degrees, Hesione was appearing, but that she did not realize that she was going to be at all like this: the character was beginning to appear so strongly that Hesione already got up and did something for which Edith was not ready. 'Don't do that yet! I find Hesione doing all sorts of unexpected things – some are right, some are not.' Yet to me, a mere onlooker, it seemed as if Edith was just exploiting her own ego. Edith, as if reading my thoughts, said, 'We can't get rid of our own egos – they have to be dragged along with us wherever we go.'

By the end of the afternoon, the other actors were a bit dishevelled as, walking like sore bears in their solitary purgatories, they tried to memorize their lines. But Edith was as fresh as a dewdrop and eager, when the rehearsal was over, to go off to have her wig fitted. 'Aren't you tired, Edith?' 'Not a bit of it. If I'm interested I can continue for forty-eight hours without a nap!'

At Gustave's, Edith's gluttony for acting asserted itself while waiting for samples of hair to be brought. She spied some 1840–60 fashion plates and sang mellifluously, 'I'd like to appear in a play in which I could wear a bonnet with plenty of ruchings.' Later, when Dolly, the wigmaker, fitted a *toile* on her head and she looked quite bald, Edith said, 'This is how I'd like to appear sometimes, looking like a Flemish Madonna. When I went to the Dutch exhibition my friends said, "These are all you – bald – with gooseberry eyes."'

At last a few wisps of black hair were produced. Edith held these up against her forehead and cheek. The effect of light on her was most harsh and unbecoming. Her eyes suddenly appeared like ping-pong balls covered with lids of chicken flesh, and one eye seemed so much lower in her face than the other. Even her complexion seemed to be coarse, with wide pores, and with alternately shiny or dry-flaked patches. Any other woman would have been horrified to see the effect in the mirror, but no – Edith was delighted. '*Ra-ther* nice!' she drawled. 'I can see that it's very becoming to my skin…!'

Edith absorbs herself entirely in her work. She could not have any other interest while rehearsing a part. To Dolly and Gus, she said, 'I'd like to fit this wig twenty times; call on me anytime you want me to come in. I'd love to work hard on it.' To me she said, 'How is it that you manage to keep your unbruised, shrewd point of view when you see so many people? You manage society so well – how is it? I'm scared of it. Those people all wanted to take me up – George Moore and the lot, but I couldn't say witty things, I couldn't compete. I became breathless and exhausted. I had to preserve myself. But you manage to see people as if for the first time. I can't do that – I can only do that with a part; I can recognize a part for the first time.'

With so much exuberance and warmth lavished on her acting, I wonder if Edith has affection for humanity or love for friends?

After an absence of a few days, I returned again to London to find that rehearsals had progressed at an astonishing pace. Already most of the characters had learnt their lines – not so Edith, who explained to the director, 'I don't want you to think I'm being behindhand in not giving up the book. I work like that – I always find I can develop my part more when I'm not fussing to find the words. I don't want you to think I don't pay any attention to this when I go home in the evenings. But I never give up my book for two weeks – it's the way I work. I'll know my part over the weekend.'

The cast, having been thrilled at the idea of playing with Edith, now began to realize the penalties of being with a great actress. Her avidity and egomania are certainly as pronounced as in most stage performers. At rehearsal she is business-like, but selfish to the degree that even when it is reasonable to hold up proceedings to discuss her own problems for a certain length of time, she hammers on with such insistency that she succeeds in falling foul of the director.

At one point she attempted to usurp a good position on a sofa stage centre. 'It's just to suggest the purely domestic thing of the married couple drifting together when anything unusual happens. Hector is sitting there – the burglar appears – wouldn't it be right that I should drift towards him and sit down holding him by the arm?' It takes a lot of strength for John Burrell to say, 'No, Edith,' in the way that he does. Edith counters: 'I stand very still for a great length of time. It doesn't look dead, does it?' When at the end of one scene Edith asked, 'Can't Ellie give me a look at that point?' John Burrell said, 'No, I don't think so, Edith.' A long discussion that was more in the nature of a war of attrition followed. Edith became very pink about the cheeks. She pursed her lips, put her tongue at one side of her mouth and held her arms akimbo with one heel dug into the ground. 'You must realize Hesione is a very difficult part – some of it almost as difficult as Shakespeare. Hesione moves from every emotion and, in many instances, with only one line to do it in. It helps me if Ellie looks at me. It makes it easier for me to weep.' 'No, Edith, it's the thought that makes you weep, not the look. Anyhow, try it again with the look.'

Edith, with a black mushroom on her head (a property wig) and a mink coat, fumed and emoted with added zest to show how much better she could act with Ellie's look. 'Well, Ellie, is that all right for you to give the look?' 'Yes,' said Deborah Kerr as Ellie. 'All right – keep it,' said John Burrell, and added, 'You're right, Edith – I'm sorry.' But that was not the end of it for Edith, who went on to the others in the cast in the same strain. 'I mean, I *know* what I can do! If they don't *like* what I do then they must get someone else. But I *do* know my job!' And, my God, she does!

For the past week I have spent a few hours each day watching the rehearsals. Sometimes the actors have been perfecting little scenes, in others just running through their parts with a parrot-like lack of emotion. Edith has succeeded with a dramatic last-minute sprint and comes in a good length in front of Isobel, who was winning all the earlier laps.

Isabel Jeans had a good training with the Phoenix Society in classical plays, but this is about the first time she has ever been in a modern play of first-class quality. Lady Utterward gives her a lift right out of the rather humdrum drawing-room comedies she has lately been associated with. When Edith heard her give an extraordinarily effective first reading Edith cocked an eye at her with intense curiosity and said, 'I think she's going to be admirable.' But Jeans suddenly discovered her part was unsympathetic and for several days went to pieces. Her distress reflected itself at the costume fittings. Although I know her clothes are going to be spiffing, Isabel became fretful and difficult. She looked in the glass with wrinkled face and said, 'What I mean is ...' but the inarticulate sounds that followed were unintelligible because Isabel is not pastmistress at completing sentences and cannot decide what specifically is distressing her.

When I asked her which costumes had pleased her during her stage career she seemed dissatisfied with the lot. 'But surely those remarkable Empire costumes designed by Aubrey Hammond in *The Man With a Load of Mischief*?' 'Nahir – nehir,' and biting her finger, and staring wildly at the floor, she threw away the remark, 'He could have done much better!'

Edith buttonholed me. 'Don't let anyone ruin my champagne satin. Remember, my champagne satin.' She is a flirt and she is easily flattered; after a long rehearsal Robert Donat twitted her with a leer, 'Let's stay behind and rehearse alone together.' She ogled back with a coy wink, 'I'm too tired today!' But she was not too tired. She is never tired; as she said, 'No one rehearses enough for me!' During the lunch interval she remains on the stage with perhaps a Thermos and a Marie biscuit to go over and over her scenes. She is never tired of acting: she acts all her living hours. She says, 'I would rehearse until I drop.'

It is fascinating to see her making little discoveries in her part and bringing the character to life, and she is astute at analysing her powers. She holds forth to the boredom of the rest of the cast about why she would like to do this and that. 'I can't falsify. My inside will become more flexible, and I'll be able to make my voice stronger later. I shan't strain. It wouldn't do to strain. You wouldn't like it, and I couldn't do it.'

I notice that she watches the director all the time he is giving the others their notes. She breathes in deep the fetid air of the theatre and it is balm to her; when others are exhausted and have aged ten years in a day, Edith, in the harsh overhead light, blossoms like a rose and begins to become a beauty.

It has been impossible to convince Edith that she should not wear black hair: yet black is too hardening to her contours. But she plonks on the thing as if it were a loaf or a hat. Then her eyebrows go up, her mouth stretches in a wide grin, 'Look, it's lovely. Look, I can wear it! I told you so – didn't I? Look, it's right with my skin!' What can one say?

Two days later I found Edith with a most extraordinary object on her head – a black, wiry mass of the stuff one finds in an Edwardian sofa. The following is the history of what happened: Dolly and Gus had succeeded in approximating a beautiful Japanese lady's wig. It was composed of strands of silken hair set in a mould of shiny perfection. Edith was delighted with it but had wished 'to get intimate with the wig'. So she took it back to Albany, back-combed it, rearranged it, had her dinner in it, rehearsed to herself in the glass in it, had slept in it, and quickly given it a little 'attention' before returning to the theatre in it.

Everyone but Edith was aghast: everyone agreed that another wig must forthwith be made. Admittedly not quite so black this time, but still giving the effect of darkness, not a Japanese wig either, but still not the interior of an old sofa! It was only when, after the dress rehearsal, Binkie told Edith that she looked sinister with dark hair and couldn't she envisage herself as a redhead, that she became upset. Edith looked tragically into the mirror and said, 'I have so many disadvantages to overcome – perhaps I'd better retire to my farm!' Nevertheless, next day her self-opinion was in no way dashed, and she was convinced again that another dark wig made of finer hair would be wonderful.

London: December

The M. of I. boys have at last decided that they want me to do the same job for them in the Far East as I did in the Near East. My first stop is to be India and they want me there quickly.

It was a bright clear day. Excellent flying conditions. Later we climbed into a Dakota that was stripped of all but the minimum equipment. One side of the fuselage was piled with our luggage and miscellaneous cargo – huge rubber tyres for aeroplanes, crates, and 'secret' packages. The pilot of the aircraft was a young fair-haired Canadian of special beauty, with high cheekbones, lean, lithe figure and a stance like a gorilla. He had pale-almond eyes and a generous mouth continuously twisted in a smile. He piloted us to our take-off point, and two hours later landed us at Land's End. Here on the icy snows, dozens of transport aircraft were lined up, having been stranded here for many days thanks to the worst weather for years.

We were all herded into an already overcrowded vast Nissen hut in which the temperature, in spite of two very small stove-fires at each end, was below freezing point. By now it was four o'clock in the afternoon. We were told that by midnight we would know if we were to 'take-off', or not. When I saw Smuts waiting amongst us I realized the seriousness of the delay. Smuts was savouring a mug of tea and looked out at the last rays of a watery winter sun.

At one o'clock in the morning we were given breakfast, a real egg and bacon too, and coffee, but the cold of the dining hut, on the edge of the cliffs, in the coldest night of the year, was even greater than in the Nissen hut mess. A pilot who was travelling with us as passenger said, 'You're cold now? You'll not know yourself when we've been flying a bit 20,000 feet up. Oh boy, you'll be conscious only of your extremities.'

The news went round that Smuts had taken off. Every chance of our leaving now – in a couple more hours. Somehow or other the time passed. Zero hour: we were taken out into the sharp blackness of the night and flare-lighted into a lorry. First stop a farm building where, in flickering lamplight, we were trussed up in boiler suits with zips – one of my zips was missing – Mae Wests and harness. These clothes added bulk without warmth and made one feel claustrophobic. When we got back into the Black Maria for our last journey to the attendant aircraft I noticed we all looked so grim and frightened that I drew up the corners of my mouth into a stylized smile.

Back in the Dakota that was to fly us through the night on our first stop to Gibraltar, I found myself sitting almost at the end of the fuselage, down by the door. As I leant against the seat there was a loud crack and it fell back lopsidedly. The sergeant steward and one of the tyre experts helped by flashing his torch and they both tried to get the seat leg back into its socket. No, no luck. 'Once we're airborne the seat will right itself,' said the steward optimistically. The dim lights were put out and we sat in Stygian blackness. It was the very positive blackness of patent leather without the highlights.

The door was locked; we listened to the roar of the engines; we trundled forward, bouncing along on the uneven icy ground.

The agony of terror that followed, though it lasted only a few minutes, seemed an eternity. Already, at the start of the run, I bowed my head in my hands and prayed very hard because I was so frightened. I prayed that if I survived this ordeal my life might be simplified, that I should resist the distractions of so many unimportant things. We were racing furiously towards the sea, then the aircraft lurched lopsidedly into the air, and banged and rattled its occupants like dice in a box. I heard a man behind me say very quietly, 'Yes that's it – now we're for it.' My terror became intense. My eyes were shut and I tried not to take cognizance of anything outside my own head. For somehow I felt that these were my last seconds of this life, and I decided that I must spend them contemplating pleasant things.

All sorts of unexpected and forgotten pictures raced through my mind, like slides on a cinematograph sheet. I saw my family when I was a child. I sensed again the excitement of getting a present at Christmas of a picture postcard of Lily Elsie in a head-dress she wore in *The Waltz Dream*. I saw a young preparatory schoolboy, Geoghegan, waiting for me to finish my school tea – as was his custom, under an arcade of chestnut trees outside the playground of my Heath Mount school. He wanted to give me a lift home on the step of his bicycle. I saw and savoured the pleasant tweedy aroma of Peter – chasing the dogs when our friendship was at its most halcyon. I had idyllic memories of the first time I fell in love, and of the soft welcoming look of Ashcombe, my house, in the height of a summer. I remembered the gaiety of certain New York winters and again could smell the hotel rooms I once occupied. I had visions of the silver-grey white trees against the blue skies of the Piero della Francesca frescoes at Arezzo. These appeared particularly Elysian and the sky such a heavenly blue that I tried to make myself visualize uglier things. This was all too pleasant; beauty doesn't consist only of pleasure. But I couldn't think of anything that was not ecstatic. My ideas worked up to a crescendo of clear, vivid thought. I was in a delirium of pleasure and terror when crash! Oh how I prayed, Oh God, oh God, oh God! I knew my worst fears had come true, that my nightmares had turned to reality. I found myself lying on a mound of parachute harness – half-way down the fuselage. I opened my eyes. Through the crack of the door leading into the cockpit I saw flashes of light. The engines were still roaring. Then the flames were everywhere. A huge tongue of blue darted down the length of the cabin. The cockpit was now an orange glow. Outside the night was lit by enormous different coloured fires. In the aircraft were patches of flame at odd places, and a bright incandescent fire centred in the extreme rear.

So this was the end. So this was Death. Any second now I should know the unknown. Meanwhile I analysed quite calmly the various stages through which I passed. No use fighting, there was nothing to be done about it. The flames approached. Everyone was very quiet in the aircraft; and even now they behaved with the polite reserve of Englishmen. I looked up to see the whole fuselage illuminated by dense, suffocating, orange smoke through which the silhouetted figures of the aircrew in their cumbersome divers' suits ran past me, groping in the fog of burning aluminium. Still no one spoke. I lay holding on to my head thinking that as soon as the flames reached us there would be panic and fighting and I should be trampled underfoot. And why not? This was it. I had accepted the worst. Suddenly someone shouted, 'Open that bloody door.' I could see various passengers hopefully and pathetically groping for an exit. The tyre expert had the presence of mind to turn his torch on the latch of the door. Its beam seemed very white in the glow of the fires. Then I understood, by some queer reflex, that the door was open. 'So they are jumping for it,' I thought, 'rather than be burnt. How high are we? Well, death is one stage farther away this way ... so here goes!' I was the last to leave the aircraft. I crawled along the floor backwards and tipped myself out head first into the cold, black night. A short drop and I was astonished to find myself, with a minor bump on the head, upside down in a grassy field covered with hoar frost and patched with snow. The air struck me as bitterly cold. Around and above me were flames.

'Get up and run,' someone shouted. 'The aircraft may explode.' In spite of a tremendous weakness in the knees, and the weight of my cumbrous harness, I ran, as we all ran, falling and getting up again and running, turning at last to watch the destruction of the plane from the vantage point of safety.

The broken monster lay spurting forth fire. Deep orange and black smoke coiled upwards in a great tower. The cockpit was diamond bright, the burning edges of the wings suggested flare paths on an aerodrome or gala illuminations on a pre-war pier. Our lungs filled with fumes, we coughed as we watched. It surprised us to find how little shocked we were. Someone said the shock would come later. It did. Meanwhile we gazed at the burning dragon as it vomited forth different coloured flames, and spat forth its distress signals of pink, mauve and golden rockets. We discussed our miraculous escape. We had crash-landed; another fifty yards and we would have plunged into the sea. But I couldn't feel proud of the negative way I had behaved: just to lie and accept death was of little help to the others, whereas the passenger pilot, who had known how to pull up an emergency lever and to jettison the locked door, had saved all our lives.

'Are you all right?' 'Are we all here?' The airfield was dotted with theatrically-lit figures. 'The pilot didn't get away,' remarked the navigator. Fumes brought tears to our eyes as we looked at the funeral pyre of the charming young Canadian. The night wind was icy and cut the scalp like a knife. Eventually the ambulance came up. And then, thank God, staggering out of the darkness, his neck and forehead bleeding, his face green, appeared the pilot. 'Good show,' the others congratulated him. 'No, no, it wasn't a good show,' he whimpered. He minded only about his responsibility to others. He was taken away in the ambulance suffering, we discovered later, from serious internal injuries: he had a broken arm and ribs; a kidney had to be removed – the stick had gone through his stomach.

In the hospital we were given tea. I was lucky enough to be given a room to myself as I was very restless, writing notes and going continuously to the loo. I kept waking to horror pictures of what might have happened if I had fastened my faulty belt and hadn't been able to get out of it. If – if – After a few hours, we were called. I could either take a midday train back to London to re-equip, or there was a transport plane going in an hour. I knew if I didn't get into that aircraft I never would fly again. (I had lost everything except my camera and films which had gone before me.)

14

The War in the Far East
1943-4

From Delhi, where he was the Viceroy's guest, C.B. visited many parts of India, photographed the Burma front, and flew over the South-Eastern Himalayas to Chungking, headquarters of the British Fourteenth Army in China. He returned home via Aden, Accra, Ascension Island, Brazil and the United States. In New York he heard of the Liberation of Paris.

Delhi: 25 December 1943

The bearer, white-turbaned and bare-footed, pulls back the curtains to let in a blaze of sun. Outside, the fountains are playing, the birds are shrieking. Cascades of stocks, carnations and petunias hang over the edges of ornamental pools. Someone is practising on a bugle, and sentries clear their throats with resounding rasps to spit, then stamp their bulbous boots on the gravel. A bearer, in scarlet tunic, comes in, salaams and gives me a parcel tied with ribbon. Another servant, in an enormous cheese-cloth puggaree, brings in a necktie wrapped in coloured paper. It is Christmas Day in Viceroy's house....

I was allowed into the War Room of South East Asia Command. The chiefs of all departments, American and English, 'breezed in' for what is known as 'early morning prayers' (a study of the latest maps, the day's reports and a short lecture given by half a dozen specialists). The Supreme Commander, Admiral Lord Louis Mountbatten, who had arrived in this theatre not long before, seemed as yet unaffected by the climate. 'We mustn't let it be a damper on effort – we've got to galvanize everyone, got to teach 'em to hustle,' he said – and he appeared to have impregnated his immediate entourage with his own robust brand of enthusiasm.

From the parapet of the Tomb of Humayan, in the precious moments of twilight, one sees India at her best. Beyond the domes of mosques lies the lilac-coloured jungle. A crescent moon appears, in silvery contrast to the few wisps of golden cloud that are hurrying to be away before the sky becomes completely dark: cranes and other large birds are flying home and their wings make a breathless flapping noise; while parrots, very small, but tightly clustered, give the impression, as they pass, of a flying carpet. Jackals come out and slink off again, horrible hang-tail scavengers. A shepherd, rather sadly, is playing on his flute; and from the distance comes the echoing call to evening prayer.

All the aids to escapism are available in Delhi. Little chance of a flying bomb; European food is plentiful; no shortage of manpower, servants galore, countless boys to preserve the tennis court and pick up the balls for the players, masses of old men to water the garden. There is little noise and the lack of traffic, except for the tinkles of bicycles at luncheon time, gives an air of leisure and prosperity.

Servants of different categories in scarlet, white and gold liveries stand like poppies behind chairs and tables, or appear in the distance of vast halls and marble enfilades looking as small as figures in a landscape.

Viceroy's house possesses its own doctor, dispensary, barber and tailor. One hundred and fifty gardeners maintain the borders and the preserves. Altogether 300 servants are employed within these regal confines, but when considering this number you must realize that, due to the caste system, at least six servants are needed to do the work undertaken in England today by one hard-working and aged peeress. Any Englishman, living however quietly and simply in India, will have at least six servants: a cook, a butler, a laundryman, a sweeper, a groom, a gardener, and perhaps one other. Even so, he will be poorly attended, his bungalow dirty, food badly cooked. The Viceroy [Lord Wavell] and his family insist on leading as simple a life as is possible in these awe-inspiring surroundings.

Friday 18 February 1944

It takes a great person not to become affected by this regal ceremonial and continuous sycophantic deference. Lord Wavell has this quality of greatness: at worst he becomes bad-tempered, but this is understandable.

After lunch I had a walk round the garden with Wavell. He said the Japs had suddenly attacked in Burma in great force. He couldn't imagine how such numbers hadn't been detected in spite of the fact that the Japs move at night, lie in wait all day, and need practically no communications. (They carry food for eight days on them.) Wavell thought it would take some considerable time before we were able to clear up the trouble in this part.

At last I feel fairly at ease with Wavell, and he seemed quite interested to hear of my itinerary and plan of campaign.

North-West Frontier

Sitting in a eucalyptus grove planted by Lutyens, suddenly I found myself surrounded by servants. Word had come that I was to leave forthwith for the

North-West Frontier. We ran in and did rough packing: within three minutes I was ready for departure. I started to give out largesse to each servant but, with typically childish amusement, they ran out with a large box. 'Servants' box! Servants' box!' They all took up the cry and, before my eyes pushed the rupee notes into the slot. Everyone was laughing, and I drove away to a cry of 'Servants' box! Servants' box!'

'This is a tough corner of the earth,' my escort explained, 'where no value is given to a man's life. You notice everyone carries a gun; robbery, hold-ups, murder and rape are not uncommon.' If the police should turn its back for ten minutes, this quarter, filled with a fermenting mass of the world's most dangerous characters, would break out in chaos. 'You never know when it will be necessary to turn on the tear gas.'

Alexander the Great and Timur the Tartar had chosen the Khyber Pass for their invasions of India; I felt nevertheless today that the Khyber belonged rather to Kipling than to any earlier period of history.

In the officers' mess, polished silver cups stand in rows against the dark oak panelling. Another round is ordered: 'Yes, we get beer from the factory at Pindi – or how about a cherry brandy?' A young subaltern comes and lays his revolver on the table, by the reading lamp with the crimson silk shade. 'Heard about old Claude's near shave? His lamp shot to blazes! Great stuff – maybe the beginning of something.'

Flying away [from Peshawar], the only passenger in a small aircraft, I noticed that the little Indian pilot was trying very hard to unwind a wheel – something to do with pumping down the undercarriage when the automatic release goes wrong. It proved too stiff; try as he might, he could not get it down. We were flying over nasty, tooth-like rocks, and into large lumps of dirty cotton-wool cloud. The Indian, sweating as he struggled with the levers, then beckoned me to join him in the cockpit. I shook my head and winked – No, I had had enough of the cockpit: I would remain with my novel! The pilot continued to beckon; it was only after a considerable time that I understood that the invitation had now become an order. The pilot was signalling for me to sit by him, to 'take the stick.'

Suddenly, flying an aeroplane for the first time, I felt like Harold Lloyd. I held on to the wheel rather gingerly, not knowing how much leeway I could allow before the aircraft reacted violently. Like a monkey, the sweating pilot crawled to and fro, among the hundred gadgets on the dashboard and the floor. The engine responded to my very tentative suggestion to climb a little higher, and I found this effort a relief.

Just as I was contemplating his having to climb out on the wings, to tie something together with string, the pilot put up his thumb with a jerk: he had mended the aeroplane.

'May I go back to my novel?'

Assam, Burma and the Arakan Front

We landed in a bowl scooped from the mountains of Imphal. The year is at its best; sun all day; cold at night; the cherry-trees in blossom, rhododendrons ablaze. Soon the vast tropical trees will be sprouting with orchids and the troops will pick the parasite blossoms and put them in their large-brimmed hats.

My first impression would have been less idyllic had I arrived during the monsoon period. This continues for nearly two-thirds of the year. The troops must exist soaked to the skin for weeks on end in an almost solid tropical rain. There is no chance of drying their clothes. In this fetid atmosphere, to wear a macintosh is to sweat so much that soon you are wet through. Boots are never dry, so that your toes begin to rot. Supplies suffer; the coarse flour breeds bugs. Mud reaches up to the thighs. Everything grows mouldy; even the bamboo poles grow internal fungus, and the smell of decay is everywhere.

Living in small holes dug in the mountainsides, supplied by a narrow mule track which zigzags up and down the mountains for over 300 miles from the nearest supply base, transport becomes impossible and essential supplies have to be dropped by air. Yet, strange as it may seem, water is often short – the mountains are so steep that the rain shoots off the sides before it can be cupped – and washing is permitted only once in three days. The enormous trees, garlanded with festoons of moss, drip heavily, ceaselessly, for months on end. Mosquitoes thrive in the elephant grass; millions of leeches appear, wagging their heads from side to side. They are small until they have feasted on human blood. Then their bodies swell to the size of your thumb. The soldiers have learnt that they will drop off if touched with a lighted cigarette; but, if you try to pull at their greasy black skin, the head remains embedded in your body and the wound becomes septic.

Jungle warfare, consisting as it does of lonely treks and skirmishes – at the most, men go out in twos and threes – demands the highest degree of courage on the part of each individual. Most men prefer desert warfare, although here there is shade, the roots and growths are a salutary substitute for fresh vegetables and a palatable addition to iron rations, and occasionally there is wild game. But the feeling of loneliness is greater; groups seldom trespass on one another's terrain. There is reassurance to be gained from fighting in numbers. Each man knows that, after a terrifying game of blindman's buff played through the coarse undergrowth, any encounter may end with a clash of knives. No quarter is asked or given. Every moment of the day each man must be on the alert; for the Jap sniper may be hidden behind that distant cliff, or in the nearest tree. There is the continual strain of listening for the sound of a footfall. Even during their sleep most men keep one ear open for the sounds of the night. They develop a sixth sense, so that they can distinguish every animal step, the calls of the birds, the laughter of hyenas, the yells of jackals, the creak of bamboo, the snapping of a twig and the Aristophanic chorus of frogs and crickets. After a time, even the most robust may show signs of nervous stress. One man, hearing steps coming closer to his *basha*, ran out in the dark and bayoneted a bear.

We were awakened in the dark; shaving in a small basin in a cold semi-outdoor was depressing. We started off for Tiddim in a fifteen-hundredweight lorry. The hearty onslaught of the captain of our party, so early in the morning, was the hardest cross to bear: he whistled through his teeth in imitation of a cockney tram conductor, and shouted abuse in four-letter English words and in Urdu to fellow travellers.

By degrees the sun had warmed the icy cold air; one side of the mountain became brilliant, the other half remaining in dark shadow. Then the sun sank behind the hills where the Japs were in occupation, and everything became pitch black. Still we motored along the small ridges, past perpendicular drops of 400 feet; sometimes a passing lorry scraped our mudguards.

Our truck bounded about in a cloud of dust thrown up by the convoy of trucks ahead. Tropical vegetation through which we passed was coated with salmon-pink dust, churned by ceaseless traffic. The bamboos, their fronds of dead branches looking like fishing-rods, rose in a perfect pure arc.

Our trucks are the least suitable vehicles for negotiating narrow ridges cut into the precipices of the mountainsides; but there was no jeep available. For hours we were tossed from one side to the other, thrown high in the air to land painfully on the little iron seat, or on the sharp edges of our baggage. We continued in semi-circles up or down a mountainside, over a surface of dust and potholes until, like Hitler's, our captain's patience was at an end. He had taken on the Herculean job of steering this heavy lorry around hundreds of hairpin bends throughout the day. We barged, crashed, thudded, ricocheted on into the night. The mountains were dotted with the small glowing fires of native encampments. After many dark vicissitudes, with distant lorries approaching like glow-worms, and passing us in a crescendo of noise and blinding light, we at last arrived, after 160 miles, on the top of a precipice covered with fir trees. We did some unpacking, sat over a fire, and waited while the sure, but very slow, black servant prepared tea and sardines and unrolled our beds.

Five thousand people live in rush-matted tents, in the encampment of Divisional Headquarters. Already by early morning the men are slick and polished as if for the parade ground; shoes shiny, everyone immaculately shaved.

The British gift of improvisation is here, fully exploited, everywhere an ant-like activity. Typewriters are buzzing, and the most elaborate systems of telephone and wireless installed. The khaki *dhobi* (laundry) festoons the branches of the trees; the 'furniture' is made of the strangest objects, and the whole picture is reminiscent of Robert Louis Stevenson. Everyone, young clerks and grey-haired brigadiers alike, wears shorts and swashbuckling bush-hats.

But living conditions are tough and work almost unending. The men sleep in fox-holes dug into the peat-like earth. After working at highest pressure all day, often another batch of work appears that must be completed after the evening meal. The day's activity starts again before sunrise.

This pressure of work helps to maintain morale. At a place so remote – it is a ten days' journey to the nearest town – there is little else to do. Everyone is extraordinarily cheerful, though it is almost more than they can bear to ask for news of England. 'What's the blackout like?' – 'Do they have enough to eat?' – 'How's the bomb damage?' – they inquire rather shyly. When I tell them that only five weeks ago I was in England, they eye me as if I were from another planet. They touch my civilian jacket and remark: 'Can't remember how long it is since we've seen tweeds.'

I handed over a package of about 250 undeveloped rolls I had exposed during the past two weeks to be sent back by air for processing at HQ in Delhi. The aeroplane which took them did not crash; the package was merely 'mislaid'. Ceaseless, but nevertheless vain, attempts have been made to discover its whereabouts. The chances are small that I shall ever be able to send the promised pictures to the men living in jungle fox-holes, firing the twenty-five-pound guns, the Howitzer teams, the Gurkhas of the 7th Regiment, the men of the Queen's Regiment and West Yorks who showed such enthusiasm and co-operation.

We came unexpectedly upon a battle. A picnic lunch in a ruined temple was interrupted by gunfire. While we climbed a flight of stone steps to discover what was happening, two over-life-size black satin crows swooped down from the magnolia-trees and carried off the remainder of our meal. So we moved on, down a disused road, through an overgrown village, once bombed, now abandoned and looking like the precincts of the Sleeping Beauty: exotic creeping plants sprawled over the half-destroyed *bashas* and summer pavilions and over the gutted motor car still parked in its neat, cement garage. At the deserted farm, provisions were dumped in a courtyard – tins of bully beef and packages of biscuits lay among hundreds of small eggs, gourds and the exotic vegetation of the tropics.

A group of young officers, with serious expressions on their sunburnt faces, were discussing the situation. During the night some Japs had come down through a nearby jungle range and had taken up their former positions which, inadvertently, we had not filled in before advancing farther. Now this enemy group was dug into the earth as snug as moles, and with a two-pounder gun previously captured from us was doing considerable damage to our rearguard. Several men had been killed, and the wounded at this moment were being brought back under fire. The stretchers were placed in the Red Cross ambulances, which the drivers manipulated on the rough roads with dexterity and compassion.

A young major appeared, his khaki battledress stained with dark, dry splashes of blood. 'We thought you'd been killed,' the others greeted him. 'Better have your arm seen to, and if you can cross that bridge, do so quickly and on all fours.'

Meanwhile, in the fields of paddy, Indian men accompanied by their naked children were still working, unmindful of the bursts of shrapnel. Bombing by air alone will send them seeking shelter.

Bombay

Less artificial than Delhi, less dirty than Calcutta, beautifully situated on the sea, Bombay cannot be considered an Asiatic city. It is the most cosmopolitan and emancipated city in India. In spite of its orchid-house climate, its inhabitants seem to possess unflagging initiative and make the town a throbbing Eastern metropolis that welcomes Western civilization. Sects, clubs, associations and newspapers are legion. Bombay is also a great town for gambling – particularly among the Parsees. Many of those present at the race meeting each Saturday have dreamt about doubles. 'Of course the favourite will win,' someone in the crowd is heard to say, 'or the stewards will want to know why....'

As the horses flash past, the crowd groans in a vast orgasm of excitement. Young women are extremely decorative in their clear coloured saris, but some of their menfolk, with tweed jackets worn over their muslin shirts, look messily indecent. The general effect, with the bright, coarse flowers set in stiff borders and a distant rainbow in the sky, has the period charm of a Manet painting.

Suddenly a violent downpour of dramatic rain disperses the crowds, not before they are soaked through. The drainage system does not allow for such a rainfall. Lawns are immediately flooded, cars are waterlogged: a few straggling Indians paddle with battered umbrellas held aloft in one hand, shoes in the other; and husky BORs, like children at play, proceed by slow degrees, climbing along with their stomachs pressed to the railings.

In the throne-room of Government House, an assortment of respectable English and Indian citizens is assembled. The inevitable Belgian Consul and his wife stand next to the huge retired colonel with high blood-pressure who must avoid the brandy. One of the Indians wears a dark green shade above his glasses, a most peculiar effect, as if he were wearing a Pullman-car reading-lamp. Some officers are in uniform; business tycoons, wearing baggy dinner-jackets of tropical weight, are accompanied by their scraggy wives.

Since there is no thought of arranging a formal dinner table such as this in any but the order of precedence, the same people find themselves, continuously and irrevocably, placed side by side. It is not to be wondered at that there is nothing much for them to say to each other and that the evening does not go with a swing.

'Will you kindly form a line along there?' suggests a rosy ADC, with only one arm and a cursory manner. 'Two rows please – come along now.' Some of the ADCs enjoy making the guests suffer. 'They don't come to Government House for nothing,' they snigger.

A long delay, long enough to make each guest fully realize what he is waiting for. At last a slight commotion is heard in the distance. 'Their Excellencies,' shouts the obstreperous young ADC.

Dinner is served on an enormous strip of table decked with bougainvillaea. The inanimate faces of the heterogeneous company are reflected in the row of silver cups.

Thirty servants, with scarlet turbans and bare feet, run around serving the inevitable banquet food. Each of the Governor's [Sir John Colville's] jokes is greeted with sycophantic laughter.

'Mercifully he seems in a good mood now,' says ADC2, sitting next to ADC3 in starvation corner. 'But I've seldom seen HE so rattled as he was this morning.'

Her Excellency personifies graciousness itself, though she, too, had a bad morning. Someone placed flower garlands round her neck at the opening of the agricultural exhibition, and they dripped down a new dress she had had copied by the *dzersi*.

The long ritual of the meal over, the company retires to the illuminated garden and sits out in armchairs and on sofas, placed on Turkish carpets. A police band plays 'Merrie Englande' and 'Poet and Peasant'. The bandsmen are in yellow and blue, with white spats.

At ten o'clock more of the European colony are let in to the sacred precincts. A further display of Anglo-Indian fashions; some of the sailors of the RIN, in immaculate white uniforms, are almost throttled by their high collars – *beaux idéals* of all novelettes.

An intellectual lady, in a taffeta picture dress with a berthe of old lace, leans forward:

'Isn't it extraordinary that so great a country as India should have fallen so low? There is nothing of promise to be found anywhere here today. No writer, no painter. The only hope for the young Indian is to go into politics; and the only hope, if the country is to regain vitality and honesty, is revolution. If Congress were to take over, they'd make the inevitable mess of it; the dishonesty and craft of the Congress leaders would soon be discovered – bloodshed and anarchy would follow – but out of that some fresh life might spring.'

An elderly industrialist leans forward and says, 'India is a feminine country, all her faults are feminine ones,' and he raises his glass gallantly.

A beautiful Indian in a pink sari says, 'Whatever those faults may be, let *us* make them. Please allow us our own headaches. India for the Indians, please.'

The ADCs move everyone around, as if in a game of musical chairs.

Under a vast electric fan, like the propeller of an aeroplane, a lady in cornflower-blue lace welcomes a newcomer. 'We were just saying that the problems of India only begin to get really confusing after the first year here.'

A young subaltern says, 'Yes, I always say it takes a year to learn to hate India.'

Two ADCs are standing apart, eyeing the guests. One holds a small printed card up to his mouth.

'HE's already had the sanitary specialist's wife three minutes. It's time we got the expert on humus heaps ready for him.'

'Oh no, Mrs Bumface gets seven minutes, she's on post-war reconstruction, but look, Her Excellency is getting a bit browned off with the Brigadier, hurry up and take that old chap over, he's the Commissioner of Police, what's his name?'

The obstreperous ADC is determined that the party shall end as soon as possible, as he has a clandestine appointment down in the hotel bar, which shuts at eleven o'clock.

Her Excellency is enjoying her talk about servants with the widow of the opium agent, Ghazipur, when the ADC interrupts.

'I think, your Excellency, that His Excellency is preparing to say goodnight.'

The guests are hurriedly thrown into line again. Their Excellencies smile with relief. It is the smile the dentist receives when his patient is freed.

'Goodnight – goodnight! – goodnight!'

The cars are churning up the gravel, especially imported from England. But in the first limousine, leaving a wake of dust and small stones, is the rubicund ADC, mopping his brow and telling the chauffeur to drive '*Jaldi! Jaldi!*'

Hyderabad: Monday 13 March

Although the heat is almost unbearable we are told to economize on electricity, so the use of the fan is frowned upon. Birds treat this house as an aviary: at night insects create a fog around the electric lights; bats rush around the matted ceiling. One gets accustomed to ants hurrying over everything, but this evening I was startled to find two frogs in the bath. Yet, all considered, this is a comfortable house.

This afternoon, while choosing, with my guide, material for an Indian dressing-gown, sirens went off shrilly and the air was rent with whistling. A few unknowing motorists continued on their way until the police cars caught up with them. With yells and curses the police cleared the road. A few seconds later the Nizam of Hyderabad sped past at high speed in a small motor car. (He has been patriotic about saving petrol.) His appearance strikes one as oddly lacking in native character. Today, unshaven and untidy, he looked like one of the porters who hang about the orange crates in any market throughout the European world.

The main thoroughfare had not for long resumed its normal clamour when, again, whistles blew to pierce the eardrums. Another motorcade came into sight, then halted. A huge yellow limousine was backing in curves from the centre of the street, and came at last to rest by the curb nearby, and I returned to the peaceful pressure of shopping. Within a few moments I heard an avalanche of oaths and curses. The shop assistant shot surreptitious but frightened glances into the street, but none would answer my inquiries as to the cause of the noise. The street was empty now but for a small crowd standing at a respectful distance opposite. 'What is all this?' I asked. My guide continued to look at silks for me as if nothing untoward had happened. From his desk a young cashier quietly answered me, 'It's Her Highness.'

Out of the elephant's breath limousine stepped an old hag. She wore her long, matted hair square at the ends, and the effect was as if she were wearing a string of loofahs. Her blue dress, with a muslin apron of pale green, was creased and messy. Her Highness stood in gold shoes with feet wide apart, hands on hips, then staggered backwards into the neighbouring shop where silver ornaments are sold. The shouting and screaming that followed was as terrifying as if knives were being drawn, and at least half a dozen fishwives were fighting to the death. But no one joined the fray. This was a solo performance by Her Highness.

Later, looking more dishevelled than ever, she reappeared and, arms akimbo, stood peering myopically into our shop. The aquiline nose, the pointed, pouting lips, the large, lean cheekbones and fierce bird-like eyes were enormously impressive in the manner of primitive sculpture. The wild appearance, though startling, even terrifying, was nevertheless on a grand scale. Magnificent, too, were the enormous drop pearl earrings and her many rows of large pearls. The grey-haired woman stood in the doorway of the shop and pointed at a blue scarf. Then she started shouting with renewed force. The young shop assistants in the tailor's shop behaved with extraordinary calm and politeness. A young boy produced the scarf for Her Highness's thorough inspection. Judging by the shrieks that followed, the young assistant's life was being threatened. Suddenly the wild woman pointed at me. I stood to attention. But the cashier whispered that I must go and talk to Her Highness, who became silent as I walked forward and bowed. As I went down the steps farther forward towards the royal lady, the screaming started again with renewed force. I had gone too near the presence. Everyone looked pained. After a scuffle the poor mad woman, for so I gathered her to be, returned to her limousine. Screaming at me from the windows, with the volume of forty dustmen, she was carried back home.

The reverence with which these shop people treated this pitiful lady provided another proof of how highly civilized and dignified they are in so many ways. Everyone in the State knows that it gives Her Highness pleasure to go on elaborate shopping expeditions. Her requests are treated with tactful acquiescence. All the purchases she has ordered to be sent to the palace are delivered, but it is known that two days later they will be returned intact.

As for myself, I believe I had somewhat of an escape, for it seems Her Highness has quite an eye for young men, and she might have ordered me to be sent up to the palace where I might not have remained intact.

Chungking: Saturday 9 April

Dazed with drugs and exhaustion I looked about me in the darkness of the Chungking night for someone to tell me where to go from here. Eventually, among the orientals, a pink-moonface came forward. 'General Grimsdale [GOC British Military Mission in China] thought you would be more comfortable staying at the Embassy than at his HQ, and Sir Horace and Lady Seymour are expecting you.' What benediction! 'Can you walk up 400 steps,' pink-moonface asked, 'or would you prefer to go in a chair?' I used my sore, stiff leg as an excuse to get into a light bamboo sedan, and be carried by two coolies up a mountainside. Half-way, two Englishmen were heard approaching: one asked my name. Yes, it was Gordon Grimsdale come to greet me. Perhaps because of the bromides I reacted strangely unenthusiastically to his welcome, for I was really grateful that these two should have descended all these steps only to mount them again, on my behalf.

The full moon shone in an empty sky, and was reflected in a widely-curving river bordered by mountains. A few twinkling lights among black trees created an effect of mystery. Perhaps it was also my rather dazed condition that made everything seem slightly dreamlike and unreal. However, I was able to register the fact that Grimsdale informed me of a tour we are to make together of the front lines. We leave on Wednesday for ten or twelve weeks on a tour of British military missions. This is a piece of luck. We may be allowed within a few miles of the forward areas, though there is no possibility of visiting the Communist areas at Yenan or Shansi.

A small Chinese soldier with a rifle saluted. He was the sentry guarding a dwarf villa. We had arrived, by car, at the top of a mountain. This was the British Embassy.

A minute hall gave on to a tall, octagonal sitting-room. The Ambassador, a lanky, overgrown schoolboy with witty eyes and a tired, but benevolent, smile on his long, donkey face, wore grey flannels. He presented his wife. She had humorous eyes, dog-biscuit complexion, and a deep, dry voice. Surprisingly, she introduced me to an owl-like Brooks Atkinson, the *New York Times* drama critic. We sat talking, maybe for an hour, in a casual atmosphere, about inflation, the Generalissimo and Madame Chiang. 'We're just picnicking here: we get, through the king's messenger, per month one bottle of whisky, a pound of butter, and a pot of marmalade, but everything is prohibitive here – especially as the black market is in a panic that it may be officially closed down.'

In this stronghold against the Japs, Chungking, the makeshift capital of China, is thriving as never before. Even the coolies are rich, earning 3,000 dollars a month: to ferry a grand piano across the river would cost 40,000 dollars. Chunking, with its rich, red earth, yields two crops a year and is self-supporting, but aid is being flown over the 'Hump' to China at the rate of one plane every two and a half minutes.

Baffling were the prices they quoted: the official rate is eighty dollars to the pound, but on the black market the pound is worth 1,200 dollars. A candle costs twenty shillings, a pound of boiled sweets thirty shillings; or, in dollars, pork costs seventy dollars a pound, a bottle of ink 200 and a gallon of petrol 900 dollars.

Sunday 10 April

By degrees, the heavy mist lifted and I could see that the place where I had spent the night was a small villa, built with centre dome and four little apses, its slate roof flowering with yellow weeds. From this vantage point a wonderful panorama stretched below: on one side the Yangtze river, and on the other the Kialing. The boats with dark-brown butterfly sails reminded me of cockle-shells.

From lower down the mountainside one could watch, at the junction of the two rivers, the tremendous life on their banks. On the steep slopes leading up to the town there is no transport: everything must be carried by primitive labour. The weights that are borne are appalling – monoliths! Both men and women wear almost permanently an agonized expression of effort: head thrust sideways, an extraordinary wriggle of the body, a swelling muscle bulging from under the yoke holding their burden.

The colonies of rickety straw houses lean in every direction. One cannot believe they can survive a storm. Yet they are not built for permanence: the occupants know that if the Yangtze should rise to a height of thirty feet, then their home will be under water.

The women are sturdy, stocky, the men have tremendous muscles. They eat their rice ravenously, gluttonously, scooping it into their mouths with the chopsticks used as shovels. The earth is valued so highly for food that there is no space made available for growing flowers: no nonsense here about the perfect peony. This part of China is as unlike the fragrant concubine, and those elegant fantasies of China that we see on porcelain plates and lanterns, as a mining town in the midlands.

Kunming

The jagged mountains of limestone, so weathered that the outline looks like the temperature chart of a consumptive invalid, are not only of great geological interest but prove that the backgrounds of Sung paintings are, in fact, true to nature.

The town is laid out with streets running in the four cardinal directions and is renowned for its gates, carved pagodas, gilded arches and old city wall (now being pulled down). Today the Chinese consider walled cities as part of an ignoble past. Instead, modern buildings, of no particular architecture, are put up hurriedly. Thus, everywhere we see bogus Spanish palaces and imitation Corbusier banks and cinemas. No rich merchant would dream of building himself a Chinese house.

The natives, until six years ago, had rarely seen a motor car but now are accustomed to lorries and jeeps jamming the thoroughfares, and to the sound of aeroplanes, which day and night fill the air as they bring in supplies from the remote outside world. But after seven years of fighting, most people seem to have grown accustomed to war and have focussed their attention on rebuilding and the interests of their family. Only professional politicians are interested in politics.

The air-raid siren sounded, the sky vibrated with the roar of aircraft, but the enemy machines were flying too high to be seen. The crowds trekked to the caves in the mountains. These warrens extend along the entire range and form an impregnable underground fortress, the whole town can shelter here. Nobody showed any sign of anxiety, in fact the occasion was treated as a picnic; kitchens were set up outside the caves and children played organized games.

We have started off on our trip [to the forward areas]! We are a company of about a dozen, including drivers. I am coupled with quiet-voiced Leo Handley-

Derry. We had hardly started when the first delay took place. A Chinese lorry in difficulties on the opposite side of a river burst into flames, and several hours passed before we could be ferried by eight coolies straining rhythmically against long bamboo sweeps. Arriving at the wartime capital of Kiangsi province, Grimsdale proceeded to call upon Chiang Ching Kuo, the son of the Generalissimo, the ruler of this town and of four other States. Learning that the great man was away, we set off again, but at the next ferry we waited another hour and a half while the coolies and a mixed crowd struggled unsuccessfully to push a heavy bus, filled with people, that was stuck between a ramp and an incline. The people inside the bus refused to help. They would wait days on end while someone else did the job, rather than leave their places. We decided to return to Kanhsien, but the hotel was full. However, the magistrate invited us to occupy the guest house of Chiang Ching Kuo, and it was a relief to find a clean lodging, even though the dwelling was built without benefit of bathroom or lavatory.

During a visit to some American Fathers in a former French mission, we listened to the radio news from Burma which has lately been disturbing. The bulletin, though very crackly, was more hopeful – the Japs driven from the Imphal plain and from Kohima ... It was strange to hear a priest saying 'What a boy!' and using Broadway slang. One, half-shaven, resembled an oversize pugilist and was a native of Pittsburgh; another, dark and bright, came from Boston.

Dinner with a Chinese General (all smiles) and an ex-minister (rather gruff) was staged in one of the best and oldest restaurants in the most ancient and dirtiest part of the town. In a room which presented an appearance of tragic poverty, with rickety stairs, peeling walls, old newspapers pasted to the ceiling to prevent the dust falling through the cracks, threadbare red cloth on the table and old faded paper flowers, we had a banquet of exquisite subtlety and refinement. Of the dozen different courses, every dish was an event. It did not signify that conversation was difficult. We ate. Particularly delicious was a fish junket (hot) with two heads and tails of fish to ornament the dish; lotus seeds hot and sweet; liver cut to look like under-the-sea plants; bean shoots, crisp and resilient; a big fleshy fish, unskinned, seasoned with fragrant herbs; and duck soup. Such a feast must have cost at least 30,000 dollars.

As we emerged, the night air was full of every sort of whiff, including opium; and a woman was buying one of the long straw tapers to light her way home into the country.

Wednesday 19 April

Leaving Kanhsien we were thrown into the vast outdoors of China. Perched high on the truck, open to the air, sun, and the varying elements, we had a ringside view of how the peasant lives in the heart of this unspoilt country. It is springtime; and the scenery looks unbelievably fresh, of an infinite variety of greens, from the pale pristine shoots of the ricefields, banked up in a succession of swirling curves, to the dark viridian squares of the rice nurseries. From the air this neighbourhood reminded me of an abstract painting by Frances Hodgkins – cocoa colour, rose-pink and pea soup green. On the ground it seems entirely green – lucid and touching greens – except for the blue distances of mountains and blue-clad peasants.

The day produced a variety of impressions: of large mountains covered with acacias, and trees with aromatic perfumes; of forests that smelt of sperm, of the very juice of spring; of peasants ploughing with buffalo the waterlogged fields of rice, the mud stretching up to the calves of their muscular legs, their thighs powdery with dry flaky mud. Occasionally we saw an old man being carried under the canopy of a sedan chair. The villages were of smoked wood and dark matting. The farmhouses, with dragon roofs curving at the eave-ends, were built simply and with beautiful proportions. Bowls of rice were eaten under the shade of a straw-plaited awning; the children had exposed behinds, and their parents, as if emptying a pot, often turned them upside down.

How the others of our party always remain so optimistic about reaching our destination in these two rackety trucks is a continuous source of admiration to me. Some part of the mechanism seems always to be giving trouble; we often run out of petrol, and must remain sitting by some deserted mountain road until, miraculously, someone appears with a camphor-smelling tin of petrol-substitute. But yesterday our truck started showing signs of ill-health soon after our dawn departure. By the afternoon it was emitting the most appalling noises, and with the approach of evening it refused to make further effort and, 100 kilometres before arriving at Pihu, emitted a series of loud bangs before coming to an abrupt halt. 'The sump has gone,' we were told. Gordon Grimsdale laughed. Soon it would be dark: better walk on, he suggested to Leo Handley-Derry, and see if there's anywhere to unroll our bedding for the night. Leo, with Bill, a breezy young cockney corporal carrying a gun, and I set forth. With the mountains a deep indigo, and the sinking sun like an enormous ripe crab-apple, the mountainous scenery was a Hokusai print, but it gave no promise of habitation. Leo smiled wryly; Bill was in high spirits, enjoying the adventure, particularly when, after we had been trudging for half an hour, he let off his gun and bagged a pheasant.

My own spirits rose when we saw, half hidden by a forest of bamboos, the dragon-tongue eaves and tiled roof of a temple. This would be quite a romantic place in which to spend the night. The temple, on closer inspection, appeared to be abandoned but for a few small chickens pecking about.

We ventured inside. Oversize gilt idols phalanxed the walls, Christian religious pictures and pictorial calendars hung on pillars, in one corner stood a harmonium while in another was an improvised dispensary. More chickens pecked around among the planks, wood-shavings and carpenters' tools which lay around on the ground, but a broken-down brass bed, Victorian armchairs and packing cases around the room showed that the temple had been converted into a huge dining-room-bedroom and storehouse combined.

Leo picked up some books and read aloud the titles of some others: *The Beat of the Heart*, *The True Jesus* and *The Analysis of the Blood Stream*. The place, he conjectured, must belong to a medical missionary.

Suddenly we heard the familiar sound of someone rasping his throat prior to expectoration, and through a wicker doorway appeared an extremely aged and shabby Chinese man carrying a tray of medicine bottles and retorts.

Leo asked: 'Are you master here?'

'No, me Wang! Master itinerating!'

Leo asked if it would be possible for us to spend the night here as our truck had broken down. Wang was overcome with laughter. I have noticed that the Chinese do not merely laugh for amusement's sake. They are apt to laugh when they are embarrassed, when they do not understand a question, or merely when they know of no other way of remaining aloof.

'Everybody welcome,' was the curt reply, but the elderly man seemed more interested in his bottles than in us.

Leo then told Bill to go back for the others, and asked Wang if there was anyone to make tea.

'No, no servants,' replied Wang. 'Servants too expensive. Cook will provide.'

Leo was somewhat baffled. Wang explained, 'Cook no servant. Cook my younger brother – but very difficult person. Cook, he heathen.'

Leo inquired, 'And you – are you a Christian?'

'I pastor,' said Wang. 'I teach the gospel with Father, but my brother heathen.'

'Is he a good cook?'

'Yes, very good cook, but very bad man.'

A small Chinese boy appeared in rags, and carrying buckets of water on a yoke. He was given Leo's packet of tea, blew his nose in his fingers and left.

Leo asked, 'Who was that?'

'That's Li.'

'Isn't he a servant?' asked Leo doggedly.

'No, Li be orphan. No servants, but plenty orphans,' chortled the old man.

At last the well-known sound of our truck horn was heard in the distance, and Leo asked if a few of Wang's orphans could help with the luggage and bedding before darkness fell.

Soon the boys came in excitedly, staggering under loads of bed rolls, basins filled with shoes and sealed bags. All the impedimenta was dumped down in the centre of the room as Gordon Grimsdale appeared, followed by Bill – with another pheasant.

Darkness was almost upon us and there was little in the way of lighting so, although our host was absent, the orderlies threw down our bedding in the various rooms at our disposal. My own room had a store of pomelo fruit in it, and it smelt the most appetizing. But 'arrangements' turned out to be next to the kitchen, as they usually are in the more primitive parts of China.

We were drinking tea, trying to dispose of a plate of sawdust cakes which Wang's brother had made for us, and discussing the missionary situation in China. It was a more or less recognized thing out here to put yourself up along the road with the missionaries, and they like it for they get very little opportunity of seeing people outside their flock. They are much respected, for they renounce everything in life, live only for others, are remarkably unselfish, and the medical ones do wonderfully useful work.

Someone was singing ecstatically in a high falsetto voice. Suddenly a small fat man with flashing eyes and pince-nez came in. He wore jodhpurs and a topi, and wheeled his bicycle in with him.

On seeing the company he reached a high 'C'. 'Why ho ho, you could knock me down with a feather! Why, for surely to goodness – can I be believing my eyes? Must I give my specs another rub? Oh, this is wonderful – company!'

Gordon trusted the little man would excuse this invasion.

'Why, my friends, I'm so delighted – so flabbergasted I can hardly put tongue to the words.'

Gordon explained our predicament and Leo formally introduced the party, while the little man explained, in an avalanche of words, that he was Father Murphy, 'a bloody neutral', and asked if we couldn't tell from his accent that he came from the west coast of Ireland. He confided, 'I was just saying to meself, "Why I can't be having visitors here for over two years!" – and goodness gracious, that was when Miss Armitage and Miss Wade from Puchang were going on furlough. God be with you – I'm surely glad to have you here under our roof for the night, though don't expect creature comforts! We live simply, mind you. We're so far away from everyone we can't get anything done for us – so we put our hands to anything, don't we, Wang?' Wang cackled. 'We make everything for ourselves. We make our own oil for the lamp: we dry the long grass for fuel: tobacco out of old tea, honey and treacle dried out – it's not the same, but it does. Prices are so terrific – why, if we had to buy *anything* we'd be destitute! We even make our own matches.'

He produced a long taper with which he tried to light a lamp. When he struck this improvised match a tremendous explosion took place.

'Our experiment has not been successful,' laughed Father Murphy as Leo lit the lamp with his own briquette.

'The great difficulty is to get drugs and medicines to carry on our work: we can't get the stuff even if we could afford it, so we have to rely on substitutes. But it's surprising what results you can get – why, we've even lanced an ulcer, haven't we, Wang?' Wang bellowed with laughter. 'You see, there's no one else in this part of the country. If they've anything wrong they come to me from miles around, and we have to do our best. It's only a mere scratching of the surface, but it all helps.'

Bill reappeared with a third pheasant. On seeing this, Father Murphy's enthusiasm almost reached the point of hysteria. 'Goodness gracious! You're just the man I want! We've got a leopard prowling around the neighbourhood. We've always wanted someone with a gun and ammunition. Several villagers have been eaten. Wang and I built all sorts of booby traps – but no success.'

Bill admitted he wouldn't like to tackle a leopard with this gun; the first shot might not kill the animal, and it was no use waiting for a second shot.

Then Father Murphy talked of another problem. 'You see that ladder? That's for Timothy O'Grady.' He pointed out a network of toy ladders and run-ways that ran up the roof and along the rafters. 'Timothy O'Grady's a seven-year-old cat, but he's all we have to catch the rats.'

'Do you have many rats?' I asked.

'Oh, many rats!' said Father Murphy, whilst Wang broke into much laughter.

Leo asked if there were any cases of plague.

'Yes,' said Father Murphy. 'Oh, many plagues,' added Wang while he and the three Chinese boys were transported with mirth.

Father Murphy told of his life here. 'Of course my real work is spreading the gospel. The Chinese make such good Christians! They love "The Bible-man", as they call me. Oh, they love the ritual – they love to kneel – they can pray for hours on end without getting tired! When I go out to tend my flock in the country all the people come out – perhaps more to see the foreigner than to hear the gospel! But you get tremendous crowds! They lift up their babies on their heads. Sometimes I can't make them go away when I want to sleep. I always get them to take a door down off its hinges, and I sleep on that – there are apt to be less foreign bodies in it than in an ordinary bed board.'

Gordon admitted that he was surprised that Father Murphy had not taken down these huge gilded effigies. Heathen gods, weren't they? Surely it made it more difficult for him with these things around?

Father Murphy was shocked. 'Oh, the Chinese are most superstitious and would be terribly upset if I took these away. They'd think it very bad luck and wouldn't come here. So we simply ignore them, that's all. The Chinese pay no attention to them either. No, this isn't perhaps an ideal place to work in, but there's nothing else in the district. You see, we were burnt out of the compound when the whole village was set on fire. That happened over a year ago.'

Gordon, surprised, asked if the Japs came as far as this.

'I'll say they did, too!' Father Murphy whistled. 'They stayed for months before clearing out, and I'll never forget that for the rest of my days. They've behaved terribly – oh, it was terrible! Our whole village was destroyed. Only twelve families escaped, the mission compound was demolished, and we've had to come here. But I'm doing all the talking! I want your news – we haven't a wireless. Our aerial was blown away in a storm, and the condenser's long worn out. Wang and I have been working on one made out of an old burnt tin, but it isn't large enough; we're waiting until another tin turns up.'

At dinner tonight Father Murphy did not, for once, live off the land. His enjoyment of our tinned foods was good to see, and he partook with relish of the contents of our flasks. His enthusiasm was so great that we wondered how we could disappoint him by ever going to our beds. He would pay no attention to any wistful plaints of fatigue, and the earliness of tomorrow's departure.

Far into the night Father Murphy talked. He wove all sorts of elaborate theories about the way the war should be fought, and asked technical questions of its progress, but he never awaited the answer.

When, next morning, we bade Father Murphy farewell, he regretted that he had not asked us about things in the old world; he had not even inquired whether we thought all that much of Lord Louis Mountbatten. 'But, goodness gracious, I've had enough to keep me thinking for months on end!'

We were happy to give him more practical reasons for remembering our visit. We were able to fix him up with a condenser and put his radio to rights, and we left behind quite a large selection of canned delicacies. Wang watched our departure with his usual gales of laughter, but Father Murphy's pince-nez were clouded over as he waved goodbye.

Saturday 22 April

Our route today took us through the mountainous paths of Chekiang province. No country could be lovelier. Gigantic gorges and vast mountains in the distance. When seen close at hand, they are covered with every exotic and strange variety of tree; ilexes in new leaf, with pale stylized foliage as in medieval tapestry; bamboos growing like pipe-cleaners; cascades of blossom; azaleas, purple, shrimp, scarlet and yellow; a mauve tree covered with waxen trumpets; the flowers of the pomelo bursting from ivory knobs, are the apotheosis of all bridal blossoms, and their perfume is positively celestial. All day, the vistas before our eyes were varied and beautiful; winding rivers, bordered with white rambler-rose bushes and flecked with white shell-like sails; neat terraces filled with gold barley or pale-green bristles of rice.

The pathways, made through the mountainsides centuries ago, are still used as short cuts by the coolies, who push their wheelbarrows, or small carts equipped with a bicycle wheel, throughout the hours of daylight. They look like souls in torment as they lumber past on their flat feet, sweating and flushed under the strain; their life is dedicated to this appalling labour. Someone said, 'It's easy for them to die, but their troubles start if they become ill.' It was a poignant and upsetting experience to watch this interminable procession of labouring humanity. Even midget children carry loads with an obvious sense of responsibility, and hop out of the way of our truck, terrified but agile. Now and then the groups of coolies in their pagoda hats and blue trousers look extremely gay and charming. But here is a ghoulish figure staggering along at a tortoise pace, his torso and arms covered with discoloured patches and spots; his yoke makes life a torture to him. It is comforting to think he may pity us strangers as mere foreign barbarians, while he is a privileged inhabitant of the Middle Kingdom, the Centre of the World.

Leo, unfortunately, pointed out to me the latrines in one village, and remarked how much the Chinese enjoy defecating in a public place while watching life pass by. After this, not only did I catch sight of hundreds of these primitive arrangements of barrels and planks under a matting roof; but a horrible stink was seldom long out of my nostrils.

Wednesday 26 April

Tropical rain all night. By early morning the compound was flooded. The river has risen six feet and the water leaked through the bamboo matting on to our papers and on to the bed. Woe is me! My stomach troubles are no better, and I have come to know the outdoor lavatory almost as well as my own room. It seems an eternity since I was internally stable; I can hardly remember what life was like when incessant visitations to an insanitary outhouse were not necessary.

Thursday 27 April

Rain continues to pour. The mill-wheel is now submerged. We cannot leave tomorrow. Everyone in poor spirits, but for myself the extra day is a relief, as I feel far from well. I got up to go next door to make a drawing of the Chinese General, but by the end of the morning was thoroughly irritated by the nagging of his interpreter – 'General Li wants you to put his stars on this way – Madame Li thinks the neck is too full – Madame Li does not want you to put flowers on her dress.' – 'Why?' – 'She says it's too flowery – Will you do another one of Madame Li?'

The rain slashes down. I became rather unnerved as the day progressed, for I had apprehension, though about nothing in particular; would I ever return to Western civilization? I visualized the possibility of being taken prisoner by the Japs and wondered how I would survive the mental ordeal. All these ruminations were founded on nothing more sensational than a telephone conversation with Leo, who rang me up from a neighbouring house to say he would discuss our plans later in the day when we met, but that it was unwise to do so now. I knew that the Jap advance was continuing and that in certain sectors the resistance was slight. However, in such a vast country there can be no precipitous invasion; progress must be slow. My qualms were the result of some form of nervous exhaustion.

A few days later

'You've got a weak tummy still; you'd better come with us.' I sat in the front of the second truck [carrying casualties]. I enjoyed, as a change, travelling with a new set of companions; nevertheless I had qualms lest our truck should break down and I should be unable to join the others at the lunch halt. We retraced our tracks of weeks ago. The azaleas were now over; double roses, *Rosa multiflora*, like ramblers, had superseded the big white rose, the *Rosa cathiensis*, of the voyage out. We caught up with the first truck at a ferry. Dr Young, the interpreter, like the shopkeeper out of *La Boutique Fantasque*, in a panama hat and white suit, was very gay, helping the coolies to row the truck across the swirling river. At this halt I had meant to get into the other truck; but at the crucial moment I was taking a snapshot. The first truck went ahead; we followed.

About half an hour later we were halted by an anxious-looking Colonel Larcom, from the first truck, standing alone in the mountain highway with an arm raised. At one side of him, a high wall of rock; on the other, a fifty-foot drop to the river.

'We've had a serious accident,' he told us. 'The truck's gone over there. The General's broken his leg.'

Scattered about on the boulders shelving down to the river lay various members of our vanguard. Bits of luggage, suitcases, umbrellas and pieces of clothing were hanging on the branches of bamboos. Some Chinese boys walked about, their faces marbled with dark dried blood; one of them looked like a prune. A Chinese soldier and Leo, quite undamaged, propped up Gordon, whose leg was giving him much pain. A few paces below him at the water's brink, on its side, lay the dead and battered truck. We were told that the truck had hit a large stone, had jerked over the precipice, before the driver was able to right the steering-wheel, and had somersaulted several times as it crashed down the rocks below. With each somersault people and luggage were thrown clear. But for a very short snapshot exposure I would have been sitting next to the driver, inside the truck, in the place occupied by Dr Young, who now lay unconscious on a crag, his suit and hat gore-blotched, his huge boots looking as if they did not belong to his body.

Bleeding Chinese were sprawled on the roadside, being sick beneath parasols. It was fortunate that a Viennese doctor, who had a huge trunk of medical equipment, was travelling with us. Bandages were applied; a stretcher made for Gordon, who was brave and smiling. How could he be dragged up the rocky slope? How to place him in a truck? How could he endure the three hours' journey back, bumping over the broken road? No, he must go by river. Someone walked miles to the nearest village to try to telephone for a boat, but returned, having found no telephone. Then someone discovered a boat to go back as far as the ferry. The wounded were piled in. At the ferry, the boatman refused to go farther. Some of our party went off to try to find other boats and boatmen. Mr Lee, the Chinese radio expert with us, managed to recruit six boatmen; but, although there happened to be fifteen sampans in the neighbourhood, no one would take the risk of allowing his boat to go on such a long journey. I was told that this refusal to help was typical of what might happen in a serious crisis.

We felt forlorn when, three hours later, the wounded were still awaiting removal from the ferry. At last everything was ready. A boat was launched. Gordon, in great pain and becoming weak and fretful, was badly bruised; he could not sit up. The Viennese doctor gave morphine tablets which did not help enough. Dr Young was still unconscious. A few minutes later the boat returned with a heavy leak. At last it was righted and sent off again.

The river was high after the rains, and was flowing fast. But it was a slow journey. When, hours later, we passed the mournful shipload in our truck and shouted from the mountainside, the replies were despairing. They doubted if they would be able to make the hospital tonight; there were rapids; the boatmen, afraid of the approaching dark, had begun to give trouble.

On arrival at the ferry, from which we had started this morning, I felt so weak I could hardly tell the story of our misfortunes. Meanwhile, night covered the unhappy boatload as it moved forward slowly among unknown dangers. We received continuous messages of its progress; it had passed such and such a village; only twenty more kilometres to go. Later, we heard shouts announcing its arrival as it passed a bend in the river, and at midnight it finally reached its destination. The recent floods had been helpful; if the river had been either higher or lower, the journey could not have been made in one day.

The local Chinese general ordered the electric light to be kept on until 3.30 a.m. when the doctors finished work. Most of the casualties are not as serious as we had feared. Gordon will have to be flown back to India to have his leg

X-rayed; but he cannot yet be moved. Some of the party will stay with him. The rest of us will continue on our return journey in a few days' time.

There were about eighteen people in our truck, when, at last, we set off this morning. Added to our usual number was a Chinese woman with her family of four small children, their nurse – a picture of gloom and despondency – their male companion, also four students who had not money enough to get to their university. The journey was uncomfortably crowded, dusty and hot; the sun gave us headaches. It was a relief when we dumped the large family at their destination, for the children had become dictatorial. The small boy aged seven had been furious when the miserable nurse drank out of the same water-bottle as himself. 'Don't you know rules and regulations?' he screamed.

Every small town and village we stay in is redolent of disease. I am bitten by fleas which, I can only trust, are not plague-carrying. Each night I go to bed anticipating visitors from the insect world. I think and dream of long baths in Calcutta. This morning the Viennese doctor diagnosed the symptoms of one of the orderlies as those of bubonic plague. Macabre jokes. 'The Plague Season is on! Have we got a Union Jack? Could we fire a volley with a machine-gun?'

My luggage has now become a pitiable mess. My bag, made for air travel, does not protect any of its contents. The vibration of the truck has caused all the tubes of cream (tooth, shaving and cold) to twist their caps and become perforated; paints have oozed on to cotton-wool, socks, ties and medicine bottles; my one pair of pyjamas is soused in petrol; no article of clothing remains undamaged.

The truck was crammed. Someone asked, 'Could we take three girl students to their school ten lee away?' 'Yes.' So ten girls turned up. Five were allowed on. Their destination, it transpired, was twenty lee away. Tomorrow, God willing, is our last day of truck travel after banging over 700 miles in this old crock, for we arrive at Laiyang, the railhead.

We ate frogs' legs and filleted eel; the bill came to 900 dollars.

Local news is bad; it seems probable that the Japs may cut China in two and capture all remaining Free China. They could even concentrate on stopping our supplies over the 'Hump'. No one is visibly panicky; the worst has been expected for so long; but everyone is secretly worried as to how the various armies will meet the three Jap thrusts.

The west of China consists of the agricultural and more mountainous provinces in which transport has always been poor and existence hard. Life in these paddy fields and small dark villages can have changed little with the passing of the dynasties. From early childhood till oldest age, from dawn until dark, every day of his life, the labourer toils for the minimum reward. The carrier-coolie, his head bent sideways, minces, like Agag, under his appalling load. The farmer, almost naked, with legs as muscular as Nijinsky's and wide apart as a wrestler's, plants in the swamps, with zealous speed, the small aigrettes of rice shoots. The water-treaders at the wheels, covered with sweat, defy by the hour the laws of gravity and cause water to run uphill. Stolid young women weed in the mire, or thresh vigorously throughout the heat of the day; children, with a wisp of bamboo, drive the herds of goats and gaggles of geese; the old women pick the leaves off the tea-trees, or tie little bags, against the onslaught of birds, over the ripening plums. The river coolies, in the rain, wearing the short capes of palm-tree fibre that, although of a design thousands of years old, are distinctly fashionable, strain at every limb as they fight the unpredictable currents and the evil spirits beneath the water.

With infinite patience, everybody battles against discouragement and dis-integration, and in the face of all disasters their spirit remains unbroken and unbreakable. When others would despair the Chinese smile with contentment, for they are of the celestial kingdom. Each farmer, coolie and soldier feels about his lot as did Shao Yung: 'I am happy,' he said, 'because I am human and not an animal; a male and not a female; a Chinese and not a barbarian; because I live in Loyang, the most wonderful city in the world.'

Simla, India: Thursday 13 July
When we woke there was a hurry to get out of the train which had arrived at the base of the mountains. Here we must change to the motor rail – a toy train that would chug its way in coils up the mountainside. First stop at 2,000 feet, another at 4,000 and, eventually, at 6,000 feet we were at the foot of the Viceregal Lodge and garden, and were welcomed by rickshaw attendants dressed in scarlet and indigo blue. How pleasant, after the drab dustiness of Delhi, to breathe in the crisp mountain air and the smell of healthy moss, ferns and palms. A brisk canter up steep asphalt drives and we were presented with the surprising spectacle of a huge, grey stone castle. It was, I believe, built by a former viceroy, Lord Minto, in the Scottish style by an Indian architect who had never left his country. The result is most bizarre. We were back among the faded snapshots of 1895: house-party groups on the porch steps and croquet on the lawn. Even the vegetation with virginia creepers winding up stone pillars and iron staircases, and cascades of Dorothy Perkins' ramblers gambolling high among the tallest pine trees, seemed to belong to the past. The well-trimmed garden beds were planted with stiff, formal salvias in formations of military precision. Old-fashioned, starch-white wooden garden seats were set against vast hillocks of harsh pink hydrangeas. Everything was damp, lush and

flourishing (the rain pours gently most nights of this month). Against this green the towering, blue Himalayas looked rather Scottish.

Inside the castle all styles were incorporated in a series of rooms that gave out of a vast baronial, balconied hall; each room was panelled and well appointed, but all the proportions were at fault, and so, too, the texture of furniture and furnishing. The eye was assailed by jaundice colours. This was a quaint monument to near-luxury that counted little in taste and charm.

Yet the comfort was almost unique in the war-torn world today: fires were crackling healthily in the grates, flowers stood stiffly arranged in ugly vases on occasional tables, and desks were well stocked with thick, crested writing paper. With as many servants and as much food and drink as we could contend with, no one, except the servants, was impressed.

Most of those enjoying the amenities of the viceregal hydro were recuperating from long ordeals in the jungle, or were recently discharged from hospital to start life again, minus a limb or a sound body. For Simla is not only a retreat from the heat of the plains but has become a great resuscitation and leave-centre, and most of its population is now wearing hospital clothes. Wandering about the garden, Peter Coats, the comptroller, eulogized Wavell's campaign in North Africa; with totally inadequate forces and only a few tanks and small supplies at his disposal, the brilliance of his feat would be appreciated by historians.

We lamented Churchill's dislike of Wavell: this had started with Churchill's jealousy after the Sidi Barrani campaign. Churchill said Wavell was like the president of a seaside golf club, and criticized him harshly in front of President Roosevelt in Washington.

Unexpectedly, we came across George Abell, Wavell's Second Secretary. He said what a great man his master was. There was nothing small in his brain: he couldn't take in petty details and only thought in broad terms: it was wonderful to work with someone like that. He said Wavell had a great gift for writing simple English, and that his letter, written to the King after he had been out here for six months, was one of the most illuminating, informed, spontaneous and vital documents the monarch could ever have received.

Discussing Gandhi's latest proposals, Abell said they were just a further attempt to blackmail his enemies, and that Wavell considers his latest utterances are those of a dying man. Gandhi was only released from prison because they did not wish him to die in captivity, but the doctor's reports seem to have been unnecessarily pessimistic, and many people now said there was little chance of his dying soon. Yet his recent behaviour had been so pettifogging that even his supporters were slightly ashamed. Abell said that Gandhi with his people was like a clergyman with spinsters.

Returning to the front of the house we joined the Wavells playing golf-croquet. Lady Wavell full of smiles, sighs, tired, untidy, and wearing a pair of really bad shoes, was coy at successfully holing out with two long putts. Sycophantic laughter from the entourage. The Viceroy, gauche and clumsy, pivoted like a top when he missed a shot.

At dinner I got HE again. Drew him on to talk of the theatre, and for a while his enthusiasm was kindled. He laughed rather wryly about certain anachronisms in plays and films, and told me about an American movie of Mary, Queen of Scots, in which a warder entered, saying, 'You're for the block, Madam.' Praising Herbert Tree, he said that he was responsible for putting Shakespeare back on the stage. He liked Tree's wit. Returning an appallingly bad play submitted by some amateur, he wrote, 'My dear sir, I have only just now found time to read your play. My dear sir!' At a rehearsal Tree, directing, had said, 'Now, ladies – a little more virginity.' I remarked that it was sad that his brother, Max Beerbohm, had become recently such a querulous old man, complaining on the radio of today's vulgarity and the way the world was going. Wavell said, 'I expect in thirty or forty years you will be deploring the lowering standards. I can hear you, as a man of seventy, regretting these old times when you sat having dinner here in a panelled room.'

The radio news told us of more flying bombs on London, and of deep shelters being opened; I felt how remote, and how horribly safe, we were here; yet, in spite of the Victorian comforts, this life is stifling and inhibiting except for the shortest of rest cures. I know that all of us are imagining the horrors that are taking place at home, and yet we can do nothing about it except to be busy on the job. Early bed (ten o'clock) a solace for the entire household.

A few days later

Have just bid goodbye to Wavell. It was rather a moving little scene. This fine man is incapable of glib sentences. But somehow he wanted to show that, although we are so many poles apart, there is something in each of us that responds to the other. We have a mutual admiration for one another, and the fact that he approves of me makes me inordinately proud. I find Wavell has a genius for cutting through the façades, and seeing people as they really are, in spite of their shyness, their alibis, and their sometimes false presentation of themselves.

As for him, although his personality is not particularly vivid or spell-binding, he is deeply impressive. He never tries to charm or hypnotize, but cannot help emanating integrity of mind, directness of purpose and unaffected simplicity of style. Indians, who are always quick to note the dominant characteristics of Englishmen, are the first to appreciate the golden goodness of Wavell. They know that he is entirely devoid of malice, deceit or guile, that he is eminently fair, and, above all things, sincere.

To be complimented by him is a reward well worth while. For in his dry and somewhat melancholy voice, and talking quietly, without moving his lips, and in a tone that is deep and easy to listen to, he says nothing that is banal. His thoughts are never ready-made, and his conversation is carefully chosen. Literature and poetry mean much to him. At dinner at Emerald Cunard's one night he recited extemporaneously Browning and Dowson at great length.

He is a taciturn man, and can be as silent in the mess as on purely social occasions. But his silences are completely unselfconscious. He has extraordinary powers of concentration: when he is thinking it is a full-time, absorbing occupation, and he is oblivious of the world. I have sometimes tried to interrupt his thoughts, and only succeeded in realizing how foolish was the attempt. Occasionally the wife of some wretched official, sitting next to him at a meal, tries frantically, but in vain, to trap him into a conversation. The woman becomes distraught. Yet, if he is interested, he can become voluble.

Wavell has just given me, as a parting present, a dedicated copy of an anthology of all the poems he knows by heart. The Wavells have accepted me almost as one of their family, and my heart is full of gratitude and friendliness for each and all of the remarkable brood. But it is the father who is on a monumental scale: merely watching him be his simple, ordinary self has been an experience which I hope may have taught me a bit about greatness.

Miami

The last five hours of the trip [to the USA from India via Africa] before arriving in Miami were the slowest, and the bucket seat became intolerably hard.

'You'll have to get priority from Washington and go commercial.' I argued, and lied in my teeth. Eventually I saw it was no good: nothing to be done until tomorrow at any rate: disappointed, I must wait the night in Miami. 'Where are you staying?' 'I don't know.' 'Well you'll never find a room at this hour of the night.'

The big hotels were all taken over by the Navy, and the lesser-known places to which the flea-bitten taxi-driver took me were not particularly inviting. Even so, with my unshaven chin and hobo clothes, I was seen as a delinquent, and not at all welcomed at the desk of several rooming houses. Yes, *I* knew my clothes stank; I was sick of every part of myself, and yet couldn't escape. I became desperate, highly critical, and somewhat hysterical. A negro, with grey stubble on his chin, taking me to a room in an evil-smelling hotel, said, 'Are you French?' 'Why?' ' 'Cos, Mister, there are some French people in dis hotel who want to talk to *anyone* who can speak French.'

Later I walked out from my furnace cell to buy an evening newspaper. The lights were blinding! Shop windows bursting with spot-lit attractions! Motor cars had headlights! Pumps were filled with 'gasoline'! Everything appeared so affluent. An old woman selling so many shiny, fat magazines and such vast, pulpy newspapers, wore a flowered silk dress that an English countess would prize for a garden party.

The women on the 'sidewalks' wore their dyed, crimped-up hair piled on top of their heads, like Marie Antoinette, the whole edifice crowned with cotton flowers, but with a long page-boy mass hanging down their back. Their brilliantly-coloured skirts were as short as tutus; their lips, from which a cigarette hung, were monstrously enlarged (in imitation of Joan Crawford) like tattooed scarlet butterflies. This Constantin Guys parade had the air of an impromptu, horrific fancy-dress party. Old white trash sat on their porches delaying the torture of retiring to an airless bedroom. Yes, this was Miami all right – the Blackpool of Florida! For me, Miami has always been the end of all hell-holes, the final stronghold of vulgarity. But Miami, out of season and in war-time! Why had I come all this way?

Connecticut

On Sunday, on my way to rest and swim at the Connecticut house of my friends, Natasha and Jack Wilson, the thoroughfares were filled with cars dashing so smoothly to the overpopulated countryside. Sexy, apricot-coloured husbands with their arrogant wives, their dyed hair blowing in the wind, paid no attention to the nest-full of children sucking goodies in the back of the car. Everyone seemed so independent and carefree, so self-assured in taking so much luxury for granted. The gargantuan Sunday joint we enjoyed would have used up a six months' ration ticket book at home.

But talk at lunch was not about the war, but of 'summer theatre' and the various Broadway stars in circuit near by. Later with coffee, we were looking through Jack's remarkable collection of theatrical scrapbooks when we came across a photograph of Geoffrey Nares. Like so many other friends, he would never return from the war. The pages were turned to reveal Rex Whistler's delightful designs for *Victoria Regina*. 'Oh yes,' remarked Jack, 'Rex [Whistler] – that's another one of our friends killed!' I let out a cry. 'It *can't* be true! When? How?' Jack looked aghast. 'I'm *sure* I saw it in the papers. Soon after the Normandy landings.' I did not need any further corroboration. I *knew* it was true! Somehow, instinct told me that Rex would be killed. There was something so indefinite and vague about him the last time he came on leave and stayed in my London house. He didn't know what he would do after the war: he didn't even know what to do with his leave. I feel somehow that people with a definite purpose are more apt to survive that awful haphazard shell ...

'Of course Rex is dead and I'm alive. It's so bloody unfair! I've been messing about doing a rotten, piddling little job that's only an alibi. I'm not capable of making any real effort as Rex has done.' I started to bellow. I was no longer in China among kindly strangers with whom one must behave with circumspection. I was with old friends. My nerves, long pent up, suddenly snapped. I blubbed. Jack and Natasha were naturally deeply upset by my tears, lamentations and hysterical cries of self-condemnation.

I remembered the evening Rex and I had spent together just before war was declared. We were sitting on his balcony in Regent's Park: Rex had already enlisted, and said he knew he had the capabilities of being a soldier, and that to accept any other job would be impossible. He made, in fact, an extremely capable officer, much beloved by his men in the Welsh Guards. The timid little rabbit became a leader. All the time he was miserable, but he never complained.

Rex, a natural talent if ever there was one, would now never be able to develop the art of painting which, he said, he felt he was just beginning to learn. His work was, in fact, undergoing a great change, and he might have developed from being a decorative painter, a muralist and illustrator, into another Turner. Now his potentials were all unfulfilled, and Rex, the person suffused with effortless charm, so romantic and youthful of appearance, with his bold, ram-like profile and pale tired eyes, would never grow old.

I wondered if Edith Olivier, nearing seventy, would survive the news. She loved him: he was everything to her – a son, a friend, her true love.

A friend wrote me of how Edith's sister had broken the news. 'It was late in the evening when Edith drove back from her many duties as Mayor of Wilton to her little house in the park. She was quite fagged out after a particularly long meeting. "I'm too tired to put the car in the garage, but I'll do it later," Edith puffed. Her sister, meanwhile, had heard the news about Rex, but did not know how she could bring herself to tell poor Edith who, at this moment, looked already so white and drained of strength. "Now come and settle down in front of the fire and have some hot tea." Edith drank three cups of tea. And I put a lot of sugar in them to sustain her. Then I told her that I'd had a wire that, alas, might be true. It was a terrible piece of news, but they had heard that Rex had been killed . . .

'Edith remained as she was – staring in front of her with a glassy, glazed look. She seemed to be peering into another world. All the remaining colour went from her face. She continued to sit, wild-eyed, staring and quite silent, utterly white. Then suddenly she started to become red around the neck. I thought I must move her, so I said, "Now we must go and put away the car." Edith whispered, "Yes, yes, we must put away the car." So we went to the garage, for I knew Edith could not go alone. Then I took her upstairs and laid her down on her bed.'

New York: Wednesday 23 August

Mercedes de Acosta, whose voice I have not heard for seven years, telephoned, as if the past had never existed, to tell me the news of the liberation of Paris.

From my hotel bedroom I could see paper flying like confetti from the tall buildings. At the Rockefeller Center ticker-tape streamers were floating in the breeze like octopuses, while sheets torn from telephone books looked like doves or miniature aeroplanes.

15

London and Paris
1944–5

The Duff Coopers were at the British Embassy in Paris; during his visits to them C.B. met old friends, put on an exhibition of photographs of Britain at war, and witnessed the visit of Mr Churchill to General de Gaulle. The war ended. C.B. designed Crisis in Heaven, *the costumes for* On Approval, *Wilde's* Lady Windermere's Fan. *He was ejected from Ashcombe on the expiry of his fifteen-year lease. He published* British Photographers *and* Far East.

8 Pelham Place, London: September 1944

The flying bombs and those beastly V2s, exploding from out of nowhere, have created new havoc in London since I left for the Far East nearly a year ago. After celebrating the liberation of Paris in New York I thought that things might be looking up a bit everywhere. But no. War in England is more total than ever, hardships always increasing. People look terribly tired and tend to be touchy and quarrelsome about small things.

Yet, in spite of all the horror and squalor, London has added beauty. In its unaccustomed isolation above the wastes of rubble, St Paul's is seen standing to supreme advantage, particularly splendid at full moon. The moon in the blackout, with no other light but the stars to vie with, makes an eighteenth-century engraving of our streets. St James's Park, without its Victorian iron railings, has become positively sylvan.

Even in the centre of the town there are aspects of rural life. While the buses roar along Oxford Street the gentler sounds of hens and ducks can be heard among the ruins of nearby Berners Street. There are pigs sleeping peacefully in improvised styes in the craters where seeds that have been buried for three hundred years have propagated themselves and make a display of purple milk-wort and willow-herb. The vicar of St James's, Piccadilly, counted twenty-three different varieties of wild plant behind his bombed altar.

Each evening at nine, everyone stops – as for the muezzin call to prayer in Mohammedan countries – for the evening news.

At Le Bourget a quick glance was enough to show how much had changed: airport completely destroyed yet nearby dwellings intact: roads almost empty: no private cars, no trams: families with their belongings crowded on the tops of lorries were being given lifts by the Americans. Lucky break for me to hitch a ride into Paris with the King's Messenger. This most auspicious and noble title belongs to a small, querulous man whose life, to me, still unnerved as a result of that Dakota crash and hating every subsequent sortie into the air, would be a purgatory of almost unending fright.

Nearing Paris, the King's Messenger noticed many more signs of life than on previous visits: markets had opened which were not there a week ago. Confectioners were empty, but bakeries' shop-windows were prettily dressed. Towards the heart of the city many bicycles. I looked for signs in faces of their domination by the Hun, but everyone appeared as before – the regard in eyes as clear and determined, showing no softening by suffering. In fact, people appeared just as ugly as equivalent English crowds would be.

When France was occupied Duff Cooper was the British Representative to the Free French in Algiers. He has now been made our Ambassador in Paris and Diana, of the love-in-the-mist eyes, samite, wonderful complexion, and glorious goatish profile, is suddenly cast in the role of Ambassadress. Diana, recently arrived, and reluctant, especially after the Arab picnic existence that she loves, to take on the burden of a formal life, wanted me to encourage her with humanizing the grandeur of the Embassy in the Rue du Faubourg St Honoré. Hurrying after her in her old velveteen pants, cotton vest, and Algerian peasant's straw hat, down the enfilades of Pauline Borghese's gilded suites, the tempo of existence accelerated. In a flash she has spread a warmth of character to these frigid rooms of state. By scattering her books and candlesticks, by hanging a favourite Victorian picture on a red cord over a mirror, by propping silhouettes, wax mask, and family photographs along a bookshelf, she has already transformed the place. And not only in matters of appearance is her love for the impromptu displayed. The rate of exchange is so crippling for the English in France that shopping is out of the question. Instead she has given enormous amusement to her staff and to herself by using the household stores for barter – exchanging soap, candles or whisky in payment for ice machines, typewriters or clothes.

This afternoon she drove me to the outskirts of Paris in her toy car. When Diana appears there is no slacking: one is galvanized into activity and sharpening one's wits: she injects life and entertainment into every situation.

Diana combines, in a unique way, a gift for using her friends, and the amenities they have to offer, with a lack of selfishness. Someone has a car at the door: 'Then can't you take us round to the garage to fetch my Simca which is being repaired?' The torrential flow of interesting conversation is not interrupted by any nonsense such as: 'You sit in the back – I'll be here.' Her instructions are given in shorthand or semaphore. No delays brooked at the garage. As she walks down the cobbled ramp she shouts: 'Hullo, hullo, hullo!' commanding immediate attention. 'You've not been able to mend the car? Well, we can't wait. Here's something for the poor box.' 'I love this car,' she says, as we rush off without horn or brakes. 'On the bat's back I do fly. You creep in and out of all the traffic – nowhere you can't go!' We dart under the mudguards of on-coming motor buses. The cross-looking man of whom she asks the way is surprised, stimulated, then amused. Likewise the *gendarme*, who at first is outraged that anyone should have the impertinence to even conceive that she could park in such a place, becomes a friend. Every expedition with Diana at the wheel has its own particular charm and excitement, for she makes her own rules of the road: a natural law-breaker, she experiments without a qualm, and thinks nothing of squeezing past a line of traffic between curb and pavement as part of her own code of right of way. Today's excursion was to visit a sub-urban, but friendly, dentist who would sell a particle of his gold supply, strictly allocated for gold teeth, in order to mend a friend's ring.

Diana is a card – a flamboyant eccentric – and a real professional extrovert in that the performance she gives is always of her best. But one must not forget that she is fundamentally a serious and noble character whose whole reason for existing is her love of Duff. Every thought is of him: everything she does is for his sake, her every action for his benefit.

When first she met and loved this comparatively unknown young man, and even faced the opposition of her beloved mother in order to marry him, she recognized his extraordinary qualities. Duff is considered by many who have a better knowledge of his potentials than I do to be one of the most remarkable men of his generation: he has political foresight, courage and wisdom that are unique. Diana knows this, and is all the time helping to make others see that, behind Duff's shyness, there is a force that could make him worthy of leading the country.

It was one of the most brilliant autumn days – a few leaves falling already, skies periwinkle-blue with dazzling white clouds gladdening the spirit. I had forgotten how beautiful Paris is. The cobble streets and silver façades, and the proportions of almost every building give an effect of consummate urban grace. Everywhere there seem to be lacy arabesques of ironwork balconies and statues luxuriously allotted in rows or in crescents. The clotted *pâtisserie* on walls and ceiling make the most modest cake-shop all the more inviting: every man in a beret in the street, every woman carrying a long loaf, seems to possess a natural reverence for *l'esthétique*.

As we drive in the wrong direction down a one-way street Diana, oblivious to the shouts, talks about de Gaulle. In answer to Duff's congratulations on the day he was recognized as Head of the French Republic the General said: '*Oh, ça finira jamais!*' Diana admits that in Algiers she found it agony to converse with the General. 'After childhood – which never fails – there's nothing else.'

Sunday 29 October

Duff, calm and immaculate, appeared by air from London. Diana, ravaged with suspense until his arrival, was then beatified with joy – also at the arrival of the Aubusson carpets from her old home. They look well in these ornate, loftily gilded rooms.

At drinks-time a few old cronies assembled in *le salon vert* to forge severed links of friendship. Although Diana takes her own unconventionality with her wherever she goes, awe of the British Embassy is obviously paramount in the minds of the Parisians. As they mounted the imposing staircase the men, in black coats and striped trousers, were excessively formal, bowing from the waist and kissing hands. All seemed to have a conservative, even ceremonial, attitude that made one realize how much more relaxed and at ease would be their equivalents in London. Little wonder that an elderly Frenchman, arriving unexpectedly early, was surprised when Diana, unbuttoning her trousers to change into a skirt, asked him point blank: 'And what can I do for you?'

The women were a curiously dressed bunch in a fashion that struck the unaccustomed eye as strangely ugly – wide, baseball-players' shoulders, Düreresque headgear, suspiciously like domestic plumbing, made of felt and velvet, and heavy sandal-clogs, which gave the wearers an added six inches in height but an ungainly, plodding walk. Unlike their austerity-abiding counterparts in England these women moved in an aura of perfume. Women and men alike were all avid for the unaccustomed bounty, now presented on a marble-topped table, of chippolatas, *petits fours* and cheese biscuits garnered from the Naafi stores. 'What we have suffered!' they exclaimed, prodding their sausages with little picks.

Sad were the ravages of time on some that I knew before. Marie-Blanche de Polignac, in a Salvation Army bonnet and widow's weeds made by her mother, Madame Lanvin, had turned into a tearful little old lady. Baba d'Erlanger-Lucinge, just before my day, was the first to bring into fashion the exotic, simian grace of the jungle and thereby created an astonishing effect of originality and allure. Today, however, she had changed her type and appeared as a conventionally well-dressed, middle-aged mother. Baba nervously told of the petty humiliations that the Germans invented in an increasing determination to show themselves masters – how the French were made to walk in the streets while the pavements were roped off exclusively for the Krauts. However,

Drian (whose etchings and drawings epitomized for me as a child the fashions of the period before the First World War) seemed as critical, caustic and mundane as ever. The years have not sweetened him, neither have they aged him. As for darling old Marie-Louise Bousquet, she does not seem a day older than when I first met her twenty years ago. Like a marionette of *La Fée Carabosse* she hobbles bravely on a stick, her hip out of joint and her back hunched, but her complexion is as sweetly pink as a dog-rose and her large eyes have all the pathos of a young hare. In a guttural croak she expresses the vitality and heart of France.

It has been said that in France a higher percentage were willing to collaborate with the enemy than in any other occupied country. Marie-Louise was saddened to discover that certain friends had fallen for the blandishments of the Germans – that they could not resist the opportunity of reappearing in the limelight and exhibiting themselves again as stars no matter under whose management.

Marie-Laure de Noailles compared the Occupation under the Nazis to being like a warm bath: soothing to begin with, but the bath became hotter and hotter so that eventually one was scalded. She described how, early one morning, a German and two French accomplices arrived in her room to search her apartment. She remained in bed, combed her hair, and called for her breakfast. After studying her family papers for two hours in an effort to discover if she were one-quarter Jewish, the strangers quit.

Each guest gave us his snippet about the appalling prices on the black market and about the *collabos*: Johnnie Lucinge, so highly cultivated and kind, told, in his rich, plummy accent, how one never knew if the ringing of a doorbell portended the last moment of liberty: most people placed a ladder against their window in case it was needed for flight: every day brought with it the possibility that one might be carried off, without a word of explanation, to camp and torture. They told us a saga of torture chambers, hot walls and electric baths, and all the other diabolical means whereby the Gestapo tried to extract secrets. A pianist had his hands chopped off: a cellist had his fingers pared as though they were pencils being sharpened. Many friends had faced their appalling deaths with incredible bravery. I noticed that not one of these people was curious enough to ask about conditions in England.

The M. of I. Exhibition of war photographs again takes me to Paris. The difficulties of finding a suitably large gallery, and then competing with the intrigues, prevarications and rank dishonesty of the owners, have now been overcome: a contract duly signed for a showroom off the Champs-Elysées to be hung with dark red velvet (hired). With a large crate of photographs I cross the Channel with Diana, who has been to London to collect provender for the

Embassy. Merely to accompany an ambassadress is enough to give anyone *folie de grandeur*: first off the ship at Dieppe – a fleet of cars waiting on the *quai* – but Diana is the last person who could ever become spoiled. She hates fuss: arriving to spend the night in a strange town she never seeks the best hotel; rather she says: 'Charm is what we're after – not revolving doors.' She is a true Bohemian; this is apparent from the clothes she wears today and in her driving: with Diana at the wheel of the van, motoring takes an insignificant place beside her conversation. With Diana talk is never allowed to flag: 'Who knows about toads? They're fascinating: they fall from the sky.' 'What is the most squalid thing you know?' 'What is an incubus or a succubus?'

Henri Cartier Bresson, who has taken a few of the best photographs in existence, has escaped after three years as a prisoner in Germany. In appearance he has become more rugged, with russet, shining cheeks, but his cherubic, almost simpleton, appearance is most disconcerting – for it gives no indication of the far from simple character of this somewhat twisted artist of the secret, prying lens. Henri told me how the farmer, on whose property he was working, always took the largest slice of meat; he, the prisoner, was allowed the second biggest – in order that he could work hard; the children next; and the mother, who nevertheless did most of the work on the place, received the pauper's share.

Henri now finds it difficult to pick up the threads in Paris where there is no unity of spirit – where everyone is suspicious of one another and denunciations are still going on all the time. And according to him there are too many political factions – all of them wrong.

It has been a great experience to meet old friends long separated, but perhaps the supreme moment of all was when, having climbed the endless flights of stairs in Number 22 Rue Casimir Delavigne, I was greeted at the summit by Bébé [Bérard] and Boris [Kochno]. Amazingly, neither of them seemed to have changed in any detail: Bébé's henna beard as long, dirty and untidy, Boris's bullet head as close-shaven. Dressed in shirtsleeves like any happy workmen they laughed, thumped my back, and vied with each other with exclamations of disbelief and joy at seeing someone straight from England. Bébé became theatrical and allowed his imagination to run away with him when describing their recent experiences. Laughingly he said the last days of the Occupation were like a de Mille production of the 1840 revolution. 'We were imprisoned for one whole week in this apartment, and the entire neighbourhood was posted with "*Attention! Ne vas être tué*": while wild citizens rushed out with bottles filled with alcohol trying to set tanks on fire – very "Victor Hugo of the Barricades".' When the 'great festivity' had taken place around the Arc de Triomphe they had overlooked the fact that there were still German machine-gun men on the top.

Bébé described the terror of living under the Gestapo. Boris's bag had been packed for prison lest at any moment, and for no known reason, he should be taken away. Yet, in spite of rules to the contrary, they had listened to the radio and done everything they were told not to do. The French went out to watch the RAF raids while the Germans remained under shelter. Bébé also told me about the swinish Hun practices that made the cruelty of the Borgias pale into insignificance: it became quite usual to hear screams issuing from buildings in the centre of the city. Max Jacob, Marcel Khill, Jean Desbordes, and so many other friends had been tortured or had died in camps. Of course the Germans had also wished to appear 'correct', and had made a great play of offering seats to women in the Métro and chucking babies under the chin, but they tried too hard to make anti-British propaganda about Oran.

The war created favourable circumstances for Bébé to abandon his more frivolous work for theatre and magazines the better to devote his great talent solely to the purpose of painting pictures. But the volume of output of painting seems disappointing though, of course, Bébé has the excuse that most of the canvases are sold and therefore he is not able to exhibit them to us. However, he showed me enchanting and tender illustrations for Colette and half a dozen other books, all beautifully produced: these were a revelation of printing after the restrictions and poor-quality paper at home. He showed also some sensitive lithographs of young girls and village children done with gutsy grace and an almost Chinese offhand understanding of draughtsmanship.

Later, when I took Bébé and Boris out to dinner, the people at neighbouring tables all joined in talk about the Occupation and gave lurid details of German cruelty. The waitress said that the French working-class man would never forgive the Boches for they had got him by the *bec* and made him hungry. The Germans had taken wine and used it for petrol in their cars. Bébé named with shame the friends who had fraternized with the Germans, but they were very few – one per cent. Chanel was cited as arch-offender, also a Russian Ballet dancer and three American women.

Dinner in this cold and poor little bistro cost £2 10s a head – but it was worth everything to see these friends again.

31 October

Jean Cocteau telephoned. Knowing I am at the Embassy he is particularly anxious to see me, because he has been accused of many crimes and wishes to be freed of guilt by being accepted by the Ambassador. When someone suggested he had not taken a strong enough line about non-cooperation with the Germans, another answered: '*Ce n'est qu'une danseuse!*'

I hurried to see Jean. We sat in his small, wine-red velvet room with black-boards for chalked memoranda notes, dates and telephone numbers and Christian names. ('Verlaine' was for some unknown reason crossed out.)

Jean called himself a phantom, trapped in Paris ('Paris is now "occupied" by the French'), despising the gossip, the bitchy wit, cynical epigrams and enforced leisure. Inactivity – the 'occupational' disease of the defeated Parisians, he said – had encouraged them to backbite and bicker but he had been fortunate to be busy writing plays and films. Now, with his friend Jean Marais at the front, he was too worried to write.

Jean boasted to me that the Germans had attacked him daily in the news-papers and for some time he remained hiding in his apartment. The young sculptor, German Brecker, he said, had saved his life – though quite how I did not understand. It is no business of mine to judge Jean's behaviour during the war, but I can imagine how difficult it must have been for him, of all ageing vedettes, to feel forgotten, and that he, more than most, found it hard to resist appearing on lecture platforms even when the auspices were highly suspect.

With his wiry, biscuit-coloured hands stabbing the air he droned on in his deep nasal voice, his lips in a pursed smile. 'Paris life today is clandestine – the reality is only whispered. The papers never give any impression of the way things are. There is still so much *politique* in Paris. Even the artists are exerting themselves too much with things outside their milieu: Picasso's being a Communist is typical. Paris provides too many disruptive distractions.' Jean considered that 'everything artistic' was dead here – one exception being Genet's pornographic novel *Notre Dame des Fleurs*. He envied my having been in India and China and living 'through different epochs'. England was united with one object – to carry on the war. He longed for England: to make films with Korda, to work in London, and to have his new play put on there before anywhere else.

We now sat at the little bistro near the cloistered Palais Royal where night after night writers, poets and painters – Colette, Balthus and others – had for-gathered for their clandestine evening meal. In my honour as an Englishman, tonight the proprietor opened a bottle of champagne and a toast was drunk to the Allies.

Jean, with his metallic violence, still possesses a fantastic youthfulness of spirit, and as an artist he manages to overrule technique by mastering it instinctively. If he has not developed his early promise as a serious poet he has become a poet in life. As for his powers of seduction – he is a real virtuoso. What wit, what manners, what brilliance! Jean excelled himself in charm for me, and put on his best performance in order to justify himself.

November

Lost somewhere under the débris accumulated in my bedroom were the odd bits of paper scrawled with addresses and telephone numbers. Who would know where I could find Picasso at his secret, unlisted address? Another search brought me near panic before the missing scrap was found. I rushed off in torrential rain to cope with transport difficulties. But on arrival at the Picasso apartment, 7 Rue des Grands-Augustins, a sad and rather sinister-looking man, perhaps a secretary or an agent, received me enigmatically. I realized that no one was conscious of my being an hour late. No one seemed to know of my appointment: 'But don't bother; there are others upstairs already.' I went up a small, winding, dun-coloured Cinderella staircase. The first room I went into was filled with huge bronze heads and squat, naked men holding animals sculptured by the painter. In the studio next door dozens of vast abstract canvases were stacked back to back. Further upstairs was a group of visitors, among them Balthus, the Polish painter, here for a morsel of shop talk, an American soldier, and two dealers. Conversation was spasmodic and cursory while they awaited the master. Picasso quietly slipped into the room. His whole ambience was calm and peaceful, but his smile was gay. He showed that he was as pleased to see me as if I had been a close friend. The fact that Hitler had been the reason for our enforced separation now made us fall into each other's arms.

'You've not changed – except for grey-white hair!' He pointed at me; he, too, had gone white. He said that he hadn't reconciled himself to his appearance. 'Have you?' he asked. 'No,' I replied, 'but there's nothing to do about it except barge on.' 'It's so unfair! It isn't as if one changed and became something else' – he screwed up his face into a childlike grin showing small teeth – 'as if a chair became a piano, for instance. No, it is merely a *dégringolade* – horrible!' But since he was not a movie actor it didn't matter a lot. But nowadays he confessed a hatred of mirrors.

Picasso has recently shown his latest paintings at the Salon d'Automne and his fame has become world-wide. At every kiosk his face stares from the covers of magazines from every country. Perhaps I am foolish to regret the passing of the blue and rose periods, the cubist, and the neo-Greek, but I find the newest works of boss-eyed women with three noses and electric light bulbs or fishes for hats of an almost appalling violence: they are doubtless diabolically clever, bad-mannered and brutal, with the effect of making every other picture pale in comparison. However, these newest Picassos have caught the imagination of the people, and Picasso said he'd heard the crowds arriving to see them were like those which file past Lenin's tomb – 'and what a strong smell those people have!'

A further posse of visitors appeared and the host talked to them in grand seigneurial manner. In fact, he is quietly delighted and amused with his success which is of film star proportions.

When the visitors departed I asked how on earth he could find time to paint with such an influx of people. 'Oh, it's the victory! It's terrible! I can't do any work since the victory – it's been too big, and all of a sudden the floods have started.' He doubted if he'd ever be able to work again. Perhaps only another war would make him work.

Later I took photographs of the master. For changes of scene we moved from one room to another, ending in the attics with sloping red tile floor, sparsely furnished with a few zebra and other animal skins thrown around – the whole of a monochrome tonality. Here he sat in his small bedroom and posed on the edge of his bath.

8 November

Picasso again. Shock to find at least sixty American soldiers and WAACs making a pilgrimage. Picasso is not overwhelmed by his popularity, and the gloomy Sabarthès and some ambiguous servants – like muses in attendance – take charge of the telephone and welcome the pilgrimages. A blonde Frenchwoman with a dashing hat over one eye, acting as interpreter, cornered Picasso in the bathroom (the warmest room in the house) and the GIs started asking questions. 'Mr Picasso, how come you see a woman with three eyes – one down on her chin?' Picasso laughed. 'Mr Picasso, why do you change your style so often?' He was amused to answer: 'It's like experimenting in chemistry. I'm always carrying out my experiments on certain subjects in this laboratory. Sometimes I succeed – then it's time to do something different. I'm always trying to make new discoveries.'

He did not excuse himself for speaking no English, and told the story of two lovers, one French, one Spanish, who lived together happily loving one another until she learnt to speak his language: when he discovered how stupid she was – the romance was at an end. Many GIs brought cameras, also books for signing. Picasso said they were like a bunch of college boys – so *naïf.*

Perhaps partly in order to get rid of them he escorted the soldiers down the street to the neighbouring studio of Adam, a sculptor and engraver. When he returned alone to his place he discovered that some of the GIs had left anonymous gifts: a package of cigarettes by the bed, a cake of soap on the rim of the bath. 'They often do that,' he smiled.

Picasso seemed far removed from the war and spoke of it in fairy-tale simplifications. But when I showed him M. of I. photographs of the destruction in London he was obviously moved. '*C'est épouvantable!* And that is happening all over the world?' I asked if I might do some sketches of him. He sat in profile and laughed that I should not make him look like Whistler's mother. Then a Hindu silence fell between us. He said: 'How refreshing not to talk! It is like a glass of water.'

British Embassy: conversation in le salon vert
Colette (like an old chinchilla marmoset sitting deep in a sofa): 'There are few people with whom I want to spend enough time even to go to bed with them, and no one with whom I want to sleep the night.'

Louise de Vilmorin: 'Oh, I'm always so alone, I adore to have someone to spend the night in my bed. And the more remote from my life and interests he is the better I like it. During the day I want excitements: during the night mystery. With the warmth of an unknown head on my shoulder I can pass an exquisite night.'

Diana: 'Listen to her embroidering upon the thought of a moment. She hasn't thought this all out before. She has all the ingenuity, flexibility and lack of plan of the Conservative party!'

November

The M. of I. Exhibition was opened formally this morning by Duff, very important and solemn. Quite a crowd and many friends turned up, mostly on bicycles. I felt very proud.

Then a great contrast: to the *Vogue* studio for my first shot at Paris fashion photographs for many years. Here again was Madame Dilé to give one a big hug of welcome. Madame Dilé, a small bird-like woman with raven's-wing hair and huge thrush's eyes, has managed the Paris *Vogue* studio and its often difficult 'star' photographers through untold phases of fashion. When first I came to Paris on assignments for the magazine I was unable to understand the language and proved inadequate in dealing with both technicians and my illustrious sitters.

But Madame Dilé at once became my friend, and no matter how perverse an editor might be to please she always had an encouraging word. As the years progressed, and my knowledge of French improved and my style of photography became ever more elaborate, Madame Dilé's task increased in difficulties. Yet at a moment's notice, and on a last-minute whim of mine, she would produce fish-nets, statues, wax-work figures, cemetery wreaths, and any imaginable assortment of objects as part of my neo-romantic or surrealistic compositions. She did not quail at the thought of going out at midnight to bring back to the studio an old seller of violets from the Madeleine, or lobster in pots from the market. Nothing ever surprised or daunted her.

Then came the war – and silence. Of course there was no fashion and no magazine: the studio was empty. But here, once more, was Madame Dilé. Today she was wrapped up against the cold in woollen shawls over woollen cardigans over woollen sweaters, a muffler covering her slightly shrunken mouth. Her hair was now grey and her dark eyes told of unspoken tragedy. But, more interested in what others are doing than in personal misfortune, she has no use for self-pity. With her deep crackling notes of sympathy and nods of wide-eyed recognition, she is one of those rare human beings who spread throughout one's adult life the feeling of comfort that has been missing since the night nursery.

After trying to instil some sort of allure into my photographs of the 'stick-in-the-mud' dowdiness of 'London's couturiers' these clothes give one wings. Balenciaga's line is very medieval and pregnant – nothing to do with the present-day travelling in *métros* so overcrowded that one has to be pushed into the train by porters – but so rich and luxurious that it is stimulating just to see.

The vegetables I asked for as props to these pictures were of great interest to those in the studio who still know hunger.

Monday

The *réveil* of Diana is like a chapter out of Evelyn Waugh which, of course, is putting the cart before the horse. Diana has woken at 7.15 am after a late night. Before the crimson curtains are pulled and her tea is brought to the vast crimson and gold bed in Pauline Borghese's crimson-walled bedroom she has already written an eight-page letter to farmer Conrad Russell, an addition to a remarkable correspondence that has continued a lifetime. Diana, alabaster-white, is wearing, tied under her chin, a tight nightcap that might have come out of a medieval German engraving. Arrival of mail: packages and parcels unfolded: envelopes and unwanted paper thrown on the floor. Follows careful – not too careful – reading of the newspapers. The bed is soon a litter of work-baskets and trays of correspondence. Then she dials a telephone number. She is trying to get an old English governess into the already overcrowded English hospital here. She makes another call: 'Have you heard the latest? This will blow your ear off. That beautiful little Laura Finch Berkeley has married an Indian snake-charmer – no, don't gasp – nothing wrong with that – I'm also charming to snakes – but listen to this. He's as tall as Emerald Cunard and completely circular – so fat, that he falls over. He's twice married and has four children ...' Now a call to the secretary: she gives instructions. ... 'That one was a brute – now I've got a nice one for you. Will you tell Sergeant Spurgeon to go to Madame Taquière and fetch a poodle – it's got long legs like arms – and take it to have its hair cut at the coiffeur and then bring it back here for life.' The telephone from the porter's lodge: 'She wants to be paid, does she? How much? Oh, she does! Well don't let her have a penny. Ask her if she'll take a bottle of whisky and some soap.' From now on the telephone is never silent. How to find a job for her son, John Julius, which will prevent his being sent by the Foreign Office to Outer Mongolia? Who could bring over from Jackson's some kippers for Duff's breakfast? The house-guests, clad in night or dressing-gowns, come into the room to hear and spread news. A black-coated man (very important in his line of antique business) arrives to help one of the guests sell a watch for ready cash; another comes in to supply bobble fringe for re-doing Josephine's bed canopy; a workman appears with a ladder to mend a chandelier and is asked his advice about new lamp-shades. An un-expected visitor places a pug dog on the bed. Mrs Portault ('the sheet woman') is announced; two girls accompany her. Soon the floors, chairs and bed are covered with finely-embroidered sheets. 'This is a "Roi Soleil" design.' Every-one is exclaiming rapturously: 'It's too lovely – too lovely!'

All the while Bloggs Baldwin, waiting to take Diana out in his car, is sewing buttons on his khaki tunic. 'Don't look at me now,' says Diana, wrapped in a bath-towel at the dressing table as she paints her face with her back to us. This is about the only privacy she demands.

When, at last, Diana is ready dressed Bloggs says: 'I'm sorry, but I can't come yet as I'm doing something that I don't think has ever been done before. I'm sewing on a back trouser button without taking off the trousers.'

The grave butler bows and shows a typewritten list. 'Coming to lunch? Sir David Keith? What can he be?' The chef comes in with his book of menus and suggestions for dinner – '*Idéal*' – and is dismissed. Finally the Ambassador appears.

Diana hands him a list of tonight's dinner guests. Duff feels in his pockets. 'What are you looking for – your glasses?' 'I can read this just as well without my glasses as you can hear without your ear trumpet.' He reads. 'That sounds rather nice!' ' 'Tisn't really – make no mistake!'

Bloggs drove Diana and me to Rambouillet to see a shell pavilion. En route we passed St Cyr and noted the precision of the RAF bombing. The destruction was entirely confined to the military target.

Rambouillet park was in a haze of mist. A child with long thin legs and long black cape walked like a character in a Grimm fairy story. Diana asked her:
'*Où sommes-nous?*'
'*C'est la laiterie de la reine Marie-Antoinette.*'
A grey stone mausoleum greeted us, the interior of marble and gold. The child unlocked another door and lo! a vast rockery with Venus among the arti-ficial rocks and fountains for cooling the milk.

The child, quiet and silent and grown-up in manner, then led us down an avenue of flaming trees to a thatched rustic house. With large keys more doors unlocked and behold! – a wonderful shell house. After exclamations of delight had echoed from shell to shell the child pulled aside a hidden door. We were now in another small room exquisitely painted with flowers and birds. Here the serious child opened some secret cupboards and some revolving dolls appeared. An atmosphere of magic.

Diana decided that this would be the place to bring Churchill for a picnic when he arrives in a few days' time.

Harold Acton and I went to *Huis Clos*, a short existential play by Sartre about hell – the premise being we make our own hell. Three characters are shown in an empty bricked-up room, here to remain intriguing and fighting with each other. The complications are infinite: misery of all sorts – including unrequited Lesbianism – and there is no conclusion. Depressing and brilliant.

10 November

The household this morning was in quite a flap preparing for Churchill's visit tonight. Candles were put in all the candlesticks – furniture rearranged once more. Diana, in pants and bandanna, delivering strange orders to the servants. 'Give that light a wash – it's got too much London on it, but it's useful: it may help us all to look a bit better.' 'Would you, what is known as, "bring this up" – it'll "come up" beautifully.' 'Place that sofa kitty-wise.' Jean moved the sofa across a corner. 'No, no – that isn't even pure-kitty!'

Saturday 11 November, Armistice Day

Churchill and de Gaulle are to lay a wreath on the Unknown Warrior's grave and watch the march past of France's war effort – including the Moroccans, Algerians, Fire Services, Post Office men, etc.

In the Embassy courtyard below bands are playing and the guard is changed. Diana calls up on the house telephone very early for she is leaving for the procession and may never be seen again. There has been great anxiety lest some of the Germans – still in hiding – might throw a bomb or bring out a machine gun.

The whole of Paris seemed to be turning out. I had no place, had made no plans, but had a great stroke of luck when I got a lift from a young officer in the bullet-proof, landmine-proof car that once belonged to Eisenhower, and we drove through the crowds, up the Champs-Elysées into the very jaw of the oncoming pageant: thus we had a ringside view of Churchill, de Gaulle and Eden laying wreaths on Clemenceau's tomb.

Almost unbelievable that, after those long, interminable years of suffering, France was once again freed. Today was a landmark in all our lives. The weight of emotion robbed one of all individuality; one became just a minute spectator of history.

The crowds, red-nosed with cold and crying, were quiet in their gratitude: some who had climbed up trees looked like black rag dolls perched without moving. When the leaders passed, the crowds shouted in unison: 'Chour-cheel!' and during the playing of 'God Save The King' they 'sh-shussed' for silence and the men removed their berets. The sky was filled with aeroplanes: a number of Spitfire squadrons were being utilized to keep any German bombers away. Even so, it was remarkable that this great mass of humanity should gather within a few miles of an enemy that was now in retreat, but, until only a short while ago, all-conquering.

Lunch at the Embassy. Mrs Churchill, feeling very cold and looking rather severe, with daughter Mary in the blush of English, pre-Raphaelite perfection in attendance, described how a Dakota had brought them from England yester-day with an escort of Spitfires. When Mrs Churchill had passed over France she wept. On arrival they had bundled into a car which at once had conked out. They changed cars and had the terror of passing others at breakneck speed in order to keep their place in the procession. On arrival at the Quai d'Orsay Mrs C. was amazed at the luxury, the grandeur of the salons, and her bedroom and sitting-room had been filled with white lilac! The hot baths in such ela-borately-appointed bathrooms had been a great event – and dinner, too – with such delicious food and so much of it: soup, scrambled eggs with truffles, followed by chicken – and as much cream and butter as you wished. Every member of the Churchill family possesses an unspoilt quality of *naïveté* that is always delightful.

After lunch Mrs Eden asked if I'd go with her to see the rooms at the Quai d'Orsay, and Mrs Churchill said she'd like to join us. It was an interesting experience walking through the crowds – none of whom recognized Mrs Chur-chill who was buffeted by *gendarmes*, bystanders, jeeps, etc. But she was thrilled to be in Paris again and, like most women, could not resist taking an interest in the shop windows. She thought the Dürer-esque hats hideous.

Outside the Quai d'Orsay the *gendarmes* challenged our approach and told us to go to a side entrance, but Mrs Churchill pleaded: 'My name is Churchill' – at which moment a jeepful of American GIs drove up: 'Say, if you're English can you tell us the way to . . . ?'

We toured these grand but monstrous apartments of the Quai d'Orsay with their oceans of Savonnerie carpet and mountains of ormolu and boule. Baskets of red, white and blue flowers had come from the most expensive florists and were in great contrast to the way in which these illustrious guests lead their lives. Nothing could have been less pretentious than the collection of toilet articles belonging to Mrs Churchill; Churchill's toothbrushes, hot-water bottle, sponge and shoddy bedroom slippers looked as if they belonged to a public schoolboy. By Eden's bedside was an Everyman edition of the classics, and the rubber dummies with which he does his exercises for shaking hands each morning.

One does not realize, when the cheers are resounding in one's ears, that the hero, acclaimed at one moment by the world, is for most of his life just like any other quiet, possibly somewhat solitary, individual.

Flying weather bad: 'Report back in an hour.' My delayed return to London was agreeably spent talking to Diana who was having a day in bed without lunch – pottering about barefoot, sorting scraps and wondering why the Embassy ran itself so badly.

Back in Pauline Borghese's huge crimson and gold bed, Diana exclaimed: 'To me, it's always a shock to hear you all saying "Bébé" to Bébé Bérard because I was always "Baby" – the baby of the family. I was terribly spoilt as it was found that I had some sort of paralysis. The paralysis was discovered when someone came from Sweden and showed us all new exercises, and Baby couldn't raise her arms above her head, or turn the pages of music in front of her. But Baby had never known anything was wrong. Baby had fallen on her face whenever Baby tripped up and was always covered with scabs, unable to raise her arms to save herself – but it didn't worry her. English doctors all said the paralysis would creep; my mother was told I had only a certain time to live so I must be denied nothing. A big ground-floor room in Arlington Street was given to me as my bedroom (I wasn't to walk upstairs). I liked the theatre. That was easy with the Trees owning His Majesty's, but I wouldn't go to matinées; I disapproved – I liked the waiting up late. I sat in the box, not allowed to clap. (Lady Tree said I mustn't clap from the box.) I went to dinner in a hansom: very dangerous – if the horse slipped in the rain you went through the window sure as fate.

'I was always eccentrically dressed – in black satin with wonderful Van Dyck aprons and collars of lace. I didn't mind that, but I was terribly embarrassed at being made to show off – at having to recite, and play the piano, and come downstairs in my "pinnie". (Mother liked the reflected lights from the pinafore on the face. We, in the nursery, thought that a pinafore was meant only to preserve the dark dress beneath and must be taken off when going in to the grown-ups.) There was always a lot of photography: at Belvoir it was dressing-up for pictures from a huge chest with old Thespian robes in it – kings and queens. We took photographs as the Five Senses – Smelling, Hearing, etcetera, or being very medieval praying in a Gothic chapel, or admiring a hollyhock. We burnt magnesium wire for lighting, and did the magic of developing and printing on POP (daylight paper). The smell of the developing dishes – the thrill of the hypo – the printing frames that fell out of the window! And then we sculpted hands. We put the guests to work and covered their hands with grease and plaster, and then the panic of the moment when the plaster dried quickly – then the breaking – would it set? It never set! Then the dipping in water – and the greased plate ... Oh, the greased plate for toffee!

'Mother never stopped finding new doctors. Eventually the paralysis was cured by galvanization – electric jerks. The muscles gradually strengthened – and then Baby had to be educated. But Baby dictated: Baby wouldn't do mathematics or German. That's why Baby's mind – not that it's been too much of a drawback – is so undisciplined today. But Baby often marvels that she could have grown up to enjoy even a modicum of success. She can hardly believe that today a woman has sent her some orchids in reply to her writing in pencil refusing to sit for a portrait. She could never believe that she could "get there". How can it be that now silly, paralysed Baby is a character, a wit – that she is carrying on this conversation in this particular room?'

Gertrude Stein and Alice Toklas have returned to Paris from their refuge in the mountains near Aix. Gertrude is much thinner and shrunken – Toklas fatter and more hirsute. Alice Toklas said, re difficulties of buying food and other scarce essentials: 'Nowadays one doesn't buy with money but with one's personality.' She described a scene in the Rue St Augustin when she and Gertrude went to buy vegetables, and suddenly some GIs shouted: 'Miss Stein, Mr Picasso wants you,' and Pablo appeared, laughing, and they all got together with the butcher in the street and he gave them extra bits of meat as a celebration.

Gertrude talks about the hordes of GIs who come to see her and Picasso. 'Why do they come to us?' She explains that for some reason she and Pablo stand for humanity: the two of them have always had the courage to fight for, and uphold, the things that they think are important. The problems of contemporary life have got out of hand: that is why so many GIs turn up to seek advice. They want to discuss their difficulties with these two people, not because they are celebrities, but because they are pioneers. One GI, however, was an exception, for he ended his conversation with Gertrude by saying: 'I think I'll go off and do a lot of hard work to become a celebrity: it seems so damned practical to be a celebrity.'

During the years of cold and shortages Gertrude and Alice became friends with a neighbour at Aix, a simple young man named Pierre Balmain, with a taste for antiques and a natural bent for designing women's clothes. In fact he made with his own hands heavy tweeds and warm garments for Gertrude and Alice Toklas to wear during the hard winters. Now he has opened a shop in Paris. At his first showing to the Press Gertrude and Alice arrived with their huge dog, 'Basket'. Gertrude in a tweed skirt, an old cinnamon-coloured sack, and Panama hat, looked like Corot's self-portrait. Alice, in a long Chinese garment of bright colours with a funny flowered toque, had overtones of the

Widow Twankey. Gertrude, seeing the world of fashion assembled, whispered :
'Little do they know that we are the only people here dressed by Balmain, and
it's just as well for him that they don't!'

Paris was cold, grey and wet today : it was a leaden day that will haunt me for
the rest of my life.

A man in the police took me on a tour of the headquarters of the Gestapo
and the prisons where the Germans, until recently, had subjected their victims
to atrocities more terrible than any conceived before in history. The chief
centres of torture were right in the heart of the city in the Rue Saussaies, the
Rue Mallet Stevens and the Rue Laurestan. At Mont Valérien, suspected
members of the Resistance were punished beyond human endurance in order
that they should give away the names of others in the movement : at least four
thousand people were done away with. The cries of the sadists' victims were
blood-curdling, yet those who heard them dare not say or do anything for fear
of bringing the same fate on themselves.

The French by now have become almost accustomed to stories of sons
tortured in front of fathers : of fathers killed by slow and diabolic degrees in
front of their families : of eyes put out : of ice-cold baths with electric currents
turned on : of hot walls, of flame jets. For me the horror was new. I heard
two women relating how the *concierge* had had to clean up the mess after Jean
Desbordes's screams had ended in a death that left blood everywhere. [Des-
bordes had been loved by Cocteau.]

On the walls of the chapel at Mont Valérien some of those awaiting their
doom had scribbled a last tragic message : 'George Maliard *mort le 26 octobre
1943.*' 'My last thoughts are of Suzanne, France and tomorrow.' Other
scrawls were terrible and bitter. '*Si jamais je crève ici Maxya, ma fiancée,
habitant 119 Rue de la Convention, sera responsible de ma mort.*'

In the Avenue Foch, in the garrets on the top of the Gestapo HQ, people
were herded together for days on end awaiting further torture or the unknown
in its most terrifying forms. Here again were pencilled last desperate messages
and testaments : '*Courage! Méfiez-vous des moutons!*' 'All is well in the best of
worlds.' '*Vive le Communisme! Vive la France!*' Terrible indictments of the
way the Germans treated their prisoners were manifest in the names of RAF
pilots and WAAF who had gone through these rooms to their deaths. Yes,
here they were, their names : 'Shelley RAF' – 'D.A. Ronden WAAF'. These
scrawled, desperate messages, written possibly in the hope that they would
come to the ears of one person, are now a writing on the wall for all the world.
They ought to be preserved so that future generations read them in order to
realize that Germans are capable of perpetrating such brutality.

For a visitor like myself, these rooms today were so haunting that even to imagine the feelings of those whom fate had arranged should be trapped here – that escape could never be – was something that would wake one with horror for nights on end.

On my way home I tried to feel thankful that such a destiny had not come my way, but my heart and whole frame were crushed that such things could be. I crawled into my bed and hoped that the pictures that insisted on asserting themselves in front of my closed eyes would one day fade away.

Ashcombe: 4 May 1945

During these long years of war the one o'clock news has so often brought disappointment or dread, that we have learned to brace ourselves for almost any kind of shock. Yesterday we were caught off guard, and could hardly grasp what had happened when we learned of the utter and complete collapse of Germany.

London

A group of us were having what should have been a quite uneventful little supper-party at Prunier's. It was given by Ti Cholmondeley whose claim to theatrical fame was that she had originated the role of Water in Maeterlinck's *Blue Bird*. After years of being happily married into the aristocracy she still enjoys the feeling that she has connections with the stage, and indeed has recently appeared in a club production of a Strindberg play directed by an unknown young man of promise named Peter Brook. Tonight her star guests were Binkie Beaumont of H.M. Tennent who, for years now, has had the monopoly of London's theatrical management, and John Gielgud. Talk was of recent play productions, and we all praised the revival of *An Ideal Husband*. Particularly delightful were Rex Whistler's last designs which he had done while he was under canvas in the army. Later, in Normandy, an enemy bullet picked him off and we were robbed of one of the greatest scenic talents the English theatre has known since Inigo Jones.

Binkie vaguely discussed the possibility of reviving some other Oscar Wilde comedy; John suggested that Isabel Jeans would be excellent as Mrs Erlynne in *Lady Windermere's Fan*. As if we were playing a country-house writing game, we all jotted down on menus the names for other members of the cast. 'Who would direct?' asked Binkie. John said that if he was wanted he'd like to take on the job. I summoned enormous courage and spurted out: 'And I will do the décor.' 'Right!' concurred Binkie. It was as easy as that.

This was the great, glorious, golden moment for which I had been waiting all my life! As a child my chief enthusiasm was my toy theatre. On that small stage the sets of *Oh, Oh, Delphine!* and *The Whip* had been re-created on cartridge paper by my water colours. The filigree of the wistaria and the rambler-rose borders had been carefully cut out with nail scissors, and the two-inch-high performers, pillaged from *The Play Pictorial* and painted with heavy make-up, were propelled on tin rods from the wings. At Cambridge I had ignored lectures and the end-of-term examinations in favour of getting up ladders with buckets of size and paint to do the décors for the productions of the Marlowe Society and the ADC.

But I had waited now a long time for a big break-through into the real live London theatre with human actors to clothe and ornament. I had so far had only the opportunity to design one or two ballets, a much-too-literary play, and an odd costume here and there. Whenever a job was going that would be an important opportunity for a designer, it was offered first to Oliver Messel, and if he were unavailable, then to Rex Whistler. For a long while I had been gathering up feelings of frustration that my chance to materialize into an important designer would never come.

All at once, I felt confident that a whole new vista was opened to me. This was a play I knew I could do well. As I walked upon air with Gielgud up the Haymarket late that night, I kept pumping him with a stream of suggestions as to how the production should look: overcharged, richly stuffed and upholstered, with a great use of *trompe l'œil* and enfilades, in false perspectives, of Victorian stucco and heavy chandeliers. Lots of parma violets, maidenhair fern and smilax, and Lady W. in apricot. He seemed a bit overwhelmed, and laughed nervously, but made no objections.

'Then can I really start tomorrow?'

'Why not?'

I got into my small Ford and drove immediately to Ashcombe, there – quietly – to put my ideas on paper. For nights sleep was impossible, for my brain was working overtime and would not quieten down. Too many ideas of decoration that had been kept in cold storage came flooding out into the glow of my enthusiasm. Things that I had remembered in childhood: the candy-striped silk of Elfie Perry, the first actress who ever came to our house; and my Aunt Cada's love of japonica pink. Then more recent impressions: the green silk walls, covered with engravings, in some London club, and the gilded garlands framing the plaques in the Bow Room at Buckingham Palace. All the ideas, like the pieces of a large, complicated jig-saw puzzle, eventually fell into place. My hands could not wield the crayons, chalks and paint-brushes quickly enough. A week later my designs were accepted.

Oscar Wilde's son is still receiving royalties from his father's plays, but it was not for this reason that Vyvyan Holland was so helpful and interesting a collaborator on our exciting project. He at once invited me to dine with him in his flat, filled with mahogany and rare books, in Sloane Street. V.H. has now become somewhat hard of hearing and his manner of speech has never been spontaneous. Age has made his mouth twitch and his eyes sag. But the more one knows him the more gentle and delightful a person he becomes.

After an excellent post-war meal with Château Yquem, *marrons glacés*, pine-apple, etc. (his wife, Thelma, is as great a gourmet as he is), he reminisced about the original production of *Lady Windermere*. Later in the evening V.H. had relaxed sufficiently to talk about his father. 'He was very good with us as children: he was great fun. I remember his saying to me he'd give me ten shillings when I grew to be as tall as his stick. One evening I stood on a footstool behind the curtains and said: "Look! I'm as tall as your stick," and he gave me a ten-bob note. But it was an appalling shock to find what complete pariahs we became after "the period". My mother and I went to Montreux, and when they discovered who we were we had to leave the hotel. I was seven at the time and it has made a terrible impression on me ever since. I can't bear even to see my name in print: it gives me the horrors. We had to change our name because everywhere we went we were hounded: people even changed the names of their dogs if they happened to be called Oscar, and in my aunts' house I came across a copy of *The Happy Prince* with the name of the author covered with sticky paper.'

Thelma disclosed that talk about Oscar Wilde was a rare occurrence and that for years this had been a forbidden subject in this household. She had just recently discovered the whereabouts of Oscar's valet. He had come to tea with her and spoken affectionately of his erstwhile master whom he had accompanied in the carriage on his last journey of freedom. When he passed his usual tie shop Oscar decided to stop the carriage. He got out and bought a new cravat.

Even the valet found it hard to find further employment when it became known for whom he had worked. It was this being scorned by the world that had killed his father, said V.H.

Lady Windermere has opened to excellent notices on its trial trip to the provinces. All portends well: it has been a comparatively smooth undertaking. Few major alterations have had to be made although until the last minute John Gielgud continued to change his direction. The most important and painful necessity and upheaval was the eleventh-hour substitution of Mabel Terry-Lewis by a younger, more forceful actress. That the frail, forgetful and irascible old lady doomed to the axe happened to be Gielgud's real-life aunt only made the situation more fraught.

Another major change: they needed an entirely new setting for Act One. For economy's sake we had ignored Wilde's directions and played Lady W.'s boudoir scene in the ballroom of Act II. But Wilde was right: the first scene calls for a more intimate atmosphere.

When a designer has used a certain chart for his colours, it is difficult to juggle them around. Gielgud and the management agreed that if Lady W.'s small gilded cage of a boudoir should be of yellow silk – very fussy and over-charged – her last act blue dress would be more suitable than the red and white candy stripes intended to be seen against the dark red walls of the ballroom. But we all reckoned without the actresses involved. Lady W. would not switch, and she was aided and abetted by Mrs Erlynne in japonica red. Binkie shrugged: 'After all, it is the actress who has to wear the clothes for the run of the play.' I was upset out of all proportion.

I did not intend to give in to defeat without a struggle that might have to continue with Binkie the entire length of the return journey to London. But as the early-morning train pulled out of Manchester station Binkie and I opened the morning papers. It was impossible to discuss theatrical trivialities after reading of the magnitude and horror of the bomb dropped the day before over Hiroshima.

Ashcombe

Surely Mr Borley wouldn't turn me out of Ashcombe after all these happy years – it couldn't be possible! And yet now I see that it is just what he has been planning eventually to do since I appeared before him as a foolish young man, willing to make a derelict ruin habitable.

When first I discovered Ashcombe – once a grand mansion but by then half-way to ruin – it was used by the landlord, a former publican of the Grosvenor Arms, Shaftesbury, and today a great enthusiast of the gentlemanly sport of shooting, as a storehouse for feed for his game. When I told him that I would like to live in such a remote spot ('Strange it appears who so'er could build a seat in so an inaccessible retreat') he eventually condescended to give me a seven-year lease. He smiled as he saw the arrival of the builder, plumber, gardener and electrician.

At the end of that lease his ferret eyes glistened and he smiled again as he made his tour of inspection and asked: 'What other improvements have you in mind?' I did not suspect his interest. 'Oh, we are going to terrace this part of the garden and make an orchard.' 'But what are you going to do about the tiles on that roof?' he asked. 'Those walls need re-pointing,' he observed, 'and the private roadway must have a new surface.' On eliciting certain promises from me, he agreed to another seven years.

Now I have been to Shaftesbury to drink a glass of South African sherry in a pitch-pine-panelled room, and have been served with an ultimatum. My lease will not be renewed, and the landlord's son will benefit by my plumbing system.

I have come away reeling from that claustrophobic Victorian villa as if gallop-
ing cancer had been diagnosed. I can scarcely swallow. I dare not be left alone
with my thoughts. . . .

Pelham Place: December

How *can* one curb the day's activity and say 'no' when interesting, unexpected,
additional jobs suddenly fall within one's reach? Now that I have no longer
a retreat in the country to retire to, the pace seldom slackens. Today it has
reached a great impetus and it was in a condition of over-fatigue, and in a mood
of self-pity, that I set off to dine with Sybil Cholmondeley. Sybil, a dear friend
of many years whom I generally see in the intimacy of her immediate family,
had explained that tonight's dinner would be just a quiet and small affair of
eight people. . . . Too bad that no taxi could be found at the last moment.
Harassed and self-absorbed, I asked the parlourmaid at Kensington Palace
Gardens if I were the last to arrive. I was. My dismay was increased to find
a most distinguished group consisting of Field Marshal Alexander, Lady Wimborne and Brendan Bracken standing in the centre of the drawing-room listening to Winston Churchill. A few moments later I pulled myself together enough
to gather that the great man was telling the company that he had been invited
to go to New York to drive through the streets, but that he couldn't do it nowadays in winter: without a hat he would catch a cold. 'I'll drive through the
city later,' he promised. This off-hand reference to being afforded a ticker-
tape triumphal reception from City Hall along Fifth Avenue, struck me suddenly as resembling an excerpt from *Alice*.

It was difficult to accept as part of everyday conversation such understate-
ments as: 'The last time I was in this street was when I drove to call at the
French Embassy, a few houses along, and there were crowds outside.' (There
were crowds for the good reason that it was VE Day and Churchill went to
congratulate the French.) Altogether the tone of this evening was so elevated
that it was hard to readjust myself to the shock of leaving so far below me the
worries and interests of my prosaic little existence. In silence I watched
Churchill holding, in his feminine hands with the pointed nails and fingers, a
glass of champagne too near his face so that the exploding bubbles tickled
him and, like a baby, he screwed up his nose and eyes to display an almost
toothless mouth. He wore cracked patent-leather shoes, and his stomach was
high-pitched under an immaculate shirt, and his heavy gold watch-chain was
like my father's. Churchill, of course, was very much the star of the evening.
He has much of the 'show-off' about him and does not brook with equanimity
rival attractions or interruption. Several times during dinner he growled:
'Allow me to continue this discussion', or: 'Please don't interrupt, Clemmie',
and indeed he knew his performance warranted rapt attention. I realized to

what a degree all in his family circle must pay him due deference. But, in all fairness, he was strictly truthful, well-balanced and impartial. At one point he interrupted himself by asking Alexander: 'Am I right, Field-Marshal?' 'No, you're wrong, sir,' said Alexander in a voice like a gun shot. Churchill was neither fazed nor angry. He 'huh-huhed' – then continued. Later he claimed that he was not a bitter political loser, that in politics you must expect everything you get ('At least they haven't been rude to me!), but during the evening several topics were discussed which showed that he was altogether somewhat disgruntled – the British Council and the recent Picasso show being particular bugbears. He was appalled by the publicity about the Nuremberg trials: 'Bump 'em off but don't prolong the agony.' He complained of photographers snapping him when he was putting a piece of meat in his mouth, and regretted the way the world is going. 'Nowadays no one is allowed their fine house. People do not want what they are given, and they are not given what they want.'

But although an occasional plaintive note could be detected from the great hero dethroned, Churchill, unlike myself, entertained no self-pity. The evening had upon me the salutary effect of making my own troubles seem unimportant. But it also made me realize with quite a shock of humiliation the limitations of my specialized existence. Here was a group of men who are uncommonly varied in their wide range of interests, yet with none of them was I able to converse with authority or ease. I realized how remote I have become from the ordinary man of intelligence. Not only in the field of politics and government, but in history, in social problems, and in the events of the day, I found myself tongue-tied and with no opinions to voice.

Churchill has never been one to put people at their ease: he is known to have an alarming effect on many. Tonight I admired him as always, relishing his turn of phrase and his wit, but I felt rather like Eve in *Howards End*: 'She was a rubbishy little creature and she knew it.' It was only when, at a comparatively early hour and wrapped in scarves and heavy clothing, Churchill was bundled off to bed by his attentive wife, that I felt able to assume even a modicum of social poise.

16

Greta Garbo
1946–8

From March 1946 for several years C.B. was preoccupied with the vain courtship of Greta Garbo. Nevertheless, he designed the films of An Ideal Husband *and* Anna Karenina *for Korda, the ballets* Les Sirènes, Les Patineurs, Camille, Illuminations, Swan Lake *and* Casse-Noisette, *and the play* The School for Scandal *for the Oliviers. He also acted in the American production of* Lady Windermere's Fan. *Edith Olivier, who had led him to Ashcombe, found him his second Wiltshire house, Reddish, in the village of Broadchalke.*

New York

The Haymarket success of *Lady Windermere* had re-kindled an interest in Wilde plays in New York, and the magnet of designing *An Ideal Husband* for Leonora Corbett drew me across the Atlantic. This project failed to materialize, but there were other tentative suggestions, including a duplication of the London *Fan*. At any rate, there seemed to be in the air the possibility of my at last breaking through the, to me, impregnable barriers of Broadway.

It was the dour, grey month of February when I eventually arrived – via a bleak and frozen Canada – in the twinkling and warm comfort of the Plaza Hotel. After the awful Atlantic crossing on a troopship filled with ugly GI brides, and their horribly seasick children, I wallowed in my old luxurious rooms. My friend Serge Obolensky, a director of this hotel, had arranged for me, on a previous visit, to live at a greatly-reduced rate in a suite decorated by myself.

Although the theatrical enterprises were all, in turn, postponed or remained undecided, almost directly after my arrival so many jobs were offered to me that it was difficult to keep an equilibrium. My photographs were said to have acquired a different quality from the fanciful concoctions of before the war: I was kept on the hop with sittings.

At last I begin to feel that the war really is over. Anxiety and nervous dread are things of the past: rationing is forgotten: the future is roseate. Of course here, as at home, the first year of peace is a period of readjustment. Here, too, it is a time of frustration – also of fear: the bogey being Russia. Everyone is scared of spies. Economically everything is in a state of flux, with continual talk of inflation or deflation or threats of further strikes. John L. Lewis has defied Truman, and can be proud that he has put a million men out of work with a loss of ninety million tons of coal. Vice-President Wallace, who in Chiang Kai-Shek in China has backed the wrong horse, has been inveighing against the British imperialistic policy in the Near East and, having done great general and lasting harm, is mercifully now in retirement. Mr Rockefeller, on the good side, has given eight million dollars towards an East River home for a United Nations building.

My doorbell rings with the printers arriving with a ballet programme lay-out for Lincoln Kirstein. At the same time a would-be producer arrives with notes for suggestions for rewrites on a play I was working on, and messengers go back and forth with manilla envelopes containing proofs of articles, type-scripts or the latest colour transparencies. Now, at last, it seems that the theatre is open to me as a designer on a big scale: it is all most invigorating. My earlier visits to New York had always seemed too fleeting. Now, with nothing specific to keep me in England, there was time to settle down and relish to the full the infinite delights that New York has to offer.

Edward James, sporting an extraordinary beard, says each day he is leaving for his habitation in Mexico on the morrow, but he goes on borrowing days, and thereby enjoying a sense of holiday. When, eventually, he arrives on his remote mountain top it will be only for a moment – for he is due back here at a certain date to continue his almost unceasing fight with lawyers. He is not so much a poet, writer, painter or connoisseur of art as perhaps he would like to be, but he is a great professional fighter. Wherever Edward goes there is trouble, yet he never seems to be unnerved. On his recent return to West Dean, the family seat in Sussex, having been away all the war, he accused his father's servants of having appropriated the linen, mislaid the stamp collection, and of generally behaving badly.

But Edward knows his own failings more intimately than anyone else. The intricate complications of his perverse mind and his startling eccentricities give him enormous enjoyment; he laughs with a high cackle at them. There is no hope for him.

Edward arranges to buy another drawing from Dali in order to induce Dali to repaint the sky of one of his earliest oil paintings which has since become ruined by mould or blisters. Edward then discovers in Mexico City the fantastic pictures of the Englishwoman Leonora Carrington. His loyalties switch. He will tell the Dalis that his lawyers have refused to allow him to buy the very expensive Dali drawing, but in order to keep the Dalis sweet he buys a piece of costume jewellery for Dali's wife Gala. It was reduced from sixty dollars to thirty dollars at Saks. Edward roars with delight. 'Gala will take it to be "expertized", and when she finds out it is false she will be furious, but I will be back in Mexico City. And if Dali refuses to repaint the sky I shall get my lawyers to sue him as it is really too bad! It's entirely his fault – he mixed the wrong varnish.'

Next day Edward forgets he has told me about the costume jewellery. 'How do you like this brooch for Gala? Pretty, isn't it? It cost sixty dollars.' 'Thirty dollars, Edward.' Edward claps his hands together, gives a leap in the air, and rushes round the room like a cat on hot bricks, yelling with fiendish laughter.

Last night dined with the Garson Kanins at the Pavillon. Margaret Case produced Terry Rattigan for them; this was a coup as Terry has scored a palpable hit with *The Winslow Boy*.

The ecstatically married Kanins (she is the redoubtable actress, Ruth Gordon) make a splendid team – both so bright, quick and humorous, they seem to spark off each other. In conversation they know how to dispense with all unnecessary impedimenta, driving right to the point, sticking to it, and brooking no interruptions.

Talk consisted mainly of the various techniques writers employ in doing their work. The Kanins start at eight in the morning (Ruth, in an aside: 'This, for an actress of many years' standing, is still quite an effort!'), and their creative work is done with the first flush of energy. After lunch the retouching and polishing of former days' efforts. They are like a couple of athletes; their training is rigorous. When on a job they do not allow themselves one drink; even a whisky and soda the night before calls for its dividend of energy the next day, they say.

Terry is by nature rather lazy, and much prefers to giggle away an evening in a haze of small talk and a little whisky. But tonight he was challenged; he was on his mettle to talk, and talk well. It was fascinating to hear him, like a business man, assess his talent. Construction is of the greatest interest to him and even the *New Statesman* admits he knows all about the well-knit play. He studies Ibsen, Shaw and Pinero for the way in which they create their effects, but he said he had learnt most from Shakespeare.

Terry is attuned to work only after long preliminaries and skirmishes. At eleven o'clock in the morning he starts, fully dressed, lying on a bed with his papers and sharpened pencils carefully adjusted around him. He retouches and buffs his play as he goes along, sometimes crossing out a line dozens of times before he feels he has the right one. But this decision then becomes final; he does not alter it afterwards. However, his most creative hours are nocturnal.

The intensity of expression on Ruth's face as she listens is so great that one can almost see the energy and dynamic force which drives her. It is typical of her and her husband that they both have much work in hand while there are five plays ready for production: Garson with a couple of film scripts and a play, Ruth with three plays. They know the hazards of the entertainment world.

Neither of them are now in the first flush of youth, but they are completely contemporary in their outlook – bored by nostalgic revivals in the theatre; it is the immediate future that absorbs and stimulates them. Their huge success is fully enjoyed by both. They are living at a fantastic rate; their extravagances (according to their great friend, Anita Loos – but then Anita has learnt to be on the careful side) are such that if both of them have a successful play running each year for the next six years they will still be behindhand with their taxes.

Their leanings politically are towards the left, but they live like royalty. They do not care to see films in the company of 'all those crowds' and prefer to wait until someone arranges for them to be shown in a private preview room. They have their own chauffeur (a rarity in New York), their meals at the most expensive restaurant. Ruth buys whole hog from Mainbocher, likewise the most expensive dressmaker. Garson showers her with presents so that she resembles a little Burmese idol, studded with bulbous jewellery. They consider money is of no use, unless spent.

I hated the hands of the clock for revolving so quickly. The bill for tonight's 'boiled dinner', followed by a *Bombe Pavillon* (an ice-cream with hot prunes, pineapple, nuts, etc., etc.), with the best wines available and liqueurs, must have made inroads into many a Kanin dividend.

Friday 15 March

Because of the continued tug-boat strike the Mayor has officially 'closed the city'. With the shortage of fuel there is only a small quota for heating or lighting large meeting-places: banks, offices, theatres, cinemas and bars are therefore shut. New York has become a village.

The most gregarious of people are the worst hit if they are suddenly faced with the reality of relying upon their own company: they do not relish the unaccustomed opportunity of remaining at home with a book. By six o'clock the solitude becomes unbearable: SOSs are sent to anyone who will come around to share the fast-diminishing supply of drink.

However, the meeting at Margaret Case's on this bitter antarctic evening had been specifically arranged – a day or two in advance – in order to bring about my first reunion with Garbo.

Ten years had passed since our first meeting in Hollywood. Although she was no longer on the screen her myth was as alive as ever, and her secretiveness as tantalizing to the public. Yet, it was said, on occasions she did abandon her hermit life to go out into the world of café society – in fact, to the most unsuitable places where she met those very people who would be most willing to exploit her and disregard her dislike of publicity. Her constant companion on these occasions was known as 'the little man'. Recently 'the little man' had discovered a delicatessen that imported caviar straight from Russia, so Garbo and her companion had invited themselves to the houses of mutual friends to drink vodka, bringing with them a pot of 'the real thing'.

Few people have done more good turns for me in my lifetime than my old friend Margaret Case, who had been one of the first to welcome me as a stranger during my initial trip to New York. By enticing 'the little man' to bring Garbo back into my existence she was performing one more – probably the greatest – coup on my behalf.

When I came through the hallway of Margaret's apartment three people were sitting around a small circular table set with glasses and plates. At the sight of Garbo I felt knocked back – as if suddenly someone had opened a furnace door on to me: I had almost to gasp for the next breath. The warmth of her regard, her radiance, her smile, robbed me of equilibrium: I held onto the back of a chair. Garbo made no definite sign of recognition but seemed to glean amusement from the mere sight of me. She took it for granted that once again I had immediately fallen in love with her. She was kindness itself, and I was flattered beyond belief to be the object of her attentions as she spread a piece of caviar on a biscuit and offered it to me pronouncing the word '*kahr-vee-yeyarr*' with histrionic flamboyance. Margaret and 'the little man' sat talking quietly in the middle-distance while I gazed at the apparition in front of me as it laughed and jabbered and waved in a frontal attack upon me.

She had changed in appearance since our first meeting. Then she had been like a large apricot in the fullness of its perfection: she was rounded, of a smooth surface. Now the apricot quality had given place to vellum. Her eyes were still like an eagle's – blue-mauve and brilliant, the lids the colour of a mushroom – but there were a few delicate lines at the corners. The face having become thinner, the nose appeared spikier which made the modelling of its tip and the nostrils more sensitive. The hair, that had appeared golden in the Californian sun, was now an uncompromising, but beautiful, cinder-mouse. I noticed that the bold, workmanlike hands were a little weatherbeaten, and her ankles and legs had the uneven, somewhat scrawny look of a waif's or of certain poor, older people: they were at odds with the grandeur of her aura but made her seem terribly vulnerable. No shadow of the conventional New York woman of fashion hovered near her: the hat could have belonged to a tinker engraved by Callot, and her shirt was that of a highwayman. In her all-grey greys she looked like a Mantegna. Although she exuded no impression of luxury one knew her to be a person of the most sifted quality.

She did the honours of the occasion in what one imagines was the theatrical style of Bernhardt: every gesture was bold and big. Conversing in a somewhat 'heightened' social manner, the content of her phrases was less important than her presence and charm which made the small gathering into a gala. She conveyed innate sweetness and delicacy of feeling as the topics changed from circus clowns to the Paris Flea Market and undergarments. She confided how much she disliked being restricted by her clothes in any way, even by garters or brassière. When she used the word 'brassière' she put her hands up to her mouth in shocked surprise at what she had said. Her voice was caressing while evoking a heartbreaking pathos. Her laugh was mellow and kindly. More caviar – more vodka. General conversation and congeniality. The companion was in good humour, making jokes and telling funny stories.

Almost imperceptibly Garbo let drop the fact that she remembered our first charming meeting. She remarked with a smile: 'I didn't wear lipstick when you knew me before.' I noticed now that her mouth was slightly too generously daubed with carmine, but the effect was charming – as if a child had been at the jam jar. With her smile so incredibly spontaneous and ever-changing expressions running across her eyes, her head thrown back to look at one from under lowered lids, it was clear that nature had endowed her. She had all the arts of enticement.

Abruptly, after she had smoked five Old Golds, it was time to leave. Panic struck me. Perhaps this was the end. Or would another lapse of ten years pass before we again met? We had had no opportunity to speak to one another in private. In desperation, and on an inspiration of the second, I implored her to come out on to the roof-garden and look at the extraordinary effect – like sticks of Elizabethan jewellery – of the lit-up skyscraper-buildings around us.

The sudden cold outside went through the body like a succession of knives, but I was determined that she should remain there until I struck a chord of intimacy. She talked – talked – talked – gabbled even harder – like an excited child – in order to cover her embarrassment at the things I was blurting out to her while discovering the knobbles of her spine and smelling the new-mown-hay freshness of her cheeks, ear and hair. Before joining the others, panic-stricken and frozen, she promised me that she would telephone me.

April

Several days elapsed without her calling. I was not permitted to telephone her, so nothing to do but wait in patience and hope. I was beginning to think she would never make the initial move. One afternoon, when least expected, she inquired without explaining who it was on the telephone: 'What are you doing?'

I gulped: 'Not a thing in the world.' Of course anything I was doing, or should have been doing, was shelved forthwith – for a miracle was about to happen and she was coming to see me right away.

She arrived, somewhat out of breath, dressed entirely in darkest blue, looking pale but even more incandescent than before. A crowd of bobbysox autograph-hunters had run after her on her way to my hotel, and they were cruel and ruthless and they upset her so much. But now she would enjoy a cigarette – calmly. We sat side by side on a long red sofa. She had not telephoned before because she had been ill: she had caught cold – doubtless by going on to that roof-top. I felt great guilt. But she explained she is an easy victim of colds, and it was foolish of her to be tempted out into the icy night winds. 'But if you had not come out on the roof with me you wouldn't be here this afternoon.' She smoked more Old Golds and drank a cup of tea remarking that cows' milk tastes so much better if it is not pasteurized, and when she pronounced a biscuit to be '*deliciosa*' I remarked: 'Then this is a festival', to which she chirped: 'Is zat so?' She talked with the excited vivacity of a child just home for the holidays, and did not look around her at my room, or show surprise or curiosity at what might be considered its somewhat startling decoration. But she did compliment me on keeping the rooms at a reasonable temperature: in fact, the steam heat was never turned on. 'Ah, fresh air!' then saluting, she cried: 'British Empire!' This was funny and somehow made sense, and I suppose I was flattered by, even in a fantasy, personifying the Empire. Garbo employed many 'service' terms and, in reply to my question as to where she lived most of the year, said: 'Oh, I follow the Fleet.' She elaborated: 'I don't quite know what that means, but I often say things like that, that only signify if you scratch beneath the surface.' But I discovered quickly that it displeased her to be asked any direct question, and she would invariably answer with some evasion.

The whole conversation had a rather wacky, inconsequential quality, but because the creature sitting by my side was so ineffably strange and beautiful one automatically and willingly accepted the idiom imposed by her. This wackiness took the place of wit and would change erratically from gay to sad. 'A doctor once looked at me very carefully and asked: "Why are you unhappy? Is it because you imagine you're ill?" Another doctor asked: "Are you bored?" I don't know why he used so violent a word!'

Another reason for my delight in her talk was that I was savouring, with a certain surprise, the still quite strong 'arckscentte' with which she spoke the English language. The tongue seemed to strike the back of the upper teeth with greater force than when a native slurs over his sentences. It gave added point to words: 'like fleet' ('*likke-fleatte*'), 'luck' ('*lukke*'), 'kid' ('*kidde*'), and 'ring' ('*wringge*'). Certain vowels were invested with unusual importance. ('Valuable' became '*vuargh-luobbhle*', 'natural'='*nahr-turrell*'; while 'o' and 'a' became 'u' – 'hospital'='*huspitulle*', 'standard'='*stundadtt*'. The Swedish version of 'known' sounds strangely Cockney ('*knewgnne*'), and 'cooler' and 'cutter' assumed quite an American blurring of the 'r's'. 'D' at the end of a word became a 't' ('*wohrt*' or '*bohrt*'). These variations on what had become the usual to me were all wrapped in a mellifluous sweetness of sound.

Apropos I know not what, she said: 'My bed is very small and chaste. I hate it. I've never thought of any particular person in connection with marriage; but, just lately, I have been thinking that as age advances we all become more lonely, and perhaps I have made rather a mistake – been on the wrong lines – and should settle down to some permanent companionship.'

This gave me the opportunity for which, subconsciously, I had been waiting. During the last few minutes I had known that – as the phrase has it – we were made for each other. Of this I was now quite certain. Not as a pleasantry, but to be taken very seriously, I asked: 'Why don't you marry me?'

I had never before asked anyone to marry me, and yet to make this proposal now seemed the most natural and easy thing to do. I was not even surprised at myself. But Garbo looked completely astounded. 'Good heavens, but this is so sudden!' She went on to soften her reaction. 'I once said to a friend of mine who invited me out to lunch: "Why, this is so sudden!", and he looked so hurt. But really, this is very frivolous of you. I don't think you should speak slightingly of marriage.'

'But I mean it. I've never been more serious.'

'But you hardly know me.'

'I know all about you, and I want to take you and teach you to be much happier.'

'But we would never be able to get along together and, besides, you wouldn't like to see me in the mornings in an old man's pyjamas.'

'I would be wearing an old man's pyjamas, too. And I think we *would* get along well together – unless my whistling in the bathroom got on your nerves?'

'You're being very superficial: one doesn't plan one's life on other people's bathroom habits. Besides, you'd worry about my being so gloomy and sad.'

'Oh no – you'd have to worry about why I was so happy, and you'd be the reason.'

'It's a funny thing, but I don't let anyone except you touch my vertebrae – they so easily get out of place.'

When it was time for her to leave, I took her down to the street. Returning to my room I wondered had she really been here? Or had I, by some extraordinary wish-fulfilment, dreamt into actuality the scene that had passed?

I looked around to see the proof that my imagination had not played a trick on me. Here was the reality: the tea cup with the lipstick, the ash-tray with the Old Gold cigarette stubs and the used matches – and the cushions against which she had leant. I would have liked to ask the hotel maid not to 'tidy' the room; I did not want her to puff out the cushions, but to preserve them just as they were now, or to cast them in bronze for always.

We have started going out for walks together in Central Park. We 'steppe outte' for miles very fast – round the reservoir then all the way home from Ninety-Sixth Street to Fifty-Ninth. During these walks over the grass, under the early springtime trees, her mood becomes euphoric. To be part of nature gives her the same elation as champagne to a novice. She strides, leaps, laughs, becomes as lithe as a gazelle. She takes deep quaffs of water at the public fountains.

Sometimes photographs are more like people than they are themselves. Occasionally, when I am walking along with Greta, I suddenly see her as she appeared in a prized photograph cut out from an old movie magazine. Today there were many such flashes; and once, when she stopped to turn and look at the new moon, I could see something that I knew intimately before I had ever met her. I watched her face in the varying lights of afternoon, and I could not help revealing to her that I had seen that particular effect before in *Queen Christina*. This sort of observation she considers unnecessary; she does not relish allusion to her film career, and I must try to avoid the subject. It was typically humble and unassuming that she remarked: 'Once in Hollywood – to mention such a distant place ...'

This afternoon the park air was so cold, but bracing, that we had almost to gallop in order to stay warm. On the spur of the moment we ran up the steps of the Metropolitan Museum to thaw and to look at the Apocalypse tapestries. Greta became so carried away that she was completely unselfconscious, as she whistled and sighed in admiration, while other visitors stared at her. She made birdlike noises of delight at the rabbits and butterflies and other small animals and insects woven into the needlework grounds of wild flowers in the 'Unicorn' tapestries. Pointing to some draperies done in reds and rose and dull pink: 'Those are now my most beloved colours. It's incredible that human-beings can do such things!' she said.

I picked up the telephone and asked for the Ritz Tower, then for her room. She answered. I asked: 'Is that my beloved?' She gasped a little, and with rather an embarrassed and happy laugh admitted: 'Yes.' I took the opportunity of asking her for the first time that very daring question: 'Do you love me?' To my astonishment she replied: 'Yes'. I was so surprised that I felt my ears could not be trusted for it was so unlike her to respond in this way. I then stretched my luck by repeating the question – and again she said: 'Yes.' And

Queen Elizabeth (the Queen Mother), 1939

Princess Elizabeth and Prince Charles, 1948

The Prince of Wales, 1968

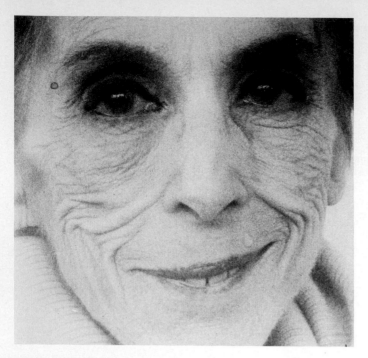

Above, Isak Dinesen; Below, Truman Capote

Above, Chanel; Below, Balenciaga

Evelyn Waugh

I went on repeating it until finally she laughed and said: 'You shouldn't ask direct questions.'

Greta told, with great humour, of how on one of her return visits to Sweden she had gone for a walk with a woman friend on a frozen lake. Greta was wearing a short fur coat and carrying a walking stick. Suddenly they found themselves up to the neck in the lake. Her terrified companion implored her to keep calm while Greta first hoiked out her walking stick, pulled herself, and then her companion, to the icy surface. But now what to do? They were miles from home – would they not catch pneumonia? Should they go to a nearby house and call a doctor? No, there would be press stories: 'Garbo Near Drowned'. 'I couldn't face that, so we decided to run. We ran all the way home, and when the woman's husband came back he found me in bed with his wife drinking hot whisky, and he laughed so much!'

One afternoon Greta started once or twice to ask a favour, then decided against it: 'Perhaps another day I'll mention it.' I was most intrigued. Then she continued hesitantly: 'If only you were not such a grand and elegant photographer ...' I finished the sentence for her: 'Then you'd ask me to take your passport photograph?' She looked astounded. 'How did you know?' Greta had told me she was planning to leave for a holiday in Sweden, and I realized it would have been impossible for her to go to any ordinary passport photographer without the results being displayed far and wide. Knowing her antipathy to publicity of all forms, resulting in her terror of cameras, I had purposely never suggested that she should pose for me. To take pictures of her has always been my greatest ambition, and this opportunity was unique. However, the sitting must be as simple and private as possible, for to have an assistant with lights would be to overload the occasion. The following afternoon a screen was placed near a window, while on the outside door of my apartment a notice was pinned: 'Passport photographs taken here.'

The sitter arrived wearing a biscuit-coloured suit and polo-collared sweater, her hair a lion's mane. At first she stood stiffly to attention, facing my Rolleiflex full-face as if it were a firing squad. But, by degrees, she started to assume all sorts of poses and many changes of mood. The artist in her suddenly came into flower. She was enjoying the return to an aspect of the métier that had been her life's work, and I could only click the trigger in an effort to capture yet another marvellous moment of her inspiration. Could I believe my luck? By degrees I was emboldened enough to ask if she would take off her habitual sweater. Then I brought out some 'prop' clothes – a pierrot's ruff and white pointed cap – that I had secreted just in case.... Greta became Deburau. A man's top hat was discarded on sight, though a Holbein tam-o'-shanter was approved once it was bashed into a Chinese mandarin's hat. Every now and again my ever-growing euphoria would be interrupted by Greta's saying: 'That's enough now – got to go.' But by the time I took her word as 'gospel' a vast number of pictures had been made.

The results formed a prized collection – though few of them were suitable for passports.

When shown the small contacts, the sitter was pleased. She pronounced them 'strong' and clean-cut and of a good quality. Together we went shopping for a folding leather frame so that I could have my favourites by me wherever I travelled. She put a pencilled cross on the back of those of which she approved and would allow me to publish in *Vogue* magazine. When the selection was sent to my good friend, Alexander Liberman, the Art Editor, he could hardly believe his eyes. Here was a precious windfall of a dozen different pictures of someone who for ten years had resolutely refused to be photographed. From the rich hoard Alex chose a laughing head to be used across two pages. Surely this did not do justice to the full range of Greta's beauty? I cajoled him into publishing a variety of moods and guises.

May

Meanwhile, Greta dropped the bombshell that she must return to the coast. Could I not join her there? No – from California she would sail almost immediately to her native Sweden. 'Could I not meet you in Stockholm?' 'Oh, no!'

Frederick Ashton wired me from Covent Garden that he had a ballet for me to design if I could return at once. I might as well go home. When I arrived back in England a telegram arrived, unsigned, from Greta, bidding me good morning.

It was only to be expected, before my photographs of Greta were to appear in *Vogue*, that word should go round in journalistic circles of the imminent scoop. I imagine 'the little man' asked why she had allowed me to publicize her. A week before the magazine was to be on all the bookstalls, Greta sent me a cable from Sweden saying that if more than one of the photographs were to appear I would never be forgiven. Frantic calls to my friends at *Vogue*: 'Stop everything!' It was too late: the copies were already bound and on their way throughout the country. Greta's telegram was later followed by a letter saying she was deeply distressed at the idea of having any costume pictures of herself published unless they had to do with her work. She was after all a serious human. It was more than ever appalling to know that, through a complete mis-understanding, it was now impossible to prevent her from feeling completely betrayed. My abject cables, letters, telephone calls, and flowers sent to her in Sweden went by unanswered.

I felt as if I had committed a murder.

New York

When *Lady Windermere's Fan* opened in Santa Barbara I was almost numb with stage fright. By the time we had moved to San Francisco I had acquired some confidence. Los Angeles audiences are notoriously unreceptive and I learned what it was to play against impossible odds – as on the night when the town's electricity supply gave out and our ballroom scene was played in semi-darkness. But once the production had been acclaimed in New York, the routine of appearing at the theatre for each evening and matinée completely delighted me. Novice that I was, I soon discovered that one must be always on the alert to what is coming from the audience: that each performance differed when at any moment some surprise element would promote an alteration of tone, voice, pitch or pace. It was exhilarating to find oneself making discoveries in the craft of acting. I wondered how on earth I had spent my evenings before this opportunity arose for enjoying myself in the most exciting and exhibitionistic way, before going out to relish that well-earned drink and supper after the performance.

We had not been ensconced in the Court Theatre on Broadway for more than a few days when Greta landed from her Scandinavian holiday. I telephoned her upon her arrival at the Ritz Tower. I was kept waiting a considerable time by the operator: doubtless Greta was talking to someone else. At last the operator said: 'She don't answer', and I suspected that Greta was hiding from me.

26 October

After many further vain attempts to speak to Greta on the telephone in Hollywood (I would call at all times of the day, and I could hear the operator being told by Greta's sad-voiced servant that Miss Brown was not at home and she did not know when she was expected back) this morning I was again fortunate enough to gain my quarry. At first she was exasperated and treated me as a tiresome burden that might as well be disposed of once and for all. 'This is no good,' she said. 'We are too different. By your action you have deprived me of a friend.' 'Who is the friend?' 'You were!' She did not wish me to telephone – she had nothing to tell me. Desperately I ad-libbed: 'But I don't want you to tell me anything – I just want to talk to you.' 'Well, we never talk on the telephone here in California – only in New York we talk on the telephone. I'm not being cruel or vindictive, but things have changed.' 'I haven't changed – have you?' I asked. 'No. I'm a very strange person,' she replied, 'and I can't change – and I don't think I want to very much either – so you had better not call any more.' I was fighting for my life. 'Then may I write?' 'What's the point?' This was pretty near to disaster for me, but by banter and repartee we eventually returned to better terms. Greta suddenly showed that she was curious – if not jealous – that someone had sent me tuber-roses to the theatre when I had my 'first night' on Broadway. 'Are you shocked with me for exhibiting myself on the stage?' 'No – not interested,' she replied, but a little later she said: 'You'd better get off that stage.' When I said that unfortunately I had to leave the cast as I was to be under contract to work in films for Alexander Korda in England, and that I'd soon be sailing home for nearly a year, she said: 'When are you going? And have you got a cow?' 'No, I haven't even a house in the country any more.' 'Well, I don't know how you'll make out.'

Pelham Place, London

When first I went to see Korda in his rooms at the St Regis, New York, it was with a certain amount of misgiving. I did not want to work in films. 'I want to buy you,' he had said. 'But I don't want to be bought – and I'm terribly expensive.' I told him of my past film experiences, working against people with no understanding of what I could give them. He looked piqued: he is not accustomed to people refusing his advances. 'Well, I think I'm the only person who can utilize all your talents and give you the opportunity to fulfil your ambitions as designer, director, photographer, writer, or what you will.' Naturally I was flattered. The more I thought about the idea, the more it seemed feasible. I went to my lawyer and a whopping great contract was signed.

Korda and I sailed to England together on the *Queen Elizabeth*. At every meeting I found him more charming, and I was surprised that anyone with a moving-picture background could be so well-read and generally intelligent. He did not seem to wish to talk about films and their making. In fact, whenever I broached the subject of my working for him he was vague and abstracted. He shrugged: 'You just do your work where you want, but when the film starts I want you on the floor with me.' At first he intended to do a film of *Salome* (Wilde), and in the preliminary discussions with his brother Vincent I saw already that we were heading for trouble. It seems to me impossible to do this period 'purple patch' in a straightforward, serious vein. 'Why not put it into a *nouveau art* frame? By making it even more curious the effect would be less ridiculous.' I had dropped such a spanner that the whole project was slowly abandoned.

Sir Alexander Korda on the telephone.

'How are you, Saisille, old boy? When shall I see you?' drawled the Hungarian voice.

'Whenever you want.'

'What about this afternoon?'

'Anytime you like.'

'What about this morning?'

'Whenever you say.'

'12.30?...Twelve o'clock, old boy, would be even better.'

When, after battling through the snow, I arrived at his office in his landering, great Piccadilly house Sir Alex was pacing up and down the large room trying to keep warm. He was wearing his overcoat: there were no lights on. We were enjoying a peak of the Shinwell winter season, and the gas and coal supply had given out.

'Hullo, old boy!' He peered at me through the gloom. 'Well, I've got two pieces of news for you. One good – one bad.'

'Tell me the bad first.' I braced myself for the shock.

'No, I'll tell the good first. You've always tried to bully me into making *Ideal Husband* as a film. Well, we're going to do it. That's the good news. Now for the bad: we start shooting in three weeks' time.'

'But that's also good news,' I said with genuine enthusiasm.

'I want you behind the camera with me – and of course to do the costumes and all sorts of odd jobs. Start right way. We'll do it entirely in the period of when the play was written – 1895.'

Out in the snow again I took up my position at the end of a long bus queue. The nineties seemed to me so much longer ago than a mere fifty years: in comparison with today's life in England under a Labour government it could have been as remote as ancient Rome. What a self-indulgent era it had been! The blessings of equality were unknown, neither had the virtues of austerity been recognized. With altogether too much pleasure and leisure most people over-ate and drank too much, and wasted hours in conversation.

One bus after another, filled to the ceiling with steaming, wet humanity, went by without stopping. The queue remained static. What a worthwhile job lay ahead – to show, by innuendo, how unenlightened in comparison to ours those old days of horse-drawn carriages had been. Snow and mud from roaring streamlined cars and motor-bike traffic spattered the still motionless queue.

At last a bus hove in sight in which I was able to find an inch of space on its running board. Holding tight to the rail I thought about Victoria as Queen of England and Empress of India, and how an empire had ruthlessly dominated the world. The bus skidded but I was thrown clear. I put up my umbrella and staggered on into the semi-darkness towards South Kensington.

Home at last, I discovered that I had run short of drawing paper: at the nearest art-store their quota of paper had given out: neither had they Indian ink in black – only orange. I did my first designs on the insides of cardboard boxes in orange ink. Two days later Sir Alexander looked at the results.

'Did the women really look like that then? How horrible!'

His brother Vincent, always depressed and always depressing, with puckered forehead was equally distressed at the sight of the furnishings of the period. 'Look at all those fussy dust-catching nick-nacks! Where can we get candles today? Hothouse flowers! Who's got hothouses? No wonder, with those side-boards groaning with ortolans and quails, so many of the Victorians had to go to Homburg or Baden to have their livers cleaned out.'

Working on preparations for the film also brought further proof of the fact that we are living in the modern world. The slips of young girls who came to portray the privileged guests in the ballroom scene in no way resembled those enormous Boadiceas, full-bosomed and well-cushioned, who could scarcely bend – so encumbered were they by their boned corsets, barbaric jewellery and dozens of yards of heavy silk. It was not easy to find among our utility materials, docketed cretonnes or nylon household-goods, anything to simulate those thick brocades, cumbrous satins and quilted damasks. Asking the wig master if he could emulate the Victorian *coiffures* by adding false hair to modern pates, he shrugged: 'Hair? We've had none for years!' We fought on manfully.

Korda did not start in three weeks' time and there were the usual delays. But much of the work of research, design, fittings, of conferences, was a revelation to me, and my enthusiasm was sustained. Then, suddenly, Korda gave me the added responsibility of designing all the costumes for *Anna Karenina*. When it became impossible to find costumiers in London who could undertake the work at such short notice, Korda suggested that the leading actress's dresses and hats should be made in Paris. Here I found that the great Madame Karinska had handed on her dress-making genius to her daughter. The confections that she created for Vivien Leigh as *Anna* were masterpieces. Likewise, Madame Paulette made free adaptations of my sketches for hats that transcended anything that I could have desired.

British Embassy, Paris: Friday
Still stricken [with a bad cold], and with a temperature, I was disappointed that there would be no *Hamlet* for me this evening. (The Oliviers had got me a ticket and I was looking forward to seeing Jean Louis Barrault.) However, Larry gave me a lot to think about as I lay in my dreary state. He trusted it wouldn't offend me to be offered second choice, but if Roger Furse, to whom he was obligated to give preference, were too busy with the film of *Hamlet* to design *School for Scandal* for him, would I care to take on the Sheridan? This is one of my favourite of all plays, so full of charm, wit and kindliness.

I would certainly jump at any such opportunity. Larry would be an interesting Sir Peter and Vivien would look adorable as Lady Teazle. My brain started working overtime with ideas for sets and costumes. I became impatient with my illness for not allowing me to get straight to work.

Saturday

Still in bed, but with throat less painful. I was able to read a lot. Larry came in and chuckled about our behaviour here in this grand house. He said: 'For the first few days I was so bloody serious because I was shy. It would be so awful to make a joke in the British Embassy and find you'd gone too far.' He said: 'I find it difficult when Duff [Cooper] comes into the room not to straighten up to attention too much or, alternatively, to be as casual as to ignore him almost entirely and finally greet him in an offhand way.' The burlesque he did of himself was quite a cameo.

After dinner the Oliviers brought up with them the two chaps who are here to work on the filming of *Hamlet* – Roger Furse (décor) and Tony Bushell (manager). They had spent the afternoon discussing plans and designs, and had thrown out two weeks of Furse's work. But they had made a valuable discovery: instead of building whole sets they would decide what would be the most suitable and pictorial background for each shot and reverse shot, then they would only build the necessary. This seems to be logical, yet is a complete reversal of the normal procedure of building an entire room, then wondering where on earth are the right angles to shoot.

'Abstract,' Larry answered when I asked how the production would look. He then proceeded to describe the film in hearty schoolboy phrases. With arms flailing he emulated with a big 'whoosh' a great curtain falling down here – a pillar 'pffutting' down there – 'a hell of a lot of smoke and emptiness all over the place'. Instead of using words that could be found in a dictionary he would illustrate his intentions by making prep-school sounds – of pops, bangs, and corks being drawn, of internal combustion explosions, 'farts', and all sorts of other coarse noises. The camera would 'raspberry' down on to the castle at the beginning of the film ('An old-fashioned idea, but then I'm old-fashioned'), and then 'raspberry' away at the end – and the castle that was shown wouldn't necessarily tally with the sets but the atmosphere would be the same. Larry is, heaven knows, serious about his career, but the project on hand is referred to only in ribald terms. No question of 'Wouldn't it be beautiful to have ...?' 'Mightn't it be extraordinary to ...?' – just: 'A great blob here (bang! bangho!)' – 'A great cowpat here (bungho!)'

It was a most gymnastic performance that we were treated to. Larry's imitations have about them something of the original clown or, at least, the essential entertainer, who can be found in some remote music hall or performing in the street outside a pub. This was the real Larry – the mummer, the ale-drinking Thespian – not the rather overwhelmed and shy cipher with wrinkled forehead that goes out into society.

I was vastly entertained and Vivien, who had joined us, sat by, amused. Larry was conscious of an excellent audience though the two chaps looked on a bit anxiously: they knew this routine of old, and their expressions of slight anxiety were inspired by the dread that the 'conference' might continue far, far too late into the night.

Sunday

Vivien spent the afternoon sitting on my bed and regaling me with stories about her stage experiences. Larry was meanwhile working with the *Hamlet* chaps in his sitting-room. Later they all came in to show me the tentative designs. They are less abstract than Larry had described, and I thought Ophelia was too positively Holbeinesque. But Furse can be relied upon always to do a thoroughly professional job, and his drawings are always sensitive and in fine taste.

While the others were out at a dinner at the Vilmorins' house at Verrières, I enjoyed looking through illustrated eighteenth-century books with Sheridan at the back of my mind. But I could wait no longer for the others to return so went to sleep.

It was not long afterwards that Larry, rather muzzy, came into the room and regaled me, in the darkness, with stories of the evening. It had not been entirely successful. Diana, furious that the men had not mixed with the women after dinner, said: 'The English have corrupted French manners!' 'The Game' (an elaborate form of 'dumb crambo') was played, the amateurs and professionals were at war. Juliet had previously confided to me how badly the actors perform in 'the Game', and tonight the professionals complained of the slowness of Juliet's reactions. 'You silly old goose – do something! Act, Juliet! Go on – oh, go *on*, Juliet!' Vivien came into the dark room, surprised at our chortles, and joined in the tirade against Juliet. 'Oh, she was so slow! She wouldn't give an indication of what she was!' When, later, Vivien and Larry were fumbling their way out of the still black room, Larry, behind the bedscreen, stumbled across the bolster which I always throw out of my bed before going to sleep. 'What on earth is this here?', and I amused him by replying: 'Lady Juliet Duff, by all that's wonderful!'

Diana said: 'Should I play the Queen in *Hamlet*?' (Larry had invited her to do so in his forthcoming production).

'No,' said Louise de Vilmorin, 'it would ruin a lovely film for me. I'd be too nervous to see it.'

Sunday

I have the days mixed, but no matter. Still in bed but decided to get up for lunch. Duff in his nicest mood. He has perhaps the most civilized mind of anyone I know: his intelligence, erudition and general knowledge make me feel inadequate. There is no subject – even photography or design – about which he does not know more than I; even after all these years I am shy with him. He can be alarming – for he does not suffer fools gladly and at any moment his temper may get the better of him – then the result is stupendous. But generally he is the most docile of people. He is never hurried and has the born writer's gift of leisure. He manages to get through an enormous amount of work, yet always seems to have time for reading. I broke into the library the other morning to find him sitting peacefully at his desk reading Horace. Diana, on the other hand, must be 'doing' something.

After lunch today, unable to relax and do nothing, she arranged for Duff to read aloud. Diana sewing a piece of black and white watered taffeta; Vivien and I listened to Duff, in dry, slow and rather sad voice, read three stories of Elizabeth Bowen. Outside a forlorn, melting snowscape.

On the Korda set

At long last we assembled, on a certain cold Monday morning, at the Shepperton studios outside London for the initial day of shooting of *An Ideal Husband*.

Clarissa Churchill, who during the past two years now has been a close friend, has recently been given a nebulous job by Korda ('You will find your own niche,' was all he explained to her) and together we went through the 'breaking in' process. Together we started off for the motor-car journey in fog or early morning mist. Soon we became exhilarated and interested in watching Korda's direction. We were full of admiration for his quickness, perception, subtlety and flair. But by his choice of cast he gave himself insuperable difficulties, and when the hard job of acting had to be faced he discovered that two of his leading actors were completely inadequate. He soon realized that Paulette Goddard, who was to be the wicked Mrs Cheveley, could not possibly play the part as an Englishwoman (her attempt to be a mixture of Lady Diana Cooper and Sylvia Ashley Fairbanks, as suggested to her by Noël Coward on the boat that brought her across the Atlantic, was really rather painful) so I was told to look through other Wilde plays for reference to Americans and we interpolated a few lines from *A Woman of No Importance* to make a joke about, and justify, Paulette's accent. Martita Hunt was called in to coach Michael Wilding, but she professed no confidence in the success of her results. 'He's too common for the part,' she said. 'All the people who see the film will be common,' said

Korda, glib in reply. But an easy comeback is a mistake. By degrees I began to realize how readily Korda excuses himself when he is in the wrong. His intention was to make the highest quality film. When I complained about a library set being particularly phoney and vulgar he shrugged: 'Well, the Chilterns are *nouveaux riches.*' That is not what Wilde intended them to be. That is not why we went to Paris for the hats, and to Wildenstein to hire Louis Quatorze tapestries.

At the time that Korda was most engrossed directing and producing *An Ideal Husband* (by no means a small production) his company directors were getting desperate to call a meeting, but Korda was busy negotiating a lawsuit in Hollywood. Suddenly, just as an *Anna Karenina* production was about to go before the cameras, Korda at last got around to reading the script which had been written by Anouilh and Duvivier (the film's director). Korda realized their efforts were unworthy.

Hell let loose. Korda again sleepless. Constance Collier, with magnificent ram's profile, important nostrils and prognathous jaw, is playing the part of Lady Markby on the *Ideal Husband* set. Today she bared her salted-almond teeth and chuckled: 'Look at the lamb: he's not with us at all. He's not directing this film – he's directing Tolstoy. Look at him reading *Anna Karenina* between shots.' Sure enough – there he was, with Tolstoy pressed close to his myopic eyes, oblivious of the electricians and grips moving dangerous equipment within inches of his head. Occasionally he would make a mark in the margin. Constance bared her salted almonds again. 'Look! He's making a few notes so he can impress them at the conference and let them know he's read the book.' After one *Ideal Husband* scene had been taken he called for a stenographer and sat on the stage, under an arc light, dictating.

When the result of this dictation appeared a few hours later it was a revelation. In spite of the conditions in which he had been working, he had written an absolutely brilliant analysis of Tolstoy's book. He pointed out where the Anouilh–Duvivier script had gone wrong, and why and where it must be rewritten.

A few days later I discovered that Korda had given his notes on the re-writing of the script to a hack-writer who has just completed a bad picture. When challenged by Vivien Leigh on the wisdom of this Alex said: 'If I give the job to Rodney Ackland, or a good writer, he'd produce *his* version of *Anna*. I want my outline to be copied faithfully.' The result – which appeared ten days later – was certainly better than the former, but naturally, since it was a 'rush job', was not really up to the mark.

May

Korda in a bad mood: all sorts of irritants make him like a bear with a sore head. Our set is teeming: over two hundred guests are assembled on stage in their expensive finery. Lord and Lady Chiltern are receiving at the head of an imposing staircase. For the fiftieth time the ghostly-looking butler rings out: 'The Earl of Caversham.' The beautiful Diana Wynyard does her extraordinarily ugly, but charming, grin: Aubrey Smith bows with as much spontaneity as if he were running through the performance for the first 'take'. Suddenly Glynis Johns cannot be found. 'Who allowed her to go for breakfast?' screams Korda, and the two men responsible for giving her leave to go to the cafeteria are given a fine display of temperament. 'Now where's Miss Goddard?' 'In the Medical Aid.' The technicians around the camera are on their guard against more disasters. One of the electricians calls *sotto voce* to an unseen figure among the lights aloft: 'Save the scoops and trim your arcs when I tell you to, for God's sake, or there'll be bloody murder.'

Without a word of warning I arrive, in full battle cry, on the *Ideal Husband* set to find the place deserted. Korda has called a halt while he flies to America to fight that lawsuit. A postponement of two weeks: complete dispersal of crew: high tension slackened.

For two weeks we are bathed in a heatwave. On the *Anna Karenina* set they are wearing furs, and laying snow on the ground to be seen through windows on which the 'prop' men are nailing icicles.

Vivien Leigh, so companionable and perky in private life, becomes sadly changed as soon as the strain of picture-making begins to tell. There is no fun any more. The difficulties are overwhelming and absorbing. I go into her dressing-room one morning, confident of finding her in a great state of elation, for the newspapers have just announced that her husband has been knighted.

I open the door. 'Oh, I'm so happy for you about the great news!' A face of fury is reflected in the mirror. 'Really, it's too stupid! Would you believe it – the dressmaker from Paris was waiting at her hotel the entire day yesterday and the studio forgot to order a car for her. Really – I've never worked on such a film as this!'

Later, Vivien instructs me: 'Please tell Clarissa how to behave when she brings journalists on the set. I don't want them turned off, but I want to have them announced first and presented.' When the message is relayed to Clarissa, she has already received it from half-a-dozen other sources.

It is difficult for me working concurrently on two large productions. There is no camaraderie between the two companies. If I excuse myself: 'I have to go to the *Ideal Husband* set,' I am told: 'Oh, leave them to it!' It is particularly foolish to plan to shoot two of the most elaborate scenes on the same day. For the *Ideal Husband* hundreds of elegant extras representing the world of fashion in Hyde Park are strolling up Rotten Row while phaetons, broughams, every sort of curricle, bicycles, and horseback riders are also on tap. There are guards parading in full dress, Salvation Army bands, horses, dogs, etc. The studio is not geared to this pitch of work. Yet on the *Anna Karenina* set fifty ballroom guests have been lined up complete with hair-do, jewels, etc.; director Duvivier snarls: 'They all look like English girls that haven't had enough to eat. (Rationing is still in force.) Get some full-bosomed girls that look like Russian aristocrats'. This criticism, coming at this time from a Frenchman, is not considered tactful by 'Wardrobe' who, having worked all weekend, has now the impossible task of re-fitting all these costumes.

'The boss is arriving! Any minute now! He's at the gate! He's here!' Korda has been met at the airport and driven forthwith to the studio. About a dozen different 'units' try to get his attention.

On the *Ideal Husband* exterior set we are waiting for a big cloud to pass: for days now we have been watching the grey skies. Each hour costs Korda an astronomical figure for the time of so many people, animals, and period carriages. The women's clothes are crushed and dirty, and their trains have trailed in the mud and the horse dung.

Everyone – society-pedestrians, coachmen, bicyclists, brass bands, platoon of guards, etc. – is ready at last, except Paulette Goddard. Her make-up girl explains the delay: 'I've been cutting an eyelash for her.'

At last the sun! A frenzied rush for the golden seconds to be used to their best advantage. Suddenly the scenes are 'in the can'. The ghost of Korda smiles.

Notley Priory: Spring

Vivien [Leigh] is away visiting her former husband: Larry [Olivier] was busy all Saturday with business plans for his Australian tour, but intended to devote Sunday to going over the details of my *School for Scandal* designs. Larry would have preferred my production to be rich and realistic with mahogany doors and built fireplaces, but, since the scenery will have to travel throughout Australia and New Zealand before coming to London, it is more expedient to use *trompe l'œil*. This gives me much more scope for invention, and I am delighted at the prospect of doing all the sets as if they were eighteenth-century engravings, even introducing the hatching strokes into the costumes.

Meanwhile, I listen to Larry and his accountant. 'We're banking on every performance playing to capacity. Now, how many are we?'

'Forty-one – that's one too many.'

'Can't we take one extra?'

'That extra fare will cost £1,000 by the end of the tour.'

'Then suppose Vivien and I don't go?'

But, in general, L. is very business-like with a minimum of jokes and interruptions. Later he talked to me about acting. 'In my opinion acting is a question of range and taste. Let me give you an example of what I mean. Margaret Leighton is a most brilliant actress: she can do anything: she does everything quite naturally. It took me two years to walk round a chair with ease: it took me another two years to laugh on the stage. I had to learn everything: what to do with my hands – how to cry. Leighton can do all those things automatically. When I was playing Buckingham I had a very short time for study. I gave a sketchy performance, and one place in particular, where I knew I was horribly banal, became quite obnoxious to me. I had to say: 'Well done – give us another song' – or something like that – and I had thought of nothing better to do than applaud. One evening I thought 'I won't do this again', and I suddenly had the idea of seeing Margaret Leighton weeping and being jovial to hide her sadness, and saying: 'Come, let's have another song' to cover up her misery. So as we sat listening to the first song I whispered: 'Weep – weep as much as you can!', and after a few moments great big tears were coursing down her cheeks. She couldn't have done that unless her range was enormous, and I consider the question of taste made all the difference to that scene.'

Wiltshire: October

Since I was thrown out of Ashcombe I have been somewhat forlornly looking for a small house in the country to take its place. But where on the entire earth could I find such another remote and beautiful a treasure as Ashcombe? 'Particulars' came from estate-agents by every post: 'Imposing Georgian-style mansion only thirty-seven minutes from Piccadilly Circus ...' 'Tudor gem – oak porch – all mod. cons. – billiard-room and solarium ...' 'Converted Gothic lodge with indoor fives court ...'

I determined to remain faithful to Wiltshire. 'No, Messrs Rawlence and Squarey, I did not fall in love yesterday afternoon with the mustard-and-pepper brick house at Quidhampton. Why? Because – well – to begin with – it's too near the railway, and those pylons make a beeline for the garden.' Eventually I became embarrassed at having to refuse so many of these 'unique offers'.

However, Edith Olivier, who eighteen years ago had found Ashcombe for me, now wrote to me of a small Wren house, not far from her in Wilton, belonging to the National Trust, and which she had heard was available for rental. Perhaps Edith could mark up a double....

The aftermath of the war has brought with it our relief and gratitude, yet few joys. We, in England, have all endured what must be one of the most uncomfortable phases in recent history. People are undernourished, yet the food prospect is dark. The financial crisis is appalling and our debt to America increasing, yet under the Labour government money is racketed away. According to Churchill, the Socialist policy, apart from 'scuttling', is to spread class warfare and to reduce us all to one vast 'Wormwood Scrubbery'. We are in trouble in Palestine and Greece, and already the Germans are cutting up rough so that our troops must remain in vast quantities and at crippling expense. Continual crises hit hard our export trade. Each month brings further humiliations: these are our last days in Burma; we have left Cairo and lost India. Mr Attlee's gang has brought disaster in practically all forms upon us, and a White Paper, just issued, prescribes no remedy for present ills. The excuses advanced for the Government's chronic mistakes are blamed on years of Tory misrule, and the only consolation offered is that we must all work harder.

To add to our winter of discontent the whole land has been suffering from a plague of cold – another ice age. Under the auspices of Mr Emanuel Shinwell the coal supply has almost completely given out: gas flickers weakly – even hospitals are without hot water. Edith Olivier and other elderly ladies have not been permitted to switch on their electric blankets, and the death rate from pneumonia has rocketed.

Not surprisingly the train from Waterloo to Salisbury on the Saturday morning was unheated. Edith had to knock the icicles off me when I arrived to find that she had still a supply of logs for her small, but hospitable, hearth. Fortunately Edith's cheerful spirits and courage were in contrast to my mood, and her rabbit-pie warmed me and gave me enough strength to set off with her on a polar expedition through the iced snow before dark enveloped us.

At first Edith's small motor car would not start; our breath made clouds of steam as, in turn, we cranked the ineffectual handle. By degrees the frozen tubes thawed; eventually we jerked and skidded over the ice towards the village of Dinton. A noble edifice, somewhat Palladian, with a magnolia pinioned to its yellow stone walls, presented itself. On closer inspection the property was altogether too grand for my taste or my pocket.

The light weakened and the thermometer dropped. On the somewhat dejected return to Wilton we passed through the village of Broadchalke. Here lived John Aubrey, the seventeenth-century antiquarian and historian. Aubrey wrote that the village possesses 'one of the tunablest ring of bells in Wiltshire which hang advantageously, the river running near the churchyard, which meliorates the sound'. Edith's car grinded to an abrupt halt in front of a miniature palace which I had often admired when living ten miles away. In fact, each time I came upon this Charles II rose-brick frontage I stopped, with screeching brakes, to admire the design of what must have been originally built for a king's *nid d'amour* or hunting lodge. Apart from its quite exceptional façade, with its elegant stone pilasters and the bust of an unknown poet in the broken pediment over the door, the house had always had added interest because of Mrs Wood, its owner and the mother of the remarkable painter Christopher Wood. Although Mrs Wood was wary of snoopers, and had an unwelcoming manner with visitors, she retained in the attic a huge collection of her late son's canvases.

Mrs Wood had recently died, and it was rumoured that the house was about to be sold. It was, therefore, with a feeling of adventure that on this cold late-afternoon Edith boldly rang the front-door bell and, after a moment of *pourparler* with an unfriendly servant, was bidden to enter.

At first, in the last light of day, the interior of the house disappointed us. The hall was cut up into several partitions comprising a gun-room, corridor, and a minute enclosure with a gate-legged dining-table. Oak beams warred with the classic lines of the exterior, and a clumsy mock-Elizabethan chimneypiece of modern red brick protruded out of all proportion. We could not understand why, in such a rambling way, rooms were placed on different levels. We shivered as we went from one disused parlour to another, then up to the dark and sinister attic where cock-fighting took place in the eighteenth century. We peered in the gloom at the pens where the prize birds were kept before being let out into the blinding light of candles to fight for their survival.

Then again we braced ourselves for the Alaskan elements in order to view the garden and terrace. The dark sky made everything appear bleak and cheerless: a dirty snow-covered hill seemed to avalanche precariously close to the house. Edith, purple-nosed, did not wax enthusiastic; neither was I, as I had been at Ashcombe, a victim of love at first sight. Nevertheless, when we had returned to Edith's hearth and were huddling over hot drinks, enough enthusiasm was kindled to suggest summoning my mother to give her opinion on the place.

On the Monday morning, for the first time in many months, the sun shone on England. Everyone's spirits soared: even one's hatred for Mr Shinwell turned to mere contempt. On the second visit to Reddish House I was elated – and my mother too. Her heart went out to the house of warm lilac-coloured brick and she loved the way it lay with the garden rising to a paddock, the long vistas of lawn sheltered by a double row of limes and elms, with the kitchen-garden enclosed with a typical Wiltshire wall of chalk topped with thatch roof. From across the village street the property continued across a meadow to a stretch of poplars and willows bordering the river Ebble, once stocked with crayfish by Aubrey and where the trout, two feet long, were considered by Charles II to be the best flavoured in England. My mother also enthused over the vast yews cut to look like plum puddings, the topiary trees shaped like chessmen, the well-established nut walk, and the clumps of beeches. Two adjoining thatched cottages, surprisingly like Ann Hathaway's with their own gardens, were also part of the property. My mother saw the possibilities of making the terrace, with its southern aspect and old-fashioned roses growing over a balustrade, into a sheltered spot for outdoor lunch or tea. In fact, we both considered that the loss of Ashcombe from which we were both so acutely suffering might be partially compensated for by this new acquisition.

Of course Reddish House did not possess the wayward romantic remoteness of Ashcombe. Instead of hiding in folds of wooded downland, it presented its extremely formal exterior on to a village street. But just as I was looking out of its old glass window panes a dogcart trotted by, and children were returning from school; the village life seemed to have a delightful Miss Mitford quality. Moreover, the house was a real house – not a fantasy, makeshift pretence like Ashcombe. This was the abode of an adult person: perhaps it would be a good thing if I started living up to my swiftly advancing age. But could I afford to buy a real house? And particularly one like this which must surely be so much in demand – small, compact, but of a fine quality? The fact that it was illustrated in early books as a gem of domestic architecture gave it an extra cachet and value.

Although I had never made his acquaintance I sent a telegram to Dr Wood commiserating upon the recent death of his wife, then boldly asked him for the first offer of refusal of his house. I discovered that the property had been left by Mrs Wood to her daughter who did not wish to occupy the house herself, yet was unable to keep her father there in solitary misery. She wished to sell her legacy as quickly and as painlessly as possible. No doubt if she had advertised in *Country Life* the house would have fetched more than the ten thousand pounds she asked me and with which, with alacrity, I bought it – only later wondering how I would find the money to foot the bill.

When my Ashcombe furniture appeared from storage out of the vans, most of it had immediately to be sent for sale in the Caledonian market, whence much of it originally came: what had been suitable for weekends of charades and folly was not suitable for Reddish. Besides, the made-over junk had not worn well. Reddish House dictated a more sober style of decoration, and its contents must be more respectful to all my predecessors whose histories I was busy piecing together from the voluminous deeds – dating from 1599 and beautifully inscribed and decorated with calligraphy and waxen seals – which came to me with the house.

New York: October

From my hotel room I telephone immediately to the Ritz Tower – to the person who has occupied my mind for the last two years. 'Miss Brown don't answer.' Why is she hiding from me again? I am in despair. How to get through the day? Are my hopes dashed? Will I never see her again? Next day I telephone Wickersham 2-5000; my heart is pounding while I wait to be put through to her room. An unfamiliar voice replies, very gay and laughing and high-pitched:

'No, I am not well. I have got sinus trouble – you can hear it in my voice.'

'It is a year and a half since I have seen you.'

'Is it really? How terrible – how sad.'

'Did you enjoy Europe?'

'Ain't going to tell you.'

'I rang you up yesterday but they said –' she interrupted me: ' "Miss Brown don't live here any more." Well, she answered today. I'd love to come and see you. Are you in the same rooms?'

'Yes.'

'Well, it can't be today and then tomorrow is Saturday.'

'You're still busy at weekends?' I asked rather bitterly, knowing that she has to be at liberty when 'the little man' is free.

'It may not be before Monday.'

'Well, I have something for you – a lot of things.' (Meaning all the letters I had written and not posted since her silence.)

November

'I am so busy!' she says on the telephone.

'Doing what?'

'Hunting. All I need is a horn and some dogs.'

'Then you are too busy to see me today?'

' 'Fraid so. You take me by surprise and get me too muddled. But I haven't had any air. Suppose we go in the park again? I haven't been there this winter. Where shall we meet? How about the Zoo? How about that archway? I'll be there at four punctually – I might lose you under that archway if I'm not on the tick.'

4 December

'Miss Brown don't answer.' It is as if I were falling through space. She cannot have left the hotel so early. I try again throughout the day. No – surely we are not back to where we were?

Has she been forbidden by 'the little man' to see me alone? Has she decided that I must be dropped? Yet she is not the sort who quickly grows tired of a friend. I am baffled and worried.

December

Mona [Mrs Harrison Williams, now Countess Martini] is one of my oldest New York friends: there is nothing I do not confide to her.

I told Mona that I felt Greta was more than intrigued by me, but the agony of never knowing quite where one was with her was almost beyond endurance. Suddenly one day Greta could not be found. Without any valid reason she had disappeared . . .

Mona gave me the advice I could only find in New York. 'You're being a dope,' she said. 'Stop it – it's not getting you anywhere. Surely you know what a bore it is to have someone waiting for you – always at your beck and call, never cutting up rough or keeping you guessing. You just play her game – behave with her in the same way that she behaves with you. Don't call her up, and when she calls you, say you've been busy. Be nice to her, of course, but be rather casual. If it doesn't work you've lost nothing, because as it is you haven't got anything. But you'll find it will succeed, believe me. I don't wish to be a traitor to my sex, but women are so much less nice than men, and you're my friend and I see her game so clearly. She knows you are just hanging about waiting on her, and if she feels in the mood she will come around, just for an hour. But you've got to get her worried: you've got to get her mind, and her mind's got to worry about what's going on in your mind. When first you see the results working, don't have any mercy. It's crucial; you can't afford to be dopey about anything that is important in your life. Why do you think I've been able to keep Harrison interested all these years? He is the arch-teaser and I knew where he was trying to get me. But I played my cards better than he did. He's guessing all the time, and that's why he is so intrigued and happy.'

Monday

I didn't telephone – my usual sentimental call of habit. I didn't telephone for four days. I was flat on my bed when the telephone bell rang. 'Can I come around now?' she asked. It was pouring with rain outside, the traffic disorganized. I didn't sound welcoming. 'It's too rainy for you to sally forth, and I've got to go out.' This refusal worked like a trick, 'I'll be right over.' The pep-talk from Mona had given me assurance: it was as if I'd employed a magic potion. The doorbell rang and, instead of hurrying to open it, I walked very arrogantly and slowly around the room in a stiff manner, amused as I watched my progress in the looking-glass over the drawing-room chimney.

'So you've been busy, have you? Well, what have you been doing?' Smiles, uncertainties, embarrassments on her part. If only temporarily – the tables were suddenly turned. G. said: 'I knew instinctively that I ought not to have waited so long.' Her fears about my being faithless had been corroborated – according to her. I sat back and smiled.

For a year and a half I had felt unsure of myself, but now I was enjoying my pathetic little victory. I mentioned that I was out until three o'clock in the morning with somebody: that made an impression. I told her I was dining tonight with Mona: that went well too. Questions were asked about other friends, and after certain admissions she said: 'You're stepping out in all directions.'

A few days later

I am dozing at six o'clock one evening when the unforgettable voice is heard again on the telephone. I perk up. 'Are you still as busy as ever?' I answer: 'Oh yes, very busy.' 'Well, I'm laid up – I'm in poor spirits.' Commiserations. More questions asked about whom I'd seen. I described Mona's beauty – her skin so blooming and in the pitch of perfection, and her hands so smooth and beautiful. G. gasped: '*My* hands are so rough and wrinkled and lined. Ask Mona what she puts on her hands, will you?' Vague plans are made for the future. She can't get seats for *The Winslow Boy*, which has been brought over from London and is an enormous success on Broadway. Have I any pull? 'Of course I have'. 'Then we'll go on Monday – and what about seeing the Royal Wedding on the screen?' We talked on the telephone for an hour. At one moment I said: 'So put that in your pipe and smoke it.' Greta said: 'You're not to use such rough expressions to me – I'm feeling down-trodden enough as it is. I'm not a bit chipper.' ('*Chippurre.*')

I do not telephone her but rather wait for her call. It makes life much happier not having to hear that death knell: 'She don't answer.' Sometimes the bell rings and I pick up the receiver: there are strange intakes of breath, muffled giggles and small squeaks, and I know who to expect on the line. My name is reiterated in a bird chirp: I no longer retort with her name. Today she would come along at five o'clock: she arrived a little before.

I accepted her compliments in silence, and whenever she asked me some point-blank questions I avoided a straight reply. She laughed: 'You're so afraid of committing yourself!' It is still somewhat of an effort to assume consciously a different role from that which one has played for the last two years. How different the state in Denmark since I arrived here when everything had been so frustrating! Now, in fun, she said: 'I think I shall have to make an honest man of you!' 'No, it's too late – you're not the marrying type,' I rejoindered, almost gritting my teeth and clenching my fists in a farcical effort to follow Mona's tuition.

Although perhaps even to confide such thoughts to paper may be unwise, there are times when I feel that the possibility is within sight that one day I might get her worked up sufficiently to rush off to a registrar. For myself I am not only willing, but desperate, and confident that we could have the infinite joy of making a new and successful life together.

I dare not feel pity for the battle is still too desperate: on so many points I'm likely to give way. But isn't it rather abominable what a difference a change of tactics has made? Greta used never to ask me to call her, and if I asked if I might, she would say: 'No, I'll call you.' Now she asks me to telephone her tomorrow to tell her about the opening of *Antony and Cleopatra*. 'Tomorrow ring me anytime – ten-thirty, eleven, whenever you want.'

I telephoned as late as possible.

Greta wanted our theatre seats to be near the stage; I managed to get them – centre front row. She was so pleased that she said: 'I think I'll have to take you to see the Minister.' Throughout the play she stared at me, and I remembered how I used to stare at people with whom I have been in love, and how annoyed they became. *The Winslow Boy* was a good choice for the play is so essentially English, and I explained that its atmosphere was similar to that in which I had been brought up. 'Did you have that sort of furniture?' she asked. I nodded. She was impressed by the English team-work acting.

On the way home, at Doubleday's bookshop, I pointed out a picture of herself in an album of cinema stars of the last decade. 'I don't give a damn,' she laughed. Then, putting her arm through mine, she chirped: 'I like you, I like you – it's not a big word, but I like you, and whenever I say goodbye I want to see you again.'

Greta suggested: 'Would you like an apple? I'll give you a couple of apples,' she said. Before I knew it, I was for the first time in the sacred precincts of the rooms in her hotel – in the forbidden Suite 26C. They were pretty, light-coloured rooms with large windows on most sides displaying a panorama of New York. Everything was better than she had described. It was fascinating to discover what books she was reading, what appurtenances of life there were about the room. She would not allow the lights to be switched on so I peered into the gloaming: there were some of her hats lying around, a few bills and package slips, and copies of *Life* magazine and *The New Yorker*, and all the mail was addressed to 'Harriet Brown'. 'I live like a monk with one toothbrush, one cake of soap and a pot of cream.' Greta went to her kitchenette and, in secret, prepared a meal. Everything was very immaculate and healthy: sweet butter unsalted, Swedish bread, ham and cheese. We drank beer and talked without restraint or inhibition. She discussed the passage of the years. 'Something has happened to time; suddenly it goes so fast, so quickly. I wish the hours were twice as long – even the hours of the night.' It was after three o'clock. We kissed one another for the thousandth time as if for the first time when, sadly, I had to leave the darkened apartment, with the two impersonal twin beds low on the ground, in their white candlewick covers.

I walked almost in a trance: for the past ten hours I have been in the highest realms of happiness: now I wondered how the present situation could be consolidated into something definite and binding. Thus it is that we always try to pin down something exquisite and ethereal. No matter what happens there will always be the memory of big eyes gazing, and the broad big smile.

What was there to stop our living the rest of our lives together? It was so easy: it was indicated. 'No, it's not easy,' said Greta. We almost found ourselves arguing with each other. 'You have not had a difficult life as I have. Everything has been smooth for you: it's easy for you to be gay and happy. Occasionally you may have been sad, when someone has not loved you as much as you loved them. But life has been difficult for me.' Greta explained: 'You must realize I am a sad person: I am a misfit in life.'

'But if you were to come to Europe, and live among creative people and congenial souls, you wouldn't be like that. You are so out of your element here with the pavements under your feet and smuts in your eyes.'

'Perhaps it was all that could happen.'

'Maybe if you had made films in Germany or France, things would have been easier. You have succeeded in spite of Hollywood taste, but it's only natural you hate everything about it.'

'I don't hate Hollywood – any more than I hate Mr Louis B. Mayer. I don't hate anyone, of course, but I don't like Mr Mayer – though I see his point and I don't blame him for doing to me what he did.'

'What did he do?' I knew that to ask such a point-blank question was extremely risky, and I waited anxiously in the interval before she replied slowly:

'Well, he made me sign a long contract – five years – and I was terrified and very unhappy for it seemed like a life-term. When I had finished the contract I said to him: "This is the end. I don't want to continue: I want to get out of pictures." He and his minions were all so worried! They had these long discussions with me, and we walked up and down outside the sound stage, and they said: 'You can't quit now: we won't let you. You're at the very peak of your career." But I was all set. I was so unhappy. And then, in 1928, the bank where I had all my money failed. That was the time of the Wall Street crash. Somebody joked that Mr Mayer made my bank fail so that he could get me back. I had to sign another contract with Mr Mayer, but I told him to do pictures that I'd like, and he agreed to pay me a cheque for half my next picture in advance. He wrote out the highest cheque I have ever seen. But I had nowhere to put it – no pocket, no bag, so I tucked it into my open shirt, and went home to Sweden while they prepared my next film, and that was *Christina*.'

Twice in her career Greta had come to the crossroads: once when she had wanted to leave, and again when the war cut off the European market and her last film, *The Two-Faced Woman*, through no fault of hers, was a complete and deserved failure.

She admitted she was still discussing the possibility of playing Georges Sand, but the script was not ready. I could see Greta wearing velvet trousers and smoking a cigar. From Joan of Arc to Christina of Sweden the idea of women in cavalier clothes has a visual aspect that is appealing to her; she would have liked to play St Francis of Assisi, also Lorenzaccio and Dorian Gray. '*Travesti*' has obviously titillated her and, since early days, she has enjoyed wearing the more romantic of men's apparel in her films. Ventriloquists' dolls and pierrots possess an ambiguity that delights her sense of the perverse. This is, no doubt, the reason why stories have been circulated about her having odd tendencies.

'Georges Sand could make a wonderful story, but it's eight years since my last film; the war came in the meantime, and there are such difficulties in the world today. My mother-country is in such a poor state – everyone's money frozen there – and in France and England there's so much unrest and lack of responsibility – perhaps the same here.... There is nothing to go to California for – just an unfurnished house with dreary rayon curtains that are too short and the ugly, ready-made sofas.'

[Tennessee] Williams is anxious that Greta should play Blanche du Bois in his *Streetcar* film. But she finds the character – a liar – a difficult and unsympathetic one. She went on to explain: 'In a way I've always been a dreamer. In my childhood I came across brutality and the result lasted with me all my life, but I'm an honest, clear-cut person and see things very lucidly. I could never be an involved and complicated person: I'm too direct and too masculine. I couldn't bear to tell lies, and see things round corners, like that girl in the play.'

Williams, obviously dejected, suggested that perhaps Greta pays too much attention to plots. She told him that since she left the screen there had never been anything that she could possibly play – all parts are too unlike her conception of life. 'The only thing I would ever like to do is *The Eagle with Two Heads*. That has an atmosphere that appeals to me, and I've always wanted to play Elizabeth of Austria.'

February 1948

Before Korda had time to tell me what he had in mind for me to work on, I suggested he should do the Elizabeth of Austria play, *The Eagle with Two Heads*, by Jean Cocteau with Greta. He was fired with enthusiasm. 'We do it right away in Shepperton in June. We shoot some of it in the Tyrol. We get any director she wants. But I don't want any vagueness. She must sign if I'm going to spend time on the project!' I saw before me a whole new vista with Greta in England.

I telephoned in great excitement to tell her the news. She was very quiet.

'All right – I'll have to think about it. I can't think about it now – I'm too tired – but I'll consider it in the morning.' Korda telephoned her twice. 'Come and see me this afternoon.' Greta complied, taking 'the little man' with her. Everything went well. They were more or less decided they would make the picture. Greta would come to England for the studio work. A lot of telephoning back and forth about a director. Such sudden activity that Greta, who was supposed to leave for California, delayed her departure by another week: such excitement that she'd not been able to sleep. However, she was convinced, this time, that the picture would be made. Greta said: 'I saw the play in all its wretchedness with Tallulah Bankhead, and I know there's nothing that can't be fixed. I'll do it, but I've got to start preparing – getting fit right away, coaxing my body back in shape, exercising my arms – and if I'm going to wear *décolletage* there's a lot to arrange. Yes, I know I'm going to do this film – I feel it. I've never been as close to anything before.'

We sat on the red sofa in my room, eating cold boiled eggs, toast, and avocado from the Frigidaire. Greta asked me questions about how she would live in England. Where was the studio? Could she rent a small house nearby in order to take long walks in the evenings? It was good that in Hollywood, after the searing lights in the studios, you could get out into the clean sunlight and walk and breathe in fresh air. She wouldn't want to live in a town while working. She wouldn't be able to see anyone while on the job; she always gave herself entirely to the project – never saw anyone. We talked of Korda, and the possibilities of the cast and crew, and we were suddenly just as matter of fact as two businessmen. Greta telephoned Korda. 'It is bad when the Empress tries to work her lover up to kill her by slanging at him like a fishwife. It should be done like an Empress.' Greta has been thinking a great deal about the part.

Beverly Hills: 3 March

I awoke early. The Venetian blinds were slatted with diamond brilliance. I let in the sun: the sky was brilliantly blue. To be here after the blizzards of New York was almost too great a contrast. I relished the rare treat of a large orange juice and egg and bacon breakfast. I telephoned Greta. A very cheery voice replied: 'I've been waiting for you – been up since early and, oh, so busy! I'll fetch you in twenty minutes. I've got to start up the buggy and sometimes she doesn't go. Meet me down by the road where the bus stops outside your hotel.'

When, in the thirties, I first came to the capital of the movie world, my dream was to make the acquaintance of its greatest star: I left without as much as a glimpse. On my second visit I did manage – on that evening that will never pale – to meet her, but now, after all these years, I was about to enter her house as an intimate friend and I would see her in a new guise, leading another life to the one we knew together in New York.

Wearing my light-weight flannel suit and feeling very spruce, I waited. I was scrutinizing a palm tree, and watching some small, dusty birds high up in its branches, when I realized a car had driven up and an intense, rather strained face was leaning forward and bidding me jump in. My heart gave one leap as I recognized the familiar features. Her hair was hanging in thick curls: she wore trousers and a jersey. We were on the way.

She, a little nervous, said: 'It's "the Dragon's" day out, but I don't know if she'll have gone yet, so let's just drive about a bit before we go into the house. But when we *do* go in, you're not to look! Promise to put on blinkers! I'm ashamed: it's awful – so obnoxious, and not as it should be. Now I'm lost – I don't know where we are.'

'Well, it's down that way. We turn off here, Benedict Canyon, and it's there.' I remembered ferreting out her house that night in her absence.

'Imagine that I've been here six years, and that you have to direct the way!'

The little buggy, champagne or dove-coloured, turned an abrupt corner. We drove under a garage roof, and the white secret door was unlocked. Expecting little, I was delighted to find myself in a pretty white-walled garden filled with sun and geraniums, everything neat and orderly: a large sun divan, covered with a white sheet, a huge umbrella, white garden furniture.

'Here, I don't expect you've had orange juice – take this.' I was as exultant as only I was when a boy on holiday. 'Now, you're not to look inside.'

'Not even a peep? I spy a baroque angel hanging on a wall.'

'Close your eyes. You see, in a way I'm a perfectionist, and this is far beneath what I would like it to be. But during the war you couldn't get anything done, and now I may sell the place. Everything's unsettled, so I feel – oh heck! let it go – what's the use?'

But I have discovered that always Greta is apt to decry anything merely because it is hers. I found later that she works in her garden a great deal, and not only does she tend the borders herself, but the Japanese gardener is permitted to work only on the front garden and is not given entrance to this, her hidden sanctum. In fact, she does the 'nigger work' – she had been mending the fence around her lawn. Often she works at it the whole day, quite naked, but she discovered that people could peer through the fence. She had bought some wood with which to fill the gaps, but it was the wrong kind and had done the job badly!

'It's hot in the sun: I'll get you some bathing shorts.'

Greta smoked an Old Gold as she lay back in a pair of tight white trunks and a brassière. We watched the humming birds in the trees and the blue jays, and I relished every detail that was part of this entourage. We lay back wallowing in sunny happiness. We were both in such a good mood for it was obvious that she was glad of my arrival.

'So you came all this way to see your girlfriend – or did you come to see Mr Hitchcock?'

'Nothing in the world would ever induce me to go and see that old show-off'.

She looked shocked and delighted. 'I was determined not to ask you to come,' she said, 'but when you telephoned I was on the point of sending you a telegram. Suddenly I get so restless.' In the brilliant light her beauty was more fine and delicate than one could have imagined: the skin of a polished flawlessness, the eyelashes like a peacock's tail. She looked furtively to the servants' quarters. 'I wonder if "the Dragon" has gone yet?' She went to a door and listened with an expression of fear on her face. It is obvious that she does not know how to handle servants and that 'the Dragon' holds her in terror.

'When may I meet "the Dragon"? So often I've heard her sad voice on the telephone.'

'Not today – tomorrow, maybe, she'll give us dinner.'

By degrees, I was allowed to see the house. In the sitting-room – a large comfortable place with huge sofas and a lot of colour – there were Impressionist paintings, two Renoirs, a Modigliani, a Rouault and, best of all, a most touching, tender, appealing 'still life' by Bonnard of a jug of poppies and meadowsweet. Again Greta deprecated the pictures. 'I bought them as investments before I knew anything much about painting. They're rather boring ones, I think.' She said she wished the Impressionists had not been so bourgeois: the objects they painted were poor in taste and their flowers coarse. Here were her bookshelves, the cupboards with the tennis racquets and the old mackintoshes, the pad with the telephone numbers written in her square, capital lettering. So this was where the '*Divina*' lived.

'I can't think quite what to do for dinner – whether to take you out to a little Italian place and look into your eyes, or whether to give you something at home.' The latter alternative was happily decided upon.

I watched as if she were performing an act of legerdemain, spellbound, as Greta prepared lamb chops and vegetables in a steam dish. Outside it was suddenly dark and soon extremely cold: the house became a Frigidaire. 'We must have some heating, however much you dislike it,' she said. The installation had not previously been turned on this year, so the rooms were filled with a stale smell of burnt metal that was the same as when the old magic-lantern let off its fumes in the nursery. The dinner, however, was good and hot, and was enjoyed sitting on a cedar-coloured sofa under the Bonnard.

A noise of dry leaves scraping together was heard from outside in the alley. Like a frightened animal Greta was on the alert, then in a flash was peering through the slats of the blind. This was a most pathetic sight, for she spends hours at the windows trying to see if anyone is about. Ever since her house was burgled, her nerve has gone, and she is in a bad state of restlessness. We went through the empty rooms to see that no one was hiding. Now I was allowed to see the series of rooms that are unfurnished, the storeroom, dining-room, drawing-room, the suites of vacant rooms. Yes, the house is much too large for her. Having peered in all nooks and crannies I convinced her that all was well.

It was still quite early, according to most people's timetable, when Greta said goodnight to me at her front door. I waved to her in the dark. Walking around her garden walls on my way home, I looked up to see her peering from her bedroom window through the Venetian blinds.

4 March

After motoring through a high winding path into the mountains we got out near the summit to walk. The afternoon sun was still hot, but quickly the day was coming to an end and, in the distance, the mountains were the blue-purple of Greta's eyes. This is one of the times when I want most to remember her, for now her beauty was at its zenith. Her fine skin had the sheen of a magnolia, her hair fell in smooth, lank bosses, her figure lithe and thin, flat haunches, flat stomach. She was in high spirits and started reciting poetry, singing old songs, and being the most companionable of human beings. When she wishes she has the capacity to talk by the hour, and her brain is alert and quick. She recounted how she used to walk alone for miles in the mountains. She would talk to herself, and shout and sing, and 'go to the little boys' room', thinking she was all alone and free of the world to do anything. But one day she saw a photograph of herself walking in the mountains, miles away from anyone – she recognized the spot. It must have been taken by someone hiding in some bushes. 'When I saw it I got such a fright. I thought maybe I'd be followed and attacked – anything might happen – and since the burglary I'm afraid to be alone. I never used to be like that – but I am now!' In that house down that mountainside a friend of hers, now dead, had lived [John Gilbert]. Once he had become drunk and pointed a revolver at her, and she had fled out into the night and gone into some stranger's house and said: 'I find I'm without a car.' They had been nice people and, although they must have realized something was very wrong, they had not talked and the story had never reached the newspapers. She reminisced a great deal about the attacks in the papers on her: of how Louella Parsons had written – merely, perhaps, because she had refused to appear at some publicity benefit – that she should be deported. As we walked we approached an isolated house which Greta had watched the inhabitants building with their own hands. A number of alarming dogs ran

out to greet her, and she was ecstatically happy patting them and playing with
them, although some were so large that they jumped up to her shoulders. Greta
said, after fondling a pet donkey: 'These must be nice people who live here
– so close to nature. People can exist like this in California if they want to –
oblivious of the movies and Miss Parsons.'

The sky grew dim and, in the distance, lay the twinkling carpet of Los
Angeles glittering in millions of lights.

We drove down the hill. We were to dine in her house, and I was to have
my first glimpse of 'the Dragon', who was preparing a dinner that was to be
a surprise. The room was filled with the pink and scarlet carnations which I
had bought in armfuls at a roadside stall. The central heating was turned on,
and the table was set with candles and mats we had bought at the Farmers'
Market. 'The Dragon' turned out to be a most refined German woman of
middle age: she obviously looked after Greta like a mother, though realizing
how difficult Greta would be to impose upon. Fortunately Gertrude, as she
is called, does not mind being alone much of the time. The 'surprise' was Irish
stew, and very well prepared it was. Greta talked about her inability to cope
with servants. When she had had a chauffeur she never knew what to do with
him in between pictures. She felt self-conscious when he was hanging about
doing nothing, so sometimes she would get into the car and tell him to drive
to Arrowhead, sixty to seventy miles away. Here she would go on the lake in
a canoe and read a book, and later she would telephone for the chauffeur to
come all the way back to fetch her. Often she would be driven to Santa Barbara,
nearly a hundred miles away. There she would go into a teashop and, after
ten minutes, return to the car and be driven all the way back – a five-hour
journey for that one cup of tea. 'What a waste of the best years of my life –
always alone – it was so stupid not being able to partake more. Now I'm just
a gipsy, living a life apart, but I know my ways and I must not see people.
Generally Gertrude serves me my dinner at six-thirty in bed, and three-
quarters of an hour later I'm asleep.'

9 March

Arrangements had been made for me to go on a long day's photographing for
Vogue at Pallos Verdes. The expedition was slow in starting, and I telephoned
later to tell Greta I'd just received a telegram from Korda. 'Is it bad news?'
I read the message that he was unable to make *The Eagle* owing to previous
commitments with Eileen Herlie [who had made such a success in the Haymarket Theatre London stage production]. But would Garbo like to do *The
Cherry Orchard* in September? Greta sighed. 'We'll talk this evening when you
return.'

I got back late. It had been an exasperating day, trying to make photographic masterpieces out of ordinary fashion-models in more than ordinary beach-clothes. Greta answered the front door wearing a white towel on her head, pyjamas, and a dressing-gown. She felt and looked 'ver varlost'. I noticed her stockings had fallen around her ankles. 'Well, it seems the Almighty doesn't want me to do a picture: every time I think I'm going to start again, something goes wrong.' If bad luck had not intervened, she would have come to England at the beginning of the war to film St Joan. She had been all set to travel on a Portuguese boat at the time of the bombing of London; but, at the last moment, Gabriel Pascal's plans with Shaw fell through. 'That was the first serious disappointment in my career – a hefty blow – after that nothing has happened. I really thought this time we would be doing Elizabeth. Oye veh! But somehow I'm never surprised by the most unexpected things; often people may be amazed – I'm never. Although I may never have imagined such things, when they happen they don't seem strange. If they're bad things, then I'm sad – but never surprised or disappointed. I'm sure I'm a reincarnation.'

'But what do you think of the Chekov?' I asked.

'It's not exciting – it's not for me.'

'Must I write that in a telegram?'

'No, let's wait. Don't let's discuss it any more.'

10 March

After our lunch, when lying under the fur rug in the garden, we discussed *The Cherry Orchard*. Apart from my own selfish wish to have Greta come to England, and to work with her (for I would insist upon designing her costumes and settings), this is without a doubt my most loved play, and I would give almost anything to see Greta as Madame Ranevska – a part that in many aspects resembles her. (The indecision, the incapability to face facts now.) But Greta felt it would not be a public success and that people would put her in another category – as a less important star. In some ways she has the urge to do more interesting plays, to be experimental in production, and yet she harks back to the safety of old-time directors and her former cameraman. By degrees, like Madame Ranevska she arrived at no decision, changed the subject and talked about last's night's party.

I persuaded Greta to go into Beverly Hills to buy *The Cherry Orchard*, so that we could read the play together. Yes – and more important still – she wanted to buy some more sacks of manure. This is really the one thing that thrills her, and she works frenetically, getting out of bed at screech of dawn to spread the stuff over the front lawn before the neighbours are awake to watch her.

We were to dine with dear old Winifred (Clemence) Dane, the English novelist and playwright, at the suggestion of Constance Collier who, with the saint-like Phillis at the wheel of her car, would lead the way to the faraway Palisades. I enjoyed the adventure of motoring through the darkness with Greta, who was somewhat alarmed at having to follow the leading car at such speed. 'It's only thirty-four miles an hour, but at night it seems to fast.' At one point she recklessly waggled the wheel of the car, which created a very funny 'dodgem' effect, and a bit later a sexily-dressed police officer appeared alongside on a motor bike and bawled out: 'You're going pretty fast, young lady!' Greta's eyes popped, and she clutched her heart.

Winifred is a huge, ebullient, adorable human being, bursting with heart and talent, always good company, intelligent and kind, and habitually sur-rounded by delightful devotees. Tonight there were many writers and painters, enormous platters of Biblical-looking food and, of course, the evening was sympathetic and entertaining. No one tells a story better than Charlie Chaplin; tonight he described his fascination for Elinor Glyn, the scarlet-haired, white-faced, romantic who wrote *Three Weeks* and looked like one of her own heroines. Reputedly Mrs Glyn brought good taste as well as sex to Hollywood. One day Chaplin saw her watching a scene from one of her pictures being played on the movie set. The lights in the early silent days were incandescent and made everyone appear as if dead. Elinor Glyn, powdered with thick paint, became bright green while her teeth, which were false, seemed mauve. Elinor Glyn was amused by the scene she was witnessing and laughed widely, the mauve enamel teeth fully exposed. Suddenly she spied Chaplin scrutinizing her, and at once she tried to assume her usual expression of enigmatic mystery, but the lips, stretched wide, would not readily close over the large, dry expanse of *ratelier*. At last, with an all-out determined twitch, she finally managed to cover the dentures and resume her role as sphinx.

Chaplin told another somewhat macabre tale of an eleven-year-old boy who, when taken out to lunch in a restaurant by his aunt, was obsessed watching opposite him a man eating alone who periodically went off into hysterical facial jerks and giggles. The boy was told not to stare as the poor man had some paralysis. Chaplin gave generously of his large repertoire of imitations, includ-ing a wry, but excruciatingly funny, ballet of Christian Scientists who, over-coming the fact that they were the lame and the halt, leapt into the air with terrible limps and in the most grotesque, but dreadfully comic, manner, per-formed their *arabesques* and *fouettées*. Greta also did imitations with an ease of manner that took me by surprise: I sometimes forget how professional an artist she is.

One particularly funny vignette she improvised was of how ridiculous Michael Duff and I had appeared when one day we took her out to luncheon in New York. I had put on some weight, and my suit was so tight for me that it revealed '*la forma divina*': I wore a sombrero. Michael Duff, in equally old and tight clothes, wore a small green pea as a hat. Blissfully ignorant of the spectacle we created, we spluttered and stuttered about the British Empire as we waited for the street lights to turn green. Then, stiff as ninepins, we strode very quickly in formation, saluting acquaintances on our way down Fifty-Seventh Street. To me, Greta's would-be English accents were not recognizable as such, but the pantomime was brilliant and received the applause it deserved.

But the evening cost Greta a great effort. When we drove home again she had little vitality and said: 'It's awful to be bored, but really for once I was. If I saw these people every day I'd perish.'

11 March

Greta had, of course, been up early to distribute the sacks of fertilizer over the lawns: she was still hard at work. I had an elaborate schedule of business dates that would occupy me until after lunchtime, but I would then call for her to go with my agent, Carlton Allsop, who had arranged for me to see Greta's old picture, *Anna Karenina*, in a private room at MGM Studios. It would be almost an uncanny experience to watch this great epic in the presence of '*La Divina*'. I had told Allsop that I would like to bring a friend to join us. 'Fine – I'll call for you.' When Greta, with scarves flying, came rushing out and I introduced her, Allsop's face went scarlet with astonishment. Greta at once became inevitably, irrevocably, so easily and honestly the seductress that Allsop was completely bewitched.

'Well, well, it takes Beaton to get me to the studios for the first time in six years!' As we approached Metro-Goldwyn, she became quite a bit flustered. It was an emotional experience for her. The studios, which one might almost say she had partly created, had been also for so long her prison: she had been unhappy there, but she owed them a lot too, and to return after such an interval made her feel self-conscious. She did not know the men at the gate any more: none of the faces were familiar: nobody moving along corridors and alleyways recognized her and, as usual, she was adept at concealing herself.

We were shown to a drab little projection room – not at all important but quite private – and the lights went out. The titles were flashed on the screen, the lion roared, the rather *schmalzy* orchestra blared Tchaikovsky, and Greta, next to me, lit an Old Gold.

During the running of the film, Greta would interject: 'Those were real Russians' – 'That's very well done' – 'Those were feathers' (apropos snow-storm) – 'A woman's crowning glory – or is it a fuzz?' (apropos her hair-do in the ballroom sequence). The telling of the story was done in a straight-forward, clear way; the scenes were suitably chosen and full of vigour. The background to the lives of the main characters was well established, so that one realized why the romance was impossible and disaster overtook Anna. Although we have condemned Hollywood for such widespread vulgarization of the classics, this popular epic possessed a great deal of the bare bones of the Tolstoy tragedy, and the superficial shortcomings were merely in the trimmings. Even more than her physical beauty it was Greta's voice that struck a note of such warmth and humanity: deep and melodious with such tenderness and such strength, with so many varying lights and shades, it comes across the sound track exactly as it is in life. Many of the sentiments expressed might have been made by her any day: the effect was uncanny.

Greta was pleased how little the picture had dated. 'When I read the script it was the first time that I was a little thrilled.' Carlton Allsop behaved with tact and charm. 'Mr Mayer would die of delight if he knew you had been to his studio today. You have become his goddess – you're a living legend.' 'Thank you – thank you.' As we emerged from the little theatre, and the operator saw to whom he had been running the reels, he tottered as if about to fall.

12 March

Grey skies – the first time I had not awoken to brilliant sun in the orange tree outside my window. It was cold and blustery. I wondered what Greta would be doing in her garden. When I went round, Gertrude shook her head and said: 'She has been doing much heavy work – cutting away the branches to keep warm.' Greta was now sweeping leaves with a fan-shaped broom. 'Oh, no other woman would do it!' She lit her 'pipe' and relaxed, but she did not appear to be in a loving mood. This morning we became two professionals discussing her business, her film scripts. Having read *The Cherry Orchard*, she did not consider Ranevska a suitable role. 'But aren't you touched by the pathos, and amused by the absurdity of human nature? There are laughs as well as tears of regret.' No: she had no enthusiasm for any of it. 'And its particular theme is so pertinent today.' 'No–ow!' she snapped. I saw the chances of our life together in England were becoming smaller. Oh, hell! What to concoct as a reply to Korda? 'Let's leave it another day.'

14 March

Brilliant sun to speed me: a turquoise sky through the orange blossoms. An anxious telephone call from Greta: she could not quite find words. 'What – what are you doing? Shall I fetch you?' I hopped into a taxi to my favourite flower-stall and bought her an armful of mixed flowers – all colours – ranunculi, stocks, gardenias, roses, orchids, hyacinths, freesias. I rushed to take them to her. Gertrude said in quite a shocked voice: 'She takes on the heaviest work!' Greta was in grey shorts, digging out the last vestiges of the root of the ivy from a deep hole where she intends planting our orange tree. I left the flowers and ran to my room, to return as soon as possible with my baggage. By the time I got back to her, there was only half an hour to spend together before I must leave for the long train-journey to New York.

We sat in the sun, and I felt rather as if I were about to undergo an amputation.

'Just take me for a last tour of the garden, and show me what you're planning to do.'

With arms linked, we walked a few paces, and then a very unexpected thing happened. I was feeling quite matter-of-fact and hard-headed when, suddenly, I realized that there was to be a break from something that had been important to me for a long time. My cheeks became wet.... Life held no immediate prospects. I knew that, in some ways, I had scored a victory over Greta: I knew that I had made her love me. Yet I had failed to give her the strength to act, to have the ability to take a more positive stand with herself. In spite of our closeness, I realized that there was nothing more concrete about our future: I had no hold over her. She had for so long designed her life to protect herself – locked up in her walled garden, with 'the little man' on duty as Cerberus to keep reality at bay – that even I could get no closer than before. I had won the battle, but the main campaign had been lost.

My sorrow was cut short by Gertrude coming out to announce the arrival of the taxi.

I shook hands with Gertrude, and turned to clutch at my beloved once again. My face was hot and red and my eyes swollen, and still a stream poured down each side of my nose. Greta stood, half hiding behind her front door, a timid child with a hand up to her mouth, her eyes wide and full of pity.

I got into the yellow cab, and pulled down one window and waved. The child waved back. The taxi moved forward and turned in a semi-circle. I pulled down the other window and waved. I could hardly see the blurred figure. The driver put his foot down on the accelerator, and we were off.

17

Home and Abroad
1948–51

While settling into his new house, C.B. wrote about his tenure of Ashcombe.
He designed The Second Mrs Tanqueray, *and wrote a play of his own,*
The Gainsborough Girls, *which was staged, but did not reach London.*
Greta Garbo visited him in Wiltshire. C.B. published Ashcombe, Ballet *and*
Photobiography.

April

I rediscovered the joys of the English countryside. It was particularly wonderful
now that I had a new house to cherish and a garden to develop. Already there
were signs of the beginnings of spring: a line of snowdrops flanked the wall
each side of the front door at Reddish, and soon other parts of the garden were
beginning to respond to the reorganization already started. The apple trees
were forming new growth, and the Victorian rosebeds disappeared almost without trace from the lawn. Inside the house, which I was growing to love, there
was a lot to be done. The Charles 11 wallpapers were just as suitable as I had
hoped for the library and my bedroom. Of furniture I had only the minimum,
but excellent things could be found if one went often enough to Mr Percy
Bates's and other Salisbury antique shops.

For almost two years I have been free-wheeling along quite pleasantly without thinking much about making any money or giving thought to my career.
Now I really must consider what most it is that I want to do. The war had
given me an incentive to step out towards new photographic horizons, and to
point my camera at more rugged aspects of life. Enough of taking fashions on
young models who survived just as long as their faces showed no sign of character, or of elderly, but rich harpies appearing as if butter would not melt in
their terrible mouths. But I would not give up photography: it was an important
part of my life. Perhaps I could be strong enough to turn down photographic
offers that were no longer a challenge, and concentrate on people and subjects
of real interest to me. I must also allow myself time to start painting seriously.
Perhaps I would have more confidence if I took a course at some art college;

I would see if this could be arranged. And there was always, at the back of my mind, the biting desire to write a play. Already I had three or four comedies relegated to the chest of drawers in my bedroom at Reddish.

However, I had long since an idea of writing a play about Gainsborough, an artist with whom I had a close rapport, and whom I felt was, in his dislike of pretentiousness and in other ways, not unlike my father. That would be of great help in developing the character. Perhaps this present lull provided the opportunity to start writing it.

But before the memories were any the less acute, I must write about my fifteen happy years at Ashcombe – that house in the downs so little distance from my new home, but which I could never visit again. Soon all other activities became secondary. Even the diary entries were spasmodic: when writing on some specific subject, my journal jottings, which I enjoy, go by the board.

With *Ashcombe* at the printers, normal existence began. Several tempting jobs were offered. Would I care to decorate a theatre? The Duke of York's was in a sorry state of disrepair, and despite post-war conditions Marianne Davis, the delightful, sporting young owner, considered it could be made to look pretty again. It could.

Would I design *The Second Mrs Tanqueray* for the Haymarket? I had never quite recovered from the beauty of Gladys Cooper whom I had seen when the Victorian play was revived in the twenties. At a time when fluffy bobbed hair was fashionable, she had parted hers in the centre and scraped it back into a large, pale honey-coloured, silken bun. Her white marble face with the noble forehead and deep-set blue eyes of a deer were of a haunting loveliness. She had worn a fashionable Molyneux dress, shapeless as a sack but as heavily encrusted with jewels as a Byzantine empress. It was as this *demi-mondaine* out of her social depths, a part that had previously belonged to Mrs Patrick Campbell, that Gladys was first considered seriously as a fine actress; the trace of a slight cockney accent gave added poignancy to her performance. Another good actress, Eileen Herlie, who had created a furore in Cocteau's *Eagle with Two Heads*, was now to be the wanton Paula.

It is a fallacy to pretend that most people look better on the stage than off. The overhead lights add ten years to create havoc with all but the most bun-like of faces. My only difficulty with the delightful Eileen Herlie was to make her as beautiful on the lit stage as she was under the one harsh 'working light' of rehearsals. Eventually we discovered that her classical features were seen at their best when – like Duse – she appeared without any make-up. It was agreed that the costumes and scenery should be done in the styles of the original, though for the second act drawing-room I went for my source to the tapestry of haymaking scenes in the library at the Dashwoods' West Wycombe Park. Although Eileen Herlie gave a performance of tremendous power, the difficulty of finding contemporary male actors with the necessary 'Edwardian' style was responsible for the revival carving no niche in theatrical history.

Other designing jobs kept me in London. Now that Sadler's Wells Ballet, with Margot Fonteyn, had become so grand and successful in its new quarters at Covent Garden, it was natural that they should revive their early success *Apparitions*, Freddie Ashton's romantic Liszt ballet, which had originally been produced on one of Dame Lilian Bayliss's thinnest shoestrings. (The fifty-pound fee I received for designing the work went back into the kitty to pay for the costumes.) But to accommodate the giant stage the sets now had to be enlarged and reproportioned. Since most of the original costumes were worn to rags they, too, had to be redesigned in a bolder conception. Having previously had the unique talent of the Russian Karinska, who had made from my original sketches confections of lightness and delicacy, it was now like being at the mercy of a plain, but wholesome English cook to have, in the wardrobe of Covent Garden, Miss Cranmer's heavy hand on the spun-sugared dresses of the ball scenes. Somehow this most exquisite of Freddie's ballets lost much of the haunting quality that made it unique on the smaller stage.

Soon my secretary, Maud Nelson, was busy putting down too many dates in the appointments book. They consisted of sittings to photograph brides, theatre people, and even members of the Royal Family. I did advertising photographs for America, often using my new house and garden as background. Although sometimes the arrangements were almost as elaborate as if for a theatrical production, and might necessitate several visits to Paris fashion houses, I made a small fortune photographing for my good friends at Johnson & Johnson.

But, most important of my projects, was the jotting down on paper of the ideas, going around restlessly in my head that, in turn, revolved about the character of Gainsborough. The more I read about the painter the more I loved him, and the jigsaw pieces of his lifetime seemed to create a picture that seemed, at least to me, to make a play. I went to Broadchalke to work, and soon became absorbed. Maud Nelson, between bouts of asthma, would call me from London only if there was urgent need to distract me from my intended masterpiece.

10 July

Emerald [Cunard] ceased to live on Saturday. For all her fantasies and foibles, she was a woman who lived *dans le vrai*. Someone as rough and rowdy as Lady Astor could never appreciate Emerald's subtlety, and quite wrongly judged her 'a pushin' American'. She was far more than a social figure. The much richer hostess, Mrs Ronnie Greville, was a galumphing, greedy, snobbish old toad who watered at her chops at the sight of royalty and the Prince of Wales's set, and did nothing for anybody except the rich. Emerald cultivated important people if she could play with them as if they were notes on a harpsichord. She had a keen eye for spotting the merits of people in most unknown places; she was a true patron and pioneer.

I particularly admired Emerald in America when, at the beginning of the war, she preferred to come back to London for the bombing. Her Grosvenor Square house sold, she took rooms at the Dorchester, where she paid scant attention to the holocaust from the guns outside her windows; but the bomb-shell that shattered her was the news of Sir Thomas Beecham's surprise marriage. She confided that only two days before, when she asked him if the rumours of his love affair with Miss Betty Humby were true, Sir Thomas had leant back and laughed: 'Oh no, no! She's impossible! Do you know, she told me yesterday that she was descended from a long line of dentists!' When Emerald read of the wedding of the man to whom she had devoted so much of her life, and upon whose musical projects she had spent most of her fortune, she was never quite the same, although she rallied bravely, and never spoke ill of the man who had treated her so ruthlessly.

By degrees, she recovered her spirits enough to fabricate a little flutter of the heart with a delightful and brilliant young man, of great promise at the Foreign Office, named Nicholas Lawford. The 'romance' was in the nature of play-acting with amusement and delight on both sides. Nicholas would hang a bunch of early-morning flowers on the handle of her bedroom door before going off to Whitehall, and Emerald would confide her tender feelings to her friends; but the romance was not serious and, in spite of her other varied interests, Emerald was a lonely Joan without her Darby Beecham.

When a friend told me of Emerald's death, I telephoned her maid, Gordon, to know if I could come and pay my last respects. Gordon, who had been at Emerald's side for almost eight weeks without more than an hour or two's sleep at a time, told me of the last scene. Emerald knew that she was dying but had no fear of death. She gave instructions that there was to be no memorial service, no publicity, and that she wished to be cremated with as little fuss as possible. For days she lay in a drugged state. Then, when they knew that the end was near, the doctor, nurse and Gordon stood by her bed. Emerald, incapable of lucid speech, kept whispering the word 'pain', 'pain', 'pain'. The doctor asked: 'Where is the pain?' Emerald shook her head. 'Pain – pain,' she repeated. Gordon gave her the new novel by Robin Maugham, which happened to be by her bedside, together with a pencil. On the fly-leaf Emerald managed to scrawl the word 'champagne'. Gordon thought it curious that she should wish to drink now, since she was accustomed only to an occasional small glass of hock. Gordon produced a teaspoon and put a little on Emerald's lips. But she shook her head again, pointed to an unopened bottle of champagne, then nodded to the doctor, nurse and Gordon in turn. They understood. She seemed to smile as they drank to her.

When asked by a friend if she would not like to die in her sleep, her reply was immediate: 'No, I'd rather be shot.' Emerald, a worshipper of beauty until the end, made her life into a work of art.

December

Happily summoned to the Palace to take the first long-awaited photographs of the heir to the throne. Prince Charles, as he is to be named, was an obedient sitter. He interrupted a long, contented sleep to do my bidding and open his blue eyes to stare long and wonderingly into the camera lens, the beginning of a lifetime in the glare of public duty.

24 January 1949

I was now about to see how my work on the Olivier production of *The School for Scandal* had materialized. The preliminary work had been extremely pleasant; in fact, everything had gone so smoothly from the moment I first showed my rough designs. Larry Olivier and Vivien Leigh had come to dinner after his day's shooting in *Hamlet*, and every proffered suggestion had been accepted with enthusiasm by him until, exhausted, Larry laid his head on the dining-table and went fast asleep.

I knew only too well what a risk it is if a designer cannot supervise the execution of his work throughout every step of the way until the last moment before the curtain goes up on the first night. Inevitably readjustments have to be made as one discovers that a certain notion does not materialize as expected, or that an actor is unsuited to a particular garment. Someone else's lighting can ruin the colours of a set, and a prop master can produce some anachronism that is so obvious that it is amazing that no one else has noticed it.

Due to Larry's *Hamlet* film having taken far longer to shoot than scheduled, and the subsequent postponement of his work on *The School for Scandal*, I had had to drag myself away towards the end of the preparations in order to fulfil a long since arranged photography contract in America. I was satisfied with the preliminary fittings for Lady Teazle's clothes which made Vivien appear an exquisite figure of Chelsea china, and fortunately the scene painters seemed to have the time and talent to paint my sets to look exactly like enlargements of coloured engravings. But I knew I was leaving with the opportunities for so many cup and lip slips. Now, having finished the first stage of the work, I had to abandon it to others; it was like leaving a child to find its way alone.

It must have been hell at the dress rehearsal when the designer was absent, and Mrs Candour wanted to change her bonnet and Sir Benjamin Backbite would suddenly like to add a muff to his costume. It was also a bloody nightmare for me – taking each theatre job as seriously as I do – knowing that the Atlantic was between me and any alterations that others were now perfunctorily thinking fit to make.

The Olivier company went off to Australia and my contractual obligation was over. It was a great relief when clippings filtered back praising my work. It was an even greater relief when the company returned to open the play in London and Larry wired me (I was still in New York) that in his first-night 'curtain' speech my name had received the greatest applause of all.

It was, therefore, a hideous surprise when, a few nights after my return to London, a comparative stranger who works in films, Anatole, known as Tolly, de Grunewald, came up to me and said: 'My God, the Oliviers are gunning for you! What have you done to them?' I was too breathless to reply, and did not wish to let this man see how shocked I was. I had felt that Larry and Vivien – particularly Vivien – were real friends, and I could think of no reason why they should both have anything against me.

24 February

John Gielgud came with me to see the Sheridan play the next time it was given in the repertory. Over an early dinner John and I had a great deal to talk about though I did not mention to him the qualms I was feeling since I had met the 'intolerable' de Grunewald. We arrived too late at the New Theatre to call on the Oliviers before curtain time, but as we crawled into our seats the lights dimmed in the auditorium and went up on stage to reveal a richly-coloured engraving of Lady Sneerwell's house with super-elegant footmen bowing, moving furniture and lighting candles. It was not surprising that I paid more attention to the decorative aspects of the evening than to the play and its performers; but I doubt if ever before have I, in the theatre, so unrestrainedly enjoyed the fruits of my own work. I was wreathed in rapturous smiles as one stage picture, and one delightful costume after another, appeared in the glow of a masterly lighting expert's effects. John, likewise, was in a condition of euphoria about the whole evening and, at the end of the performance, together we went backstage to congratulate all concerned. Rather than visit each room together we decided to go our separate ways, John starting off with Larry while I tapped on Vivien's door.

On going into the leading lady's dressing-room, in spite of the de Grunewald story, I expected the usual backstage superlatives, the 'darlings', the hugs and kisses. I met with a view of Vivien's back; she did not turn round to greet me. I kept up a hollow flow of flattery, filled with green room jargon, in praise of her performance and her appearance. Vivien's eyes of steel now stared at herself as she rubbed a slime of dirty cold cream, a blending of rouge, eyeblack, and white foundation over her face. Not one word did she say about my contribution to the evening. She broached no other subject, and answered any question with a monosyllable. Somehow, after a short while, I managed to extract myself from the room. Phew!

Now I must face Larry and, possibly – though why I knew not the reason – the same frigid reception. It was worse than I could have expected: no smiles, no back thumping, and no 'old mans' or 'old cocks'. Larry had some elder relation with him – a cleric to whom I was not introduced – who naturally monopolized his time and interest. I remained silently in the background, like a recalcitrant schoolboy waiting to be given a severe 'dressing down', by the 'govenor'. As soon as the clergyman was the other side of the door, in a panic to avoid a silence, I let forth an avalanche of praise about the production: about how right he was in his portrayal of a middle-aged, not a senile Sir Peter; about the prettiness of Vivien, the polish of the teamwork, and the charm of so much 'business' that he had invented – such as the cascade of bandboxes arriving at the front door as an indication of Lady Teazle's extravagances. But no re-action: even the most fulsome compliments failed to thaw the temperature. I suppose I should have asked Larry quite bluntly why he and Vivien had suddenly adopted this extraordinary attitude – in fact, it must appear incomprehensible that I did not – but I am always anxious to avoid a row if it is possible to do so. I know, in the theatre, that great explosions of temperament take place on an impulse; appalling things are said in the heat of the moment. Wounding, vile insults are thrown around when the adrenalin rises. But everything is forgiven and forgotten on arrival at the theatre next day. Some people enjoy these blood-lettings: I do not. In fact, if I have to be subjected to an unpleasant scene, or someone is wounding to me, it is likely to be a very long time before the scars are healed.

Larry's dresser now became the focus of his attention: whispered instructions given about his clothes . . . Then the dresser left, and still Larry addressed no word to me. The silence was broken by John Gielgud coming into the room. I don't know if John noticed anything peculiarly cold about the atmosphere, and I did not mention it to him when, a few moments later, together we left the theatre. But once outside the confines of 'backstage' my indignation rose to the surface. I knew that, such is my unforgiving, unforgetting nature, no matter how hard the Oliviers might try, one day, to make up for this evening's affront, I would have no further interest in them – let alone feel that we were friends. They were both out of my life for ever.

Winter

A vicious attack of the prevalent flu felled me completely. For several weeks I tried from my bed to carry on with writing, but I knew I was working under an impossible disadvantage: I seemed to make no progress. When my kind neighbours, Juliet Duff and Simon Fleet, sent me a telegram from the south of France to say Willie [Somerset] Maugham would like me to join them and recuperate in the winter sun, I was soon on an aeroplane.

My friendship with Willie had only recently started. A few days before taking a ship in New York to return to England, I met another fellow passenger, one of my oldest and most delightful New York friends, Monroe Wheeler, an erudite and entertaining director of the Museum of Modern Art. He told me: 'Willie wondered if you would care to have your meals on board with us?' Not only was I delighted to be with two such excellent conversationalists, but I was pleased to have this opportunity of perhaps getting to know Willie a little less formally.

My first acquaintance with him had been when, at the start of my professional career as a photographer, he came to my parents' drawing-room to be photographed for *Vanity Fair*. He was shy: I was shy. The sitting did not become alive. I gave him cursory instructions as to where to place his arms and hands. He obeyed: 'Thus?' or 'So?' As a result the photographs were completely static. Although we then became acquaintances over a long period of years, he never seemed to thaw – certainly not towards me. I doubt if this had anything to do with the fact that his wife, the effervescent Syrie, whom he detested, became a particular friend of mine.

On the first day of the Atlantic crossing Willie at dinner said: 'Sissel, I hear you've written a very good play. I would like to read it; have you a copy on board?' I lied. I wished to do a lot more rewriting on it. Couldn't I send him a copy later? Then, of course, I realized that there would surely never again be such an opportunity to benefit by his advice. I owned up to my lie, and sent the play to his cabin.

At luncheon next day Willie said: 'I have read your play, and I will tell you what I think of it at some more suitable time, and in private.' I was full of nervous anxiety at the prospect of the acid test. Of late I had been becoming increasingly dubious about the merits of this gigantic opus; but if I am to go ahead and put it, as I hoped, before the public, it would be asinine to flinch at hearing the opinion of a dramatist who really knows what he is talking about.

The following day I was pacing the deck with Monroe when he said: 'Willie was in wonderful form before luncheon. He came down feeling rather crotchety after a sleepless night. He asked me to take the air with him, and he told me he was worried about what he was going to say to you about the play. Then, proceeding to tell me what he thought of it, he warmed to the task, and when his thoughts were formulated and straight in his head, he said: "Now I think I'll sit down and have a drink." The relief of having got off his mind all he had to say to you was so great that his spirits then began to soar. He was unusually comic – never been in better form!'

At luncheon in the restaurant we talked about Willie's collection of Zoffanys and his other theatrical pictures, about the Old Vic company, a comparison of Noël's and Terry's dramatic talents – but never a word about my play. Eventually I asked when could I have the interview?

'This afternoon at three-thirty.'

Precisely on the moment he appeared: 'We had better go into the dining-room: it is quiet there.'

It was as if I were 'up to the head beak'; I was terrified.

'Well, Sissel, I've read your play with a great deal of interest. It is extremely well written and constructed, and the story is very moving. The characters are excellent, and it's dramatic.' (My heart beat with relief and joy!) 'But there is one thing that worries me very much indeed: you must explain it to me. Why do the characters of Gainsborough and the auctioneer, Christie, talk in a quasi-eighteenth-century manner but then address one another by their christian names?' Willie recommended Jane Austen and Fielding and that I should read *Clarissa Harlowe* and Sheridan to give the play a far more authentic eighteenth-century flavour. Or perhaps I would prefer to use a contemporary dialect? Then it would be correct to use such phrases as "a place in the sun" which was said by Germans before the last war. "Giving someone a lift" is entirely modern. You must make up your mind which idiom you are going to use.'

I confessed to ignorance and slovenliness and an inattention to detail. Willie also told me he thought the ending could be strengthened. 'You want your final curtain to be something that will make your audience sit up: yours is too arbitrary.' He made the suggestion that I should bring back the dashing young Lord Angus to buy his own portrait, and when the two daughters, both of whom had so disastrously loved him, saw him again, neither could recognize him. Poor, dotty Mary, who has been seduced by him, might ask: 'Who was that man?'

I agreed gladly with everything Willie told me. The criticisms seemed so unimportant compared to my fears that he might say that my play was split down the middle, that it contained some irrevocable fault of construction. What a relief to feel that basically the workmanship was sound, and comparatively little wrong that could not be remedied. Willie stuttered: 'I d–don't know w-whether or not you are prepared to go to all this t-t-trouble; but if you don't you'll have people laughing at you for these an-an-anachronisms.'

Life at the Villa Mauresque is ideal for the semi-invalid: breakfast in bed; the garden below the balcony a sea of magenta and blue cinerarias; no need to put in an appearance before midday. The large salon, with french windows opening on to a terrace, is impressively decorated with a huge sunburst of gilt carving, much golden gesso, huge sofas, and eighteenth-century paintings in carved frames. On the terrace the lunch visitors assemble: maybe witty, delicious and slightly scatty Lady Kitty Lambton with piercing eyes and iron-grey curls, the raven beauty Muriel Wilson who had been part of King Edward's coterie, renowned for organizing amateur theatricals, and who owned the famous nearby 'Maryland' garden. One day that old silenus Marc Chagall appeared with an astonishingly young and pretty wife. For me the special treat was the arrival of Graham and Kathy Sutherland. He is still working on the drawings for a portrait of Willie, and those I've seen are brilliant. Graham does not spare any horses, and he has made Willie as sour as a quince – yet Willie seems delighted.

It is odd that Willie seems to dislike the company of his fellow writers, and finds people who have not been able to succeed with the difficulties of old age anathema to him. He was grateful to poor, dithering, bleating, stuttering Eddie Marsh for proof-reading some forthcoming publication of his, and felt he should be invited to stay for a fortnight. Juliet [Duff] agreed that it would be a treat for Eddie, who was finding time going slowly for him. 'No,' decided Willie quite suddenly, 'I couldn't stand it! I'll send him a case of brandy.'

Perhaps we go to a picture gallery where Willie has bought many of his post-Impressionist paintings which grace the walls of the dining-room. But although he professes to be a connoisseur, I am cad enough to feel that he has no real understanding or love for it. It is more in terms of an investment, or as a status symbol, that I see him as a collector.

The early evening is when the garden is at its most magical. The sound of the crickets in the olive trees drowns even the birdsong. For someone coming from the bleakness of winter in England it is incredible that here tuberoses and sweet peas are flourishing out of doors; at this hour of dusk their scent is all-pervading.

Willie prides himself on the variety of his menus. He says anyone can provide a good dinner, but his aim is never to repeat the fare during the length of his guests' visit. Juliet and Simon, who have been here longer than I, have not twice been offered the same dish. Meals are treated with the reverence they deserve. Willie holds forth for a short time on a topic of his choosing: he selects his words with care. Then bridge, and an early night.

Willie Maugham, at the age of seventy-four, knows exactly what he wants to do with his remaining years. They are ordered with a mathematician's accuracy: so many months for travelling, six weeks for visits to England, and March to September in his Riviera house. At the Villa Mauresque everything is arranged with military precision. Woe betide anyone who puts a spanner in the running order so that an appointment is delayed; a guest who is late for a cocktail on the terrace learns not to be late a second time. My darling Lily

Elsie, the original 'Merry Widow', now, like so many of us, past middle age, found the foreign currency restrictions made her holiday seem alarmingly expensive. Willie invited her to lunch at the Villa Mauresque, but omitted to send his motor car for her, deciding that she could hire a taxicab from her Monte Carlo hotel. But Lily Elsie decided to save her precious francs by taking a bus which deposited her at the bottom of the Cap Ferrat hill. Unfortunately, the bus was late, and the great heroine of musical comedy who, in the phrase of the time, 'had all London at her feet', arrived, distraught, sweating and tired, twenty minutes late. Willie was furious that lunch was kept waiting. 'She was always a stupid woman,' he said.

Tangier

Truman Capote has also added to the variety of this holiday. He has been lured here by the delights I promised him, but he is disappointed. He and a friend, Jack Dunphy, are living on a mountain top under a corrugated-iron roof. It is hellishly hot and altogether unattractive, but he cannot afford to move and he is good at making the best of a bad job. Also staying in the same compound are Jane and Paul Bowles, so it has become an interesting writers' community.

When first I became friends with Truman two years ago, he was fluttery and wraith-like, enjoying many affectations and frivolities. Now he has developed considerably; he doesn't think of himself as a pretty little kitten any more, and pays only a minimum of attention to his appearance, which has become comparatively rugged. For days he will go without shaving, for months he lets his toenails grow; his rooms become untidier, the dogs make messes on the floor; he will never write that telegram at the right moment, or send his suit to the cleaner. He takes little notice of the less important exigencies of life, for he reserves all his energies for his creative work.

At twenty-six years old, Truman still looks so young that bartenders are likely to consider him under age and refuse to grant his request for 'a martini – very dry and very cold'; here the Arab urchins treat him as a child and are apt to taunt him.

During his short span Truman has known many aspects of life, during which various vicissitudes he has spent his time learning, absorbing, and remembering. His knowledge and interests are extraordinarily varied: his horizons stretch wide. In whatever part of the world he may happen to be, he knows exactly what is going on in other parts of the world. (I've seldom seen him read anything but newspapers and magazines – *Time* magazine from cover to cover – yet at some time he has read all the classics.) The training to read, given him when he was working on *The New Yorker* where he had to scrutinize thirty newspapers a day in order to pick out stories that might be worth developing in 'The Talk of the Town', has enabled him to get the gist of every article at a glance. People of all kinds become the keen objects of his study, and their secrets are laid bare under the microscope of his eye. He has the warmth to draw them out, and little do they realize that whereas he may be sympathetic to them, he is also vastly indiscreet. But it is surprising to discover that much of contemporary life, and many of the interests of civilized people, pass him by. Whereas it is unexpected that he knows much about finance, and has admiration for those in big business, he is totally uninterested in painting, works of art, classical music or architecture; wild horses won't drag him into a museum.

Chantilly: November

It was a relief to take the train, in torrential rain, to Chantilly to stay the night with Duff and Diana [Cooper].

Suddenly the atmosphere was of a celebration. 'You've missed such beauty! There was a *panne d'électricité* and we had everyone in here in candlelight – it was too beautiful!' Diana was exultant. 'And you've missed the hunt service this morning. We got to Rambouillet by ten, and the congregation was all in pink coats, and they blessed the hounds. And you've missed such a wonderful row going on upstairs. The Cabrols missed the Ghislaine Polignac–Chuck Basildon car which had their lunch in it, and have arrived wet through, exhausted, starved, and they're fighting it out now – it's wonderful!'

I sat in Diana's bedroom while she dressed for the evening's festivity – a local hunt ball. While doing her hair in the glass she remarked: 'My face looks terrible.' Half an hour earlier, wearing a scarlet tricorne, she had struck me anew by her beauty. Now, meaning to indicate my recent astonishment at her continued beauty, I lamely replied: 'Well, it didn't,' to which Diana, with a wry laugh, concurred: 'No, I know it *didn't*!'

Duff came in and, apropos the morning hunt service, Diana asked him: 'Why should the Church celebrate the killing of a stag?'

Duff, a dry martini in his hand, said: 'The Church isn't against hunting. There's nothing against hunting in the Bible. A stag has to be destroyed,' he continued; 'the damage it can do is appalling. It can eat a whole field of turnips.'

'But that's no reason for the Church to bless the killing of it.'

'Why not?'

Diana: 'We all know adultery's charming, but we don't have a church service for it!'

'But the Bible is against adultery, and anything the Church is not against can be celebrated by a special service.'

'Well,' I interpolated, thinking of the horror I'd left behind at the theatre, 'I don't see why we shouldn't have a service to pray for a successful ballet season?'

'Certainly not – a very good idea!' said Duff. 'But do be quick, Diana – we're already late.'

'Now do stop worrying me, Duffie – you know the others won't be ready for hours!'

By degrees the guests assembled: the men in knee-breeches, pink coats, yellow and purple and green coats – very pretty. Diana, wishing to appear *à la chasseuse*, decide to wear a red cape – but what to put with it?

'This is just like dressing for an Albert Hall ball. What about this top worn with that bottom?'

The impromptu was made into an art medium. To a swarthy maid Diana confided: 'Oh, Naomi – I do love you! You've altered that button beautifully.' Naomi giggled, and proffered her choice of separate tops and bottoms.

'No, I'm going to wear this skirt. Mr Beaton likes it, and he's the arbiter of taste in England.'

'But this is France,' replied Naomi.

Dinner very noisy. Everyone in good spirits and I think, like me, felt they had come to the end of a long day and an endless week and could now enjoy themselves.

Later, as we were assembled in the hall to leave for the ball, Duff rushed past the guests with eyes popping like an owl and shouted at the cowering Naomi: '*Où est Jean?*' Naomi didn't know or care. His Excellency, with fists clenched, leant so far forward towards Naomi that I thought he would lose his equilibrium.

'*Où est Albert? Où est Bertrand?*'

At last the missing Jean was produced: he appeared greener of visage than ever. Duff had words to say to Jean, though to me they were incomprehensible: yet somehow in the frenzy I gathered that Duff '*sonnéd*' so many times, and there were four servants in the house, and why couldn't there be someone to help the guests with their coats? Why could none of the servants ever be relied upon? '*Salauds – salauds!*' spluttered Duff. Jean, by now emerald of face, answered indistinctly: 'Very well, Your Excellency, I'll go.'

'Yes, go tomorrow!'

The guests were appalled. We filed into the cars, and the princes and princesses, dukes and duchesses, barons and baronesses, counts and countesses all said: 'How does he manage to keep the servants? We wouldn't dare lose our tempers like that! He behaves as if it were before the war!'

Duff was soon in the sweetest of moods. The ball at Royaumont was a noble sight with fine French furniture, crystal chandeliers, and yellow chrysanthemums with orange or green centres – and the ladies dressed to kill. All the Fulde-Springer family have instinctive taste and a great knowledge of works of art. Max, tonight's host, is no exception, so it was not surprising that the festivities were outstanding and continued until dawn.

Next morning I slept late. Diana in the adjoining room busy telephoning.

'May I come in?' I asked.

I walked in, wearing pyjamas. Diana, in her pink-flowered sheets, wore her nightcap like a baby's bonnet. Enthusiasm typical of Diana: 'The new bride is coming! Anne and Michael Tree!' It is always a birthday morning with Diana. Jean, still very green in the face, was by the bedside and gesticulating with long, bony fingers to inquire how many for luncheon?

'Eighteen. The Windsors and sixteen other people.'

Jean likes notabilities so he was quite pleased about the impending party but, of course, had to show his displeasure of last night's scene.

'It is not my fault if His Excellency cannot find his shirt studs. There is no order in his methods and he does not let me take control. Why blame me if there was not enough partridge or pheasant for dinner? It was those two extra guests.'

Diana: 'You know, Jean, it wasn't either of those things that irritated His Excellency. It was the fact that not one of you four servants were anywhere to be found when we wanted to leave. He rang and rang, and you had shut the door of your room so you could eat in peace. He was extremely displeased – and with good cause.'

'All the same, it's no use being taken for a "*salaud*".'

'No, Jean; but we've been into all that. There will be eighteen for lunch.'

'Very good, my lady.'

Door shuts. Diana's eyes up to heaven. 'Lord! I've been dreading it all night – couldn't sleep a wink! I was so afraid he really would go!'

Duff appeared two moments later. Eyes very much askew, he was fully dressed in a smart grey suit, with a protruding stomach and bottom and shining shoes. 'Well, how was it?' he asked.

'All right – I think good will come of it; but you must take a high line.'

Duff and Diana are a loving and extraordinary couple: they understand one another completely. Of course it would have been beside the point for Duff to excuse his outburst to Diana.

'Well then, now, Duffie – about lunch.'

Evelyn [Waugh] has arrived for a few days. Diana admires him immoderately. She is a true friend of his, though I cannot imagine how she, the most straight-forward, unpretentious person, puts up with Evelyn's snobbery. When I criticize Evelyn – whom I find intolerable – Diana defends him, but admits she can't bear his 'showing off', being so boringly pompous, and pretending to be deaf.

Of course I am prejudiced. That wise old marvel, Morgan Forster, wrote somewhere that even in later life one can never forgive the boys who tormented one at school. During my first morning at Heath Mount day school in Hampstead the bullies, led by a tiny, but fierce Evelyn Waugh, at once spotted their quarry in me during the morning 'break' as, terrified, I crept around the outer periphery of the asphalt playground.

After Evelyn's novels had brought him fame, he lived in a large house in the West country, with his coat of arms carved in the pediment over the front door.

There was another reason for my dislike – and it was mutual. Both Evelyn and I now moved in more exalted spheres than when we lived in Hampstead and Highgate. In our own way we were both snobs, and no snob welcomes another who has risen with him. My particular snobbery was more in the nature of wanting to become part of the world of the 'culturi'. I was magnetized towards the Sitwells, Gerald Berners, Lady Ottoline Morrell, Viola and Iris Tree, Raymond Mortimer, and certain of the Bloomsbury set. Evelyn was attracted by the foibles of those who lived in large, aristocratic houses. He cultivated the Lygons at Madresfield, got elected to the 'best' clubs (where he taunted newer members or visitors), and fostered a fascination, though in many ways despising it, for the highest echelons of the Army and military etiquette. He drank port and put on weight, and attempted to behave in the manner of an Edwardian aristocrat. He was very conscious of what a gentleman should or should not do: no gentleman looks out of a window, no gentleman wears a brown suit. In fact, Evelyn's abiding complex and the source of much of his misery was that he was not a six-foot tall, extremely handsome and rich duke.

We seemed to have certain friends in common and, since we met quite often, it was expedient to put the old hatchet away. Its burial was only temporary. However, for a time a truce was enjoyed. Evelyn seemed to find me amusing, laughed full-bellied at my jokes, while I found his observations about people and general perspicacity quite wonderful. His novels were written in a prose of which I was never tired. Ostensibly we were friends, Evelyn sent me inscribed messages of good will on the front pages of his latest works. But I was always aware that I must not let him find a chink in my armour.

As fellow guests of Duff and Diana at Chantilly, we played a subtle game of cat and mouse. I flattered Evelyn by taking him around the precincts and photographing him in every conceivable posture. (The most significant snap was of Evelyn scowling, with outsize cigar, as he leant on a gate marked 'Défense d'entrer'.) Then, to show how versatile I was, I bade him sit still while I made a crayon sketch of him. I knew that Evelyn, sitting back, pot-belly proffered, was peering with incredibly bright popping eyes and vivisectionist's knowledge, awaiting like a tiger the opportunity to tear me to shreds. But I was never off guard. When he saw the result of the sitting he exclaimed: 'Oh, that's cheating! Anyone can do a passable drawing with a red pencil.'

Evelyn has a talent for making a complimentary word sound suspicious. A mutual friend, Bridget Parsons, gave a cocktail party at which the sudden rush of guests appeared to be overwhelming. Clean glasses ran out. Bridget asked one or two of us if we would take the 'dirties' into the kitchen where they would be washed. As I passed, Evelyn, standing warming his rump in the fireplace, remarked to the man enjoying the pleasure of his company: 'What on earth is he doing with those glasses?' I shouted into his ear trumpet: 'A buttling job.' Evelyn sneered: 'How extraordinarily *kind*!' After Evelyn had been to a small dinner at my house, he referred to me for some time as 'an extremely *hospitable* person'. Somehow he managed to convey that my chief role in life was to entertain people, and most certainly for some sinister, ulterior motive.

I wonder if Evelyn ever really likes anybody? I believe his second marriage to be an exceedingly happy one, but I cannot imagine his ever loving anyone. Diana says she loves him though she is fully conscious of the unkind and cruel things he does to people. Once the two of them were motoring together through Marlborough. At some traffic lights they came to a stop, and an anguished pedestrian put his head through the car window and said: 'I've got a train to catch. Can you tell me the way to the railway station?' Evelyn gave him elaborate instructions. The man ran up the hill in a muck sweat. Diana put her foot on the accelerator.

'How clever of you to know where the station is.'

'I don't,' said Evelyn. 'I always give people the wrong directions.'

I have heard Diana and Evelyn being appallingly rude to one another – really vilely, squalidly rude – and yet Diana is deeply touched by him. Today, however, Evelyn did get Diana's goat. He had the impertinence to criticize the breakfast tray: he said it 'wasn't fully furnished'! Diana, even several hours later, was still exploding with wrath. 'There was I, trying to get the trays ready for everybody – with Marguerite in bed ill having her you-know-whats. I was doing my best in my nightgown, bare feet and bald pate. Well, I let him have it. I said: "Really, Evelyn, it's too much to put on such an act!" and I gave him the full benefit of everything that I'd been bottling up about his pretentiousness. It really rankled with him – but it'll do him good!'

8 June 1951

At last things seem to be moving. Unless some catastrophe such as a general strike overwhelms us, or war is declared (and the threat never, never seems far distant), I feel that my play is really going to be produced.

God, it's been a long time! I can't even remember now when I first started to write the bloody thing. Perhaps the seeds germinated when I was still at Cambridge and enjoyed looking at that Gainsborough *Conversation Piece* in the Fitzwilliam. Then I read a life of Gainsborough and was intrigued by those poignant little children – his daughters – whom he painted chasing butterflies, and who posed for many of his 'fancy pieces'. Coming with their father, from the countryside which they all loved, to make his way in the grand world of London, the bright lights went to the children's heads. After serious setbacks in love they both ended up as dotty old maids – so snobbish that they ennobled the tradesmen who were their only visitors; thus the milkman, before he could leave the milk, announced himself as the Duke of Churn.

The first time I read my completed script was in America when, one Friday night, I was staying with those two stage-struck enthusiasts, the actress Ruth Gordon and her playwright husband Garson Kanin. Anita Loos was also there, and I could not believe it when, soon, my audience of three started to ripple with laughter, and react in a far more enthusiastic manner than I had ever hoped for.

Of course that night I could not sleep.

After torturing procrastinations, the American firm of Aldrich & Myers decided that they would present the play in England. If the trial run of the provinces was successful, then the entire package would be shipped immediately to the US. Aldrich & Meyers employed Henry Sherek, who had previously turned down the play, to put the show on for the firm.

The most important step was to get the right director. Peter Brook had long since gone to greener pastures; Peter Glenville had shown enthusiasm for a while, then also disappeared to the US. Then Norman Marshall, with a long list of worthy theatre successes behind him, showed willingness to launch the leviathan.

Brighton: 28 July

I am writing in the hotel bedroom in which I have spent many unhappy hours since I arrived here, so full of expectation, two weeks ago. As the train bringing me to Brighton stopped at outlying stations I craned to see if there were any billboards bearing the name of my play; the sight of the first large poster was a thrill. The welcome at the familiar hotel was warm, as it was, too, at the jewel-box of the little Theatre Royal. The set was already up, Sherek in high spirits, while everyone else was impatient for the lighting to be finished before the dress rehearsal.

By the end of the evening the anti-climax was appalling: the play had never come to life. A few people in the audience made no comment. Joyce Grenfell appeared like a lightning-struck sheep, and added not one word. My agent

looked even more like a ruined pudding than usual; he merely cleared his throat.
Mrs Myers, the wife of the American producer, when asked if she would like
a sandwich, said: 'I would like a taxi.' A strange chemical reaction took place
in me; suddenly I was robbed of all hope. But perhaps the dress rehearsal disaster was a good sign: it was said to be. Next day I worked non-stop in the
theatre on set, costumes and script changes; but the cast was not sure enough
of their lines to be given the cuts I now suggested.

But I didn't realize how much cutting was necessary until the audience was
there – a terrifying first-night crowd of London friends and critics. A steel-
like curtain of defiance seemed to go up between them and the play. The first
act went without laughs. Later things warmed up, but never were the laughs
as I had hoped for. At the end of the play there were a number of curtain
calls, but no great enthusiasm. At the party afterwards my friends tried to give
me the impression that the evening had been a success.

As usual, I was awake very early next morning, too pent-up and overtired
to be able to sleep. I called for the papers, and with no exception the reviews
were bad. 'Trite dialogue.' 'So much good material in it, and it often almost
achieves its purpose.' 'Much charm, some lightness, a certain amateurish flatness in the writing, trace or two of gaucherie, and a rather agreeable and affect-
ing sentiment.' 'Heavy disappointment. Enchanting to look at.'

For two weeks I had had a feeling of sickness in my stomach, but now I
was aghast. I felt as miserable as one only does when one falls unhappily in
love. My mother and Baba were in the next bedroom. I had to wake them
with the news that the reviews were bad: I felt more queasy than ever. It was
like telling them of a family death: they did not know how to comfort me. What
was there to do? Try and swallow the cold breakfast.

I got out the script again, for the thousandth time, and I started to make
cuts so that, by the next evening, the changes would be made. We had a midday
conference in the hotel: Sherek, Myers and Norman Marshall. Dick Myers
said he still has faith in the play, but a lot of work must be done on it, that
Angus was a stick, and should be made the central figure of the play.

Under great duress I worked in my hideous hotel room, and managed to
find a typist to take down a new scene. It was rehearsed and put into being:
but none of it was fun any more. The critics had written failure over my play,
and I couldn't get rid of this horrible feeling; I turned even against my scenery
and costumes.

However, the cast worked hard, and Norman was very persevering. That
sweet man, Duff Cooper, penned me a note from White's, saying that he
thought the critics had been unduly harsh, that often resentment was built up
when people had had success in other fields of activity and took to something
new.

We continued as if the play were a success and, after the first night, audiences seemed really to enjoy themselves. There was always a lot of laughter and many curtain calls. For two weeks here we have been doing business that Sherek says is 'wonderful'. What will happen in other towns I do not know.

One afternoon, in order to escape from the atmosphere of the theatre, I took a bus and went to Firle to call on that most stimulating and entertaining of all human beings – Lydia Lopokova, the dancer. When I first discovered Diaghilev's ballet, the minuscule Lopokova was one of its wittiest adornments.

After suffering from a bad heart for ten years, Maynard [Keynes] died recently, leaving Lopokova his remarkable collection of pictures and, if little cash in hand, three places in which to live.

When my bus deposited me near her house on the Downs near Lewes, Lydia rushed out to meet me wearing a mercerized silk skirt of cream leaf pattern, cocoa-coloured stockings, woollen socks, straw boots, an apron, and about three different sweaters over a silk blouse. Her head was tied in a maize-coloured handkerchief: a pale grey, shiny face without make-up, but freckled and sunburnt at back of neck.

Tilton House proved to be typical of the Bloomsbury taste when the Omega workshop ordained that nothing brighter than terracotta could be used among the clay, oatmeal and slate colours of their domineering palettes. But Lydia's own personality was very apparent, for everywhere was a mess of all the things she is interested in: yellowing snapshots, bits cut out of the newspaper – how to stop snoring, a review of Roy Harrod's book on Maynard. The chimneypieces, the occasional tables, sideboards, even the piano, were all stacked with tins of food, cardboard boxes of provisions, matches, serried jars of pickles; everything on view. Surprising it was among all this litter to discover, skied high on the walls, a marvellous collection of Modiglianis, Cézannes, Seurats and Picassos. 'Oh, they don't belong to me,' said Lydia. 'They were Maynard's, and they're only loaned until death.' What other woman would disclaim ownership in this modest way? But such humility is typical of Lydia; the impression she creates on the world means absolutely nothing to her.

The widow chuckled, and exclaimed in her thick Russian accent: 'I have to ask the trustees for every half-crown, and for a hand-basin for my bedroom, but I don't really want for anything. I live well. I drink wine with my meals; I have here a garden with peas in it, the rooms in Gordon Square, and a flat at Cambridge. When Maynard died I thought I could never live without him, and I suffered a lot. But now I never think of him.' She is utterly absorbed by her new life. 'I go into the raspberry canes and I imagine I'm in the jungle, and I bend my body and it gives me such a feeling of freedom – and I picked these peas for our lunch.' ('Will you have sausages or cold ham?' She rushed off and shouted to a hidden servant: 'He wants ham!') 'Yes, I'm blissfully happy here. I have a married couple whom I gave this nice home to, and in return they do the cooking for me. I can't cook. Oh, it's too much of a bore – too messy! But sometimes I try to experiment – and the other day I ate a squirrel! It tastes rather like a bird – it lives on nuts and apples – and it's delicious, and next time I'll eat half a dozen! But I always make my own bed; I like that, it gives a rhythm to life. And I go for walks, and I read a bit, and the days aren't long enough; twenty-four hours aren't long enough at this time of the year.'

During my visit today Lydia, looking like the Widow Twankey, danced the 'Valse des Fleurs' of the *Casse-Noisette*. She did imitations of the way that Michael Somes moves, leaning slightly forward as if sand was falling out of his behind, and proved in a thousand different ways that there are no disadvantages to old age when one is as completely lacking in self-consciousness, is as interested in as many aspects of life as she continues to be, and is able to laugh as much as ever.

Lydia has taken to English country life as if born to it, though she has never been able to master the language. Describing how much she enjoys riding, she says: 'Of course it is hard on the two halves, but my feet have never come out of the hooks, and I never lost my horse morale.'

Reddish: July 1951

David Herbert, good at gardens, when asked for his advice about improving my terrace, suggested first of all that it would be an improvement to rid the lawn rising to the paddock of that heavily wired, rose-covered fence that was the sole means of preventing Herbert Bundy's horses and cows remaining decoratively in the semi-distance. 'The eye should stretch to that distant row of trees, so you could feel you are at one with nature – that your garden is part of the countryside.' Of course, of course – how could that suburban-looking fence have been allowed to exist all these years? When once someone has pointed out an obvious fault one cannot imagine how it has been overlooked for so long. One must set about improving the state of affairs immediately. Not a second to be lost!

But the problem of how to keep out Farmer Bundy's animals was a difficult one. A 'ha-ha' would necessitate building a sunken brick wall, and this would cost much more than I could afford. But, in any case, the hill sloped the wrong way and the cows would fall into the trench, or the horses leap across the dyke to enjoy trespassing on my juicy plots. Farmer Bundy suggested an electric wire, but no one else much cared for that idea.

After much consultation the offending fence has been removed, and we now have a barbed line stretching neatly from posts, camouflaged green, placed at intervals. The effect is not quite as one hoped, but with luck one can now imagine the paddock as being almost a continuation of the garden. The evening sun slants across the grass up to the deep shadows of the trees; the cattle graze, the horses frisk about, and the white mare gallops across the view like a Delacroix. The effect is good.

This late summer evening I sauntered into the paddock, and wondered if we could not have a series of posts with roses trained between each to form a string of garlands. This would be more fitting than the barbed wire, and would serve as protection, too; I must think seriously about this. Meanwhile, on up to the end of the garden.

This is the time of year I most enjoy: I must savour my enjoyment to the full. I walked on past the herbaceous things: the stocks, phlox, daisies and evening primroses, and into the kitchen garden. It was dark green at this quiet time of the evening. The lettuces in rows were looking orderly and appetizing, the radishes rosy ... But, to my great chagrin, and as a result of the discarding of the fence, a young rabbit hopped across my path; then, frightened, ran among the French beans, and finally took refuge under the potato leaves.

Back after Anthony's long convalescent holiday, and once more involved in high politics, the Edens come down to the doll's cottage in the Corot-like valley behind the watercress beds in Broadchalke. 'Rose Bower', which my mother found for Clarissa, has become important in their lives. At first Eden hit his head on doors and ceilings, and had to come down to my library to use a telephone with a scrambler for secret conversations, but now he has a great affection for the cottage and considers it his home. Here, free from the turbulence of Whitehall, he can get on with the contents of 'the boxes' without interruption.

When Clarissa drove over to lunch with me, leaving the Edens, *père et fils*, to look after each other, I noticed the changes since that morning when she sat on a chair in my bedroom and confided that she was going to marry. At that time Clarissa had seemed so independent and capable of living by herself, that one wondered at her ever deciding to 'settle down'. When first I knew her, with her long, corn-coloured hair hanging like bells, she was a most romantic character; a friend of James Pope-Hennessy and the eccentric Gerald Berners, and of publishers, writers and painters. This news came as a tremendous switch.

At the time of the engagement Anthony Eden was so busy, so many were his commitments, that, ridiculous as they admitted it to be, there was no chance of the marriage taking place for several months. Meanwhile, total secrecy. It was amusing to be with Clarissa in Bond Street one morning when, after choosing some hairbrushes to be initialled 'AE' at Cartier's, she popped the letter announcing her engagement to her Aunt Clemmie who was, at that time, abroad in a clinic. On receiving the sensational surprise, Clemmie Churchill returned home immediately, and Randolph then 'took over'. Clarissa described the news of the engagement, and the press onslaught, as being in the path of a typhoon. Clarissa, beautiful yet unphotogenic, became a public figure. She was too occupied to see old friends, but when occasionally we met, everything seemed wonderful for her. The vistas were endless: she could help to do so much for the arts, she could wield power in the right direction.

Whenever I met her husband, a wave of what I had hoped was long-forgotten shyness would again overwhelm me. Anthony, by nature, himself is shy, Clarissa too. So we made an agonizing trio: three people, all wanting to be nice to one another, stumbling about in the mire. If only for the reason that Anthony had become my great friend's husband, I wanted to be friends with him. I happen to admire his character: his honesty, courage and fairness. But we shied from one another. Clarissa obviously found it difficult to treat me with the insouciance of old times, for she has changed in many ways. Before, when Clarissa passed by my house on her way to and from 'Rose Bower', she would come in unannounced by the back door. Sometimes I'd get a great shock to find her standing silently, like a ghost, in the library. Today when she came to lunch, she drove her car up to the front door and rang the bell – though, typically, did not wait until it was answered before coming in. She no longer wears leather jerkins, trousers, and does not appear as someone from 'another part of the forest': she dresses in a more conventional style. Yet, after a while, she relaxes into being the marvellously sympathetic person I love.

'I can't tell you what fun it's all being: much more interesting than I'd ever imagined. It's fascinating all the time, and there are new developments every day. I'm loving my tea parties for the Ambassadresses, and I get such wonderful notes, putting me wise, from Marcus Cheke, the Marshal of the Diplomatic Corps. He tells me not to sit Ecuador next to Esthonia as they're not on speaking terms, and I must not mind if the Nepalese never raises her eyes as it's the first time she's been out without a veil.'

Clarissa amused me with a story of Anthony Eden, just returned from the Palace where he had to introduce a new Ambassador who was about to present his credentials to the Queen. It seems that a disregard for on-the-dot punctuality is something our present Queen may have inherited from Queen Alexandra. On this particular morning Her Majesty was a bit late for the audience during which several matters of state had to be attended to before the Ambassador (who arrives in a horse-drawn coach) could be shown in. Suddenly Anthony Eden said: 'I think, ma'am, we must hurry through this as the Ambassador has been here some considerable time.' The Queen said: 'Oh yes, and we can't keep the horses waiting?' She saw the joke and laughed.

I suggested that Clarissa write a diary. She gave a wry smile, said she would, and I believe she has written for an hour each night before going to sleep.

Although we did not talk intimately, my impressions are that she is much in love with Eden, has a great maternal feeling for him, and is perfectly content to devote herself entirely to his welfare. But, in spite of the enthusiasm of the moment, I don't think she is interested in politics and politicians. She says, with pride: 'I haven't opened the papers today' (they are full of yesterday's Tory rally), and it is obvious that she is not going to bother to do so. I'm sure she will do the present job well, for she is exceptionally efficient about anything she undertakes; in order to achieve her ends she could be utterly ruthless. Yet, in some ways, she is an unhappy person – always in search of something denied her. I daresay she will suffer a great deal all her life, and it is certain she will not end her days in the milieu of politics.

After lunch I went back with her to the cottage where the Edens were sun-bathing on a patch of lawn that was out of the shade. I was amazed to hear her say to her husband: 'I've brought Mr Beaton back here for a walk.' How *could* she be so formal, and how could she inflict such a burden on all of us? I'm sure a walk in my company was the last thing her husband wished for, and I felt an immediate urge to flee. But Anthony suddenly made a great effort to be friendly.

October

Bandy-legged old Mr Gould is, apart from being a local publican, a farmer and a car-hire driver. Ever since I came to live in Broadchalke it has been in his old boneshaker that we arrived at and departed from Salisbury station. So great is Mr Gould's enthusiasm and interest in all aspects of rural life that the road in front of him cannot confine his attention even when at the wheel, and in order to see how Mr Gilling's crops are faring, or whether there is a chance to run over a stray pheasant, his eyes must dart in all directions. Often his head is pivoted almost back to front the better to tell us, in his broad Wilt-shire accent, of some neighbourly event: how farmer Bundy's cows were elec-trocuted, of Mrs Bundy's sow's record litter, or of Captain Dale's accident resulting in his old Rolls being a 'write-off'. Yet, although others in the locality have found themselves head-on to some runaway tractor and propelled over a hedge, Mr Gould boasts that he has never yet had a road accident.

In the darkness, and without so many distractions, Mr Gould's driving is no less fanatical. Tonight he was to take me further afield than usual – as far as Southampton, where I was to take the tender out into the darkness to meet the giant ocean liner, the *Liberté*, on its way from Cherbourg to New York.

Among its passengers was Garbo who was disembarking at Southampton in order to stay with me. The future was as bright as this enormous, illuminated structure which suddenly towered into the night – all her funnels spot-lighted, each deck a brilliant glow, every one of her portholes a twinkling star.

Greta, wild-eyed and seemingly somewhat terrified, was waiting, among empty glasses, with her 'little friend' in the restaurant. They did not smile on seeing me: it was as if I were coming to make the final transaction of a business deal. The general atmosphere was so grim and overladen with tension that I wondered if, at any minute, one of them would suddenly inform me of a change of plan. Without allowing time for such an opportunity, and with an impatience that was quite ruthless, I snatched my friend by the arm and, in my best Lochinvar manner, guided her down the gangway into the waiting dinghy. It was with the greatest feeling of relief and happiness – too good yet to be true – that I looked back to see the golden illuminated liner receding into the distance.

For several minutes we sailed in silence on the dark liquid waves towards the cold blue light on the jetty. Here we were on English soil – safe at last! But even now I did not find that Greta seemed fully conscious of my presence: not one look or one word of intimacy. But once in the smelly old local car Greta was intrigued by Mr Gould's broad Wiltshire accent. She asked him to repeat certain phrases, and soon, throwing back his head and roaring with laughter, he was completely conquered by the unseen passenger at the back of his car. Even though he is accustomed, in his role behind the counter, to meeting all sorts of unexpected types, he sensed that this was someone quite out of the ordinary. He was obviously very amused and struck by her, but it was many days before he discovered the identity of the lady in the dark.

Mr Gould was only one of the local personalities who at once became friends with Greta. Soon she was on the best of terms with the vicar, the butcher and the gardener. George and Lily Bundy, the general storekeepers, and farmer Herbert Bundy and his pig-keeping wife Olive, were also trusted with her friendship. Greta was surprised and grateful that everyone in the village treated her as an ordinary private individual and that no one, even in the Salisbury market where we went to buy gum-boots, fish or potted plants, would stare at the stranger in their midst.

It was a revelation to watch her coming to life, and loving nature and simple things, and taking to Wiltshire ways as if this was where she belonged. For me it was marvellous to see that the transformation which I had hoped for, was, in fact, taking place.

Greta became totally relaxed and lost many of her inhibitions; she was seldom cautious about being on view or in other ways exploited. She became her true self: she blossomed.

The only worry to our peaceful coexistence was the press. On the very first

morning of relaxation in the green quiet of Broadchalke, the telephone rang
a few inches from Greta's ear. I stretched for the receiver and we both listened
to inquiries from the *Evening Standard* as to Miss Garbo's plans, and were
congratulations in order for Mr Beaton? Greta did not smile. This was my
baptism into the ways the press can hound its quarry when it considers the
pursuit is worth its efforts. The experience was alarming. Within a short space
of time, nice, rustic and somewhat *naïf* journalists in old tweeds appeared, on
instruction from London, from the offices of the *Salisbury Times* and *Western
Gazette*. Two hours later, city-suited professionals arrived from Fleet Street
for only a brief interview with Miss Garbo. At first polite smiles and refusals.
Then an ominous note was heard. Greta, unseen in the background, would
not yield an inch. Therefore the campaign intensified outside. A large, black,
urban limousine remained waiting in the village street for days on end. Shop-
keepers and rustic folk maintained a canny secrecy, and gave away nothing
about the luminary in their midst. Once, however, while climbing a steep wood-
land arcade, we were taken completely unawares by a flashlight photographer.
A whacking great ulcer exploded in my stomach, and I tried to hide the *Sunday
Express* from Greta next day. But she is a realist, and demanded to see the
picture which she perused with the corners of her mouth turned down in the
ultimate expression of dissatisfaction.

Perhaps more than a month after her arrival, when the press had lost interest,
an unexpected reporter called while I was in bed reshaping on my Gainsborough
play. The cook, unused to the wiles of reporters and easily flattered, had given
away the information that Miss Garbo had gone for a walk by herself over
the hills past Mr Bundy's pig-styes. When I heard this, I rushed out in my
pyjamas in cold and windy pursuit. In the distance I saw the lone figure
approaching. I signalled violently to Greta to return by the woods above the
house, and thereby avoid an unwelcome confrontation.

It was not surprising that my mother should become upset that her son who
remained, at middle age, unmarried, and whom she had come to rely upon
to look after her for the rest of her life, now appeared as if he might be making
plans to make a painful change. She was resentful. My mother has never been
one to hide her feelings; when she met Greta for the first time her welcome
was far from warm. Greta took no time to notice this. A 'situation' arose that
made things extremely difficult. I was exasperated. How was it that one couldn't
expect support and help from one's nearest, if not – at this moment – one's
dearest? I was told that my mother even sank to the melodramatic level of
referring to 'that woman'. However, after a while, my mother decided to relent.
One cold winter's evening she came home with a pale translucent, green and
white bunch of the first hot-house lilies-of-the-valley, and as Greta said: 'No
one can resist lilies-of-the-valley.'

My birthday was celebrated by the arrival of sisters, aunts and cousins for a family dinner party. Apparently everyone else was at ease, and treating Greta as if she were already one of them; there was much joking and laughter. But on this occasion it was Greta who disappointed; she made no effort to put on at full voltage her powers of fascination. Even in appearance she seemed drab. Perhaps, although it was sad for me, it was more suitable for the occasion, and, by not outshining the female members of the coterie, she showed once more her powers of intuition. But for me, the evening was so charged, so fraught, that I felt like one of those tragi-farcical Chekov characters who suddenly rushes out of the room while the slamming of the door is followed by an abortive pistol shot.

When Greta decided to come to London by far her greatest delight was to watch the Changing of the Guard at Buckingham Palace or the sentries on duty at St James's Palace. In front of any of these men she would lose all self-consciousness as, incapable of keeping still, she imitated the swing of the arms, the rhythm of their heavy steps, the jumping to attention. Unaware of passers-by watching her in surprise, she would lean forward in utter attention, then quiver with shock and delight each time they presented arms. She was completely rapt. 'Oh, look at the swing of their coats! *Quel chic!*' She would scurry after a retreating sentry marching across the cobblestones of King's Yard, and then be almost frightened out of her wits as he stamped his boots and about-turned to face his childish devotee.

One morning I went into Greta's room. She was serious: she had had a letter from 'the little man'. 'He's very clever,' was all she said; but later she admitted that he wrote: 'There's nothing left now but to announce your good news.' However, the question of marriage did not seem to become any more positive than before. Whenever I brought up the subject, Greta would cast it aside or make a joke of it. None the less, I was not unhappy – in fact, the reverse. The fact that we got along so well together …

Christmas approached. What to do? Michael Duff invited us to stay in Wales at Vaynol: it would be a real festivity. Yes, she would enjoy that. Then, for no more reason than that she wished to buy a certain cashmere or a pair of brogue shoes, Greta insisted that we should go to Paris.

We stayed at the Crillon from whence I took her to museums and galleries, dress collections, theatres, antique shops and restaurants. Sometimes the shopping was a trifle embarrassing, for Greta would leave a shop, where everything had been turned upside down for her, with a 'Well, we'll come back later'; she was happily unmindful of the attitude of the rather surly assistant. After a few weeks the routine became somewhat monotonous.

But suddenly, without explanation, Greta decided that she would fly to New York next week. I knew there was no influencing her.

18

The Beginning of a New Reign
1952–3

C. B. designed the ballet Picnic at Tintagel *for the New York City Ballet,
Truman Capote's* The Glass Harp *and a revival of Lonsdale's* Aren't We
All? *He witnessed the new Queen's first opening of Parliament. He designed
Coward's* Quadrille *for the Lunts. He attended the Coronation, and took
the official photographs. When in August 1953 Eileen Hose came to work
as C. B.'s secretary, he acquired a friend who would not only run his household
but supervise every detail of his business affairs. He published* Persona Grata
*with a text by Kenneth Tynan. He went back to school and entered the Slade
as a student.*

The Queen, it was said, wished to give her encouragement to the London
theatre by paying one of her rare visits to a play. She didn't particularly wish
to see anything of Brechtian gloom, or adapted from the French, or even an
American importation, so this 'old-fashioned rubbish', as the critics recently
called *Aren't We All?*, received the honour.

Such is the effect of Royalty that, although the play has been running for
a hundred performances, the entire cast was nervous. Even the old professionals, like Ronnie Squire and Marie Löhr, were saying: 'Oh, we'll be too
keyed up to give good performances,' and everyone was a bit too intent on
putting their best foot forward. The women insisted that the wigmaker should
re-dress their hair, their dresses were sent to the cleaners, and Marie Löhr
told me she had walked for four hours to try, in vain, to get a champagne-
coloured bow that I had suggested she should put at her stomach. Everyone
behind the scenes was giving an extra spit and polish to their job. Paul Anstee
hurried off with all the hydrangeas to have them given a certain dye-spraying
as the blue had faded in the strong lights of the arcs.

The streets around the Haymarket were lined with people held back by a
concourse of policemen. The audience had to be seated half an hour before
'the Royals' arrived. It sat cheerfully talking. There was the usual air of expectation. The Royal Box was decorated with hideous, small, bronze and yellow

chrysanthemums. The first thing to be seen was the approach of a bouquet. 'God Save The Queen.' Everyone stood to attention; the Queen quizzed the house out of the corner of her eye, not looking at all self-conscious at being stared at. The Queen Mother appeared, preceded by another bouquet and a bosom draped in white tulle. Then, without a tiara – perhaps with the wish to appear different – Princess Margaret. With precision the two Queens, having been politely cheered, sat down, the house lights were lowered, and the curtain went up.

Throughout the performance the regal Box was being surreptitiously watched by half the audience, so that the play received scant attention; but the general atmosphere was uncritical and good-natured, the display of manners and loyalty impressive. It was very interesting to note how the Royal Family seem to have acquired a communal manner of behaviour. They have developed an instinctive self-protection so that they should not bump into each other or stumble down a step. They move in slow motion with care and a fluid grace: their technique is so perfected that it appears entirely natural. No doubt but that much of this charm and grace is very special to the Queen Mother. The reigning Queen has developed independently but her charm and interested wonder is inherited from her mother's genius.

The Queen sat relaxed and hunched, with head cocked backwards to listen concentratedly to the play. Princess Margaret had straight neck and back, and perhaps a more artificial interest in the stage performance. But the Queen Mother is an exceptionally bright woman, and tonight was in her most jovial mood, enjoying every nuance of the play's humour with a hearty relish, and alert to all the complicated twists of the mechanical plot. She was having a 'night out', and in such good spirits that she chuckled at many things that the audience would take for granted, and roared at the things that amused her most. In the first interval, when Freddie Lonsdale and I were presented, she said: 'We're having such a good time.' When talking to Royalty I am apt, perhaps out of nervousness, to do an imitation of them to their faces, talking to the Queen Mother in the same wistful tones with wrinkled forehead. 'It's delicious, enchanting,' are her favourite words, and I find myself repeating them. I was being wistful, hesitant, and much too sycophantic when I heard, with admiration, Freddie Lonsdale just being himself. In his somewhat offhand manner, he was saying just the things that he would say to Gilbert Miller or Henry Luce. 'Oh, we are enjoying it so much – it's delicious!' one of the Royal ladies would say. 'It gets better,' said Lonsdale.

'Oh, but that's surprising! It isn't generally like that! The last act's always the trouble, isn't it?'

'My last acts are the best.'

Roars of laughter.

I thought perhaps the Queen Mother would be bored talking politely about the evening's entertainment, and suddenly I found myself asking: 'Did you have a good holiday?'

'Oh, I've bought a villa [the Castle of Mey, on the northernmost tip of Scotland] in the most remote part of the world!'

'How brave of you to have nothing between you and the Atlantic.'

'I've taken this villa to get away from everything; but I don't expect I shall ever be able to get there.'

Hearty laughter. If the Queen Mother were anyone other than she is (ridiculous supposition) would one come so readily under her spell? Would one admire quite so much those old-fashioned, dainty movements? The sweetly pretty smile, with tongue continually moistening the lower lip? Yes – whoever she were, she could not be faulted. As it is, everything about her adds to her fascination. Even her professed enjoyment of good Scottish oatcakes only adds to her comeliness. What matters it if her tip-tilted nose is not specially delicate in its modelling, nor the teeth as pearly as they used to be? It is important that she has such style, subtlety and humour, but it is her empathy and her understanding of human nature that endears her to everyone she talks to.

I wish that I could make a better impression on the Queen – not because she is the reigning monarch, but because I admire her character – her fairness and her judgement – so much that I reproach myself for something inadequate within myself if she does not respond favourably. Yet I find her difficult to talk to. The timing always seems jerky and inopportune. I know I am at fault. As for her appearance, one would wish her to wear her hair less stiffly, or to choose dresses that would 'do' more for her; but one must admit that all these little alterations would make no real difference. The purity of her expression, the unspoilt childishness of the smile, the pristine quality of her pink and white complexion, are all part of an appearance that is individual and gives the effect of a total entity.

Princess Margaret has more than a certain kindness and understanding, and she can be extremely amusing with a good turn of phrase and an appreciation of wit in others.

In the second interval the company was presented. Jolly jokes, graciousness: everyone had his proud moment. The final curtain. The cast bowed and curtsied to the Royal Box. Then the Royal party left. Cheers, hands waving to the gallery. The Queen Mother gets her special round of applause. Exit. Police in control. Sudden release of tension. Shouts, laughter, eyes wild, bouquets, flashlights. For the people responsible, an evening of great achievement. For the Royal Family, no doubt a pleasant enough excursion: one to be discussed very little on their return, and forgotten completely in the busy events of tomorrow.

4 November

At the kind invitation of Rock [the Marquess of Cholmondeley] and Sybil Cholmondeley, I went to the Opening of Parliament. It was the first time that this
ceremony was to be performed by the young Queen.

Rock, being the Lord Chamberlain, has a strategically-situated box in the
Royal Gallery (which is raised only a few inches from floor level) from which
its occupants can have an intimate view of almost everything – from the moment
the leading personalities make their entrance up the main staircase before processing into the House of Lords.

I had to get up at sparrow-fart since ingenious arrangements had been made
for me to take photographs connected with the forthcoming Coronation. It
seems, and in any case robes (or tunics) are not allowed out of the building,
that dignitaries are loath to dress up for a special sitting, so my camera was
hidden in the robing rooms the night before, and I would be allowed to take
some shots before this morning's proceedings. After I had photographed Black
Rod in his small room, which smelt strongly of the apples labelled with their
different names – Blenheim orange, Cox's orange pippins, Beauty of Bath,
Charles Ross, Codling, Bramleys and Anne Elizabeth – in cardboard boxes
hidden behind a screen, George Bellew, put on the same costume that his
ancestor had worn three hundred years ago.

'Big Ben is exactly 10.24. You had better go now, Beaton, for they lock the
door to the Royal Gallery.' I was one of the last of the populace to arrive, and
felt abashed at having to walk the length of the Gallery between the serried
rows of spectators. The Beefeaters lined the blue carpeted route, and I had
never felt a carpet more silken and soft beneath my feet. The Gallery, with
huge picture-book murals, and Gothic wallpaper of gold and dark green, is
a mess of golden Victoriana and, although not in itself beautiful, gives the effect
of grand ugliness or ugly quaintness.

Suddenly I found myself surprisingly and happily placed next to the cosy,
adorable Lynn Fontanne, so all terror and anxiety immediately vanished. I
always enjoy watching my fellow human beings; but now, in their traditional
fancy dress – a fancy dress that has been tried, developed and improved until
found to be flawless – the show could have gone on for ever. Ancient men with
tired eyes, wrinkles, thinning hair, and all the sad outward aspects of age,
appeared perfectly cast as unique and remarkable characters, in these marvellous scarlet, black and white clothes. Grand soldiers or officers of state were
stiffly encumbered with gold thread embroideries as if they were in their natural
everyday habit.

The arrival of parakeetish Princess Alice and the yeasty Duchess of Beaufort
was somewhat of a shock, for they bustled through the Gallery on their way
to the Robing Room wearing half-length fur coats that savoured too much of

the pedestrian life outside this strange and glorious world. No – the women altogether were not ceremonial enough: jewellery, however important, on badly-made, creased old evening gowns, was not good enough. They lacked 'hauteur'. It was the masculine gender who won today's prizes.

I am completely ignorant of the various offices of those near to the Crown, but realized that most of these people had been brought up to do these particular duties, so it was only natural for them to carry the Crown or Sword of State with such consummate ease. It made me realize the futility of trying to be someone one isn't: a lesson to go about one's life-work immune from any false note of pretension and snobbery. In what other country could people dress themselves up at this early hour, with such ease and naturalness, and never be in danger of making fools of themselves? The only impostors here were among the women: those who by some devious means had trapped a man into a marriage which technically gave them a foothold here. That tiresome, pushing little Lady Waverley was still wriggling her way up the ladder; with her innate vulgarity of yellow, frizzy, musical comedy curls and sycophantic flattery she stuck out a mile.

Exactly on the appointed minute the various bodies walked slowly through the Gallery to await the Queen's arrival. There was something quite casual about the whole thing. No one appeared nervous – for no one was. The procession of the Heralds, in complete silence, brought vivid touches of scarlet, blue and gold. There was something quite haunting about one, a young man whose name I discovered to be Frere. His hair was sand-coloured, his complexion colourless, his eyes tired. With his pale, lovelorn face he seemed to be burnt out by some romantic passion. Now nothing was left to him but to materialize – as he did – a perfect work of art, in his quartered tunic and sombre stockings, as he held the two Sceptres in pale ivory hands.

The Black Rods, in their lamp-black stockings and pumps with silver buckles, seemed to come from the insect world of Grandville. Brian Horrocks, with his long parchment face and thickly-covered head of carefully-combed grey hair, was a subject for Tintoretto – and yet, perhaps, something an English master could better interpret.

With a tinkle of swords against spurs, the Queen's Bodyguard followed with more military precision. An aged warrior, in cock-feathered helmet and dashing uniform, was made more poignant by the contrast of his having to walk with a stick – no doubt the result of some injury in long-forgotten wars; was it possible that he had survived the Charge of the Light Brigade? It was he who now gave the word of command as his company – all tall, in splendid feathers – clanked forward.

Up the carpeted stairs came a playing card from 'Happy Families', the 'Pig King' as personified by the Duke of Norfolk, with sadly surprised eyebrows and bags under small, tadpole eyes, impertinent, aggressive snout and sulking pout. His scarlet-vermilion cloth cape was in need of pressing; but I was told that these garments must be thrown into a linen bag to be brought out only for each occasion, and that there is great feeling that they should never be ironed.

The Duke of Beaufort appeared – superb in his tightly-filled kid trousers, enormous shining black boots, and scarlet jacket. His red face winter-weather-beaten, his chin blue with continual shaving; by wearing a pair of steel-rimmed spectacles, the sort that one only sees on elderly countryfolk or in medieval portraits, a note of reality was added to this fairy-tale grandeur. By his side, even taller, and wearing the same impressive uniform, was Queen Mary's brother, Lord Athlone. With his clear-sky eyes, fresh rosy complexion, crisp, thick white hair, and overbearing physique, he presented an awe-inspiring elderly figure.

Bobbety Salisbury, whose large cranium, pale eyes and aquiline features made of vellum, gave the onlooker an immediate impression of his general intelligence, worldly wisdom, and profound experience of life, moved in staccato jerks and dashes that caused the white satin ribbons to flutter at the shoulders of his long crimson-lake cloak. Rock Cholmondeley, as svelte as a fishing-rod and a-glitter with medals upon gold and silver embroidery, a Pelion-on-Ossa effect, appeared holding the Crown. This precious symbol was placed on a cushion so close to where Lynn and I were sitting that, without leaning forward, it would have been possible to touch the Koh-i-noor and the acorns made of pear-shaped pearls in their husks of diamond. Lord Alexander, with his eyebrows and long cloak properly adjusted, came in with a perhaps too dramatic, dedicated expression on his face, holding the Sword of State.

Princess Margaret appeared with her aunt, the Princess Royal, with the white-skinned Duchess of Gloucester in black velvet at her side. The Princess, her eyes bright and inquisitive, looked from side to side as she walked forward with rolling gait and head slightly thrust forward, and her kid-gloved arms held with prominent elbows. The Princess Royal, without make-up of any kind, her face and lips equally white, with her crown of diamonds lodged in a hard, wiry coiffure of curls like a lawyer's wig, was of the right scale: her dignity innate.

Indoors all quiet until suddenly, outside the high windows, various rumbling noises told one that the Queen was arriving. The cheers of the people sent a tremor through the bloodstream. One expected, but did not hear, an organ to roll out a volume of noise. It was the continued insistent silence that made all the more impressive the moment when the tall double doors were thrown open to reveal the young Queen standing with her gloved hand held high on that of her Consort. A moment's pause, then in a slow, ambling march the procession passed towards the Throne where the young lady would make her first speech to Parliament.

The Queen wore gold and stolid white. The long red velvet train, miniver-edged, splendid against the gold and scarlet setting, her stance, with the rigid little head and the well-curled hair around Queen Victoria's Crown, was marvellously erect. She has inherited many of her mother's graces, but, most important of all, she has acquired her frank serenity: her eyes are not those of a busy, harassed person. She regards people with a recognition of compassion – and a slight suggestion of a smile lightens the otherwise cumbrous mouth.

There was nothing formidable about the general mood, which encouraged an ease and sense of relaxation in the spectators, and the procession moved so slowly that one felt tempted to talk to those passing by. The Duke of Edin-burgh appeared somewhat hollow-eyed, his complexion pale, and hair beginning to thin.

The Queen Mother's Mistress of the Robes, the Duchess of Northumberland, gigantically tall with wonderful jewels, wore a Knightsbridge horror of a dress, a crinoline of coarse, Parma violet nylon-tulle with self-same sausages, that was so daring in its bad taste that the effect was wonderful. The two Women of the Bedchamber in oyster satin were not looking their best in this cold, unbecoming light of winter.

When the procession moved out of sight, one could only imagine the ritual when Black Rod, with the ebony hand at the end of his wand, shouts: 'Open, open!' to allow the doors of the Chamber to give entrance to the Queen.

From where will Clarissa be watching her husband, the Prime Minister? And Mrs Churchill?

Then we hear the relayed voice of the Queen, in high, childlike tones, thanking the Lords and the Members of the House of Commons for their sympathy expressed on her Sovereign father's death. She hopes to follow her father's example, being sure that Her People would accord her the same loyalty and understanding. In the year to come she hopes to visit some of Her Colonial Empire, prays for an early armistice in Korea, promises that Her Government would take full share in the work of NATO, aims to strengthen the unity of Europe, and considers the scheme for Federation in Central Africa. The task of placing the national economy on a sound foundation, curbing inflation and reducing expenditure, must also be undertaken, while every encouragement shall be given to the fishing industry. She prays that the blessing of the Almighty may rest upon Her Government's Councils.

Then, no doubt greatly relieved that her vocal ordeal is at an end, she smiles with added sweetness as the procession returns. Smiles to left and right, and the sea of spectators billows down in curtsies and bows. The Queen and her Duke are through the double doors from whence they came; the doors are shut.

A moment's pause. Two tall officers of venerable age appraise the Crown, once more reposing on its cushion within a few inches of my grasp. They speak to one another with an offhand perfection of manners. There is a bond, or link or understanding, that goes much deeper than mere *politesse*. None of these people are looking for slights, for grudges, neither are they surprised or impressed. They live on terms with each other, and do not need the framework of formality that is part of social exchange in other echelons. These people do not need to meet each other at given times at lunch or dinner in answer to an invitation. They come across one another casually in the course of duty or pleasure – in their study, corridor, palace or club. They go about their jobs with ease, knowing their like are not jockeying for position or trying a little knifing in backs. This is the reason for the prevailing mood of generosity. One of the officers of venerable age says casually to the other: 'I'll look after it now, and when the Queen leaves, you can come back and fetch it.' 'It' is the jewelled Crown of State.

The Queen is now bidding goodbye to the Lord Chancellor, to Lord Alexander of the super-arched eyebrows, to vellumy Bobbety Salisbury, to ramrod Rock. Broad smiles; it is now all very gay. The Duke of Edinburgh makes some jolly jokes. The Queen departs. A clash of steel, horses' hooves, and again the distant thundering of cheers from the people lining the streets.

The old fur coats are helped on to shoulders of skinny peeresses. Some wrap their trains round their goosefleshed arms, and the party breaks up. The wives of Labour peers are now dressed to go rat-catching. Lynn Fontanne says: 'Isn't it lovely to be in a crowd that doesn't push!' Rock Cholmondeley, already changed into stovepipe trousers, black overcoat and white scarf (no doubt to hide the fact that he had no collar on), has a broad grin on his face. He is delightedly congratulating the police and the Boy Scouts on the smooth running order, and receiving from his guests the compliments that are deserved.

London was in its usual blue haze; the bare plane trees dripping with tassels like Victorian bobble fringe. Big Ben struck twelve, military orders were shouted in rasping, retching voices, guards sloped arms, a brass band brayed, the crowds jumped on their toes, nannies ran with their charges to follow the bobbing sea of bearskins, and the ordinary flow of traffic, so severely inconvenienced, again began to move. Already the newspaper men were selling the earliest editions with their posters, 'The Queen's Speech', and the photograph of the Monarch in her coach, laughing and jerking her hand at the crowds. The flashlight had caught the brilliance of the Queen's laugh, the glitter and the movement of the coach exemplified by the pear-shaped pearl swinging at her ear. This radiant photograph, much admired by Winston Churchill, had the greatest and most deserved fame; a bulls-eye of journalistic photography.

New York

My first taxi drive from the hotel after my arrival took me to the Lunts for tea. Alfred Lunt and Lynn Fontanne, at the height of their stage glory, were among my first professional photograph 'sitters' when first I came to New York in the early thirties. Lynn later said that they wanted to like me, but they had such difficulty in getting through my shyness. However, they succeeded, and when each winter I arrived in New York, no matter how busy they were, they always managed to give me ham and eggs while we sat through the night exchanging confidences. I did some drawings of Lynn, and she always urged me to discontinue my photography in order to devote my time entirely to painting. But it was as a stage designer that I really wanted to work, and although we talked of one day 'doing a play together', the opportunity did not arise.

I had unexpectedly received a cable to the boat saying: 'Terribly excited your arrival,' and the moment I came into my hotel room the baggage boy answered the telephone and Lynn was piping a request for me to go round immediately.

At their East Riverside house, Alfred and Lynn both appeared in bubbling spirits. 'What are your plans? Are you very busy?' they asked. 'What do you think would be a pretty period to design a play for? Do you like bustles?' I said I liked all periods of costume. 'But why do you ask? Have you any play in mind?' I inquired. 'No,' said Lynn, 'but I feel that something might drop out of the blue.' She just had the right feeling – something was in the air – she felt it in her bones. I left a bit baffled, but we had made a date to see one another again in a few days' time.

Meanwhile, on the next boat from England Noël Coward arrived. Word soon got around that, straight from the docks, he went to read his new play, *Quadrille*, to the Lunts and that they were enchanted with it. I was most impatient to hear the next move. Would I be asked to design for it?

At last the offer came. The play, set in the year 1866, was sent to me, I loved it, and from that moment on there was nothing but smiles all round. I have never known a production go forward so smoothly, with so few setbacks. Polaire Weissman, Head of the Costume Department of the Metropolitan Museum, showed me all her authentic clothes of the period, and lent Lynn corsets and bodices. Alfred was enthusiastic about the men's beards, tall bowler hats and travelling cloaks. On the boat back to England, Lynn, Alfred and I had long talks in their cabin about the forthcoming production.

London

At a meeting at Noël's house in Ebury Street I showed the finished designs for sets: the scene builder held no objections. Binkie Beaumont, the manager, seemed quietly satisfied. Noël was delighted. Lynn, without any reservations, was thrilled by her clothes. Alfred was also happy.

In spite of an early start, once more, as with every theatrical production, we were 'up against time'. Rehearsals started. I had hoped to have Lynn's dresses ready before then, but due to the aftermath of war difficulties we had trouble in getting certain stuffs. A particular candy stripe was needed, but it was 'out of stock'. Binkie would not have it painted: not practical – it would not clean. At last some firm was willing to weave the material. Two weeks later the loom broke down, so the dress had to be hand-painted at the eleventh hour. When the costume was at last finished, Noël came to me in trepidation: 'I'm afraid we don t like it.' 'Neither do I', was my – to him – surprising reply. 'Let's give it to Marian Spencer.' We did, and it suited. In other ways the production went forward ominously smoothly.

I would have liked to spend more time watching the way the Lunts create their stage characters, but there was too much else to do. At the end of one long day's rehearsal Lynn and I went home in a taxi. She put her feet up and laughed: 'Why do we do this – all in the name of fun? It's never fun. It's damned hard work, and we'll fight a lot; but it's interesting and exciting, and if we win through, it will all have been worth while.'

When, at last, we arrived in Manchester for the trial run, the atmosphere was so electric that one felt there must be an explosion any minute. Alfred wanted me in his dressing-room. He felt lonely, he said: he was strung up. But I was too busy to sit and talk. There were calls from every direction. Bessie, Lynn's dresser, tapped on Alfred's door: 'Miss Fontanne would like to see Mr Beaton a moment.'

'Darling, what about my wedding ring? Will you choose one because I can't wear this: it's so thin and modern. And what about Alfred's ring?'

Then: 'Could Mr Beaton see Mr Lunt a moment?'

'Cecil, this tie – it's a bit puny, isn't it? And how about this watch-chain?'

Again Bessie: 'Mr Beaton, Miss Fontanne.'

'Darling, I wondered what you meant about my eyebrows being thicker?'

Back to Alfred.

Watching the play unfold for the first time before an audience was a revelation. Noël is nothing if not a craftsman, and he knew just how to make his play come alive. Many of the laughs came as a pleasant surprise. Whereas, in the dressing-room, Lynn had looked adorable in her Empress Eugenie bonnet and bustles, now on stage she had assumed consummate beauty. She has the dignity of the true artist. Alfred is that rare thing – a genius of the theatre.

Throughout the provincial tour the Lunts continued to develop aspects of their roles as well as perfecting the production as a whole. After three weeks on the road it was quite extraordinary to note the difference in the playing.

The performances acquired tremendous pace; Lynn and Alfred managed to discover many more varieties of mood. Before, the effect of the play had been brittle and crisp; now a deeper emotion had crept in to certain scenes that made them extra poignant and touching. If the play were to run for two years, I knew that Alfred and Lynn would continue making inventions and minuscule improvements right up till the last performance.

Before catching a train to go back to London, I went in to pay my respects to the Lunts. They were making towards the stage, preparatory to their entrances. Alfred turned back and said: 'What a risk you took with the sets, and wouldn't it have been awful if they hadn't worked! Aren't you glad this all turned out so marvellously well?' And Lynn, kissing me, said: 'Thank you for your dear patience.'

Spring 1953

I realize I am exaggerating when I write the following, but there is more than an element of truth when I say that I did not realize how life can be ruthless, even to queens. We all know what happened to Henry's six wives, and certainly today we have become a bit more civilized; but still human nature can be pretty base. Through a sad break of fortune Queen Elizabeth loses her husband at an early age, and from that very moment her position in life is changed completely. Although she is undoubtedly treated with great love, consideration and sympathy by her daughter who is now reigning monarch and living at Windsor Castle, nevertheless, no doubt unknown to the present Queen, her mother is suddenly given quite casual treatment by many at Buckingham Palace.

The Queen Mother is being taken care of by a 'skeleton staff', and when I went to take the first photographs since her widowhood, the lady-in-waiting confided that they were 'picnicking' here, and that a palace was a very uncomfortable place in which to picnic. Some of the rather higher-up Palace servants let it be known to my assistants that they 'couldn't think why the Queen Mother stayed on here so long – not that she will relish the move to Clarence House for there won't be the number of servants there that she's accustomed to'.

When I passed by the Queen Mother's old rooms there was a strong whiff of decorator's paint, and I saw that the walls were bare and the furniture taken away. Electricians whistled as they walked down the Picture Gallery. The rooms in which we were to photograph were so cold that, even though it is said that the Queen Mother, after her healthy Scottish upbringing, is impervious to the elements, I felt that this below-freezing temperature was beyond a joke. I asked for a vase of flowers to use in my photographs. The lady-in-waiting returned later saying that there was not one in the whole palace.

The 'sitting' augured badly. Nothing went right. A camera shutter was jammed, my feet were leaden. The dark-red curtains I had brought for my background would not, when draped, assume any grace or vitality of form, and what there was of daylight came through the windows with an ugly winter-rawness.

Our preparations were not finished before the Queen Mother's arrival was announced. Her smile and warmth of sympathy made it seem as if the sun had come out. She manages to disperse anxiety and care, even makes it seem impossible that people should ever behave badly, or that things could go wrong.

Of course there is something of the great actress about her, and in public she has to put on a show which never fails, but it is her heart and imagination which guide her. She will always say just the one thing that puts people at ease and make them feel a glow of happiness, because she understands and appreciates the reality of any situation – whether it be tragic or gay.

The photograph session lasted just the right amount of time. When it was over the Queen Mother remarked on the speed at which I operated, and how all her family always enjoyed being photographed by me. This gave me the pat opportunity to ask if I might be allowed to take some pictures of the new Queen.

'Oh yes, I must speak to her. I would like that so much. She's looking particularly well just now. She has such a lovely quality of youthfulness. Yes, she has youth on her side, and an extraordinary calmness and serenity which will come in very useful in the years ahead.'

On my way home I stopped at my favourite florist. For once I would be as extravagant as I wished. I took enormous care to choose a bouquet of all the first spring flowers to be sent to that adorable human being living in that cold, bleak Palace.

May

Have been wondering if my day as photographer at the Palace is over. Baron, a most unexpected friend of Prince Philip's, has been taking all the recent pictures, so the call saying the Queen wanted me to do her personal Coronation photographs comes as an enormous relief. Another lease of life extended to me in my photographic career. 'Would you please not tell anyone about it yet as, when the news gets out, so many people will ring up to know why they aren't being asked, and the Queen wants you.'

The same night that this message was relayed to me, at a ball at the American Embassy, I saw the Queen for a brief moment and thanked her. 'No, I'm very glad you're going to take them,' she said, 'but, by the time we get through to the photographs, we'll have circles down to here' (she pointed halfway down her cheeks), 'then the Crown comes down to here' (to the eye), 'then the court train comes bundling up here, and I'm out to here' (sticks stomach out). 'There are layers upon layers: skirt and mantles and trains.' She spoke like a young, high-spirited girl.

I also had a short opportunity to thank the Queen Mother for what I am sure must have been her help in bringing about this 'coup' for me. She laughed knowingly with one finger high in the air.

Coronation rehearsal: 31 May

I have not yet learnt to ignore worry – to say 'it may never happen'. An almost continual feeling is with me that things may go wrong. The knowledge that much of my suffering is of my own self-making does not mitigate the pain. Others have the knack of only doing the things they want to – and evade unpleasant responsibilities. Why do I take on jobs that are often fearfully alarming to me?

Why must I so often have to wake soon after dawn to take an aeroplane to foreign parts when, as a result of the Dakota crash in which I miraculously escaped during the war, I am still terrified of the air? These thoughts, strangely enough, come to the surface at my being bidden to the Press Gallery for the dress rehearsal of the Coronation ceremony. This is a coveted invitation, and I should feel grateful that the intention is to make my job of sending in drawings and articles subsequently, as well as taking photographs, easier, by having a previous glimpse of the scene in the Abbey. Instead I am suffering from another attack of anxiety. No doubt my imbalance of mind is due to too much stress and activity at home. I have to cope without any help as Maud Nelson, my secretary, is always away ill. No doubt Maud worries that she is not capable of coping with all my affairs and this nervous stress brings on another bout of asthma. Yet she will not allow anyone in to help her. It is being a difficult time for me.

My taxi drove up at the wrong entrance of the Abbey. Instead of, as I expected, hurling abuse at me for my stupidity, the policeman opening my cab door smiled tolerantly and said: 'All right – you can get out here. It's only a short walk along to "J".' At 'J' I was directed to pass through an awninged passage of new canvas, pungent and peculiar-smelling, at the end of which a figure in a cocked hat and black velvet knee-breeches gave a superior look at the sketchpads and inks I was carrying, then with a grave and silent nod allowed me to pass. I went on down a passage, up one or two steps, then turned sharply into a pitch-black cavern. It was a Kafkaesque experience. I stumbled and groped: in the darkness I felt dreadfully alone. There was an inevitability, a finality, about what I must do: no turning back now. Soon all the things I feared would start happening to me. Probably even the scaffold?

I must admit that my dogged determination to continue is often rewarded – as it was at this time. I lurched on without anything appalling happening to me, until suddenly I was in lightness and two Goldsticks were kind to me. I'd never, in fact, encountered such beautiful manners before. It was as if I'd attained the Heavenly Kingdom when after an old colonel had taken my ticket, brought it to within an inch of his left eye, smelt it, then barked 'Wheel right,' I found myself in the triforium. Soon the rehearsal for the Coronation started . . .

After two days' quiet respite in the country cosseting my nervous system, I drove back to London on Sunday night. In the boot of the car were several baskets containing the roses and clematis that I had picked for the Queen's photographs. I had the idea of making some pictures in the Winterhalter manner, with real country flowers on a side-table instead of the usual palace display of hydrangeas and gladioli. As we neared London the same unflattering photographs of the Queen decorated every shop and public building. I felt I must do better than these, and remembered reading how Carlyle had become so sick of the face of Queen Victoria plastered all over the city at the time of her Coronation that he left London. Soon I began to feel again highly strung and tense at the thought of the intense effort soon to be made. For not only must I write two articles on the ceremony – one to be telephoned in cable-ese for Australia – and do illustrations, but the photographic side not only comprised taking pictures of the Queen in her Crown and robes, surrounded by her entourage, but the Press representative of the Palace, Richard Colville, had compiled a list of each group of the Royal Family with their attendants to be taken together and individually.

I have found that when any Royal sitting is involved there are more arrangements involving telephone calls than one could have believed possible, and so many contingencies to cope with, that one might be organizing a vast crowd scene for an early Cecil B. de Mille moving picture. But in the movies there are trained technical crews of electricians and technicians, wardrobe assistants, and numberless people to call upon. Never having, by preference, had a studio with full-time assistants of my own, I found myself at this particular time in a predicament. However, Pat Matthews, a good friend from *Vogue*, volunteered to come along and organize a technical staff.

The day before the Coronation we started to set up special backgrounds at the Palace, the electricians having spent the morning preparing the light cables. When I arrived early in the afternoon to make final arrangements, and went unescorted down a long labyrinth of unfamiliar corridors, to the Green Drawing Room, I could hear that I was getting nearer to a hubbub of voices. I saw some fur stoles and ladies' handbags lying on gilt chairs. Knowing how many visiting Royalties were in the Palace I guessed that some sort of lunch party must be in progress.

Not until I came face to face with myself carrying a huge blanket bundle of garden roses and clematis in front of a pair of mirror-doors at the end of the Picture Gallery, and peered through a small crack, did I realize that I was about to intrude into an enormous luncheon for the Commonwealth Prime Ministers. Luckily I did stop for, if I had proceeded further, it would have been to run smack in front of the Queen with a dozen distinguished old men lined up in military formation each side of her, to be fired at by *The Times* photographer. I pried at the proceedings. Jolly jokes were made. The photographer asked: 'Another one, please?' as he let off a flash. 'Another one,' repeated the Queen in her high, fluting voice. Giggles, laughter: the Queen quite obviously elated at being the delightful, gay and attractive cynosure of all. She wore a pale, dove-fawn coloured dress, with handbag to match, and her hair curled like a child's for a Christmas party. The excitement, nourished by the newspapers, mounting every day, has obviously affected her spirits and she seemed to be in an exultant mood with a blush of triumph in her cheeks. She has, about her, a certain humility and slow shyness but, at the same time, innate dignity, and one senses a quality of kindness. The Queen is really the one person of whom we cannot say that she has the fashionable inferiority complex.

The dark-skinned men in the group stood stiffly to attention: a hoarse shout was raised when the flashlight went off, and the group then dispersed to the Music Room where a large concourse was smoking cigarettes and cigars: Churchill standing and glowering with his legs apart; the Duchess of Devonshire with head earnestly thrust forward; Princess Margaret, intent with sharp head movements, Hanover-turquoise eyes and cigarette-smoke-exhaling nostrils.

In the Green Drawing Room step-ladders stretched half-way up to the gilded ceilings, but my backgrounds still lay unrolled in a corner; with much anxiety I noticed that the electricians and other assistants had made little headway. Their jobs were of a highly technical nature, and I found myself useless and unwanted, with nothing to do but continue to take a furtive glimpse of the Commonwealth party scenes from behind a huge set-piece of splayed flowers that Constance Spry must have created for the occasion. The Palace was *'en grande tenue'* and a great mass of hydrangeas, rubber plants and sweet peas gave a 'special occasion' look to the huge, gilded, often dead-looking rooms. Enjoying a 'Bisto Kid's' view of grand life, I was amused to notice how conventional in pattern, and formal in behaviour, all human beings appear when enjoying enforced entertainment. Artificial smiles that are real, heads cocked, jokes that suffice. The Duke of Edinburgh, never far from his uncle Dickie Mountbatten, with his eyes screwed up in intensity, conversed with Indians whose clipped, bird-like pleasantries brought back vividly my days in Government House in Bombay during the war.

I was surprised when Martin Charteris, the Queen's Private Secretary, spied me and came across, saying: 'Oh good, you're here! Now I can give you the information about dinner tomorrow at our house. We're going to be about thirty. Arthur Koestler is our star, and later we're going to roll up the carpet and dance to the gramophone.' He is the most delightfully casual, efficient and unimpressed of courtiers.

The afternoon continued and still the setting-up of lights and cameras seemed to make no progress. The electricians, after they had knocked off for a break, had been forced to wait for two hours before they were allowed upstairs again. (I suppose for fear of running into the Commonwealth Prime Ministers.) Now all hands must work desperately hard to get electric cables running with juice, and backgrounds and curtains and various 'blow-ups' in place.

On the way home, I noticed that the wind and gusts of rain had dispersed the summer crowds who, hoping for some preview glimpse of the Queen, had been sheltering all day in the improvised stands. How cruel if such wintry weather were to continue tomorrow! My stage fright at the thought of my responsibility tomorrow returned with renewed force, and at dinner I drank more than I should. Early to bed, I slept fitfully, and when I was called before five o'clock I was suffering from a hangover and my vitality count was low.

Coronation Day

The birds had started to sing and the sky was pale grey; already a few electric lights were on in the bedrooms of the houses opposite. An angry wind blew the branches of the cherry tree in the next door garden, and despite the heavy sheets of rain people were already going off cheerfully and hurriedly to take their places in the crowds. I watched a genteel woman, with her husband and small child, scurrying off, complete with umbrellas, macintoshes and sandwiches; they were utterly respectable and charming, and a complete, happy little unit. I felt a great lump in my throat: I don't know why they were so poignant.

With passes, journalists' Press permits, cards and instructions clutched tightly, and with sticker on the hired car, and my grey topper filled with sandwiches, indian ink and gadgets for my drawings, I was off on my way.

Remarkably smooth traffic regulations. Already at this early hour motors were bumper to bumper in front: it was fun to peer at the old men, bad-tempered and sleepy at this hour, in cockaded hats with lace jabots, their womenfolk having had, before dawn, a hairdresser to their houses to set their coiffures.

Goldsticks stationed around the cloisters showed us on our way. They were already frozen blue. One of them asked me if I had heard the good news that Hunt had climbed Everest. The iced wind blew in circles round the winding staircase that took me to the rafters, and I felt much sympathy for Hunt. My allotted seat was just near the pipes of the great organ. It was by no means an easy place from which to make drawings: only by peering somewhat precariously over the edge of the balcony could the activities below be seen.

But I discovered that, without disturbing my fellow journalists, it was possible to move about fairly freely, and a vantage point from my rook's nest was discovered from which I could not only see the arrivals coming down the nave, but much of the activity in front of the high altar.

Feeling nervous, cold, and rather sick, I buoyed myself up by eating barley sugar and chatting to nice Christopher Hussey of *Country Life*.

One has seen many woodcuts, and pictures of all sorts, of the earliest Kings and Queens being crowned; particularly detailed are the prints of the first Queen Elizabeth's procession. In all periods, painters have had a shot at recording the ceremony; with the improvements in the technique of photography the scene has become almost familiar. Yet this spectacle today transcended all preconceived notions. The ceremonial seemed to be as fresh and inspiring as some great play or musical event that was being enacted upon a spontaneous impulse of genius. Perhaps it was the background of lofty vaulted stone – like a silver forest – that made everything seem so particularly surprising.

The words of the service struck one's ears with an impact that had the pure audacity of a poem by Rimbaud. The music sounded pristine.

The colours red, gold and smoke-blue always beguiled one's eye by the unexpected. The brilliant gold carpet was the perfect floor-covering for the slippered feet of the pages, the train-bearers, and the scarlet, blue and gold-clad heralds, for the bishops and clergy in white and gold. Black Rod made way for a messenger; a mote of light caught a gold sequin fallen on the carpet, or a jewel in a bishop's ring; the sun came out and lit up a posse of scarlet uniformed Goldsticks. It was all living and new: it was history, but of today and of the future. It was something that is pulsating and vital to us, and an essential part of the life we believe in.

The guests presented great contrasts in their national and traditional garments. The peeresses *en bloc* the most ravishing sight – like a bed of auricula-eyed sweet william – in their dark red velvet and foam-white, dew-spangled with diamonds. Lady Haddington and the Duchess of Buccleuch in huge diamond 'fenders' were particularly outstanding; but, most beautiful of all, was young Debo Devonshire, sister of Nancy Mitford, with her hair dressed wide to contain the Edwardian cake-like crown, in Georgiana, Duchess of Devonshire's eighteenth-century robes, quite different in cut with the straight line from shoulder to shoulder.

Willie Walton's *Orb And Sceptre* blazes out on the organ as the other Royalties arrive and the procession begins: the minor Royalties, and the foreign Royalties and Representatives of States. Norway, Greece, Nepal, Japan, Ethiopia, Morocco, Thailand, Peru; the Sultans under Her Majesty's protection;

Queen Salote of Tonga, a great big, warm personality. Is Russia here? Then the Princes and Princesses of the royal blood: the mother of the Duke of Edinburgh, a contrast to the grandeur, in the ash-grey draperies of a nun. The manipulation of the long velvet trains is in some cases too under-rehearsed: Princess Marie Louise, agonizingly old, but still athletic, is obviously very angry with her fatuous lady-in-waiting for making such a balls-up with her train. The Gloucester boys, too, give their mother a moment or two of anxiety as they tug and mishandle her train. Likewise the attendant of Princess Alexandra is at fault; for that matter, so is the Princess's dressmaker, for he has made a confection that is far too fluffy and unimportant for the occasion. Her mother, the Duchess of Kent, has the dignity of a carved wooden effigy. The Mistress of the Robes to the Queen Mother, of towering height, is minimized by the enormous presence and radiance of the petite Queen Mother. Yet in the Queen Widow's expression we read sadness combined with pride.

A posse of church dignitaries portends the Queen's procession followed by the Knights of the Garter and the Standard Bearers. After them the Prime Ministers of the Commonwealth and the Lord High Chancellor. The dour old Scot, Canning, with his lean face, exposed skull and dark crimson cope, does not intend to play second fiddle to anyone; yet, quietly and legitimately, the Archbishop of Canterbury overshadows him with consummate tact. That great old relic, Winston Churchill, lurches forward on unsteady feet, a fluttering mass of white ribbons at his shoulder and white feathers in the hat in his hand; Mrs Churchill, close by, grimaces a recognition as Montgomery and his page, Winston Junior, pass her by.

Then, most dramatic and spectacular, at the head of her retinue of white, lily-like ladies, the Queen. Her cheeks are sugar pink: her hair tightly curled around the Victorian diadem of precious stones perched straight on her brow. Her pink hands are folded meekly on the elaborate grandeur of her encrusted skirt; she is still a young girl with a demeanour of simplicity and humility. Perhaps her mother has taught her never to use a superfluous gesture. As she walks she allows her heavy skirt to swing backwards and forwards in a beautiful rhythmic effect. This girlish figure has enormous dignity; she belongs in this scene of almost Byzantine magnificence.

She moves to the Chair of State. Then the Archbishops and Bishops, having placed the Bible, Chalice and the Regalia on the altar, come to present the young Queen for recognition to the east. '*Vivat! Vivat!*' shout, surprisingly, the boys from Westminster School: trumpets sound to split the roofs and shatter the heart. Then, likewise, the Queen faces her people to the south, west and north. '*Vivat! Vivat! Vivat!*' and each time the trumpets blow the recognition as the solitary figure bows humbly at each shattering volley.

The Queen takes the Coronation Oath, kisses the Bible, and, after the Creed and the Communion Service, the Archbishop says the Prayer of Consecration. The choir begins the marvellous anthem 'Zadok the Priest' during which the Queen is divested of her crimson robes, her Diadem and Collar of the Garter, and, in preparation for the Anointing, puts on a simple white shift. Four Knights of the Garter hold a canopy of cloth of gold under which the Archbishop anoints the Queen with holy oil in the form of a cross. Then the presentation of the Spurs, Sword and the Orb, and, on the Queen's fourth finger of the right hand, the Ring. The Queen's hands are those of an artist, a ballerina, a sculptor or surgeon. When the Sword has been presented, then offered to the altar, Lord Salisbury redeems it for a bag containing one hundred silver shillings, and thenceforth holds it naked and erect.

The crowning is superbly dramatic: the expression on the small face of the Queen is one of intense expectancy until, with magnificent assurance, the Archbishop thrusts down with speed and force the Crown on the neat head. At this moment the hoarse shouts of 'God Save the Queen' break out. The peers put on their coronets and caps of State, and the peeresses, with long, gloved arms looking like wishbones, hold up their coronets. A fanfare of trumpets, a blaze of violins, an eruption from the big organ, and the guns are shot off from the Tower down the river. This is a great moment, immediately to be followed by the enthroning and glorification of the new monarch. While anthems are sung, homage is paid by a strange concourse of old and young alike. As a simple communicant rather than as Queen of England, she kneels to take the holy wine and bread. Thence she goes to St Edmund's Chapel where, divested of the garments delivered to her during the solemnities, she is arrayed in the robe of purple velvet.

Long delays, pauses and waits, but always something occupies one's attention. A new arrival of uniformed dignitaries. A procession forms, and Mr Winston Churchill comes from his pew to line up for the final exodus. He turns on his heels to admire the peeresses. 'Yes – a very fine bunch of women, a most magnificent sight,' he seems to be saying as he gives them his appraisal. He turns back to see if things are ready. No. Again he turned towards these wonderful women. Also waiting to take their allotted place are the great figures of the war, Lords Alanbrooke, Halifax and Portal.

There is an unfortunate hold-up when the Queen Mother is about to proceed from the Abbey. Someone has mistakenly allowed minor members of the clergy to go before her; a herald is sent to inform her of what has happened. She smiles patiently as she waits.

Rain had fallen solidly throughout most of the ceremony. Uniforms were soaked, horses champing; the Golden Coach was now waiting in Dean's Yard in a downpour. The men in cockaded hats and livery were making little effort to keep out of the rain. I made my getaway before the traffic started.

Back home, I found my mother listening to the radio announcer's banal, genteel, rich-fruit-cake voice: 'On this, this great day ...' I rushed upstairs, took a fistful of aspirins, then off with my clothes and I was able to sleep for nearly an hour before dashing again to the Palace for the photographs.

I awoke minus my headache and much relaxed. Again managing to avoid the crowds, within a comparatively short while I found myself at the trades-men's entrance of the Palace, to be shown up to our now almost familiar haven in the Green Drawing Room. My sister, Baba, who in the inevitable absence of Maud, my secretary, had kindly offered to help arrange the trains, presented a miserable spectacle, chattering with cold and rain-soaked. Thank God the others – the electricians and assistants – had also contrived to be here. Pat Matthews was calm and reassuring. From the balcony of the inner court-yard we watched the return of the carriages. Baba was proud that David Smiley, our brother-in-law's brother, was the Field Officer commanding the Escort.

Every window framed the faces of Palace servants, and a group of them raised a tremendous cheer as the Queen Mother came back, waving and smiling as fresh as a field flower. Then, to the sound of distant roars, drawn by eight grey horses the bronze gold State Coach, with its Cipriani paintings and dark-strawberry padded silk, bowled through the central arch and back to home. The Queen looked back over her shoulder and appeared somewhat dazed and exhausted.

Not long after, girlish voices were heard at the end of the Picture Gallery. 'Oh hullo! Did you watch it? When did you get home?' From the mirror-doors of the Green Drawing Room I spied the Queen with her ladies, her excited children; the family asking questions, jokes, smiles, laughter, the high-pitched voices of the Queen and Princess Margaret heard above the others. The Duchess of Gloucester was leaning forward from the hips with almost perilous intent. The Duke of Norfolk, his duties successfully carried out, lolled behind one of the mirrored-glass doors. George Bellew, Garter King-at-Arms, leant against the brocade walls. The fair, good-looking Duke of Hamilton beamed.

It was now time for the Queen to be on her way to the Throne Room to be photographed by *The Times* – then she would come to me. I started taking family groups. The Queen Mother, dimpled and chuckling, with eyes as bright as any of her jewels, and her younger daughter, with pink and white make-up and a sex twinkle of understanding in her regard, was now sailing towards me, her purple train being held aloft by her four pages; Prince Charles and Princess Anne, who were running around to try and get a hold of it, eventually had recourse to climbing under the purple velvet. No time to lose! Please turn this way, now that; a certain shape was formed, a picture came to life. Quick,

quick! All sorts of Royalties popped their heads in on me: Prince Bernhard; then the Duke of Edinburgh put his face through a door. 'But you must come! You're keeping the whole group waiting!' Exit Princess Margaret and the Queen Mother. Through the mirrored doors I watched the guests in the long Picture Gallery.

Then the return of the Queen Mother in rollicking spirits, and slow voice asking: 'Do you really want to take a few more?' Suddenly I felt as if all my anxieties and fears were dispelled. The Queen Mother, by being so basically human and understanding, gives out to us a feeling of reassurance. The great mother figure and nannie to us all, through the warmth of her sympathy bathes us and wraps us in a counterpane by the fireside. Suddenly I had this wonderful accomplice – someone who would help me through everything. All at once, and because of her, I was enjoying my work. Prince Charles and Princess Anne were buzzing about in the wildest excitement and would not keep still for a moment. The Queen Mother anchored them in her arms, put her head down to kiss Prince Charles's hair, and made a terrific picture. Then, ashen-faced and like the wicked uncle in a pantomime, Richard Colville, who deals so sternly with all of us who are in any way connected with the press, appeared prematurely and, as if to sound my death-knell, informed me: 'The Queen has already been kept waiting. You must take the Queen now!'

In came the Queen, with her ladies, cool, smiling, sovereign of the situation. I asked her to stand against my 'blow-up' Abbey background. The lighting was not at all as I would have wished, but no time for readjustment: every second of importance. Yes, I was banging away and getting pictures at a great rate; but I had only the foggiest notion of whether I was taking black and white, or colour, or giving the right exposures. The Queen looked extremely minute under her robes and Crown, her nose and hands chilled and her eyes tired. 'Yes,' in reply to my question, 'the Crown does get rather heavy.' She had been wearing it now for nearly three hours.

The Duke of Edinburgh stood by making wry jokes, his lips pursed in a smile that put the fear of God into me. I believe he doesn't like or approve of me. This is a pity because, although I'm not one for 'Navy type' jokes, and obviously have nothing in common with him, I admire him enormously, and think he is absolutely first-rate at his job of making things comparatively lively and putting people at their ease. Perhaps he was disappointed that his friend, Baron, was not doing this job today; whatever the reason he was definitely adopting a rather ragging attitude towards the proceedings. However, I tried in the few seconds at my disposal (like a vaudeville comedian establishing contact with his audience) to keep the situation light and full of movement so that no one could adopt any definite attitude: like a juggler I moved the groups about. Photographs of the Duke alone; he looked extremely handsome. Once

I replied in a cursory manner to the Queen's: 'What shall we do now?' 'Will you go into the corner?' 'Go into the corner?' She looked at me with wide eyes and a wide smile. No time for explanation.

Now to the other side of the room: The Queen and her Maids of Honour. Quickly, quickly, because this was just about the end.

'You must be tired, ma'am.'

'Yes, but this is the last thing we have to do.'

While the entire family retired to watch the 'fly past' of the RAF from the balcony (which we watched, too, from the inner balcony), Baba and my assistants toasted the Queen from a glass of champagne from which the monarch had only taken one sip.

A panic-stricken page came in: 'Where are the Orb and Sceptre?' They had been left here on a cushion.

Other groups then appeared. Princess Marina, romantically beautiful and remarkably distinguished but sad, and incapable of keeping her children in a vein of seriousness: they all joked and made staccato noises. It was difficult not to get exasperated with my delightful friends, but they, poor things, were at the end of a long, tiring, possibly unnerving day; they confessed their feet hurt.

It is hard enough to give instructions when taking large groups in circumstances like these, but when one is challenged, and asked for a reason why one's instinct has prodded one to say: 'Move over there,' then chaos ensues. The Gloucesters came in with the two boys pulling their mother's train in every direction. The Duke, in his crown, red and shining of complexion, looked like an Alice in Wonderland character.

'Will you stand on that step, sir?'

'But won't I look too tall?'

'Yes, sir, you're perfectly right. Won't you stand down there on that step?'

'Well, if the others are going to be there, won't I look too short?'

I then suggested that perhaps he might open his cape to let me see more of his uniform.

'I don't think I could do that.'

'No, sir?'

'Well, as a matter of fact, I've got the wrong ribbon [wibbon].'

'Which ribbon, sir?'

'This wibbon wight across here.' His eyes protruded and lips quivered.

But the Gloucesters were chivvied off quickly for the Queen was available again for a few more pictures to be taken, this time, sitting at a table on which were placed my by-now rather sad-looking 'Etoile d'Hollande' roses and the wilting Jackmanii clematis from Reddish.

Now that's all.

For better or worse I'd had my chance.

I felt somewhat dissatisfied; the sensation of achievement had escaped me all day long. Now I wondered if I had got any worthwhile pictures. Except with the Queen Mother and her grandchildren, I felt I'd never become airborne. The bulk of my pictures had been a smash and grab affair; I couldn't imagine they would be successful. Not only was I depressed, but rather alarmed. If the results weren't sensationally good, the press would attack me bitterly for having failed with such a fine opportunity. Yes – an unique opportunity had been afforded me. Had I misused the trust?

The rain poured. Still the crowds roared and the Queen reappeared on the balcony. Baba and I went home utterly whacked. But I had now to wire a description of the Abbey proceedings for syndication to Australia and Canada. Luckily I had written a considerable amount of local colour material beforehand; even so, the chore took me longer than expected, and the cables were late relaying through my accounts. No sooner were these sent off than Siriol Hugh Jones arrived with a shorthand-typist from *Vogue*. Siriol suggested an article was not necessary: that 'Notes from the Abbey' would be more spontaneous. I agreed with relief. When the 'Notes' were finished, we drank champagne and talked over the day's events with excitement. After midnight I went to the Massigli party at the French Embassy. I ate enormously: I drank a lot. At three o'clock in the morning I rang up the studio to hear that they were delighted with the colour pictures of the Queen; they thought I, too, would be pleased. I went to sleep relieved.

Early-morning visit to the studio to be surprised to find that so many of the pictures were excellent. A heavy morning's work selecting the best and getting them to the Palace; by midday a number of them were passed for publication. The rest of the week was a complicated nightmare trying to supply to the press the requisite number of pictures. Messengers were waiting in the various rooms of my mother's house for another messenger who never arrived. I talked myself hoarse on the telephone, and only by a fraction of a minute did I catch the Friday evening train to make my getaway to the retreat of the country. I bought an evening paper at Waterloo Station and one of my pictures of the Queen was printed across the front page of the *Evening News*.

23 July

Elizabeth Cavendish was to call by for me at ten minutes past eight, together to take the night train to Wales. At seven o'clock I awoke, strangely anxious, depressed and dazed from 'forty winks' of a most debilitating, even quite sinister kind. Why had I not the strength to attempt to snap out of my introspection by jumping into a taxi and going for half an hour to meet, for the first time, Audrey Hepburn? Anita Loos and several other friends have told me how delightful a creature this young actress is, and how full of talent. Recently she had been given the leading part in a film called *Roman Holiday* which, it is said, will put her at the top of her profession. The clock ticked on for fifteen minutes; still I hadn't made up my mind. How silly always to be in such a rush! Even if I *should* go, by the time I got there I'd have to leave. Better remain on the bed. Then, quite suddenly, I decided to go. In the cab I chafed at the traffic congestion that always follows a rainstorm in London on a summer evening.

I was the first to arrive at Miss Hepburn's flat in South Audley Street; I would be the first to leave. I talked to the mother, Baroness Heemstra, a lady with a rather charming rolling accent, who told me that her daughter was dressing, was always late. Wouldn't I have some hors-d'œuvre, a martini? The guests, like all film people on social occasions, were unconsciously late. Mel Ferrer arrived, a charming, gangling man resembling a coarser Peter Watson, who, no doubt as a result of his theatrical career, has developed a slightly professional charm of manner. He described A.H. to me as 'the biggest thing to come down the turnpike'.

At last the daughter appeared – a new type of beauty: huge mouth, flat Mongolian features, heavily painted eyes, a coconut coiffure, long nails without varnish, a wonderfully lithe figure, a long neck, but perhaps too scraggy. Today's stars are brought from a different strata of life. A.H.'s enormous potential cinema success, with attendant salary, seems to have made little impression on this delightful human being. She appears to take wholesale adulation with a pinch of salt: gratitude rather than puffed-up pride. Everything very simple about and around her: no maid to help her dress, or to answer the door to the guests who had now started a slow trickle into the room.

In a flash I discovered A.H. is chock-a-block with spritelike charm, and she has a sort of waifish, poignant sympathy. Without any of the preliminaries I felt that she cut through to a basic understanding that makes people friends. Nothing had to be explained: we liked one another. A chord had been struck and I knew that, next time we met, we would continue straight from here with no recapitulation of formalities. This was a unique occasion.

But the point of this brief précis is to try and explain that, after half an hour, I had become completely immersed in such a very different and new atmosphere that, when I returned home a short while later, I was feeling entirely differently about my life. The tempo had heightened again. My morbid mood had passed; I was pleased that I had made this onslaught into another world. How many suicides could be prevented by a change of scene!

A little while later Elizabeth and I were sitting in a sleeper compartment on our way to Bangor to stay for a large weekend party of interesting types. 'Here we are,' I remarked, 'at the outset of an experience. The slate is clear at the moment, but surely the portents are that something will happen, and something very positive, by the time we return home on Monday. Someone will have fallen in love or have had a row.' 'Yes,' said Elizabeth, 'that's what's so lovely.' Few people enjoy life as much as Elizabeth, who all the while is experimenting, and going off to meet it in its many varied forms.

We were going to stay with Michael Duff in his large, rambling, white house, Vaynol, in a large park of rhododendrons overlooking Snowdon. It had been the scene for such a number of greatly enjoyed house parties in the 'old days' before the war. There had always been the most stimulating assortment of people – some of whom would never have tolerated each other if they had not come under the spell of Michael's magic wand. He made everyone appear at their best: sympathetic, cosy, brilliant, or merely physically attractive. So many times I had stayed here for Christmas, and there had always been dressing-up, charades, wild dancing, exciting games taking place all over the house.

It was here that poor Gerald Berners, so late in life, had found his greatest love. It was here that Natalie Paley posed for my early photographs covered with the best roses from a sunny wall.

Michael's mother, Juliet, who lives within a few miles of me at Wilton, has with the years become an ever closer friend. But when first Juliet introduced me to her son, we looked at one another with mutual suspicion: in fact, one could say it was a question of hate at first sight. Mother and son talked together as if they were the most formal of strangers; I considered this more unnatural on the part of the son than of the parent. With his ramrod back and nape, his stiff manner and staccato stutter, Michael struck me as being the pompous ass I called him to his face as he spat back some equally unpleasant expletive at me.

But I learnt my mistake. Somehow, somewhere – I have forgotten the circumstances – Michael and I suddenly became real pals, and my friendship with him has brought me much joy, fun, and even a little more understanding of people.

Michael once told me of the first time he ever went abroad. As a boy in his teens, he arrived at Victoria Station, full of expectation for a marvellous excursion to Paris with his mother, whom he considered he saw only too rarely. But, to his dismay, he was greeted with derision. The sight of her twelve-year-old son was too much for Juliet, for Michael was wearing a brand-new tweed suit of ginger plus-fours, topped by a bowler hat. Juliet was unable to make light of the situation; Michael's chagrin lasted long after that weekend. In fact, when he came of age, and his mother suddenly discovered she had given birth to a much sought-after and attractive *parti*, she decided to cultivate him, but it was too late for Michael.

It is sad when parents cannot understand or sympathize with their offspring.

It is sadder still that, in cases where the children have most suffered from lack of parental empathy they, in turn, are unable to communicate with their own offspring. Juliet's mother was the distinguished and brilliant Lady de Grey (later Lady Ripon) who, perhaps more than anyone, can be given credit for mixing people from all worlds at her parties. It was she who brought Diaghilev's ballet to London, and then invited Nijinsky to meet Queen Alexandra. Lady de Grey had high hopes for her daughter, but she was disappointed. She told her friends that she would have her gangling daughter so well educated that no one would realize she was a goose. Although Juliet admired her mother, and perhaps even loved her after her death, yet she had no real intimacy with her; and, in turn, Juliet was incapable of understanding her own children, while they in turn...

Michael is handsome, tall of stature with wistful blue eyes. His classical features are those of a very conventional Ouida guardsman, and there is certainly a twinge of the military in his rigid deportment. But Michael is unlike his appearance. He is, in fact, a true eccentric, and this he would consider the greatest compliment. His point of view is always original, his mind full of fantasy, and his intuition uncanny. When in form, I know of no one who can be funnier; he is master of the anecdote, with an instinctive knowledge of the value of the pause, and the stutter adds enormously to the dramatic effect.

Michael remembers people's characteristic movements as if he were a choreographer always on the lookout for inspiration. He does an imitation of how the hostess, Lady Colefax, while talking of 'H.G.' (Wells) or 'B.B.' (Berenson), would be rearranging the salt and pepper pots, the spoons and forks, the toothpick and cigarette boxes, and all the objects in front of her on her dining-table. Lady Granard would send the silver boxes flying the length of her polished table; Lady Crewe was continually dusting her mouth with a sideways pendulum swing of a chiffon handkerchief. Michael also relished the fact that Lady Crewe, out of shyness, would never wait with the other patients in a dentist's waiting-room. Arriving on time in Harley Street, she would send in her chauffeur to inquire if the dentist was 'running a little late', or was he ready for her appointment? If not, the car would drive her ladyship around the squares until, eventually, she could be shown straight up to the dentist's chair.

Michael is a godson of Queen Mary, and there is surely no one who knows more than Michael about the private lives of any reigning family, in no matter what country; in fact, it can be said that he is 'royalty struck'. He collects stories and gossip about any royal personage, and treats his hierarchy with a mixture of complete reverence and a realization of how ridiculous their more exaggerated characteristics can become. He appreciates fully the qualities of his Royal godmother while being conscious of her gaucherie – her never being able to smile in public or look anyone straight in the face. Yet when she is alone and amused by some item of gossip, the old lady will laugh until she has to produce a handkerchief to wipe away her tears. Michael may be summoned to have tea and tell the Queen 'all that is going on', and he watches with fascination while the Queen cuts her cake into small squares, then, one by one, throws them, not to a dog, but into her own mouth. In fact Michael's highest compliment for his adored 'old Dutch' is that she is 'doggy'. Michael's feelings of love, admiration and awe for the old Queen prevent him from ever laughing at her, and though he knows his anecdotes about her are highly amusing, he is too intent and serious himself to smile.

He is amused that 'Old Doggie' refers to 'my woman Shaftesbury' (her lady-in-waiting, Lady Shaftesbury), and that, in fact, all those in waiting are 'women'. Michael relishes their names: Bertha Dawkins, Pussy Milnes-Gaskill, Maggy Wyndham, Lizzie Motion. While relating these incidents, Michael subconsciously punches the air with her inexpressive hands, or prods the ground with the point of an imaginary umbrella. His description is hilarious of how Queen Mary and he were crammed into a small lift on the way up to pay a call on Michael's mother in her Belgravia flat. Michael, nervous at not wishing to touch the Royal bosom, pressed the wrong button. As the Queen and he shot to the roof, Lady Juliet Duff was seen, in a flash on the landing as they went higher, doing a deep curtsey, but with a look of utter astonishment in her eyes.

'Did you know that at Marlborough House her wash basin is surrounded by the most marvellous jewelled toilet set given to her by the Tsarina? Isn't it odd that she should have a sunken bath let into the marble floor, and that her loo is covered with red velvet and is like a throne?'

The old Queen's knowledge of *objets d'art* and furniture was more of a pleasure to her than to the King who once, at dinner, heard the Queen ask Michael if he had bought anything lately? Whereupon King George angrily thumped the table and said: 'There you go again, May – always furniture, furniture, furniture!' In fact the King could become extremely exasperated with his consort, and is said to have sent her out at a Sandringham shoot with the beaters. Once Michael heard the gruff German tones evoking her: 'May, *will* you rattle your brolly!' No one was more amused than Michael when, one day, Queen Mary sent a note through her lady-in-waiting to say she was sorry she hadn't recognized him when, a few days earlier, she had been visiting Batsford's bookshop in North Audley Street. The explanation was that, since Michael was not wearing a hat, the Queen had mistaken him for one of the shop assistants.

Michael finds his most charming topic in Queen Alexandra who adored his grandmother, Gladys de Grey. After the birth of her second son the Queen became deaf, and this affliction made her an even more difficult companion, for she had never been able to master the English language well enough to string sentences together and would gruffly point and say: 'Screen – table – dog – woman,' etc. In spite of her deafness she enjoyed sitting at the opera, and some said she learnt to lip-read the singers. When, two years after her marriage, she discovered the infidelities of her husband she packed a bag and, in the middle of the night, started down the main staircase to leave Windsor Castle. But Queen Victoria, though sympathetic, forbade her to go. 'You are Princess of Wales. I know what you are suffering, but you cannot leave.'

One evening at dinner, Queen Alexandra noticed that Lady de Grey was scrutinizing Queen Mary, her daughter-in-law, across the table. The Dowager Queen leant across to Lady de Grey and, in a voice enlarged by her deafness, shouted: 'Ugly old thing, isn't she!' Lady de Grey used to bring back to Queen Alexandra, from her visits to Paris, a great selection of false jewellery which the Queen preferred to the Crown jewels. She was once on her way to the Opening of Parliament when a long row of artificial pearls broke. Although she was, as usual, late for the proceedings, she insisted on remaining in her carriage until every bead had been found.

The Vaynol weekend (a Royal one, for Princess Marina was there to launch a lifeboat at Llandudno) ended with the inevitable practical jokes, and 'ghost figures' found elaborately bedecked in the Royal bedroom. But the wholesale jollity, the wild exuberance of youth, was missing. Neither had there been the element of the haphazard, the great surprise. Sadly Elizabeth and I had to agree, on our return railway journey, that no one had either fought or fallen in love.

Portofino: August

The corrected galley proofs of my *Glass of Fashion* had been sent to America, and I left England to stay with Truman in Italy in a state of unusual happiness, for a smiling, kindly and totally delightful Eileen Hose had been 'sworn in' as my efficient new secretary. I left her to sort out the appalling mess of my business affairs and knew that for the first time my life was being properly looked after and all important things taken care of.

At Santa Margherita Truman Capote met me with yells of laughter. 'Oh, you're going to have the most marvellous time here! You're going to love every minute of it – the bathing, the people. Yes, everyone's waiting for you.'

The steep paths up the hinterland are laid with cobblestones, and only at night, when the port is seen in a warm apricot glow of low-powered lights, is the sound of busy clogged feet muffled.

The first days were as if in a sanatorium. I slept from one o'clock in the morning until ten, and again for several hours in the afternoon. For long periods I lay resting, too drowsy to turn over on my bed, or stretch for a book. At first my dreams were anxious, unpleasant ones, and the moments of half-consciousness were full of vague fears; but, by degrees, the *angst* of my London existence faded, and my mind when both asleep and awake was only filled with happy thoughts.

Soon I had abandoned myself completely to the pleasure of Truman's company; going out in a boat with him, sunbathing and swimming, for days on end we talked.

I found Truman's authoritativeness very refreshing and salutary. He can clear the air with a word; sometimes he even slaps people down in order to get some sense into an argument. Put him with a group of people who are far removed from him in interest, and he will, after they have recovered from the first shock of his appearance and manner, find themselves utterly beguiled and impressed. But Truman himself does not consider whether or not he is making an impression. He doesn't mind if there should be hostility, is quite willing to make a disturbance if necessary. He is frightened or awed by nobody: he has courage.

Truman appears to have few worries. He enjoys good food, lots to drink, and gets it. He loves his dog, Bunker, and enjoys leisure as much as the bright lights of café society. He is avid for gossip. His obvious enjoyment of a good story, and his hoarse, hearty laughter always make everything seem a little better than you had thought it.

Truman has perfected an American use of the latest slang; there is no catch-phrase that cannot be pigeon-holed for effective use in the future. He utilizes current phrases as a brilliant Broadway librettist might. Also he uses with a toughness that is healthy and refreshing all sorts of extremely crude and indecent phrases: 'Oh, he's my dream trade.' 'He's on my shit list.' If, for instance, a typically selfish Italian motorist barricades the road, he will eventually be treated to an astonishing vocabulary from Truman who, as the Goncourts pointed out, like many artists whose thoughts are in the clouds, comes down to earth now and then with a salutary thud.

In some ways I feel anxious lest Truman, like Bébé Bérard, may not survive to make old bones. I am slightly scared that someone who lives so intensely, so warmly, so generously, may be packing into a short span more than many people are capable of enjoying or experiencing in a long lifetime. Truman seems to attract drama: he has violent reactions to everything, and the moment comes when total fatigue takes over. Then he sinks into a death-like, sensual sleep from which you feel he will never recover. When, however, he does eventually surface to a deep, drowsy awakening, he seems reborn to all the wonders and surprises of life.

If Truman, Jack and I should need extra divertissement there are plenty of interesting people in the offing. Rex Harrison and Lilli Palmer live on the top of the mountain. A group of theatre people assemble on the terrace of their villa: John Perry, Binkie Beaumont and John Gielgud. Max Beerbohm is close by at Rapallo. There are sudden yacht arrivals: the *Sister Anne* came bringing Daisy Fellowes and her prisoners; another yacht brought the Windsors. Wallis on meeting John Gielgud at dinner for the first time, said: 'You know England made a great mistake in getting rid of the Dook. He's a very valuable addition to the country, an interesting person. You know, after sixteen years I am still fascinated by all sorts of things he has to tell me – after sixteen years! And yet I suppose you think of me as the devil with horns!'

16 September

In appearance offstage John Gielgud looks, at first glance, anything but an artist. But, by degrees, one senses his poetic quality, his innate pathos. The large bulbous nose is a stage asset: the eyes, though tired, have a watery blue wistfulness that is in the Terry tradition of beauty. He is not altogether happy that he has inherited so many family characteristics, and praise of his mellifluous voice and superb diction embarrasses him.

With the good manners that come from his true spirit, and not only on the stage, he has the grand manner. Unlike his rivals he does not know the sensation of jealousy; he will always plan to do the best for the project as a whole, rather than as a means of shining brightly himself. This has often led him to playing small and ineffective roles, and even obliging someone else by doing the wrong thing for himself; however, in his case the 'wrong thing' only adds to his reputation for his innate devotion to the cause of the theatre.

Once, when I was designing for him a revival of a very poor Edwardian comedy, *The Return of the Prodigal*, he sent me a thirteenth-hour SOS to alter the construction of the scenery because, at one point in the play, he was to lie in a hammock. Although, a month before, he had given the 'go-ahead' for the ground plan, he now considered he would not be in a sufficiently prominent position for an important scene. He was not being so much the 'star' as a 'realist'. He knew that it was he that the public would come to see and therefore it was necessary to rebuild the set.

Something about John appeals very directly to one's sympathy. Often he appears to be deeply unhappy, and seems to make life hard for himself. Then one wonders if he does not take from the parts he plays on the stage the compensatory life he misses in private. One of his most disarming aspects is his knowledge and devilish enjoyment of his own shortcomings. 'I'm spoilt, I'm niggardly, I'm prissy. I come home in the evening and count the books on the shelf to see if one is missing.'

John is the first to admit that actors are often vapid and stupid people, yet he spends most of his time, most happily, in unworthy green room gossip. He relates how, during the war, on some ENSA tour, he was sharing a bedroom with Binkie Beaumont and John Perry, and they talked until dawn about a prospective theatrical venture. Only complete exhaustion silenced them. But the moment John awoke in the morning he carried on the conversation where it had been interrupted, by asking: 'And do you think Dolly [of Gustave's, the wig-makers] can be trusted with the wigs?'

Here at Portofino John has appeared wearing a ridiculous white linen hat, sitting bolt upright in a rowboat as formally as if he were at a board meeting. John is always the first to realize how comic a picture he presents, and in no way resents our amusement; in fact, his eyes twinkle with the fun of the absurdity as, unmindful of waves or splash, he continues, in his rich, foghorn voice, to extol the work of Granville Barker, or where he went wrong with *Hamlet*.

For Truman and myself this was to be a working holiday (Truman was desperately late with the script for his play *The House of Flowers*, and I was still struggling with my Gainsborough play), so when John suggested to us that we should motor with him to Sermione, where he had just been offered a part in a Shakespeare film, we were both loath to interrupt the quiet continuity of our labours. But John badgered us. He hated having to go alone; wouldn't we join him just for a few days? But since Truman and I – unlike the star actor – would not be guests of the film company, and rooms were scarce everywhere at this peak time of the year, would John please be certain to arrange our accommodation in advance?

Once on our way, in the film people's hired motor car, John confessed he hadn't felt like telegraphing for rooms for us, and in any case it was too late. On arrival at Sermione it was discovered, as we had feared, that there was only one room available for John. Truman and I were crushed. John, ebullient, asked airily: 'Will it cost you very much to go on by car to Verona?' He then disappeared into the arms of the *Romeo and Juliet* company.

When eventually John suggested coming with Truman and me to Venice we now had the upper hand, but we relented and gave him a seat in our car. Each morning at breakfast John would appear fully attired and, in his beautiful *voix d'or*, talk out of the window. 'Really, Venice is excessively ugly in the rain: it looks like King's Cross.' When discussing the theatre he expanded with real feeling: 'I'm sick of doing old plays, and don't have much interest in the younger generation. Perhaps I'm tired.' John has a writer's use of words: talks of the 'mutinously bored cast', and says someone has a talent with pencil-sketches 'as if to touch the bar of heaven'.

'Max will be pleased to see you for tea at four o'clock.'

Max Beerbohm's companion, Elizabeth Jungman, telephoned the welcome news through to us in Portofino, adding the cautionary information that of late the venerable master of *belles lettres* had not been sleeping well and could, without becoming overtired, only receive a few visitors for a rather short time. The previous spring he had had a close shave with influenza. The heat of Rapallo summer was bad for him, so they had removed to the summit of a nearby mountain.

Truman drove me in his little boneshaker around the dusty, circling road to Montellegro. Then we wound our way through sweet-smelling trees and fresh green slopes, and we were excited at the prospect of seeing, at the summit, Sir Max Beerbohm, that rare and wonderful link with the Victorian past. A half-century ago he had already become immortal – the gentle and unassailable creator of *Zuleika Dobson*, the master of fable, satire and caricature.

He was considered one of the greatest conversationalists of his time, and his gift for describing the physical exterior of his victims was so vivid that one knew exactly what they must have looked like. The youthful Churchill had dry hair like a waxwork, no wrinkles, and the pallor of one who has lived in the limelight. He also had hereditary bad manners, was courteous and brutal alternately. Shaw had a temperance beverage face, and Beerbohm hated the naked look of the back of his neck. Balfour was girlish and seemed dazed. Oscar Wilde he likened to an Assyrian wax statue, effeminate, but with the vitality of twenty men. His heavy shoulders, and his fat, white hands jewelled with huge rings, made him also look like a feather bed, an enormous dowager schoolboy. He had a way of laughing with his hand over his mouth. Of Lord Curzon, Beerbohm said he was 'Britannia's butler'.

Miss Jungman materialized as a pepper-and-salt-haired woman of immense vitality with a strong German accent. She took us into a cool, impersonal dining-room where, hunched at a table set for tea, sat the somewhat crumpled, but dandified little figure to whom we had come to pay homage.

Today, on his mountain peak, Sir Max, of whom Oscar Wilde said he had the gift of perpetual old age, was still, in spite of his eighty years, the perennial dandy. He was wearing a smart pale-grey suit speckled like a moorhen; a black silk tie; a white shirt buttoned at the old-fashioned, rounded ends of the collar and cuff, with quite a large expanse of white showing above his wrist. On his long, pointed fingers he wore a bunch of heavy rings that drew added attention to his remarkable and almost inhumanly pale hands. They might have been made of old parchment or fine ricepaper – the nails dry and horny, the skin freckled and blotched. Bird-like hands, sensitive and expressive, they added distinction. The hair on his domed head grew in long, white wisps at the temples and above the collar. His complexion was clear and waxen, with a blush of transparent pink on lean, shiny cheekbones; he was immaculately shaved around the white moustache that graced the somewhat simian, thin-upper-lipped mouth (his lower lip more pronounced than that of my father). The eyes were still his most dominant feature. The lids were more hooded than my father's ever became, and the muscles below his left eye had relaxed revealing a red pocket of flesh; he seemed self-conscious about the anomaly. Nevertheless, his eyes communicated a lovely wonder and wistful surprise. They had a bird-like intensity, love-in-the-mist blue, and changed noticeably as he switched his memory from the past to the present.

We sat at a small rickety table. Before us were two plates of fancy biscuits, some very strong Indian tea that our host did not drink, and a bottle of red Chianti wine from which he poured himself a glass. The dining-room was empty. Its ugly cream- and salmon-coloured walls and red-tiled floors resounded to the echoes of children shouting or crying at play; rather a lot of flies were being restless.

When we first settled down at the tea-table, there was an instant's silence. What were we comparative strangers to talk about? How were we to begin? Hesitantly, I broached the subject of Sibyl Colefax.

Sir Max ruminated: 'Yes, Sibyl was a reliable, helpful friend, and she seldom missed a year without making a pilgrimage to visit me here. She will certainly go down to posterity through countless memoirs. No one could have imagined, herself least of all, that she would figure so largely in the history of her time.'

It was evident that Sir Max had an extraordinarily exact and precise memory. Never once, during our afternoon's visit, did he fumble for a name or a date.

We talked of cabbages and coronations, though Truman kept a restful silence: he was busy imbibing every nuance.

His voice was quiet, leisurely and gentle, perhaps a trifle quavery. Yet he articulated every word with precision, giving such emphasis to his syllables that we marvelled at how rich in its effect the English language could be.

I ventured upon the theatre as a safe topic, since here was the man who had been one of our outstanding drama critics. Sir Max complained that, from a certain moment onwards in theatrical history, it was almost impossible to hear what was being said upon the stage. He gave an amusing imitation of the breathless gasps, pantings and half-finished exclamations that certain latter-day actors employed in order to express emotion. But even in the old days of great bravura performances that involved much 'ranting', his brother, Sir Herbert Beerbohm Tree, always had trouble at His Majesty's Theatre with Row H. Somehow, those sitting in Row H could never hear the actors, however loudly they bellowed: the acoustics were such that the sound always went straight to Row I. Experts were brought from far and wide. 'Herbert tried everything, but it was all to no avail.'

In any case, Sir Max went on, His Majesty's Theatre was always too large for comedy, even for Shakespeare. The ideal theatre was the Haymarket. 'With only a few people on stage you could always give the effect of a crowd.' But it was in the congenial intimacy of the St James's Theatre that Sir George Alexander did the Wilde comedies so well, 'with conventional scenery but good furniture'. Sir Max recalled that the author, after the first night of *Lady Windermere's Fan*, congratulated the audience on its enthusiastic performance.

What did he think of Harley Granville Barker? Sir Max's bushy eyebrows were raised wistfully. Barker had been an excellent impresario for Shaw, Ibsen and Strindberg, but never appreciated the inner rhythms of Shakespeare's verse. His actors just rambled on, breaking up the metre in a dreadful massacre. 'For that matter,' our host added, 'few actors know what they are doing with Shakespeare.' Gielgud and Olivier are exceptions, and he thought they should have a good influence.

He expatiated on Tree's production of *A Midsummer Night's Dream*. 'Yes,' the old critic concluded, 'it was very pretty with all those little people fluttering about – really *féerique*. But Barker's production had gold fairies! Absolutely wrong! From what little I know about the subject, I am positive fairies were never made of gold. That is an earthy affair entirely.' Certainly very little gold has come the way of Sir Max. Although few writers have acquired his réclame – he has since his first success had a legendary quality – yet his books were sold in very small quantities and today are out of print. It is rather terrible to know that the successful Somerset Maugham criticized Max as being someone whose shirt-cuffs were generally dirty.

At length Miss Jungman perceived that Sir Max was becoming a little jaded, so she instigated a walk for Truman and me round the mountain top. We looked down on vistas of olive-clad hills, distant gorges, and the huge expanse of opal-coloured sea towards Lerici, where Shelley drowned. Miss Jungman explained that she had been friends with Sir Max and Lady Beerbohm for many years. There had been a 'little secret agreement' with him: 'If anything should happen to my wife ...' But Miss Jungman had never let him finish the sentence, for it was unnecessary. And when Lady Beerbohm became ill for the last time, Sir Max had summoned her. She came post-haste from Oxford, arriving two hours after his wife's death to take on the duties of companion. [Miss Jungman in fact became Lady Beerbohm a few days before Sir Max's death.]

When we came back from our mountain walk, Sir Max was sitting on a parapet sunning himself, his cane held gingerly in one hand and a boater straw hat cocked jauntily to one side. He looked, for a moment, like one of those dapper monkeys that are dressed up to sit on the street musician's hurdy-gurdy. I could not help taking advantage of the situation, and when he turned towards us with lowered head and upward glancing eyes, he saw that in spite of his earlier demurs I was photographing him.

Sir Max seemed amused and even pleased when I said how delightful he looked there. 'Mayn't I take one more?' He beamed, posed for a moment, and turned his head so that his left eye would not be visible. Encouraged, I took several more snapshots. Then I asked him if he would show his hands, as they were such beautiful hands. By way of response he held one arm straight towards the camera, fingers splayed and stiff.

'Now no more, please. It's too late, and I look dreadful.'

I closed my camera.

'But you will let me see them, won't you? And you'll destroy any that are horrors?'

I promised that I would. 'It is almost time for his dinner,' Miss Jungman whispered. 'Max dines at six-thirty.'

We said goodbye, and the lady companion took us into the hotel dining-room to collect some parcels. As we came out on the terrace again, Sir Max could be seen from our vantage point under the tendrils of vines, walking slowly down the steep hill. A dandified little figure, with his cane and straw boater worn at a rakish angle, he looked as if he were sauntering down St James's on a summer morning in 1904. He did not know we were watching him, and as he walked examined one of his hands to see if it were really as beautiful as I had said it was. He turned it around, stiff and fishlike, to admire it from every angle.

September

To those who used to bemoan the fact that no young hostesses follow in the tradition of Sibyl Colefax and Emerald Cunard we now advocate Anne [Fleming].

This week she gave a dinner to celebrate the fiftieth birthday of Cyril Connolly, and the small group she collected had unity and character. A lot of talent, brilliance and erudition was gathered here between 'Empire patterned' walls. They were people, born in all sorts of different strata of life, enjoying the fruits of success in the company of others they respected or had most in common with. The talk was on target: no one wasting time in banalities.

I had been to a ballet, met Lucian Freud and Francis Bacon at Wheeler's, and we had come on together to find Anne's party at its height. Cyril was radiant and feeling very warmhearted at such a genuine display of affection. His heart and greed were equally overflowing at the tributes given to him. Clarissa (Churchill) Eden, very white and taut: I asked if such talk was not rather impressive after her summer spent looking after Anthony in the US. She admitted that when Maurice Bowra held forth, she had difficulty in following the flow. Stephen Spender, hair ruffled, white locks on end, tripping over as he went upstairs to pee. Freddy Ayer vociferating, and Peter Quennell benign; when Peter is in a good mood he can be the most polished and delightful conversationalist in the world: lovable too – but woe betide you if he is in a bitter mood.

Anne was enjoying the success of the party so much that she wanted her beloved husband, Ian, to savour every nuance of it. She was disappointed that, at two in the morning, he had disappeared to bed. Anne had stars in her eyes until the last guest stumbled out after dawn.

October

I have gone back to school. Perhaps it should not be considered a return for, apart from the spasmodic sketching classes at my public school, art tuition never came my way. At Harrow our drawing master, an aggressive, white-haired, little lion cub, was W. Egerton Hine, and I was his most promising pupil. In fact, I learnt to paint water-colours of bluebell woods, farmyards and manure heaps, in exactly the same manner as my master. Although this was considered the ultimate achievement at the time, I found that, even a lifetime afterwards, when faced with any landscape I could not stop producing – with ample use of raw sienna and Prussian blue on Whatman hot-pressed paper – imitation Eggie Hine, and this became somewhat of a handicap.

Perhaps it was partly for this reason that I decided to come to the Slade. Also I have always felt the lack of tuition in draughtsmanship and wished to learn the use of oil colours.

Suddenly the rhythm of my life changed. In order to do a full week's work I came to London from the country for five, and not two days a week. Instead of scrambling out of Pelham Place, after a busy morning's work, into a taxi for a luncheon appointment, I now must be in the Underground by nine-thirty (Art Schools do not start early: no complaint there!), so the usual coping with letters, messages and making arrangements has now to be organized with Eileen before that.

At first it hit me head-on when I arrived in a building teeming with fellow students a third my own age. My old shyness and uncertainty came back with a bang. I was reminded of my first day at St Cyprian's boarding school; but, unlike the Eastbourne preparatory school, this place was well heated, and the students were not hostile. With their beards and long hair, they appeared like the artistic personages in that vast group of the nineties painted by Fantin-Latour. It was a bit comforting later to discover that a certain timidity was also felt by other first-year students. Yet coming as an interloper into a quiet room in which a number of young people are silently working, while live figures are sitting motionless without their clothes on, was a bit uncanny. The brown and buff room with growing green plants, and fish floating in tanks among the plaster heads and torsos, was less alarming. In this room a kind, grey-haired, sepia-eyed man named Townsend gave me a 'position' facing a model of a

Greek youth with a sliced-off cranium. He also found an easel for me, and then, tactfully, left me to my own resources. I tried to comprehend my newly-acquired equipment. First, to pour a little liquid into one of the dishes on my spruce palette. But panic seized me: I could not even unscrew the top of the bottle. I was desperate: what kind of a guy was this who couldn't even get at his own turpentine? I knew that I would create an atmosphere of abject hopelessness if I asked one of my neighbours to help me. The veins in my forehead swelled as I made a Herculean effort – and won! Next – the battle with the easel. Of course one leg was far too short: how to lengthen it? It was completely unyielding: nothing would budge it. Could I shorten the other two? One leg moved easily, but not the others; and, in any case, my easel would then be in a position that, if I wished to paint, necessitated my kneeling down or lying on the floor. I tried once more to raise the legs. Appalling noise as canvas and easel, palette and paints collapsed. Oil and turpentine everywhere. Fortunately Mr Townsend reappeared to put chaos to rights.

Slowly I discovered that I had been far too ambitious in selecting such a vast canvas as I had to stretch to put a stroke even half-way up the picture, and it was quite bewildering to see what was appearing on it. After a few days I realized that my still-life, done in warm tones of Devonshire cream and burnt sienna, was definitely Hine-haunted. How could I exorcize Eggie's ghost? I wanted to put my signature to a picture that was undeniably and positively my own. These doubts, when relayed to the kind Mr Townsend, brought a slow, knowing smile to his face. 'Don't bother yet about painting a picture. Just get on with the problem of showing the contrast of the highlights on that thigh with the darkness of the plants in the background, and the half-tones of the figure in shadow.' Although it did not look like a 'Beaton' (and what does?), my large canvas, when completed a week later, was to me quite an achievement.

I was now ambitious to go into the life class room, but Mr Townsend insisted upon my remaining longer doing drawings and oil studies of other plaster casts. Only after several weeks was I allowed to face a real live nude. Mr Townsend gave me a 'front-row' position facing an enormously fat, naked lady, who sat bolt upright on an Indian-patterned sarong. One of her baby-fingered, dimpled hands was placed meekly at her side, the other half-covering her sex. On her face this kewpie Eve maintained an expression of the utmost affectation with eyebrows raised superciliously, lids lowered, and a mouth twisted to one side in the most exaggerated pout. She was doing an Oliver Messel imitation of herself.

Being surrounded by folk so much younger than myself makes me realize, with amazement, that I really am now an elderly person. No matter what I may feel (and I suppose I kid myself for much of the time that I'm still a 'bright young thing'), the fact remains that nearly fifty years have passed since my birth, while many of these students were mere boys at the beginning of the last war. No matter what I imagine about myself, these youngsters know that I am a very different person from them; this is something I have got to face. I realize how much more realistic the younger students are in respect to formal manners and artificial conventions. When needs be, they are ruthlessly critical and unsentimental, yet deep and sincere is their respect for those whose work they admire.

Suddenly a young man of twenty-three (whom I am beginning to think of as a contemporary) said to me: 'You don't know what you mean to our generation. You stand for all the gaiety and exuberance' (these not his words – I forget his) 'of a period that seems so utterly remote to us: the personification of a life that we all admire.' I was surprised. I had thought of myself only in private terms – coping with my own difficulties, never thinking that maybe others were conscious of the results of my previous efforts. I found it easy to talk to this young man, and extremely interesting to hear his views on contemporary painters such as Lucian Freud and Francis Bacon. ('Yes, I can answer that – I've thought a lot about that one,' he said, when I asked why he thought Francis had such an influence on the younger generation. Answer: 'They've had aesthetics, sensitivity, but never before a breaking down of all the rules and associations, a revolution in accepted creeds and standards of painting.') I was somewhat abashed when he said: 'Why, you must have known all the painters. What sort of a man was Bonnard?' It was as if he had asked 'What was Leonardo really like?'

Started on a head – an easy job compared to last week's elaborate composition. I tried to see the face in the round so that a fly crawling over it would know it was not flat and would have to hop over its various surfaces. I would not have imagined it possible to spend two weeks on a face. But at the end of the first week there was still a tremendous way to go before the painting would be taken to its ultimate conclusion. One old professor, no doubt in an effort to encourage me, said: 'Yes, yes, you have a distinct talent for getting a likeness. After all, this is a rare enough gift. You should do well in the line of portraiture among your friends.'

After these weeks I have perhaps gleaned a bit through my ears, but not enough through my eyes or with my mind. Professor Rogers remarked that I had not simplified a face enough, that I had put in too many shadows and that those that were darkest were unreasonably so. 'That face is a pale mass against a dark background. Now I'm going to do a cad's trick,' and he painted a white layer all over the face. The picture never recovered, but it was an effective way of bringing to my mind the important fact of simplification. (In my

Audrey Hepburn on the Ascot set of *My Fair Lady*

Noel Coward, 1972

Rudolf Nureyev

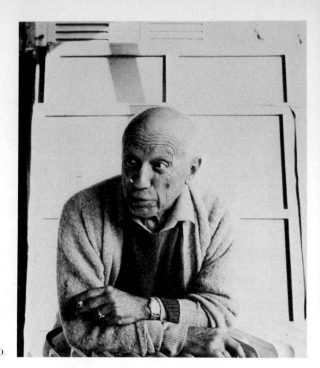

Picasso.

C.B. drawing Picasso in his studio at Mougins

C.B. at Reddish House, Broadchalke

Lady Diana Cooper

drawings, caricatures and other painting media I am quite adept at the knack of omission.)

13 December

The term is suddenly over. When I took William Coldstream [Slade Professor of Fine Art] out to lunch he asked me if I felt 'it was beginning to work'. I had to admit that I didn't think it was. Perhaps it was not to be wondered that I haven't yet begun to master the medium: it really needs another year or so of hard perseverance. Coldstream said: 'The other students come to us every day for three years!' Nevertheless, the big, rousing shock has been to realize what a serious business it is! There are no alibis, and even if one thinks it possible to avoid a hurdle, one is soon found out trying to by-pass it.

19

Lecture Tour
1953-4

During the winter of 1953-4 C.B. went on a lecture tour which took him to seventeen cities in the United States, as well as Montreal. In the course of this he celebrated his fiftieth birthday.

My hotel in Norfolk, Virginia, was just another name on the itinerary. But it became a name that I shall never forget, for in it I spent one of the most gothic nights of my life. A very ugly gentleman, carrying a briefcase and noisily chewing Beech-Nut gum, had filled the so-called limousine from the airport with the synthetic odour of mint. He reached the hotel desk before me, and patiently I waited my turn. When at last I gave my name, there was a slight delay about the key. The clerk consulted the bellhop, the bellhop went into a lengthy discussion with the clerk.

'Well then, give Mr Bayton room 462.'

A strong smell of breakfast food being cooked was an unusual assault on one's nose at nine o'clock in the evening. The elevator took up the theme with more cooking odours. In the corridor, which smelt of cement, bits of plaster had fallen like indoor snow on to the carpet. The paint on the door to my room was in a state of chipped desuetude, and the bellboy unlocked the door to reveal habitation large enough for little more than the bed, with its peasoup-coloured covering smelling strongly of disinfectant.

Well, if this was what the traveller's fate had planned for me, I was too tired and uncomfortable to ask any questions. A few minutes later the telephone sounded. It was a woman representing the local radio station.

'Mr Beaton? this is station VIRG.' Could she come up and bring her tape recorder with her, in order to interview me?

'Have you ever set up a tape recorder in a prison cell?' I expostulated. 'There's barely room for one person here!'

We passed through some tribulations, but finally it was arranged for the lady to be given the temporary use of a suite. In half an hour, I found myself gossiping intimately into a microphone with a complete stranger.

Afterwards I returned to my room, feeling a grim kinship with America's vast cell population which, in a million hotel rooms at that very moment, lowered the blinds, turned on radios and took baths.

A bath? Yes, a rousing hot bath would bring me back to life. I tried the hot-water tap, but the water was tepid.

I picked up the telephone. 'Can you send me a Scotch and soda?'

Crisply the reply came back, 'Sorry, this is a dry state.'

Returning from a late dinner, I put, with undue optimism, a 'Do Not Disturb' call through to the operator until ten o'clock the following morning. My lecture was in the afternoon at the Irene Leache Memorial Museum, and I was looking forward to a late rising, followed by reading and writing in bed.

Then the crisis began, building slowly at first. The squawk of neighbouring radios kept me awake for a long time. Oblivion had just been achieved (the oriental's bliss) when I started up in bed at the sound of a conscientious rattle on my door-knob. It was the night watchman.

I settled back on the pillows, but shortly there came another noise at my door. 'Who is it?' I sat bolt upright in bed. There was no reply.

Back to the horizontal I went, tossing and turning like a milkshake in an electric machine. Outside, the tomahawk whoops and screams of high-spirited sailors gave one the feeling of being in a fort rather than a hotel. My watch told me it was one o'clock in the morning.

As an antidote to my sleepless discomfiture I opened a book by Colette. What was this world of good food, delicious smells, warm fleshly comfort, and all the sensualities that were now so lacking? I turned out the light.

Other noises took up the nocturnal concert. There were such groans from the man in the bed on the other side of my green wall that surely the death rattle would come at any moment. The door-knob rattled instead. It was my friend the night watchman, back on his rounds again. Belatedly, the hot water began to circulate with confidence in the pipes. I had wanted a bath and now was the time to have one. But the flesh was too weak to make the effort. Wide awake and madder than a hornet, I took a masochistic pleasure in sorting out the noises. Added to the hammer-like banging of the pipes, there were bumps and there were screeches, the ticking of my watch, catcalls in the street, hoots and whistles, and honks and beeps and toots and smacks and claps and raps. Hard on the nocturnal ear came slam, bang, thump, plump, gurgle, plash and guggle. A car backfired in the street.

At length I rose from my bed of pain, took an aspirin and stuffed cotton wool in my ears. The light of dawn had barely crept into the window when the ceaseless taps from the hot-water pipes were joined by a stomping cavalcade in the corridors, by neighbouring radios, and, incredible as it seems, by six o'clock maids who tried in vain to open my door and make up the room.

The hot-water pipes really began to get up steam. It sounded as if Vesuvius were about to erupt, or that Paracutin would rise up from the floor of my room, as it did in a Mexican cornfield several years ago. Now for the explosion! The walls began to reverberate with such force that the tiles in the bathroom would surely fall.

Bang! Bang! My door was rammed as though the Gestapo had come to take me away. I opened it and stuck a wild head round the door. Enlightenment came: a demolition squad, already hard at work, had begun to pull down a wall outside my room. I yelled furiously at this group of nonchalant workmen whom I could barely discern. They were wearing biscuit-coloured overalls, and stood in a cloud of cement dust like that of a London fog. They paid no attention to me, and as soon as the door was shut again they rammed it with great iron girders.

Still early morning and many hours before my breakfast time – I went stubbornly back to bed. More cotton wool was stuffed into my ears until the drums were pushed in. I would sleep in spite of everything.

Industry triumphed. Defeated, grovelling and whimpering for mercy, I ordered my tea and toast and unlocked my door. A coloured maid asked, was I ready to have my room made up?

A new wave of obstinacy swept over me, giving me strength. Let them blast with dynamite, let them drop nitro-glycerine under my nose, but I would carry out my intention of staying in bed all morning. With a thick Turkish towel round my head, I sat in bed and summoned the shades of the Stoic philosophers to counsel me. I would will out of existence the terrible anvil noises, the bangs, the hammering and sawing that went on the other side of those paper-thin walls.

To some extent success was mine. Only occasionally was the mind distracted from the most monumental effort of concentration ever practised by a Westerner with no knowledge of Yoga discipline. At moments, a great explosion of noise and a quivering of walls would intrude upon my consciousness. I would then meditate upon the noise, my thoughts drifting off into fantasy. If the wall should in fact fall in, conking me on the head with great slabs of plaster, how much could be got out of the hotel by suing for physical hurt, nervous stress, non-appearance at my lecture performance, and lawyer's fees? Perhaps a hundred thousand dollars; then I could retire from this racket. 'Beaton awarded highest damages ever paid in an American court; result of injuries sustained while on lecture circuit in Norfolk, Virginia, hotel catastrophe.'

By late forenoon, it was the workmen's lunch time. Comparative peace reigned at last. I was able to progress with my work for an hour. But the return of the demolition squad outlawed my brief paradise of silence. With renewed vigour, they beat a devil's tattoo on the walls. I would admit defeat!

There was a long wait for the elevator. Then the elevator door, of frosted glass illuminated from within, rushed half-way up to my floor, hesitated, and went down again without picking me up. The last straw! I kept my hand pressed on the bell for an eternity, but the lift never returned to take me out of my misery.

Escape! The word made my temples beat. Panicky, I dived for the nearest stairway.

My sponsor had arrived in front of the hotel to take me to my lecture. She remarked soberly, 'I feel that something is going to go wrong today. Do you ever have that feeling?'

'Yes, indeed,' I assured her. And in a burst of sudden confidence, I described my adventures since my arrival.

'That hotel you complain of is practically the only one in town,' she explained. 'It's owned by a firm of bankers who discourage rivalry. But now there's another hotel which is going to be remodelled because it wasn't very respectable. Your hotel feels the pressure, and *it* must do something, too. That's why they're pulling down the wall outside your room.'

My sponsor continued her monologue, sketching in a picture of her home-town for me as we drove to the museum.

'Norfolk is one of our oldest American cities. Some of our people here can trace their family tree right back to the earliest settlers.'

'The city doesn't look that old,' I countered.

'Ah, that's because it was entirely burnt to the ground in the Revolutionary War. We've nothing earlier than 1800. This' – she indicated the avenue along which we were moving – 'is the only street where there are any residential buildings. There aren't many of them, either. You see, we don't have any people living in large suburban houses. Norfolk isn't a well-to-do town like Richmond.'

We arrived at the museum. My sponsor remarked wryly, 'The lame and the halt are beginning to arrive, you see.'

Sure enough, old ladies with hearing aids and bad legs were struggling to get out of their motor cars. The head of the museum showed somewhat obviously that he did not enjoy the human onslaught on lecture days. The influx soon threatened to break all previous records of attendance. Never had the hall been so full, they said, and more chairs were brought in shoulder high.

Perhaps it was thoroughly unprofessional of me to mind late-comers; they are something every performer must take in his stride. But today's tardy arrivals were very insistent upon asserting their personality; or so it seemed to me, for the sleepless night had left me highly strung and very keyed up. I could feel my body reacting like a Geiger counter to all disturbances.

Two women swopped seats with others, elderly people would try to open windows, fail, and have to call for help. It was with great difficulty that I refrained from asking if I couldn't oblige.

At last the ordeal was over. The applause was generous, and during the hand-shakes and politeness that followed, I was quite mellowed by the warmth of the nice, kind and good, cheerful and open-hearted people who had perforce to live in this horrid place. Yet one woman said, 'Oh, I wouldn't live anywhere else for anything in the world!'

Back at the hotel, the workmen had now gone home, their noise-making was at an end. I sank on my peasoup bed-cover and started to sleep, then sat up. Perhaps, after all, I could get a plane out of Norfolk tonight?

I rang the airways. 'No, I'm afraid we can't help you. There's a flight in an hour, but we've been booked solid since early this morning. Now if only you'd called sooner.'

It just wasn't my lucky day or my lucky town. I went back to the green bed-cover. Much later the telephone bell rang. A drunken woman from Virginia Beach was calling. She had known a friend of mine in Calcutta, where she had lived for many years. 'Is he married again? Oh, I love him, but we won't go into that now,' she added.

'All right, we won't go into it,' I said.

She wanted to apologize to me for not having organized any social activity while I was in Norfolk, but her young daughter had developed the mumps. Was it too late now to arrange something?

'Yes, I'm afraid it's too late. I intend to leave tomorrow and frankly, it'll be a relief to leave this hotel.'

'I know just how you feel,' she soothed me drunkenly. 'That's why I want to do something about you. We've got a real nice little group down here at the beach.'

Unless a firm line was taken, the talk would go on forever. 'Well, you're kind to think of me and I'll certainly look forward to accepting your hospitality the next time I come to Norfolk.'

Then my heart almost broke. The drunken, drawling voice changed into that of a startled, wistful child. She screeched, 'Do you really think you will ever come back here again?'

My insincerity had been taken at its face value. So much was implied in the high-pitched, incredulous change of tone. 'Do you really think you'll ever come here again?' It seemed to indicate a regret for Calcutta, for the love of our mutual friend, for the fact that she had to drink a lot of whisky to keep going. And then there was the excitement of her daughter's mumps. If I was fortunate, I would be able to escape tomorrow. But the drunken woman from Virginia Beach had to remain here with her 'real nice little group'.

I slept the sleep of the dead. However, soon after dawn, the telephone brought me to life. A cablegram was on its way up to me. The telegram was to wish me 'Many Happy Returns' of my fiftieth birthday.

This was surely the last nail. One does not become old by gradual stages; a series of ugly jolts makes one realize the passage of time.

The bell rang again. This time the local reporter and a press photographer had come to see me. It is possible to respond with enthusiasm to anyone who asks pertinent or even impertinent questions. But this early morning, there was hardly a pretence that the reporter was in any way interested in me. The photographer likewise showed only routine curiosity and I couldn't blame him. I caught a glimpse of myself in the looking glass that gave me no assurance. I looked awful, green and ruffled. Once, I used to love having my picture in the paper. I was young and vain. The pleasure is indeed mitigated now. (Worms feed on Hector brave.)

'Now what can we take that's different?' the photographer asked, producing his flashlight. I looked baffled. He hit upon a rare notion.

'Have you brought your camera with you?'

'Oh please! I so much dislike a picture of a man trying to look as if he were taking a picture. What about my reading my lecture?' I suggested brightly, fondling my script.

The photographer moved his hat to the back of his head. 'No!' he said. 'What about standing here? – No, that won't do! – Or here? – No! That's no good!' At last he decided to take me looking out of the window at the blank grey wall a few feet away.

'Now smile!' he said.

Here I was, in Norfolk, Virginia, and fifty years old. It was no smiling matter.

20

A Statesman's Farewell

1955

Duff Cooper died. Lady Diana was with C.B. at Churchill's farewell party at No. 10 Downing Street. C.B. published The Glass of Fashion, *and designed* Love's Labour's Lost *for the Old Vic.*

New York

Kind and considerate and faithful as ever, Mr Sirest of the Condé-Nast publications travel department came to meet me on the docks and escorted me through the Customs in record time. Before I knew it, I was back at the hotel telephoning friends and exchanging news. And what news! Little Truman Capote had had to fly from Paris as his mother killed herself by taking an overdose of sleeping pills. Many other friends had died suddenly, but to me the most shocking of all was Duff Cooper's death. While I had been filling my mind with him and his book on board ship – a wonderful document – he had died at sea on a slow boat en route to Jamaica. Duff must have known he would die: his life was rounded, fulfilled. A perfectly satisfied, contented man, he had always had good luck, and he died the way he wanted – with no protracted suffering.

Duff had always made me feel inferior: he knew so much more than I did even about my own subjects. However much he tried, he could not help making me shy; but he said I had guts.

All Diana's fears and anxieties were now a reality. The thing she had dreaded for so many hours each day, for so many years had, in fact, happened. I wondered how she could have the strength to live without her Duffie. Everything she had done was for him. A little while later a letter arrived from her on her way to Greece.

In spite of the lecture tour the winter had not been financially successful: no stage jobs had come my way, and my *Vogue* work was severely criticized. I did no drawing at all – in fact, never brought my paint things out of the cupboard. It had been a pleasant enough visit, but once the ship on which

I was sailing shot past the downtown skyscrapers of Manhattan my existence of the past four months slid painlessly and quickly into limbo.

London

The invitations did not suggest it was to be a 'Goodbye to No. 10' party, although all friends knew that this, in fact, was the chief reason for forgathering. The cards informed us that 'Sir Winston was "At Home" to celebrate the anniversary of Lady Churchill's birthday'. Indeed it was her birthday, and all family friends and supporters and every old crony who had been bidden were determined not to miss this very particular celebration. I was impressed at being sent a card which, I am sure, was inspired by a reminder of my existence from a mutual friend, the beautiful lady, Rhoda Birley, with whom I dined before the festivity. For many years I have been friends with at least some members of the Churchill clan, but, since they have so many acquaintances, I was surprised to find myself among the chosen.

Rhoda is very Irish and very vague. This evening she seemed to be in another world. She was a man short for dinner, and said her day had been a nightmare – everything wrong. She had cooked the dinner herself (she is a painter, but also an artist in the kitchen), and thrown the dessert over her head. Guests: Jock Colville, for a considerable time the Private Secretary of Churchill, and his redoubtable mother, Lady Cynthia of prison reform; the Hamish Hamiltons; Tortor Gilmour, gaunt, of ivory bones; gentle and smiling Lady Lascelles, wife of the late King's Private Secretary, who bought from my father our house in Hyde Park Gardens where we lived before difficulties caught up with us all. An unusual, yet pleasant enough party. The men lingered in the dining-room talking about Burgess and Maclean so that we were late arriving at Downing Street, where the large and lofty rooms were already crowded.

The public servants (or are they old Churchill servants? – I doubt it) seemed much more familiar and friendly than at most social gatherings. They beamed, and their eyes twinkled a welcome, for they knew and liked almost all the guests, and the announcer at the top of the staircase did not need to ask many names before sending forth, in stentorian tones, the latest arrivals into the *mêlée*.

A buzz of excited conversation and pleasant laughter. A flooding of light. An impression of flowers. All the years rolled by. To think that this gathering was being given by someone whose face already went back into history. It was part of the Boer War, a face, still young and calf-like, that showed such intelligent anger among the other bland leaders of the First World War. It became the smiling face that knew defeat, that scowled in eclipse, and came out into the brilliance again to guide us during the last terrible years. At a time when Churchill could promise us nothing good but ultimate victory, he was the rallying point. Without him we might have been defeated. For a long lifetime now we have taken for granted this figure in our midst. Almost as familiar is the face of his wife: her Grecian profile, the deep-set, pale-blue eyes, have changed little with the years. She was always gaunt and elegant: in her bridal dress, in 1914 'tailor-mades', and in the ubiquitous bandanna kerchief of the last war. These two faces have together travelled through many epochs in our personal history. Tonight was a private goodbye.

Churchill stood alone by the door, immaculate in his sagging evening dress – very pink and rose-buddy. Although still stunningly like his image carved in memory, he appeared smaller than one remembered. A cigar was held in tapering pink fingers, and he wore a look of acute amusement in his eyes. Between spasms of newly-arriving guests he would sit down on a chair with his legs planted well apart, a hand on each knee, resting.

Lady Churchill was dressed in black lace with orchids at the waist, and her eyes were focused to other distances. Nevertheless, she could still throw out a few *mondanités*, and answered some stupidity of mine by saying it was not surprising that they had made the rooms look 'lived-in' considering that this had been their home now for so long. It was said that Lady Churchill was tonight suffering agonies from phlebitis; but there is still fire and dash in the consort of the old warrior.

These noble rooms of good Georgian proportions have been poorly decorated by the Office of Works. The imitation silk curtains, of meagre quality, are not full enough, have shrunk, and hang five inches from the floor. Sofas are upholstered in timid, puky pea-greens, almonds and beiges. Yet the effect tonight was splendid, the English portraits making an effective background, the fine chandeliers of Bristol glass sparklingly clear. Friends and well-wishers had sent so many flowers that every ledge and table was adorned with offerings of different shapes and sizes. There were luxurious baskets with sprays of peach blossom, roses and orchids: others were more humble precursors of spring with early daffodils. The personal touch was supplied by portraits of the family by Orpen and Birley, some refined, good taste 'still-lives' in muted colours and bevelled frames by that most sensitive and beautiful painter, William Nicolson, and rows of framed snapshots of the family.

But the guests provided the chief interest of the evening. Proust said that it is possible to get a vivid impression of the quality of a party by reading only a few of the names published in a newspaper. One look at this assemblage and one could tell that this was of a fine vintage, mellow and restrained. By the omissions one could tell as much as by those present. These people were not necessarily of the aristocracy, nor of politics; few of them were involved seriously in the arts – though literature was represented; but the gathering represented a quality that is above distinctions; that, unmindful of what the world thinks, has its own code of merit. Neither did beauty, or rare good looks, play a preponderant role – no one was invited for their renown. In this household Royalty is certainly highly respected; but this was a private occasion, an occasion apart, and the presence of Royalty, which always creates a tension, would be contrary to the effect desired. So no Royal personage was invited, but relations, friends, and the confederates who went back into the very earliest years were relaxing together in affection and friendship.

Churchill's doctor was among the favoured; but none of his professional allies were invited unless they happened to be friends too. Ghosts of former Governments abounded: reminders of Asquith in Lady Violet Bonham-Carter, with Etruscan profile and scared donkey's eyes, tonight surprisingly *décolletée* in bright pink satin – surprising because, with her great intelligence and intellectual interests, she has seldom shown an interest in chiffons; and Cynthia Asquith, looking sadly stolid instead of the pre-Raphaelite sprite that she always will be remembered as. Still recognizable as having been a great Edwardian beauty was old Pamela Lytton, curved and bent, but pink and white in black lace. It is said that the young Churchill admired her above others, and there was a question of an engagement. How astonished she would have been if I, a complete stranger, had gone up to her and asked why, when she went to that Empire Day Ball given by F.E. Smith and Lord Winterton in 1911, dressed as Pavlova as 'The Swan', she had worn a long skirt instead of showing her legs in a tutu! How could she guess that this interloper enjoyed gleaning such pieces of useless information as a precocious schoolchild from the society magazines? I remembered also the early photographs of Anita Leslie, a descendant of the Leslie clan, as a tall, shy child. Now she was looking just as surprised as ever with her raised eyebrows, but she had suddenly become mature – a matron. How impersonal and beastly is the disguise of old age! It reduces the individuality of the most vivid personalities: even Margaret, Lady Birkenhead, with aquiline features and bright, bird-like eyes, whom one imagined would always challenge the years, now looks rather sad and perturbed in old age. Margaret was one of my first upholders, and she occupies a large place in my heart. She always judged people by her own standards, never accepted ready-made opinions or acknowledged reputations decided by others. Gipsy-like, unconventional, utterly unsnobbish, she wore very lightly the burdens of her husband's high office; tonight she brought to the gathering her own craggy bonhomie and the aura of the great F.E.

I doubt if white-haired, but ageless and indefatigable Sylvia Henley, Venetia Montague's sister, a tremendous Churchill prop, ever looked much different – but then I've only known her for twenty years. Apart from the immediate family there were masses of Romillys, and naturally Mitfords. There, with red bobbed hair, was Molly Long, known as 'Marmalade Moll'; she exudes the friendliness and sympathy of a firelit tea in winter, and her voice is like the crunching of toast.

Many important relics of the last war were on view. Sir Archibald Sinclair, who used to be so handsome in a romantic Victorian mould, has now become diminished of stature and the fiery black has turned to cinders. His wife, by his side, is now twice his size – an enormous grey-haired matron. Another figure from the past: that horrid old snob, Professor Lindemann, now risen to be Lord somebody. Faces known by caricature and political cartoons acquired an extra dignity this evening as they came out of retirement. Lord Ivor Spencer Churchill always presents a most remarkable appearance, aristocratic and refined, with the pursed, cherubic features of his American mother, Madame Balsan, famous for the Boldini and Helleu portraits, and his expression that denotes that he, quicker than anyone, realizes the sadness and amusement of the fact that he will never appear grown-up. Clarissa and Anthony Eden – successors to this house – were conspicuous by their absence in Manchester.

This was no occasion for an exchange of darts, for political, social or any other warfare. People stood about, drinking a glass of champagne and displaying their nicest moods. Although happy at receiving this cheerful hospitality they knew that, although nothing has been announced, the resignation of the Prime Minister is imminent. The Churchills had left Chequers for the last time this weekend, the Queen comes to dine here on Tuesday, and it is assumed that the resignation will be given next day. So this was the end of an epoch, and everyone present realized it. There was much unmentioned sadness.

We wandered into the small dining-room where the host cut the birthday cake. Juliet Duff suggested that Winston should make a speech. 'My days of speech-making are almost over,' he said. 'Someone else can do it,' and he pointed to Lord Goddard. 'Why not he who sends bad men to the gallows?'

Randolph was emotionally upset and carrying on a feud against the world; one's heart went out to him in his suffering. Later he led me up to sit and talk with his father while Diana Cooper was having her half-hour with the great man. I was extremely diffident of encroaching as, with certain people whom I most admire, I would rather run a hundred miles than be forced *vis-à-vis*. I found that the two were talking about modern painting and Winston raged against his portrait by Graham Sutherland. 'These modern chaps! You're in their power. They make some drawings, and then go away and do their damnedest: they like to make a fool of you. I *hate* this thing! And I wouldn't be surprised if no one got the opportunity of looking at it after my day. It's a horrible portrait – a horror and vile in colour!'

The first time I had ever met Churchill was at a party Venetia Montague had given for his birthday at a time when he was still in eclipse. Supper was served for about a dozen of us around a large table; there was iced champagne, hot oysters, a very special dish that I believe Venetia had had sent in from the Embassy Club, and a great reverence for the great 'star' of the evening. I became paralysed with fright, and was incapable of speech.

Tonight I peered at Churchill at the end of his long and glorious career. His pale eyelashes were blinking, his thin wisps of delicate white hair were combed neatly back, and I noticed the very peculiar, flat end to his bulbous nose which appeared as if cut off straight with a knife. Churchill sat hunched up, his shirt-front rose in a high big roll, and his waistcoat seemed almost 'Empire' in cut. He sucked on the end of a long cigar without pretence of smoking it. He made a few jokes that showed that the old spirit had not deserted him and our laughter was a little exaggerated with relief; but his delivery is so high in Gibbonian style, with long pauses for effect, that every remark is given added pith when delivered in such a grandiose manner – or conversely, when thrown away in his own inimitable offhand style. Churchill, aged eighty-one, looked fit – a very, very healthy baby – but he was somewhat deaf and hated being shouted at by kind friends who were gallantly doing their best to amuse him.

Winston does not enjoy having to accept the inevitability of old age. He said, rather sadly, that if he were to loose the reins of responsibility, and leave the fate of the country in the hands of others, he would, at any rate, have leisure for his painting. But, although he feels groggy some of the time, he knows that in fits and starts he is more alert and experienced than anyone else.

I left the gathering with Diana. She was very sad. Trying to comfort her, I made some ridiculous remarks about the Churchills going out on a high wave. Diana listened hardly at all to my imbecilities: she was deep in her own thoughts. Duff had been such a friend ... his whole life – and their life together – so closely linked with Winston ... Diana was inconsolable.

21

The Daily Round
1955–60

Work took C.B. backwards and forwards between London and New York, as well as to Paris. There were holidays in the South of France, in Venice, Rome, Switzerland, Spain and Greece, and he made a journey to Japan with Truman Capot, from which he returned by Hong Kong, Bangkok, Angkor Vat and Honolulu. C.B. designed for the stage, The Chalk Garden, My Fair Lady, Saratoga *and* Tenderloin; *for the Metropolitan Opera House, Barber's* Vanessa; *for the screen,* Gigi. *He published* It Gives Me Great Pleasure (*about the lecture tour*), The Face of the World *and* Japanese. *Peter Watson died. C.B. was appointed a Commander of the British Empire.*

Paris: Summer

No one knows the real age of Elsie Mendl; some say it was over a hundred years ago that she was born in America. Until recently, she gyrated like a galvanized monkey and in order to maintain her physical flexibility exercised herself each day in a most frenetic fashion. These acrobatics were watched by her awed friends and admiring staff who applauded the climax, a *pièce montée* when Elsie stood on her head. However, one day disaster overtook her. At least one vertebra was wrenched out of place, and the poor old girl was never to be the same.

Looking extremely delicate, Elsie is lying on a velvet leopard-skin-covered sofa in the bathroom of her Paris apartment. It is a room filled with orchids in crystal vases, glass objects, mirrors and mirror-screens behind one of which is her *chaise percée*. Elsie seems to be getting smaller every month and is certainly prettier – prettier than she has ever been before. Not until she was eighty did she learn to smile; it is now a sweet smile.

Soon a bachelor from the United States is shown into the room, and kisses are exchanged. The confirmed bachelor explodes: 'Well now, my dear, I've got some news for you!' The usual flapping and confidential gestures and grimaces. 'I'm going to bring Mr Getty into your life, and he's so rich you just can't believe it!' Elsie's health is at once restored. Bolt upright, she asks: 'But can't we get him to buy my Coromandel screen?'

I photographed Elsie this morning. She has just recovered from her last face-lifting operation (only a month ago). The bruises are no longer Stephen's ink blue and dark red, and the stitches hardly show, but no one is yet allowed to kiss her on the cheeks. It was a major operation, and only an incredible old bird like Elsie could undergo such a shock voluntarily, and through sheer discipline be able to withstand it.

For her photographer Elsie wore an elaborate new ball-gown with a white tulle crinoline skirt. The hairdresser, Antonio, had done his best with the few remaining strands of hair – had dyed them mauve, fluffed them into corkscrews, and filled in with spangled bows. The chauffeur, upstairs for orders, was invited in to admire the result of so much time, energy and expense. Elsie paraded in front of him like a mannequin on a wire. She asked: 'Don't you think it's pretty, Léon?' Léon, the driver, truthfully said: '*Och, mais c'est un miracle!*'

Elsie telephoned from Versailles to invite me down to dine. Her accent was as strongly Bostonian as ever (which sounds, in her case, like Brooklynese – a 'doity-doid' for 'thirty-third'), but her voice was sad, frail and crackling. 'My dear, I didn't *know* there was so much human pain to be endured in this world. It's the spine, you see, and they can't take out the spine of a very old wummun. They can't do nothun but drug you, and I've never been much of a druggist.' When I arrived the butler told me she was sleeping.

I decided to go for a walk in the park of Versailles. The Hubert Robert avenues of vast dark trees were a triumph of symmetry; at certain points one came to the junction of eight avenues stretching to the statue-adorned horizons. Surely the French in the eighteenth century had reached their peak in ordering nature to current fashion? Returning to Elsie's entirely green garden, I wondered if she had not beaten even the eighteenth century at its own game? The lawns were like billiard cloth, the overhanging trees were 'set' in place by a great scene designer so that not a branch dare move. But the *clous* of Elsie's topiary garden were the trees cut into the shape of oversize elephants. These green animals were Elsie's last defiance at the contempt with which the Germans had maltreated her garden during the Occupation.

I remember coming down to see the house directly after the enemy had left, in order to report to Elsie, in her Californian refuge, on the damage that had been inflicted to her pinchbeck palace. Against the boiseried walls, where Elsie's carefully-chosen Jacob and Cressant pieces had once been placed, it was a travesty to see modern brothel-furniture, and a naked electric-light bulb hung where rock-crystal chandeliers had been. The cellar was ransacked, but I remember finding in a cupboard a mountain of Elsie's scrapbooks.

I came in from the garden and my forest walk. The other dinner guest, the American Howard Sturgess, had by now appeared. We awaited the imminent arrival of Elsie. Various white-gloved servants came in to alter the placing of a chair or squirt the flower-scented air with more oriental perfumes. In the distance a parrot squawking, a great rattle over parquet floors, and Elsie, at very high speed, was wheeled in sitting like an idol in her chair.

Elsie is magnificent – and knows it. She squeaks with pleasure at our compliments about her coiffure, her sparkling jacket, her new necklace. We drink dry martinis immediately served on small silver trays with the same biscuits that Maxine Elliott patented in the South of France. Elsie's food is always imaginative and unusual. She makes rules – never any soup: 'Don't start your dinner on a lake!' An exquisite meal is served at a small circular table decorated with, paradoxically among the silver gilt and crystal, some rustic branches of nasturtiums.

Later Elsie confessed: 'I've outlived my time. I realize it: I'm too old now. I ought to have died before the war; I've just been hanging on since then, and for someone who's led such an active life as I have, it's terrible to retire and take things easy, and try to preserve a little vitality.'

Elsie showed us tonight, in many little ways, something of the experience she has gained in a long life of hard work. Yet, up to the last, she has brought amusement and activity with her.

When the evening had come to an end for her – it was to be the last time that I was ever to see her – she bade us remain and drink another glass of wine as the night was young – except for an old lady. She was then lifted up to bed by the chauffeur, Tony. The sincerity of the demonstration of love on the part of the servants was a tribute to her qualities. The servants were not merely in attendance on a rich old woman whom they knew would soon die and, maybe, leave them a fat present; they were grateful that such a remarkable character had treated them with the greatest fairness and consideration over a long period.

Howard Sturgess (he too, like Elsie, to die so soon) in his foghorn voice said: 'Elsie was wonderful tonight. I shall always remember her in that little jewelled jacket, with the butterflies in her hair, sitting against the green of the garden in the twilight.'

Tony, the gloomy chauffeur, driving me to the station to return to Paris, said: 'She may have been wonderful tonight. That's because you were there and gave her an incentive, and she hopped herself up, but in the morning she won't feel so good. She'll 'ave a 'orrible 'angover!'

Venice: September

When Venice was comparatively new to me, twenty or thirty summers ago, the Italian aristocracy continued to congregate as they had done since the days of Canaletto, in St Mark's Piazza after the heat of the day was over. With eighteenth-century flourish they continued to greet one another with exaggerated nods and smiles.

I remember the buzz of excitement and the whispers: 'There's the Morosini!' as an elderly lady with dazzling white complexion, flaming hair under a large, hard hat, dressed in a pale salmon coat-and-skirt, grinned and bowed to left and right like a mechanical marionette. To a few fortunate ones she gave a brief audience; these remained at attention while she, grimacing, conferred upon them the accolade of her approval.

The Morosini was said to have been more admired than any woman in Italy, and to have had many important lovers, amongst whom was the German Kaiser who, at the time she was living at the Ca d'Oro, had addressed one of his letters to her simply:

> To The Most Beautiful Woman
> In the Most Beautiful House
> In the Most Beautiful City In The World.

The letter is said to have reached its destination.

Brando Brandolini intimated one morning recently that nothing would be easier than for him to take me to meet the Morosini, and that it would amuse him to see my reactions to her. Since the former beauty now never emerges from her *palazzo*, having had the misfortune to break a femur, and must remain in an invalid's chair, she has become to the outside world even more of a legend.

At the end of a great hall on the *piano nobile* of a *palazzo* overlooking the Grand Canal, with shining, polished stone floor and high, echoing walls, there came an extraordinary series of parrot-like screams. As the volume of sound increased at our approach, a white-haired, painted woman with cherries and cream complexion, in black taffeta, was seen in the distance, waving and gesticulating wildly from her perch.

'Who are you?' she screamed in English. 'Who is this? Six of you – what a lot! ... Brando and Charlie Bestigui? ... And who are you? ... Oh, Ode de Mun and Freddie Cabrol and Daisy ... And who are you? ... Oh! – are you the English photographer who took the Coronation? Oh, you're very chic, very elegant!' Gales of convulsed laughter.

The aged beauty, eighty-nine years of age, wielded a stick and fluttered her large, black fan like a great actress who knows that the curtain is up and that the Goldoni comedy is under way. She relayed the tattle of Venice. Gossip is her passion and keeps her going: from early morning until two o'clock each day she is busy screaming into the telephone. She knows who is leaving, who is arriving, and not only who is sleeping, but who is dining with whom; it is a life of eighteenth-century intrigue and plot.

Footmen poured glasses of raspberry or redcurrant juice, or tipped cream into coffee. An incessant stream of visitors arrived. The old lady gave the impression of merry sweetness and loving kindness. But at no time had she been particularly endowed with either of these qualities; always she had shown a healthy respect for important people and an inflexible indifference to others. She could always laugh at herself and was the first to relate how, in a desperate attempt to improve the service in her house, as soon as she heard of the death of one of her best friends she telephoned to the butler, before the cadaver was even laid out, to know if he and his first footman would come into her household. It was after her fifth call that the butler ordered the telephone to be taken off the hook.

The Morosini continues to flash her fan above the splashing waters of the Canal. Perhaps only now has she reached her apotheosis. She has everything she needs; happiness exudes from her. She has acquired an audacity of speech and a frankness that comes with either extreme youth or partial senility.

Mouton (Rothschild): November

It is winter in England but it is like summer here – flowering Judas, chestnut, cherry and laburnum trees, wistaria rampaging, flower-beds spilling bachelors' buttons and pansies.

My bedroom: *Louis Seize* bed painted white, *toile de Jouy* upholstery on white-painted furniture. Chinese pots containing lilac, plants in earthenware pots and saucers.

Through the shutters the sun pierces and makes incandescent the silver inkpot, the strips of brass inlay on the writing table, and discloses the work of a small spider whose silver thread is weaving a pattern attached to the lilac.

The sound of hundreds of doves on the huge, sloping roof cooing with content, the clapping of their wings (applause in flight), deep guttural voices of those working in the stables and vineyards, a saw wheezing, a hammer on wood. Someone, in a burst of whistling, crunches over the gravel.

The vineyards have been kept for three thousand years. The stony earth sprouts fresh, strong shoots of vine. A Roman villa stood where Mouton now stands. With its cellars, its outhouses, stables and barns, it had been converted in 1922 from the seventeenth-century *caves*.

The little villa-house where Pauline and Philippe de Rothschild live today was built in 1890; with its tall Gothic stone walls, it is like a child's illustration to Walter Scott. Inside it is crammed with Napoleon III decorations, bead pictures, bead cushions, gold drawing-room furniture upholstered in scarlet brocade, flowered rugs on red carpets and coloured glass panes in the verandah porch.

Huge trumpet-shaped vases, filled with blossom, stand on the floor and there are pots of calceolarias and ferns. Miniatures in jewelled frames are mounted on velvet and displayed on easels.

There are many dogs. Philippe says: 'A dog in the home is a piece of moving furniture.' 'What's the time? Oh, only an hour-and-a-half before dinner. That's not enough for pottering about my room and I must read the last act of a play,' says Philippe.

Bravo! Robert! The applause is for the flower decorations on the dining table. A raw-boned youth in white, starched jacket gives a twitch of pleasure and a subservient nod. Philippe says he always insists on having a different arrangement of flowers on the table for every meal. Another youth brings in a freshly-ironed napkin, unfolds it with ceremony, lays it on the floor, then brings in the dog's dinner and places it on the napkin. M. le Baron, in claret velvet jacket and white satin tie, is robustly appreciative of the *petits soins*. Pauline asks: 'What are these called?', flicking a delicate hand towards the embroidered tablecloth which has been dotted for the occasion with sprigs of bridal wreath and laburnum surrounding a centrepiece of iris and chestnut blossom. It is a work of imagination. 'And he's just a simple peasant boy from here. He's never been further than Pauillac,' says Philippe, rubbing his out-stretched hands as he settles down to his place at table.

A miraculous meal is served. 'To be greedy in this house is considered a form of politeness,' Philippe says, but unfortunately he must ignore the *soufflé*, so too the other dishes. His doctor forbids him to indulge. Elaborate dishes are taken from the table minus only one spoonful. Pauline toys with some water-cress salad. It is the ritual that she enjoys and the opportunity for serious con-versation. Tonight the subject is Izak Dinesen, Baroness Blixen, the one and only great literary star in Denmark 'who has all the Danish assets'. According to Pauline no woman writes about men as well as she. Her dialogue is always convincing. Dinesen seems to dislike women. Sometimes she invites seven men to dine. Yet, according to Pauline, although she tells an anecdote extremely beautifully in a man's deep voice, there is something less interesting about her personality than her writing. When she left Africa after having lost her lover, her husband and her money, she told a friend that she could do three things: she could cook, write, or become a tart. (Pauline considers forty to be an excellent age for a tart.) Dinesen decided that writing was the least hard work.

To some, Pauline seems affected, but her affectations have become com-pletely natural. She has a rare capacity for concentration, and she expects others to listen to her with the same intensity that she would give to them.

She is direct and purposeful. When one is not following her, she challenges one and proceeds to contradict if one's reasoning is hazy.

Pauline has come to rest in a well-lined nest. She has had a life of great contrasts – an unsuccessful marriage, a period of selling jerseys in Formentor, and various romantic attachments which led her to all parts of the earth and to no particular world. Yet Pauline has always known what she wants. Others may not have wanted Philippe, but Pauline was certain she knew he was for her. When she was introduced to him, she said with reverence: 'Not the poet!' and that flattered him above all else.

Pauline still has signs of independence. In Paris she lives in her bachelor apartment away from her husband's house in the Avenue d'Iena. She goes to Rome to learn how to draw; she has a model to pose for two months in the same position; thick portfolios are filled with drawings of the same subject. 'You can't have a teacher for this sort of thing: you must work things out your own way.'

Yet Pauline is deeply enmeshed with her husband's interests. Her eyes look meltingly at him; she laughs at his worst jokes, ignores or does not notice his interruptions. Philippe drops a fragment of food on to his dinner jacket, scrapes it off and eats it. She becomes tired; Philippe's vitality is excessive, but that is no complaint; Pauline, besotted, smiles.

Pauline is never hurried, never impatient; she loves to idle, to sit on a stone wall and watch the antics of her terriers. Meals are late: luncheon at two, tea at seven-fifteen, dinner nine-thirty. She is impervious to the passage of the months. A sofa, a room, an apartment, or a new building will take a long time to finish – a year maybe – but she has a five-year plan, a seven-year plan, a ten-year plan. She is not afraid of the future, or of loneliness; she takes her design for living for granted. If it is too exquisite, too refined for more earthly mortals, it has its own reality. She is an artist in life. She has the variety of an actress's inflections in her voice, sometimes so lightly skimming over the parenthesis then hitting the important word hard. Her gesticulations and arm movements are over life-size.

On board ship

I'm tired of seeing Margaret [Duchess of Argyll] about 'everywhere'. She always looks wonderful, but always the same, with her dark eyes and nut-brown hair, her pink and white complexion, her bandbox fresh dresses chosen with impeccable restraint. There is nothing of the private faces in public places about her. There is a dull inevitability and monotony about her beauty.

I was leaving New York once more by ship, and there was the usual dockers' strike. Going up in a luggage lift in the company of a bunch of fellow passengers, I was appalled to find myself standing next to Margaret. Oh, God! Would I have to be her companion for the next five days? I was a bit taken back when she asked if we could eat together during the voyage in order to escape the boredom of certain of her friends. What on earth could one find to talk about all the time? I believe it was the late Lord Wimborne who said of Margaret: 'She don't make many jokes, do she?'

Soon after the hooting and moaning of sirens, and as we were slowly passing 'downtown' Manhattan, I ran into Margaret sitting upright at a table, watching through a dirty window the skyline of Wall Street passing away from us. She had about her an extraordinary air of leisure and self-completeness.

'I always love to watch New York like this. Even if we arrive at six in the morning I come up to watch. I *love* New York. I feel so well there; it's a tonic for me. I'm always sad at leaving. But [surprised and startled] these windows are dreadfully dirty. Do they realize they haven't been washed for days? That's not too good, is it?'

I was amused at her apparent shock. Today most smart ladies are no longer surprised to see dirty windows. When I told Margaret I had intended to economize and have some of my meals in the dining-room and not pay extra each time I go up to the Verandah Grill, she was equally shocked.

'Oh, but I love sitting with the sun shining and all the windows on to the sea. I can't bear eating during the day in electric light! Promise me to be in the Verandah Grill at one!'

Margaret was already sitting, cool and serene, when I went up. She was surveying the sea with a certain wide-eyed amusement. I discovered she has the capacity to be 'on' to herself.

I have known Margaret since she and my sisters were schoolgirls together, but I have never spent much time hearing her talk. I discovered that her idiom of speech is extremely fashionable. Her language is quite strong. Some particular man she described as the 'President of the Shit Club'. She explained: 'There's no nonsense about me. Oh no, I'm earthy: you can't fool me. I'm shrewd and have lots of commonsense which is very rare. Why do they call it "common" when so few people have it? No, I'm master at calling people's bluff, making them come off their perches; but I can't keep my great mouth shut. It's terribly hard for me not to contradict even when I know it's no good to do so, and I'm always putting my foot in my mouth. Queen Gaffeuse.' She admitted her clothes are the result of inordinate care and thought, that she buys them in New York because they're better value, but goes to Paris to keep her eye in. 'I love the way American women look – that neat, clean, simple look – but I couldn't be that. The overdressed type, that's me.'

Margaret must be one of the few left today who still feels impervious to the approach of the common man. Her money has given her a sense of security, and she is one of the rare examples of someone who has used it well.

'I'm a very good housekeeper. I run my home beautifully. I entertain a lot, but I don't think any woman should spend more than five minutes a day talking about the arrangements; it's too dull. But men hate the fact that I do it all so quickly. I talk to my cook on the house telephone each morning, but I wouldn't dream of going down to the kitchen. She knows that I can't boil an egg, so what would I tell her? I hate it in America where nowadays your hostess puts on an apron and says she is going to fry a steak. I want other people to do the cooking, and I can't bear it [apropos a visit to a Cabinet Minister] when people mow the lawn. They should get others to cut back the roses and dig.'

I discovered Margaret has quite a talent for observing her particular sort of existence, and drawing definite conclusions. 'American women are too sure of their husbands: Englishmen too sure of their wives.' 'French women spend their days sitting on the *bidet*.' Poor-little-rich girlisms: 'I love to dance, better than to eat.' 'I love camellias, but I don't like to see them growing.' 'Oh, do look at Lady Rosse with amber necklace and diamond bracelets and sapphire brooch. Oh dear, she hasn't thought that *parure* out!' When her husband, while on honeymoon, was 'putting on the dog' in Seville (in Holy Week), complaining of their poky bedroom to the management and saying: 'After all, I am the Duke of Argyll', Margaret chided him later, saying: 'Sweetie, don't try that one; in this town dukes are two-a-penny. If you want to get results just start crackling a few crisp dollars!'

New York: November

This year, instead of staying in the cushioned unreality of a luxury hotel, I rented the apartment of a Sicilian friend, Fulco Verdura: unkind friends said that in taste it was Poor Man's Charlie Beistigui. To me it was extremely pleasant, with avalanches of good art books and long-playing records of the classics; a mixture of Mannerist paintings, seventeenth- and eighteenth-century engravings, and sketches by Bérard; nice bits of china, palm trees and dark green walls, an effective if slightly sketchy attempt at interior decoration. A bell rang downstairs: a fastener on the door was a safety-valve against unwelcome visitors. 'Who is it?' A voice answered my shout: 'It's the garbage man', or 'Any roaches to be got rid of?'

Even before I had unpacked I was totally engrossed with work. I was soon at such fever pitch that the coloured servants were incredulous and said: 'Do you always keep it up like this?' Some evenings I would come back so tired that I could hardly stagger up the short flight of iron steps to my first-floor apartment, and I would fling myself on the day bed, soon to recover energy after at least three or four cups of tea from a thick, chipped-spouted, yellow earthenware teapot.

My immediate job was to assemble the furniture, props and a thousand little details for Enid Bagnold's *The Chalk Garden*. Work on this had already been going on for many months in London. It has not been an easy assignment and I would be called up late at night to talk about rethinking the whole visual conception. At weekends, too, I had to be on duty. It was not an agreeable experience, and I cannot think why I had not decided to break my contract, and be free – free – free! However, now I had more or less finished my designs, the workshops were busy building the sets and, apart from costume fittings, I was able to find time for correcting the proofs of a comic book, my experiences of a lecture tour on the blue-rinse circuit. Although the eventual possibility of production seemed more remote than ever, I also tried to do a bit of polishing to the last scene of my long-deferred Gainsborough play. Also I did designs for a small ballet, *Soirée*, for the Met. with Karinska making the costumes.

Three whole months had gone by in an incubator of work.

It has been a Garbo-less visit. I was deeply hurt. She sent a message through Truman Capote that she wanted me to call her, that she wanted me to take her to Jamaica, but I reckoned, sadly, that she reacts more favourably to a negative reply.

The Ambassador Hotel, New York: 16 March 1956

Through my windows on Park Avenue a winter scene presented itself, and a pretty violent one it appeared to be but, fortunately, my work confined me to the rooms. These I have decorated myself (and for the hotel!) in a Japanese *nouveau art* manner. Since I have ceased to work for *Vogue*, I have been doing quite a lot of sittings for the deadly rival, *Harper's Bazaar*. The editor, Carmel Snow, despite all these years on the staff has never lost her innate enthusiasm and lettuce-crisp enjoyment. She is an inspiration. It gave me a new lease of life to discover the offhand way in which she whipped up her confectionery with the slightest effort. She worked with the minimum staff, and seemed to enjoy the impromptu.

However, my main photographic work was a book for George Weidenfeld, to be called *The Face of the World*. To my strangely decorated rooms came a procession of personalities – Dr Suzuki, the great Japanese philosopher; Eudora Welty, sad and sensitive; Mary Macarthy, by whom I am determined not to be alarmed, and many other varied personages.

Jim Benton, with dark monkey-fringe for hair and a slow, deep voice, came to do a few secretarial chores for me. By degrees work became hectic, yet Jim proved himself a master-hand at keeping things under control with the ever-ringing telephone and the various chores that now kept me indoors most of the day and night. He would buy necessities for the ice-box, be messenger, look after the vastly increasing hoard of photographs which I was collecting for the book. He gave me a perspective on the glamour potential of some of my sitters or visitors. He made, for instance, a sitting with Joan Crawford into quite an event. Very seriously he said: 'Why, she hasn't had such a distinguished workout in years!' He was less impressed by the personality of Callas, who was one of my most difficult photographic subjects. However the tornado visit of Marilyn Monroe was the greatest fun. Although one-and-a-half hours late, Marilyn was instantly forgiven for her disarming, childlike freshness, her ingenuity and irresistible mischievousness. The cupboard where the photographs were kept suddenly became full to overflowing; the bills mounted appallingly but, fortunately, so did the invoices that Jim sent out.

Working on the production of *The Chalk Garden* had been for me so deeply disturbing that I felt disinclined ever again to work for the stage as a designer. I was lucky to have had the offer of another play, which turned out to be one of the happiest productions of all time.

When that most delightful, witty and loyal of all friends, Herman Levin, had rung me in London to say Alan Lerner and Frederick Loewe were doing a musical of *Pygmalion* for him and that they wanted me for the costumes, I had not been enthusiastic about the project. Some years back the Theatre Guild had come to me with the same project. Gertie Lawrence was to be 'Eliza' and I was thrilled at such a prospect, but all had fizzled out.

There was another reason for regret: Oliver Smith had already been signed to do the scenery, and although I am devoted to Oliver, I had made a rule that I would never again participate in only one of the facets of what I considered should be a visual whole. However, I went to Claridge's and listened to Fritz Loewe strumming the music on a piano while Alan Lerner croaked his lyrics. No sooner had they given their rendering of 'The Rain in Spain stays mainly on the Plain' than I knew the venture must be a dazzling triumph. Of course I would do the costumes – better than nothing. My decision had been fortunate.

In New York I had spent five weeks working on the costumes and then returned to England where Rex Harrison's clothes were to be made. Rex is a perfectionist and demands minute attention. I had taken him to my tailor and made quick decisions about what he should wear: I work like that. If too many alternatives are suggested, I am likely to become waylaid, and even influenced for the bad. Rex is like a dog with a rat and will 'worry' details at enormous length. If given the opportunity, he will work himself up into a state of nervous alarm. I cannot say that Rex is the easiest boy in the class. But he has good taste and knows when something is not right for him. If it is wrong, he can become wild. One morning, he ripped off in anger his first-act long coat because it was tight under the arms. The seams split and the expensive stuff was frayed. The 'strait-jacket' was thrown to the floor.

But Rex is a martyr to indecisions and doubts. About this time, one evening after dinner at my house, he suddenly decided that as he had not signed his contract he did not after all wish to play the part of Henry Higgins. 'They wanted Gielgud – they'd better get him.' I telephoned in a panic to New York. Rex soon changed his mind.

One morning we had been choosing shirts, pullovers and ties in Burlington Street and, on the way to his hotel, Rex suggested I should go back with him and talk over our choice. 'It might be better if instead of the buff colour...' He was very put out when I suddenly hailed a taxi for home.

Berman's did the right thing by the clothes that Stanley Holloway wore for Doolittle – a sweet man, gentle, unassuming and what an artist! I am ever grateful to him for giving the performance of a long lifetime.

At this time it was customary to dress almost all period musicals in the styles of the 1900s. It had become a cliché. A certain amount of opposition met the proposal that I should use the fashions of 1914 – those of the time when Shaw originally wrote the play. 'Surely they won't be sexy!' I promised they would be sexy. There was also scepticism about my idea of doing the Ascot scene in black and white. I remembered the pictures of 'Black Ascot', after King Edward VII's death, and the effect was stunning. But for this particular scene perhaps the women would appear too much like vultures. The 'magpie' effect was the solution. Moss Hart, the director, was in agreement with me and the other chiefs shrugged their shoulders and said: 'Well, all right.'

Here at last was the opportunity to put on the stage all the memories stored up since my early boyhood. My mother's grey ostrich-feathered hat would suit Mrs Higgins at Ascot. My Bolivian Aunt Jessie's enormous cartwheel hats were remembered, and Elfie Perry, the first actress I ever met, wore a striped dress that would now be given to Eliza.

At the first reading on Broadway before the assembled company everyone was keyed up, convinced that they were participating in something exciting. Each number was spontaneously applauded. The atmosphere was electric.

I doubt if any major musical production has been brought to the stage with less difficulty. Of course it was damned hard work for all concerned, but apart from cutting a whole ballet and writing in an important scene there were the minimum of changes. Moss Hart, the captain of the crew, was brilliant, professional and tireless.

It was a happy day when Helène Pons said she would undertake to make the clothes. A dark little Russian with bruises under her eyes, a pretty mouth and a nose finely sculptured, this heroic woman worked with a sensitivity and delicacy of touch only equalled by the strength of her staying power.

Returning to New York I was now in the midst of the excitement. I was out of my hotel rooms for most of the day. (My wrist became severely strained by having to push so many times a day the heavy door of glass at the entrance of dressmaker Helène's studio building.)

Julie Andrews, an almost unknown girl who had the talent and luck to land the whopper of the part of Eliza, was almost unbelievably *naïve* and simple. She was angelically patient at the many fittings of her clothes and never expressed an opinion. One day, due to exhaustion at rehearsals, she keeled over in a dead faint while fitting her resplendent ball-gown. A Dixie cup of cold water was enough to revive her and she reproached herself that her mother, back home in Walton-on-Thames, would be ashamed of her. 'Oh, Mummie, what a silly girl I am,' she kept repeating.

One evening when we had seen enough of Julie's performance to know that she was absolutely perfect for the role, I rather impertinently said that she must try always to remember this most wonderful moment in her career, when she was just about to burst on the world as a star. It was typical of Julie's modesty and professionalism to say in a somewhat Eliza-like phrase: 'The only thing that matters is if I do it right.' She did!

Nothing could have been more exquisite than Cathleen Nesbitt's little cameo as Mrs Higgins and she never suggested for a moment that I had overdressed her. Bob Coote was totally effective as the waffling Colonel Pickering.

Rex Harrison was by now extremely tense; never having appeared in a musical before, and doing something so utterly different, he felt he could not rehearse enough. The chorus-girls, long since exhausted, lay on the floor or were sprawled in the stalls, while Rex repeated, over and over again, certain phrases of 'I've grown accustomed to her face'. At length, when he was playing the last-act fight scene with Liza and she threw the slippers in his face, the entire chorus applauded from the stalls.

No doubt Rex was right. He knew his performance was more important than the impatience of thirty chorus-girls and dancers. However, Rex's continuing egotism upset me to such an extent that only by a miracle was I prevented from making an ugly scene. I was so steamed up to fury on some now forgotten account, and was just about to burst into his room to tell him what I thought of him – an idiotic, pointless and impertinent thing to do in any case – when I was interrupted by the stage manager: 'Moss wants you immediately at the back of the stalls.'

The dress rehearsals in Newhaven were long-drawn-out and complicated. Yet the unions did not prevent their continuing until near dawn. By dint of Moss's brilliant organizing and with help from the stage manager, Bud, the show was able to open in extremely smooth shape.

The news of the success of *My Fair Lady*, as *Pygmalion* was at last named, spread from Newhaven to New York. I had never before worked for a big Broadway musical and I only now realized what it meant to participate in a grand opening.

The performance of the first-night audience was as brilliant as that on the stage. Every joke was appreciated, every nuance enjoyed and the various numbers were received with thunder-claps. The success was beyond all expectation. I did not understand how great it was until next day, while saunter-ing up Park Avenue. I came across someone whom I knew very little for he had never seemed to acknowledge my existence. I was, therefore, extremely surprised when he said: 'Hullo, Seesil, good to see you. You really are quite a guy!'

Success on such a scale now seemed easy, and I wondered why it had never happened before. It had taken such a long time to achieve. It had not come too late, yet I was, perhaps, a bit bitter that some of my friends in the theatre (if there is such an anomaly) did not have confidence in my talent twenty years before. None the less it was pleasant to enjoy it now.

On the last lap of my stay a snowstorm blanketed New York, and its com-muters were isolated. Everything at a standstill for two days; appointments cancelled; I had to delay my sailing by a week. In this time I was able to squeeze in most of the pressing urgencies, including the designing of a set of modern clothes, based on *My Fair Lady*, for a Seventh Avenue wholesale firm.

The telephone seldom stopped ringing, and messengers arrived with pack-ages, or people arrived by appointment. Now the various jobs of work are finished. There are no visible signs of spring in Central Park but those definite vibrations are in the air. I'm impatient to get home, and to see what, in my garden, has survived the great frost.

I arrived at the dock too late for any further visitors to come aboard. I waved to Margaret and Jim and others who had appeared. Hooting – an eerie sound. I went to my cabin and I lay on the bunk. I felt I was on the crest of a wave and must enjoy the ride.

New York

My last meeting with Greta had ended on a high emotional note. The scene had taken place in her rather too ornate apartment. I had drunk vodka cocktails. When Greta mentioned a twenty-year-old score – something about her having no heart – I became uncontrollably angry. 'If after all these years you can't forget that, then I'm a failure and our friendship means nothing!'

I banged out of the apartment. She came to the elevator to stop me. 'Then you won't marry me?' she joked. But it was no joke to me.

When I had got back to England I wrote her one long, serious, sad letter. Then I decided on silence. When I came back to New York I did not call her.

I did not answer her messages sent through Truman. I went home again and I still did not write.

On my return to New York I waited before telephoning her. She was contrite and sweet. We were friends again, and yet the relationship was different. I had consciously put a brake on my emotions.

On the day before I was sailing, we lunched together at our accustomed table. Unfortunately I had to leave directly after to pay my taxes.

That evening I went to say goodbye to her in her apartment. 'Life is such a compromise! I wanted to live in such a different place from this, and yet one must have tables and chairs! But these are not what I like.' Only her most unfurnished dining-room, where there is a great, solid table that could have been Queen Christina's, looks as if it belonged to her. The ormolu, the bound volumes (never opened), the bits of china were all bought under the influence of 'the little man'. . . .

But suddenly she said that she had been wanting to answer my 'serious' letter. She had wanted to say: 'I do love you, and I think you're a flop! You should have taken me by the scruff of my neck and made an honest boy of me. I think you could have been the Salvation Army.' 'Thank you for telling me that,' I murmured.

Sunday 6 May

I lunched with Peter [Watson] at a branch of Wheeler's restaurant that is near to his Institute of Contemporary Arts in Dover Street. Peter was busy hanging an exhibition of garden schemes from Brazil and could not spare time off to get back to my house for lunch.

We talked, as always, very animatedly. He had survived the rigours of winter though he had been feeling terribly ill and had gone to my Dr Gottfried. He spoke with such gusto and intelligence that I was very happy to listen and admire his point of view; his ever-sensitive appreciation for so many aspects of art and life. I thought that he was a completely fulfilled, integrated person; someone who has been through many vicissitudes and has now discovered himself.

Peter is an independent, courageous person, on terms of absolute honesty with himself, with the world, and with everybody he talks to.

Tony del Renzio, whom I had seen with Peter at the ICA a few days ago, telephoned. I let out a moan that was like that of a bull in agony. I could not speak and I asked him to wait until I had given myself fresh energy to face the dreadful fact that Peter was dead.

Nearly thirty years I have known Peter . . . here a painting of Ashcombe we had found together – so many books – so many memories – snapshots taken in every part of the world – America, Mexico, Austria, Germany, France. I dressed like Peter and I behaved like him.

Later he wore awful mackintoshes – his hair, once so sexily lotioned, was on end. He was a real bohemian – gone the elegant clothes and motor cars. He had become thinner and more gaunt and of a bad colour.

He had edited *Horizon* with Cyril Connolly and become a serious art patron in a quiet, unobtrusive way. He was deeply interested in music, painting, sculpture and poetry. He read books in many languages, and thought a great deal about politics. He was intensely single-minded. Sometimes I would watch him as he talked with such concentration and he would look like a ruffled old chicken, his complexion yellow; he had become very sloppy about shaving and generally had a few cuts around the face. But however awful he looked, he had a quality of beauty. He relied less and less on charm; but his smile was so disarming that people could not but like him.

Paris

Chanel has been the most important influence on fashion since the 1914 war. Her romance with the rich Duke of Westminster became notorious. The duke gave her a block of property in Mayfair, a mill where she designed her particular brand of English tweeds, and a gold-mine in jewels; she was seen in the hunting field with rows of pearls swinging on her habit. Her temperamental scenes and extravagances were violent. It was said that Chanel was the one woman who was never sycophantic or subservient to this incredibly spoilt man. He gave in to her every whim, even setting up a workroom for her at Eaton Hall, complete with her French staff, rather than have her return to Paris a month earlier to make her season's collection. When she was displeased, and the duke tried to placate her with offerings of jewellery, she was likely to stamp on them or throw them through the porthole of his yacht.

Her business continued to prosper with each year. Then came World War II. France under the Occupation became prison; fashion dead.

Now, after an interval of fourteen years, French friends and acquaintances seemed vague about whether or not Chanel still existed. They had positively no idea of her whereabouts since, during the war, she had taken a good-looking husky German as a lover. Certainly, she had long since given up making clothes; the windows in the Rue Cambon still displayed bottles of '*Numéro Cinq*'. However, it was not really difficult to discover that the 'pariah' was still to be found in the apartment at the top of her dress shop. She would be delighted to see me.

Paris seemed empty during that weekend. It was almost an uncanny experience to enter the deserted Chanel building, to walk past row upon row of display stalls long since covered with dust sheets, then up flight after flight of the mirrored stairs, eventually to arrive at a door that opened on to her private apartment and into an Aladdin's cave of oriental splendour; an unbelievable richness of Venetian glass mirrors reflecting lacquer screens, gesso tables and Tang horses.

Strains of Wagner wafted from a hidden gramophone through the expensively-scented atmosphere. An eminent-looking businessman, with a folio of papers under his arm, greeted me in whispers, and in pantomime invited me to accompany him. 'Come here – quick, quick!' With a magician's gesture, he bid me behold: '*Voilà!*' Chanel was asleep on an enormous suede sofa. She was fully dressed, wearing a hat, with a sable rug thrown over her; she had assumed a pose of graceful abandon.

But I felt guilty that I had intruded. It was as if I were looking at someone dead; so, after a moment of admiration, I retreated to the hall while the businessman decided to wake her. Moments later the 'outcast' rushed from the corridor to greet me. It was as if a whole box of fireworks had suddenly gone off: splutters of squibs, diamonds from sparklers, pops from jumping Jacks, and even the whoosh of a rocket. Chanel was talking, laughing, gesticulating, grimacing – in fact, being herself.

After the first pyrotechnic onslaught had successfully won the audience to her side, I realized what a strange and extraordinary sight presented itself; a sunburnt old gipsy was thrusting her unbelievably raddled face within an inch of my nose. One could see that her cheeks had been pulled up to the ears by a violent surgeon, and there were deep lines from the great gash of her almost lipless mouth to the incredibly wide nostrils of her toadstool nose.

The flashing smile and over-brimming vitality soon became hypnotic; the darting blackbird eyes were never still; the rich, creamy croak from deep down her larynx was urgent, confidential, conspiratorial. This *jolie laide* still played her games of attraction expertly. Her welcome was so warm and spontaneous that I felt I had regained a long-lost relation.

Wearing a buff-coloured coat and skirt trimmed with leopard-skin, Chanel had arrived years ago in my mother's drawing-room to be one of my first professional sitters. I was easily alarmed by strangers, and found her particularly difficult to approach. When, years later, she came to New York, and appeared as the very quintessence of Parisian chic at a candle-lit supper party given by the dressmaker, Charles James, she was overwhelmingly attractive, but she seemed to swat her admirers as if they were so many obtrusive flies. How different the reception today!

Back in the sitting-room I now had the opportunity to scrutinize a little of the Golconda collection: the crystal chandeliers, Chinese screens and tables, life-size gazelles and antelopes, the gold objects, the precious stone animals, so typically mixed with classical Greek statues, Italian carvings and

Japanese junk. Chanel apologized that the flat was not finished, that no curtains were hanging at the tall window; but, nevertheless, she preferred living in unfurnished rooms. 'It gives a feeling of life – vitality.' She likes her things to be put around in an impromptu manner; nothing to be arranged or set.

Although she has not designed clothes for many years she appeared today to be ahead of fashion, so incredibly spruce she was, in a Beau Brummell way – yet totally French – in navy-blue serge over white linen blouse. Every detail was of an exquisite refinement and immaculate quality. The simplicity of her perfectly-tailored suit was paradoxically overwhelmed by a fantastic array of jewels; strings of pearls hanging in cascades among chains of rubies and emeralds and gold links around her incredibly thin, stringy neck, and her mushroom hat and a lapel of her coat were each adorned with a vast sunburst of diamonds.

Her appeal for friendliness, her frank lack of reserve, her wide-apart legs with continual flexing of knees, gave one the impression of an attractive young schoolboy, and yet her grace and appeal are entirely feminine. Her hands, without nail varnish, are a young girl's hands and the skin is satiny and unwrinkled.

In her deep, gruff, catarrhal monotone she jabbered non-stop, but it was up to me to try to dam the torrent and start work on the drawing for my book. Her enthusiasm was untiring. Such vitality is irresistible; I could well see why so many remarkable men and women had found her devastating.

Chanel had nothing to do. Now that she wasn't working she had leisure. She was living the life she'd always been unable to live; at last she could meet young people, travel and read; she realized, a little, what was going on in the world. She protested perhaps too much that one must not think of the past, but become part of the changed world. She complained of bores, and was disloyal to her old friends. Apropos of fashion, she said that it had died with the last war and no longer existed or had become entirely commercial: 'Fashion is now in the hands of American Seventh Avenue and the pederasts.'

It is unattractive when older people are poisonous about their rivals. Chanel pronounced opinions that most other women would not have dared to voice. Yet somehow one could not believe in her display of hatred and jealousy; it was as if she were acting the words without feeling. A lot of conversation was geared to the fact that she wished to rehabilitate herself in the eyes of the very Parisians she despised and who, because of her 'collabo' reputation, had dropped her cold. There was an extra reason why she should put herself in a good light for me. She was far too subtle to mention the subject of her 'disgrace', but it was important that she should get word through to Winston Churchill to tell him what a lot she had done for England. Churchill had known her in the South of France before the war; but recently he had not replied to her letters, and it was vital that the British Embassy here in Paris should see to it that he received her messages. Was there anything I could do?

Newton Ferrers, Cornwall

It is doubtful whether anyone will write a life of that most retiring of men, Bertie Abdy, for he has always courted anonymity and would certainly give no active help to his biographer; in fact, he would be as uncooperative, stubborn and difficult as only he knows how to be. Bertie's lack of compromise has reduced his list of friends to the minimum. To a very carefully-sifted little group, who love him for his peculiarities, Bertie has always been irresistible.

Although his father disliked anything connected with the arts, Bertie became passionately interested at the age of ten in the aesthetic world. Later, when he inherited his fantastic fortune (he owned a large slice of the London Docks), he was able to cultivate his ambition to almost unlimited lengths. He denigrates his penchant for the pretty: 'I suppose everything I like is "chocolate-boxy", but look at this Fragonard – isn't it lovely? Every rose bush a Cadbury!' Yet he is surprisingly catholic in his tastes; he is a collector of Renaissance bronzes and was among the first to introduce to London such painters as Degas and Kokoschka. But when even Bertie could not afford to buy more statuary, paintings, books or *objets* for himself, he bought for others. He became expert in advising Chester Beatty, Gulbenkian and other rich collectors in the world. When most of his dockland property was destroyed by fire, he went into business to the extent of advising and finding rare items for such firms as Wildenstein, Seligmann and Partridge.

Bertie is incapable of being a shrewd businessman and feathering his own nest. The essence of integrity himself, he is never embittered when tricked by crooked agents. But his honesty and his lack of tact have made him many enemies. One of his usual sallies is to give advice that is not welcome. Once I showed him a painting of mine that had gone wrong. He told me that there was nothing to be done but fly immediately to Spain to see how Goya would have tackled the problem in an entirely different way. Few people relish his outspokenness. He called Sir Joseph Duveen a mountebank; and when Mrs Neeley Vanderbilt showed him her Fifth Avenue house and explained. 'This is the *Louis Seize* drawing-room', Bertie asked: 'And what makes you think so?' On another occasion a Chilean friend, Tony Gandarillas, bewailing the fact that his elderly dog had become frail and possibly could not live much longer, said he would like to take him to Brighton to see the sea before he died. Bertie inquired: 'Wouldn't it be better if you took him to the Wallace Collection?'

Bertie's standards are so high that he even designated the Kent furniture made specially for the Double Cube Room at Wilton as 'so coarse, it'd be all right for a circus roundabout'. He dismissed the taste of the interior decorator Elsie de Wolfe as 'ribbons and rubbish'.

I have come to stay with Bertie in his rough-hewn stone house, Newton Ferrers, in Cornwall. A catastrophic fire gutted one whole wing that contained many of his greatest treasures; none the less, in other parts of the house a collection of rare books, pictures and sculptures remains unscathed, and the garages, stables, and other out-houses are still filled with terracottas, old-master drawings and Boulle furniture, which he cannot bear to sell.

Bertie, blinking through huge tortoiseshell-rimmed glasses, climbs a step-ladder in his library and hands down a slim volume to be admired. 'What could be prettier than this binding with the Bourbon arms, 1753?' Look at this – no one in England ever did anything to equal this sort of thing!' His long, white, cheese-stick fingers falter along the tops of gold-tooled volumes. 'This is a pretty book for wig-makers and hairdressers of the eighteenth century.' His voice seems even sadder. 'Now this beautiful binding just shows how civilized they were to honour a book on how to make two hundred and fifty different *méringues*! This machinery is for blowing the icing sugar.' A few steps higher on the ladder and Bertie points out the calligraphy of the Dauphin's prayer book. 'Madame de Behargue offered me a thousand pounds for this! I bought it in London for a song. Ah, but mine's only a child's collection!' moans Bertie, coming down the ladder and thinking of the things he would have liked to buy.

Then, unexpectedly, Bertie's face breaks into a thousand pieces as he laughs, takes off his spectacles to polish them with his handkerchief, and explains: 'I'm so hard up I can't afford to go to London any more.' His face becomes ashen and grave again. 'Eleven shillings for a meal – it's preposterous! And uneatable too! That's why I go to Lyon's for a bun and a cup of milk.'

'You can't find anyone to do anything for you nowadays. I used to travel a lot to see dealers and works of art. I'm not a manager, and I don't know how to look after myself. Edwards, my man, used to do everything. I don't care if he stank of my sherry – he looked after me. I'd say: "Get me to Brussels" and he'd manage it. Once, going to Vienna, I found myself on the wrong train; Edwards realized it, and somehow he got on to it and fetched me back. Edwards had a sense of the art of living. He enjoyed his work. He'd spend hours boning my boots. Who has his boots boned today? And each time I put on my clothes they had been ironed – underclothes and pyjamas always ironed! And that man did all the silver! Have you ever tried to clean silver? And the porcelain – every bit he had to wash himself. I used to give Edwards tips – a cheque for one hundred pounds if business was good, and fifty pounds at Christmas. When he left I gave him five hundred pounds because he was worth it.'

At Newton Ferrers today there is no one to valet Bertie (he wears old game-keeper's clothes during the day and green velvet suits at night). He still orders a thousand more flowering cherry trees to blossom in his 'surburban garden of pink veils' ('a million cherry trees and never a cherry'), and once a month he can't resist buying, however small, a Fragonard or a Rouault.

Once in the railway carriage he settled down to talk about Horace or the merits of wine. The doors open. In a stage whisper Bertie moans: 'Oh, two more women with unwashed hair!'

One of Bertie Abdy's more recent possessions is a bronze torso by Henry Moore. This piece of sculpture has been very much in the news. It is said to have been inspired by Moore's first visit to Greece and is considered a work of importance. In fact the Directors of the Manchester Art Museum were interested in buying it, but at the last moment the voting went against them, resulting in newspaper headlines and controversies. The piece has now been placed temporarily by Bertie at Newton Ferrars in Cornwall in a position dominating his elaborately cascading water garden. Henry Moore was due, at any moment, to give his advice about where best it should be permanently placed.

Out of the local taxi bundled hurriedly a little businessman in rough tweeds with a North Country accent. He had, I thought, a rather anonymous appearance; plain pudding-face, weak eyes, pale blue, watery but bright, a beaky nose and irregular, somewhat parrot-beak teeth and a high forehead with receding hair laid flat and lifeless across the dome. No time to be lost before taking him down to the water garden to try and find Bertie. He talked in staccato, jerky sentences and struck his words with insistent hammer-force. He seemed to be trying to overcome an innate nervousness and shyness (and I too).

It took us both a few moments to realize that we shared that particular fraternity of feeling that is common to most people who practise in the world of the arts; we were soon talking as if we had known one another of old.

But if I felt Moore and I had struck a chord of sympathy, it was nothing to the soaring harmony of understanding and genuine recognition that was sparked off the moment that Henry Moore met Bertie. Henry Moore became immediately and completely at ease; Bertie, whose views are not readily understood by many who are practising artists, found at once that he had a soul-mate.

Bertie showed the sculptor the possible sites from which the figure could be seen at good advantage. The three of us marched up, down and around beside the cascades. Finally Henry Moore was convinced that the site chosen by Bertie, at the fount of the water display, was the most effective. We celebrated the decision.

In the railway carriage on our way home we kept up continuous conversation. Henry was unable to contain his enthusiasm for the beauties of the springtime landscapes of Somerset. He kept jumping to his feet to point out as it rolled by some particular vista or phenomenon bathed in blue mists.

Henry considered carving to be soothing work, not too strenuous either physically or mentally. It was more exciting than digging in the garden, but not so exhausting. Much of the time the work was automatic; he could work for eight or twelve hours a day. But drawing, or inventing new shapes in small model form, was creative and took a greater toll.

By the time the train had arrived at Salisbury, where I had to leave the party, I noticed how Henry's face had quite transcended its contours. It had become lively and sparkling, rippling with laughter, the hair blown into a natural shape, the mouth no longer parrot-like.

August 1957

The sun of Beverly Hills was shining above the sentinel palms and through the Venetian blinds into my bungalow. The stillness was broken by large blue birds which darted from scarlet hibiscus to emerald blades of the banana tree and back to the feathery heads of a nameless tropical plant.

Six months previously Arthur Freed had asked me to design the musical film version of Colette's novel *Gigi*. Alan Lerner was to write the book and Fritz Loewe the music. I was well aware that it would be Colette's own world that I should have to re-create, and by degrees I began to see with her avid eyes; the colours and the atmosphere should be hers, not mine. Little girls in tartan dresses, in *broderie anglaise* with black boots and stockings, and great jewelled ladies supping at Maxim's or airing themselves in all manner of *équipages* in the Bois.

Together with Vincente Minnelli I drove to the Musée Grevin, to the Skating Rink, to the Parc Monceau and other landmarks looking for locations. 'This is where Gigi might have lived!' Minnelli mused and pointed to a tall seventeenth-century house overlooking La Cour de Royan. An *'art moderne'* building suggested Aunt Alicia's apartment. Gaston, with his sugar-merchant parents, most likely would have inhabited the grandiose Victorian mansion that now housed the Musée Jacquemart-André.

Preparations were exhaustively detailed. Major additions had already been made to the cast of stars. We winnowed from a crowd of Folies Bergère girls and fashion models the beauties who were to portray *demi-mondaines*. We searched among the army of extras for the warts, wrinkles and noses that would give an authentic Sem character to the ensemble.

I returned to England with a sheaf of notes about Minnelli's requirements.

'*The Bois:* 150 people, dogs, prams, respectable family, two or three aristocratic men on horseback, two women in habits, twelve children.'

'*Maxim's:* 20 characters, caricatures, nobility, actresses, Indian, Polaire, Lady de Grey?'

'*Trouville:* Bathing machines, tennis, diabolo, alpaca swimming costume, etc.'

During May and June I was busy at work on the pinchbeck life of Paris and Trouville of half a century ago. Time was short and I dabbed paint on a hundred drawings as if I were a Japanese factory-worker. Then almost before the paint was dry I would fly off again to Paris to present the designs to producer and director before handing them on to the costumiers. Customs and Passport authorities got to know me well during those weeks.

As a result of the tests, I began to avoid certain dangerous colours. Experience showed that most bright reds became claret colour; greys inexplicably turned to Prussian blue; chartreuse yellow wound up like a Jaffa orange, and turquoise blue predominated with such force that it had to be labelled 'for external use only'.

Previous experience had shown me that designing for films is quite different from theatre work. Seldom, for instance, is a costume seen full length in the average motion picture and elaborate ornamentation on a hem is wasted effort. It is the same with the scenery. The focal point on the screen is inevitably about eye level. Yet no detail may be left to chance. The camera not only picks up shoddiness but it detects lack of sincerity or shallowness of feeling. This applies ubiquitously to the work of director, performer or designer.

By the end of July, when all had been set for an August 1st 'opening day', we discovered that in Paris the summer holiday is taken very seriously indeed. Madame Karinska had been persuaded to make more costumes than she had ever intended, but at a given moment, her hordes of Russian helpers vanished.

To add to our stress, Paris was now suffering from a fierce heatwave. The Parisiennes who were being fitted into wine-glass corsets were unable to breathe. When Madame Karinska, with artistic ardour, pulled the strings to her satisfaction, the actress would swoon. A tumbler of water and a patter of smacks on the face would not succeed in 'bringing round' the fallen lady before a heavy thud proclaimed another victim – '*Encore une autre est tombée!*'

At long last, after the last detail had been worked out, the first day's shooting was scheduled.

It was a brave new world of indomitable spirit that forgathered in the Bois de Boulogne at dawn's early brightness. Producer, director, cameraman and huge technical crew, together with a vast sea of extras, had been waiting expectantly in a roped-off section of the park.

It was an historical scene. There were *calèches* of every sort, men and women on horseback, crowds of passers-by in 1900 costume. Cameras moved by on cranes, while megaphoned instructions added to the din.

By evening, the 'take' had been re-shot countless times. Carriages bowled by with clockwork precision, *grandes cocottes* looked like empresses in their elegant barouches, Chevalier continued to greet the passers-by with the same grinning spontaneity. Assistant director Bill McGary, in shirt-sleeves and turned-in shoes, shouted himself hoarse. 'Send for the Stock Girls! Give us a dozen cocottes!' Grand ladies in huge hats would materialize. 'There's one cocotte missing!' 'Anybody seen a cocotte?'

Another part of the Bois was decorated with bunting and flags. A dozen carriages, entirely covered with real and artificial flowers, stood waiting for the Battle of Flowers.

It proved to be another kind of battle. A strong August wind blew hats off in every direction. Angry bunches of lilies swayed ominously, leaves fell from the trees to give warning that summer was near its end. But nature was ignored while a windblown director and crew, on high with moving camera, followed the procession of carriages.

As Queen of the Carnival, dressed in a tall muslin bonnet, a beauty sat in a lily-bedecked carriage. By way of homage, someone heaved a huge bouquet of roses into her lap.

Abruptly, ominous clouds blanketed the sky. A deluge was at hand. The fashionable crowd made tents of newspapers and took refuge under the streaming trees. Spartan horsemen were soaked while still in the saddle. The Battle of Flowers ended in a waterspout.

Locations varied daily, but at the end of each day's shooting we would motor to St Cloud to see the rushes of the previous day's work. Far from being anxious and serious, the atmosphere in the projection room was one of jocularity. A democratic audience of technicians and performers would jeer and shout unflattering things about each other's efforts and appearances.

As part of 'la belle époque', Maxim's was closed to the public for four days while bright lights transformed its mellow 'art moderne' interior into a background for rich French bankers, gay ladies, zouaves, Egyptians, Ouida guardsmen over from London, and the moral refuse to be found in the best restaurants of the world. Supper-table roses wilted in the arc lights. Extras drooped or fell into sprawling attitudes of sleep during the intervals between takes. The confusion, noise and heat in this inferno continued until all participants were prostrate with exhaustion.

The heatwave that had enveloped Paris had given way to a spell of icy cold winds and the company found itself suffering from la grippe. A doctor went the rounds giving injections. Nevertheless on the appointed hour the miracle happened. Maxim's was once more open to the public, and the Gigi company was suddenly on its way to do the remaining interiors in Hollywood.

We had, while working in France during these past three months, completed nearly half of the film. But now the most important dramatic scenes were to be shot in the comparative calm of the Californian Sound Studios. A week later I found myself in Hollywood.

It was strange to come back as an employee to this city within a city, where, twenty years before, I had been a zealous sightseer. In my film-fanatic enthusiasm I had dogged the publicity staff, and a young man named Howard Strickling (now head of the department) had arranged interviews and photographic sittings with some of my favourite stars. When he took me to the studio cafeteria for a club sandwich and ice-cream in the company of medieval peasants, cowboys, ladies in white wigs and crinolines, German spies and the entire Barrymore family, I felt I was really seeing life from the inside. Little did I expect that one fine day, as set and costume designer for the musical version of *Gigi*, I would eat my Elizabeth Taylor salad or Cyd Charisse sandwich here each noon for weeks on end as a matter of course.

Perhaps now the greatest impression, as a newcomer, was of the distances to be covered during the course of an average day's work. Women's Character Wardrobe and Men's Wardrobe were long distances apart, though Wigs and Makeup were conveniently situated in the same building. The sound stages were often half a mile from the Art Department or the 'Still' Camera Depot and Publicity, while the outdoor locations on Lot 2 were impossible to reach on foot. Even the warehouses, where furniture of all periods, china, glass and every sort of 'property' are stored, were like vast hangars, and a man who wore a pedometer on his ankle discovered he had walked ten miles in a morning. Few people realize the value of the contents of these warehouses. I discovered a Golgotha hoard of riches dating back to the great days of extravagance. Here was Sèvres porcelain and real Louis xv furniture that had been brought back from Europe by special envoys scouting for Norma Shearer's *Marie Antoinette*.

There were specialists in charge of jewellery and of buying materials and there were those who knew precisely how dirty to make a certain costume. The 'property men', too, responsible for everything the players may use in the course of a day's acting, have developed their craft so that they have come to be relied upon as magicians.

Once I mistook a turning and found myself on the Pacific Ocean front at Santa Monica, twenty miles off course. Nevertheless at the end of the day's work I enjoyed driving, with the radio at full blast on the dashboard, towards Beverly Hills, purple in the fading light.

Leslie Caron never allowed herself to be hurried or cajoled into making a decision she had not long thought out for herself. Typical of the new Hollywood leading lady, she despised flamboyant behaviour or 'glamorous' off-screen appearances and reserved her temperament for her performance.

Isabel Jeans was always good-tempered, however arduous or disappointing her days might be. Often ready 'made up' after a dawn call, she would wait upon bad weather or a delayed schedule until dusk without appearing before the cameras. But then when the time came she gave as spontaneous and distinguished a performance as if it had been rehearsed for months before.

Maurice Chevalier, the complete professional, was never out-of-sorts or inconsiderate and had a broad smile for all....

By now we had shot the Trouville scenes on the Pacific shore and they had appeared successfully like paintings of Boudin.

12 January 1960

The late fifties were fortunate years for me. I was riding on the crest of a high wave. Although working hard, even to the point of exhaustion, things seemed to go easily and I was pleased with my output and its quality. I suffered from strain and pressure but was never positively ill.

With the success of *My Fair Lady* and *Gigi*, my self-confidence enabled me to ignore small setbacks. However, at the end of last year, disappointments and reverses began to rain down on me.

Everyone working on *Saratoga* was confident this would be the biggest success since *The Music Man*. In spite of it being the brainchild of the same director, this was not to be. *Saratoga*, after five successful weeks in Philadelphia, was roasted by the New York critics. No success to chalk up here.

Paris: February

Often I am foolish enough to arrive in Paris without warning anyone of my visit, and sometimes for the first day or two I do not seem able to forge into the life of the city. (I dislike having a meal by myself in a restaurant and I am certainly not adventurous in touring the night spots alone.) However, on this occasion I had warned dear old Marie-Louise Bousquet beforehand of my impending appearance. Awaiting me at the hotel was the typically generous note from this most loving of all friends, saying: 'I am free – free – free. I await you at your convenience – at drink time – or for any dinner – all my lunches are free – free – free.' Before I had time to unpack the telephone rang. It was Marie-Louise saying that Cristobal Balenciaga would like us to dine.

Cristobal is a quiet, calm, even serene person; as soon as one arrives in his apartment one comes under his spell. There is no greater pleasure than being in his company.

When we arrived, he was sitting in front of the fire, dressed all in black as is his wont, absorbed in the details of Camus's 'unnecessary' death in the evening paper. Obviously it gave him quite a shock to be brought back to the present, but by degrees he surfaced enough to tell us that Ramon would be with us soon. He fixed the dry martinis and we talked generalities.

His flat, decorated in dark greens and pale greys, was furnished in a bold style typical of him: heavy candlesticks, solid fire-irons, a huge lump of crystal on the low table, the very chaste *appliques*, the two large bushes of azaleas, one white, one pink, in porphyry pots. It is a phenomenon that the son of an ordinary Spanish boatman, a poor boy with no opportunity to glimpse the grand world, should be born with such innate taste. Now his clothes influence the entire world of fashion, and he has a highly-refined sense in all forms of art. This apartment was proof of his purity of vision. He admitted how much he enjoyed going out to antique shops and discovering finds: yet his rooms are so sparse and uncluttered that you know that everything has been chosen as the result of ruthless elimination and complete discrimination.

Marie-Louise, by way of conversation, informed Cristobal that I had recently decorated a show in New York with over one hundred and fifty costumes. Cristobal winced, shut up his face like a sea anemone, and said: 'What a terrible work! How *tired* you must be! That must be such a tremendous nervous strain: it must take so much out of you!' In fact it doesn't take all that much out of me; I happen to be overtired at this point for the foolish reason that I had undertaken to do too much for too long. I am aware, too, of the enormous amount of vital energy it takes for Cristobal to create his clothes: that is why they are so good; they are the result of depth of thought, intense concentration, even physical suffering.

Marie-Louise observed that I was now going to lead a clinical existence in Switzerland. Cristobal perked up to his favourite subject: it appears his hobby is the snow. He talked about the calming influence of mountains in snow, the effect of the quietness on the nerves. Cristobal said that it was necessary for him to spend at least one long holiday, if not two, in the winter, calming down in the mountains. He described the pleasure of sitting in bed with the window open to the cold or to the sun, and the luxury that was provided in these dazzling heights: hothouse flowers and fruit, cherry jam and croissants, and caviar with hot potatoes.

Cristobal's friend, the young Ramon, came into the room, smiling and swarthy. Marie-Louise began to tease him. He looked somewhat embarrassed. Cristobal smiled his crinkled surgeon's smile. Marie-Louise's ribaldries are refreshing to this solemn, monk-like Spaniard. No one else behaves in her outrageous manner in this reserved, quiet apartment.

Marie-Louise gave a virtuoso's performance: she became a witch throwing her head back in hollow, hoarse laughter. She bubbled with pure fun and French wit.

One always has the feeling of privilege when one is with a person who sees few people. One feels proud at being the exception to the rule. Tonight I realized that although Cristobal refuses to see anything of the *monde* and never faces his clients, he knows all the latest *potins* and scandals almost before anyone else.

An exception to his rule was when he made a dress for someone to wear at a gala. He told us of it: 'It had huge panels hanging loosely back and front, and a tight tube underneath.' (He goes through the motions of a snakecharmer.) Two days before the gala, he went to the fitting-room to see the lady, who turned triumphantly to him: 'Don't you think it's beautiful what I've done to the dress?' The panels had been sewn together and shaped to follow the line of her waist, and they had been covered with expensive embroidery. 'Don't you think it's beautiful?' Cristobal leapt at the dress, tore it to shreds and said to the *vendeuse* (who was a particular friend of his): 'And you will pay out of your own pocket for all that embroidery!'

Reddish House, Broadchalke

The creakings of the floorboard on the landing have become a new, but important element in the life of the house. It is something that I will always remember with a certain dread and sadness. Quite recently my mother has become even more restless, and one of its forms is that she will not remain in her bed for more than a few minutes. Exhausted by walking up and down the stairs and along the kitchen corridors in search of an apple, sandwich or drink of lime juice, she becomes affected by the phenobarbitone tablets and at last settles down again to sleep. The apparition, in the pink and blue nightgown, is a haunting one – Shakespearean in its sense of doom: her nocturnal walk like Lady Macbeth. Withal she is dignified and beautiful.

Diana Cooper, having refused all invitations for the Wilton Ball, now decides she'd like to see its glories. But she says she must stay with someone who lives nearby – 'I last longer when I know I can escape.' Since all houses in the vicinity are now full, Diana asks for a caravan so she can sleep in the park at Wilton. Sidney Pembroke, on hearing this, winces and makes a face as if he'd bitten a lemon: 'I *can't* have any eccentricity in the park!'

Rome

Diana, the beauty of her generation, has become with the years one of the great characters of our time. So strong is her personality that she has countless imitators who try, with far less wit and success, to emulate her 'come off it' attitude to life. But Diana, in turn, has been greatly influenced throughout her life by the Herbert Tree family and by Iris in particular. Iris, the youngest Tree daughter, is here in Rome with us now.

It was the eldest, Viola, whom I first got to know and to worship. She was everything that a young man struggling to break through the barriers of convention could admire. Viola was like a young zephyr, incredibly tall and coltish, she had the quality of a child even when her face became drawn and drab with illness. She was a mistress of the impromptu and a brilliant mimic – but only for one performance. She was never professional enough to meet the challenge of repetition and she could not duplicate some little cameo of observation on the stage. As an actress she was, considering her parenthood, surprisingly ineffective. Having started out with only the highest ambitions, it was sad to see her at the last, in a noble attempt to pay for the education of her sons, having to capitalize on her height by appearing in a grotesque part in a musical comedy.

I loved being with Viola when she came to stay with me at Ashcombe and loped over the downs and drank water from the boles in the tree-trunks. I loved her in Soho when she would go into a grand florist and unselfconsciously buy one long-stemmed rose because that was all she could afford. I loved her answering the door of her Bloomsbury house in bare feet. She was for ever an overgrown child of nature, and it was only after she was cruelly struck down with cancer that I came to know her more exotic-looking sister.

Iris just escaped being an albino. With great cunning she made her whiteness an advantage, and cut her flaxen hair with shears to look like a sort of 'Till Eulenspeigel'. At an age when it was daring to look anything but extremely conventional, she strode about in highwayman hats and cloaks, or in dirndl skirts worn with brilliant flower-embroidered blouses. She became a poet, her life Bohemian in the extreme, and in the many countries where she found herself her friends were mostly artists or writers. She married first the delightful Curtis Moffat, whose unusual photographs inspired me in my formative years, then, later, Count Friedrich Ledebur, who is still one of the best-looking, and certainly the tallest, men I have ever seen. For a long time Iris and Friedrich lived in a caravan in northern California, then Iris acted and studied in the Tchekov School in Carmel. Only occasionally would the nomad return to Europe; but now, for some time, she has settled in Rome.

Iris has a remarkable pristine quality. She never could be spoilt, for she takes nothing for granted. If she is more exaggerated in her manner than Diana it is because perhaps she is the more assured. Both have a fundamental shyness, but Iris somehow makes an asset of what is to Diana and others a great disadvantage. When these lifelong friends get together (they have met only seldom in recent years) they become like greyhounds straining at the leash to run after the hare, so great is their enthusiasm for each other. Not that they gush or enthuse – far from it : they contradict, they argue, but they laugh uproariously and applaud with great glee each other's witticisms and eccentricities.

Throughout these years Iris has never been bored and today, when she turned up at the 'cheap little restaurant round the corner' which Diana prefers, she brought to the occasion a youthful enthusiasm for the pleasure of 'lunching out', of sitting at table and being served with wine and unusual foods. Diana was equally game. Iris was accompanied by a huge dog which suddenly barked and startled everyone in the restaurant. Whereupon Diana shouted : 'I wish he wouldn't do that – it's so common!' (Meaning, I discovered, it is so common to possess a badly-trained dog!)

Diana then proceeded to encourage Iris to do an imitation of a colonel whom Iris and her husband once met many years before on an Atlantic crossing. The Colonel had become a figure of fun in their circle ever since. Obediently Iris gibbered like an ape and was extremely funny. Diana's nose screwed up in howls of laughter. The waiter did his usual trick of interrupting. Diana, the chairwoman, in Viennese accent said: 'Come on now – quickly! "Concentrate, choose and order" as Kaetchen Kommer used to say.' 'Wouldn't you like fungus? Or kidney cooked with sage – or those little birds with bay leaves? I won't have them because of my anger at their killing anything so small. But you could have goat – kids – very Biblish and a good taste. Let's get this over! What to end with? Pear and Parmesan? Good! Now that's over! Now then – where were we?'

Diana leant forward in her blue spectacles: 'The Colonel – you were doing the Colonel.' 'The Colonel' started to talk most inexplicably about the Knights of the Round Table. He treated the Knights as old boys of the same club: a hilarious impersonation.

'Now, Iris, do Friedrich!'

Iris obliged with an imitation of her husband in a very deep voice: 'Now – er – what – er time is it?'

'I don't know, Friedrich. I haven't got a watch.'

'No, I mean – er what – er – er – day is it?'

'I think it is Wednesday.'

'No – I meant – er – what time of the year – what month is it?'

'January.'

'Oh, good!'

Iris then scored with an imitation of the Terrys in *The Scarlet Pimpernel*.

In spite of the imperfections that age must necessarily bring and a ridiculous hat she wore today, Diana still appeared to me utterly beautiful. The line of her forehead and nose and the placing of the eye in profile reminds me of a goat, and today she ate goat with gusto.

Chantilly

Today Diana bought a house in Little Venice in London. It has been hard for her to decide to leave Chantilly after so long and with so many memories of Duff. Beautiful as her little St Firmin château is, it is a witch of a place, luring her to further expenses and complications, needing more and more servants, more doing to the garden, and then, at best, giving the impression of being an impermanent folly.

Diana has come to detest the French race, and she says she leaves few friends behind. It is better for her to live on a smaller scale in a city she loves, where she is surrounded by adoring, faithful friends, wonderful family, and many cultivated interests.

I arrived at Chantilly for an evening alone with her; I knew that it would be stimulating, but, even so, I had forgotten just how remarkably integrated a character Diana is. She is un-snobbish. She is quick to recognize quality in its many surprising aspects. She has a lively interest in history. At dinner, at a small card table, she talked about Napoleon's humiliation on St Helena as if it were Winston going through those appalling experiences. She was reading a life of Bonaparte and, although she does not approve of him as a character, she feels so sorry for him that she cannot sleep.

Diana has strong feelings about the servants, about her garden, and, above all, about her grandchild Artemis, who was here in dressing-gown to greet me. Diana does not treat the seven-year-old as a child. She talks to 'the light of my eye' as an intelligent grown-up, and pumps her with all sorts of information. 'Who was Medusa?' 'Never say bye-bye!' 'What is seventeen minus two?' Diana brings out a series of books written to educate negroes. She talks to Artemis with complete frankness about everything – including nature in its more basic forms, and about the child's looks: 'You've got a podgy, smudgy face that's good; it will improve with age.' (Her own did!) 'But you must realize your hair isn't good, and you've got to do something about it. Mustn't wear your hair scraggy!'

22

Sitting for Two Portraits
1960

C.B., who had sat to Bérard and Tchelitchev, posed for Francis Bacon and Augustus John. Neither portrait satisfied him. Between the two sittings he spent a holiday with Truman Capote in Spain.

February 1960

Bébé Bérard did a remarkably fine portrait of me and I think of it as my definitive likeness. It is as I would like always to be. Alas, twenty years have passed since then.

It would be pointless to sit to the usual portrait-painter. But I did like the idea of Francis Bacon trying his hand at me. He had recently done an interesting 'portrait' of Sainsbury, the art collector. The sittings would doubtless be highly enjoyable for Francis is one of the most interesting, refreshing and utterly beguiling people. He is wise and effervescent and an inspired conversationalist.

Francis Bacon has been a good friend for many years now. Graham Sutherland was the first person I heard talk of him, when we were having a discussion on 'taste'. Graham surprised and intrigued me by saying that Francis Bacon's studio nearby in South Kensington had a strong individuality. He described Bacon's penchant for huge pieces of heavy mahogany furniture, and Turkish carpets, the antithesis of all that the painter had once created in the days when he was a designer and decorator of furniture. Graham went on: 'He seems to have a very special sense of luxury. When you go to him for a meal, it is unlike anyone else's. It is all very casual and vague; there is no timetable; but the food is wonderful. He produces an enormous slab of the best possible Gruyère cheese covered with dewdrops, and then a vast bunch of grapes appears.'

When I met Francis we seemed to have an immediate rapport. I was overwhelmed by his tremendous charm and understanding. Smiling and painting simultaneously, he seemed to be having such a good time. He appeared extraordinarily healthy and cherubic, apple-shiny cheeks, and the protruding lips were lubricated with an unusual amount of saliva. His hair was bleached by sun and other aids. His figure was incredibly lithe for a person of his age and occupation, wonderfully muscular and solid. I was impressed with his 'principal boy' legs, tightly encased in black jeans with high boots. Not a pound of extra flesh anywhere.

I don't know much about his background, except it is said that at a very early age his father sent him off in the care of a rider to hounds who immediately attempted to seduce him.

Of his many qualities I admired most his independence. I envied his being able to live in exactly the way he wished, and I was impressed by his aloofness from the opinions of others. We went out 'on the town', but I am not good at pubs, drinking clubs and late hours and would fade away just when Francis was about to enjoy himself.

Recently he came to stay, and although I believe he does not care for the countryside, he could not have been a more sympathetic, appreciative and delightful guest.

Francis began the painting of me two years ago. He had just returned from a winter in Tangier where he had been too harassed and ill to paint. But he was then recovered and full of the joy of London life. He was bursting with health and vitality, in his extraordinarily messy, modest drawing-room studio in a most unlikely block of scarlet brick flats in Overstrand Mansions, Prince of Wales Drive, Battersea.

He showed me an enormous black-paint-covered canvas, and said he hoped I wouldn't be alarmed by the size of it but that the portrait would be cut down, if necessary, when he had finished it.

Francis started to work with great zest, excitedly running backwards and forwards to the canvas with gazelle-springing leaps – much toe bouncing. He said how enthusiastic he was at the prospect of the portrait which he said would show me with my face in tones of pink and white. He did not seem interested in my keeping still, and so I enjoyed looking around me at the incredible mess of his studio – a converted bedroom no doubt: so unlike the beautiful, rather conventional 'artist's abode' that he had worked in in South Kensington when I first knew him! Here the floor was littered in a Dostoevsky shambles of discarded paints, rags, newspapers and every sort of rubbish, while the walls and window curtains were covered with streaks of black and emerald green paint.

Francis was funny in many ways, slightly wicked about pretentious friends, and his company gave me pleasure. The only anxiety I felt was that there might be some snag which would interrupt the sittings that were to follow. Sure enough, a telegram arrived putting me off the next appointment; indeed, for anyone less tenacious than myself, there would never have been another sitting.

I went to America, came back, saw Francis once or twice, and he came to dinner, but no mention of the picture from me or from him. Eventually, an opportunity presented itself and I asked Francis if he'd *hate* to go on with the painting of me.

Francis Bacon's name has now become even more renowned. He is acclaimed by the younger generation which, it seems, considers Picasso to be old-fashioned. Francis, bubbling with amusement, smiled and with his usual marvellous manners said nothing would give him greater pleasure than to finish the picture that he'd long had of me in his mind. An enormous black canvas, the only one with its face not turned to the wall, depicted a monster cripple – a nude figure, with no apparent head, but with four legs. It was painted with brushes that had been allowed to slide around in the manner children are taught not to employ. The forms were so gauche that when Francis pointed to the picture and said it was a failure, I was somewhat in agreement. But Francis explained that he wanted more than anything else to be able to do something of that same cripple who had inspired Muybridge, that great photographer at the end of the last century.

Francis showed me a huge canvas covered with emerald green dye-paint. Again he said my picture wouldn't be as large as that when finished, but that all the works for his next exhibition were going to be on these green backgrounds. I had imagined myself as a sort of Sainsbury floating in stygian gloom and wondered what an emerald green picture would look like in any of my existing rooms. I sat on a kitchen chair placed so, and according to instructions turned my head a bit this way. 'No – further! That's it.' Francis started to work with energy, but he seemed to look harassed, not at all happy. I asked: 'Would you prefer if I looked more this way?' 'No – it's fine – and I think if it comes off, I'll be able to do it quickly. The other didn't start off well – but this is fine.' Would I mind his exhibiting the canvas as the Marlborough were screaming at him for more pictures?

Francis works without apparent difficulty and keeps up a running conversation that is illuminating and inspiring. I noticed, among the rubbish of old discarded suede shoes, jerseys, and tins on the floor, one or two very costly art books on Egypt and Crete. Francis tried to describe to me the beauty of two painted figures about three feet tall – a man and woman sitting side-by-side, in cream and white. He said how he longed to take a trip to Assuan later this winter to see the carvings before they are flooded. He thought Egyptian art among the most beautiful in the whole world: 'Those early heads are *amazing*, but, of course, it's because of the sun that they're so beautiful.'

He then laughed: 'You mustn't look at my mouth. I'm just recovering from having a tooth knocked out. My face was in an appalling mess.'

Francis had spent the winter in Cornwall. But it hadn't worked out as there had been such terrible quarrels and he got behind-hand with his work. It was the same in Tangier: such upsets! rows and getting thrown out of the window!

He had done no work. Then a talk about Tangier – Francis's Tangier, a close intimacy with the Arab world, with the brothel life, and the freedom that can be found only in certain Mediterranean countries where access to women is difficult.

Occasionally Francis would sit down on an old chair from which the entrails were hanging and which had been temporarily covered with a few French magazines and newspapers. His pose reminded me of a portrait of Degas. He curved his head sideways and looked at his canvas with a beautiful expression in his eyes. His plump, marble-like hands were covered with blue-green paint. He said he thought that painting portraits was the most interesting thing he could ever hope to do: 'If only I can do them! The important thing is to put a person down as he appears to your mind's eye. The person must be there so that you can check up on reality – but not be led by it, not be its slave. To get the essence without being positive about the factual shapes – that's the difficulty. It's so difficult that it's almost impossible! But that's what I'm trying to do. I think I'm closer to it than I ever have been before.'

With Francis the air is mountain fresh: one feels invigorated. I used to go to his studio before taking the train for Salisbury. As the weather was particularly cold, dark and foul, I would be dressed for the country in a very warm, brown suit. Francis was all radiance, even if he said he had been appallingly drunk on vodka the night before. He would expatiate on those evenings: though he didn't really remember much about them, but he'd left an American who had 'passed out' before dinner, gone on to Soho, turned up at his usual 'Club' and didn't know where the rest of the night had gone.

One morning I asked Francis: 'Does it matter my being in a different suit?'

'No – that's a lovely colour. But I want you to put your hands up on this extra chair like this. Anyhow, it doesn't matter.'

During the morning I purposely moved the position of my hands several times to see if Francis would ask me not to change their position. Once he said: 'The hands are splendid like that.' But never again did he ask me to go back to the same pose. Neither did he seem to mind if I moved my head. 'But that's what's so awful about having to sit to Lucian,' said Francis. 'He makes you sit by the hour without moving an eyelash, and I find sitting very unnerving, exhausting work.'

Francis had, during his drunken haze last night, caught a glimpse of Lucian Freud. Lucian had returned from Sweden where he had gone to paint Ingmar Bergman for a cover of *Time*, but there had been too many interruptions for Lucian to produce any result, and he now hated *Time* magazine, Bergman and Sweden. We then talked of Lucian's latest painting – how he seemed, in an effort to paint quicker, to have lost some of his intensity. Lucian was intelligent enough to know that his painting up to now was not a complete expression of himself. He now found himself in the awful predicament of having to try and discover himself again. That, for someone of Lucian's vanity, was a difficult thing to do.

We discussed Lucian's intellectual brilliance, his complete independence and strength as a man who knew exactly what he wanted out of life. But we admitted that Lucian was no angel. After a row, his wife Caroline had said: 'If you want to know what Lucian is like, just see him drive.' Mercifully, Lucian has now been forbidden to drive, for he is reckless at the wheel.

I admitted I found if difficult to be loyal to Lucian all the time. I could not understand the mentality of gamblers, and it worried me that Lucian should lose so much so readily.

Francis said the Bérard portrait of me was a great likeness. (In many ways the two painters resemble one another: both ignoring convention, and living in their own purity – uncontaminated by the asphyxiating cocoon of respectability.) He considered people didn't appreciate Bérard nearly highly enough as a painter at this time. One day they would, since he was definitely one of the great. His use of paint was never thin in quality even if it was spread lightly over the canvas: maybe he had learnt that from Vuillard. How lovely some of the late Vuillards were! And painted with quite a lot of oil. At one time Vuillard and Bonnard were almost indistinguishable, but they went on in their separate ways getting better and better. From the piles of rubbish on the floor Francis extracted a colour reproduction of a Bonnard he had cut out of *Paris Match* and stuck on to a piece of cardboard. The colours were vivid: oranges, reds, red-browns, brilliant blues, enough colours for three pictures. 'I don't know what time of day it represents, or is it night?' With outstretched arms, Francis enjoyed the picture to its fullest. 'You see, people don't appreciate paint today; that's why nobody sees how absolutely marvellous Rembrandt is.'

Suddenly, as he sat, head cocked looking at the picture, his eyes lit up as he said: 'I'm very pleased with this portrait. I think it's going to be all right: one of the best things I've done. Next time you're here, I'll show it to you because it doesn't need much more work on it. When they go well, they go very quickly.'

Francis opened the door, smiled and said: 'The portrait's finished! I want you to sit in that chair over there and look at it.' I walked towards Francis's degutted chair in the corner, not glancing at the canvas on the way. I turned round square and sat to get the full effect. It was as well that I was sitting, otherwise I might have fallen backwards. In front of me was an enormous, coloured strip-cartoon of a completely bald, dreadfully aged – nay senile – businessman. The face was hardly recognizable as a face for it was disintegrating before your eyes, suffering from a severe case of elephantiasis: a swollen mass of raw meat and fatty tissues. The nose spread in many directions like a polyp but sagged finally over one cheek. The mouth looked like a painful boil about to burst. He wore a very sketchily dabbed-in suit of lavender blue. The hands were clasped and consisted of emerald green scratches that resembled claws. The dry painting of the body and hands was completely different from that of the wet, soggy head. The white background was thickly painted with a house painter's brush. It was dragged round the outer surfaces without any intention of cleaning up the shapes. The head and shoulders were outlined in a streaky wet slime.

Francis expected that I would be shocked. He was a little disconcerted. He said it gave him a certain pain to show it to me, but if I didn't like it I needn't buy it. The Marlborough Gallery would want it. I stammered: 'Well – I can't say what I think of it. It's so utterly different from anything of yours I've ever seen!' To me the picture was of an unusual violence. The brushwork, the textures, the draughtsmanship were against all the known rules. Francis suddenly exclaimed: 'Oh, I unearthed these beautiful Egyptian figures for you to see. Look, here they are! How beautiful they are! They're only three feet tall, but the way the faces are painted ...' But what did that signify now to me?

Francis could not have behaved more typically gallantly and charmingly about the fee d'amis for the painting. 'Take the picture, and if you don't like it, or your friends object, send it back in time for it to be sold in the Marlborough show.'

I was baffled. Could I ever hang the canvas in any place that I live in? The harshness and ugliness would surely give me a 'turn for the worse' each time I saw it. But I'd gone to Francis for a painting because I genuinely considered him a unique painter. If this was what he felt like doing at this particular moment I must respect it, even if I could not understand or appreciate it. If the Marlborough Gallery would give him so much more for it than he had asked me, then perhaps it would be an investment. I asked him if he'd mind if after I bought it and found I didn't want to keep it, I could sell it again? 'Of course! It's yours to do what you want with.' I took a gulp and said I would like to have it.

I came away crushed, staggered, and feeling quite a great sense of loss. The sittings had been so harmonious; we had seemed to see eye to eye. I had hoped that many of Francis's theories about life, art and beauty were going to be incorporated in the portrait.

No sooner had I written the above than the telephone bell rang from London. It was Francis. In an ecstatic voice he said: 'This is Francis, and I've just destroyed your portrait.' 'But why? You said you liked it? You thought it such a good work, and that's all that matters!'

'No – I don't like my friends to have something of mine they don't like. And I often destroy my work in any case; in fact, I've destroyed most of the pictures for the Marlborough. Only I just wanted to let you know so that you needn't pay me.'

It seemed little to Francis to waste all that work. He seemed jubilant at not getting paid, at *not* finishing a picture. He said that perhaps one day he'd start again, or do one from memory: 'They often turn out best,' he said.

I don't really know what is at the back of Francis's mind. I am sorry that the canvas is destroyed and that there is no visible result from all those delightful, interesting and rare mornings.

From Broadchalke to Fordingbridge

I hated having to take myself out of my warm house. The rain poured in buckets and the windscreen wiper had gone wrong. It was a horrible journey in the dark. However, on arriving in front of the pretty façade at Fryern the dining-room was lit up like a doll's house and the scene inside, with the long table covered with food and litter, looked inviting. As always, I was delighted to bask in the rare and sympathetic atmosphere of the John household. Dorelia explained that the curtains were new and appeared too violently red when drawn, so they had to keep them pulled back.

Dodo seemed less worn, less tied down with household chores and responsibilities than usual. She was thrilled that they now had a gardener (three days a week) who was 'making all the difference'. Augustus was in his studio painting by artificial light on some huge murals intended for exhibition at the next year's Academy Show. (I fear they will never be completed.) Dodo sent the Italian servant-boy to fetch him, but confessed her inability to communicate in his language.

Augustus came in holding a pipe in gnarled right hand. As he shook hands with me a sharp pain nearly caused me to shout. A thorn had gone into my first finger – how or why I can't imagine. Perhaps, in a hundred-to-one chance, a splinter from his match had just struck at the right angle. The pain forgotten, we sat talking about Augustus' desire to do a portrait of me. I told him that Francis Bacon had painted me looking like a piece of raw offal against an emerald green background. 'You deserve it for sitting to him,' Augustus said and then, with infinite sarcasm: 'These idiosyncrasies are the prerogative of genius.'

I told him that I had recently read a description in my diary of his being at the Eiffel Tower with a lot of young girls dressed as lesbians. 'I love lesbians,' said John as the door opened to his natural daughter, Amaryllis Fleming, the cellist, a glorious figure of a woman with tumbling curls. Talk then switched to her mother. The triangle of Mrs Fleming, Lord Winchester, and Miss Bapsy

Pavry, the Indian, is infinite in its variations on the theme of love, marriage of convenience and divorce.

Dodo is not an easy person to know. Yet she must have realized with the years my enormous admiration for her. Not only am I spellbound by her Luini-like beauty, but I love her calm and dignity. She is mysterious, or perhaps I should say she is one of the few women I've known who possess a sense of mystery. I don't know anything about her antecedents; she is Scottish, she wears clothes unlike anyone else, she is completely amoral. She looks after her hordes of children, and it does not seem to worry her that some are illegitimate. She leads the life of a wife, busy in the kitchen, bottling things, going to Salisbury market; and withal she has a quality so that one knows that she is unlike other women.

With a patience that shows itself in her deep brown eyes, she tends Augustus with the greatest devotion. It is not an easy task. Augustus is selfish, wild and bad-tempered. He loves Dodo, he loves the children, Tristram, David, Romilly, Robin, Edwin and Kaspar [First Sea Lord], Poppet and Vivien – but they are often terrified of their father. Friends and strangers too can be alarmed by Augustus. Fryern used to be like an island surrounded by a dangerous sea. Only the most intrepid visitors were able to make a landing. When I regretted to David Herbert that I had not spent more time in the John colony when I lived at Ashcombe, David replied: 'But they didn't want us!'

With the years, Augustus has become gentler, more mellow. This evening he was positively benign.

I left, full of red wine, to battle my way home through the cloudbursts, with the happy feeling that both John and Dodo were weathering the winter extremely well and that they were in better health and spirits than they had been for some years.

Palamos, Spain: May

One of the pleasures of my visit to Truman at this tiny fishing village was that we could talk uninterruptedly without his being diverted by the activities of unrewarding café-society personalities. We discussed the difficulties of writing – he with particular reference to his new work *In Cold Blood*. Truman complained that not more than a few hundred people appreciated the merit of his writing. He was not jealous of the success of hack writers, but it appalled him that his own publishers did not recognize the quality of his work. He felt it was created out of such loneliness, such painful concentration, that sometimes he exhausted himself. His paragraphs were constructed with great care, immaculate punctuation and never a repetition of words or sounds.

During the days on the island Truman and I managed to do quite a bit of sightseeing as well as work. One afternoon we made an unexpected discovery of the house that once belonged to Sert, the Spanish painter of murals. The house was unoccupied, but it still showed the simple yet luxurious taste of its former owner. It was decorated in white – white walls, muslin curtains, white or indigo linen chair-coverings and dark Spanish furniture polished like glass. It brought back to my mind all sorts of forgotten impressions of the extravagance of the thirties. The house was no doubt built with the proceeds from the murals he had done in houses in Florida at a time when they were almost regarded as an essential decoration in the homes of millionaires.

June

Augustus sent a message through McNamara that he was serious about wanting to paint me and when could we start. The proposal is flattering but somewhat appalling too, for the chances of the picture ever being finished are slight. Augustus must be over eighty. Even at the best of times he was apt to ruin his pictures by going on too long; lately he has chalked up few successes. If only he had asked me when I was a neighbour at Ashcombe he could have done something quite wonderful. For then I was less unworthy of being painted. Instead of this dreary grey creature, I was in the pink of romantic perfection; and I had all the time in the world. Now I work so hard that it is difficult to find time. But in the Ashcombe days Augustus and Dodo were an alarming couple and they did not encourage visitors. Augustus would sometimes come over to me but never suggested my going over to him. Now his two studios at Fryern are filled with discarded portraits and murals. The portions that have not been repainted a dozen times are quite beautiful, but he seems incapable of making up his mind even about the position of legs or arms, and in his indecision, or due to his dissatisfaction, has even taken to embellishing the compositions with silver paint.

Augustus himself realizes that he is 'through' – that he cannot overcome the onslaught of old age. Yet the other day Ralph Pitman managed to salvage a portrait of his daughter Jemima before it was ruined. Augustus, although angry at first ('What business is it of yours if I ruin it?') was later grateful; in fact, so moved at having completed a portrait that he burst into tears.

I went over to Fordingbridge in my panama hat and almond suede coat and without more than a glance at me the old boy began to scratch noisily at a large canvas with a piece of charcoal. For an hour he grunted stertorously. He looked like an elderly porpoise staring at me with an expression of desperation in his wild eyes, enlarged by his spectacles. His mouth, under the tobacco-stained moustache, hung open. Every now and again he gave a little jump in the air and landed heavily. His determination to some extent seemed to conquer his inabilities. The first morning produced quite a good, but slight, drawing.

On arrival for the second sitting the charcoal had been wiped into a misty mess, and Augustus started to do another more finalized rendering on top of the original. He took a long time to decide what colours to use; then at last he bashed on a bit of paint. His jargon is 'old student': 'Shall we have a go?' 'Another dodge is to put a curtain there'; no theorizing about his intentions and beliefs. Although Augustus has a keen intellect, real understanding about painters and painting and had a classical training at the Slade (where he won a prize for a composition that is one of the school's proud possessions), he is an intuitive painter and he does not, I suspect, know why he works the way he does. It just happened that at a certain time his taste and dynamic strength produced canvases, based on Rubens and sometimes influenced by Greco, that created a shock in the twenties and thirties. Today he is an 'old master'.

I returned next morning and sat without moving an inch for two hours. Augustus liked my hat. By the end of the morning he shouted, 'We'd better stop!', and for good reason: he had started daubing the sensitively painted face with green. Maybe he will right the damage, but the turgid, solid green is of that particularly unpleasant variety that they use to paint cricket pavilions. I realize I have let myself in for a painful experience and one that is a time-waster.

As I drive round the gravel path to his house I can see the old boy, his beret on the back of his head, glaring up at my portrait from his corner of the large studio window. Today he was talking to himself as I went in. It is sad to see this great man in his dotage. The coiled wire of his hearing aid loops like a worm and it seems the apparatus is useless, sometimes emitting a low hum that angers him so much that he flings the delicate contraption to the floor. His skin is pitted with dirt and blackheads, his fingers holding the brush between first and second fingers, the fourth discarded like an old banana, and the palette rattling in his shaky left hand. He spills ash and turpentine on the floor, and his box of matches becomes covered with paint on his palette. Augustus does not notice the electric stove on the floor and falls over it – 'Damn!' He tries clumsily to knock the keys into the back of the frame with a hammer. It is remarkable that he can achieve anything effective under such physical disabilities. His life has become one long struggle against odds.

My portrait continues to make slow progress. I suppose it is taking its inevitable course. But frankly I don't know what Augustus is trying to do. I feel his sense of colour – never his best point – is strangely erratic. One day the green paint on my face is dominant, then the face becomes orange, but when he suddenly finds a very violent blue, he makes this the background for my green coat and pink shirt. It is all very haphazard.

My criticism of the painting is its flatness; it is like a large cartoon or poster.

Today Augustus asked me if I'd been to the theatre in London, and when I told him how impressed I'd been by Finch in the film *The Trials of Oscar Wilde* he reminisced about Wilde. 'I knew him quite well; lunched with him every day for two weeks or more. It was when he'd just come out of prison and he was in Paris. Such a nice chap, so full of fun and a delightful conversationalist. But I didn't think so much of his entourage, and sometimes I crept away. They sat around adulating Wilde and getting him to show off. Who were they? Oh, anybody who'd buy Wilde a drink. He had no money, you know, but he never complained – never about his punishment, never mentioned prison. They'd cut his hair, you know; that was a pity. Yes, he was a bit fat – flabby, I'd say: the skin hung a bit loose. But he was so full of fun. He'd say about Robbie Ross: "He'd defend me within an inch of my life." All the time the trouble was on, Frank Harris had a boat waiting; he wanted Wilde to escape. But Wilde said he couldn't face the prospect of being alone on a boat with Harris; anything was preferable to that!' Augustus gave his rich, fruit-cake laugh.

He talked of Picasso – 'The finest draughtsman in the world today' – but when Picasso was painting the *Demoiselles d'Avignon*, Augustus asked him what he was trying to do as he could not understand it. Picasso replied: '*Je cherche la liberté.*'

I look at the accumulation of muck on the window-sill; I see the discarded goblets of milk and brandy (his medicine), the mound of paint-brushes. I look at the discarded portraits of the twenties and thirties. I am reminded of Mary Alington, so luscious, so kind, so full of charm; Lord Tredegar, very birdlike and spiky; the Duveen daughter (a brute of a painting, this).

Monday: another morning given up to sitting. There has been, in the meantime, the gaiety, noise and abandon of the party surrounding the Wilton ball. After the long, quiet period that my house has known, with my mother and myself making only sporadic attempts at conversation, the dining-room (without its carpet since the storm and flood) reverberated from the stone floor to the vaulted ceiling with the chatter, hilarious screams and yells of six outspoken friends. The ball is now over, but the memory will remain of the Double Cube room filled – but not overfilled – with a sea of dancers watched by the ancestors painted by Vandyck.

Now, once more, back to the picture. Today it was as if every aspect of the picture was closing in on him for attack. He looked suddenly like a bewildered old bull. It was one of his deaf days.

He gave up early. 'Come back tomorrow.' Weakly I said I would. But I warned him that I have only a few more days before I go to the United States. 'I think we can finish it in that time.' He has no sense of time whatsoever. Augustus is great and grandiose, like a figure in the Old Testament. He has completely the manner of any artist. He can be lustful and he can drink to excess, but he never uses bad language. He is a gipsy but he is also a great gentleman.

23

A Busy Year
1960–61

C.B. stayed with Frederick Ashton in Suffolk; witnessed a confrontation of Harold Macmillan and Nikita Krushchev at the United Nations; entertained the newly-engaged Princess Margaret and Tony Armstrong-Jones, as well as Greta Garbo, at Broadchalke; stayed with Countess Cicogna in Tripoli, where he visited the grave of Baba's husband, Alec Hambro; designed Turandot *for the new Metropolitan Opera House; refused to design the film* The Sleeping Prince *for Laurence Olivier; saw Nureyev for the first time; dined in the company of Mrs Kennedy; attended Barbara Hutton's ball in Tangier and Countess Volpi's in Venice. He published the first volume of his diaries,* The Wandering Years.

Suffolk: July 1960

The weekend was painfully wet. Fred Ashton's sad eyes greeted me from the shade of an umbrella. It was particularly sad for him for this was his only holiday and for most of the time it had rained. I, however, was content to bask in the summery atmosphere of his pretty 1800 Gothic house with roses in Victorian vases, on china and on chintz. The house is like the house of an old aunt or of the girl in *Spectre de la Rose.*

Elizabeth Cavendish was the other guest. We were fortunate to enjoy Freddie at his best. He has become not only portly in frame, but has acquired with the years weight of character. He speaks with great authority and seriousness combined with a frivolous cynicism. He is never hurried, knows his limitations and does not try to do too much. He does not attempt to read many books, but those he does he imbibes with intensity. Things that impress him are never forgotten. Freddie gets on surprisingly well with the common man or woman. He chuckles delightedly when there are family rows and shocking language is used. His eyes fill with amusement: 'It's so human!' When I told him how much I envied him his sense of leisure, he said: 'It's merely laziness. I'm the laziest person in the world: I like to do nothing. When I'm alone my mind isn't meditating – it's merely a blank. I like looking at the ceiling, and when I have to work hard it is just in order to get through it as quickly as possible.'

At dinner on Saturday (a meal which started at about ten o'clock at night) Freddie talked of his favourite, the adored Pavlova. Once or twice he rose from the table to do an imitation, to run as she did, take a pose for the photographer or make an entrance in her grand manner. Despite his plumpness he was able to impersonate the first ballet dancer to make thinness admired; his eyes conveyed his intention so forcibly that one imagined one was witnessing the original. These were moments of real genius. He told us that from today's point of view, Pavlova was technically not a good dancer; that she had no strength, and that half a dozen of today's Covent Garden ballerinas could dance her off her feet. She had poor taste in her choice of composers and in the quality of her ballets; for instance, *The Gavotte*, danced to the most hackneyed of tunes, and *The Christmas Doll* were of appalling banality. Nevertheless, her showmanship was so remarkable that the audience were given the impression that they were seeing more than they were. She might dance for three minutes on end, then take five minutes for curtain calls. She would suddenly appear from an unexpected entrance on the stage, or leap from behind the back curtains, run forward at great pace, or merely subside by the side curtain. He described how the arc-light trembled on one spot while awaiting her arrival on stage. In *The Christmas Doll* she was seen to stand motionless for a long time but, in order not to appear dead and inanimate, she would occasionally breathe enough to encourage the sequins to glint on her tutu, or she would flicker her eyes. Those eyes were magnetic and wild, and were the focal point of her gaunt, birdlike face. In many ways Freddie judged she was inferior to Karsavina, but superior in that she did possess genius.

It was the greatest thrill of his career when as a young choreographer his work had been singled out by her and he was bidden to Ivy House to see the great star.

He was talking to her husband, Monsieur Dandré, in the drawing-room when he saw those elongated eastern eyes looking at him above the shutters of the window. She came in. She looked old but marvellously preserved, the skin stretched tight over the bones of her face; and no matter where she stood or sat, she instinctively took up the most wonderful poses.

She took his hands and blessed him. 'You will have great success, one day. It may take a long time, but it will come,' she told Fred. She said that she would like him to arrange dancers for her when she returned from her next tour. She never returned. She had a bad cold, caught pneumonia while changing trains at night and, in those pre-penicillin days, she died.

Pavlova had been one of my enthusiasms since that memorable, unforgotten Saturday evening when, suddenly, my father realized that her latest season was ending, and that there was only this one last chance to take his whole family to see her. Of course all the seats at the Prince's Theatre were sold except, miraculously, for a box. It was situated very high on the 'prompt' side of the stage from which only a bird's eye view could be obtained; that was better than nothing, and if we were to occupy a box we must all dress for the occasion. As it happened, the cricket match at the Hampstead Cricket Ground, in which my father was playing, continued later than usual. My impatience to embark on our journey to theatreland turned to exasperation with the rest of my family and their last-minute delays.

Long since trussed-up in my first dinner jacket, and in an effort to pass the time, I wandered into the garden. There I picked some of my mother's standard roses which thrived so well in our clay soil; I would take these roses to the theatre and perhaps be able to throw them from our box at the star of the evening. These roses became somewhat wilted by the time they had been clutched in my hot hands during the excitements that followed.

Of course I knew nothing about the technique of great dancers and dancing – could not tell an *arabesque* from a *fouetté* – but my father now informed us we were being taken to see 'the greatest dancer in the world'. I knew from the newspapers that she gave garden parties and danced on the lawn for her guests behind those high walls of 'Ivy House' behind the Spaniard's, not far from where we lived on another side of the Heath. But my parents now passed us little snippets about the temperament of the Russian dancer, and regaled us with 'inside' information, widely known, for example that such was Pavlova's rage and jealousy of her partner, Mordkin, that, on one occasion, she had taken a bite out of his ear.

For me, Pavlova was the epitome of all that was rare and mysterious. From the moment that evening when she appeared on the stage, with her big beak of nose, the V-shaped smile, and the long spears of blue painted eyes which gave her the head of a peacock, she was to me the personification of magic. Her fakir-thinness, her mask-white make-up, her stylized, quivering gestures, rather than her flowing grace of movements, sent me into transports.

At the end of that evening, after Pavlova, in the lilac-blue circle of the following spotlight, had danced 'The Death of the Swan', she embarked upon the lengthy ritual of accepting her applause. This was one of the great features of all Pavlova appearances and was known to last as long as her actual dancing upon the stage. But on the last night of the season it had extra significance. The more the audience howled its approval, the more the dancer conceived new devices for eliciting even more adulation. She darted off into the wings on one side of the stage, while the audience, under the impression that, by sheer volume of sound, it could 'will' her to come forth from whence she had flown, yelled its delight at seeing the star appear, and rush forward, with arms outstretched, from the depths of the opposite side of the stage. Pavlova then received yet another bouquet of long-stemmed, dark red roses. She reappeared almost immediately in a shower of flowers which rained down from the gallery. The ovation increased until the ballerina was again sacrificed to her public amidst a new welter of magnificent hot-house blooms – no doubt from Solomon's in Piccadilly, that most *recherché* of florists.

The applause and the curtain calls continued. The cheers became hoarse; the palms of a thousand hands were burning and painful, but still the clapping went on. The star figure materialized before the curtains at longer intervals and, though the plaudits were as generous, the flower shower became more of a trickle. Now surely this must be it – this must be the final curtain call of the miraculously revived 'Swan'! Yes, once more Pavlova curtsied slowly, the arms weaving, the eyebrows raised, the eyelids lowered: the tremulous, flickering smile was a tragic goodbye, followed by another farewell kiss to all out there in front. Not a flower was left to throw – except my *roses fatiguées*. This was my moment. In spite of my appalling embarrassment I stood up in the box and threw with all my strength. Caroline Testout fell limply through the air, followed slowly by Madame Abel Chatenay. Down, down, down they went, and miraculously they landed at the pointed toes of the *ballerina assoluta*. An electric current ran down my arms, my spine, my legs. I could hardly believe it when, from among the Solomon relics on the stage, the thin white hands went out to my home-made offerings and clasped my mother's roses. An incredible sense of intimacy went through me. It was as if I had established a sexual rapport with Pavlova and it had been watched by the whole audience. The fact that my family laughed and cheeringly congratulated me only made me feel more embarrassed. But I left the theatre in a daze of fulfilment.

For weeks on end I scribbled likenesses of Pavlova on any scraps of paper lying about our house. The telephone pad was a maze of that precious, birdlike profile and sleek cap of black silken hair. A few months later, at Harrow School, I submitted my interpretations of Pavlova taking her curtain call as 'The Fairy Doll' for the end-of-term competition. When a stranger to the Arts School offered half-a-crown for its purchase, I was extremely flattered and felt enriched. It was the first time I had sold a painting.

Broadchalke

Oliver Messel has been cast to play the role of my rival over a long period of years. At the beginning of my career I felt that he had everything I longed for – a niche in the theatre, and in London life, and a group of doting friends and lovers. We became friends. I adored him but I was always envious of his success. He was avid to guard every aspect of it, and in fact so ambitious for more that not only was he a dog-in-the-manger about wanting to keep jobs from others but tried to hang on to those that he was unable himself to fulfil. Recently I felt the competition was over and that it had been won decisively by me. It was, however, a wry stroke of fate that in my photographic career my only serious rival should be Oliver's nephew. Tony Armstrong-Jones suddenly had enormous success – and indeed deserved it. For his photographs were vital and he himself was a young man of great liveliness and a certain charm. The fact that he moved in the second-rate world of magazines and newspapers sullied him, but I personally think that he has survived with his freshness pretty well intact.

At the show of silk designs that Oliver, Graham Sutherland and I had done for Seker, Princess Margaret came up to me and said, 'I've been faithless to you.' I knew at once that she meant that she had had her photograph taken by T.A.J. This was a blow, but I thought it extremely honest and frank to tell me before the pictures appeared. I showed great tact by muttering, 'I'm *so* glad. He's such a nice young man and deserves his success. If I have to have a rival I'm glad it's him and not Baron.' 'And what are they like? Are they formal?' 'Oh, heads mostly – all sorts.' Our talk was then interrupted.

Mark Boxer told me that he'd been invited to dine in Tony's riverside slum dwelling and Princess Margaret would be there. When I arrived at Broadchalke for a weekend's work with my assistant Alan Tagg, and Eileen telephoned the news that Princess Margaret was going to marry T.A.J., I had not received such a bombshell of news for many years. I tried to analyse why I felt upset. I telephoned various friends in amazement. I then thought how wonderful that from one day living in a basement in Pimlico he could be transported by love into Buckingham Palace. I did not for some time work out that in fact this extraordinary phenomenon had enhanced the social status of a photographer! The engaged couple were photographed together at Royal Lodge, they were cheered in the Royal Box at the Opera, and appeared at a race meeting at Newbury. Then they were photographed motoring away for a weekend at the Jeremy Frys' beautiful gold stone house in Bath.

On Sunday morning Tony telephoned to me. Couldn't I go over and have lunch with them. Eileen and Alan would not mind being left alone, and I set off in high excitement and good deal of anxiety at the difficulty of finding the way. Crowds outside the house – policemen, journalists, bumpkins. The door was opened by T.A.J. and Jeremy Fry and we stood talking in a most informal atmosphere in the hall that was hung with the most modern of pictures. In the next room a babble of voices and more violent pictures; and young men with long hair and jeans, young women with equally long hair and sweaters – an artistic group, all very unpretentious and most sympathetic. Tony, very blue-eyed and alert, was full of quiet excitement and vitality. Jeremy Fry an absolute offensive of charm. I found myself engulfed by him and was not able to cope with his wife, a charming blousy girl in the hugeness of pregnancy, who wore ballet slippers and long straight hair. In the midst of this milling party group, looking very simple and homey, was the bride-to-be. She was smoking a cigarette in a holder held in a podgy little hand that had an engagement ring on it and wore a puny little diamond wrist-watch. Her complexion was exquisitely pink and white (with a lot of rosy rouge on the cheeks) and her hair was chic enough to differentiate her from the others.

I made a speech to Princess Margaret saying that I thought she had found the most delightful solution for me as to how, most charmingly, to get rid of a rival photographer. She roared with laughter and asked me to repeat the sentence to Tony. But I bungled it – should never try to repeat anything. Then I was shown the first communal wedding present. One of the painters present had given them a large picture of a great number of hysterical-looking naked figures milling together in what appeared to be a blue haze or an earthquake or a trench scene of the 1914–18 war. Princess Margaret said, 'They're all dancing.' I took a gulp of champagne and said, 'Oh, I'm so glad it isn't a disaster.' Princess Margaret laughed so much that she had to lie flat in an armchair. The arty crowd left the party and I took my friend Elizabeth Cavendish into a corner.

The lunch that followed was simple and delightful. Food the usual English Sunday fare – beef, with uncooked carrots, heavy apple tart – and Tony helping round with the vegetables. Coffee drunk from mugs without saucers. Tony's piercing eyes occasionally transfixed on his affianced one, in a trance of love. In an undertone he would call her 'my pet'. She seemed like a ripe peach, all bloom and rosiness. The whole atmosphere without any formality was extremely refreshing. The Frys are both completely at ease and unimpressed. One felt that one had known them for years, that they were the greatest of friends, and that there was absolutely no pretence about them. The party had the charm of a picnic.

The house was under siege from the Press. Tony confided – 'We're hemmed in here – we'd like to go for a walk and get some air – could we come over to you this afternoon? Otherwise we don't know where to go.' I was delighted, but when I tried in vain for half an hour on end to ring the house to warn them of the impending invasion, there was no reply. Someone must put the bed-cover on my bed, and clear up the 'Turandot' designs from the drawing-room floor. My mother, Eileen, Alan, Nick and Mrs Talbot should be in the house. But still no reply.

Elizabeth and I were to motor together – following the others out of town, then leading the way to Broadchalke. But we got lost and were resigned never to catch up with the car in front although I put my foot on the accelerator to such a speed that we were not so much motoring as flying. It was not until the white bridge at Bowerchalke that at last I overtook the others – and arrived at the house half a minute before them. The telephone call alerting the household had eventually got through only quarter of an hour before, so the rush had been hysterical. But everything seemed to be reasonably tidy.

The party toured the garden – which was looking very wintry with only a few signs of spring; then the lovers went off for a walk – Tony in his shirt sleeves doing a Sir Walter Raleigh act as Princess Margaret got over the barbed-wire fences to climb to the downs. The others admired the house and the Winter Garden which was at its best with clouds of jasmine smelling like the tropics. Here later Tony took snapshots saying rather sadly, 'I haven't used my camera for so long!' When photographing me he asked Princess Margaret, leaning forward to look at the goldfish, please to remove her head out of the picture. She did not show the slightest sense of irritation.

I was too restless to make jokes, but I think the others enjoyed themselves. Jeremy Fry certainly seemed his usual contented relaxed self, while his wife oozed satisfaction like a great domestic cat. Mummie in large stage asides to Eileen said, 'When are they all going to leave?'

New York: January 1961

The first night of *Turandot* was electrifying. Never has there been a more charged atmosphere at the Met. The standing ovation for Stokowski's appearance on crutches was thrilling and throughout the performance the audience applauded enthusiastically at every opportunity.

My evening, however, was ruined by one chorus-woman coming on in Act I in the costume I had designed for her to wear in Act III. It was a particularly unfortunate accident as the hundreds of dresses in Act I were specifically designed to be dark blue and other drab colours in order to create the necessary sinister atmosphere. Suddenly this 'trespasser' appeared in an orange skirt, meant for an entirely different scene later on. All eyes were drawn to her. I was dumbfounded and could only hope that she would somehow fade into the background. But no, she was always in the forefront of the stage. When the chorus lay on the floor, the orange bottom was the biggest and most prominent. Then when she went to the side of the stage and stood in an arc-light, my rage exploded. I darted up the length of the aisle gathering more fury with speed. I rushed backstage and pushed my way through the crowds round the back of the set until I came to the wings where the orange could be seen in full glow. Here the chorus-master helped me to signal the woman off-stage, although even when the guards indicated with their halberds that she must come off-stage, she moved further forward in the light. Eventually she was pulled backwards. Whereupon, in silent fury, I tore at her skirt. I went on pulling at it in an ever-growing frenzy, but it would not give way. I was beside myself in a manner that surprised me. At last I heard a rending screech of a tear. I pulled downwards in spite of 'Mr Beaton!!' coming from the startled chorus-master. At last the lady was standing in her BVDs with an orange skirt in tatters on the floor around her. Then I rushed back to my stall. But to enjoy no peace. I almost had a heart attack. I sat with my face in my hands completely exhausted.

In the first interval, just as I was about to escort Suzy Parker to have a drink in the Opera Club, I was approached by John Gutman and Bob Herman. 'Do you want the show to go on? Unless you make a public apology to the female chorus, there will be a strike. The Union will close the show!' I was frogmarched backstage. I felt what it was like to be handcuffed and taken off in the Black Maria. I was hurried to the dressing-room in which forty angry, half-naked women were changing. A little 'Minnie Mouse' was sitting mopping tears with Kleenex papers rolled into a ball. She wore Chinese make-up and a dressing-gown.

'I've come to apologize for what I did. I didn't know I was capable of behaving so badly. It was inexcusable and I can only say in my defence that we've been working so hard for three months to get the blues just right and to see this orange figure was just too much. But I should never have lost control and I'm extremely sorry. Please shake hands to show you have forgiven me.' The little woman never spoke a word – shook my hand and dabbed away another tear.

Then an angry woman from the chorus said: 'And, another thing, these sandals are all coming apart.' The day was won – Guttman took control of her. We fitted out Minnie Mouse in blue for the last act and, terrified, I returned to the appalled Suzy. For one hour I was alternately overcome by remorse and laughter.

The orange woman had ruined my first night. But despite this I gradually realized what a success the evening had been for me as well as for all concerned. The after-party at Nin Ryan's was unique in that it needed no build-up – all the guests arrived in a state of elation. Noël Coward was adulatory and made a very funny remark about Corelli who is known in Italy as the man of the golden legs. 'Well, I wish he'd shown us his fleece.' Adlai Stevenson said, on hearing of my backstage exploits: 'I've known people get worked up about a word or a phrase. I did not know that one colour could be of such importance!'

Rudolf Bing became human, all shyness disappeared. He roared with laughter about the orange skirt: 'I can't imagine this calm, collected Britisher, this photographer of the Royal Family ...'

The Ambassador Hotel, New York

The telephone rang. It was Larry Olivier just arrived from London at the New York airport. Could he see me immediately? What was I doing for lunch? I was working desperately hard with Waldemar polishing a last draft of my first volume of diaries for an impatient publisher. Waldemar and I had, as usual, planned to have the Room Service bring in a sandwich so that no valuable time should be lost 'breaking for lunch'. For some weeks now I had turned off the telephone and arranged no appointments during the day, and I did not feel now like breaking this routine. I had not forgotten Larry's cruel reception of me in his dressing-room at *The School for Scandal* and we had not spoken to one another since that awful evening. What did he want of me now, I asked? He would not tell me on the telephone, but said it was important. I relented. He could come and have a quick lunch with me downstairs in the hotel restaurant, while Waldemar, by himself, would have a sandwich and a glass of milk upstairs.

Larry appeared, looking a bit travel-strained. He was *chétif* in manner, edgy and nervous. He made no reference to our earlier 'situation' and seemed incapable of spitting out the object of our meeting. We were already half-way through the lamb chops, broccoli and mixed salad with Roquefort dressing when I took the conversational bull by the horns. 'What's all this in aid of?' I asked. A lot of flicking of the head, clearing of throat and darting out of the tongue presaged the 'top secret' information that he was going to do a film of Rattigan's *Sleeping Prince* and wanted me to do the costumes for Marilyn Monroe.

I believe Larry was disappointed that I was not more impressed. But when I saw the play in London, I disliked it intensely. I considered the evening's only distinction came from Martita Hunt's quite historic performance as a Grand Duchess – a part in which she had completely eclipsed Olivier and which she was not now being asked to repeat on the screen. I love Marilyn Monroe and would put up with a great deal of trouble, delays and indecisions for this adorable person, and the pre-World War I period is one that I can hardly ever resist, but probably, under the circumstances, this time I could.

I went back to my room and to Waldemar, and we immediately took up where we had left off and worked long into the night. Only next day did I ring Arnold Weissberger, my friend and attorney. I told him to ask the highest fee that any designer in the history of entertainment has ever been given. As I never heard another word from Larry – and not even a thank-you for the lunch – I imagined my demands were considered insufferable.

London: 11 June

The Jackie [Kennedy] evening was interesting in some ways. It was to be the one informal evening in a week of triumphant European official visits for the wife of the American President. Jakie Astor and his wife Chiquita gave a small dinner party for her (apart from the Radziwills, just the William Douglas-Homes and me). Stella, their schoolgirl daughter, rushed excitedly up and down the stairs and backwards and forwards to the window in her nightgown and with one bedroom-slipper missing, because some photographers were outside and knew of their 'secret' guest.

Jackie appeared to be very much an over-lifesize caricature of herself. Huge baseball-players' shoulders and haunches, big boyish hands and feet; very dark, beautiful receptive eyes looking roguish or sad – sometimes they pop too much – mouth very large and generous, with a smile turning down at the corners in an inverted laugh; a somewhat negroid appearance; the suspicion of a moustache, and very black hair.

Jackie's manner is affected, with deep southern drawl. To the word 'marvellous' she would give great weight. She adopts a slight hesitancy which is good because it makes her appear modest and humble.

Jackie was outspoken and impolitic, telling of the rough talk between Jack and Mr Krushchev. Mr Krushchev had said: 'When I was forty – your age – I was a clerk in an office, and I've grown to be the head of my nation, which shows what wonderful opportunities there are in the Soviet Union.' To which Jack replied: 'I can become President at the age of forty.'

About the flowers and the taste of the festivities at the Versailles banquet, she was ecstatic. About dinner with the Queen last night she said they were all tremendously kind and nice, but she was not impressed by the flowers, or the furnishings of the apartments at Buckingham Palace, or by the Queen's dark-blue tulle dress and shoulder straps, or her flat hairstyle.

Jackie had been criticized for wearing Paris dresses, but she just laughed and seemed to have no fear of criticism. She enjoys so many aspects of her job, and takes for granted the more onerous onslaughts of the press.

The evening ended early as Chiquita was only just recovering from a nasty car accident, and Jackie was tired too. She laughed a lot when I said: 'When you bugger off, we're going to have a wonderful post-mortem.'

Tangier: August

The gilt-edged invitation cards summoned the privileged guests for 10.30 in the evening. By 11.30 a hundred ill-assorted people of all ages wandered aimlessly from room to room wondering when the hostess would appear to greet them. The house is almost too oriental in its excess of latticework tiles, painted and carved woods, and divans piled with velvet cushions. David Herbert had arranged a great number of flowers, but somehow there was nothing to surprise or delight, and quite a lot of the more distinguished, older guests sat around winking or making veiled comments of disapproval.

Trapped by consuls' wives or ex-ambassadors, I revolted. This was not what I'd come to Tangier for. I sought out Ira Belline who, turbanned and bepearled, looked beautiful. She conducted me to the roof-terraces, which were splendidly transformed for the night. In cleverly-arranged shafts of light there were scarlet and orange tents. Orange and magenta cushions of Arabic designs in brilliant colours were everywhere. Obelisks, balls and Archimbaldo figures were made of marigolds, zinnias and sunflowers. The effect was made more remarkable by the night scene of Tangier's inhabitants peering from the neighbouring white houses, and in the distance the silhouette of the old town.

Suddenly the hostess was on view, dazzingly illuminated in a greenish light. The performance was to be given only for tonight. The real emeralds, as big as prunes, were embedded in a great fillet of real diamonds. The egg-size pearls at her neck had an unholy brilliance; her dress was heavily embroidered in diamonds. It was a little Byzantine empress-doll. Her gestures of greeting and affection, her smiles, the look of surprise or delight, were all played in the grand manner. An arm was extended for the hand to be kissed, a graceful turn of the head to greet a Moroccan 'big-wig', a wide, open-armed welcome to an old friend, head thrown back with lowered lids and a move of the mouth – every sort of smile and coquetry.

I watched, as did quite a number of others, as if she was in reality playing a scene on the stage. She seemed quite oblivious of the stares, or of the photographic flash-lights. In her gladioli tent with the brass tray table at hand for her champagne glass, she received the most important Tangerines until, suddenly, she decided to leave her igloo to go to a higher roof to watch some local dancing.

I would have liked an opportunity to talk to her during the evening. But, by now, she was too euphoric to be able to communicate except by pantomine, and to do spasmodic little dances *à la Bali* with neck shaking from side to side, and a wriggle of her shoulders. Standing behind a belly dancer, we watched not the performance but Barbara's reaction to it.

As the evening progressed, she overplayed her role. She was in need of a director to tell her that she was forcing her effects too much. None the less, I was fascinated.

This perfect oval face was seen at its best with the Helen of Troy hair-do and the fillets above. I could not discover why I did not think she looked utterly beautiful. Any minute the curtain might come down for ever. But, meanwhile, the delicate little child's hands applauded, and the exquisite little feet, shod in the tiniest Cinderella sandals, were beating time ineffectually, with the toes turned in.

Venice: August

Flying towards Venice in the late afternoon one saw the shape of this small, sea-surrounded town as one never can when living in its labyrinth of canals and twisting streets.

An hour later in the grand Palazzo on the Grand Canal, Brando [Count Brandolini], my host, said we were all to be taken to the Villa Maser to hear some *cinquecento* madrigals. At once one was involved in a highly civilized eighteenth-century way of life that does not exist in many places today. It is probably the last place where footmen in white gloves and family livery help with the cold buffet of game and salmon, truffles in rice, and wines produced on the estate.

The Villa Maser, brightly lit in the motionless night, came alive as the guests arrived to be greeted by a screaming hostess; a token drink, a *canapé*. The guests were bidden to the terrace to listen to the music against a Palladian background. The sounds created there were of great subtlety and perfection and one marvelled at such exquisite dedication to an art form that, to most of us, may seem rather remote.

The news of a further nuclear test by the Russians, and the sealing of East Berlin seemed rather an empty menace here in Venice where the merits of the latest contribution to film art, *L'Année Dernière à Marienbad*, the interpretations of the Zeffirelli Old Vic production of *Romeo and Juliet*, the exhibition of the Albertina drawings at St Giorgio and the modern abstractionists at the Palazzo Grassi were being discussed vehemently. And who could bother about Mr Krushchev when that great impresario, Lili Volpi, was about to give her annual ball?

Lilies were being placed in obelisk form or in garlands; the tuberoses splayed in glass tubs on the floor (*très goût courtisane!*), floral tributes sent by well-wishers. Would the hostess raise her hand to some uninvited guest and shriek '*Sortez! Sortez!*' as she had done in the past?; or perhaps sack all her servants on the spot so that two days later she would be weeping in a completely deserted Palazzo?

Chez nous, the hairdresser in Cristiana's [Countess Brandolini] bedroom was attending a scurrying bevy of beauties: Graziella was under the dryer, the Duchess of Alba against her will was having her yellow hair dressed downwards. 'But I wanted it up! I'm always being a victim!' The queue for attention was frenzied, and the result was that the other guests assembled for the large dinner party were all kept waiting. Daisy Fellowes, who, in spite of her weak heart, climbed the stairs with serenity, was now beginning to get fractious. 'I'm hungry. The Rothschilds are always *très en retard*, but they don't mind!'

The motor-boats puff and throttle at the door. The waves lap over the gangplanks, as other boats rush by on the way to the midnight rout. 'If the wind blows my head, I'm done for!' the loud cries are squawked.

A red carpet had been laid on the planks outside the Palazzo, where dozens of husky servants helped the helpless guests on their unsure feet. That social institution, that pillar of all that is decadent, La Maxwell, looked like a terrified buffalo as she was aided to the entrance. She was dressed in gold-bead embroidery of a magnificence that should belong to a Calpurnia or a Volumnia.

The great assemblage was exactly the same group of Venetian society as it was last year and all the years before. All the hairdressers and costumiers had been at work, and hundreds of people involved. Yet there was no note of originality. No dress was outstanding. Only Lili Volpi's beehive hair-do was remarkable in the boldness of its proportions.

She looked bored as she wandered around or sat in positions of abandoned relaxation, leaning on a massive elbow or slumped against the back of a chair. Occasionally she exerted herself to give hell to the servants in the dining-room. The head steward looked miserable; any minute his head may fall. She moved a screen in front of the servants' entrance in her own rich arms. She supervises the scene in the ballroom – '*La chaleur! C'est raté mon* party – the band is *épouvantable*! My silly daughter, Anne Marie, is responsible. I told her this band would be a flop but she insisted, the stupid, stubborn girl. She's always making mistakes. No wonder her husband has left her! To have married him in the first place was an error!'

The cold buffet was a triumph of the chef's art with huge octopi made of lobster; a gondolier rowing a decorated ham, two bleeding mountains of cascading beef; crawfish filled with crevettes, and pinnacles of shrimps.

Back at the Palazzo Brandolini, where Wagner wrote *Tristan*, a charming scene of relaxation. Most of the ladies have unfastened their waists and bodices. 'At last I'm free! My dress was killing me!' Now they are guzzling ripe figs. The men's shoes are off and strewn about the oriental rugs. The funny vignettes of the evening are discussed. Cristiana says, 'It was a horrible bore. I hated every minute!'

London: November

The curtain went up to the music of Scriabin. The huge stage was empty except for the scarlet-shrouded object standing centre. A crack of applause broke from the audience. Here was the exile of the Soviet Union, subdued no longer. Suddenly the cloak moved more swiftly than the eye could follow, and was violently whisked away to reveal a savage young creature, half naked, with wild eyes on an ecstatic, gaunt face, and a long mop of flying, silk hair, rushing towards the footlights. The force and dynamic power of this unexpected figure was shocking and compelling.

The dance upon which he had embarked was so strong in its impact that the theatre became an arena of electrified silence. The wild, faunlike creature, with the parted pout, was darting round the stage, dipping and weaving like a swallow, then turning in screws like a whiplash. Then he began slowly to weave, like the leaves of water-plants, but always with metallic resilience and strength.

I am incapable of appreciating the intricacies or subtle technicalities of the dance. Even more inadequate am I at describing them. But as I held my breath for fear of disturbing my rapt attention, even I noticed the marvellous precision with which his feet were returned from space to the boards of the stage. The feet, slightly heavy and large, were like blobs of metal attached to a very resilient wire. These legs were strong, but not over-muscular like Nijinsky's; they moved with molten glass fluidity as he made smooth leaps high into the air.

The torso was broad-shouldered, and rather narrow at the waist; the arms were strong and long, and swayed with an ineffable grace and strength. The hands, too, did everything that a sculptor in mobility would choose if he happened to be a master of the ultimate taste and refinement.

Here was something almost perfect in the taste of today. Diana Cooper, next to me, whispered: 'He's better than Nijinsky!' This boy – a peasant until seventeen when he won a scholarship to be trained as a dancer – looks like all the young Beatniks of today. What we were now seeing was the culmination of the development of dancing since it began. Genius is not too strong a word to describe his quality and talent.

Nureyev's wild, Slavic poem came to an end. The audience was for a moment stunned. Then, recovering, it produced its storm of lightning and thunder applause.

The boy responded with charm, dignity and superb Russian pride. He was obviously pleased and touched by such friendliness. His obeisances were lengthy, leisured, and completely relaxed. This twenty-three-year-old creature from the woods was now, beatnik hair and all, a Russian emperor imperviously accepting the acclaim of his people.

When I was introduced to the young faun at Margot's cocktail party afterwards, I kissed him on cheek and forehead in gratitude.

24

Fond Farewells
1962

C.B.'s mother, with whom he had shared his homes in London and Wiltshire for so many years, died in February 1962. C.B. designed A School for Scandal *for the Comédie Française. He visited Denmark, and saw Karen Blixen for the last time.*

Reddish: 15 January 1962

Generally Dr Christopher Brown has said: 'Physically she's fit, she's not in any pain, she does not suffer. She may go on like that for a very long time.' But tonight this kind, intelligent, very human young man paused quite a long time. Then he said: 'I think you ought to know that she is failing very fast now and it may not be very long before her life is over. I must say she is quite comfortable. Her restlessness is a thing of the past and she is now dozing most of the time.'

The coal readjusted itself in the grate. The library looked very dark and serious. I remembered an incident that occurred just before Christmas. I had been attending to some last-minute detail of the festivities, when I saw my mother standing at the top of the flight of five steps. She looked bewildered at the thought of having to manipulate the further stairs. When she saw me she made a gesture which I shall remember until my dying day. She lifted her arm high and yearned towards me with her thin hand stretching in desperate supplication. All the years of my life seemed to be cast away as I ran towards her and tried to give her the support that she had given me as a child.

23 January

Somehow or other this slow process of dying was different from what I had imagined it to be. Death has always seemed sinister – it had elements of cruel mystery, something to be ashamed of. This was sad, but no more frightening than the crumpling up of a flower, or the weakening of a bird.

She scrutinized her hand a great deal and seemed surprised that her wedding-ring now slides loosely on her fingers. She likes to have me sit by the the bed holding her hand. She looks very beautiful.

23 February

I had to go to Paris for two hectic days of work. It was at the end of the second day that at last I lay down on my bed at about 6.30 in the evening. The telephone bell rang. Since we had already discussed all the business in hand, I was surprised that it was Eileen. She told me in a very calm, offhand way that my mother had died at 3.30 that afternoon, that it had been most fortunate that Nancy had been with her, also Mrs Talbot and Doctor Brown; that she had died very simply and quickly – no pain – very peaceful. I took the news so calmly that I could only wonder at my lack of emotion.

Broadchalke

I rushed out into the garden, and blubbing like a fool, walked up and down the lawns in the cold air. I wanted to die of my grief. After a time Nancy came out and, her arm in mine, told me how marvellously peaceful the end had been; how fortunate that it had been so painless and dignified. How Mummie had given Nancy two seraphic smiles then turned on her side, and breathed like a child, and then no longer breathed. 'You must go and see her. There is nothing frightening about it. She looks beautiful.'

Mummie lay in her darkened bedroom very low in her bed. I was surprised to see how small she was; her head had been tied with a white cloth under the chin. On her chest Nancy had put a little bunch of flowers that she had picked from the garden – pink azaleas, violets, snowdrops, primroses and jasmine. She looked vulnerable and trusting. Her forehead was so cold. I hurried from the room.

I could not wait at the church lychgate after the Broadchalke service for the usual politenesses – the shaking hands, and commiserative smiles. I bolted. I rushed back shivering to my bed, and remained in a daze.

Wiltshire: 14 April

Juliet [Duff] is not having a holiday this August. 'I've had so many expenses. The wall fell down in the kitchen garden and the greenhouse needed repairs, and we had to have the hall recarpeted because of the dog stains. Everything costs so much that we've had to send a bit of jewellery up to Sotheby's'.

In spite of her strong personality, she is a weak character, gutless and apt to change her opinions according to those of others. But the fault that has increased with age is her scattiness.

Tonight Juliet was on her mettle as Lady Churchill was staying for the weekend; Raymond Mortimer was there too. Like the Edwardian hostess that she is, Juliet was determined to stage-manage her little party and to give her chief guests an opportunity to shine. Somehow she managed only a few interruptions, but these were easily parried by Lady Churchill, who is a good talker and accustomed to holding the stage.

Clementine Churchill told us about her friendship with Walter Sickert whom she knew first when she was a gangling, fifteen-year-old schoolgirl at Dieppe. She said that he was a most wonderful-looking man, living in lodgings that were owned by a Madame Villain, who had several children running around with a marked resemblance to him. But of course as a schoolgirl she had no idea that the rather possessive housekeeper was anything more than just that.

'Which is Mr Sickert's room?' the young Clementine had asked.

'He's out!'

'But he asked me to come and see him!'

The landlady smiled in an enigmatic way. 'You can go in and see if you don't believe me.'

The bedroom that confronted the visitor was in an appalling state. The bed had not been made; there were unattractive sights under the bed; and there was a fish skeleton on an old plate on the window-sill. Clementine described how she cleared up the room; she made the bed, covered it with a counterpane (pronounced 'counter-pin') and with delicate fingers tossed the fish remains into a convenient dustbin which she found outside the window. When Sickert came back a little later he was not at all pleased to find that his *'nature morte'* had been destroyed.

Sickert had never painted his ardent young admirer, but once, when she arrived red-faced and radiant from a hockey match, he took a red-hot poker from the fire and burnt on wood a caricature of her, thin and beaky-nosed, with the hockey stick. 'That is to show you how you look.' 'It was a most excellent likeness,' the sitter conceded.

Four years later the young girl was told by her mother that she could go to Paris with her governess and stay as long as they could on £25. By eating little they managed to stay for two weeks. While they were there Sickert called most unexpectedly one morning at eight o'clock, with a bag of brioches, to take the nineteen-year-old girl out to see Paris and some pictures. (The governess was delighted to have the day off to visit relations.) Sickert and Clementine went to a café in the Champs Elysées for breakfast of beer and brioches. The beer was not paid for, but marked up as being another debt that Sickert owed.

Sickert appeared to have no money, and they walked everywhere. First to the Louvre, where Clementine was asked which was her favourite picture. She pointed out Sargent's *La Carmencita*. 'That shows your bad taste,' said Sickert. 'Now look at this Puvis de Chavannes!'

'Oh well, that's a classical picture,' retorted the defiant girl. From the Luxembourg gardens they walked all over Paris until past lunchtime. Again Sickert was not able to pay for their meal, and a chalk mark was put up on a board.

'Now I'll take you to see someone you'll never forget,' and together they went to visit Pissarro, who sat wearing a large black hat, surrounded by his enormous family. As the night approached, Sickert said: 'And now I'll show you a fashionable painter,' and, wisely enough, they dined with Jacques-Emile Blanche, for he provided excellent food and wines.

The young girl's infatuation with Sickert did not burgeon. Later in life the two seldom met, and she grew to have rather a poor opinion of the great man for 'He was, I think, without doubt, the most selfish human being I've ever come across.'

Paris: May

The experience of working on *The School for Scandal* for the Comédie Française has been in great contrast to some of the jobs I've had in the theatre on Broadway and even in London. Each department is headed by an artist, someone who understands the difference between thirty different colours of grey. The tailor spends a morning finding the right silk for a lining or button for a waistcoat; the wig-maker spends infinite time annotating one's wishes; and the head of the scene painting says, 'You must be sure and tell us if you're disappointed with the work and think it should be done with more refinement.'

As for Karinska *fille*, to work with her is to feel that it is easy to design and make beautiful costumes.

Raymond Gerome was always so calm and polite I found it hard to understand that excellent work could result with a display of so little temperament.

As for the authors, Barillet and Grédy, they were enthusiastic and sometimes critical aids to a final effect, and the Administrator, Monsieur Escande, gave forth a flow of gracious compliments that could not fail to gladden my heart.

It is a delightful world of creativity and my last three visits to Paris have centred around those descendants of the seventeenth-century theatre who work in those eighteenth-century attics by the Palais Royal, doing the classics as if for the first time. My new Paris celebrities are M Chaplain, the *perruquier*, who smells strongly of fish after lunch, his wife, with her white Gainsborough pomeranian lying by her side as she works through thick glasses on a front piece of hair; the head cutter, Ernest, with feminine hands, who lovingly smooths a perfectly-cut hunting coat; and Mr Hoff, in charge of the stage.

Food of all sorts is expensive enough in Paris, but the fruit is so superb in quality that one does not mind paying for a pear or an apple as if it were a jewel. I ordered eight pears and while they were being packed up was able to admire to the full the marvellous display of fruit on counter and window.

This year spring has been particularly late in appearing and this made the 'out-of-season' fruit arrayed in tiers seem even more remarkable. There were enormous, globular bunches of pale-green grapes, wonderful symmetrical pale-green artichokes, ceps of all shapes and colours, heavy custard apples, mangoes and aubergines like bolsters. Even the oranges and tangerines not only tasted better than all other oranges and tangerines but looked as if they did too. Passers-by outside would stop and smile as they gesticulated at the marvellous sights, the most remarkable of which were the two boxes which contained half-a-dozen bright, ruby red strawberries that were as big as fir-cones.

The fruit and vegetables *chez* Fauchon are treated with the care which they deserve, and the white-haired duchess who attended me arranged that my pears should be beautifully wrapped for the aeroplane. The procedure tòok a great deal of time. While I waited my gastronomic juices were working overtime as I admired the best of every sort of sausage, pâté and cheese. It was a busy time of the morning and there was quite a *va-et-vient* in the shop.

Suddenly an old, old woman, all in black, a black shawl over her head, and carrying in one gnarled hand a large, cracked black leather bag, appeared in the doorway. She was the very essence of old age and the essence of France. Everyone in the shop watched her and there was a moment of quiet. Whether the lull was created by shock or embarrassment I do not know. The ancient woman hung for support on to the glass of the door. She was bent forward and her face was solid and pink; although not particularly lined one knew she was ancient; she must in fact have been eighty-five years old. But although she looked healthy enough, she had outlived her strength. She knew she could move only with great care, and the effort of coming into this shop was almost more than she could manage. Yet the habit of a lifetime is strong, and she knew instinctively how to preserve herself from falling. She stood peering with a dazed gaze into the interior of this grand emporium.

One of the assistants called cheerfully, '*Entrez, Madame*', and gave the old woman a present of some appetizing meat and wrapped it in shiny paper. The old woman could not say thank you, she merely stared with large, incredulous eyes peering from her rosy, rough-hewn face. She had a drop at the end of her nose, and her stockings were twisted round her 'shrunk shank' like a gnarled tree. She was like all the French peasants one has ever seen; she had the earthy ruggedness of Van Gogh's early paintings.

I wanted her to know how friendly we all felt towards her, and so I stood meeting her bewildered gaze with a forced smile on my face. But she did not understand anything. Another assistant ran to put a large tangerine in her cracked old bag, and I managed to put a coin in her hand. Lurching forward, she slowly turned with enormous dignity towards the door again, to take herself out into the bustle of the Madeleine.

Eileen was there at Pelham Place, smiling and calm, to attend to all that was piled on my desk. She is indefatigable, impeccable; and the fact that it was a Sunday afternoon and that she must cope with all these last-minute nonsenses in no way upset her. It took the two-and-a-half hours at our disposal to do all the packing, letters and photograph instructions, and it was only when the hired car was ready to take me to the airport that I suddenly faced up to the fact that I was going to Denmark.

'Here is your ticket and passport and this little map and book will show you where you're going. You see, there is Copenhagen; to get to Fyn you take the train east across country and you cross the sea and land at Nyborg.'

'And what money do they use? What are these you've given me?'

'Kroner – about twenty to the pound!'

At dinner one evening with Philippe and Pauline de Rothschild the talk was on the subject of cocottes who survived the 1914 war and until 1924 were about the last of their profession in our time. It was inspired by a discussion about the remarkable Jeanne Toussaint, the designer at Cartier, who is now the widow of the Baron Elie d'Orsel. Philippe had known her as a cocotte when her name to intimates was Pom Pom. She was painted by Helleu. She had great taste and that is why Mizza Bricard admires her. She copies the way Pom Pom decorated her rooms in beige, her Greek and Louis XVI furniture and her method of stringing pearls together.

Said Philippe: 'It's a pity I didn't write about them, but I didn't know they'd ever be interesting. I was just having fun with them. For years I lived with Charlotte Bouquet; she was a remarkable woman. Her father kept a hotel in Toulouse and she had an ugly sister who lived with her in her apartment (very Jansen!) on the Quai d'Orsay. The sister was called Blanche Bouquet, but it was smart to have English names at that time of the shingle and the short skirt, and to be rather masculine in appearance, so Charlotte Bouquet became Charlie Brighton. They weren't beautiful, these cocottes. They were clever and witty. They made you laugh and Charlie was like Mistinguett with a big mouth and too many teeth. But she had such style! She wore Chanel clothes, and none knew more about the way to please a man! Charlie always had the best men in Paris – always six-footers and very rich. I shared her with four others. Only once in five years did I ever run across any of the other men by mistake. It was beautifully managed. The morning was taken up with the dressmaker and the hairdresser. Then the afternoon was given up to her men.

'In the evening we always had the best table at the best restaurant. Charlie said that, when making an entrance, one must walk as straight as a die to one's seat, never looking to the left or to the right, or greeting anyone you knew. The *maître d'hôtel* had great respect for these women; they knew more about the men they were with than the men knew themselves, and they knew all the dealings in the banks and stockmarkets.

'Of course *coucheage* was always at the back of your mind, and that came later, but the cocottes were essentially amusing and their trump card was intimacy. They hardly ever gave parties, and when they did they were always flops. Honor Corbett, the last cocotte in Paris, who could be so amusing, tried to give respectable parties but they were always terrible.'

I asked Philippe how it was arranged that you paid these ladies for their entertainment. 'Very easy. They just asked for a cheque. They said, "How do you expect me to live? Do you think I live on air? Who pays for my clothes, the apartment, the meals?" If you didn't pay enough they just tore up the cheque, and you'd have to think again. Thank heavens that never happened to me.

'And the interesting thing is that these women never became absorbed into society. They knew their place. They never wanted to be part of the world. They always remembered their beginnings; although Pom Pom eventually created a new and successful career for herself as Jeanne Toussaint, she would never invite Pauline to her apartment unless Pauline suggested that she should.'

August

I remembered that I had told Karen Blixen that I would get in touch with her again on my return from Fyn. I lifted the telephone receiver. After a moment I heard the familiar sepulchral voice.

'Oh, you're leaving so soon? Then can you come out and have *lunch* with me today?' 'I can't because my aeroplane leaves at four and I'd have to leave you by two o'clock.' 'Oh, I'm very sad about that. You said you'd come. Well you won't see me ever again, that's certain!' My heart stopped. I tried to remonstrate with her but she hung up. I knew I must rush to her immediately. Karen was a rare and wonderful woman whom I had admired for a long time. We were friends and I was proud of that. The last time we had met was in New York. She had appeared so ill and thin that I was convinced she would return to her native country to die.

No sooner had I arranged to have a hired car take me out to her house, three-quarters-of-an-hour away at Rungsted, than the telephone rang again. 'I wanted our conversation to end on a happier note.' 'I'm coming out to see you now. The car will be here in a few moments.' 'Well, you see, now you've arranged to go out to lunch with an old infirm woman.' 'But I'll be there before 11.30.' 'Oh well, that will be very nice. I am glad. We'll have a little drink together.'

I motored through the suburbs of Copenhagen on the way to Elsinore. At one small town I stopped to buy her some flowers. The florist was very sympathetic as he let me choose a flower here, and there, to make a bouquet of apricot and salmon pinks.

Karen was sitting in a large room on a white Biedermeier sofa against the sun, seemingly surrounded by white muslin curtains. She had an aura of extraordinary beauty. I wondered if this was created by the colour of her pale, made-up face, lavender hair and blue sweater, or by the expression of the smiling, heavily blackened eyes. Her eyes have never appeared so shrunken, so small. She was even more wrinkled and thin than the last time I saw her – a gesticulating cadaver.

Karen welcomed me in her deep booming voice. 'Oh, I'm so glad to see you. It's so *good* of you to come.' She was delighted with the flowers.

'How young you look, Cecil! Come and talk. You see how thin I am. My arms are like sticks.' Only too readily she lifted the sleeve of her huge, thick jersey to reveal arms that were indeed matchsticks.

'I'm so weak, of course. I can't write. It's intolerable! The newspaper here wrote that I was now so thin that I'd got down to the cranium! I don't know if you would have liked to photograph my cranium?'

I was relieved to be asked just at that moment when the sun was coming so felicitously through the curtains. Her sweetly-smiling face was sad, and the wrinkles looked like lacework. This woman who knows the whole of *King Lear* by heart carries the wisdom of the world in her eyes. 'You know I *can* walk if you'd like me to move to that other banquette.' I gave her a hand, and I could feel her elbow like a wishing bone. She smiled grotesquely. In some positions she looked like a scarecrow. But she was really beautiful, and I was excited to be given the chance to take such pictures.

'We must drink your health. Can you open that bottle of fizz?' I helped myself greedily to some excellent foie gras, and we were joined by the companion, kind, good, utterly devoted Miss Svenson, who had been with Karen for years. But the presence of this grey-haired, robust spinster somewhat prevented us from having a serious conversation. I thought the remark made by Karen on the telephone could be an opening to her views on meeting her saviour, and her regrets at quitting this life. Instead Miss Svenson recalled all the times we had met in New York.

'Do you remember when Mrs Selznick went to a lunch party by mistake? Mrs Paley said, "You've come on the wrong day," but Mrs Selznick didn't leave. And do you remember the time when we all went to Carson McCullers'?' Karen recalled the time when we had all stayed at Stratford, and had seen three Shakespeare plays in succession. She had not been too tired to go with Gielgud to see that lovely garden – Laurie Johnson's. But I had been exhausted by the intellectual effort and had hardly been able to concentrate on the last play.

We talked non-stop, and I did a sketch of her. But the time was passing.

'I must stand up to say goodbye to you.' I clasped her in my arms. The littly bony body was nothing but a skeleton beneath the thick sweater and the grey flannel trousers. We kissed fondly and fervently; then I hurried out to the hired car. Karen came to the door to wave. Miss Svenson had tactfully disappeared so I had a last glimpse of this great person standing alone in the doorway, waving slowly and sadly. The chauffeur was proud to have seen this distinguished and well-known figure and he bowed low to her.

As we drove away from her she seemed to be peering into the distance. Her eyes became black holes in her face; a beautiful phantom that I shall always remember. I feel she cannot survive much longer. I hungrily looked my last, as the tiny figure turned to go out of my life for ever.

25

The Film of *My Fair Lady*
1962–3

After designing Ashton's Marguerite and Armand *for Fonteyn and Nureyev, C.B. had to leave its final realization to Alan Tagg. He spent most of the year of 1963 in Hollywood enjoying what he called 'the greatest creative experience that anyone working in the theatre can enjoy'.*

London: Tuesday 11 September

The market was almost deserted this evening except for a few policemen hanging around in the empty, reverberating arcades. George Cukor, Gene Allen and I were wandering round Covent Garden, looking for locations and 'local colour', before having a squint at the evening performance of *My Fair Lady* at nearby Drury Lane. I wanted Cukor to be impressed by everything he saw in order to overcome his dislike of making pictures in England ('They're always breaking for cups of tea'). I felt so positively that many scenes, particularly the cockney ones, must be photographed within the sound of Bow Bells. George said: 'Yes, yes, we will certainly shoot some of the scenes here,' but he seemed to be in need of extra conviction. I tried my hardest to stage-manage the outing, but the lack of market life at this hour struck me as a personal affront. Moreover, as often happens when one assumes a responsibility for everything that one is showing off, I even had trouble in locating certain favourite landmarks: 'I *think* St Paul's church is at the end of this arcade, but just in case it isn't, I'll ask this policeman.' 'You're a fine guide,' said George. But he was impressed by the scale of the columns of St Paul's while I noticed, with certain misgivings, that they had recently been so cleaned that they no longer looked as if they were made of the droppings of a million pigeons. Gene Allen, a former policeman, stocky, apple-faced, with a bullet head and child's starry eyes of wonderment, agreed that an effective shot could be taken of the Opera House façade, with the green wrought-iron framework of the market buildings alongside. My fears that the real London might not be used were momentarily allayed. By degrees, the semblance of a beginning for the film formulated itself. Watching *My Fair Lady* tonight was for me like witnessing the laying-out of a friend. After playing for five years all life had gone from the performance; there remained a tired old show with seemingly too few musicians in the orchestra pit and not enough people in the chorus to furnish the stage. Even the lights seemed to lack their former lustre. Zena Dare, who at the age of seventy has clocked in at almost every performance for the entire run, was having a fortnight's holiday. Many of the cast were understudies of understudies, and while waiting for their big opportunity, appeared to have grown disastrously old. Eliza had wilted, and when she was arriving at Ascot it seemed as if her feet hurt. Mrs Pearce, the housekeeper, was the only character who gave any reality to what she was saying. It was particularly painful for me to see that the clothes, over which so much trouble had originally been taken, and which were chosen according to each actor's personality, had not only been sent to the cleaners until their goodness had long since departed (some of the materials were as shiny as lacquer), but were being worn by a cast that had changed so often that no resemblance remained to the originals. The capacity audience fortunately did not share my disappointment. They responded just as they were meant to, but the laughs came, not from the wit of Shaw's lines, but from some awful 'business' that had been interpolated in the absence of a director: Doolittle tripping up on his first entrance, squashing a bug with his foot, Higgins catching a flea and indulging in tasteless horseplay when showing embarrassment.

The life of a play in any one production is always limited. Comes a moment when the bloom is off. This particular production was long since dead except, of course, at the box office. The funeral parlour activities on stage produced in me such chronic physical discomfort that I begged permission to leave after Eliza's success at the ball.

15 February 1963

It seemed strange to find myself packing possibly for a whole year in California while London remains blanketed with snow and ice. The whole day was feverish. Earlier, with traffic around Covent Garden almost at a standstill, I had been caught in a taxi. Got out and ran to the Opera House where I was finishing work on two productions simultaneously, an opera and a ballet. Across the road in the Wardrobe, Nureyev had arrived for his final fittings. We anticipated difficulties because Nureyev had not ingratiated himself with the staff and had quarrelled with an equally temperamental tailor. In the morning I had to be in the scene-painting shop for vital, last-minute decisions about *Turandot*; unexpectedly, Margot Fonteyn had burst in, wearing fur-topped boots and wondering, with an innocent expression, if, after all, her country scene dress had not better be made of a different material? I blanched at the difficulties but sought solace in the fact that the day was a red-letter one since Princess Margaret came to lunch.

Hollywood: Monday 18 February

The police cop at the auto gate at Warner Brothers' Studio laughed and waved wildly at George Cukor who drove me, in his shining black Rolls-Royce, to the éclair-coloured bungalow on the lot which I was to share with him. But this was to be for me, also, a day of warm receptions. Gene Allen, the Art Director, materialized almost immediately with his bright, twinkling eyes, sparkling teeth and well-scrubbed cheeks. He seemed like an old friend after our days looking unsuccessfully for locations in London some months back.

Then George Hopkins, the Set Decorator, appeared. Lanky and Grant Wood-looking, he has a deep voice like gravel and the quick eyes of a cockatoo. His domain comprises the vast warehouses full of furniture of every period, the carpenter's shop where more furniture is made, and 'Upholstery' where, at his word, thousands of yards of material are made into curtains, bed, chair or sofa covers. Would I like my rooms done up? They once belonged to Harry Warner, but they are kind of gloomy now. 'Great!' 'What colour?' 'White.' 'Will do. And new curtains?' 'Orange, please.' 'Will bring patterns. And what colour carpet?' 'Grey.' When, by noontime, two painters in white overalls had already started work on the walls, I realized with what irrevocable speed things can be done in a studio.

Introduction to Joe Hiatt, in charge of 'Wardrobe', a dark florid-faced giant with the eyes of a Renoir child. Little wonder that in such a vast factory as he showed me, they are anxious to make all the clothes for the picture.

'Research' was like a University library. I wondered why, with all this brilliant documentation and with solicitous scholars at hand, most moving-pictures ignore authenticity. Mr Carl Millikin and his Viennese assistant, Gusti Adler, proceeded to send me every book they had on the pre-1914 war period decoration and fashion. Meanwhile, what could they order for me?

It was difficult to realize that any work was being done as George, Gene and I, lolling around feet up, talked in a desultory manner. But, in fact, we were going through the script, scene by scene, deciding how to do the ballroom scene, or how to differentiate the houses of Mrs Higgins and her son. 'How would you react to my doing the ballroom in trellis? It was very fashionable in 1912 and would be a welcome relief from the usual gold and cream "Grace Kelly" sets.' Books arrived forthwith from Research, showing Elsie de Wolfe salons and lobbies done in 1910 in the fashionable lattice work. Gene, enthusiastic, produced a ravishing *treillage* room from Schönbrunn.

Jack Warner's eyes popped with apparent incredulity when he first caught sight of me, but he appeared relieved when I turned out to be more or less human, after all, and laughed at his jokes: 'Hah, I've got a new audience.'

His shining teeth stretched wide, his eyebrows high in youthful surprise, his complexion clear and tanned, his hair shining, nut-brown, he caressed the length of his silk tie with well-manicured fingers. He is an amazingly agile figure, and holds himself with such a straight spine that sometimes he appears almost to be toppling backwards. In his yachting jacket and sportive shoes, he has something about his swashbuckling style that reminds me of Douglas Fairbanks, Senior, and the great era of silent movies. In fact, he is the sole remaining partner of Warner Brothers and, in spite of the aura of the vaudeville theatre in which his career started, the jocular gags with twirling cigars and schoolboy jokes, one sees that for every good reason he is still the head of one of the few great film empires to survive.

'Now, first we've got to tie Alan Lerner down. He's a difficult boy to get hold of, and we have to know when we can expect a finished script. If we don't start soon, time will envelop us. How's that for an ad-lib? I like that bit. Time will envelop us.'

At lunch in the executive room Warner gesticulated in the grand manner. 'This used to be Marion Davies' bungalow when W.R. [Hearst] kept putting her in films, and we made them for him. He was like a Louis, that W.R. Did you ever sleep in Cardinal Richelieu's bed up at the ranch? Yes, he was a Louis all right.'

Sitting next to Warner I made desperate attempts to talk on subjects that might interest him. I took pot-shots at Dali, polo, the Aga Khan and the old Embassy Club days in London. Warner's eyes were flashing towards the far end of the table, and his smile encompassed everyone, but I managed to keep him talking about James Dean. Jack Warner is foremost a tough businessman ('I may forget names but never a sum of money') but he showed that, in spite of all the chaff and nonsense, he recognized greatness. 'That kid Dean was a natural actor. He gave us a lot of trouble, but it was worth it! He only made three pictures, yet he had the biggest appeal of anyone at the box office. He was surrounded with stars in *Giant* but we believe he was twenty-five per cent responsible for the success of that picture! But boy, was he difficult! He slept in his dressing-room here, wouldn't quit. And he'd have broads in at all times of the night, and the police objected and said we were not insured against having people live in this "place of business", so we told Dean to quit. But he wouldn't. He was rather tight with his money. Then I said I'd pay his hotel, and still he wouldn't go, so we had to force him out physically. Then suddenly he started to become hysterical: he said he must return for a few minutes. Well, the police had to accompany him. When he was back in his room he put his hand in a pot and pulled out a thousand-dollar bill, and then another, and then another. He'd forgotten his money there.'

Thursday 11 April

To design fifty new costumes for Ascot or the Ball is no problem, but at this point in the operations it often takes considerable time to devise just the right costume for a principal in a certain scene.

I showed George the designs for Gladys Cooper's costumes. We have decided not to make Mrs Higgins into the conventional Mrs Rittenhouse–Marx Brothers' dowager, but into quite an 'original', a Fabian, rather an aesthetic intellectual (for, after all, she is the mother of the young Bernard Shaw). To suggest the character is quite a tricky technical problem.

I wrote to Diana Cooper, asking what her mother, the Duchess of Rutland, would have worn at Ascot. The Duchess was an aesthetically-inclined beauty and a member of the 'Souls'. She dressed in a picturesque manner. Diana wrote: 'Certainly *cream*. A straw hat trimmed, of course, by herself, with little bits of bird's breast and/or ribbon in dirty pink, wide-ish brimmed and fairly shallow because of the Grecian back-handle, and the Sarah B. fringe in front. I don't suppose she ever set foot in a milliner's shop. She would have been dressed from the old clothes cupboard with cream skirt to the ground, and cream shirt, and lace scarves around the neck held with paste brooches, a tortoise in enamel, and a bay leaf. The whole rag-bag camouflaged over by a *démodé*, once good, three-quarter length coat of beige, lace or brocade, inherited from sister Marjorie, perhaps. Good suede gloves (beige and long). Very high-heeled shoes she hoped didn't show. Parasol, of course.'

George's reaction to the sketches was positive and constructive. He said: 'You've gone way-out on the first one. We shouldn't see her as a freak: we must realize, by degrees, that she is intelligent, a woman of character. You've made her too altogether arty. Gladys must look lovely.'

New York: May

The evening at Diana Vreeland's was a joy. Diana's new wig-like hair-do was unbecoming. But her important responsibilities as Editor-in-Chief of *Vogue* do not seem to have got her down in the least. In fact she was soaring higher in more fantastic upward spirals than before. Truman brilliantly related his latest experiences with the two murderers he had been to see in 'Death Row' [and about whom he wrote *In Cold Blood*].

Truman is quite changed in appearance. No longer is he the elfin waif; he has become a solid man of parts. It has always amazed me how much at home he is in the world, able to talk with anyone on his own terms, with no reserves or apologies. He told us how he had come to possess the grimmest document that one could imagine. As his horrifying saga unfolded, he unconsciously revealed the magnitude of his development as a story-teller, the wealth of his experience and the strength of his imagination.

In the terrible prison Truman had not been able to summon up the courage to ask Perry if he could be present at his hanging. He felt that although Dick was not as good a friend, he could ask him. He produced his fountain-pen; Dick wrote the appalling sentence, then put the pen in his sock and refused to give it back. Dick then started to taunt Truman. 'I've never liked you. Perry was your friend and I've hated you for the five years you've been around and if I give you your pen it will be through your heart.' 'What good would that do you?' 'Justification! Do you realize that before you could call the guard, with that pen I could put out both your eyes?' 'And what good would that do?' 'Satisfaction!' By showing no sign of panic, by telling Dick that it would not help his last appeal, Truman proved his supremacy and Dick threw back the pen at him. 'I Dick ... hereby in respect of $250 being paid to my mother, appoint Truman Capote to be my official witness at my hanging.'

Truman asked us, 'Do you think I was justified in getting that permission from him for such a small amount of money?' He had explained that a well-known lawyer had said it would be impossible for him to be present at the hanging as the leading magistrate did not like him.

Truman also told of other murderers he had come across in this prison – two very beautiful young men who had gone through five states murdering for kicks as they went; both strangling respectable housewives with bull whips while performing the sexual act.

Monday 6 May

Back in Wardrobe, where seventy women, having progressed from Covent Garden to the magpies of Ascot, are now starting on opal-coloured costumes of the Ball scene.

'Anyone want to see me?' 'No, not today,' smiled Barbara. Louise and Lucia, too, were engrossed in their work, so I stopped to confer with Agnes Koschin, who was born in Siberia, escaped with her husband from Russia three years after the revolution, to live seventeen years in China before coming to California. Although much too young to have lived in it, she has a remarkable instinct for the period we are re-creating.

Occasionally we have a bad day, and some dresses are a disappointment. We battle against odds. However, the average is high. The 'feel' of this production is different from the stage.

All in their own ways, the fitters have their excellencies. Louise, like Mother Earth, is a fine tailor. Carol, so pretty, with her grey hair and star eyes, must have been too beautiful to need talent as a young girl, yet had developed a great sense of design and knows instinctively when something is lacking. Lucia, who is Italian, is past-mistress at manœuvring frothy, light lace. Barbara looks worried and persevering, but she knows her *métier* as well as any. Helen, a handsome Duchess with white hair, is terribly nervous with me, but need not be because I'm delighted with everything she does. Mr Morris is a sentimental little owl, and his voice is so packed with emotion that he seems as if he is weeping. 'Oh, I like to work on that. It's a pleasure!' he beams unctuously. 'I don't want to put any fur on it. It's far better as it is.' The tailoring of his coats is impeccable. His latest creation is a silver cape that Helen wore with such pride and shyness. Everyone complimented her on her appearance. 'If only I were young!' she said. An Italian, Filomena, with her spectacles worn on her head, the better to give unhindered winks, is full of sly fun.

Most of the laughs are to be found in the millinery corner. One hat looks like a weather-vane on which half a dozen crows are trying to alight: another is a large chauffeur's cap made of most unsuitable materials, while yet another is just an upturned bucket with a cascade of ostrich feathers. The work girls take off their spectacles and pose in the most outrageous millinery. But this is not merely a fun-fair. These are great artisans whose craft is apparent in so many delicate nuances of understanding and experience. If these hats were made by a heavy hand, they would be vulgar, ugly and impractical.

Leah's enthusiasms come from doing something that is, perhaps, the best she has ever done. 'Oh, this makes me flip,' she says, as she puts on a Gothic monster of black spikes. This is a *tour de force* on her part, for she has fashioned it with the subtlety of a piece of modern sculpture. Recently my designs have become more and more 'difficult'. Yet, to date, they do not seem to be a stumbling block. To see the drawings and designs, made in a hurry two months ago, suddenly brought to fruition is a real thrill.

On Stage 2, Higgins' house – based on a genuine house in Wimpole Street – is being built. It is a most intricate and ingenious arrangement with the three floors and their staircases built side by side on the sound stage instead of one above the other as in a real house. In spite of the difficulty of the staircases being cut off sharp, half-way up- or downstairs, it now begins to take shape. Many aspects of the transplanted house – the nodes and crannies – are so familiar to me that I feel that Dr Gottfried will materialize at any minute to give me an injection.

June

Hitchcock, whom I've always loathed, was a fellow guest [at dinner with Edie Goetz] and said to David Selznick (apropos of the Profumo case) that it had cut England down to size. The English were so arrogant – didn't this serve them right? Didn't I think the British were arrogant? Without knowing why, I have been gunning for Hitchcock for many years. There is nothing more unattractive than a man decrying his own country in another one. He did not know what had hit him when I burst out at him, 'Of course the English are arrogant, and with good reason! I love them for it. I love arrogance!'

Hitchcock said that films should be made to give pleasure to people who weren't interested in films as an art form. 'The films are not an art form. It's selfish of people who make films for their own pleasure and interest.'

Then we started to fight about artists in films – like Fellini. Hitchcock brought the subject round to himself. He said he was the father of the avantgarde in France; that all these young people were doing very badly. They all called on him for help. 'I hope you give them money,' I remarked.

'That's very rude,' said Mrs Goldwyn on my right.

'Aren't fathers there to do just that?' I answered. The evening was nightmarish, but good to laugh about afterwards.

27 June

The evening was interesting in that it was spent at a party given for Rudi Nureyev. I never know in what mood he is going to be and was quite expecting him to be cold and disdainful. But, no, he was slightly drunk and very coy. I made a great play of flattery and he fell for it with every dimple in his thin cheeks. We hugged and kissed and displayed a great love for one another and I proposed that he should come and live with me. It was all very agreeable and an amusing comedy. But in between the lines he threw me a few home truths. People have been very mean with him; he will continue with them, but they must pay him. He will do TV work here in New York, but the US Government takes all in taxes. I felt sorry for him. He is, for all his fame, a lone wolf.

The party was one of Hollywood's most select but, like all Hollywood parties, it had no homogeneity, no atmosphere, and an awkward wait before any food was served.

On my way out I went to find Nureyev in his bedroom. 'Rudi? Rudi?' I found him sitting in his great bedroom dangling a loose shoe. 'What are you doing here? Are you sad?'

'Yes, and very lonely – this awful house – you suffer so. Maybe I have five days in Paris with my friend, but we have been travelling a month without meeting; and when you love you are apt to be sad and there's no hope for us. We can't work together. It is *always* travelling for me; always on the road – without a window.'

'You see ballet people are so silly. They do as they're told. They never think. Nobody understands me, perhaps Margot a little from time to time, and Freddy's nice, but he offers me nothing, and they hate me. But I don't care.'

I tried to cajole him, to make jokes; I told him of the beauties of being in love if one did not suffer too much; and how lucky when it happened painlessly. But Rudi is a Russian and I don't expect he loves painlessly. He came out to the car. 'Would you like to go for a ride with me?'

'No, I must stay here. The others will be arriving from the ballet.'

My feelings about the ballet *Marguerite and Armand*, on which I had worked so hard, were mixed. The auditorium dwarfed the set, the curtain did not stretch to the sides and the lighting was very rough. The orchestra played an introduction with chiming bells that I thought poor in quality, but once the ballet started I was carried along in a transport of emotion. It is a remarkable work despite what the critics said. It is packed with drama and one sits tingling, on edge in case one misses a nuance.

I was very pleased with my contribution and considered that it hit exactly the right note. The ballet conveyed, in fact, just the atmosphere that we had hoped that it should. Margot's performance is her best and she shows herself to be another Duse. The taste she displays is amazing and she is made a beauty through the quality of her spirit. Nureyev, too, is the quintessence of all romantic passion; smiling in the early scenes and like a tragic clown (even to the red nose and pale eyes) at the last. Fred Ashton's work is inspired, and it is everything that I like in ballet.

It was a thrill to see that the result of our labours had turned out as we had hoped. The audience screamed. But it was good to hear George Cukor yelling himself hoarse. He said, 'I never remember shouting in a theatre before, and the thought is painful for me, but your work is beautiful!' My mind was in a state of elation. This should have been a happy evening.

I had watched Audrey [Hepburn] during the tests, wearing almost no make-up and being photographed in a somewhat flat light. One took for granted her charm and vitality, but it was only when the result was magnified hundreds of times, that one realized that, as Jack Warner said, 'She is one in a million'. Somehow, the celluloid accentuates her expressions of tenderness, humour, fun, *hauteur* and plaintive childishness. Her nose and jawline do not conform to the golden rule of Praxiteles yet add enormous character to the photographed result. After seeing herself without eye make-up Audrey pleased me by saying that, in the future, she was going to soft pedal its use. The 'Flemish' look, without any eye make-up, is going to be a surprise. Suddenly, one realizes what a hard look the black liner gives the eye, and how its effect is to close up, and make smaller, the white of the eye. Audrey's appearance without it will be quite a revolution and, let's hope, the end of all those black-eyed zombies of the fashion magazines.

On the Covent Garden set, they were working on the cobblestones on the uneven ground, but they were not just stamping the shapes from a mould as they usually do in a studio. Each pebble was made with individual care. This makes all the difference between something that is mechanical and something that is vibrant. The effect, if not seen, is definitely sensed on the screen. Gene is to be complimented on attending to these important details. By encouraging the painters to put layer upon layer of different coloured washes he has managed to get them to give the stonework of the church and the arcades a real patina and quality of depth. He is also responsible for the refinement of the brass work: advertising plates, polished signs and gas lamps.

Geoff Allan, a burly, somewhat top-heavy-looking youth from the outskirts of London, has become an expert at 'ageing' clothes. Today he was breaking down Eliza's little jacket in which she first visits Higgins' house. Everyone who had seen the coat in a test agreed that the black velveteen appeared too elegant and rich-looking. In an effort to save the garment, Geoff decided to take drastic measures. He asked me, 'Suppose it doesn't survive?' 'Go ahead. At worst, we'll have to get a new one.' Geoff put the coat in a boiling vat. After a few hours the black velvet had become a cream colour. Geoff now started to make the coat darker, many shades darker. Putting a spoon in dye, he smeared its surface, leaving light patches where the sun might have faded the collars and shoulders. He purposely left paler the material at the edges and in the creases. The coat was then dried out in a furnace. To me, it now looked like something found in an ancient Egyptian tomb: it was as hard and brittle and brown as poppadom. With blazing eyes, Geoff then brought out a wire brush and gave the garment a few deft strokes, saying, 'This bit of pile will soon disappear.' It did. Later Geoff said, with avid enthusiasm, 'I'll take the thing home tonight and sew frogs on it again – coarsely, with black thread, and I'll sew them with my left hand. Then, with my right hand, I'll rip them off. Then I'll knife the seams open here as if it's split. Afterwards, with coarse thread, I'll patch it. Of course, the collar will have to be stained a bit as if Eliza had spilled coffee on it (no, she would drink tea ... it will have to be tea stains), and there must be greasy marks on the haunches where she wipes her dirty hands. Naturally the skirt will have to be made muddy around the hem, because, you see, she sits when she sells her violets, and the skirt, and petticoats also, would seep up the wet'.

Monday 15 July

A group of extras, supposedly epitomizing the grand world of opera lovers, appeared dressed in what we considered our most stately clothes. Disaster! All the care, patience and love expended so lavishly seemed to have gone for nothing! Each person was strong enough in his or her own brand of anonymity to kill any costume dead. The glittering capes were for tall women who should have looked like birds of paradise. Here was a dreary gang of runts. They might have been dressed from any old, tarnished rag-bag. What bathos! Something will have to be done about this! From now on, we must take these beautiful garments and allow them to wear the person who is within them. We will have, perhaps, as many as twenty different fittings, each time discarding the wearer until we find a nice suitable body to fit into our finished product.

Wednesday 18 September

Today 'close-ups' were being re-taken of 'Wouldn't It Be Loverly' and 'Why Can't The English?' This puts the schedule behind one day. Here again, as if life had stood still, there turned up the same old recalcitrant extras. Their reappearance brought back to mind the hectic tension of the first week's shooting. Luckily, that sort of frenzy has to die down eventually.

Rex sang his song over and over again with such perfection that one could not but be amazed at his technique. The range of sound that he produces is extraordinarily varied: there are deep notes that have survived since his first days of stage training, and he is not afraid of becoming almost falsetto. He knew he was performing well and was highly keyed. He was unaware that he was surrounded by people, yet submitted like a prince to the titivations of the make-up and hairdressers. After every take his sweating brow was mopped, then the mirror placed in front of him while absorbedly he replaced his hat.

At one moment we were all alarmed to see sparks and flashes of light issuing from the outer periphery of the set; an electrical fuse box had caught fire. Thirty workmen ran in the direction of the blaze, smoke went up to the skies. I envisaged the incendiary of the whole of Covent Garden, and a stampede to the doors. But Rex went on looking into the glass, patting his tie, and with great gravity asking, 'Is the camera reloaded?' Fortunately, the fire was put out before the cyclorama went up in flames – for this would have been serious – and Rex continued to sing without a 'dry'. During these long takes Cukor swayed backwards and forwards with a wide, beatific grin on his face, and indeed anyone with appreciation for artistry of a very high order cannot but have been impressed by Rex's virtuosity. His phrasing is masterly: with the emphasis and 'throw away' lines so perfectly balanced, the line is firm and as delicately trod as an expert tight-rope acrobat. This surely was Rex at the very peak of his career.

The fire alarm was soon forgotten but the climate on the set itself continued to be quite inflammable and, since I deemed it unwise to start any photography today, I beat it.

I knew, when taking on this assignment, that it would mean exiling myself from the rural countryside of Wiltshire for at least the whole of one spring, summer, and autumn. But this large-scale venture was one worth making great sacrifices for. I would have been extremely upset if any other designer had pocketed this particular plum. And I am being paid well.

Why, then, is it that I am in a mood where I know I must 'slog on' long past the point of enchantment? The work never fails to be interesting; the talent, kindness, and willingness of my assistants never fails to astound. Nothing but enthusiasm and gratitude emanates from Jack Warner and his office. How have I failed my Director? He does not complain of the quality of my work, or that it is behind schedule. Yet if I had perpetrated something so ugly that it jeopardized the work of all connected with the picture, and each piece of furniture or length of wallpaper I had chosen was an offence, my presence on the set could not create an atmosphere more fraught with tensity. This is a disappointing state of affairs. A gut-grinding pain seldom leaves me, even when spending the evenings with friends who sense my preoccupation yet are loth to mention it; their secret commiseration for something they know nothing of only causes me further distress which haunts me during the night.

To brave the opposition on the set becomes more and more of an effort the longer I delay putting in appearances.

10 October

The first real day of shooting Ascot. My presence was essential, but still no croak could emerge from my throat, so I went about with a notice pinned to my coat: 'Laryngitis, sorry cannot talk.' In this smog-ridden vicinity this is a commonplace illness, and no one seemed surprised at my enforced silence. In the middle of the crowds of racegoers Audrey (who is known by the Frank Sinatra group as 'The Princess') appeared to be tested in her ballroom dress and coiffure. Never has she more lived up to her name, and never was her allure more obvious than now as she smiled radiantly or shyly, flickered her eyelids, lowered her lashes, blinked, did all the tricks of allure with enormous assurance. She gyrated in front of the camera while two hundred extras watched. She was vastly entertained that some of them were scrutinizing her through their race glasses. The glistening ball dress is like ice on trees in Switzerland, and her new coiffure is certainly startling, but I wish I could have prescribed something a little more of the period.

11 October

Slept for twelve hours. Still no voice on waking. This gives me cripple complex.

On the Ascot set only a half-strength crowd had been summoned for the dialogue scenes between Rex and others. Audrey, according to the Wardrobe Plot wearing Costume 13 ('Eliza is a success until she forgets herself during race'), was resting on a lounging board. I asked her in dumb crambo if she would come to the side of the set to pose for a photograph while they were arranging the next shot. This she did with pleasure. Buck Hall, the Assistant Director, then asked us not to get in the way of the cleaners who were polishing the floor. 'Could we move down here?' I gesticulated. Buck gave the 'OK' sign. 'You're sure it will be all right here?' I whispered, then nodded my thanks. In pantomime I gave suggestions to Audrey as I took a black and white roll of her posing among the trellis work. I was about to change to colour film when Buck Hall returned. 'Would you please not take Audrey off the set.' Without a voice I croaked: 'But we are not "off the set" and you said it would be all right!' 'Mr Cukor doesn't want you to take pictures of Audrey while they are fixing the lights.' 'Then when can I?' I wheezed. 'Mr Cukor doesn't want Audrey to get tired. He wants her to be thinking about her part; he does not want you to photograph her on the set during any of her working days.' I had little voice in which to say: 'Then there's no other opportunity to photograph her: all her days are working days and I have been waiting a month for this opportunity.' Looking very pained, Audrey argued in secret with Buck Hall, who was most anxious that Mr Cukor's sugar should not ferment. For the moment I felt no pain. Audrey said: 'I can't be in the middle of this, but try not to be too upset.' She, meanwhile, smoked a cigarette outside while waiting to be summoned. I was later told that it took George Cukor two hours to recover from his displeasure with me enough to continue.

November

My contract is up. There were times when I doubted if I would ever reach the end of this stint. I went to pay my bill and collect my diaries from the hotel safe; seven notebooks have been filled since my arrival. For the last time I took to the freeway with its larva-like mountains rising forlornly each side of the eight parallel lanes of cement and tarmac.

Back for the final round-up in my office. My baggage was bulging full and tight, extra packages had been done up to be sent air freight. Now I scribbled notes of goodbye – written messages often take less time than telephone calls. Then a farewell visit to the adorable people in the Wardrobe: Agnes' eyes melting; Louise, the salt of the earth and looking like Mother Earth; Carol, calm and cheerful with starry eyes. Anne Laune, with wrinkled forehead and eyes brimming over; Betty Huff, sweet and giggly and shivery; and Leah, a bulwark. In this Department I had spent the happiest moments since arriving. Here there was no one to say me nay, or interfere or put a damper on my activities. Here, only the most stimulating help. Joe Hiatt was beaming with pleasure at the nice things his staff were saying about me. He has always been my chief support.

To say goodbye to all these friends cost me much in emotional energy. But now I must muster the strength to go down on to Stage 7 and say goodbye to George Cukor and his Assistant Director, to thank Gene, and to take a fond farewell of Audrey.

They were shooting the scene where Eliza returns to Covent Garden Market after the row with Higgins.

22 November

Betsy, my beloved secretary, came back with her nose twitching in its habitual way like a rabbit. 'There's the most terrible news. President Kennedy has been assassinated in Dallas, Texas. He was shot while driving in a motorcade.' My blood turned to a pale liquid; I felt I was rushing through space down a lift shaft. The switch from life to death, the waste, the tragedy for his family, for the country, for the world, appalled me. There was a great sense of shock. I could only grieve for Jackie.

Jack Kennedy's wit, style and courage, his kindness and feeling for humanity, and his sense of humour were his chief qualities. That this young man, at the height of his power, and holding out such promise for his country, should be violently struck down now was an unfathomable tragedy. We were all completely stunned.

26

Here, There and Everywhere
1963–7

C.B. had never been busier. He published Royal Portraits *and* Images. *He visited Nigeria, Kenya, Tanganyika and Madagascar. He designed* La Traviata *for the Metropolitan Opera House, published* Cecil Beaton's Fair-Lady *and the second volume of his diaries,* The Years Between, *photographed incessantly, travelled in France, Italy, Turkey, Morocco, on a yacht in the Mediterranean, and in Poland. Much of England was unknown to him, and he set out to explore the country with his new friend from California, Kin Hoitsma. Together they motored west to Devon, north to Scotland and east to Norfolk, visiting cathedrals and the great country houses of Kedleston, Haddon, Chatsworth, Hardwick, Marchmont, Lambton and Houghton, as well as C.B.'s mother's birthplace at Temple Sowerby in Westmorland, on the way. C.B. made new friends, such as Mick Jagger of the Rolling Stones; his appetite for new art forms, new trends and new faces was undiminished.*

11 December 1963

Exercises at eight o'clock were quite an effort with a hangover. Decided to give up work for the day. Lunch with Patrick Plunket. Highly-sophisticated fish food at Wilton's, served as in a nursery. Jokes, high spirits, followed by tour to Bond Street, strange frantic shoppers; on to crowded David Hockney exhibition. He is undoubtedly an original, and his engravings for *Rake's Progress* are beautiful. This Bradford boy with the yellow glasses, yellow dyed hair and exaggerated north-country accent was accosted at vernissage by an irate lady. In a loud voice she challenged him for drawing his nude women in such a distorted manner. 'Can you really imagine that is the way the arm comes out of the socket? Look at their bosoms – they're nowhere near where they should be. Have you ever seen a naked woman?' 'A dorn't knogh ars ah harve!'

Reddish: 21 December

The Crichel boys came to lunch. The 'boys' [Raymond Mortimer, Eddie Sackville-West (Lord Sackville), Patrick Trevor-Roper, and Desmond Shawe-Taylor shared a house at Crichel in Dorset] are all elderly men now. Eddie, a lord, cannot and need not work. His taxes make it simpler not to earn. Desmond Shawe-Taylor exploded with rage when I asked if he'd approve of a *Traviata* country scene taking place in a stable. 'You can't write notes in a stable – she's got to have a desk.' His eyes shot red flames. I felt unable to concentrate upon Trevor-Roper's diagnosis of imaginary or non-imaginary pains as I was too busy clearing the table, and with the dining-room reverberating more than I realized, I found myself hard of hearing and sadly missed a lot of the conversation on the subject of Stephen Tennant's eccentricity and young Julian Jebb's longing to make the pilgrimage to his house at Wilsford.

9 February 1964

Simon Fleet had arranged a pub-crawl of the East End, a dozen of us in three cars; a Chinese restaurant; only faintly amusing décor in the pubs; amazing to see the prosperity of the dockers, all well dressed, wearing starched collars and blue suits. The beat-look out. Dancing the Shake; no one minding anything or anybody.

The real thrill was seeing the Christopher Wren house at midnight on Cardinal's Wharf. This exquisite tall grey-stone house looks on to a miraculous view of the river, with barges beached at low tide and hazy St Paul's in the distance. The monochrome scene of liquid lights, black cranes, silver and mist, was unbelievably mysterious and romantic.

New York: March

Half-way across the Atlantic, Pelham Place had receded into the distance and the readjustment to New York had started.

The arrival had its own character. A man from the Metropolitan Opera House met me with a car, and gave me good news of the production of *La Traviata* that I was to work on. Messages had been left for me at the hotel, and before I had unpacked an excited Alfred Lunt was on the line. Could we go immediately to the opera house? Before many minutes in the company of Krawitz, Wrong and Bing, my colleagues in this venture, I began to feel I had always been there. The old problems arose: not much money; little rehearsal time; and too many productions in too short a time. But Alfred, smelling of beer, said his piece, and apologized for talking too much. He is sweet and understanding and a good man, and I pray to God that I will always love him. Alfred took me home in the afternoon but I was too keyed up and exhausted to sleep.

At eight o'clock I went to the dinner he and Lynn were giving for me. Truman was there, the Joe Alsops, Madeleine Sherwood and others, and soon I was involved in local gossip.

Truman came back with me to the hotel. We talked over whiskies and sodas until I realized that by English time it was 7.30 in the morning.

When I woke I spoke for one hour on the telephone to Diana Vreeland. She inspired me, and gave me impetus to carry me through my non-stop day. Diana has learnt not to be pressurized. She's never in a hurry, though she knows there are dozens of people waiting for her to hang up the receiver.

Lunch at the Met., followed by Zeffirelli's *Falstaff*, then, in the evening, *Dolly* with Margaret Case. To end the day, a snowstorm. It gave us such a surprise when we came out of the theatre and prevented our finding a cab. So we had to trudge through the tornado and were soaked through by the time we got back to the hotel.

Stratford-upon-Avon: April

To Stratford to see the exhibition celebrating the quatercentenary of Shakespeare's birth. This proved to be Dicky Buckle's triumph! Absolutely thrilling, mysterious, surprising, shocking, full of contrasts; and, above all, imaginative. Pop art and Nicholas Hilliard, rare Elizabethan revelry and modern junk; music, sonnets, and scent coming out of the ether to greet one. The Elizabethan London of Timothy O'Brien evoked in terms of today; Elizabeth being cheered as she passed in her chair the burnt corpses of the plague; among the squalor, a huge hunk of bleeding meat hanging in mid-air. Alan Tagg's work was subtle and sensitive; a long gallery of authentic Elizabethan portraits and a clever, fascinating model of the Globe Theatre. The Jean Hugo murals were old-fashioned but, I suppose, a good contrast.

At the theatre there was a marvellous production of *Richard II*. All the actors in this company have a mastery of style, a reverence for the poetry and none of the ranting of the old ham. David Warner's interesting portrayal of Richard II was offhand, and his obsequious attitude utterly contemporary.

London: May

From the moment the group assembled themselves in the white oasis in front of the camera, the pattern seemed to form and the lighting proved as luminous as we had hoped. Moreover, the infant showed bonhomie and an interest in the activity that was going on. His behaviour pleased and amused the Queen, who was in a happy, contented and calm mood, and smilingly obeyed my instructions.

Prince Andrew was determined to be in every picture, and behaved like a professional, adding the charm of the too-young-to-know-really-what-it-is-all-about.

I found myself rushing up and down a step-ladder with the celerity of a mountain goat. The Queen remarked on the speed with which I cranked the camera: 'He's much quicker than I am!' I noted that sweat was running down my torso. But such effort was justified. Sometimes I click with desperate speed, hoping that some fluke will evolve. This time I felt that good results were being got immediately. The Queen's wide grin dominated the picture, and other felicitous elements were provided by Andrew's blue, wistful, little-boy eyes and those of the infant who was alert, curious, and already a character.

The day was dark and grey, with lowering clouds, but there was enough light and we moved to take pictures around the crib in which the Queen, Princess Margaret and all her children had lain. Thence to the blue porphyry columns, and to the blue brocaded drawing-room next door. These pictures were more banal, but I was elated at having chosen white-paper backgrounds, as the gilt and heavy marble columns, though impressive to the eye, have been overdone and appear fussy and old-fashioned.

Andrew, the dominant figure, remained cheerful, the baby continued to hold its own, and each time I asked the Queen if she had had enough, she was *just* willing to continue a little longer. 'Look, his eyelashes are all tangled!' she said, admiring the latest addition to the family. 'It's most unfortunate that all my sons have such long eyelashes while my daughter hasn't any at all.'

I seldom notice the presence of Mrs Cartwright, who has been a faithful member of the Pelham Place entourage for many years now. She is quiet and tactful, and although I try to treat her as a human-being I am generally so absorbed in writing a letter or choosing the best poses out of a hundred negatives while she is tidying the room, that there is seldom more than a cursory exchange of politenesses. Mrs Cartwright is rather shy and tentative. Only once did she overcome her reserve: she tried to comfort me when I was sitting at my desk convulsed with tears at hearing the news that Peter Watson had been drowned.

I have heard, through Eileen, that Mrs Cartwright has strong dislikes. At one time she got on extremely badly with Cornelius, the cook; although she has a bawdy sense of humour she can be easily shocked, as when she saw a set of nude photographs I'd taken and covered them up as they lay on my desk.

Eileen, arriving in my bedroom at the start of another busy day, is always treated to a short account of the previous evening's happenings before the telephone interrupts us; and the awful, harrowing, unnerving rush to get to my first appointment starts.

My dinner party had portended well. I had brought up from the country, with great care, three beautiful bottles of rare claret – Rothschild 1928 and 1921. These were for the benefit of Cyril Connolly, who was coming to London in order to have dinner with me. I had invited Cyril and his wife, Deidre, Bertie and Jane Abdy, and Martita Hunt. But I had to confess to Eileen that although the intentions of the guests were friendly, the atmosphere had been indefinably spiky. I did not quite know why, but neither the Connollys nor the Abdys seemed to be playing on my side. Maybe it was my imagination, but Cyril seemed aggressive; perhaps it was his way of trying to cover up the lateness of their arrival. No sooner had he appeared than he was baiting Bertie, who was fatuously 'poohpoohing' Cézanne and saying his importance was only fabricated by women and dealers; Bertie's theories about nobody caring about art, only about the money that art can provide, become more ridiculous.

Bertie then said to me: 'May I be perfectly frank? I don't think you should have these rugs on this lovely floor. You should get rid of them.'

Talk had been so intelligent that later Martita told me she had not felt equal to joining in. However, she did hold forth later on as a connoisseur of food, and where to get the best in London. This she did with consummate style and she displayed her flair and taste in the way that justified her presence.

A day later Eileen arrived in the country. As we sat in the drawing-room after dinner, she said: 'You know, you were right about what you said about your dinner party not being quite easy. Mrs Cartwright had noticed it, and told me all about it. She said that she sensed it from the moment the Abdys arrived and Sir Robert asked her, it being quite a lovely summer evening, "Are we dining in the garden?" ' Upon entering the drawing-room he had asked me the same question in a rather bullying tone. I could not remember my reply, but Mrs Cartwright had and had thought it was rather good: 'No, and I'm afraid it's too late to get a nightingale from Berkeley Square.'

Unaware to me, Mrs Cartwright had gone back to Streatham with her head full of interesting impressions of an evening that I knew was not at all cosy, yet which, but for her, would soon have been forgotten.

1965

Alan Tagg used to be so timid that it was impossible to hear his whispers hidden behind a curtain of fair hair. Now he has blossomed, and when given a sympathetic audience he can be devastatingly funny for long leisurely spans of time.

He has been beguiling us with anecdotes of his recent visit to America and each story is told with such exactitude of dialogue, and is in itself so carefully chosen and individual, that one gets the very essence of his experiences. Likewise, when he described his ecstasy of amusement at the play *Sin*, and described the evening's entertainment, we might all have been present at the performance.

A delightful aspect of Alan's humour is that once something has struck him as funny, it is always funny and can be enjoyed over and over again with pristine relish. Suddenly he will explode with mirth and in explanation tell us that he has just remembered something he heard one woman say to another in a bus ten years ago. 'What was it, do let us share the joke?' 'Well, one woman said, "I washed it for her when she was eighteen, I washed it for her when she was twenty-one, I washed it for her when she was married, and I washed it after her first-born, but I'm never going to wash it for her again."'

We were talking of John Gielgud who had directed a little family comedy for which Alan had done the décor. John has always been tactless, and has developed the art of saying exactly what is on his mind to the most farcical extent. In his deep, throaty, almost military, staccato voice he keeps up a flow without ever noticing the reaction it may have on others. At one rehearsal he says: 'You're beginning to be very good. I'm *very* pleased with you all, except, of course, Berty – you've got it all wrong – no good at all.' Berty explodes into noisy tears. John, stricken with embarrassment and avoiding a row at all costs, is not seen for dust.

One poor girl does not see that a piece of scenery has been placed in her way, falls over it with a painful thud. 'Oh, Dilys, do be graceful!' remarks John.

Reddish House

David Hockney arrived (to be painted) on his way from Bristol. He turned up in his car wearing the thinnest of synthetic windbreakers over a T-shirt. 'Noh, I'm nut corld. Is it corld outside? I get into my car and the heat's automatically on and I get out at the plaice I arrive at. You may think this cappe is a bit daft, but I bought ert at Arrods because I wasn't looking whaire I was gohin and I knocked over all the hat stall and I put the mun to so mooch trouble, I thought ah moost buy sommut!'

Likewise, nothing seems to surprise him. A boy from a humble family in Yorkshire, he arrived to learn to be a 'paintah' in London without any misgivings. 'It was most extraordinary at the college. After a bit they wouldn't give me any more cunvass, or paints, because I hadn't got any munnay, so that's how I got interested in engraving. They let you have the stoof free, but even so they said I was waaistin their copper plates because I did static isolated line drawings of figures they said I should use up all the copper by covering it with pattern. Before someone came and gave me a prize (for that picture you bought), they never thought anything of my work. Now I paint twenty pictures a year and Kas [Kasmin, his dealer] sells the lot; and I teach. I luv America and I teach there quite a lot. They can't paint a sphere, so I set the class to paint a door. They all got canvases the size of a door and painted as realistically as possible and we had an exhibition of all the doors down a corridor. It looked naice. But I couldn't get oop in the mornings. I was supposed to start at eight-thairtee, but I'd paaint at night and then go out to the poobs until they closed and that'd be two o'clock, and perhaps it was three or four before I got to baid, so I couldn't get up at eight o'clock, so I'd go in at ten-thirty and stay till one, but no one seemed to caire.'

It staggers me how this young man can be so at home in the world. When *I* first went to America, I was too scared to ask a policeman which was up or down town. Not David! He arrives in Los Angeles without knowing a soul. He gets arrested at three in the morning for jay-walking; he makes a lot of friends and goes off in a truck with one to try and get a driving licence. 'Where's your car?' 'I haven't got one, but this is my friend's trook.' He drives it around with the instructor, who thinks him mad – quite understandably because David had never driven before – but who nevertheless gives him his licence. Hockney then buys a car and starts to drive it on the St Bernadino freeway. He can't get off it, so has to drive on and on until he comes, four hours later, to Las Vegas. He stays there for an hour then comes all the way back. 'It gives you confidence to be driving for ten hours on end.'

28 April

It is strange that, at my age, I should work myself up into such a nervous condition at the idea of photographing Picasso. I was certainly extremely on edge, I remember, when I first photographed him in the Rue de la Boétie in the early thirties. At that time I could speak very little French. In the meantime every photographer in the world, and thousands of amateurs too, have had a field day with him; I remember Alexander Liberman saying it was tiresome that once one had photographed Picasso, he had never had enough and begged one to come back tomorrow.

I sent a telegram as from le Petit Beaton from London to warn him of my arrival. I was in a state of anticipation by the time I arrived at the Grand Hotel, Cannes. Five minutes later I was on my way in a taxi to the Notre Dame de Vie at Mougins.

I realized what a tremendous number of canvases must have been sold to pay for this long, winding drive that circled to the top of the mountain. Suddenly a closed gate, with a bell. The driver rang. No answer. I would not have been surprised if they had not answered. It could have been like the end of *Washington Square*. But, suddenly a voice asked who was there. 'Mr Beaton? Mr Cecil Beaton?' 'Yes.' 'Then wait.' The door eventually opened and we were suddenly in a courtyard filled with brilliant mauve wistaria and being welcomed by Madame Picasso.

Madame Picasso is squat and short-necked. She wore a blue silk coat and white trousers, hair immaculate. She was very polite. 'Pablo says it is twenty years since he last saw you. Please come in.'

A great welcome from Picasso. 'Oh, I am *pleased* that you are here. We must embrace.' I kissed him on two, soft, cleanly shaven cheeks.

Also present were Monsieur and Madame Gomez (she specializes in the works of Balthus) and the room was a kaleidoscope of brilliant objects and colours against a sunny white background.

Picasso, sad to relate, had aged and it had taken the form of shrivelling him. There was something melancholy about his eyes, which had lost some of their brilliance; before they were black, but now they seemed a light brown. His skin was pale cigar-leaf and his hands and pointed fingers, rather heavy, were a darker shade; the teeth like old ivory and the whites of the eyes parchment. In fact, in his several sweaters and velvet trousers, he was altogether a symphony of brown, beige and mushroom. There was a gash of green paint on one arm and a sleeve was worn to tatters, a hole also in the black stockings; neat white leather shoes.

Lots of fun about the passage of the years. Yes, he remembered my photographing him like Whistler's mother and featuring the toys on his mantelpiece. No regrets about the dead or the past. We must go on even if it was madness. The numbers of paintings he did! Sometimes eight in one day. We must see everything there is to see. 'Come!'

We left his sitting-room for another white, simple drawing-room with such a mass of letters, pottery, drawings and stacks of canvas that it was impossible to take in more than an occasional detail. Past the dark dining-room with the long table covered with parcels, pictures, books, sculpture, and pictures stacked against the wall, to the hall, full of packing cases and canvases. Down to the basement (formerly the hall in the Guinness' time), now just a cemetery of modern statuary, some lifelike, others abstract constructions of wire, steel, painted tin. Picasso wandered about turning on extra lights for the photographs; he enjoyed being taken, was amused and flattered; he had a semi-queasy expression on his face. He gazed at the camera with wildly staring eyes, and I took a lot of pictures as we continued our tour of the house.

The amount of work by Picasso was utterly staggering. But there was more. 'Come, you must see everything. This is nothing.' Madame Picasso was self-effacing and managed to be out of the camera line all the time, and when I did try to take her, she seemed genuinely unhappy and shy. We then climbed a white circular staircase to one huge painting-room after another. Each was filled with pictures, some not finished and still wet, everywhere large daubs of the shapes we have become accustomed to; but to me the latest work seemed to have lost exactitude. The line was not good; the brush stroke coarse and rubbed. A lot of curious painting with every sort of trick employed; sometimes he dipped a cork into the paint and pressed that on to the canvas; a smell of Ripolin and everywhere stacks of tins of paint. Even on a huge glassed-in terrace, with a superb view of distant purple mountains, there were masses of blue canvases, mostly of monstrous women, all somewhat indecent according to Victorian standards.

The sun poured through the shutters which, because of the high wind, slashed backwards and forwards. I clicked and clicked, hoping for the best in my excitement; I moved a piece of sculpture that I thought was made of card and found it was of iron; points dug into my thumb and the blood poured. Nothing to do but suck and forget. Some of the time the sun came through on to the floor and enabled me to take good patterned compositions, but much of the 'work' was pretty humdrum stuff and God knows if I got the exposures right.

Back in the first sitting-room we sat around the circular table and talked happily. In the centre of the table there was a bowl of deep-pink roses from the garden, and around the room in odd pots delightful little posies of daisies, tulips and small, bright, wild flowers. I went on taking pictures.

When I felt I had taken enough I got out my sketch book; but I found that after the intensity of taking photographs my energies were too dissipated for drawing. I kept turning the pages. Picasso rushed from his chair. 'You do what Degas did and have pages that are transparent, so that you can turn over and trace the good bits and ignore the bad.' He was tremendously enthusiastic about this idea and his eyes popped. It was another facet of his extraordinary display of vitality.

At one point he demonstrated to M. Gomez the advantages of the modern (Knoll) swivel chair he sat in. He almost twirled himself into space. All his actions were quick ones; his arms raised in a jerk; his body too nervous and tense to be graceful. Generally when he turned his head, his body turned too. He jumped from place to place like a boy skipping. He talked of his working at night. Then it was quiet, with no one to disturb him. Sometimes it was three o'clock before he stopped, so he got up late in the morning. He didn't need much sleep but liked to rest and read. When someone complained that they hadn't been able to sleep, Picasso said: 'So much the better for you. Sleep is a waste.' He is strong; he is accustomed to moving sculpture. He did an imitation of his mother in her working chair. Her feet could never touch the ground. He asked Madame Gomez why she was here. 'Specially to see you.' That reminded me that Alice Toklas arrived one day and said she had come especially to see him. 'Now you've seen me, you can go.' Alice was not amused. But Picasso is fond of Alice and is still helping her through the financial difficulties she was in after the death of her friend Stein. Picasso sometimes stared very intently at me and his regard still has the power to intimidate. He laughed at me holding four sharpened pencils in my hand and said: 'Aren't you going to paint me?' He said he thought I *was* a painter. I had the eyes of a painter, like Chardin or Fragonard, but not of a photographer. Most photographers had eyes like lenses. Photographs were too mechanical. Drawings were more alive, and colour photographs added nothing to black and white.

Madame Gomez went into the next room to talk business with Picasso, and Madame Picasso told me that she still found Pablo someone that she could never take for granted. She had been married for eleven years and each day was more impressed by his honesty and naturalness. He was so great that she felt it was a privilege to be with him and take care of him. It is clear how much she loves him. Her eyes linger on him. She dashes forward in distress if, the wind blowing one canvas on to another, they have smudged. She wraps his jumper across his chest when he comes out into the open. She brings him a large glass of milk.

Jacqueline Picasso admitted she would like to go to Paris; that they seldom went out here, not even to the bull fights any more. Pablo only liked to work; his world was here on the mountain top. He had already made three new studios and he wants to fill a fourth. This at eighty-four is not bad! She is obviously perfectly happy to look after this man and has no ulterior motives.

Time to go. 'I have to paint,' said the master. It is marvellous that he has such gaiety at his time of life.

I had been somewhat suffocated by too many neo-classical heads and tortured buttocks and graffitiesque twats; and there were too many photographs of Picasso around. But he had been kindness itself to me.

'So good to see you looking so well,' I said and he ran to touch wood. He does not like the process of getting old. 'Come back again in twenty years, but come back sooner as well.' Eyes melting with amusement and friendliness, he waved as we circled down the mountainside.

July

For many, many years Juliet Duff has been a great figure in my life, and has had a certain influence on me. Her taste, inherited from her mother, [the Marchioness of Ripon], has always impressed me, and she has an elegance and a sense of eccentricity that is appealing. But I have never really liked her, nor has she me.

At first she was very undecided as to whether she would 'take me up' or not. At the time of my 'first appearance' in London she was an intimate friend of Diaghilev, sitting in his box at the first night of the new ballet season. It was to a large supper-party in her Belgrave Square house that she first invited me. The fifty guests were already seated at a long table in the dining-room; marble swans looked on. Everyone was drinking pink champagne, a drink always served by her mother. Most of the men guests were in dinner jackets. I, arriving late, had to walk the length of the room to greet my hostess. I was in a tail coat, having come on from some other beano that warranted such apparel. Emerald Cunard on seeing me created a little rumpus of displeasure, for only a few days before she had thrown on to the fire and put a poker through my recently-published *Book of Beauty* declaring that I was a 'low fellow'. Juliet was now in a quandary. As hostess she must be polite to her *invité*, but although she never liked Emerald she did not necessarily want to incur her wrath. With one gracious smile I was bidden to sit out of earshot and sight of Emerald, and from that day on Juliet has been a constant friend.

As the years pass, Juliet's once enormous income has diminished; she has had to retrench, and her innate meanness has taken a severe hold. The slate mines have been doing badly in Wales, so she must sell a Fabergé ornament or a Boilly painting.

Sunday

Today, however, Juliet was at her best; she sat back and listened to the talk, which was racy. Occasionally she made a contribution about someone she considered eccentric and interesting. Simon, rather tipsy, was in his most delightful vein and at the end of the evening he ran his hand down Juliet's arm and said: 'You've looked so pretty in your rose-coloured dress.'

But lately we have become alarmed, for Juliet's health is very poor. She has fallen several times and although Dr Gottfried has reduced her blood pressure from the danger point, she does not look as if she will be long in this world. Then one day she keeled over getting out of bed. The doctor was called and she was ordered to rest. The next day she had a brain haemorrhage, lost consciousness, and died.

Although in many ways Juliet and I did not get on, I know I shall miss her.

July

Kin's exit was as if to an execution [Kin Hoitsma, the new friend from California]. In my pyjamas I watched him go. He had two heavy bags to carry. He gripped his lips tightly and looked very serious. I like to think that it was as bad a moment for him as it was for me. The taxi came. His outstretched hand was stiff and taut. I went back to bed, not to sleep, but to moan at my loss and feel desperately sad.

London: 10 September

What a very different opinion Balanchine holds on Pavlova. He told me he thought she was awful. 'She had bad taste and chose dreadful music. She liked Hungarian composers and dainty, tippety-tip dances. Ta, Ta, Ta, Ta, Ta, Ta;

Dimty, Dimty, Dimty – Turn! And her feet were ugly, such large, lumpy shoes. And her dresses! She'd dress up as a *marquise* with a beauty spot and do the gavotte. It was terrible, but the audiences loved it. They didn't know any better in those days. They loved the *Dying Swan*, just for one reason, there are only about two movements in it and the hands go flap, flap, but the audience know she's going to die, so they're all waiting for it to happen. But she wasn't an artist. She didn't get along with Diaghilev; she was selfish. Yes, I knew her. She wasn't interesting. She didn't inspire men.

'Nureyev came to see me shortly after he fled from Russia, but he wanted to dance "on circuit" and make extra money. He wanted to be the star. He didn't want to be part of a ballet. He is too selfish and a dancer cannot afford to be selfish. You will soon spot a selfish dancer. Nureyev will end up badly, you'll see. He'll be like Pavlova.'

11 April 1966

So Evelyn Waugh is in his coffin. Died of snobbery. Did not wish to be considered a man of letters; it did not satisfy him to be thought a master of English prose. He wanted to be a duke, and that he could never be; hence a life of disappointment and sham. For he would never give up. He would drink brandy and port and keep a full cellar. He was not a gourmet, like Cyril Connolly, but insisted on good living and cigars as being typical of the aristocratic way of life. He became pompous at twenty and developed his pomposity to the point of having a huge stomach and an ear trumpet at forty-five.

Now that he is dead, I cannot hate him; cannot really feel he was wicked, in spite of his cruelty, his bullying, his caddishness. From time to time, having appeared rather chummy and appreciative and even funny (though my hackles rose in his presence), he would suddenly seem to be possessed by a devil and do thoroughly fiendish things. His arrogance was at its worst at White's. Here he impersonated an aristocrat, intimidated newcomers and non-members, and was altogether intolerable. But a few loyal friends saw through the pretence and were fond of him.

Reddish: January 1967

After six months of *pourparlers*, a lorry drove up with a lot of ancient stones. These are the beginning of our new plans for the garden. We will pave over some of the flower-beds and have fewer bedded-out plants.

The trees for 'Little Japan' arrive next (the prunus and flowering fruits that are to dot the hill opposite my bedroom). We are planning for posterity. It is an act of faith, and I wish it had been done before.

The only thing that prevents my making other major alterations is money. I never know my financial situation. Eileen is in charge. I rely on her to warn me when we have spent too much. I'd like very much to improve the guest rooms, and give each its own bathroom. But Eileen says we must not do this for another two or three years. How she knows this I do not know. But here's hoping there will be no cataclysm! One can be poor when young, but never later on in life.

Marrakesh: March

On the Tuesday evening I came down to dinner very late, and, to my surprise, sitting in the hotel lobby, discovered Mick Jagger and a sleepy-looking band of gipsies. Robert Fraser, one of their company, wearing a huge, black felt hat and a bright emerald brocade coat, was coughing by the swimming pool. He had swallowed something the wrong way. He recovered and invited me to join them all for a drink.

It was a strange group. The three 'Stones': Brian Jones, with his girlfriend, beatnik-dressed Anita Pallenberg – dirty white face, dirty blackened eyes, dirty canary drops of hair, barbaric jewellery – Keith Richard in eighteenth-century suit, long black velvet coat and the tightest pants; and, of course, Mick Jagger, together with hangers-on, chauffeurs, and Americans.

I didn't want to give the impression that I was only interested in Mick, but it happened that we sat next to one another as he drank a Vodka Collins and smoked with pointed finger held high. His skin is chicken-breast white and of a fine quality. He has an inborn elegance. He talked of native music; he had heard a local tribe play pipes like those used in Hungary and Scotland. He liked Indian music too. He said he would like to go to Kashmir and to Afghanistan, in fact to get right away from England, which he considered had become a police state, with harassment and interference. Recently twenty policemen had invaded the house of his drummer in the country looking for dope. The newspapers had published completely false accounts. He was going to sue the *News of the World*. He maintained that he had done nothing to deprave the youth of the country. Here in Morocco people were not curious or bad-mannered. He liked people that were permissive.

By degrees the shy aloofness of the gang broke down. We got into two cars; the Bentley I was in had been driven from Brian Jones's house in Swiss Cottage to here, and the driver was a bit tired. The car was filled with pop-art cushions, scarlet fur rugs, and sex magazines. Immediately the most tremendous volume of pop music boomed in the region of the back of my neck. Mick and Brian responded rhythmically and the girl leant forward and screamed in whispers that she had just played a murderess in a film that was to be shown at the Cannes Festival.

We went to a Moroccan restaurant – tiles, banquettes, women dancers. Mick considered the style of decoration gave little opportunity of expression to the artist. He is very gentle, and with perfect manners. He indicated that I should follow his example and eat the chicken in my fingers. It was tender and good. He has much appreciation, and his small, albino-fringed eyes notice everything. 'How different and more real this place is to Tangier – the women more rustic, heavy, lumpy, but their music very Spanish and their dancing too.' He has an analytical slant and compares everything he is seeing here with earlier impressions in other countries.

Mick liked the new ballet *Paradise Lost*, but was bored by Stravinsky's *Les Noces*. He is limited in his field of music to what he had studied since he was eleven years old and which is the kind of music he plays now.

'What marvellous authority she has,' he said, listening to a coloured singer. 'She follows through.' He sent his arms jerking about him. I was fascinated with the thin concave lines of his body, legs and arms. The mouth is almost too large; he is beautiful and ugly, feminine and masculine: a rare phenomenon.

I was not disappointed and as the evening wore on found him easier to talk with. He asked: 'Have you ever taken LSD? Oh, I should. It would mean so much to you; you'd never forget the colours. For a painter it is a great experience. One's brain works not on four cylinders but on four thousand. You see everything aglow. You see yourself beautiful and ugly, and other people as if for the first time. Oh yes, you should take it in the country, surrounded by all those flowers. You'd have no bad effects. It's only people who hate themselves who suffer.' He had great assurance. 'If you enjoyed the bhang in India, this is a thousand times better: so much stronger – good stuff. Oh no, they can't stamp it out. It's like the atom bomb. Once it's been discovered, it can never be forgotten, and it's too easy to make.'

We walked through the deserted, midnight streets. Mick admired the Giacometti-like doorways; was sad at the sleeping bundles of humanity, and had not seen such poverty since Singapore. He loved the old town with its mysterious alleyways.

By the time we reached the hotel it was three o'clock and my bedtime, but they were quite happy to go on. Never a yawn and they had been up since five o'clock this morning.

It is a way of life very different from mine and I enjoyed being jerked out of myself. Mick listened to pop records for a couple of hours, and was then so tired that he went to sleep without taking off his clothes. He woke at eight, undressed and got into bed to sleep for another couple of hours.

At eleven o'clock he appeared at the swimming pool. I could not believe it was the same person walking towards us. The very strong sun, reflected from the white ground, made his face look a white, podgy, shapeless mess; eyes very small, nose very pink and spreading, hair sandy dark. His figure, his hands and arms were incredibly feminine.

None of them was willing to talk except in spasms. No one could make up their minds what to do, or when.

I took Mick through the trees to an open space to photograph him in the midday sun. I gave his face the shadows it needed. The lips were of a fantastic roundness, the body almost hairless and yet, surprisingly, I made him look like a Tarzan by Piero di Cosimo. He is sexy, yet completely sexless. He could nearly be an eunuch. As a model he is a natural.

Their wardrobe is extensive. Mick showed me the rows of brocade coats. Everything is shoddy, poorly made, the seams burst. Keith himself had sewn his trousers, lavender and dull rose, with a band of badly-stitched leather dividing the two colours.

Brian, at the pool, appears in white pants with a huge black square applied on to the back. It is very smart, in spite of the fact that the seams are giving away. But with such marvellously flat, tight, compact figures as they have, with no buttocks or stomach, almost anything looks well on them.

April

Have been reading Volume II of Harold Nicolson's *Diaries* with as much pleasure as I read his first. I wonder why, in spite of being told again and again by his friends, James Pope-Hennessy and others, what a fine fellow he is, I've never liked the man.

Once more he shows himself to be an honest, good character, sensitive to others, candid about himself. He is never vulgar, and always has an eye for the comic. Often he is able in the written word to move me; in fact I finished this book in a blur of tears.

But when scrutinizing the photographs I again see that I am as put off by his physical appearance there, as I am in life. How unfair this is. But the Kewpie-doll mouth, the paradoxical moustache, the corpulence of hands and stomach all give me a *frisson* and there is no getting over the fact that I could never get to know him well enough to become a close friend. Sad, because he could have been a help and guide and an influence for the better.

Reddish: June

Monday morning my breakfast is brought in – tea, charcoal biscuits, yoghourt and the papers. I am looking out of the window at the green scene when I hear that war has started in the Middle East. Israel and Egypt are each saying the other was the first to be the aggressor.

The awful sinking dread surged through from the nape of the neck to the solar plexus. At once one thinks, not of the suffering, the pain, the killings in the far land, but selfishly of home and oneself. If the war spreads we are liable to become involved, even if only remotely, by, say, the rationing of fuel. It seems such a little time ago that we were doing all we could to scrounge an extra can of petrol. But the continual dread ... the encroaching anxiety.

Miraculously the Israelis have overthrown the Egyptians. Against all odds, with brilliant tactics and fierce fighting, they have brought about in three days a complete reversal of the Middle-East picture.

No one can be more delighted than our neighbour up the valley – Anthony Eden.

There was quite an extraordinary atmosphere of joy and celebration in the pretty Georgian house at Alvediston that Clarissa and Anthony have recently bought. Despite his plastic duct and continuous fever, Anthony had reached the age of seventy. It was his birthday and the events of the last week were a wonderful present. They have meant that, in principle, Anthony's much-criticized policy on Suez, and his distrust of Nasser, were correct. Clarissa, generally so cold and reserved, admitted this evening that she was 'stewed'. She was enchanting in her gaiety and, in an aside of happiness, said: 'I never thought Anthony would live long enough to see himself proved right.'

Anthony, sunburnt and wearing a marrow-coloured velvet dinner-suit, seemed the picture of health and radiance. He was surrounded by his loyal *confrères*, and a few members of his family. Bobbety Salisbury made a speech that was eulogistic but neither embarrassing nor sentimental. Oliver Lyttelton, whose desire to amuse has increased with the years to the extent that he is a real bore, made one funny joke. The evening was a great success. A surprising group: the Lambtons motored from London; Lord Scarbrough came from Yorkshire; Nicholas and other young Edens; Lord Brooke; Ronnie Tree; Anthony and Dot Head; and the Hoffs [Raimund von Hofmannsthal and his wife Lady Elizabeth] (whom I brought).

Nicholas handed round tulip-shaped glasses of Elizabethan Kümmel! This was real dynamite! It tasted like aquavit, and took the breath away as it went down the throat. Bottles of champagne popped, and the gathering was very English, understated and poignant.

June

Old age creeps upon me in many indefinable ways. In spite of exercises and massage from Charlotte Gaffran, and being stretched and manipulated by Svenson, my back aches and I am apt to walk upstairs more slowly. I realize I am not as young as I was. Fewer things seem to give me pleasure. Lately I have felt a restlessness that is most unwelcome. I have noticed on the faces of older people the terrible look of empty boredom. Is this coming my way? The only thing to dispel it is work and, thank heavens, I have my painting (and sometimes my writing) to keep the heavier hours at bay.

As a snobbish boy I was always disappointed when my mother's request for tickets to the Royal Enclosure at Ascot were turned down. But the slap in the face came back again and again from Lord Churchill on behalf of the King. However, nowadays anyone who can pay the few guineas necessary is welcomed, and with the opening of the flood-gates that allowed in Jack Hylton, Binkie Beaumont and any little starlet, I was given the OK. But it was too late. By the time I got there the grand ladies in their fantastic dresses and the exclusiveness had all gone.

The Ascot weeks that I spent, in the pleasant company of Mrs Nancy Lancaster, were really rather an effort. I know nothing whatever about racing, and I was soon bored and tired.

The rules have now changed. You need not buy a Royal Enclosure ticket for a whole week. So, for one day, I thought it might be fun. I went under the best auspices, with Jakie and Chiquita Astor, whom I love. He, as a member of the Jockey Club, can make things easy. We had a delightful lunch at their flat. The car journey was enjoyable until the queue started, half an hour away from the course. Then all sorts of forgotten snobberies rose to the surface; unimportant things assumed importance; our eventual arrival on the course was perfectly timed so that we saw the royal procession coming towards us. Some people with a banner were running in front of the oncoming horses. 'Stop the murder in Vietnam.' The police, like bioscope cops, were slow off the mark.

The colour of Royal Ascot has changed – Edwardian Ascot must have been entirely pastel-coloured. But this was a transformation that I enjoyed. Everywhere there were large touches of brilliant magenta, orange and viridian. The Maharaja of Jaipur in a marvellous turban of ochre and scarlet. Yet the retina-irritant mutation of the plastic and the nylon looked crummy in the outdoors; the crocheted shift, the mini skirts and little-girl fashions were hardly right. But then I was not right.

Loelia Westminster gave me a look of surprise. 'What are *you* doing here?' She may well ask. I suddenly realized I wasn't enjoying myself and that I was only pretending. It was tedious to go into that Holy of Holies, the Jockey Club restaurant, for a short drink of iced coffee and to hear Lady Sefton abuse her husband. The only diversion was losing £1 each way on Mrs Englehard's horse. The sight of the French Ambassadress wearing an *art nouveau* picture-hat adorned with water-lilies was the only fashion note that gave me a slight tremor.

But I was not diverted in any way and all I could think of was getting away and leaving before the last race in order to miss the worst of the traffic.

Corfu, on the Wrightsman yacht: July

The Greek royal family came on board for lunch. (Evelyn Waugh once wrote that the presence of royalty was like heavy thunder in the air.)

The King, very boyish, with puppy fat, came from Athens. He was grateful to be asked to take off his coat. His Queen, pretty complexioned, but as yet too young to show any character, was dressed in a most uneventful way. I have Queen Frederica on my left and her giggling daughter Sophie on my right. Sophie is easy to talk to, with bulging low cheeks, silken hair, drooping eyelids, button-mushroom nostrils, baby teeth, and pretty eyes. Her unmarried sister Irene is the more serious of the two and is a good pianist. Queen Frederica is deaf but I have her better ear. She talks of her vegetarianism. It started because she had seen so much suffering, and did not wish to inflict more on animals, fish, or anything that loved its mother. Much laughter. What about whitebait? She was surprised at our reaction, but has the sense to laugh at herself. 'I did not like my mother,' she added. She said that taking drugs was like having a glimpse of heaven, but paying with shoddy money. It should only be done in isolation. She said she had been called Fascist yet had worked on our side against the Germans during the war. The British papers had been monstrous, but she thought the people were sympathetic.

The Queen related being 'set upon' while walking with Princess Sophie outside Claridges and how shaken they had both been. As she walked on in a dignified way, her daughter had told her what was happening. 'Two are on the ground and now they are closing in on us.' They walked faster and only when in the mews at the back of the Italian Embassy did they run and ring a doorbell. This was how Marti Stevens, the actress whose doorbell it was, learned the story of the life of the Queen of Greece. The police and embassy attachés had eventually come to their rescue.

August

I have not allowed my mind to be trained, or my interests to broaden. I am in many ways the same person I was forty years ago. But with a slowing down. I can't take in as much as I could. I learn nothing new. I get tired more easily, and bored. Even my ambitions are less than they were. I don't seem to have any plan to do anything that I have not tried before. If I survive, I may publish more diaries, but the fount of inspiration for an original book seems to have dried up, and the chances of writing for the theatre are becoming rarer. I may possibly do a bit more painting. However much I am interested in today's phenomenon there are positive signs that I have become part of an older generation with its tired attitude and approach.

I don't really feel that I am ever going to come into my own, to justify myself and my existence by some last great gesture. I am likewise certain that nothing I have done is likely to live long after me.

I have got to the point where I know I should relax, calm down, read more, and prepare for retirement. But I realize how little accustomed I am to living without surface excitements. The whole problem of the future is one of anxiety.

The other day when discussing with Eileen the problem of whether or not to spend £2,000 on an addition to the house in the country I said: 'I'd like to have the benefit of the change as soon as possible because God knows how many years I will be spared. Any minute I may get an unpleasant shock and a tax man come along. . . .' Eileen said: 'You've probably got another twenty years.' How appalling! I don't necessarily want to take my own life, but I don't want to have to hang on patiently bearing the humiliations, the loneliness, the discomforts of decrepitude.

Yet perhaps this is not for one to decide. My father was sad, bored and alone in his late sixties, and my mother was brave about all the physical disabilities she had to put up with until she was nearly ninety. I am glad that, unlike poor Rex Whistler, I was allowed to survive the last war, but I don't really find myself enjoying life today as much as I did before.

Randolph Churchill, looking old and grey, like a haggard hawk, has been on the brink of death for three years. The other night he told me that he was now happier than he had ever been. He was at last doing something that justified his life – his book on his father, the best thing he had ever done, his contribution to the world; the fact that he was no longer restless was balm to him. I am sure he was being sincere, but it is hard to believe. His eyes look so abysmally sad.

September

Chrissie Gibbs is a delightful, intelligent and extremely well-informed young man.

When he asked me to have dinner I thought it would be a quiet one with him. I returned to Pelham extremely late, in a state of near collapse, having been out all day. I rang to ask if it would matter my being a little late. 'Not at all – take it easy.'

On arrival I found Jane Ormsby-Gore, with her baby, Saffron, lying in a shopping basket. She was calm and sad about the tragic accident that had killed her mother four days before. She spoke sympathetically about the misery that her father must face each time some new aspect of his loss occurs. The snapshots that he took on that last Sunday's tea-party, at which I was a guest, will one day be returned from the printers. Chrissie hustled about his dark panelled rooms doing nothing in particular and certainly never settling down to talk. Half an hour later Michael Wishart, freshly out of a nursing-home, came to call for Jane. She snatched up the basket and they disappeared. 'Mick's coming to dinner,' said Chrissie, 'bringing Marianne Faithfull, but I can't think where they are.' At 10.15 they appeared. Mick was in a gold brocade coat with tight, coffee-coloured trousers. He shrugged a bit, made no pretence of manners, and settled down to look at a picture book. Marianne, with white suety face, the usual drowned-blonde hair and smudged eyes, her dress torn under the arm, fluttered, and made 'groovy' conversation. Also present, by now, was Prince Stanislas, or some such name. I remembered seeing him two years ago at a freak Dufferin party as a huge white and black Hamlet, wearing, in spite of the heat, a heavy, black cape. He looked extremely self-conscious and po-faced. Tonight he was still dressed as Hamlet, with strips of sequins on his blouse and his sleeves painted psychedelically in silver, magenta and gold. He showed a large, white decolletage, a vast Adam's apple, huge white hands covered with rings, Byzantine-black page-boy hair, white face and potato nose. Throughout the long evening he spoke not at all.

In spite of the impediment in his speech, the most articulate person there was Robert Fraser. He has the usual pallor, the five-o'clock shadow, the tie badly in need of a pull up, and hair.

At 11.30 pm we went off in taxis to the Bagdad House restaurant in Fulham Road. Here, in the club-like atmosphere of the basement, we found others of the gang. Mark Palmer, more rodent-like than ever with his greasy blond hair over his nose; Michael Wishart, looking as if he needed to go back to the nursing-home; the youngest Tennant girl dressed like an aged 1920s figure with dark glasses, frizzed hair, a mini skirt over thick, purple, woollen stockings and rows of clairvoyant's beads. Also now present were Jane Ormsby-Gore with her husband, Michael Rainey. He was asleep, 'out', with his head on a shoulder; nearby, oblivious of the flashing lights and roar of a juke box, was the baby, Saffron, in the shopping basket.

I tried to talk to Mick. He shrugged, twitched his eyes, contorted his mouth and screwed up his face. He was hungry. He wanted 'fewd'. Little plates of mush were brought. He put a cake of pap into his huge mouth. I was, by now, in a trance of fatigue. Robert Fraser extolled the virtues of Andy Warhol's *Chelsea Girls* film. Wouldn't I like to come and see it? He had it at home. It runs for four hours. I wondered if I should be a devil and make a night of it. But no, I hadn't the strength. I said: 'If you'll excuse me.' It was one o'clock when I left to walk home up the deserted Fulham Road, leaving the night to the rest of them to turn into something or nothing.

September

I'd never met Princess Alice, Countess of Athlone before, but lately, going through early bound magazines, I had seen pictures of her at her wedding. I was struck by the tininess of her waist and the *potelé* little bosom and rounded hips that were pushed out from the corset. Now today the Princess, playing croquet under the cedars of Lebanon at Wilton, was disguised as an eighty-year-old lady.

The remains of beauty are still there, though the waist has gone; together with her porcelain complexion.

But unlike most royalty, and perhaps she has the advantage of being very 'minor', she has a directness that is healthy, and her shyness is well under control.

The Pembrokes keep up the tradition of the Edwardian house-party and had assembled twelve for this weekend, which was now, on Sunday evening, at a low ebb, half the guests having departed. The croquet over, we were relaxing in the library having a drink before changing. Princess Alice talked on her 'Topic A' which was Queen Victoria.

The following points interested me. The Queen's children were all very much in awe of this fearsome little figure. Since it was always being drummed into them that they must behave well in front of her, when she appeared they quaked. But she was easy and good-humoured, laughed a lot and had two long, birdlike teeth in front that appeared whenever she was amused. Princess Victoria, known as 'The Snipe', inherited them.

The Queen was very clean and always smelt refreshingly of rose-water. She was often making a hat, plaiting straw together, and the Princess Alice was furious at having to wear this hat which she considered hideous.

The Queen had no figure, just an avalanche of basalt black with little, white lawn collar and cuffs that were immaculate. I think the word for the neckpiece was 'tucker'. She did not wear it high round the neck in the fashion of the time, but was quite *décolleté*, and therefore dowdy.

At Windsor, Balmoral and Osborne there was always too much food. The sideboards were heavy with cold and hot meats, fowls and capons. There were always two soups, clear and thick; fish and eggs, and so much for the servants to take away. Such a waste!

New York: November

Eileen has a great deal more patience than I have. She has many uses for it, being victim, on the telephone, of the vagaries of the rich and spoilt people who speak more bluntly to her than to me. But even Eileen got exasperated with Margot Fonteyn.

Months ago Diana Vreeland, editor-in-chief of *Vogue* magazine, said she wanted a pictorial feature showing the greatness of the dancer 'as a woman'. The article to accompany the pictures was to be written by Marguerite Duras. But Margot kept postponing the engagement with me. She is, admittedly, tremendously busy. She knows her days of retirement are not far off, and she is making as many appearances as she can possibly fit in in all parts of the world.

It is a bore to be photographed. But the prevarications were endless. Margot would be in Paris between the 3rd and the 19th, if I'd come over, but she couldn't pose on the 4th, 5th, 6th, 7th, 8th, 11th, etc., etc. Then she was going to Sweden, then Texas, but she didn't know when that would be.

Suddenly she was completely out of touch. Eventually we tried to reach her through her mother and through her chauffeur. I then sent a frenzied telegram to Diana in New York.

Vogue paid the fare for Margot to come from Dallas and sent a car to the airport to meet her, by which time I was in New York too. She rang to know if she could be photographed in the home of Trumble Barton where she was staying, but this was not allowed.

Margot arrived at my hotel quite punctually, very staccato and jolly. She said she was sorry I'd got the impression she didn't particularly want to be photographed by me; more than anyone else she wanted me.

Margot, at over fifty, still possesses the line and movement of youth. Her legs are long and straight, and go into ballet positions which look odd when she wears a very 'way out' St Laurent evening dress. Her spirit shines through like a blade of young grass.

27

Apotheosis
1968–71

When Roy Strong became Director of the National Portrait Gallery, he decided to include photographs along with paintings, and he arranged through Richard Buckle for C.B. to give a number of portrait prints to inaugurate the collection. Buckle designed a retrospective Beaton exhibition to mark the occasion. The record-breaking show was regarded by members of the profession as the official acceptance of photography as an art. Moreover, it made clear to C.B.'s public how the war divided the fantasy of the early portraits from the classic simplicity of the late. C.B. designed the musical Coco, *and the film* On a clear day you can see forever, *published* The Best of Beaton *and the third volume of his diaries,* The Happy Years, *and travelled in Australia, the Pacific, Bolivia and Peru. He witnessed the Carnival in Rio de Janeiro and stayed with the Carcanos and the de Hoz in the mountains of Argentina. Improvements were made to Reddish House.*

5 January 1968

The building alterations at Reddish were considered to be of a minor character until the men started to hack down an inside wall. Then one thing led to another. It seems that if the alterations had not been done, i.e. the creation of a 'landing' library, and the addition of guest bathrooms, the landing floor would sooner or later have caved in anyway; the boards had become rotten and were resting on the water pipes. The cisterns in the attic were about to burst and had to be replaced. When the faulty ones were brought down they were found to be filled with the bones of rats, birds, cats, and other animals, and with horror we realized that for years we have been drinking the water in which these bodies had been decomposing.

Now, when the main work is nearing its end, we are told that the roof above the garage may fall in any day, that certain walls are being pushed out too far, and that a perilously leaning chimney-stack must be dismantled, brick by brick, and put back again.

All of this is a very boring way of spending a lot of money at a time when the country has been brought to economic chaos, and we are all fearful of what the new Labour Chancellor may introduce in the way of taxes, squeezes and restrictions.

I am advised about my finances by an old man who must surely be left over from the time of Dickens. He does not seem to me to have the sort of fighting qualities which I would have thought necessary in such a difficult taxation time. I am in the hopeless condition of knowing nothing about my own money affairs.

I rely upon Eileen to be level-headed enough to say when I am in a really serious jam. As it is, it is a battle to make money enough to pay the income tax. This year has been a poor one financially. The result is that I now feel extremely wary of spending even the ordinary cash for everyday expenses. In comparison to some, I suppose I am well off. But by the standards of most solvent people, my existence is pretty precarious. With God on my side, I may continue to make enough to keep going to the end. But it takes a jolt like a transatlantic journey to make one realize that one can lose sense of everything except one's immediate surroundings. Other people's currency seems remote, and values are merely relative to one's immediate needs. Thus a peseta is a windfall to a starving Spaniard, while a hundred thousand bucks is chicken feed to a Hollywood agent.

Bora-Bora, Pacific Ocean: January

When I saw the Tahitian bungalow of bamboo and palm fronds in which I was to stay alone for three or four days, I felt utterly lost. Why had I come all this way to be trapped? Like many people I have a certain fear of being alone, although sometimes I like time off from people in my own house. However, the time passed quickly and agreeably, thanks partly to the calming atmosphere of this tiny, humid, tropical island in the middle of the Pacific, but mainly thanks to Jane Austen. Each time I returned from an expedition, or on the translucent sea, or returned from a meal of fruit, I became absorbed in the Bennet family. Their problems and their characteristics are so real that I am amused and fascinated, and not a little moved from time to time.

All the lush, plummy vegetation makes the island look exactly like the eighteenth-century engravings done at the time of Captain Cook's voyages. The mountains are of basalt and have now acquired, after millions of years, very peculiar sawn-off, rather hideous, shapes. The grey summits may be in cloud, but the mountainsides are sunny velvety green, covered with flowering trees, palms, bananas and mangoes, and bushy with coffee and vanilla.

The white coral reef seems miles away; inside the lagoon the waters are quite still and one can see the wonderful rainbow colours of the forests of coral and seaweed below.

My first morning glimpse was of an idyllic shore with white sands, a tangerine, lilac and rose sea, the blue sky filled with circling, shrieking white birds – the terns, so named by Cook's botanist, Sir Joseph Banks. The water was almost rippleless, in fact it engulfed one like a caress. I ventured on a plastic floating mattress with a peephole to the deep through which I watched white and yellow fish darting in and out of the coral. By snorkelling extraordinary magical mysteries below the surface were revealed to me. The coral forests were of every variety of tree, some like firs, some windswept conifers, others yellow spiked, some dappled with purple, some like nuggets of gold. The pale grey and blue were like white icicles. At one's approach a complete cloud of brilliant blue fish with black spotted backs panicked and hurried for safety.

Pelham Place: April

Last time I was honoured in this way by having the Queen Mother to lunch, Edith Sitwell was the *pièce de résistance*. Truman Capote had arrived an hour early and together with Eileen we had watched from a top window as a huge ambulance drove up to the house, and a pair of stalwart men moved to bring the poet out into the daylight. A pair of very long medieval shoes appeared, then a muffled figure and finally a huge, golden melon of a hat. Edith was wheeled into place and given two strong martinis. This time the mood struck me as much calmer.

The other guests arrived: Roy Strong in a psychedelic tie; Kirsty Hesketh, hatless and dressed by Courrèges like a child's idea of a primrose; Leo d'Erlanger, mundane in a black coat and wearing a hat which he subsequently forgot; Jakie Astor; Irene Worth, just right in non-colours; and Diana Cooper, casual, as beautiful as ever, with her habitual basket occupied by Doggie, the chihuahua.

The Queen Mother's huge limousine arrived and out stepped the smiling, delightful, familiar figure. She was dressed in a brilliant puce and magenta. 'The last time ... poor Edith,' the delightful hesitancy, wistful eyes. 'How nice and warm your house is. I'm cold from sitting to Mr Ward. Sitting produces its own coldness doesn't it?'

Introductions: I suddenly found myself nervous and stumbling over my words. Roy calm-headed. The topic was the lack of painted portraiture today. Would Graham Sutherland be good to paint the Queen? 'Why not you?' the Queen asked me. Controversial subjects such as Lord Snowdon and his documentary film about old age were avoided; Prince Charles eulogized, and perhaps just a suggestion of criticism for his father sending him to a tough school. 'Now he doesn't need to be toughened any more.'

The Queen applauded the reappearance of the old *Tatler*. I described the attack on its existence by the *Observer*. 'What's this I hear?' asked Jakie, ready to defend the family honour, and conversation became general. Leo spoke the English language in a flowery manner that is seldom used by Englishmen today but which is utterly delightful. The Queen, on hearing a particularly well-planned compliment, said: 'I must remember that.' Now, Diana, Doggie nestling in a shiver at her bosom, with vodka and wine under her belt, did a virtuoso piece on spending the weekend with the 'Horse', Harold Macmillan, and described how Ava Waverley had been *'décommandé'*. The fact that Macmillan was continually referred to as the 'Horse' added to the Queen's enjoyment.

The Queen's car had arrived. It was ignored. Half an hour later the Queen asked Jakie the time. 'I must go!' As the Queen stood in the street, while a few onlookers gawked, I managed to speak out: 'I want to thank you for being always such a support and good friend to me.' The car drove away – smiles, bows, waves....

The party was soon over, for the other guests were late too. But it *had* been a whizz, hadn't it, said Diana.

May

A horrible summons to New York shatters the peace. I *have* to make a certain amount of money to go on living in the way I do (two houses a great burden). So I *have* to jump at an opportunity to do a big New York production, but as bad luck has it, this always happens in the summer so that the garden I've longed for all winter and spring has to be abandoned, and my tranquillity of mind upset.

Reddish: June

There was the nice friendly driver from the car hire service to meet me at the airport and drive me to the quiet realm of Broadchalke. Never have I been more pleased to return to my haunts.

Incredible standard roses were growing in the gardens of the ugly villas on the way; every village was a bower of flowers, the meadowsweet lamp-post high. Everything is burgeoning in this marvellous spell of sun and heat. It was the best time of the year and as we drove up I could see the house bedecked with apricot rose fronds. Eileen ran out in a state of euphoria. For two days she had been savouring to the full this peak moment. 'Look!' I was ravished by what I saw. In the interval from last Sunday every rose had come out; it was a plethora. I had never seen so many cushions of pale blossoms. After twenty years, the garden seemed at last to look as I want it to look.

In pleasurable mood I walked round every corner and twist of the garden and gradually the strain of the past week was forgotten. And what a strain it had been! The air trip to and from New York, the delays caused by the 'go slow', the three long conferences to discuss the project on hand, a musical about Chanel.

Then the return to London to cope with chores there before going off to Paris, and the terrible strain of listening to Chanel talk about herself without stopping from 1.30 to 5.30. Never once was I allowed to ask her a straight-forward question, so really the exercise was fruitless, except to make 'friendly contact'. But the whole week was a rush against the clock, meetings and dinners, a visit to the osteopath, and the British Embassy Ball; too much to fit in, let alone remember, in such a short time. But miraculously I returned all in one piece (as the Queen says) and able for two days to relax and savour summer.

August

When I think of Princess Marina I remember her deep, serious voice, and her sad smile of compassion. I remember her shock at being greeted in the street in Florence where she was never recognized as at home in England, and she was suddenly reminded that she was not just an ordinary private individual. I recall the many photographic sessions in the garden at Coppins with her husband and children, and, at the studio, when she would arrive with a picnic lunch-basket and boxes containing Greek national dress and her formal gown complete with orders and decorations. I can see now the expression of intense concentration as, with dust sheet on the sitting-room floor, she worked with crayons and pencils at her easel. I remember her amusement at Vaynol in North Wales when slowly and ridiculously I fell into a lake fully dressed; and after a dance at her country house when she and her sisters, in nightgowns, laughed with the other house guests about the incidents of the evening.

Brought up by her mother with a deep regard for tradition, and steeped in ritual, she was the most simple of human beings, at her happiest in informal surroundings. It was characteristic that, throughout her life, she preferred to serve her friends herself at lunch at Kensington Palace, or better still at an outdoor picnic. Her parties lacked grandeur and possessed a delightful atmosphere of the impromptu, although there was never anything casual or offhand about her. She paid impeccable attention to details. In spite of all that she had to do, she never permitted herself to be hurried or thoughtless.

Her sense of fun sometimes made it difficult for her on official occasions, and she was the first to laugh at herself in some situation which she considered 'och, so stupid!' She loved to give herself up to uncontrollable laughter. Sometimes her amusement was caused by jokes of a quite basic nature.

Beautiful and romantic princesses are a rare phenomenon today, and their mere existence enhances. Even those who saw her only a little were warmed by the knowledge that she was there; with Princess Marina's death that particularly lovely glow has gone from the land.

October

The plane (from New York) is delayed. But I *do* land early morning in England – very exhausted, deflated, on edge.

I rush off to Westminster Abbey for Princess Marina's Memorial Service. The traffic is at a standstill. I get out and run three-quarters of a mile, arriving out of breath, dishevelled, to find myself importantly placed in the nave. Tremendously impressive proceedings – the Charles II copes in mint condition of silver embroidery on grape velvet – and today the addition of the Greek clergy, the Bishop in jewelled crown, an old priest shuffling like the Fairy Carabosse with loud heavy tread, a stick and a protruding bottom. A shock to see some near contemporaries for the first time in so long, particularly Noël [Coward]. He has become a fat old turtle with slits for eyes – no upper teeth – the lower lip bulging outwards – hunched – bent – the lot. How sad. He was once the very spirit of youth ...

But I must hurry on to the National Portrait Gallery to see what was prepared.

A tremendous thrill and a real *cri de cœur* of joy went up when I saw Dicky had almost finished the exhibition and it was *marvellous*! The first glimpse of the 'Studio' made me exclaim. The rack of Stars is triumphant – Real excitement. Dicky was pleased.

4 November

The Apotheosis is over. It went well. Really very few disappointments and much to be thankful for. There were still outstanding some photographs to take specially for the exhibition of Dicky, Prince Charles, and the Queen in colour. The Prince is a simple, nice, cheerful adolescent of nineteen years. He has a gentle regard, a disarming smile and the tip of his nose is delicately modelled like a Gainsborough. He has obviously no great flair – is badly dressed but at any rate his hair is long – and that is a triumph of independence over the influence of his father and others at court. As I drove to the Palace people were going off to work in the dark glossy rain-sodden early morning (I was being given an hour between 9.30 and the Prince's attending his Mother's Opening of Parliament). I had just time to see that Geoff was installed in front of the huge gloomy grey windows and to go to pee, when on coming out of the lavatory I faced the Prince. We talked of Cambridge ADC and Marlowe Society and it reminded me that he was next week appearing in an Orton play ... very advanced. He seemed jolly, yet sensitive and rather a dreamer. He seemed to look around the rooms we were in as if seeing them for the first time. Sometimes I did not feel like interrupting his reveries.

Dicky was on top form for his sitting. He was dressed in black and white and wore a garland of elephants' tusks round his neck. His hair had been beautifully coiffeured in Early Elizabethan style and his eyes were bright with gleaming joy. It really did one good to see such relish … The Fortnum & Mason trestle tables arrived – the white lilies, the smilax. The *Vogue* hosts appeared and soon a great crowd of people. They not only seemed pleased to see each other but they paid attention to the photographs. It was a rewarding sight to see the enthusiasm of June Osborn, Diana Cooper, Noël Coward and Gladys Cooper looking at catalogues and the exhibits on high. My sisters were surprisingly lively and appreciative and a great number of old friends turned up to cheer. All our little jokes seemed appreciated and the effects were work-ing. The 'Studio' a very lively spot with the revolving PC stand of Marilyn Monroe, the flashing lights, the huge plaster hat and the stove a lively scene. Django Reinhardt's jazz and Julian Bream playing Dowland, the incense burn-ing, the lights flickering.

But no lying in next morning. Back to NPG for the Press View.

In the afternoon went to the gallery to show poor bereaved Princess Olga around on a very private back-door visit. 'So those are hippies – great heaven! So they've taken their clothes off!' She nevertheless telephoned the Queen Mother and said she had been touched – the show was very nostalgic …

As we stood by the awning awaiting the royal car's arrival, Roy Strong said, 'Oh, the excitement! I think this is the most thrilling thing that has ever hap-pened to me!' The rain came down in torrents. Rush-hour traffic was at a standstill. But the maroon limousine appeared, and the Queen Mother in puce and magenta.

A very charming and sympathetic tour. 'Oh yes, Freda – I remember that well. Paula – she died, didn't she?' (It was no good contradicting.) 'Oh, I remember that sitting (her own). It was really the end of an epoch. And Gertrude Lawrence – she was unlike anyone – she was quite unique. I'm glad you've given her a whole group to herself. Dear Rex Whistler – what a talent he had – so spontaneous. What a loss! Oh, and the frieze. Yes I remember that Hesse diadem. That's one of the best of Marina. She was beautiful up to the last. And look at Marie Louise – what a character!' Laugh. A careful look at the Windsors. 'They're so happy, and really a great deal of good came out of it. We have much to be thankful for.' I did not over-egg the pudding by saying, 'We have to thank them for you', but merely responded, 'We have *much* to thank them for.' Then the War Room. Dicky took over to explain. I came back in the Scene II 'Studio'. Much appreciation for the Broadchalke characters. 'What a good face the gardener has!' Interest in the new picture of the Queen. 'Yes, she told me I'd be surprised by it. It's very different, she warned me.' 'Do you like it?' I asked. 'Yes, I do. It has great character! The Prince of Wales. How *delightful* – such a nice boy – I'm so glad you liked him.'

Then, after the tour, to the Board Room. A line-up. Nancy disguised as a young dowager in red velvet and chinchilla. When I introduced her as a guinea pig, sister Nancy's upper lip became very straight and she talked with pursed lips but she *adored* the evening. After an hour and a half the Queen had to leave.

Now to the main Private View party. Already the rooms were full. Museum friends this time and the general public. The same interest in the pictures, the effects and the décor. The great sunshine was a visit from Broadchalke of Mrs Betts and Mrs Prest. When the latter was seized by the arm by Eileen, her eyes filled with tears. Lots of Ambassadresses, Rosemary Olivier, John Betjeman, Anne and Michael Tree, David Herbert from Tangier, and a great cross-section … Refugees from the storm continuing to arrive till past eight o'clock when I had to participate (without having had time to pee) in the most boring dinner given by the Chairman, Lord Kenyon, in Roy's nice room …

Next morning all the papers (except mother *Times*) carried huge pictures of the Queen in the Boat Cloak.

Dicky telephoned in high glee and embarrassed me by talking of 'the Beaton Magic'. He said the show was being a great success – interest mounting – 1,000 people had been through on Saturday and 1,500 people today Monday. All day long there was a queue. He said that it was fascinating to watch the rapt faces of the public – that he couldn't keep away – and the young looked at the pictures of the thirties as if they belonged to some long-forgotten world of Fragonard or Watteau, and at the pictures of the dressed-up beauties with an incredulous smile on their faces. One young man in a white mackintosh had remained standing on the same spot for ages, and Dicky wondered if he was probably just listening to Django Reinhardt. Dicky went off to his bank to cash a cheque and when he came back the young man was still there in the same position. Dicky reported that the old museum had never known such liveliness and that everyone there was going about wreathed in smiles. Roy, particularly happy, felt that they'd get their expenses back in the first week. Of course I take a lot of this as exaggeration but … I am most surprised.

London: Easter 1969

I arranged to take the recently widowed Sybil Cholmondeley to the première of the film *Oh What a Lovely War*.

There are few people who still manage to have the aura of pre-1914 luxury about them, but Sybil Cholmondeley is one of them. During winter, she is likely to wear a tuberose pinned by a pear-shaped diamond brooch to her dress. Tonight she provided a marvellous half-bottle of champagne and smoked-salmon sandwiches and, fresh from Norfolk, her keepers had sent three plovers' eggs.

'Now you must do what my brother Philip taught me to do with them. You must redistribute the yolk. Now, my hand is quite clean, open the palm flat, place the egg with the flat base in the centre – now be brave! Bring the other hand down on it very suddenly and hard – slap – like that – the egg suddenly becomes a poached egg, flat and with the yolk seen through a film of white jelly.'

I felt I had had a glimpse of another world – the world I had yearned for as a child.

Reddish: Whitsun

It was the first time that David Hockney came to stay. For three days I have been studying him while he savoured all the impressions of Wiltshire and, monkey-like, squinted or grimaced up at me, then down again to his drawing pad. He has been asked to do a drawing of me for *Vogue* and since I admire his work, I was willing to sit until Domesday if he needed that time to get a good result.

To begin with I was utterly appalled, having remained in some romantic but extremely uncomfortable pose for a great deal too long, when I saw an outline in Indian ink of a bloated, squat, beefy businessman. He laughed. No, it wasn't very good, and he embarked upon another which turned out to be just as bad. About eight horrors were perpetrated while the days advanced until, finally, something rather good emerged. He was encouraged. He was enthusiastic. Would I sit again tomorrow all morning and then again after lunch. He eventually decided to draw me in pencil rather than in ink and the result was different and better.

Poor Roy Strong did not seem to have much attention given to him, and he had recourse to doing watercolours in the conservatory and garden. David, tireless, continued with his drawing with infinite care and precision. I marvelled at him as he sharpened the pencils (having discarded the pen) for the hundredth time. I realized what a very different sort of an artist he is from myself. He has a great technical flair. He knows about cars, he can open unfathomable locks, he knows how to put things together; how paint and pencils work under certain conditions. He is an engineer, but he is also that strange thing, a phenomenal genius.

It is always fascinating to see someone as remote from oneself working in the same field. I was intrigued to see him admiring things that I like from a completely different point of view. We could not be farther apart as human beings and yet I find myself completely at ease with him and stimulated by his enthusiasm. For he has this golden quality of being able to enjoy life.

He is never blasé, never takes anything for granted. Life is a delightful wonderland for him; much of the time he is wreathed in smiles. He laughs aloud at television and radio. He is the best possible audience, though he is by no means simple. He is sophisticated in that he has complete purity. There is nothing pretentious about him; he never says anything he does not mean. In a world of art intrigue he is completely natural.

He was born in Bradford on the day that Michael Duff and I gave our elaborate *fête-champêtre* at Ashcombe. His family were poor and had little interest in art, though David's father surprised the family when years later he saw a reproduction of the Leonardo cartoon which the National Gallery were appealing to buy, and said : 'Oh yes, I've done that; it's called "Light and Shade".' (He had had some art tuition.)

David had three brothers and one sister, and his mother never went for a walk in the country without picking everything she knew to be edible in the hedges. Nettle soup was a great favourite and in a huge, yellow bowl she made very intoxicating nettle beer.

David, inspired by the pictures in the *Children's Encyclopedia*, knew by the age of ten what he wanted to be. At sixteen he left school determined to be a commercial artist, and he took his portfolio around Leeds with no success.

During his National Service David showed his independence of thought by becoming a conscientious objector. He helped bring in the harvest for Sir Richard Sykes whom he refused to call 'The Master'. He then worked in hospitals, at first in the medical wards where bronchial cases were treated. He saw many people die of heart attacks. He became an orderly in the skin-disease ward. One particular, pot-bellied old man whom he loathed had to be dabbed with calamine lotion. Standing up naked in front of David he would say, 'Don't forget the testicles, David.' David was then give the job of shaving and washing corpses. The thing he disliked most was washing the mortuary floors.

In 1953 he went to the Bradford School of Art. After four years he went on to the Royal College of Art in London. During the first term he finished four drawings. He lived for four months on £30; but in 1961 had saved enough to buy a forty-dollar ticket to New York with a hundred dollars in hand. He lived there for three months and dyed his hair 'champagne ice'.

When I went to the college to take a few lessons, David and his friends were referred to by the professors as 'the naughty boys upstairs'. I visited them up there and found David at work on a huge Typhoo Tea fantasy. Everyone seemed to be doing what they wanted and loving it. The school at this time boasted Allen Jones, Ron Kitaj, Peter Phillips, Derek Boshier, and

Pat Caulfield. I bought an indecent picture, 'Homage to Walt Whitman', by David who brought it round when Pelham Place was in the throes of building alterations. The workmen were startled at his appearance.

David is a meticulous worker, never hurried. He seems to have infinite leisure. He has a great taste for literature, having as a boy got books from the public library. He devours the encyclopedias and remembers everything he has read.

His Bradford lilt gives a melodic and touching quality to his sentiments. His voice, though low, has a great range of sound. He can touch one's heart with his euphoria. His words are carefully chosen and often unexpected. For instance, he says that someone is 'not immune to the oddity of a situation'.

October

On my way to London Airport I got a great thrill seeing a procession of out-riders in white helmets, the cavalcade of motor cars and all the panoply of power that usually goes with the arrival of royalty to our shores. The 'Moon Men' had come to England. In one of those cars were the perfectly nice, ordinary men who had made that incredible journey. I thought of the extra-ordinary experience it must be for them, having spent ten days in those unreal conditions and now to process through the capitals of the world, cheered and fêted wherever they go; and, quite rightly, treated as super-heroes.

It must be very different from anything they have known before! Tonight they are being received by the Queen in the Palace.

January 1970

On arrival in Hollywood at the huge 1920s cement apartment block which Mae West owns, I was surprised to find how small her personal quarters are. To begin with I was fascinated; white carpets, pale yellow walls, white pseudo-French furniture with gold paint, a bower of white flowers, huge 'set' pieces of dogwood, begonias, roses and stocks – all false.

The piano was painted white with eighteenth-century scenes adorning the sides, a naked lady being admired by a monkey as she lay back on draperies and cushions. On the piano was a white, ostrich-feather fan, and heart-shaped, pink rose-adorned boxes of chocolates with nothing inside but the crinkled brown paper. A box of Kleenex was enclosed in a silver-lead box. Lamps were converted from huge Victorian china figures of lovers. There was a great display of photographs of Mae West retouched beyond human likeness all in silver frames. Dust was covering everything. In a nearby lavatory, for instance, a discarded massage table looked grey and it was only when I put my finger on it that I discovered the dark red, artificial leather underneath.

Perhaps Miss West likes to preserve every dollar she has earned. She seems quite contented, or so it appeared from my short glimpse of her during the afternoon photographic session. Miss West's entourage consisted of about eight people from the studio, her own Chinese servant, and her bodyguard, Novak, an ex-muscleman. She was in the bedroom. She had 'finished her eating' and was feeling 'most uncomfortable'. She had put on weight over the holidays and her dresses would not fit. She was rigged up in the highest possible fantasy of taste. The costume of black with white fur was designed to camouflage every silhouette except the armour that constricted her waist and contained her bust. The neck, cheeks and shoulders were hidden beneath a peroxide wig. The muzzle, which was about all one could see of the face, with the pretty capped teeth, was like that of a nice little ape. The eyes, deeply embedded and blacked, were hardly visible. She smiled like an automaton. She gurgled at the compliments. She seemed shy and nice, and sympathetic. When I told her that Lady Sitwell had seen her at a party dressed all in white looking like a vestal virgin, she pretended to be shocked.

She moved very slowly into the living-room and stood – she could not sit – on very high heels. She stroked her yellow fronds of borrowed hair with fat, pointed fingers on which a dozen false diamond rings sparkled: her fingernails grown to several inches in length. She preened and her audience gasped with admiration.

'Oh, Miss West, you have never looked so beautiful – the lighting is so soft.' Miss West chortled.

As a prop, a young Adonis, a former athlete from the local university, Tom Shelleck, had been corralled from the film studio to be included in the photographs; a more outrageous combination could not be imagined, this beautiful, young, spare, clean, honest specimen of American manhood, and the *pourriture* of this old 'madame'.

She has a sense of humour and is able to laugh at herself. I liked her twinkle; and her vulnerability.

When the whole thing was over she started to walk, but teetered and I caught her just in time. By now, the apartment had become too cloying and airless and I escaped.

The most important thing about Mae West is her genuine belief in herself. She is not putting on an act. Lying on her bed and looking up at herself in the ceiling mirror, she says: 'You can see that you are a queen,' and she believes she is a queen.

She looks after herself well, living on health foods, and has become interested in the occult. She says she has extra-sensory perception. She has a few intimate friends who depend on her.

Recently the young generation has discovered her films and she has had a tremendous 'come-back'.

I told her Prince Charles had thought her 'Chick-a-Dee' was the funniest thing he'd ever seen. 'What a pity he saw me with W.C. Fields! I wish he'd seen me in something else. Well, goodbye, dear, and I hope we meet again.'

Reddish

Diana Cooper arrived for the weekend with Doggie hidden under her jacket and though stiff-kneed was able to walk around the garden. She kept up a pretty good running commentary for the lunch guests, and at dinner gave a *va et vient* of brilliance, quoting Donne. After dinner she reminisced about the time before the 1914 war. She talked of the Casati with great sympathy.

Next day Stephen Tennant made a spectacular entrance for lunch having 'rested' all winter; he had not been out of his bed. I saw this extraordinary figure being helped across the hall. He had a long white beard, was incredibly fat, and under layers of coats and jerseys wore a red cotton, bobble-edged tablecloth as a skirt. As George, his chauffeur, assisted him upstairs, it fell round his ankles, much to Stephen's embarrassment. The cloth was being used to cover up the fact that he could not get into his trousers; an enormous gap displayed a pregnant stomach. Once I was accustomed to seeing Stephen as an elderly man, I found the beard gave him nobility and distinction. He looked handsome like St Peter and it did not matter that he had no teeth.

Diana, who knew him but little, met him square on and would take no over-fine phrases – 'Oh, Diana, you are as beautiful as ever!' 'Oh, come off it, Stephen. Don't over-egg the pudding. You're hiding a big stomach. You can't do up your flies?'

The two sparked one another off; Stephen reminisced about Pamela Grey (his mother), Margot Tennant, Harry Cust ('My father,' said Diana), Pavlova, Karsavina, Lady de Grey. Talk was so rapid that it was difficult to follow.

At one point Stephen asked Diana to sing some early songs as he knew she never forgot a lyric. This set Diana off on to Gilbert and Sullivan. Stephen lowered the tone by singing, 'If you knew Suzie as I knew Suzie, ooooooh what a girl!' Then Diana told how she, Cynthia Jebb and the Duke of Wellington once motored from London to Marlborough and sang the whole way.

At dinner at Reine Pitman's, Diana continued to be eloquent. She never becomes fuzzy and always remembers names, dates, and quotes. She was very graphic in word and gesture about twice being bound up by burglars.

Windsor Castle: May

Because I was still in hospital after an operation I wondered if I would be prevented from going to the Ball. As it happened I was given permission by the doctors.

It was one of the most beautiful moonlit nights of a wonderful summer.

Windsor looked lively at this hour of the evening with crowds coming out of the theatre and the pubs. The castle was floodlit. Little posses of people stood around watching the guests arrive. Policemen and yeoman of the guard were at every point.

Surprisingly informal in a rather cavernous light, the Queen received her guests at the top of a small flight of stairs. As I got nearer I could see the marvellous sheen on the Queen's skin, her teeth, her lips, her hair. She was dressed in white with some sparklets round the neck and her hair a bit stiff. I have never in my life seen such a marvellous regard or such a look of interest and compassion. I was thrilled.

The silence after 'Good evening' was broken by 'Are you better?' Prince Philip asked: 'What's all this about?' I explained that I had left hospital to come here. He laughed, as much as to say: 'You must be mad' or 'What else is new?' He would have liked to bully me but I moved on. Patrick Plunket told me to go to the long Gothic gallery where the guests were gathering and a buffet stretched the length of one wall. The party was to celebrate the seventieth birthdays of the Queen Mother, the Duke of Gloucester (he's too old to appear), the Duke of Beaufort, and Lord Mountbatten.

Prince and Princess Paul of Yugoslavia were there, and a lot of German royals, and all sorts of young, including several long-haired young men. Ava Waverley looked like a drawing of an old woman by Dürer, her mouth fallen open and her eyes popping. Her hair was like the fluff of a five-day-old chick. Diana Cooper was a *tour de force* of aristocratic beauty in white.

The Queen Mother was wearing pale moth-coloured chiffon with pelisses covered with solid sequins, a big pearl and diamond necklace and tiara. Princess Alexandra looked ravishing, long tendril curls, a dark red satin dress and a sheen on her skin; the most adorable of human beings, she exuded beauty. Princess Anne, with wild hair, was fascinated by all she saw and heard. Prince Charles with crab-apple-red cheeks and chin and nose, healthy, full of charm, and intelligent. He asked me if I was still photographing, which gave me a great opportunity to talk about the recent visit to Royal Lodge.

I sat with a neighbour, Mary Pembroke, and the Hopes; was visited by Sybil Cholmondeley, Chiquita Astor and others who pretended that I looked well. I ate a bit of supper and drank two glasses of champagne.

Patrick Plunket then took me to the Charles II rooms to see the new decoration and the pictures which had recently come from Buckingham Palace. Some of the wall coverings are a mistake but in general the improvement is immense.

Patrick has been responsible for doing all the flowers. Instead of the carnation–sweet-pea arrangements, he got the gardeners to grow vast quantities of green zinnias, tobacco plants and alchemilla mollis to fill the golden candelabra on the buffet and to decorate four huge cones. There was a vast edifice of white eremurus, white delphiniums, and white peonies. Patrick had arranged for a whole syringa tree in flower to be cut down and put into a great malachite pot in the supper-room.

The evening was obviously being a success; everyone enjoying themselves and in good mood and the reason was that the election results had returned a great Tory victory. We had been expecting to put up with Wilson and his lot for another five years but quite dramatically all was changed and here was the new leader in person. I didn't see Heath, but he was there and when he appeared, a cheer went up and I was told that he blushed to his collar.

I felt I had better leave before my strength gave out. I had enjoyed myself and the evening for me was more than replete. The return journey seemed to take no time and at the hospital two giggling Irish nurses were waiting by the front door for me. I felt like a prisoner happy to return after his parole outing. I slept better than I have for nights and woke up next day with temperature normal.

8 June

E.M. Forster died yesterday aged ninety-one. He was a sweet man; gentle, self-effacing, kind, with great moral courage and a determination to fight for what he believed in.

His last novel was written as long ago as the early twenties. Altogether he wrote only five novels and the fact that he is considered one of our greatest writers proves that quality is better than quantity.

A delightful friend, the last time I saw him was two or three years ago when the Italian ambassador and Madame Guidotti gave a gala for his having encouraged an understanding of Italy at a difficult time. He was invited to stay at the Italian Embassy in London and to receive a gold medal at a special lunch in his honour. When he left Cambridge he got into the wrong train; the limousine sent to meet him at the station waited in vain, and he eventually arrived bedraggled and out-of-breath.

I had always liked to think of him still living in his rooms at King's.

September

Went to the house in the beautiful Bois de Boulogne to have tea with the Duchess of Windsor. On arrival in this rather sprawling, pretentious house full of good and bad, the Duchess appeared at the end of a garden vista, in a crowd of yapping pug dogs. She seems to have suddenly aged, to have become a little old woman. Her figure and legs are as trim as ever, and she is as energetic as she always was, putting servants and things to rights. But Wallis had the sad, haunted eyes of the ill. In hospital they had found she had something wrong with her liver and that condition made her very depressed. When she got up to fetch something, she said: 'Don't look at me. I haven't even had the coiffeur come out to do my hair,' and her hair did appear somewhat straggly. This again gave her a rather pathetic look. She loves rich food and drink but she is now on a strict diet and must not drink any alcohol.

Wallis tottered to a sofa against the light in a small, overcrowded drawing-room. Masses of royal souvenirs, gold boxes, sealing wax, stamps and seals; small pictures, a great array of flowers in obelisk-shaped baskets. These had been sent up from the Mill, which will be sold now the Duke is not able to bend down for his gardening.

We talked as easily as only old friends do. Nothing much except health, mutual friends and the young generation was discussed. Then an even greater shock; amid the barking of the pugs, the Duke of Windsor, in a cedar-rose-coloured velvet golf-suit, appeared. His walk with a stick makes him into an old man. He sat, legs spread, and talked and laughed with greater ease than I have ever known. At last, after all these years, he called me by my Christian name and treated me as one of his old 'cronies'. He has less and less of these; in fact it is difficult for him to find someone to play golf with. There were moments when the Prince of Wales' charm came back, and what a charm it was! I noticed a sort of stutter, a hissing of the speech when he hesitated in mid-sentence. Wallis did not seem unduly worried about this and said: 'Well, you see, we're old! It's awful how many years have gone by and one doesn't have them back!'

We talked of the current trends in clothes, hippies, nudity, pornography, 'filthy' postcards, etc. The thought struck me that had it not been for the sex urges of their youth, these two would not be here together today. But they are a happy couple. They are both apt to talk at once, but their attitudes do not clash and they didn't seem to have any regrets. The Duke still talks of his investiture as Prince of Wales, and asked me to find out where the crown is that he wore at Caernarvon. He got to his feet (with stick) to look out some illustration in a book and talked of the old 'characters' – Fruity Metcalfe, Ali Mackintosh, Freddie Cripps, Eric Dudley.

An hour passed quickly enough, but I felt we were perhaps running out of small talk when I looked at my watch and realized I must leave for an Ionesco play. The leave-taking was lengthy, due to many red herrings on the way. The Duchess leaning forward on tiny legs, looked rather blind, and when an enormous bouquet of white flowers and plants arrived, she did not seem able to see it. She leant myopically towards it and asked, 'What's that? A tuberose? An arum lily?' The man corrected her – 'An auratum' – 'Ah yes, will you tell them how beautifully they have done them.' I watched her try to open the card to see who this incredibly expensive 'tribute' had come from. I'm sure it cost all of £75! 'Who is it from?' asked the Duke. 'Don't be so full of curiosity,' said his wife trying to read without glasses. 'It's from Jane Englehard!'

The two old people, very bent, but full of spirit and still both dandies, stood at the door as I went off in Lilianne's smart car. Through the passage of years I had become one of their entourage, an old friend, and the Duke even said to me: 'Well, between these four walls...'

Reddish

Cathleen Nesbitt is the most delightful companion. I have always admired her on the stage and considered her a romantic personality. She is beautiful, decorative, and easy about the house. She embellishes the garden and every room she sits in, and her talk is of the best literary quality.

Cathleen shows a rugged sense of reality that no doubt she has learnt in the theatre. She alludes to Willie Maugham as a bastard. She talks freely of the functions of the body. She is clean-living and clean-thinking, but realizes the importance of the sensual passions. Rivals have surpassed her in the theatre; she has no regrets and is not bitter in any way. She is generous, kind and unselfish; and she has an inner contentment.

It is incredible to think that she is eighty-two years old. Her brain is still quick and alert and her ability to quote at great length from poetry and literature is impressive. She is seldom at a loss for a name from her distant past, and can even put a date to a long-forgotten play. She always has a feast of reminiscences about the theatre and is full of good anecdotes about stage celebrities and occasions. Cathleen is also a wonderful audience and throws her head back in raucous laughter.

She is still wonderfully natural. Her face is bright and clean in the moment of waking as others are after hours of preparations. She leaps out of bed, runs upstairs, and does exercises like a child. Without much money she manages to be delightfully dressed. As Dot Head said, 'She is the perfect example of how to grow old, and proves how wrong it is to make too much effort in the ways of artifice.'

It was only when I was driving her to the station for her return to London (and a diet of cream cheese) that I popped the question of whether she would have married Rupert Brooke. 'Yes, I suppose we would have married if it had not been for the war. You see, I only knew him for three years and during two of those he was in America and that's why there were so many letters. I keep them in a cardboard box and should preserve them more carefully. But, you see, we were both recovering from unrequited love affairs. I had had that girlish crush on Harry Ainley with whom I was appearing on the stage, and he was having an affair with another woman. Anyhow, Rupert was studying for some Naval Reserve course at Dartmouth, and I went down there to see him; sometimes he came to see me when I was touring. We read poetry to one another, I reading Donne to him, and he reading his poems to me. Rupert said he thought he ought to be thinking about making a will, and he supposed we'd better get married. And which would I prefer – to be left his rather small possessions, or the rights to his poems? Then he went on to say he thought perhaps as he had just started a poetry magazine with Lascelles Abercrombie, de la Mare and Gibson, and he would like it to continue, it would perhaps be best to leave the copyrights to the three of them. After Rupert's death Mrs Brooke, his mother, said it was quite *frightening* what a lot of money came in from the poems; that all England was mad about "If I should die think only this of me ...", when the other sonnets were far better.'

Cathleen described Rupert's stocky body but graceful, quick movements, the marvellous colouring, the jutting, unclassical nose, and how he had, by dying so young, achieved lasting fame. A young poet dying in a war is always the stuff of legend, but what if he had lived? Would he have developed as a poet? Rupert had wanted more than anything to be a playwright; he had written two plays, but they weren't any good. Would he have become embittered? What would he have looked like today as a man of eighty-four?

I asked Cathleen about Bernard Shaw. She did not know him well, but he had directed the taking of photographs of the production when she played Perdita and he said, 'No, that's the wrong side of your face.' When she told him she would like, for once, to play in comedy, he said, 'No, your jaw is too pronounced. People should have no chins for comedy.' Once, soon after she came over from Ireland and wanted to be an actress, she was invited to lunch with Sir John and Lady Lane. 'I don't know why, because it was all above my station.' She said Shaw should have been present but he was ill. Henry James, however, was well enough to be present. Cathleen wondered what could be the engrossing topic in which Mrs Shaw and James were so intent. She discovered it was entirely about the stomach troubles of Shaw and James.

When Cathleen played Mrs Dubedat she wrote asking Shaw what she should wear; he answered in minute detail about clothes and character. Cathleen again wrote to the now great man when she wanted his permission to do a play of his on radio. Shaw refused. 'They disturb the voice,' he said. 'They made me sound like a bloody Irishman, when everyone knows I haven't a trace of an accent.'

I never came across a woman who has lived so intelligently in such a variety of circumstances and has overcome all the disadvantages, putting them down to part of life's experiences. Perhaps all the sad things that have happened to Cathleen have made her face all the sweeter.

28

Life Goes On
1971–4

In the New Year's Honours List of 1972, ten years too late to give pleasure to his mother, C.B.'s name occurred among the Knights' Bachelor. C.B.'s sister Baba and several old friends died. School friends, such as Cyril Connolly, were celebrating their seventieth birthdays. C.B. travelled to Egypt and to Guatemala. He published the fourth volume of his diaries, The Strenuous Years. *He made a new water garden at Reddish.*

Reddish: April 1971

This Good Friday was as cold, raw, windy, wintry and bleak as it is possible to be. Nothing to do but stay indoors. Fortunately for me Alan Tagg was staying, and we took the opportunity to change the furniture and effects in the dining-room, winter garden, and other rooms. Alan has a wonderful eye and sees things that are no longer valid and that I, through living with them daily, miss.

Easter Saturday brought out the sun, and people's spirits were revived. Alan went for a walk before breakfast, and the day was spent out-of-doors discussing with Smallpiece the construction of a lake – of all things – across the road which David Offley says he can fashion for us. Then, at Alan's suggestion, we went for a walk 'to see the village', the cottage gardens, and the spring that bubbles so clearly and coldly to the watercress beds. Faces at windows were as interested in us as we were in them.

The wintry sun was now at the end of a long span of light. We watched a beautiful barn owl, dove-biscuit coloured with a huge wing-span; it flew along the valley, flittered, soared, prospected then landed; it walked, it rested, then it was on the wing again. We saw a rabbit hurrying over a steep hill to safety.

Alan's quick-as-a-flash eye discovered some blue flowers that were rare, with dotted leaves.

Reddish: 30 May

A big change has been brought about by a huge prehistoric mechanical digger which has bitten into the soggy marshland at the bottom of the field opposite the front door, and has created a lake with an island all for my very own benefit.

It is extraordinarily exciting to see, at night, from my bedroom window the remnants of the light in the sky reflected in the winding ribbon of water. It brings a whole new interest to life here, the element of water.

Even in the appallingly muddy condition with which the landscape is at the moment disfigured, I can tell that this will be a lovely place to look at, with fish and all sorts of birds that are different from those on the terrace of the house. Already there are moorhens, ducks have visited and swans have been seen. . . . As for the trout, it seems I could spend my old age being a fisherman. King Charles said these were the best trout in England.

The house itself is now seen proudly standing in a paved forecourt. Instead of a gravel path of uneven design, we have a very formal slice of green lawn with paving-stones coming to the edge of the box and the yews. It is a great improvement and is a delight not only to me but to passers-by. All that is needed now is some herb growing between the cracks of the stones and things like white foxgloves and valerian sprawling in clumps at the edges of the drive and steps.

September

Margaret Case was my first friend in New York. I had arrived late for a large lunch at Condé Nast's apartment and she was impressed that I had already seen the Grecos in the Hispano Museum. She showed a friendliness that few others did, and by degrees she became a very important person in my American life. She maddened me. I hated much that she said. Often her reactions showed that she did not understand what I really meant. But, my God, she was a hardworking friend. If I asked her to buy a dozen presents to take back to England, the telephone calls would continue until I was sorry I'd ever asked her. If I was in trouble she would be terribly upset. I remember when my career was threatened as a result of the Walter Winchell row, I was hard and metallic and difficult in the face of losing everything. She, the first to come round to my hotel room, sat weeping on a sofa. She realized, more than I did, what a blow had befallen me, and she was helpless to do anything for me.

Margaret was always the first person to telephone on my arrival in New York. She it was who got theatre tickets for me, reserved the table at the restaurant and was always 'at the ready' at the last minute.

Now she is dead. Perhaps in her melancholy she took an overdose, though, being a strong Roman Catholic, this does not seem likely; but whatever the reason, New York will never be the same for me. I will miss her more than I realize, and it says well for her that maybe twenty other people feel the same way.

The sad news of her death is followed by the manner of it. It seems the unhappy soul jumped from the window of her bedroom on the fifteenth floor. One cannot imagine the misery of mind that caused her to have such terrifying last seconds.

That she suffered so much unhappiness was a shock, for Margaret seemed to have a great deal to keep her interested. I know she was upset by what was happening at *Vogue* and disturbed by the direction things were taking there; but she read a lot and she saw all the new plays. As for people, she never stopped making new friends and continued to be most loyal to her lifelong cronies. However, they obviously did not make up for the emptiness of her life; she no doubt felt that she was going round like a squirrel in a wheel, and in any case was not in a fit state to withstand any cruel blows.

The picture of her recently published is a wonderful character study of her in a benign, amused, interested mood, as she arrived as chic as-be-damned in spite of her ugly face, at some exhibition. The cameraman could not have known what emotion his picture would create in so many hearts. The sight of it went through me like a stab.

Went to two excellent plays last week; or I should say one good play, *Butley*, and one wonderful entertainment, *The Changing Room*. David Storey, who wrote the latter, used to fly up to Manchester at the weekends to play football while studying at the Slade. He is now not only a successful novelist, but a playwright.

His subject is the behind-the-scenes at a football match, an enormous cast. I cannot think it would read well, but Lindsay Anderson has made characters of each individual, and has made it into a sort of choreographed play. The effect is stunning, for Storey knows just how to make his theatrical effects. The evening is an effective *tour de force*.

Butley is a most articulate play, in fact one I would like to read, and is made momentous by the performances by Alan Bates and Richard O'Callaghan. Bates has invented an original sense of humour. It takes a while to realize what he is up to, but by degrees one is overcome by his tongue-in-cheekness and self-mockery. He has grown his hair very shaggily long. This is obviously to compensate for the width of his neck which has now become almost inhumanly large. But what a marvellous find for the theatre he is. He came in on the new wave of John Osborne and has gone from one peak to another: a real artist, modest, determined and utterly charming.

Chanel is dead. One can no longer take for granted the feeling that she and her talent are always with us. She was unlike anything seen before. She was no beauty, but her appearance in the twenties and thirties was unimaginably attractive. She put all other women in the shade. Even in old age, ravaged and creased as she was, she still kept her line, and was able to put on the allure.

She used to spend most of the time complaining in her rasping, dry voice. Everyone except her was at fault. But you were doing her a service by remaining in her presence, for even her most loyal friends had been forced to leave her. You tried to leave, too, for your next appointment, but she had perfected the technique of delaying you. Her flow of talk could not be interrupted. You rose from your seat and made backwards for the door. She followed. Her face ever closer to yours. Then you were out on the landing and down a few stairs. The rough voice still went on. Then you blew a kiss. She knew now that loneliness again faced her. She smiled a goodbye. The mouth stretched in a grimace, but from a distance it worked the old magic.

I found myself outside the shop a few weeks ago. I had not seen her since the musical *Coco* and thought I'd pay her a call. She looked older than ever. No gipsy had ever looked so old. The hair was like black wool; eye-black smudged; no make-up would remain on the dark skin. Her hands appeared enormous at the ends of long, stringy arms. The chest was almost concave. She never ate anything; one felt it was only her spirit that kept her going. Her servants and the others who work for her were cowed. But she knew that she would always have the whip hand.

I always wanted to get to know Coco, but she was very forbidding. She never had any feelings of friendship for me, so I am not disloyal when I write of her venom, her lack of generosity and her disloyalty.

For fifty years she went on proving that her taste was impeccable. She had a strong, daring, sure approach that made others fade into insignificance; never anything extraneous and fussy; she believed in utter simplicity. She was a female Brummell. Just as the Beau got rid of frills and furbelows overnight, so too Chanel demonstrated that nothing was more chic than fine linen, navy-blue serge and lots of soap. She had an eye to quality and proportion that was unbeatable. She had daring, freshness, authenticity, conviction. She was exceptional and she knew it. She was unfeminine in character, but totally feminine in her ability to entice, and she had great sex appeal. Chanel had qualities and talents that are very rare. She was a genius, and all her faults must be forgiven for that one reason.

London: Saturday 18 December

It is very seldom that I am in London at the weekends, but I wanted to go to the memorial service for Gladys Cooper on Saturday.

The service was beautifully arranged. Stanley Holloway read from the *Pilgrim's Progress*; a Shakespeare sonnet on 'Love' was read by Celia Johnson;

a serenade from *Hassan* played; Robert Morley's comic and evocative address gave great relief to the congregation and prevented the atmosphere becoming morbid. A prayer, a blessing, then two minutes of silence in which we were all to remember, in our own way, our friend Gladys.

For myself, I remember Gladys since, as a faltering schoolboy, I went up to her when she was having lunch at the Carlton Restaurant with Gertie Millar. I remember the sweetness with which she acceded to my stammering request, and said I must of course also ask for the signature of her friend. Her complexion was of a white and pink marshmallow perfection, her hair fair silky fluff and eyes the bluest.

Gladys – I could now write a book about her. She was one of the recurring enthusiasms in my life. She has meant a great deal to me. I was full of admiration for the way she could be *utterly* herself on all occasions. Few people have had such strength of character. Gladys had her share of disappointments and tragedies, but she accepted everything with a wide-eyed courage.

As Sybil Thorndike was about to be driven away from the church, I told her how beautiful she had become, more so now than at any time in her life. 'Don't be such a fool! Don't be so silly!' she said, but was pleased. Then she said, 'I hope my service will be as gay as this one. It won't be long now; you know I'm nearly ninety!' and waving and leaning back and cackling, away she went.

Kitty Miller during a dragging conversation said: 'I knew Proust.' Suddenly everyone was on the edge of their seats. 'Tell us what was he like?' Kitty answered: 'Ghastly, darling!'

January 1972

'Sir' is a romantic title. It sounds so unlike me, so much less personal than 'Mr Beaton'. 'Sir' on envelopes seems to take away some individuality, but I felt proud, and sorry that my mother was not alive to share my pleasure.

Luxor, Egypt: March

The climate is ideal. Yet I am not at all content. It is awful to see a country that is going to the dogs, that is living in and on the past. Tours by calèche, bus, and boat have shown us the best of this country. But having spent most of the morning battling with hall porters and tour guides and being bitten by flies while I wait in dreary offices and undergo infinite humiliations, I have become disgruntled. Perhaps I hate too much.

Paris: 28 May

I woke early to hear Lilia Ralli's familiar chirp announcing the death of the Duke of Windsor. I felt callously indifferent, no pang of nostalgia. Certainly he had been a great figure in my adolescence, full of charm and dash, glamorous, and a good Prince of Wales. Then the sensational abdication and marriage. As a photographer, I came into that scene in a big way, but throughout the years the Duke had never shown any affection for or interest in me. In fact, perhaps rather presumptuously, I felt he disliked me. It was only at the last meeting when I went to have a drink with 'Darby and Joan', and all his men friends were dead, that he thawed towards me, and talked about the 'old times'. He was always cold in his friendships, and could cut them off overnight. He was inclined to be silly. When James Pope-Hennessy told him he was writing a book about Trollope, he roared with laughter and turned to Wallis saying: ' 'E's writing a book about a trollop!'

Windsor

The Duke's funeral was noble and dignified. The military knights in their scarlet uniforms, medals clinking, marched with a loud stamp-shuffle. The slowness and the muffled metal sound was impressive, and the fact that these knights were all aged, with clear pink skins, made it that much more remarkable.

The coffin, borne by eight sturdy Welsh Guardsmen, arms linked and heads bowed, was draped with the Duke's personal standard, and covered with a huge trembling mass of Madonna lilies. Members of the Royal Family followed; the King of Norway, extra tall; the Duke of Edinburgh, grey and drawn and yet emitting strength; the delightful, charming young Prince of Wales; the young Kents and Gloucesters; and Lord Mountbatten.

The service was short and poignant. An anthem. Prayers. Another hymn, then a dramatic moment when Garter King of Arms read out the Styles and Titles of the late Duke: Knight of the Garter, Knight of the Thistle, King Edward VIII of England, Ruler of India ... and the ribbons and badges of the orders were carried on cushions. One was reminded of Shakespeare's kings and princes.

Majorca: August

Am really sorry for myself. So far I've enjoyed more than average good health, but lately a blight has been put on my existence by my not being able to read or write without being punished with a nervous head pain that stretches over my left eye, over the head and down the nape of my neck. It puts such a damper on my activities. I live by my eyes. It is being particularly annoying during the holiday when there is little to do but read.

Dr Gottfried does not seem optimistic. He says that the headache is caused by the arteries to the brain getting tight, due to brain fag and overstrain. I have been many times to excellent oculists and they say there is nothing wrong with my eyes, that eye strain does not exist. However, I do know that if I have

used my eyes more than average, the pain strikes. It is very hard to know what
to do, especially when I had hoped my old age would be spent reading and
writing if not painting.

Montreux: September

I had heard about Noël [Coward]'s Swiss retreat. 'It's very typical of him, lots
of signed photographs, a house that might have been brought from Eastbourne.'
It is true the house suits Noël perfectly. It has no real character, is ugly, is
decorated in the typical theatre-folk style, but it is warm and comfortable and
it works.

I found Noël in a scarlet jacket hunched and crumpled in a chair, looking
very old and resigned and fatter. He seemed a bit surprised to see me although,
no doubt, as he later said, he had been looking forward to my visit. A glass
of brandy and ginger-ale was within reach and the cigarettes at hand. Noël
is only a bit more than seventy. He suffers from a bad leg; the circulation cannot
be relied upon and if he walks he can be in great pain. As a result, he doesn't
walk, and spends most of his time in bed. This is not good for anyone. But
Noël has aged into a very nice and kind old man. He is really a darling, so
trim and neat, his memory unfailing. His intelligence was as quick as ever and
within a few moments we were enjoying each other's jokes and laughing a lot.

You know that when Noël gives an evaluation of someone else's talent or
personality, he will be absolutely 'on the ball' and never prejudiced. There
are certain types that he despises. He has no time for amateurs, or people that
tell lies or are phoneys. But he is incredibly generous in his appreciation of
most people, particularly those who have succeeded in the theatre.

Naturally we reminisced about the first times we met; how he gave me a
deserved 'going over' during a return journey from America, and more recently
about the production of *Quadrille*. He complimented me on my professionalism
and said I was a most direct and workmanlike designer.

Later in the evening it was wonderful to hear him singing in a quiet but
musical voice the songs that had meant so much to him since he was a boy.
Noël still remembers all the lyrics; Vesta Tilley songs, Albert Chevalier songs
from a terrible Jack Hulbert musical called *The Light Blues* in which Noël had
learnt to tap dance, and snatches of songs from long-forgotten musicals.

I asked Noël to tell me about the stars he had seen from the pit when taken
to the theatre by his mother on birthday treats. 'Lily Elsie, the way she moved,
very slowly, but with incredible grace; those long arms and never a coy gesture.
She was such fun too – a darling! And her voice true.' Of Gertie Millar: 'She
could dance like a wisp, with those long legs, and she was a star and like all
stars she had vitality. No one without vitality can have any glamour.' He talked
lovingly of Gertie Lawrence, as someone with whom he could never quarrel

for she was such a perfectionist. He had great praise for Maisie Gay, whom he considered more a brilliant dramatic actress than a comedienne. She played each part as if it were written by Chekhov.

It was time to go to bed. In the lift, recently built for Noël's comfort, he plopped himself down on the stool and said, 'It's awful. I'm so old!'

Vaynol, Caernarvonshire: October

Vaynol used to be the centre of much frivolity and inspired gaiety; charades, improvisations, elaborate dressing-up, practical jokes, youthful gaiety of all sorts. Now two wings of about thirty rooms have been pulled down. It has become more and more difficult for Michael to maintain the place as in the old days.

Michael has a very busy life attending to his various responsibilities, so, because he was at a meeting, we were met at the station by the old chauffeur; an old butler came out of the front door as we drove up, made a little speech regretting Michael's absence, and then said that the first time he had seen me was in 1936! Patrick Procktor on hearing this was staggered, as it was the year of his birth, and I could not believe that forty years had passed since I first came to this house. So the visit took on the colour of a journey into the past.

Soon Michael appeared and cheered us with the readiness of his interest, his curiosity, his humour. For someone who started as a backward child, he has come a long way and has made a very interesting life for himself. He and I have shared so much of the past together that we necessarily veered towards subjects that we had both enjoyed.

In the house there were many bibelots and pieces of furniture that had belonged to Michael's mother, Juliet. Juliet's scrapbooks were brought out and I was astounded that the well-remembered events here recorded had taken place so long ago. It seemed to me as if they had happened but yesterday. It was with a haunted fascination that we looked at those old milestones. People who had to us seemed so old and decrepit then, now appeared to look young, and even beautiful.

Michael gave me a feeling of strength. He has survived well, so why shouldn't I? He had no regrets, so why should I feel sad. Maybe it had all been frivolous, but it had been a creative frivolity, and it must have taught one something about certain aspects of life. Anyhow it was no use sighing.

Hawarden Castle: March 1973

As the doctor prophesied, Baba's condition has slowly deteriorated. She has come up to be with her beloved daughter, Rosamund, for the last time. She is desperately weak but she has not given in, and it makes her angry that she is not strong enough to come down to lunch, write her name, or light a cigarette.

She looks incredibly beautiful; so thin as to be hardly recognizable; the bone formation of her face is marvellous, high cheekbones, noble nose and brow, and her forehead is without wrinkles.

I am somewhat comforted to see that death need not be as terrifying as one feared. The sedatives make the withering away less tragic; her fading out will be like that of a plant which suddenly becomes sick.

Sunday 11 March

I steeled myself. The first thing that struck me on entering her room, and I saw her lying asleep with her face turned towards the window, was that her hair had fallen on to her forehead. This somehow added the final touch of poignancy to the picture. It affected me deeply.

I stared at Baba. She lay, a small steel-grey piece of sculpture, and I left the room in a state of complete breakdown.

Almost a week later

Rosamund telephoned early in the morning. Baba had died at 4 am. Goodbye, Baba, who was always so independent, so lithe and graceful; always with a pet dog, so athletic and country loving.

Goodbye my most beautiful first, home-made model. Goodbye to so much of my own life. Goodbye to Baba.

Reddish: 16 June

The summer weather is so unbelievably beautiful that I only wish my sense of delight and enjoyment was stronger. Perhaps, after a day or two's rest, I will regain my zest. Already I feel less tired, and have been out in the early-morning sun walking barefoot on the dew-covered lawns. The birds are having a fine time (the pigeons very destructive!) and the doves seem to have made a haunt of this place. There are chaffinches and yellow-hammers. The garden is at its peak. Just *before* its best, Clarissa [Avon] came and had tea under an awning on the terrace, and thought she liked the garden best now when you could see the shapes before all the colour. The terrace is a mass of roses, and I only trust the summer will continue till next weekend when the garden is open!

I watched on television Marlene Dietrich's successful performance staged at Drury Lane. The quality of the photography was extraordinarily exact, and I felt I saw more and heard more than if I had been a part of the wildly enthu-siastic audience. As for Marlene, aged seventy (actresses are always said to be older than they are), she was quite a remarkable piece of artifice. Somehow she has evolved an agelessness. Even for a hardened expert like myself, it was impossible to find the chink in her armour. All the danger spots were disguised. Her dress, her figure, her limbs, all gave the illusion of youth. The high cheek-bones remain intact, the forehead good, the deep-set eyelids useful attributes, and she does the rest.

Not much of a never-musical voice is left, but her showmanship persists. Marlene has become a sort of mechanical doll. The doll can show surprise, it can walk, it can swish into place the train of its white fur coat. The audience applauds each movement, each gesture. The doll smiles incredulously. Can it really be for me that you applaud? Again a very simple gesture, maybe the hands flap, and again the applause, not just from old people who remembered her tawdry films, but the young, too, who find her sexy. She is louche and not averse to giving a slight wink.

Marlene has created another career for herself and is certainly a great star, not without talent, and with a genius for believing in her self-fabricated beauty.

Her success is out of all proportion and yet it is entirely due to her perseverance that she is not just an old discarded film star. She magnetizes her audience and mesmerizes them (and herself) into believing in her.

I sat enraptured and not a bit critical as I had imagined I might be. The old trooper never changes her tricks because she knows they work, and because she invented them.

London: 11 September

Cyril [Connolly] was only told the *venue* at the last minute as the car turned into Regent's Park and went on to the zoo. Because of the heatwave, his friends gathered to celebrate his seventieth birthday outdoors at the members' club drinking champagne. John Betjeman, with trousers too short, walking like a toddler on the sands; he only lacked a bucket and spade. Alastair Forbes, Anthony Powell, Hamish Hamilton, eight people from *The Sunday Times* and Raymond Mortimer, in old age looking beautiful with long wavy silver hair. To comfort those of us who are reaching the age of seventy, Raymond said that he had been happier during the last five years (he is seventy-five) than at any other time of his life. He certainly looks contented, serene, unworried.

Philippe de Rothschild, Anne Fleming, Antony Hobson and Tania were there, and, of course, Deirdre. Deirdre told me that Cyril reads in bed almost all day. He hardly ever goes out and at Eastbourne they see no one. Cyril's life is entirely centred round his books, but it seems an interesting, satisfying life.

Cyril looked calm, pretty as a celluloid cupid in a bath, with no apparent nervousness, and although he says he has never made a speech, did in fact deliver himself of a spontaneous one. It was a typical piece of Cyril embroidery about his having an unhappy childhood (only son) with ill-assorted parents, how as a schoolboy he went to St Cyprian's, 'where a younger boy, Beaton, he was only called Beaton, taught me about painting and we ate gooseberries together – when the black ones were finished, we ate the green ones. When the unhappy only son of ill-assorted parents went on to another school, here he attained puberty and he admired the shell-like ear of a boy with black hair, Noel Blakiston, and he's sitting over there, and then I won a scholarship for Eton and I became friends with Kenneth Clark, sitting over there. Then I worked in J.C. Squire's office and was helped by J.B. Betjeman – and he's sitting over there; and Tony Powell helped me and he's sitting over there.' We thought he might be going through the whole thirty-odd guests and making it a 'This Is Your Life', but it was perfectly timed and not a sentence too long. It was funny, pithy, satirical, well dramatized – Cyril at his best; a lovely celebration.

King's College, Cambridge: December

I had seen Dadie [Rylands] two weeks ago at Raymond Mortimer's at Crichel and was struck by his healthiness, his freshness, vigour, and purity. I thought him wonderfully rare and uncontaminated by the rush and squalor of contemporary life. Only occasionally does he take wing from his life of books and study, but whenever he does make friendly forays, he always shows a childlike enjoyment.

Extraordinary as it seems, Dadie is now over seventy. He still appears to me, even if a bit thinner on top, to be the young bullocky blond that he was at King's when I was unhappily at St John's.

Dadie was, with his pale-blue eyes, blue tie, pink-and-white complexion, and canary quiff of hair, a spectacular figure. A great friend of all the Bloomsbury group, the names of Lytton, Duncan, Vanessa, and Clive were seldom off his lips. He was loved and passionate; his reputation was most enviable. He played the Duchess of Malfi, a role that I could have performed if only I had not been so tiresome and difficult, and it was the best Duchess of Malfi I have seen, out of at least a dozen. Dadie was dignified like a unicorn, neither male nor female.

Now Dadie, in boyish open neck, welcomed Jakie Astor and me in his kitchen. I have seldom seen anything so ordered in the clutter of his rooms, a magpie's hoard of silver, china, and twentyish paintings. Mercifully everything was extremely well dusted and polished. Nevertheless, the effect was peculiar, a mixture of a Victorian old lady's taste and donnish severity; mahogany bookcases, china cabinets, and a hangover of Bloomsbury décor. Carrington had painted typical and pretty panels on the doors and cupboards, and his smaller sitting-room was liberally sprinkled with 'dated' nudes against a noughts-and-crosses background.

Dadie made the tea, produced hot buttered buns and macaroons. He asked about Jakie's 'arable land', gave information about what all the Cambridge celebrities were doing and how they had achieved eminence in other fields. He was quick and trenchant and showed a wide range of interests; his little beady eyes popping and his lips pressed in a pout as he listened. One felt that time had in no way impaired the sharpness of his brain. He talked about Thomas Hardy, quite a close family connection there; about Siegfried Sassoon, and Stephen Tennant, Victor Rothschild, and Raymond Mortimer, all of whom he described in a very true way.

Jakie sat in amazement. I felt that Dadie had mellowed and that he must be a very happy man. But no, it seems he is extremely lonely, feels the lack of grandchildren, finds the hour of waking and the early morning appallingly depressing. He is happier when, after seven or eight cups of tea, he lies in bed reading. Three o'clock in the afternoon is his most difficult time and whisky at six o'clock helps him to continue.

His eyesight is perfect, so he can indulge in his favourite pleasure of reading for the rest of time.

The telephone rang. He answered it in his very poor and small little bedroom with the chamber pot under the wash-basin. 'They've called it off?' he asked; his dinner engagement was off. He would cook eggs or sausages for himself on his 'Little Belling', and he would get through the washing-up and clearing away in ten minutes flat, and then the long evening would be in front of him.

25 January 1974

The various news items on the television come and go so rapidly that one wonders at times if one has heard aright. My heart missed a beat as I learnt that James [Pope-Hennessy] had been severely beaten up, and stabbed. A photograph of James's poetical face was shown on the screen, and before I could take in the horrible fact that he had died as a result of the attack, the news moved on to Ireland or to a football match.

I was struck by an overwhelming sorrow and horror that did not leave me during the night. When I woke and the breakfast tray came in with the news-papers and letters, my hopes that the news-flash might have been a mistake were dashed when I saw the same beautiful face in a photograph on the front page. I looked at my letters. Surely this envelope was written in James's hand? I opened it and a most tender, friendly, sweet letter from him pierced me to the heart. James was thanking me for a present I sent him at Christmas, which he had found on his recent return from America where he had been interviewing friends of Noël Coward for his forthcoming biography, and he longed to meet me again.

James came into my life at the beginning of the last war with a new and fresh sort of appeal. He had 'quality', was intelligent, and intellectual, and serious, and yet good company. I delighted in him, and we became fast friends. We did a book together, he the text and I the photographs, on the bombing of London. Our expeditions to the city were dramatic, often tragic, but agreeable. Sometimes after exploring the still-smoking ruins, we went to the Strand and ate a good lunch in a restaurant.

James introduced me to Clarissa Churchill, who has remained a close friend, and to many others whose company I enjoy.

I remember seeing James from a taxi as he got out of another taxi in front of Batsfords. He was late, he was panicky, his arms full of books. As he descended, his hat hit the top of the taxi, hat and books went flying. I saw in that glimpse myself.

Later James began to be rather difficult. He drank too much. He made friendships too easily with the 'rough trade'. This was dangerous and extremely boring for his other friends, who often said: 'Unless he's lucky, one day James will find himself murdered.' James lost his looks, became bellicose, devilish and impossible. Maybe drugs, as an antidote to drink, did improve the situation. 'You do spread your friendships thin,' he once taunted me. I was hurt. Every time I returned from America I brought him a present. I was always the one to ring first. He seldom took the initiative and then there would be a long silence; and now this.

Reddish: February

The water-garden has become one of the most magical places in the garden. To visit this place of babbling water, and birds, is like being in a different country. To think that all these years I was hardly conscious that a river did go past my property! Every sort of bird seems to congregate here, quite different from those that come to the terrace. We are surprised often to see a heron or two on the lookout for fish. But the greatest excitement is a kingfisher – a rare enough streak of blue, yet suddenly I saw one, and the sight gladdened my fading spirit. Kingfishers fly so quickly that by the time one says 'Look!', they have gone.

London: 13 March

Yesterday I went to the Imperial War Museum, not my favourite place, to see the collection of photographs that I had taken during the war for the Ministry of Information. They have all been put into over thirty albums and, to my amazement, I find there are thirty or forty thousand of them.

It was an extraordinary experience to relive those war years; so much of it had been forgotten, and most of the people are now dead; the Western Front, where at least three hundred of my pictures were unaccountably lost, Burma, India, China. It was fascinating to see the scenes in old Imperial Simla, the rickshaws drawn by uniformed servants, the grandeur of the houses, the palaces, the bar scenes, the men on leave swigging beer, and to wonder how I had been able to 'frat' with such unfamiliar types. The horrible war had taken me to beautiful landscapes I might not otherwise have seen. I had not realized that I had taken so many documentary pictures, some of purely technical interest. Looking at them today, I spotted ideas that are now 'accepted', but which, thirty years ago, were before their time. The sheer amount of work I had done confounded me.

It was a thrilling but upsetting morning, for I felt that I was dead and that people were speaking of me in the past. 'The greatest collection by one person of any subject in our museum.'

I went out into the grey dreariness of Lambeth today. It had been a particularly revolting week with strikes, power cuts and epidemics. Despite the dark grey skies I was buoyant and would not believe that my life had lost any of its old fire and zest.

Index

Note: CB refers to Sir Cecil Beaton